PRESIDENTS

of the

CHURCH

Second Edition

THE LIVES AND TEACHINGS
OF THE MODERN PROPHETS

edited by CRAIG MANSCILL, ROBERT FREEMAN,
DENNIS WRIGHT, *and* MARK D. OGLETREE

PRESIDENTS

of the

CHURCH

Second Edition

◆

THE LIVES AND TEACHINGS
OF THE MODERN PROPHETS

Craig James Ostler · Charles Swift · Paul Nolan Hyde
Lawrence R. Flake · Arnold K. Garr · Craig K. Manscill
Kent R. Brooks · David F. Boone · Mary Jane Woodger
Blair G. Van Dyke · Clyde J. Williams · Matthew O. Richardson
Timothy Merrill · John P. Livingstone · Cynthia Doxey
Lloyd D. Newell · Michael A. Goodman · Mark D. Ogletree

CFI
An imprint of Cedar Fort, Inc.
Springville, Utah

© 2008, 2015, 2019 Craig K. Manscill, Robert C. Freeman, Dennis A. Wright, and Mark D. Ogletree

ISBN: 978-1-4621-3633-9

Published by CFI, an imprint of Cedar Fort, Inc., 2373 W. 700 S., Springville, UT 84663
Distributed by Cedar Fort, Inc., www.cedarfort.com

The Library of Congress has cataloged the first edition as follows:

Manscill, Craig K.
  Presidents of the Church / Craig K. Manscill, Robert C. Freeman, Dennis A. Wright.
    p. cm.
  Includes bibliographical references and index.
  ISBN 978-1-59955-163-0 (alk. paper)
  1. Church of Jesus Christ of Latter-Day Saints—Presidents—Biography. 2. Mormon Church—Presidents—Biography. I. Freeman, Robert C., 1959– II. Wright, Dennis A. III. Title.

BX8693.M36 2008
289.3092'2—dc22
[B]

                    2008014857

Cover design by Shawnda T. Craig
Cover design © 2019 Cedar Fort, Inc.
Edited by Annaliese B. Cox and Nicole Terry
Typeset by Angela D. Olsen and Kaitlin Barwick
Indexed by Gary Gillum

Photographs in this publication are used by permission of The Church of Jesus Christ of Latter-day Saints, with the exception of those used by permission of Lori Tubbs Garcia and Rachael Van Syckel-Pancic in the President Thomas S. Monson chapter, and those used by permission of the Nelson family in the President Russell M. Nelson chapter.

Printed in China

10 9 8 7 6 5 4 3 2 1

Printed on acid-free paper

ACKNOWLEDGMENTS

A volume such as this cannot be created without the talent, energy, and patience of many wonderful individuals. Sincere thanks are expressed, first and foremost, to the individual authors whose collective expertise has allowed our publisher, Cedar Fort, to produce a book unlike any other. Each chapter represents dedicated research and writing of the individual authors, several of whom have studied the prophets they are writing about for many years. This team of experts has been very patient over the several years that it has taken to see this project through to publication. We are likewise grateful to Cedar Fort for their interest and vision in helping this project come to a fruitful end. The talented leadership and staff at Cedar Fort were available at just the right place and at just the right time to help this effort see a successful conclusion.

Additional appreciation is conveyed to Bruce Pearson at the Church Visual Library, to Bill Slaughter at the Church Historical Department, and to their talented staffs, who assisted greatly in gaining both access and the duplication of photos and other images. Thanks also to the Church Museum of Art and History for their assistance in similar ways. Much of the text editing, photo selection, and text preparation has been accomplished by research assistants from Brigham Young University, a group of energetic students to whom we owe a great debt of gratitude. Thank you to BYU Religious Education and to CES for their support. In addition, sincere thanks is expressed to Dr. Richard Holzapfel and his staff, who provided helpful suggestions and published abbreviated versions of several of the chapters included in this volume in the Religious Studies Center's *Religious Educator* at Brigham Young University. We are also deeply grateful to the Office of the First Presidency, which allowed author access and approval to use and duplicate key materials and photos relating to the lives of Presidents Gordon B. Hinckley and Thomas S. Monson. Finally, we are grateful to President Russell M. Nelson and his family who were so willing to help with the photographs and interviews.

Abbreviations

CR   Conference Reports of The Church of Jesus Christ of Latter-day Saints (Salt Lake City: The Church of Jesus Christ of Latter-day Saints, 1898 to present).

HC   Joseph Smith, *History of The Church of Jesus Christ of Latter-day Saints*, ed. B. H. Roberts, 2nd ed. rev., 7 vols. (Salt Lake City: The Church of Jesus Christ of Latter-day Saints, 1932–51).

JD   *Journal of Discourses*, 26 vols. (London: Latter-day Saints' Book Depot, 1854–86).

MFP   James R. Clark, comp., *Messages of the First Presidency of The Church of Jesus Christ of Latter-day Saints*, 6 vols. (Salt Lake City: Bookcraft, 1965–75).

CONTENTS

INTRODUCTION

On the date of the organization of the Church, there was no formal office of the President of the Church or of the First Presidency. At that time Joseph Smith, along with his associate Oliver Cowdery, were identified only as Apostles of the restored Church (see D&C 21). It was not until three years later that the office of Church President formally came into existence. In response to the Lord's instructions as found in sections 81 and 90 of the Doctrine and Covenants, Joseph Smith led the Church as its first President from the spring of 1833 until June 1844, when he was murdered at Carthage Jail. Of the over ninety Apostles ordained in the latter days, seventeen have been called to lead the Church in this dispensation, including our most recent President, Russell M. Nelson.

Each successive President of the Church has been the Lord's key representative and the presiding high priest, called for a particular purpose and season in time. For example, President Hinckley's unique talents and experience prepared him to lead the Church through a period of unprecedented temple building. His expertise in the areas of public and media relations helped the Church immensely as Utah, home to Church headquarters, hosted the world during the 2002 Winter Olympic Games.

The chapters in this volume highlight the unique character and divinely instilled traits of leadership that were vital for the time in which each particular President served. Each prophet is discussed in a separate essay that outlines the pivotal life events of the prophet and then presents stirring profiles and his key teachings. Adding to the distinctiveness of these essays are the many photographs and other images relating to the lives and leadership of these great men.

The beloved hymn "We Thank Thee, O God, for a Prophet" reflects the gratitude we feel for these leaders. Truly, they are the Lord's anointed, and each President has served as a beacon to the world in our commotion-filled dispensation. President Gordon B. Hinckley said, "How thankful we ought to be, . . . how thankful we are, for a prophet to counsel us in words of divine wisdom as we walk our paths in these complex and difficult times. . . . We either have a prophet or we have nothing; and having a prophet, we have everything."[1] We add our voices of appreciation for each of these leaders who were most certainly prepared from the foundations of the world.

NOTES

1. *Ensign*, January 1974, 122–24.

Chapter One
JOSEPH SMITH

LIFE AND TIMES

1805	December 23	Born in Sharon, Vermont, to Joseph and Lucy Mack Smith
1820	Spring	Received First Vision
1823		Instructed by the angel Moroni concerning the Restoration of the gospel and the plates of the Book of Mormon
1827		Married Emma Hale; received the Book of Mormon plates and began their translation
1829		Received keys of the Aaronic Priesthood from John the Baptist as well as the keys of the Melchizedek Priesthood from Peter, James, and John
1830		Published the Book of Mormon; organized the Church of Christ at Fayette, New York; began inspired translation of the Bible
1831		Moved to Kirtland, Ohio; traveled to and identified Jackson County, Missouri, as center place of Zion
1832		Sustained as the President of the high priesthood; received vision of the wonders of eternity (D&C 76) and later was tarred and feathered by a mob
1833		Served mission to Upper Canada
1834		Traveled as the head of Zion's Camp to aid Saints who had been driven from their homes in Jackson County, Missouri
1836		Dedicated the Kirtland Temple
1838		Arrived in Far West, Missouri, after being forced to flee for his life from apostates in Kirtland, Ohio
1838–39		Imprisoned in Liberty, Missouri
1839		Settled in Commerce (renamed Nauvoo), Illinois; traveled to Washington, DC, and met with President Martin Van Buren to seek redress for the Saints' Missouri persecutions
1842		First administered the temple endowment in the room above the Red Brick Store in Nauvoo, Illinois
1844	June 27	Martyred at age thirty-eight in the jail at Carthage, Illinois

BIOGRAPHICAL HIGHLIGHTS

Joseph Smith was the first President of The Church of Jesus Christ of Latter-day Saints. He was "called a seer, a translator, a prophet, an apostle of Jesus Christ . . . through the will of God the Father, and the grace of your Lord Jesus Christ" (D&C 21:1). No prophet has been greater in revealing and declaring the gospel.

Born in the mountains of Vermont to a humble family of noble religious heritage, Joseph was chosen to lay the foundation of the Church of Jesus Christ in the dispensation of the fulness of times. In the spring of 1820, he saw and conversed with God the Father and His Son, Jesus Christ. Other heavenly messengers tutored him in his calling as a prophet of God and restored essential truths and priesthood keys through him. He married Emma Hale of Harmony, Pennsylvania, who shared his life and testimony of the Restoration. In 1836 he dedicated the Kirtland Temple, where the Savior again appeared to him. He endured great persecution because of his valiant witness of Jesus Christ and died as a martyr, sealing his testimony with his blood.

CONTRIBUTIONS

The Prophet Joseph Smith bestowed the foundational writings of the Restoration. He translated and published the Book of Mormon. He received revelations that are published in the Doctrine and Covenants, worked on an inspired translation of the Bible, and translated the book of Abraham. Joseph oversaw the compilation of the *History of the Church* and the *Lectures on Faith*. As the first prophet of a new dispensation of the gospel, all ordinances performed in the kingdom of God trace to the restoration of priesthood keys conferred upon him. Joseph organized the Church of Jesus Christ and set in order the organization of the priesthood, including the various rights and responsibilities of each priesthood office. Perhaps the crowning contribution of the Prophet Joseph Smith is that he restored temple ordinances that seal families for eternity and prepare individuals to enter the presence of God.

TEACHINGS

The Prophet Joseph Smith taught that God is a "Man of Holiness," in whose image we are created. Further, he testified that Jesus Christ is the Son of God and the Savior of the world. Joseph emphasized that the gospel of Jesus Christ has always been the same from before the foundation of the world. Further, Joseph's teachings gave purpose to existence. He taught that as spirits we lived before dwelling on the earth. He explained that God had an eternal plan to bless His children and that mortality is essential to that plan. Joseph testified that life continues after death and that each individual will be judged according to his obedience to the laws and ordinances of the gospel. In sum, Joseph taught the fulness of the restored gospel of Jesus Christ.

LIFE OF
JOSEPH SMITH

◆

It is most probable that more individuals have borne testimony of the divine call of Joseph Smith as a prophet, seer, and revelator than of any other prophet who has lived on this earth. Joseph is the primary witness of the restoration of the fulness of the gospel of Jesus Christ. He was appointed before he was born to hold the keys of this last dispensation and was given the responsibility to prepare the earth for the Savior's return preceding His millennial reign. He was commissioned by Moses to lay the foundation of a greater work in gathering Israel than Moses himself had accomplished.[1] He fulfilled many of the prophecies of Isaiah and was the means through which came more divinely inspired scripture than even that great revelator gave to ancient Israel. His forefather, Joseph who was sold into Egypt, spoke prophetically of him as "a choice seer" (2 Nephi 3:6).

John Taylor testified, "Joseph Smith, the Prophet and Seer of the Lord, has done more, save Jesus only, for the salvation of men in this world, than any other man that ever lived in it" (D&C 135:3). Yet, while orienting some newly arrived Saints in Nauvoo, Illinois, Joseph himself stated, "I told them that I was but a man, and they must not expect me to be perfect; if they expected perfection from me, I should expect it from them; but if they would bear with my infirmities and the infirmities of the brethren, I would likewise bear with their infirmities."[2] On another occasion, he graphically characterized himself and the opposition he faced: "I am like a huge, rough stone rolling down from a high mountain; and the only polishing I get is when some corner gets rubbed off by coming in contact with something else, striking with accelerated force against [wickedness] . . . and corrupt men and women—all hell knocking off a corner here and a corner

there. Thus I will become a smooth and polished shaft in the quiver of the Almighty."[3]

Joseph knew of his divine call as a prophet of God and also of his own weaknesses. He placed his life and character in the hands of the Lord to be directed and molded into

Description of the Prophet Joseph Smith

Parley Pratt said: "President Joseph Smith was in person tall and well built, strong and active; of light complexion, light hair, blue eyes, very little beard, and of an expression peculiar to himself, on which the eye naturally rested with interest, and was never weary of beholding. His countenance was ever mild, affable, beaming with intelligence and benevolence; mingled with a look of interest and an unconscious smile, or cheerfulness, and entirely free from all restraint or affectation of gravity; and there was something connected with the serene and steady penetrating glance of his eye, as if he would penetrate the deepest abyss of the human heart, gaze into eternity, penetrate the heavens, and comprehend all worlds.

"He possessed a noble boldness and independence of character; his manner was easy and familiar; his rebuke terrible as the lion; his benevolence unbounded as the ocean; his intelligence universal, and his language abounding in original eloquence peculiar to himself—not polished—not studied—not smoothed and softened by education and refined by art; but flowing forth in its own native simplicity, and profusely abounding in variety of subject and manner. He interested and edified, while, at the same time, he amused and entertained his audience; and none listened to him that were ever weary with his discourse. I have even known him to retain a congregation of willing and anxious listeners for many hours together, in the midst of cold or sunshine, rain or wind, while they were laughing at one moment and weeping the next. Even his most bitter enemies were generally overcome, if he could once get their ears."[1]

The Prophet Joseph Smith.

Sharon, Vermont, birthplace of the Prophet Joseph Smith, December 23, 1805. A memorial was erected near the site of the Smith cabin. The obelisk ascends 38½ feet into the heavens—one foot for each year of the Prophet's life.

a pillar of strength and as a testimony to the world of the Restoration of the fulness of the gospel of Jesus Christ.

HUMBLE BEGINNINGS: BACKGROUND AND HERITAGE

The Prophet Joseph Smith was born into a family who possessed little of the world's goods but who maintained a rich and noble religious heritage. His father, Joseph Smith Sr., for whom he was named, and his mother, Lucy Mack Smith, were honest, God-fearing people who turned to the Lord for strength and raised their family to appeal to the Bible, rather than man, for knowledge of God. They believed that God could answer prayers by dreams. Both had their hearts prepared for the Restoration by dreams that revealed that the

day would come when they would be blessed with the true gospel of Jesus Christ, not found on earth at that time.

Joseph Sr. was a man of sincere faith. Although he did not associate with organized religion before the Restoration of the gospel, he was one of the first to be baptized the day that the Church of Christ was organized on April 6, 1830. He was called and ordained as the first Patriarch to the Church, in which calling he served to the day of his death. Lucy had dedicated herself to God as a young mother and defended the Restoration of the gospel to the end of her life. Though small in stature, she stood toe to toe with men and women of the day in zealously correcting any persons within her earshot that demeaned the divine calling of her son Joseph.

As a descendant of Abraham, Isaac, and Jacob, through Joseph, son of Jacob, and Joseph's son, Ephraim, Joseph

Joseph Smith Sr. and
Lucy Mack Smith.

Joseph Sr. and Lucy Mack Smith

The Prophet's father, Joseph Smith Sr., was tall, strong, energetic, and compassionate. The Prophet wrote that his father "was six feet, two inches high, was very straight, and remarkably well proportioned. His ordinary weight was about two hundred pounds, and he was very strong and active. In his younger days he was famed as a wrestler, and, Jacob-like, he never wrestled with but one man whom he could not throw. He was one of the most benevolent of men; opening his house to all who were destitute."[2] On another occasion the Prophet wrote that his father "was a great and good man. . . . He was of noble stature and possessed a high, and holy, and exalted and virtuous mind. . . . I now say that he never did a mean act, that might be said to be ungenerous in his life, to my knowledge."[3]

The Prophet's mother, Lucy Mack, was not quite five feet tall, as judged by her preserved clothing. A grandson assessed that "there never was a more earnest and social body . . . than Grandma Smith."[4] She was "possessed of a high sense of duty," a woman of action who "sometimes took weighty matters into her own hands and carried them through to successful completion."[5] The Prophet affirmed concerning his mother, "Blessed is my mother, for her soul is ever filled with benevolence and philanthropy."[6] The Prophet Joseph Smith recorded, "Words and language are inadequate to express the gratitude that I owe God for having given me so honorable a parentage."[7]

Smith came into mortality inheriting the covenanted promises that God made with his faithful forefathers. In America, Joseph's ancestors were from New England. Seven of them sailed to America on the *Mayflower*.[4] They were among those that Nephi saw in vision, whom the Spirit of God would inspire with courage and resolve to seek religious freedom (see 1 Nephi 13:13–14). Among his ancestors was the early colonist and religious reformer John Lothrop. John left his homeland of England because he could not agree with the state-run church. Upon coming to America, he served from 1635 to 1653 as pastor of the Congregational Church in Barnstable, Massachusetts. For the most part, the Prophet Joseph Smith's ancestors were known for their dedication to the Lord and for their integrity, often sacrificing for their religious convictions. They were also given to spiritual insight and promptings. His grandfather, Asael Smith, "predicted that there would be a prophet raised up in his family."[5] Asael later received the Book of Mormon with gladness and read it through before his death. He and his wife, Mary Duty Smith, believed that Joseph was the foretold prophet that would be their descendant.[6] Lucy's great-grandfather, John Mack, sailed from Scotland to America. Her father, Solomon, settled in Gilsum, New Hampshire, where she was born. The Smith and Mack families eventually moved to Vermont, and it was there that they formed a union through the marriage of Joseph Smith Sr. and Lucy Mack. Joseph and Lucy were blessed with eleven children, nine of whom lived to adulthood.[7]

As a young boy, Joseph lived in the New England states of Vermont, New Hampshire, and Massachusetts. In 1813, while living in West Lebanon, New Hampshire, typhus fever spread though the region. All of the Smith children were soon afflicted with this dreaded disease that threatened to take their lives. One day, when nearly recovered from typhus fever, Joseph, who was at the time a mere seven years old, "suddenly screamed out with a severe pain in his shoulder."[8] A doctor was called to the Smith home to examine a large fever sore between Joseph's left breast and shoulder. Upon lancing the sore, the pain "shot like lightning (as he said) down his side into the marrow of his leg bone on the same side"[9] (the tibia bone of his left leg). The leg began to swell and caused intense pain for three weeks before the doctor returned and made an eight-inch incision between the knee and the ankle, which alleviated the pain somewhat. The young boy became so weak that Lucy carried Joseph in her arms throughout the day, attempting to calm and comfort him until she, too, became unwell from exhaustion. At that time Lucy recorded, "Then Hyrum [thirteen years old], who was always remarkable for his tenderness and sympathy, desired that he might take my place. . . . We laid Joseph upon a low bed and Hyrum sat beside him, almost incessantly day and night, grasping the most painful part of the affected leg between his hands and, by pressing it closely, enabled the little sufferer the better to bear the pain which otherwise seemed almost ready to take his life."[10]

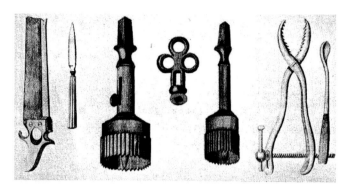

Drawing of surgical instruments.[9]

Eventually a team of doctors came to the Smith home and determined that Joseph's bone was so infected that to save his life it was necessary to amputate his leg. Mother Smith pled with the surgeons to make one more attempt to save Joseph's leg. They agreed to attempt to remove only the diseased portion of the bone and ordered that Joseph be bound to the bedstead for the painful operation. When the young boy refused to be restricted, the doctor insisted that he drink some wine to deaden his senses to the pain. Joseph again refused, but consented to be held in his father's arms while pieces of bone were broken loose with the medical tools of the day—trephines, or hand drills, and bone-grasping forceps.[11]

The surgery was successful and Joseph began to recover. His parents sent him to live in Salem, Massachusetts, with his uncle Jesse Smith, hoping the sea breezes might promote his health. Soon after returning home, Joseph and his family moved to the village of Norwich, Vermont, which lies a mere nine miles from Lebanon, New Hampshire, across the Connecticut River. They remained there for three years, each year suffering crop failure. The last year, 1816, was known in New England as "the year without summer," when snow fell in the second week of June and temperatures plunged below freezing.[12] It is apparent that Joseph Sr. and Lucy were prompted to move from their home to the area appointed by the Lord—Palmyra and Manchester, New York, near the Hill Cumorah. Here the angel Moroni had secured the ancient Nephite record, known today as the Book of Mormon, nearly fourteen centuries earlier. This land became the spiritual schooling ground for Joseph, the latter-day seer.

Joseph Smith's Heritage

Speaking of the Prophet Joseph Smith's heritage, President Brigham Young declared, "It was decreed in the counsels of eternity, long before the foundations of the earth were laid, that [Joseph Smith] should be the man, in the last dispensation of this world, to bring forth the word of God to the people, and receive the fulness of the keys and power of the Priesthood of the Son of God. The Lord had his eye upon him, and upon his father, and upon his father's father, and upon their progenitors clear back to Abraham, and from Abraham to the flood, from the flood to Enoch, and from Enoch to Adam. He has watched that family and that blood as it has circulated from its fountain to the birth of that man."[8]

PREPARATION OF A PROPHET

While living in the region of Palmyra, New York, Joseph matured physically, and his spiritual talents and deep desire to find truth were manifested. Physically, he grew in stature, reaching a height of over six feet. He also began to exercise the muscle of spiritual development that led to his profound understanding of the gospel of Jesus Christ. Under the Lord's tutelage the Prophet Joseph Smith gained a depth of gospel understanding that places him shoulder to shoulder with the greatest of the prophets. A key to understanding Joseph's keen gospel insight is that he was prepared for his mission before he was born and "reserved to come forth in the fulness of times to take part in laying the foundations of the great latter-day work" (D&C 138:53). President Joseph F. Smith saw in vision that he was "among the noble and great ones who were chosen in the beginning to be rulers in the Church of God . . . [and] received [his] first lessons in the world of spirits" in preparation for his mission on earth (D&C 138:55–56).

In the early 1800s, religious teachers targeted Palmyra, New York, and surrounding communities for spiritual renewal and revival. While yet a young teenage boy, Joseph sought to learn of God and the salvation that He offered His children. Joseph joined with those attending the various camp meetings, at which people of the area gathered to listen to preachers for days on end. At a joint revival meeting between the Baptists, Methodists, and Presbyterians, the question arose as to which Church the newly converted individuals should join. The only sect among the three with a meetinghouse in Palmyra was the Presbyterian church, and Reverend Stockton suggested that the new converts should be under his care.[13] Joseph's mother, his brothers Hyrum and Samuel, and his sister Sophronia, joined with the Presbyterians. On the other hand, Joseph wrote that "in process of time my mind became somewhat partial to the Methodist sect, and I felt some desire to be united with them; but so great were the confusion and strife among the different denominations, that it was impossible for a person young as I was, and so unacquainted with men and things, to come to any certain conclusion who was right and who was wrong"

(JS—H 1:8). Reverend Lane, a Methodist minister involved in the aforementioned revival, gave a sermon on the subject of "what church shall I join?" In that sermon Reverend Lane cited the text that Joseph recounted he later read, pondered, and reread—James 1:5, "If any of you lack wisdom, let him ask of God, that giveth to all men liberally, and upbraideth not; and it shall be given him."[14]

After much deliberation and reflection, Joseph determined to ask God. "I retired to a secret place in a grove," he explained, "and began to call upon the Lord; while fervently engaged in supplication, my mind was taken away from the objects with which I was surrounded, and I was enwrapped in a heavenly vision, and saw two glorious personages, who exactly resembled each other in features and likeness, surrounded with a brilliant light which eclipsed the sun at noon day. They told me that all religious denominations were believing in incorrect doctrines, and that none of them was acknowledged of God as His Church and kingdom."[15] In answer to his humble prayer, God the Father and His Son, Jesus Christ, taught Joseph face to face in open vision. When Joseph left the grove of trees near his home in Palmyra, New York, even though he was but a lad of fourteen years, he knew

Palmyra, New York. Restoration of Joseph Smith Sr. log home, where young Joseph lived at the time of the religious revivals, the First Vision, and the angel Moroni's visits. As a young boy, Joseph retired to a grove of trees near his home in Palmyra, New York. Today this wooded area behind the Smith log home is referred as the Sacred Grove.

Religious Revivals of the Early 1800s

Joseph wrote that "there was in the place where we lived an unusual excitement on the subject of religion" (JS—H 1:5). It is likely that the young Joseph attended camp meetings promoted by Methodists to spread their faith. "These meetings were usually held on the edge of a grove of trees or in a small clearing in the midst of a forest. After traveling many miles along dusty or water-logged roads, the settlers would locate their wagons and pitch their tents on the outskirts of the encampment. Farmers' markets and grog or liquor shops often sprang up near the camp grounds, thereby providing some farmers with unusual economic opportunities. The meetings frequently continued for several days, and sometimes one session would last nearly all day and into the night. Ministers would rotate preaching assignments so that one minister would immediately be followed by another, and at times two or three ministers would preach simultaneously in different parts of the camp ground. Itinerants not only preached lengthy sermons but devoted much of their time to counseling and to directing prayer circles and group singing."[10]

Joseph's account seems to describe a similar series of meetings in which the clergy promoted "this extraordinary scene of religious feeling, in order to have everybody converted" (JS—H 1:6). It was not uncommon for there to be enthusiastic and emotional demonstrations, including falling to the ground and crying out for mercy. Years later Joseph told a group in Nauvoo that at one of the revival meetings, his mother, brother, and sisters got religion. "He wanted to get Religion too, wanted to feel and shout like the rest but could feel nothing."[11]

more concerning God and His designs for mankind than any other mortal then on earth.

Three years later, when Joseph was seventeen years old, the angel Moroni appeared to him, and during the next four years mentored Joseph in preparation for translating the plates containing the Book of Mormon. During those times of instruction, Moroni informed Joseph concerning the Restoration of the gospel. In addition, President John Taylor explained that the Prophet Joseph Smith was in communication "with the ancient apostles and prophets; such men, for instance, as Abraham, Isaac, Jacob, Noah, Adam, Seth, Enoch, and Jesus and the Father, and the apostles that lived on this [the American] continent, as well as those that lived on the Asiatic continent. He seemed as familiar with these people as we are with one another. Why? Because he had to introduce a dispensation which was called the dispensation of the fulness of times, and it was known as such by the ancient servants of God."[16]

During his life, the Prophet had many moments of instruction from on high. One of the most poignant occurred when he first went to the Hill Cumorah and saw the Book of Mormon plates. After locating the spot where the plates were buried, he found a stick that could act as a lever to lift the stone lid of the enclosure. After opening it, he reached in the stone box that held the plates to remove them, when, to his surprise, he received a violent shock. He made a second attempt but was shaken more forcibly than before. He made a third attempt and failed once more, at which he audibly exclaimed, "Why can I not obtain this book?" To his amazement a voice answered, "Because you have not kept the commandments of the Lord."

The angel Moroni stood before him, and the angel's instructions from the previous night were vividly brought to his mind. He recalled that he had been unfaithful to the angelic charge that he was to have no other object in mind for obtaining the plates than to glorify God. Yet, as he had traveled to and ascended the Hill Cumorah, he had allowed his mind and heart to muse on the possible monetary value of gold plates for himself and his family. This resulted in a lesson that Joseph never forgot.

"At that instant he looked to the Lord in prayer, and as he prayed darkness began to disperse from his mind and his soul was lit up as it was the evening before, and he was filled with the Holy Spirit; and again did the Lord manifest his condescension and mercy: the heavens were opened and the glory of the Lord shone round about and rested upon him. While he thus stood gazing and admiring, the angel said, 'Look!' and as he thus spake [Joseph] beheld the prince of darkness, surrounded by his innumerable train of associates. All this passed before him, and the heavenly messenger said,

Restored upstairs bedroom of the Smith log home in Palmyra, New York, where Joseph would have slept at the time that the angel Moroni called him to prepare to receive the Book of Mormon plates.

'All this is shown, the good and the evil, the holy and impure, the glory of God and the power of darkness, that you may know hereafter the two powers and never be influenced or overcome by that wicked one.' "[17]

Joseph's training and growth continued as the Lord had foreseen and had wisely prepared means to teach the youthful Prophet. While the Prophet and his wife, Emma, lived in Harmony, Pennsylvania, during the early days of translating the Book of Mormon plates, Martin Harris, a friend and neighbor in Palmyra, New York, aided Joseph as his scribe. At the insistence of his wife, Martin asked to take the first 116 handwritten pages of translation back to Palmyra. Upon inquiring of the Lord about Martin's request, Joseph was warned not to allow Martin to take the translation. Nevertheless, Martin would not accept that answer, and he persuaded Joseph to inquire of the Lord again and again. In the end, Joseph allowed Martin to take the manuscript to his home in Palmyra, New York. Sadly, although Martin made a solemn covenant and signed a written agreement to show the translation to only a few close family members, he broke that promise and eventually wicked men stole the translation.

Joseph had feared man more than he had feared God, and, as a result, he lost the translation.

The Lord chastened the young Prophet by taking the plates, breastplate, and Urim and Thummim from him. The angel Moroni appeared to Joseph and advised him, "If you are very humble and penitent, it may be you will receive them again; if so, it will be on the twenty-second of next September."[18] Joseph lost the power to translate and was left to himself to determine the depth of his dedication

The Book of Mormon plates were buried near the crest of the hill on the west side of the Hill Cumorah.

to the will of God, regardless of the persuasions of others. Fortunately, Joseph learned his lesson well, never again placing the will of man above the Lord's will. From that time forward Joseph trusted in the Lord's counsel. In addition, Joseph learned that the Lord's wisdom was greater than the cunning of the devil and his servants who were seeking to destroy God's work in bringing forth knowledge of the Savior through the testimony of the Book of Mormon (see D&C 10).

The Lord sent Joseph another scribe after the incident with Martin Harris. A young man by the name of Oliver Cowdery learned of Joseph's work to bring forth the ancient record of the Nephite nation while he was teaching school in the Palmyra, New York, area. At the end of the school year, he traveled to Harmony, Pennsylvania, to meet Joseph and immediately became a scribe for the translation. He continued to aid in this work until the publication of the Book of Mormon in March 1830. Another significant aspect of Joseph's preparation and mission was that of receiving priesthood authority under the hands of heavenly messengers. It became evident in the translation of the Book of Mormon that baptism by the proper authority, which had been lost in the Apostasy, was essential to perform ordinances recognized by God (see 3 Nephi 11:21–12:2).

On May 15, 1829, Joseph and Oliver retired to a wooded area near the Susquehanna River to pray for understanding. The veil was parted and an angel introducing himself as John (known as John the Baptist in the New Testament) conferred upon them the authority and keys of the Aaronic Priesthood. He laid his hands upon their heads and declared, "Upon you my fellow servants, in the name of Messiah, I confer the Priesthood of Aaron, which holds the keys of . . . baptism by immersion for the remission of sins" (JS—H 1:69; D&C 13:1). Soon afterward, Peter, James, and John, chief Apostles during the Savior's earthly ministry, appeared to Joseph and Oliver, conferring upon them the Melchizedek Priesthood and the necessary authority to build up the kingdom of God on earth. This included the right to confer the gift of the Holy Ghost by the laying on of hands, as administered anciently. With the priesthood restored, Joseph was prepared

and authorized to organize the true Church of Christ on the earth once again.

FIRST ELDER AND PRESIDENT OF THE CHURCH OF CHRIST

On the day that the Church of Christ was organized, April 6, 1830, Joseph was set apart for the work that would continue the remainder of his life. Those gathered in Fayette, New York, at the Peter Whitmer Sr. home, sustained Joseph as the First Elder of the Church. On that day the Lord called Joseph to be a prophet, seer, revelator, translator, and Apostle of Jesus Christ (see D&C 21:1). The Savior also instructed Church members: "Thou shalt give heed unto all his words and commandments which he shall give unto you . . . for his word ye shall receive, as if from mine own mouth" (D&C 21:4–5). At that time Joseph was twenty-four years old. The newly restored Church grew rapidly, and less than two years later the Lord revealed that Joseph should be ordained presiding high priest and President of the Church of Christ.[19] He served as the presiding priesthood leader of the Church until his death on June 27, 1844, at the age of thirty-eight. Thus, he was younger at his death than any of the subsequent Presidents at the time they were first set apart to preside over the Church. The fact that he was able to accomplish so much of the Lord's work in such a short time at a relatively young age stands as a witness of divine intervention in his life.

The Lord revealed through the Prophet Joseph Smith more scripture than by any other individual in recorded history. Each of the standard works of the Church has come to us through him. The first book of scripture to come forth through Joseph was the Book of Mormon, another testament of Jesus Christ. During translation of the Book of Mormon and thereafter, many revelations were given directing the Lord's work, including revelations pertaining to the organization and governing of the restored Church of Christ on earth. Many of these revelations are published in the Doctrine and Covenants. The Lord also directed Joseph to make an inspired translation of the Bible. Many plain and precious truths taken from this sacred volume were restored and clarified in the prophet's translation. Excerpts from the

Joseph married Emma Hale on January 18, 1827.

inspired Bible translation of Genesis are published as the book of Moses in the Pearl of Great Price. Joseph also translated writings of Abraham from scrolls purchased in a collection of mummies and papyri and published them as the Book of Abraham. Excerpts from the *History of the Church* have been printed as Joseph Smith—History and the Articles of Faith, also in the Pearl of Great Price. Through the Prophet Joseph Smith, the Lord laid a firm scriptural foundation upon which later Presidents of the Church have built.

As the head of the dispensation of the fulness of times, Joseph organized the Church of Christ and revealed and set in place the responsibilities of various priesthood offices—apostles, bishops, patriarchs, seventies, high priests, elders, priests, teachers, and deacons. He also directed the work of spreading the gospel through the eastern United States and Upper Canada. He commissioned missionaries to travel to the British Isles proclaiming that the fulness of the gospel was once again on the earth. Toward the end of his life, he dedicated time to instructing the Saints concerning the necessity of building temples wherein sacred ordinances of the gospel could be performed.

MARRIAGE AND FAMILY

Joseph met his future bride while looking for treasure of another sort. In 1825, Joseph and his father accepted employment from Josiah Stowell of South Bainbridge, New York. The Smith family were enduring some financial difficulties and welcomed the opportunity for extra income to help pay for the annual mortgage on their farm. Mr. Stowell had heard rumors that Joseph "possessed certain means by which he could discern things invisible to the natural eye,"[20] and he hoped that, in addition to muscle and hard work, Joseph might be able to aid him in finding an abandoned Spanish silver mine that was thought to be in the area. Joseph labored for two weeks in the Onaquago Mountains near Harmony, Pennsylvania, and then, after discouraging Mr. Stowell from continuing to search for the mine, remained to work on his farm. During this time Joseph and the other hired hands boarded at the Isaac Hale farm in Harmony, Pennsylvania. Although he was not able to help Josiah Stowell in his quest for silver, Joseph did discover a treasure of his own—Emma Hale, Isaac's daughter. Joseph found a helpmeet who would stand by his side through the joys and sorrows of life.

Sadly, the Hales opposed their daughter's relationship with Joseph. Thus, it was against their wishes that the beautiful, dark-eyed, and determined young woman with a rich soprano voice became Joseph's bride on January 18, 1827. On the other hand, Joseph's parents were much more accepting of Emma. Joseph told them "he thought that no young woman that he ever was acquainted with was better calculated to render the man of her choice happy than Miss Emma Hale, a young lady whom he had been extremely fond of since his first introduction to her. His father was highly pleased with Joseph's choice, and told him that he was not only willing that he should marry her but desired him to bring her home with him, that we might have the pleasure of her society."[21]

The newlyweds first lived with Joseph's parents in Manchester, New York, and later moved back near Emma's parents in Harmony, Pennsylvania. It was while living in Harmony that Emma joyfully announced she was expecting their first child. Unfortunately, once born the child lived only three short hours. Emma remained so ill afterward that it appeared that she would join her child in death before she began to recover. Joseph attentively cared for his sweetheart for the space of two weeks, scarcely sleeping. They would face such difficulties many times during their life together. In 1831, near Kirtland, Ohio, while living in a log home on the Isaac Morley farm, Emma gave birth to twins who died that same day. Near that time, Joseph and Emma adopted twins, a little girl and a little boy, named Julia and Joseph, whose mother died in childbirth. The small family moved from Kirtland to live with John and Elsa Johnson in Hiram, Ohio. By the end of March 1832, they had placed little Joseph in a cold grave. Later, while living in Nauvoo, Illinois, Joseph and Emma

Harmony, Pennsylvania, site of Joseph and Emma's home, where their first child was born and much of the translation of the Book of Mormon was accomplished.

The Family of Joseph and Emma Smith

Alvin (June 15, 1828)

Thaddeus (April 30, 1831)

Louisa (April 30, 1831)

Joseph Murdock (April 30, 1831–March 29, 1832; adopted)

Julia Murdock (April 30, 1831–September 12, 1880; adopted)

Joseph III (November 6, 1832–December 10, 1914)

Frederick Granger Williams (June 20, 1836–April 13, 1862)

Alexander Hale (June 2, 1838–August 12, 1909)

Don Carlos (June 13, 1840–September 15, 1841)

Stillborn son (February 6 or 7, 1842)[14]

David Hyrum (November 17, 1844–August 29, 1904)

A Caring Husband

Joseph was a caring and attentive husband. Jesse W. Crosby related:

"Some of the home habits of the Prophet—such as building kitchen fires, carrying out ashes, carrying wood and water, assisting in the care of the children, etc.—were not in accord with my idea of a great man's self-respect. . . . [on an occasion when Joseph returned a sack of flour he had borrowed] I reminded him of every phase of his greatness and called to his mind the multitude of tasks he performed that were too menial for such as he; to fetch and carry flour was too great a humiliation. . . . The Prophet listened quietly to all that I had to say, then made his answer in these words: 'If there be humiliation in a man's house, who of that house but the head should or could bear such humiliation?'

"Sister Crosby was a very hardworking woman, taking much more responsibility in her home than most women take. Thinking to give the Prophet some light on home management, I said to him, 'Brother Joseph, my wife does much more hard work than does your wife.'

"Brother Joseph replied by telling me that if a man cannot learn in this life to appreciate a wife and do his duty by her, in properly taking care of her, he need not expect to be given [her] in the hereafter."[15]

buried two more children. A baby boy, Don Carlos, died in 1841, a few months after his first birthday, and a stillborn son was buried less than five months later.

Tribulation and separation challenged Joseph and his family, but it also brought them closer together in love. While on Church business in New York City, Joseph wrote to Emma, "I returned to my room to meditate and calm my mind and behold the thoughts of home of Emma and Julia rushes upon my mind like a flood and I could wish for a moment to be with them. My breast is filled with all the feelings and tenderness of a parent and a husband."[22]

Six years later, while being held unjustly in jail at Liberty, Missouri, Joseph wrote, "Tell little Joseph, he must be a good boy, Father loves him with a perfect love. He is the eldest [and] must not hurt those that [are] smaller than him, but comfort them. Tell little Frederick, Father loves him with all his heart. He is a lovely boy. Julia is a lovely little girl. I love her also. She is a promising child. Tell her, Father wants her to remember him and be a good girl. Tell all the rest that I think of them and pray for them all. . . . Little Alexander is on my mind continually. Oh, my affectionate Emma, I want

you to remember that I am [a] true and faithful friend, to you and the children forever. My heart is intertwined around yours forever and ever. Oh, may God bless you all."[23]

It must have been with great joy that Joseph learned that family relationships could be eternal, if sealed by priesthood ordinances and the Holy Spirit of Promise. Joseph and Emma were sealed for eternity by the authority of the priesthood on May 28, 1843.

MISSION

Although the entire life of the Prophet Joseph Smith may be considered a mission, it appears he served only one full-time proselyting mission, which lasted for one month. The area of his service was Upper Canada. He left his home in Kirtland, Ohio, on October 5, 1833. He traveled a little over three hundred miles to reach the area of Mount Pleasant, Ontario, Canada, on October 18. He had two companions in his journey and work, Elders Sidney Rigdon and Freeman Nickerson. Like many missionaries today, the Prophet missed and worried about his family during his absence.[24] During his journey the Lord revealed to the missionaries, "Your families are well; they are in mine hands" (D&C 100:1). The Prophet

Joseph's Family

"Joseph enjoyed his family. There are dozens of references in his official diary that read like this one of March 27, 1834: 'Remained at home and had great joy with my family.' Indeed, according to a distant cousin, George A. Smith, one convert family apostatized because, when they arrived in Kirtland from the East, Joseph came downstairs from the room where he had been translating 'by the gift and power of God' and began to romp and play with his children.[16] In their view, this was not proper behavior for a prophet! The Prophet's journal mentions going with his family to musical concerts, the theater, circus performances, and taking excursions on Mississippi River boats."[17]

experienced both the highs and lows of missionary work. He recorded that on the journey some doors were opened to the elders, where the inhabitants received their testimony with joy, and they reasoned with others "but to no effect."[25] He noted that in Mount Pleasant "the people were very tender and inquiring."[26] He recorded with joy that on Sunday, October 27, 1833, he baptized twelve new members of the Church, and the next day two more were baptized.[27] The time came all too quickly for Joseph to return, and he arrived home in Kirtland, Ohio, on November 4, 1833.

This missionary experience left Joseph Smith with a special love for the Saints in Mount Pleasant, Canada. "I remember Brother Freeman and wife," he later wrote to them, "Ransom also, and Sister Lydia, and little Charles, with all the brethren and sisters. I entreat for an interest in all your prayers before the throne of mercy, in the name of Jesus. I hope the Lord will grant that I may see you all again, and above all that we may overcome, and sit down together in the kingdom of our Father."[28]

A MAN FOR ALL SEASONS

Prophets are real people with interests and passions who often love to engage in social activities. "Joseph Smith favored music, drama, debating, hiking, boating, athletics, and parties, dancing, and picnics. He liked to go for long walks, horseback riding, and to get out into the beauty of nature."[29] He described himself as possessing a "native cheery temperament" (JS—H 1:28). He understood his holy calling as the Lord's mouthpiece on earth, yet he did not ascribe to sanctimonious piety. For example, his journal entry for February 8, 1843, reads, "This morning I read German, and visited with a brother and sister from Michigan, who thought that 'a prophet is always a prophet;' but I told them that a prophet was a prophet only when he was acting as such. After dinner Brother Parley P. Pratt came in: we had conversation on various subjects. At four in the afternoon, I went out with my little [son] Frederick, to exercise myself by sliding on the ice."[30]

The Prophet Joseph Smith enjoyed physical labor and athletics. "It was not uncommon to see him involved in sports activities with the young and vigorous men of a

Playing with the Children

One associate shared, "At that time Joseph was studying Greek and Latin, and when he got tired studying he would go and play with the children in their games about the house, to give himself exercise. Then he would go back to his studies as before. . . .

"He was preaching once, and he said it tried some of the pious folks to see him play ball with the boys. He then related a story of a certain prophet who was sitting under the shade of a tree amusing himself in some way, when a hunter came along with his bow and arrow, and reproved him. The prophet asked him if he kept his bow strung up all the time. The hunter answered that he did not. The prophet asked why, and he said it would lose its elasticity if he did. The prophet said it was just so with his mind, he did not want it strung up all the time."[18]

community. He is known to have wrestled, pulled sticks, engaged in snowball fights, played ball, slid on the ice with his children, played marbles, shot at a mark, and fished."[31] On February 20, 1843, he oversaw about seventy brethren who "sawed, chopped, split, moved, and piled up a large lot of wood in [his] yard. The day was spent by them with much pleasantry, good humor and feeling."[32] The wood warmed not only the Prophet and his family, but also those many individuals and families that applied for help at his home.

Joseph knew that recreational activities can be wholesome and refreshing even to a prophet. Joseph was a true prophet of God and did not try to fit into the mold of sectarian sternness cast for supposed men of God. He taught by example that tenderness and joy in living are part of a righteous life.

FAITHFUL IN PERSECUTION

A man often reveals the innermost core of his soul when placed in difficult circumstances. Joseph's heritage as the servant of the Lord was to be opposed by wicked or self-righteous individuals and mobs at every turn. As a young man, age seventeen years, the angel Moroni warned Joseph that his "name would be had for good and evil among all nations, kindreds, and tongues, or that it should be both good and evil spoken of among all people" (JS—H 1:33). Later Joseph would record, persecution "has been my common lot all the days of my life" (D&C 127:2). Joseph related that as a young man he soon discovered that his testimony "excited a great deal of prejudice . . . among the professors of religion" (JS—H 1:22). Over his lifetime he truly learned firsthand the Savior's admonition: "Rejoice, and be exceedingly glad: for great is your reward in heaven: for so persecuted they the prophets which were before you" (Matthew 5:12).

Joseph endured well in tribulation and became purified like gold in the refiner's fire. Throughout his life he had to endure numerous trumped-up lawsuits and slanderous lies. When the minions of evil resorted to physical violence, he wept for those who were his associates in persecution and his prayers ascended to heaven in their behalf. He stood above the hatred and malice that were strewn in his path. Among the many occasions when Joseph was bitterly opposed is that of the evening of Saturday, March 24, 1832, while Joseph and Emma lived in Hiram, Ohio, with John and Elsa Johnson. That evening Joseph and Emma had been taking turns caring for the twin babies that they had adopted from John Murdock when his wife, Julia, died in childbirth. The children were seriously ill with the measles. Emma had nursed the babies, and Joseph was asleep in the trundle bed with the little boy. A mob of men

Hiram, Ohio, home of John and Elsa Johnson. Joseph and Emma lived with the Johnsons September 1831–September 1832. A mob dragged Joseph from his bedroom on the lower left of the photograph, tarring and placing feathers on his body.

from the community broke into the room, dragging Joseph out into the darkness of the night. They choked him nearly unconscious, beat him, applied tar and feathers to his stripped body, and left him. After he had recovered sufficiently to return to the house, the night was spent scraping and removing the tar and washing his body that he might be clothed. The next morning, being the Sabbath, Joseph spoke to those who had gathered for worship, including some who had been in the mob the night before. "With my flesh all scarified and defaced," he recorded, "I preached to the congregation as usual, and in the afternoon of the same day baptized three individuals."[33]

He sorrowed over the injuries suffered by his friend and companion, Sidney Rigdon, during the attack that same evening. The mob had dragged Elder Rigdon by his heels, causing his head to be severely lacerated by the ground and leaving him in a state of delirium. Possibly even more difficult for the Prophet was that his newly adopted infant son, already sick with the measles, caught cold in the chilly evening draft and confusion, and died the following Friday. Yet, three days after the boy's death, in obedience to a previous commandment, Joseph and a group of Church leaders left to meet with the Saints in Jackson County, Missouri (see D&C 78:8–10). He was deeply committed to following the Lord's commands, finding strength in opposition.

Joseph was humbly courageous even in the midst of severe persecution. In the autumn of 1838, Joseph was living in Far West, Missouri, which was the place that the Lord had appointed for the Saints to gather after they had been driven from Jackson County, Missouri, and northeastern Ohio. Many Missourians hated the Saints at that time. Tensions escalated to a boiling point when, under the command of the Missouri Governor, Lilburn W. Boggs, the state militia had been ordered to drive the Mormons from the state or exterminate them. When Joseph met with militia leaders to discuss terms of a peaceful resolution to the problems, he and his companions were placed under arrest and taken to jail, first in Richmond and then Liberty, Missouri. While held as a prisoner at Richmond, Joseph lay in chains on the floor. Some of the men commenced in braggadocio fashion to tell of their exploits against the Mormons. Elder Parley P. Pratt, who was also imprisoned with the Prophet, related:

Liberty Jail. (Inset with painting *Joseph in Liberty Jail*.) The Prophet Joseph Smith was unjustly imprisoned in the jail at Liberty, Missouri, for a little over four months from November 30, 1838, until April 6, 1839. While held here, he penned a letter to the Saints who had escaped to the banks of the Mississippi River following Governor Lilburn W. Boggs's extermination order against the Mormons.

"In one of those tedious nights we had lain as if in sleep till the hour of midnight had passed, and our ears and hearts had been pained, while we had listened for hours to the obscene jests, the horrid oaths, the dreadful blasphemies and filthy language of our guards, Colonel Price at their head, as they recounted to each other their deeds of rapine, murder, robbery, etc., which they had committed among the 'Mormons' while at Far West and vicinity. They even boasted of defiling by force wives, daughters, and virgins, and of shooting or dashing out the brains of men, women and children.

"I had listened till I became so disgusted, shocked, horrified, and so filled with the spirit of indignant justice that I could scarcely refrain from rising upon my feet and rebuking the guards; but had said nothing to Joseph, or any one else, although I lay next to him and knew he was awake. On a sudden he arose to his feet, and spoke in a voice of thunder, or as the roaring lion, uttering, as near as I can recollect, the following words:

"'SILENCE, *you fiends of the infernal pit. In the name of Jesus Christ I rebuke you, and command you to be still. I will not live another minute and bear such language. Cease such talk, or you or I die* THIS INSTANT!'

"He ceased to speak. He stood erect in terrible majesty. Chained, and without a weapon; calm, unruffled and dignified as an angel, he looked upon the quailing guards, whose weapons were lowered or dropped to the ground; whose knees smote together, and who, shrinking into a corner, or crouching at his feet, begged his pardon, and remained quiet till a change of guards."[34]

Of all the trials that shaped and purified the Prophet, those at the jail in Liberty, Missouri, stand above the rest. From December 1, 1838, until April 6, 1839, Joseph and his companions were held prisoners in the most depraved of circumstances. They were incarcerated in a wooded prison-pit that allowed very little light or warmth to penetrate its walls. The sentence of death was passed upon them by the mob-like Missouri militia leaders. They awaited their day in court while the correspondence the prisoners received concerning the Saints reported the destitute situations of family and friends being driven from the state "under the most damning hand of murder, tyranny, and oppression" (D&C 123:7). It was by the hands of apostates, those that had partaken of spiritual refreshment with Joseph, that these dire circumstances had befallen the Saints. Apparently, it was only with great effort that the Prophet was able to purify his heart of ill feelings toward his enemies.

While in Liberty Jail, Joseph penned a letter to the Saints that stands as a monument to his prophetic inspiration; it comprises Doctrine and Covenants 121–23. The light from heaven found in the letter refused to fight its way through the darkness until Joseph rid his soul of impurities. Letters from Emma and other Saints encouraged the Prophet's heart and opened the door to let out whatever pent-up feelings might have yet been harbored in his soul. He wrote that one token of friendship can work so that "all enmity, malice, and hatred, and past differences, misunderstandings and mismanagements are slain victorious at the feet of hope; and when the heart is sufficiently contrite, then the voice of inspiration steals along and whispers, My son, peace be to thy soul; thine adversity and thine afflictions shall be but a moment; and if thou endure it well, God shall exalt thee on high."[35]

The lessons of forgiveness and love learned in Liberty Jail continued to guide the Prophet until his death. Joseph was a different man when he left Liberty. He was a good man before that time, but there was something more refined and tender about him after that experience. It was not just the freedom from the confinement of the prison walls that influenced his life, but rather, the triumph of the heart to love and forgive his persecutors.

MARTYRDOM OF THE PROPHET

On June 27, 1844, Joseph "sealed his mission and his works with his own blood" (D&C 135:3). Some time before the fateful day that he and his brother Hyrum were shot and killed by a mob in Carthage, Illinois, he had premonitions that he would be taken. "We were in council with Brother Joseph almost every day for weeks," related Elder Orson Hyde of the original Quorum of the Twelve Apostles.

"Says Brother Joseph in one of those councils, there is something going to happen; I don't know what it is, but the Lord bids me to hasten and give you your endowment before the temple is finished. He conducted us through every ordinance of the holy priesthood, and when he had gone through with all the ordinances he rejoiced very much, and says, now if they kill me you have got all the keys and all the ordinances and you can confer them upon others, and the hosts of Satan will not be able to tear down the kingdom, as fast as you will be able to build it up."[36]

Joseph and Hyrum were ordered to report to Carthage, Illinois, to answer to charges from apostates and enemies of the Church that they had illegally directed the destruction of a newspaper press. Accompanied by seventeen friends, they surrendered themselves to a constable for trial and were subsequently placed in the jail at Carthage, which was contrary to the law. Thomas Ford, governor of Illinois, promised to protect them, but he left for Nauvoo and charged their enemies, the Carthage Greys, to guard them. John Taylor reported, "When Joseph went to Carthage to deliver himself up to the pretended requirements of the law, two or three days previous to his assassination, he said, 'I am going like a lamb to the slaughter; but I am calm as a summer's morning; I have

A Forgiving Heart

One of the causes for the incarceration of Joseph and his companions in Liberty Jail was the betrayal and apostasy of William W. Phelps, a former close associate and member of the Far West Stake presidency. Brother Phelps became one of the Prophet's most bitter enemies, testifying against him when Joseph was held as a prisoner in Richmond, Missouri.

Later, Mr. Phelps felt the prodigal and desired to return to fellowship with the Saints settled in Nauvoo, Illinois. To this end he wrote to the Prophet requesting forgiveness. Joseph's response was filled with compassion and mercy. He acknowledged that Phelps had contributed to the bitter cup he drank during those dark months in prison and that he added to the sorrow of the Saints being driven from their homes. However, like Joseph, who was sold into Egypt by his brothers, the Prophet extended the hand of friendship to his repentant brother and took joy in his return. He closed his reply to Phelps, "Believing your confession to be real, and your repentance genuine, I shall be happy once again to give you the right hand of fellowship, and rejoice over the returning prodigal. Your letter was written to the Saints last Sunday and an expression of their feeling was taken, when it was unanimously resolved, that W. W. Phelps should be received into fellowship. 'Come on, dear brother, since the war is past, For friends at first, are friends again at last.' Yours as ever, Joseph Smith, Jun."[19]

The jail at Carthage, Illinois, where Joseph and his brother Hyrum were martyred June 27, 1844.

a conscience void of offense towards God, and towards all men. I SHALL DIE INNOCENT, AND IT SHALL BE SAID OF ME—HE WAS MURDERED IN COLD BLOOD'" (D&C 135:4).

The afternoon was sultry as Joseph, Hyrum, and their companions, John Taylor and Willard Richards, stayed in the jailor's personal upstairs bedroom for their comfort. Joseph requested John Taylor to sing one of the Prophet's favorite songs, "A Poor Wayfaring Man of Grief." Given the circumstances of that moment, the song was aptly and poignantly meaningful. The song relates the attempts of an individual to help a suffering stranger, who after asking for the ultimate sacrifice, that being if the provider would die in the unjustly condemned stranger's place, reveals himself as the Savior. About 5:20 PM, Thursday, June 27, an armed mob of men with blackened faces surrounded the jail, a few rushing inside and up the stairs. In a matter of moments they forced the door to the bedroom, firing a ball that entered through the door into the face of Hyrum and killing him. Joseph, seeing that John Taylor lay severely wounded after attempting to escape through a window, turned and leaped through the same window. He "was shot dead in the attempt, exclaiming: *O*

Lord my God! Joseph and Hyrum were both shot after they were dead, in a brutal manner, and both received four balls" (D&C 135:1).

The life of one of the greatest of all prophets had come to an end. He lived faithfully to the finish of his mission. "Many have marveled because of his death," revealed the Lord, "but it was needful that he should seal his testimony with his blood, that he might be honored and the wicked might be condemned" (D&C 136:39). "I used to have peculiar feelings about his death," reflected Elder Wilford Woodruff, "and the way in which his life was taken. I felt that if, with the consent and good feelings of the brethren that waited on him after he crossed the river to leave Nauvoo, Joseph could have had his desire, he would have pioneered the way to the Rocky Mountains. But since then I have been fully reconciled to the fact that it was according to the programme, that it was required of him, as the head of this dispensation, that he should seal his testimony with his blood, and go hence to the spirit world, holding the keys of this dispensation, to open up the mission that is now being performed by way of preaching the gospel to the 'spirits in prison.'"[37]

TEACHINGS OF PRESIDENT
JOSEPH SMITH

Because of the gradual restoration of gospel principles, the teachings of the Prophet Joseph Smith were developmental in nature. That is, he received heavenly born truths line upon line, unfolding the panorama of the plan of salvation and restoring the house of Israel to knowledge of the true Messiah. Joseph testified that the canon of scripture is not closed and that God speaks once again to prophets as He had done anciently. As the seer chosen to restore the gospel to the earth, the Prophet Joseph Smith spoke and wrote on a multitude of topics. The foundational principles for every truth that we have received in the Restoration of the gospel came through the Prophet Joseph Smith. That which follows is but a brief summary of a few of his teachings.

THE GODHEAD

It was the mission of the Prophet Joseph Smith to reintroduce the world to the true and living God. During the Apostasy, knowledge of God's correct nature had been lost in an array of false beliefs, most teaching that Deity was without body, parts, or passions. All biblical references to man being created in God's image or to God's fatherhood were taught to be mythical and symbolic terms to explain the unexplainable. In the spring of 1820, as a simple boy walking from the grove of trees near his home, the Prophet Joseph Smith knew that the sectarian God of Christianity was an apostate myth espoused in creeds of uninspired men and that the true God is an actual living being (see JS—H 1:17–19). Joseph later taught, "That which is without body, parts and passions is nothing. There is no other God in heaven but that God who has flesh and bones."[38] Indeed, the first authoritative declaration that Joseph made concerning religion was that God the

Father is a real being, who hears and answers prayers. For this simple teaching he was accosted, possibly by the very individual who had a few days previous exhorted those at the religious revivals to seek God in prayer. Following his first vision, Joseph reported, "I happened to be in company with one of the Methodist preachers, who was very active in the before mentioned religious excitement; and, conversing with him on the subject of religion, I took occasion to give him an account of the vision which I had had. I was greatly surprised at his behavior; he treated my communication not only lightly, but with great contempt, saying it was all of the devil, that there were no such things as visions or revelations in these days; that all such things had ceased with the apostles" (JS—H 1:21). Each truth revealed through the Prophet met with opposition, but like the fearless seers who had preceded him, Joseph courageously put forth to a corrupt world the

The Prophet Joseph Smith conversed with God the Father and His Son, Jesus Christ, in what is referred to as the First Vision.

truths communicated to him by the voice of God, angels, visions, and inspiration by the power of the Holy Ghost.

Joseph was a witness that God the Father and His Son, Jesus Christ, are two distinct beings with bodies, in whose image we are created. Although we do not have record of all that Joseph was taught during the appearance of the Father and the Son in the spring of 1820, Joseph later intimated that he also learned of the distinct nature of the Holy Ghost at that time. "Any person that had seen the heavens opened," he explained, "knows that there are three personages in the heavens who hold the keys of power, and one presides over all."[39]

Joseph continued to reveal the nature of God the Father to those he taught. During his last general conference of the Church at Nauvoo, Illinois, in April 1844, he delivered what has become known as the "King Follett Discourse." In many respects it is the climatic point of Joseph's teachings regarding Deity. He explained: "God himself was once as we are now, and is an exalted man, and sits enthroned in yonder heavens! That is the great secret. If the veil were rent today, and the great God who holds this world in its orbit, and who upholds all worlds and all things by his power, was to make himself visible,—I say, if you were to see him today, you would see him like a man in form—like yourselves in all the person, image, and very form as a man. . . . It is the first principle of the Gospel to know for a certainty the Character of God, and to know that we may converse with him as one man converses with another, and that he was once a man like us; yea, that God himself, the Father of us all, dwelt on an earth, the same as Jesus Christ himself did."[40] Thus, Joseph taught that the Father is an exalted "Man of Holiness" (Moses 6:57).

TESTIMONY OF JESUS CHRIST

The Prophet Joseph Smith is *the* special witness of Christ for the dispensation of the fulness of times. He knew more about the Lord Jesus Christ than any other mortal being living on the earth. Joseph taught that Christ presides over this earth under the direction of the Father. He testified that Jesus Christ truly lives and is not an absentee master. The Prophet's initial special witness came from the answer to his humble boyhood prayer in a grove of trees near the Smith log home in Palmyra, New York. Joseph testified, "I saw two Personages, whose brightness and glory defy all description, standing above me in the air. One of them spake unto me, calling me by name and said, pointing to the other—*This is My Beloved Son. Hear Him*" (JS—H 1:17). From that early moment of heavenly revelation, Joseph taught that Jesus Christ was appointed and commissioned by the Father to represent Him.

Joseph removed the mists of darkness shrouding the mystery of the Lord Jesus Christ's nature as Father and Son. The Prophet taught that previous to His birth in Palestine, Jesus was known as Jehovah to prophets and peoples of Old Testament times. As the God of Israel, He appeared to them as a premortal spirit being. He was known as the Father because the Father had given His firstborn spirit son, Jehovah, of His fulness. Further, Jesus was known as the Father of heaven and earth due to His work as the creator. He became the Son because He was born into mortality as the literal Son of God in the flesh (see D&C 93:4). It was as a mortal being that Jesus atoned for the sins of the world. He died and His body was placed in the tomb, while His spirit visited the spirit world and preached the gospel to those spirits of men awaiting resurrection. After three days, He rose triumphantly from the tomb with a resurrected body of flesh and bones.[41] As the prophet, seer, and revelator, Joseph clearly testified and clarified the doctrine of Christ.

"The Son," Joseph explained, "who was in the bosom of the Father, is a personage of tabernacle, made or fashioned like unto man, being in the form and likeness of man, or rather man was formed after his likeness and in his image; he is also the express image and likeness of the personage of the Father, possessing all the fulness of the Father, or the same fulness with the Father; being begotten of him, and ordained from before the foundation of the world to be a propitiation for the sins of all those who should believe on his name, and is called the Son because of the flesh, and descended in suffering below that which man can suffer; or, in other words, suffered greater sufferings, and was exposed to more powerful contradictions than any man can be. But, notwithstanding all this, he kept the law of God, and remained without sin; showing thereby that it is in the power of man to keep the law and remain also without sin, and also, that by him a righteous judgment might come upon all flesh, that all who walk not in the law of God may justly be condemned by the law and have no excuse for their sins. And he being the Only Begotten of the Father, full of grace and truth, and having overcome, received a fullness of the glory of the Father, possessing the same mind with the Father, which mind is the Holy Spirit, that bears record of the Father and the Son."[42] Many have declared that they never could understand God, Christ, and religion until they were taught the revelations received by the Prophet Joseph Smith.

In February 1832, while living in Hiram, Ohio, Joseph and Sidney Rigdon bore witness: "And now, after the many testimonies which have been given of him, this is the testimony, last of all, which we give of him: That he lives! For we saw him, even on the right hand of God; and we heard the voice bearing record that he is the Only Begotten of the Father—That by him, and through him, and of him, the worlds are and were created, and the inhabitants thereof are begotten sons and daughters unto God" (D&C 76:22–24). The full implications of this witness were later clarified by the Prophet in poetic form. He wrote:

And I heard a great voice, bearing record from heav'n,
He's the Saviour, the Only begotten of God—
By him, of him, and through him, the worlds were all made,

Even all that career in the heavens so broad.

Whose inhabitants, too, from first to the last,
Are sav'd by the very same Saviour of ours;
And, of course, are begotten God's daughters and sons,
By the very same truths, and the very same pow'rs.[43]

Joseph testified that the atoning sacrifice was unlimited in its comprehensiveness. That is, Jesus Christ atoned for the sins of those individuals who live on worlds beyond this earth, extending throughout all of His creations. Truly, Joseph bore witness that the sacrifice of the Son of God was infinite and eternal. Further, from this vision Joseph learned that the atoning power of the Savior would save all except the sons of perdition. The Prophet declared that the salvation of the Redeemer is so extensive that three degrees or kingdoms of heaven are prepared in which individuals inherit glory through Jesus Christ according to their obedience to His gospel (see D&C 76).

With an eye looking forward, the Prophet taught that before the great day of judgment, Jesus Christ will return to the earth in glory accompanied by the angels of heaven to usher in a millennial era of peace. He explained that the gospel was restored as a forerunner to the Second Coming of Jesus Christ. Thus, we are preparing for the Savior to return and reign with His Saints in righteousness upon the earth for a thousand years (see D&C 29:11; 43:29–40).

The upstairs room of the Johnson home in Hiram, Ohio. The Prophet Joseph Smith and Sidney Rigdon used this room as an office where they worked on the inspired translation of the Bible. It was here that they saw the Savior, Jesus Christ, in vision, and were shown the celestial, terrestrial, and telestial glories.

FAITH AND SACRIFICE

The Lord revealed that he called the Prophet Joseph Smith to restore gospel truths "that faith might increase in the earth" (D&C 1:21). From the Prophet's earliest revelations and further teachings through the end of his life, he emphasized that faith is "the first principle in revealed religion, and the foundation of all righteousness."[44] While in Kirtland, Ohio, the Lord directed Joseph to preside over a school, in which the elders were to meet to learn of the doctrines of Christ. Later the discussions within the classes were written in lecture form and published with the revelations received in establishing and regulating the Church. The volume was titled the Doctrine and Covenants and the seven lectures were designated as the *Lectures on Faith*. As recorded in lecture three, Joseph taught of the importance of knowledge to exercise faith sufficient to lead to eternal life. "Let us here observe," he explained, "that three things are necessary in order that any rational and intelligent being may exercise faith in God unto life and salvation. First, the idea that he [God] actually exists. Secondly, a *correct* idea of his [God's] character, perfections, and attributes. Thirdly, an actual knowledge that the course of life which he [the individual] is pursuing is according to his [God's] will."[45]

Joseph made clear that faith is the motivation behind all human action. In addition, he taught that all faith is not equal. "Let us here observe, that a religion that does not require the sacrifice of all things never has power sufficient to produce the faith necessary unto life and salvation; for, from the first existence of man, the faith necessary unto the enjoyment of life and salvation never could be obtained without the sacrifice of all earthly things."[46] Thus, Joseph emphasized that faith was founded on behavior, or living the gospel, and not simply centered in verbal professions of belief. The latter-day heritage of the Prophet's teachings regarding faith is found in the works that the Saints undertake in response to the Lord's commands. That is, true religion is practical religion. True faith is manifest in service to God and through serving humankind. From the Prophet's teachings, the Saints have sacrificed to build temples, wherein they continue to labor for the salvation of the living and dead; left home and family to travel the globe preaching the fulness of the gospel; traversed mountains and plains to establish Zion in the deserts of the western United States—many coming on foot with their belongings stored in wagons or in handcarts; dedicated innumerable hours fulfilling various callings within the Church; and strived in faith and hope to keep the commandments of Jesus Christ.

MISSIONARY WORK AND THE ESTABLISHMENT OF ZION

The Prophet Joseph Smith knew that the Restoration of the gospel would extend to the far reaches of the globe and taught such from the earliest days of the Church. He testified that The Church of Jesus Christ of Latter-day Saints was the stone cut out of the mountain without hands, spoken of by the prophet Daniel, which will roll forth until it fills the whole earth (see D&C 65:2–6).

Although Joseph did not live to see the gospel go forth to all the nations of the earth, he knew that such would be the case. In 1842, he wrote a letter to Mr. John Wentworth, editor and proprietor of the *Chicago Democrat*. He informed Mr. Wentworth that the gospel had been planted in nearly every state of the Union and also spread to England, Ireland, Scotland, and Wales. "Our missionaries are going forth to different nations," he continued, "and in Germany, Palestine, New Holland, Australia, the East Indies, and other places, the Standard of Truth has been erected; no unhallowed hand can stop the work from progressing; persecutions may rage, mobs may combine, armies may assemble, calumny may defame, but the truth of God will go forth boldly, nobly, and independent, till it has penetrated every continent, visited every clime, swept every country, and sounded in every ear, till the purposes of God shall be accomplished, and the Great Jehovah shall say the work is done."[47]

Similarly, Joseph taught that members of the Church were to establish and build up Zion in every nation. The establishment of Zion became one of Joseph's main concerns and topics, and he exhorted the Saints, "We ought to have the building up of Zion as our greatest object."[48] He taught additionally that the Saints must become a Zion people to receive the blessings

A Prophet's Vision

During the early days of the Church in Kirtland, Ohio, the priesthood brethren gathered on Isaac Morley's farm and shared their testimonies. Afterward, Wilford Woodruff, who was present at the meeting, reported that the Prophet observed, "Brethren, I have been very much edified and instructed in your testimonies here tonight, but I want to say to you before the Lord, that you know no more concerning the destinies of this church and kingdom than a babe upon its mother's lap. You don't comprehend it. . . . It is only a handful of priesthood you see here tonight, but this church will fill North and South America—it will fill the world. . . .

"It will fill the Rocky Mountains. There will be tens of thousands of Latter-day Saints who will be gathered to the Rocky Mountains, and there they will open the door for the establishing of the gospel among the Lamanites, who will receive the gospel and their endowments and the blessings of God. This people will go into the Rocky Mountains; they will there build temples to the Most High. They will raise up a posterity there, and the Latter-day Saints who dwell in these mountains will stand in the flesh until the coming of the Son of Man. The Son of Man will come to them while in the Rocky Mountains."[20]

reserved for those who lay the foundations of that society. He received revelations that indicated that the Saints were to gather together in one body for strength and to combine their efforts to build Zion. To this end Joseph taught the Saints to gather to Jackson County, Missouri, which was designated by the Lord and dedicated as the center place of the city of the New Jerusalem. At the heart of this city was to be a complex of twenty-four buildings dedicated to the Lord—temples of the Most High. Joseph sent instructions with a plat map to lay the city out in sections of straight roads, each with blocks divided into lots of property to be deeded as stewardships to those who had consecrated their properties to the Church of Christ.[49]

This was the law that was to govern Zion and exhibited the dedication and commitment of soul that the Saints had in establishing the New Jerusalem. Likewise, Joseph taught that the Saints were to gather to areas designated as city stakes of Zion, where a temple would be in the center of the city and roads and properties laid out in similar fashion as that of the New Jerusalem. Joseph taught that a Zion people were a community of individuals united by the law of the celestial kingdom in consecrating their lives to God and imparting "of their substance, as becometh saints, to the poor and the afflicted among them" (D&C 105:5). The first of these city stakes was organized in Kirtland, Ohio. Other city stakes were established in Far West and Spring Hill (known as Adam-Ondi-Ahman), Missouri. During the 1840s, Joseph directed the Saints to gather to the area of Nauvoo, Illinois, which the Lord designated as "a cornerstone of Zion" (D&C 124:2).

TEMPLE WORK

Joseph restored knowledge of true temple worship and ordinances. He dedicated land for five temples, only one of which was completed in his lifetime. He designated Independence, Missouri, as the center place of the New Jerusalem and, as previously mentioned, instructed the Saints that a complex of twenty-four temples would be built upon the land dedicated as Zion. The first house of worship built under his direction was in Kirtland, Ohio. He dedicated that temple to the Lord on March 27, 1836, which was the only temple that he was

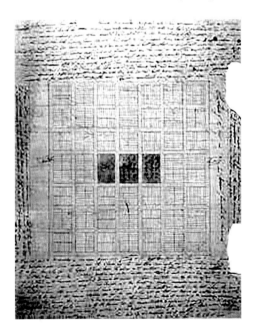

Plat map of Zion.

privileged to see finished. He later dedicated ground for temples in Far West, Missouri, and Nauvoo, Illinois.[50]

The temple in Kirtland was built as a place of instruction and for the Saints to receive an endowment of the Holy Spirit. The ordinances of washings and anointings were administered and keys of the priesthood were restored by the ancient prophets Moses, Elias, and Elijah. Later, while the Saints were building the Nauvoo Temple, Joseph explained that the purpose for that temple was to build upon the foundation laid in Kirtland and to restore the "fulness of the priesthood" (see D&C 121). In addition, the Prophet taught the important concept that the priesthood has the authority and responsibility to perform essential gospel ordinances in behalf of the dead. First, Joseph addressed the need for baptism for those who did not receive this ordinance for their own persons in the flesh. Two sections of the Doctrine and Covenants are letters of instruction from the Prophet to the Saints regarding baptisms for the dead (see D&C 127–28).

He further instructed, "The declaration this morning is, that as soon as the Temple and baptismal font are prepared, we calculate to give the Elders of Israel their washings and anointings, and attend to those last and more impressive ordinances, without which we cannot obtain celestial thrones. But there must be a holy place prepared for that purpose . . . so that men may receive their endowments and be made kings and priests unto the Most High God. . . . There must,

The Building up of Zion

The Prophet Joseph Smith's teachings filled the Saints with anticipation of fulfilling prophecy in establishing Zion in the latter days. "The building up of Zion is a cause that has interested the people of God in every age," he wrote to the Saints in Nauvoo. "It is a theme upon which prophets, priests and kings have dwelt with peculiar delight; they have looked forward with joyful anticipation to the day in which we live; and fired with heavenly and joyful anticipations they have sung and written and prophesied of this our day; but they died without the sight; we are the favored people that God has made choice of to bring about the Latter-day glory . . . when the Saints of God will be gathered in one from every nation, and kindred, and people, and tongue, when the Jews will be gathered together into one."[21]

Kirtland and Nauvoo Temples.

however, be a place built expressly for that purpose, and for men to be baptized for their dead. It must be built in this central place; for every man who wishes to save his father, mother, brothers, sisters and friends, must go through all the ordinances for each one of them separately, the same as for himself, from baptism to ordination, washing and anointings, and receive all the keys and powers of the Priesthood, the same as for himself."[51]

Among the most consoling and stirring of all the Prophet's teachings connected with the temple is that family associations may continue after death and resurrection. Joseph explained that the power of the priesthood to bind or seal in heaven that which has been bound on earth included marriage and sealing children to parents. Further, Joseph emphasized the importance of temple ordinances and faithfulness to the covenants made in the house of the Lord: "Except a man and his wife enter into an everlasting covenant and be married for eternity, while in this probation, by the power and authority of the Holy Priesthood, they will cease to increase when they die; that is, they will not have any children after the resurrection. But those who are married by the power and authority of the priesthood in this life, and continue without committing the sin against the Holy Ghost, will continue to increase and have children in the celestial glory."[52]

THE PLAN OF SALVATION

Joseph Smith's teachings unfolded the purpose of human existence to a world that had lost the truths of eternity. Joseph himself learned line upon line the truths that he revealed. The foundation of the Prophet's teachings was laid in 1828–29, during the time that he translated the Book of Mormon. That record restored knowledge of divine purposes underlying the Fall of Adam to provide mortal bodies for God's children

Eternal Nature of the Family

In the winter of 1839–40 the Prophet Joseph Smith visited Philadelphia, Pennsylvania, where Parley P. Pratt was laboring in the mission field. A close associate of the Prophet, Parley wrote about his feelings and joy in being taught the doctrine of eternal families:

"During these interviews he taught me many great and glorious principles concerning God and the heavenly order of eternity. It was at this time that I received from him the first idea of eternal family organization, and the eternal union of the sexes in those inexpressibly endearing relationships which none but the highly intellectual, the refined and pure in heart, know how to prize, and which are at the very foundation of everything worthy to be called happiness.

"Till then I had learned to esteem kindred affections and sympathies as appertaining solely to this transitory state, as something from which the heart must be entirely weaned, in order to be fitted for its heavenly state.

"It was Joseph Smith who taught me how to prize the endearing relationships of father and mother, husband and wife; of brother and sister, son and daughter.

"It was from him that I learned that the wife of my bosom might be secured to me for time and all eternity; and that the refined sympathies and affections which endeared us to each other emanated from the fountain of divine eternal love. It was from him that I learned that we might cultivate these affections, and grow and increase in the same to all eternity; while the result of our endless union would be an offspring as numerous as the stars of heaven, or the sands of the sea shore.

"It was from him that I learned the true dignity and destiny of a son of God, clothed with an eternal priesthood, as the patriarch and sovereign of his countless offspring. It was from him that I learned that the highest dignity of womanhood was, to stand as a queen and priestess to her husband, and to reign for ever and ever as the queen mother of her numerous and still increasing offspring.

"I had loved before, but I knew not why. But now I loved—with a pureness—an intensity of elevated, exalted feeling, which would lift my soul from the transitory things of this groveling sphere and expand it as the ocean. I felt that God was my heavenly Father indeed; that Jesus was my brother, and that the wife of my bosom was an immortal, eternal companion; a kind ministering angel, given to me as a comfort, and as a crown of glory for ever and ever. In short, I could now love with the spirit and with the understanding also.

"Yet, at that time, my dearly beloved brother, Joseph Smith, had barely touched a single key; had merely lifted a corner of the veil and given me a single glance into eternity."[22]

and setting before them choices between right and wrong. The central message of the Book of Mormon is the power of the Atonement to overcome spiritual and physical death initiated by the Fall of Adam, and forgiveness of individual sins upon conditions of repentance, baptism, spiritual rebirth, and obedience to God's commandments.

Joseph's early teachings centered on the theme of the Restoration of the gospel, including angelic visitations to guide the work and restore priesthood authority. These teachings were accompanied with the message of the first principles and ordinances of the gospel—faith in the Lord Jesus Christ, repentance, baptism by immersion for the remission of sins, and the gift of the Holy Ghost by the laying on of hands. During the inspired translation of the Bible in the summer and fall of 1830, Joseph learned and afterward revealed that God's work and glory is "to bring to pass the immortality and eternal life of man" (Moses 1:39). Added to the revelations regarding the premortal existence of mankind, Joseph learned from the translation of the book of Abraham that mortality is a time to receive a body of flesh and bones, like our heavenly parents, and to be tested regarding our obedience to God's laws. He taught that "the great principle of happiness consists in having a body"[53] and that the spirit and the body are the soul of man (D&C 88:15).

Later, in the Nauvoo era, Joseph instructed the Saints further regarding judgments that attend our choices in mortality. He explained that God the Father and the Savior, Jesus Christ, laid out plans for our salvation before we were born on earth. He wrote, "The great Jehovah contemplated the whole of the events connected with the earth, pertaining to the plan of salvation, before it rolled into existence, or ever 'the morning stars sang together' for joy; the past, the present, and the future were and are, with Him, one eternal 'now.' . . . He knew the plan of salvation and pointed it out; He was acquainted with the situation of all nations and with their destiny; He ordered all things according to the council of His own will; He knows the situation of both the living and the dead, and has made ample provision for their redemption, according to their several circumstances, and the laws of the kingdom of God, whether in this world, or in the world to come."[54]

Earlier, in March 1832, while yet engaged in translating the Bible, Joseph and Sidney Rigdon were shown in vision that all humankind will be judged according to their acceptance of the gospel and valiance in the testimony of Jesus Christ, as well as their response to prophets and receiving the everlasting covenant (see D&C 76). In subsequent years Joseph taught of the universal nature of salvation for all of God's children, excepting those that commit the unpardonable sin against the Holy Ghost. "The great designs of God in relation to the salvation of the human family," the Prophet wrote, "are very little understood by the professedly wise and intelligent generation in which we live."[55] Joseph cited the eternal condemnation that each sect and religion places on those not of their faith and clarified, "But while one portion of the human race is judging and condemning the other without mercy, the Great Parent of the universe looks upon the whole of the human family with a fatherly care and parental regard; he views them as His offspring."[56] Accordingly, Joseph introduced the doctrine of salvation for the dead as an essential component of God's plan to bless His children. That is, toward the end of his life, Joseph's teachings often centered on the wisdom of God in setting apart a time after death, before resurrection and final judgment, during which all of His children may be taught and receive the ordinances of the gospel while in the world of spirits.

Further, Joseph explained the equity of judgment, which allowed all mankind to determine, by covenants and obedience to gospel laws, the level of salvation that they will enjoy in eternity. As he saw in vision, Joseph explained that there are three major degrees of salvation, each with their laws and qualifications, which we may choose to inherit according to our willingness and ability to abide by the laws of each kingdom—celestial, terrestrial, or telestial (see D&C 76:50–112; 88:17–35). In one of his last discourses to the Saints, May 12, 1844, Joseph testified: "There are mansions for those who obey a celestial law, and there are other mansions for those who come short of the law, every man in his own order. There is baptism . . . for those to exercise who are alive, and baptism for the dead who die without knowledge of the Gospel. I am going on in my progress for eternal life. It is not only necessary that you should be baptized for your dead, but you will have to go through all the ordinances for them, the same as you have gone through to save yourselves. . . . Oh! I beseech you to go forward, go forward and make your calling and your election sure."[57]

After the Prophet's death the Lord sanctioned Joseph's work: "I did call upon by mine angels, and by mine own voice out of the heavens, to bring forth my work; which foundation he did lay and was faithful; and I took him to myself" (D&C 136:37–38). The firm foundation laid by the teachings of the Prophet Joseph Smith has been built upon by each subsequent President of the Church, thus continuing the Restoration of the gospel of Jesus Christ until the day that we will have all truth revealed in its fulness.

Craig James Ostler

Professor of Church History and Doctrine, PhD
Brigham Young University

NOTES

1. See Jeremiah's prophecy in Jeremiah 16:14–15.
2. *HC*, 5:181.
3. Ibid., 5:401.
4. These include Edward Fuller and wife, and son, Samuel, who brought with him a chest of surgeon's instruments; John Tilley and wife and daughter Elizabeth Tilley, who married John Howland, another youthful *Mayflower* passenger and ancestor of the Prophet. See Archibald F. Bennett, "Solomon Mack and His Family," *Improvement Era*, 58, no. 10 (October 1955): 713. The name of Edward Fuller's wife is unknown and the name of John Tilley's wife is uncertain. It appears that John may have been married several times since various wives' names and marriage dates are given in the family history records currently available.
5. *HC*, 2:443.
6. Ibid; see also George A. Smith, "Memoirs," manuscript 2, cited in Richard Anderson, *Joseph Smith's New England Heritage* (Salt Lake City: Deseret Book, 1971), 112–13, 215.
7. Joseph and Lucy lost their first child, an unnamed son, in an untimely birth between the middle of 1796 and the spring of 1797, and another son, Ephraim, in 1810. See Richard L. Bushman, *Joseph Smith and the Beginnings of Mormonism* (Urbana and Chicago: University of Illinois Press, 1984), 198, note 65.
8. Lucy Mack Smith, *The Revised and Enhanced History of Joseph Smith by His Mother*, ed. Scot Facer Proctor and Maurine Jensen Proctor (Salt Lake City: Bookcraft, 1996), 72.
9. Ibid., 72–73.
10. Ibid., 73.
11. Dr. LeRoy S. Wirthlin has written on the medical procedure proposed by Dr. Nathan Smith of Dartmouth College, in Hanover, New Hampshire, a few miles north of the Smith home in Lebanon. The hand of the Lord is evident in the Smith's move to Lebanon, since Dr. Smith is the only surgeon known to have performed the limited removal of the infected bone described in Lucy Smith's narrative rather than amputate the leg. See LeRoy S. Wirthlin, "Joseph Smith's Boyhood Operation: An 1813 Surgical Success," *BYU Studies* 21.2 (Spring 1981): 131–54.
12. Bushman, *Beginnings of Mormonism*, 40.
13. Interview with William Smith, *Zion's Ensign*, Independence, Missouri; printed in the *Deseret Weekly* (Salt Lake City: Deseret News Publishing Company, 1894), 48:179.
14. Ibid.
15. *HC*, 4:536; see also *Times and Seasons*, vol. 3, no. 9 (March 1, 1842).
16. *JD*, 21:94.
17. Oliver Cowdery, *Messenger and Advocate*, 2:198.
18. Lucy Mack Smith, *History of Joseph Smith by His Mother*, 174.
19. See D&C 107:65–66, 91–92; *HC*, 1:243.
20. Lucy Mack Smith, *History of Joseph Smith by His Mother*, 124.
21. Ibid., 126.
22. Dean C. Jessee, ed., *Personal Writings of Joseph Smith*, rev. ed. (Salt Lake City: Deseret Book; Provo, UT: Brigham Young University Press, 2002), 253; spelling and grammar standardized.
23. Ibid., 368; spelling and grammar standardized.
24. *HC*, 1:419, note.
25. Jessee, *Personal Writings of Joseph Smith*, 18.
26. *HC*, 1:422.
27. Ibid.
28. Ibid., 1:442–43.
29. Leonard Arrington, "Joseph Smith and the Lighter View," *New Era*, August, 1976, 13.
30. *HC*, 5:265.
31. Richard L. Bushman and Dean C. Jessee, "Joseph Smith: The Prophet," *Encyclopedia of Mormonism*, ed. Daniel H. Ludlow (New York: Macmillan Publishing Company, 1992), 3:1338.
32. *HC*, 5:282.
33. Ibid., 1:264.
34. *Autobiography of Parley P. Pratt*, edited by his son Parley P. Pratt (Salt Lake City: Deseret Book, 1938, 1985), 179–81.
35. *HC*, 3:293.
36. Orson Hyde, *Times and Seasons*, September 15, 1844, 651.
37. Wilford Woodruff, *JD*, 24:54.

38. Joseph Smith, *Teachings of the Prophet Joseph Smith*, sel. Joseph Fielding Smith (Salt Lake City: Deseret Book, 1976), 181.

39. *HC*, 5:426.

40. Ibid., 6:305; also published in Smith, *Teachings of the Prophet Joseph Smith*, 345–46.

41. Ibid., 4:425.

42. Joseph Smith, comp., *Lectures on Faith* (Salt Lake City: Deseret Book, 1985), 5:2.

43. Joseph Smith, "A Vision," *Times and Seasons* (February 1843) 4:83.

44. Joseph Smith, *Lectures on Faith*, 1:1.

45. Ibid., 3:2–5.

46. Ibid., 6:7.

47. *HC*, 4:540.

48. Ibid., 3:390.

49. For an explanation of the plat of the city of Zion and deeds for consecrating property and receiving stewardships; see *HC*, 1:357–68.

50. See D&C 115:7–12 and *HC*, 3:41–42, regarding the temple in Far West, Missouri; cf. D&C 124:26–28, 42–44. In addition, there is some indication that Joseph may have anticipated building a temple at Spring Hill or Adam-ondi-Ahman, Missouri. See *HC*, 3:36; wherein Joseph visited the area for the purpose of "laying off a stake of Zion." Alvin R. Dyer noted that "the city of Adam-ondi-Ahman was similar in design to other cities layed out by the Latter-day Saints: (Kirtland, Ohio, The City of Zion at Independence, Missouri, and Far West, in Caldwell County, Missouri). All had temple sites, the center square of the city, which usually included a temple site, storehouses, places of worship, schools, etc." See *The Refiner's Fire* (Salt Lake City: Deseret Book, 1968), 164.

51. *HC*, 6:319.

52. Ibid., 5:391.

53. Andrew F. Ehat and Lyndon W. Cook, ed., *The Words of Joseph Smith: The Contemporary Accounts of the Nauvoo Discourses of the Prophet Joseph* (Salt Lake City: Bookcraft, 1980), 60.

54. *HC*, 4:597.

55. *HC*, 4:595.

56. Ibid.

57. *HC*, 6:365.

SIDEBAR AND PHOTO NOTES

1. *Autobiography of Parley P. Pratt*, 31–32.

2. *HC*, 4:191.

3. *HC*, 5:125–26.

4. Mark L. McConkie, *The Father of the Prophet* (Salt Lake City: Bookcraft, 1993), 64.

5. *Journal of History*, 12:108; Mary Audentia Smith Anderson, *Ancestry and Posterity of Joseph Smith and Emma Hale*, 74; cited in Vivian M. Adams, "All Prophets Knew, Testified of Him," *Church News*, May 14, 1994, 11.

6. *HC*, 1:466.

7. *HC*, 5:126.

8. Brigham Young, *JD*, 7:289–90.

9. *BYU Studies*, vol. 21, no. 2, 142.

10. Milton V. Backman Jr., *Joseph Smith's First Vision* (Salt Lake City: Bookcraft, 1980), 71–73.

11. *Alexander Neibaur's Recording of Joseph Smith's Testimony*, cited in Backman, *Joseph Smith's First Vision*, 177.

12. *HC*, 5:107.

13. Lucy Mack Smith, *History of Joseph Smith by His Mother*, 249.

14. Linda King Newell and Valeen Tippetts Avery, *Mormon Enigma: Emma Hale Smith* (Garden City, NY: Doubleday & Company, Inc., 1984), 103, 324, note 29.

15. Recollections of Jesse W. Crosby, reported in "Stories from the Notebook of Martha Cox, Grandmother of Fern Cox Anderson," LDS Church Archives; published in Hyrum L. Andrus and Helen Mae Andrus, comp., *They Knew the Prophet* (Salt Lake City: Bookcraft, 1974), 145.

16. George A. Smith, *JD*, 2:214.

17. Leonard Arrington, "The Human Qualities of Joseph Smith, the Prophet," *Ensign*, January, 1971, 37.

18. "Recollections of the Prophet Joseph Smith," *Juvenile Instructor* 27, no. 10 (May 15, 1892): 302, 472.

19. *HC*, 4:163–164.

20. G. Homer Durham, comp., *The Discourses of Wilford Woodruff* (Salt Lake City: Bookcraft, 1969), 38–39.

21. *HC*, 4:609–610.

22. *Autobiography of Parley P. Pratt*, 259–60.

Chapter Two
BRIGHAM YOUNG

LIFE AND TIMES

1801	June 1	Born in Whitingham, Vermont
1804		Family moved to New York
1815		Mother died of tuberculosis
1823		Joined Methodist Reformed Church
1824		Married Miriam Works
1830		First saw the Book of Mormon
1832		Baptized into the Church; wife died of tuberculosis; traveled to Kirtland to meet Joseph Smith; left on mission to Canada
1834		Marries Mary Ann Angell; marched with Zion's Camp; worked on construction of Kirtland Temple
1835		Called to Quorum of the Twelve Apostles
1840		Left New York for mission to England; became President of the Quorum of the Twelve
1844		Death of Joseph Smith; the Twelve sustained by the Church as leaders; Nauvoo Temple dedicated
1846		Left from Nauvoo for the West; directed formation of Mormon Battalion; established Winter Quarters, Nebraska
1847		Arrived in the Great Salt Lake Valley; ordained as President of the Church
1849		Divided Salt Lake City into wards; elected governor of provisional State of Deseret
1850		Established the Perpetual Emigrating Fund Company
1852		Plural marriage publicly announced
1853		Broke ground for the Salt Lake Temple
1858		Directed evacuation of Northern Utah settlements; arranged for peaceful settlement with U.S. Army
1867		Reorganized Relief Society
1868		Established University of Deseret (later called University of Utah)
1869		Organizes Young Ladies' Cooperative Retrenchment Association
1871		Dedicated St. George Temple site
1875		Organized Young Men's Mutual Improvement Association; organized Brigham Young Academy (later called Brigham Young University)
1877		Dedicated St. George Temple; dedicated site for Manti Temple
1877	August 29	Died at home in Salt Lake City at the age of seventy-six[1]

BIOGRAPHICAL HIGHLIGHTS

Brigham Young was born in 1801 in Vermont to a farming family. Brigham acquired the ability to work hard early on, and his practical skills and perspective helped him throughout his life. He eventually married and, after years of religious study, learned of the restored gospel and was baptized.

He was a dedicated member of the Church from the moment he came out of the water, always loyal to the Prophet Joseph Smith and committed to building up the kingdom of God. Eventually, Brigham was called to be an Apostle and, later, the President of the Quorum of the Twelve. When the Prophet Joseph was martyred, the Quorum of the Twelve guided the Church under President Young's leadership. He organized and headed the Saints' westward exodus and was ordained President of the Church in 1847.

President Young was Church President for thirty years, overseeing the tremendous settlement of the Great Basin and the growth of the Church. He passed away in his Salt Lake City home in 1877.

CONTRIBUTIONS

President Young's great spiritual capacity was complemented by his amazing organizational skills. He led the trek west, making certain the necessary plans were made and then personally traveling with the Saints across the plains. Additionally, during the trek he established the Mormon Battalion to help in the war effort for the United States and to bring much needed income to the families of the Church.

A remarkable colonizer and Church President, President Young helped the Saints settle the Great Basin. In a relatively short period of time, he was elected governor of the provisional State of Deseret, sent settlers throughout the Basin, established the Perpetual Emigrating Fund Company, and broke ground for the Salt Lake Temple. Missionary work remained paramount in his administration as he sent missionaries throughout the world.

One of his greatest contributions was his counsel to the Saints. He gave hundreds of sermons on a wide range of topics, always willing to help the people in any way he could. President Young provided the leadership the Church needed to help it thrive during a very difficult period of history.

TEACHINGS

Before he was converted to the restored gospel, Brigham Young was often frustrated by what he saw as inconsistencies in other religions. He was committed to finding and living the truth, and yearned for a church that abided by the teachings of the New Testament. Once he joined the Church, he rejoiced in its teachings and loved to explain to the Saints how the restored gospel encompassed all truth.

His teachings were not limited to the strictly spiritual, however, for he saw the spiritual and the temporal as one. President Young taught his people not only how to pray, read the scriptures, and keep their covenants, but he also taught them about proper ways of preparing food, how to manage financial concerns, and what children need from their parents. His counsel was wise and often ahead of its time.

Committed to Christ above all else, President Young's greatest teachings were conveyed through the manner of his life. He cared for people and wanted nothing but happiness for them—and he knew that the highest form of happiness comes through living the gospel.

LIFE OF
BRIGHAM YOUNG

◆

GROWING UP

Brigham Young was born in Whitingham, Vermont, on June 1, 1801. He was the ninth of eleven children born to John and Abigail Young. Abigail suffered from tuberculosis and had to rely on the children to care for each other and help with the many duties around the house. The family struggled to make a living off the land and, in 1804, moved to central New York in hopes of finding better land to farm. The family was large and poor, so Brigham diligently labored to help with all the chores that had to be done and later remarked that there were times when he worked in the "summer and winter, not half clad, and with insufficient food until my stomach would ache."[2]

When Brigham was only fourteen years old, his mother lost her struggle with tuberculosis and passed away. Her death, combined with the rigors of a life so dependent upon the land, helped the boy grow quickly into a man. The children were left in the care of their father who, though a good man, was often very strict. Brigham would later say of his father that "it used to be a word and a blow, with him, but the blow came first."[3] His father would sometimes have to leave the children on their own for days while he worked or got supplies. One time Brigham and his brother were so hungry, with nothing but maple sugar in the house, that he resorted to shooting a robin so the two boys could have something to eat.[4] It was not long after his mother's death that his father told him it was time for him to leave home. "When I was sixteen years of age, my father said to me, 'You can now have your time; go and provide for yourself;' and a year had not passed away before I stopped running, jumping, wrestling and the laying out of my strength for naught; but when I was seventeen years of age, I laid out my strength in planing a board, or in cultivating the ground to raise something from it to benefit myself."[5]

Brigham left home and became an apprentice carpenter, painter, and glazier.[6] Over the next five years he gained a reputation for being a capable and hardworking man. He eventually met and married a beautiful young woman, Miriam Works, and the couple was blessed with two daughters.

A carpenter's tools. Brigham Young was a fine carpenter by trade.

FINDING PEACE IN THE RESTORED GOSPEL

Brigham's parents belonged to a branch of the Methodist Church and raised their children in a strict religious environment.[7] But despite the fact that young Brigham was raised in

Visionary Man

In the fall of 1827, Brigham Young and his wife observed for two hours remarkable lights that marched across the moonless night like men in the formation of great armies. Several miles away, members of his family and others also witnessed the same amazing spectacle in the skies. Heber C. Kimball even reported that he heard guns and swords. For years this experience was a vivid memory for Brigham, but he and his family did not know what meaning to ascribe to it. Later he was to discover that the very night he marveled at the lights in the night sky was the night the angel Moroni delivered to Joseph Smith the gold plates.[1]

such circumstances, studied the Bible, and meditated upon deeply spiritual questions, he did not belong to any church for quite some time. His resistance to the religious teachings of his day was not born of arrogance; he recognized that there was truth in some of what the churches preached, but he wanted to "reach the years of judgment and discretion" so he could judge for himself.[8] Brigham tried to live a good Christian life of morality and high integrity, conscientiously studying the Bible and applying its teachings, but he simply could not find a church that appeared to be founded upon those teachings. Finally, about the time of his marriage, Brigham joined the Reformed Methodist Church. He insisted on being baptized by immersion even though his new church did not believe the method of performing the ordinance was important.[9]

In 1830, Brigham's older brother, Phinehas, purchased a copy of the Book of Mormon from Samuel Smith, the young missionary brother of the Prophet Joseph. Phinehas, as well as other members of the Young family, read the book and quickly proclaimed their acceptance of it. Brigham, on the other hand, took more time, carefully studying the book and the church behind it. While he had studied a number of different religions, this new religion struck him as something very different from all the others. This religion went deeper for Brigham than the others he had examined; it answered his questions and made sense to him. He was careful, however, to not rely only on his practical approach of studying nor on the commitment to the new church that others in his family

were willing to make. He wanted to pray and feel right about each important aspect of the religion before moving forward.

After studying the Book of Mormon and Bible, meeting with missionaries, and even traveling to Pennsylvania to observe a church meeting, Brigham firmly decided to be baptized. "I examined the matter studiously for two years before I made up my mind to receive that book," he later said. "I knew it was true, as well as I knew that I could see with my eyes, or feel by the touch of my fingers, or be sensible of the demonstration of any sense. Had not this been the case, I never would have embraced it to this day; it would have all been without form or comeliness to me. I wished time sufficient to prove all things for myself."[10]

On a snowy day in April 1832, Eleazer Miller baptized Brigham in his own mill pond. The next day Brigham's close friend, Heber Kimball, was also baptized, and within three weeks their wives were baptized as well.[11] Eventually all of Brigham's immediate family would join the Church. Brigham had found the restored gospel and with it the joy that comes

Brigham Young, about 1846.

through living it. "Our religion has been a continual feast to me. With me it is Glory! Hallelujah! Praise God! instead of sorrow and grief. Give me the knowledge, power, and blessings that I have the capacity of receiving. . . . Give me the religion that lifts me higher in the scale of intelligence—that gives me the power to endure—that when I attain the state of peace and rest prepared for the righteous, I may enjoy to all eternity the society of the sanctified."[12]

SERVING THE LORD AS A NEW DISCIPLE

Brigham demonstrated his commitment to the restored gospel by his unwavering willingness to diligently serve the Lord and His Church. He devoted much of his time to preaching the gospel, including going on a mission—by foot—to Canada. He met with personal tragedy once again when his wife, Miriam, passed away from tuberculosis, leaving him with their two young daughters to care for. Despite the challenges he faced, he was completely dedicated to the gospel and felt no hesitancy to do what he could to serve in his new religion. "I hear people talk about their troubles, their sore privations, and the great sacrifices they have made for the Gospel's sake. It never was a sacrifice to me. Anything I can do or suffer in the cause of the Gospel, is only like dropping a pin into the sea; the blessings, gifts, powers, honour, joy, truth, salvation, glory, immortality, and eternal lives, as far outswell anything I can do in return for such precious gifts, as the great ocean exceeds in expansion, bulk, and weight, the pin that I drop into it."[13]

One especially significant event that happened to Brigham was when he had the opportunity to meet the Prophet Joseph Smith. Brigham, his brother Joseph, and Heber stayed with family in Kirtland, Ohio, and soon made their way to the Smith home. They were informed that the Prophet was chopping wood. "We immediately repaired to the woods," Brigham would later explain, "where we found the Prophet, and two or three of his brothers, chopping and hauling wood. Here my joy was full at the privilege of shaking the hand of the Prophet of God, and received the sure testimony, by the Spirit of prophecy, that he was all that any man could believe him to be, as a

Clothing belonging to Brigham Young.

true Prophet."[14] Brigham would always be a true friend to the Prophet, loyal without question.

In 1833, Brigham gathered his two daughters and moved to Kirtland. "When I went to Kirtland," he later said, "I had not a coat in the world, for previous to this I had given away everything I possessed, that I might be free to go forth and proclaim the plan of salvation to the inhabitants of the earth. Neither had I a shoe to my feet, and I had to borrow a pair of pants and a pair of boots."[15] At that time Kirtland was a village of about thirteen hundred people, set in a beautiful location of rolling green hills near the Chagrin River. While there he grew closer to the Prophet Joseph, continuing his gospel education. Brigham met Mary Ann Angell, a native of New York who was then living in Kirtland, and the two married on February 18, 1834.[16] Though Brigham labored in building homes, he spent most of his time preaching.

While the Prophet Joseph and many of the Saints resided in Kirtland, there were about twelve hundred members of the Church who had settled in Jackson County, Missouri, to help with the establishment of Zion. There were many difficulties in Missouri for the Saints, however. "There, an angry mob, led by a militant minister, destroyed the Mormon store and printing establishment, tarred and feathered the bishop, and finally, in November 1833, drove the Saints from their homes with whippings and plunder. Many houses were burned, livestock was killed, and furniture and other domestic property were seized and carted away."[17] Daniel Dunklin, the Missouri governor, promised to help the Saints get their homes back if they would provide him with help in doing so. The Prophet decided to recruit a group of men, called Zion's Camp, to help. Always a staunch supporter of the Prophet, Brigham was one of the first to volunteer for the camp; he and Heber were chosen to be captains of their respective companies.

The march to Missouri was extremely difficult with little sleep, poor roads, hot weather, and unsanitary eating and drinking conditions. Many of the men complained to the Prophet about their circumstances. "We had grumblers in that camp," Brigham said. "We had to be troubled with uneasy, unruly and discontented spirits. . . . Brother Joseph led, counselled and guided the company, and contended against those unruly, evil disposed persons."[18] By the time the men made it to Missouri, the governor had backed away from his promise and decided not to help the Saints recover their homes.[19] The men of Zion's Camp encountered threats of mob violence against them and were even spared one evening when an attacking mob was stopped by a terrible storm within two miles of Zion's Camp and had to turn back. The company of Saints saw the hand of the Lord in this and was grateful for His protection. It was just a matter of days later, though, that cholera spread throughout the camp. Sixty-eight members of the camp were afflicted and fourteen died. Joseph called the men together and told them that if they would humble themselves and covenant to follow his direction, the epidemic would be stopped. The men covenanted to be obedient and the Prophet's promise came true. On July 3, 1834, Joseph discharged the group without their ever having to go to battle.[20]

The Prophet had promised Brigham that if he would follow him to Missouri and keep his counsel, he would come back unharmed.[21] Sadly, there were those who did not return. But the Prophet later spoke of how he had a vision in which he saw the men who had died in Zion's Camp and how the Lord had cared for them. "Brethren, I have seen those men

Friend and Defender of the Prophet

Even when other leaders of the Church spoke out against the Prophet Joseph, Brigham Young always remained loyal to his spiritual leader and friend. "I feel like shouting hallelujah, all the time, when I think that I ever knew Joseph Smith, the Prophet whom the Lord raised up and ordained, and to whom He gave keys and power to build up the kingdom of God on earth and sustain it."[2] Elder Young stood up to apostates plotting to remove Joseph from his office and helped other Church leaders remain loyal. Late one night he heard a man running through the streets of Kirtland, speaking out loudly against the Prophet. President Young explained what followed: "I put my pants and shoes on, took my cow hide, went out, and laying hold of him, jerked him round, and assured him that if he did not stop his noise, and let the people enjoy their sleep without interruption, I would cow-hide him on the spot, for we had the Lord's Prophet right here, and we did not want the devil's prophet yelling round the streets. The nuisance was forth with abated."[3]

who died of the cholera in our camp; and the Lord knows, if I get a mansion as bright as theirs, I ask no more."[22]

In the eyes of some members of the Church at the time, Zion's Camp had failed in what they thought was its purpose. However, it proved to be an important education for many men who would later be leaders in the Church. "Ask those brethren and sisters who have passed through scenes of affliction and suffering for years in this Church, what they would take in exchange for their experience, and be placed back where they were, were it possible," Brigham said years later. "I presume they would tell you, that all the wealth, honors, and riches of the world could not buy the knowledge they had obtained, could they barter it away."[23] Brigham gained much from closely associating with the Prophet during this trying time and considered it an important beginning for his learning how to lead the Saints. Regarding those who would question the benefit of Zion's Camp, Brigham proclaimed, "I told those brethren that I was well paid—paid with heavy interest—yea that my measure was filled to overflowing with the knowledge that I had received by travelling with the Prophet. When companies are led across the plains by inexperienced persons, especially independent companies, they are very apt to break into pieces, to divide up into fragments, become weakened, and thus expose themselves to the influences of death and destruction."[24]

LOYAL MEMBER OF THE TWELVE APOSTLES

In February of 1835, just a few months after Zion's Camp had returned to Kirtland, Joseph Smith gathered together the veterans of the camp, along with other Church leaders, and announced that it was time to organize the Quorum of the Twelve Apostles and the Quorum of the Seventy. Joseph called upon the Three Witnesses, Oliver Cowdery, David Whitmer, and Martin Harris, to select the Twelve, and they called both Brigham and Heber to be members of the Quorum. Since the first Quorum of the Twelve was organized according to age, Elder Young was the third in the Quorum with Elder Heber C. Kimball being the fourth. Nine of the twelve men called to the Quorum had served with the Prophet Joseph in Zion's Camp.[25]

Over the next few years, Elder Young divided his time between missionary work and attending to his family. During the summer months he would serve missions in the eastern United States, and for the remainder of the year he would help build up the Church in Kirtland and care for his wife and children. He was intimately involved in the painting and finishing of the Kirtland Temple, working on the windows and helping supervise the exterior masonry work; later he was able to participate in its dedication. Such devotion to the building of the first temple in this dispensation was not without sacrifice: Elder Young found little time to financially support his family and had to rely on the Lord and the help of others. At this time he was also involved in the School of the Prophets, where he received instruction in the gospel and other subjects such as history and languages.[26]

Despite the great blessings that flowed from having the temple in Kirtland, a troubling spirit of fierce contention spread throughout the village. Many members of the Church believed that Joseph was unwisely combining the spiritual with the secular and should not allow the Church to be involved in temporal affairs. They blamed him for "meddling" with a financial institution (the Kirtland Safety Society Anti-Banking Association) that ultimately failed.[27] Always loyal to Joseph Smith, Brigham Young defended him and his inspired role as head of the Church against all critics—even certain members of the Twelve. He knew Joseph was not perfect, but he also knew he was a prophet. The unrest and resentment toward the Prophet and those who supported him became so severe, in fact, that Elder Young had to leave Kirtland under the cover of night for his own safety.

It was not long before the Prophet, Elder Young, and many other Saints began settling in Far West, Missouri. Then when governor of Missouri Lilburn W. Boggs issued his infamous extermination order,[28] the Saints fled to Nauvoo, a

Man of Sacrifice

When it was time to leave with his good friend Elder Kimball for their mission in England, Elder Young was so ill that he could not walk short distances without assistance. He had to leave his ill wife, Mary Ann, tending their three-week-old baby and their other children who were also sick. After he was taken to the Kimball home, his wife was carried in a wagon to the house so she could take care of her husband until he had to leave for England. Elder Kimball and his family were also very ill, so it was tremendously difficult for the men and their families to have to part in such a trying circumstance. Elder Kimball wrote about the ordeal:

"It was with difficulty we got into the wagon, and started down the hill about ten rods; it appeared to me as though my very inmost parts would melt within me at leaving my family in such a condition, as it were almost in the arms of death. I felt as though I could not endure it. I asked the teamster to stop, and said to Brother Brigham, 'This is pretty tough, isn't it; let's rise up and give them a cheer.' We arose, and swinging our hats three times over our heads, shouted: 'Hurrah, hurrah for Israel.' Vilate, hearing the noise, arose from her bed and came to the door. She had a smile on her face. Vilate and Mary Ann Young cried out to us: 'Goodbye, God bless you.' We returned the compliment, and then told the driver to go ahead. After this I felt a spirit of joy and gratitude, having had the satisfaction of seeing my wife standing upon her feet, instead of leaving her in bed, knowing well that I should not see them again for two or three years."[4]

new gathering place for the members of the Church designated by the Prophet Joseph. After a short time, Elder Young and other members of the Twelve left for their mission to Great Britain. Elder Young was extremely ill but would not listen to his sister's pleadings for him to wait until he was well. "I was determined to go to England or to die trying," he said. "My firm resolve was that I would do what I was required to do in the Gospel of life and salvation, or I would die trying to do it."[29]

In April 1840, the Apostles in England "formally and unanimously" sustained Brigham Young as the President of the Twelve, a role he had been filling since 1838.[30] He quickly led his brethren in an extensive program of missionary work, publishing, and preparing to help the English Saints immigrate to America. Among their publications were the Book of Mormon, a hymn book, and the *Millennial Star*.[31] After a year of hard work and continual spiritual development, President Young and his brethren had baptized thousands of people. The positive effects of this English mission for the Twelve would bless the Saints for years to come. "As a result of the mission to England, the Quorum of the Twelve Apostles came of age precisely at the time its support and strength were needed most. Under Brigham Young's direction the Twelve had achieved unprecedented proselyting success and, for the first time, had become an effective agency of ecclesiastical administration."[32]

After their mission to England, the available members of the Twelve were called together by the Prophet. He announced that it was now time for that quorum to take additional responsibilities in overseeing the affairs of the Church. It was also during this period of time in Nauvoo that the Prophet instructed the Twelve on four new doctrines and practices: baptism for the dead, plural marriage, the full temple endowment, and the sealing of children to parents.[33] As always, President Young supported the Prophet and followed his teachings, but he found that the doctrine of plural marriage was an especially difficult concept. "I was not desirous of shrinking from any duty," President Young would later say about first hearing of the new practice, "nor of failing in the least to do as I was commanded, but it was the first time in my life that I had desired the grave, and I could hardly get over it for a long time."[34] After weeks of study and prayer, President Young accepted the doctrine and, with his wife's consent, married his first plural wife, Lucy Ann Decker Seeley, in June 1842.[35] He would marry a number of other plural wives throughout his life.

As President of the Quorum of the Twelve, Brigham Young was a very influential man with many responsibilities in Nauvoo. He was president of the quorum that had been charged by the Prophet to take care of such things as "directing missionary work and the work of the gathering" of the Saints, "managing the temporal affairs of the Church and assisting in the building of the Nauvoo temple."[36] Around March 26, 1844, Joseph conducted a solemn meeting with the Twelve in which he pronounced that something important was going to soon take place—perhaps he would even be murdered. He bestowed upon them all the keys and powers that he held,[37] thus ensuring the authority needed for the future leading of the Church. Just three months later this sacred meeting would prove to be a priceless treasure to the Saints and their future.

RECEIVING THE MANTLE OF THE PROPHET

President Young was away on a mission in Boston when he found himself deeply sorrowful while sitting in a railway station on June 27, 1844. Though he did not know the reason for his "depression of spirit" at the time, he would learn weeks later about the martyrdom of the Prophet Joseph and his brother Hyrum.[38] He returned to Nauvoo as quickly as he could, only to find Sidney Rigdon trying to persuade the Saints that he should lead the Church as its "guardian." Sidney was a member of the First Presidency but had become unsupportive of the Prophet and had moved from Nauvoo. President Young did not wonder about the next course of action, however, for he understood that he and the Twelve held the priesthood keys necessary to lead the Church.

A miraculous event occurred when President Young stood to address the gathered Saints and many there received a "divine witness" that the mantle of the martyred Prophet had fallen upon him as he spoke.[39] Many thought President Young sounded and even looked like Joseph as he spoke. In

Shepherd of the Flock

During the long trek west no wagon was allowed to stop unless the entire train was stopping for camp. This rule prevented individual wagons breaking the procession and increasing the risk of Indian attack. Near the beginning of the journey, Lucy Groves, a woman weak from having given birth just ten days earlier, slipped when she attempted to leave the wagon while it was in motion and fell in front of the front wheel, breaking three ribs and a leg. President Young immediately came to her aid, setting her leg and giving her a blessing that she would arrive in Salt Lake in good condition. Lucy's bed took up all the room in the wagon, so her children had to continue the trek on foot. After several days, with her leg mending well, her daughter accidentally tripped over her mother and broke the injured leg a second time. This time the pain was so severe for Lucy that she cried out every time the oxen took a step. Eventually she had to ask her husband to pull the wagon off to the side. As soon as President Young saw that their wagon had stopped, he ordered that the entire train stop while he made his way back to the Groves. Lucy explained what was happening and insisted that the train move on, leaving her behind in the wagon. President Young would hear nothing of that, however, and decided to have everyone camp for the night. While others were resting, President Young sawed off the legs and tops of Lucy's bed and attached it to the wagon bows so that it could swing freely, like a hammock. He then renewed the previous blessing, promising her that she would live for many years. The wagon train proceeded in the morning, with President Young riding beside the Groves' wagon for the next several days to make certain that Lucy's needs were met.[5]

fact, there are at least 101 "written testimonies of people who say a transformation or spiritual manifestation occurred."[40] As one of the witnesses to this amazing event, Benjamin F. Johnson wrote, "President Brigham Young arose and spoke. I saw him arise, but as soon as he spoke I jumped upon my feet, for in every possible degree it was Joseph's voice, and his person, in look, attitude, dress and appearance was Joseph himself, personified; and I knew in a moment the spirit and mantle of Joseph was upon him. . . . I knew for myself who was now the leader of Israel. New confidence and joy continued to spring up within me."[41] The people voted to sustain the Twelve as the leaders of the Church.

Though the Prophet Joseph was gone, his influence would forever be with President Young. President Young wrote one of his daughters about feeling Joseph's presence in spirit though not in body: "This much I can say—the spirit of Joseph is here, though we cannot enjoy his person. Through the great anxiety of the church, there was a conference held last Thursday. The power of the Priesthood was explained and the order thereof, on which the whole church lifted up their voices and hands for the twelve to move forward and organize the church and lead it as Joseph had. This is our indispensable duty. The brethren feel well to think the Lord is still mindful of us as a people."[42] Not only did President Young rely on the experiences he had with the prophet's

Brigham Young with hat in hand in about 1864.

teachings and character, but he also received counsel from him in spiritual experiences. In one dream, for example, the Prophet Joseph appeared to President Young and taught him the importance of the people being humble and following the Spirit. "Tell the people to be humble and faithful," the

Founder of the Mormon Battalion

"With regard to our going into the wilderness," President Young told the Saints, "and our there being called upon to turn out five hundred able-bodied men to go to Mexico, we had then seen every religious and political right trampled under foot by mobocrats; there were none left to defend our rights; we were driven from every right which freemen ought to possess. In forming that battalion of five hundred men, brother Kimball and myself rode day and night, until we had raised the full number of men the Government called for. . . . The boys in that battalion performed their duty faithfully. I never think of that little company of men without the next thoughts being, 'God bless them for ever and for ever.' "[6]

A statue of Brigham Young in downtown Salt Lake City. This work reflects the leader's attributes as a leader and colonizer.

Prophet told him, "and be sure to keep the spirit of the Lord and it will lead them right. Be careful and not turn away from the small still voice; it will teach you what to do and where to go; it will yield the fruits of the kingdom. Tell the brethren to keep their hearts open to conviction, so that when the Holy Ghost comes to them, their hearts will be ready to receive it."[43]

LEADING THE SAINTS TO THE GREAT BASIN

The increasing hostility toward the Church made it clear that the Saints would not be able to stay in Nauvoo much longer. Joseph Smith had spoken of finding a place for the Saints to dwell peacefully west of the Rocky Mountains[44] and, after much study and discussion, the Twelve decided to lead the Saints in an exodus to the Great Salt Lake Valley. Believing it imprudent to wait, President Young led a group in the snowy cold of February 1846. In leading his people on such a dangerous exodus, he did not remain aloof from them and travel in comfort. He worked closely with the other Saints and did all he could to help them. "I would not go on until I saw all the teams up," he wrote about when they left Nauvoo. "I helped them up the hill with my own hands."[45]

During the difficult journey west, having just seen his people forced out of their homes without governmental protection, he received word that U.S. President Polk had authorized the enlistment of five hundred Mormon men to serve as soldiers in California as part of the U.S. war with Mexico. President Young realized that this was not only an opportunity to serve the country but also to receive some much-needed funds for the exodus west. He personally visited men and boys to encourage them to volunteer for what would be called the Mormon Battalion.[46] While the Mormon Battalion are honored today for "their willingness to fight for the United States, for their march of some two thousand miles from Council Bluffs to California, for their participation in the early development of the West, and for making the first wagon road over the southern route from California to Utah in 1848," they were also honored at that time by President Young himself for being such a blessing to the welfare of the Church.[47]

After staying in Winter Quarters (in Nebraska) for the winter of 1846–47, President Young headed for the Salt Lake Valley with an advance party. Because of illness, he did not arrive in the valley with the advance party but came a few

Founder of the Perpetual Emigrating Fund Company

In 1849, President Young established the Perpetual Emigrating Fund Company (PEF) to help provide much-needed monies for Saints traveling from England and other countries to join their new brothers and sisters in the Great Basin. The PEF was an independently administered arm of the Church, relying upon contributions of the faithful Saints and repayment from those who had benefited from the fund. Many of the emigrants received credit toward their PEF loans for doing such work as helping construct buildings and roads. President Young devoted much of his energy toward encouraging the Saints to contribute generously to the fund and was himself very liberal in his offerings, donating cash from his savings, from his salary as governor, and from the sale of some of his own land and buildings. The fund blessed not only the lives of the thousands of people who received help in their emigration, but also all of the Saints in the Great Basin whose lives were improved by what the new settlers accomplished.[7]

days later. On July 24, 1847, he saw the valley and confirmed that it was the right place for the Saints to settle. He identified the spot where the temple would be built and began directing the settling of the valley in such endeavors as farming, surveying, and building. In August, President Young led a group of men back to Winter Quarters to help the families there prepare for the trek to the Great Salt Lake Valley. Later, President Young would take no praise for this great accomplishment of guiding so many people so far: "I do not wish men to understand I had anything to do with our being moved here, that was the providence of the Almighty; it was the power of God that wrought out salvation for this people, I never could have devised such a plan."[48]

After President Young returned to Winter Quarters, the Twelve met several times for "lengthy discussions and prayer sessions" concerning how the leadership of the Church should be organized. After much deliberation, the Quorum of the Twelve Apostles decided to organize a First Presidency, with Brigham Young as President, in December 1847. They also sustained his selection of Heber Kimball and Willard Richards as counselors. Three weeks later the Iowa members of the Church sustained the new First Presidency in a hall large enough for the gathering. [49]

Though President Young had presided over the Church as the President of the Twelve, now he presided over the

Beehive House. The principal residence of Brigham Young and his family during their years in Utah.

Loving Husband

Though President Young was always in the public eye because of his many governmental and ecclesiastical responsibilities, he did have his private moments with his family that reveal more about his depth of character than any sermon he gave. He cared deeply for his family, watching over the welfare of his wives and children. Always respectful and solicitous to his wives' needs, he earned their admiration, love, and loyalty. His young plural wife Clara Decker accompanied him on the first journey across the Plains to the Great Basin and grew to almost reverence her prophet-husband as she observed the kindness with which he treated her, despite the hardness of the journey and his serious illness with the Colorado tick fever. The women he married possessed strong spirits, and he respected them as individuals. He tried to lead his family in kindness and decided that if he had to quarrel with any of them in order to get them to do as he wished, then he wouldn't say a word.[8]

Church as its President. Years before, when Brigham Young was a new convert to the Church, the Prophet Joseph made what must have seemed to be an amazing prophecy at the time. The Prophet said that "the time will come when brother Brigham Young will preside over this Church."[50] Similarly, Levi Hancock bore his testimony that "one day he was chopping a Beech log with Joseph and saw Br Brigham for the first time. Joseph remarked to him before Brigham came within hearing 'There is the greatest man that ever lived to teach redem[p]tion to the world and will yet lead this People.' "[51]

PRESIDENT OF THE CHURCH

One of the greatest challenges President Young faced was the need to settle the Great Basin area and thereby establish a place for the Saints to gather. "We came to these mountains because we had no other place to go," he said. "We had to leave our homes and possessions on the fertile lands of Illinois to make our dwelling places in these desert wilds, on barren, sterile plains, amid lofty, rugged mountains."[52] His great strength as a leader and organizer proved invaluable in meeting these challenges. He led the wide variety of efforts needed to successfully bring in the newly arrived Saints and establish the many programs and systems they needed to start their new lives. And always, despite his many heavy

Portrait of Brigham Young at about age sixty-four.

Dedicated Father

President Young was a kind and affectionate father who was concerned about not only his children's proper upbringing, but their youthful happiness as well. President Young provided a school for all of his children and plenty of area for playing. He built a recreation room that included a stage for family theatrical productions, and outside he constructed a large porch that could serve as a gymnasium, complete with ladders and horizontal bars, jumping ropes, roller skates, and swings. He even provided a family swimming pool for his children near one of his homes.[9] Though he believed in helping his children to be well-disciplined and could be firm when he felt it necessary, he did not subscribe to some of the disciplinary approaches others might have found justifiable. "Solomon said, 'He that spareth his rod hateth his son,' but instead of using the rod, I will teach my children by example and by precept. I will teach them every opportunity I have to cherish faith, to exercise patience, to be full of long-suffering and kindness. It is not by the whip or the rod that we can make obedient children; but it is by faith and by prayer, and by setting a good example before them."[10]

responsibilities as President of the Church, President Young was a caring father and husband, actively participating in all the facets of his large family's life. One of his daughters, Clarissa, shared a particular account of what it was like to have Brigham Young as her father: "Father usually discussed the topics of the day, and then we would all join in singing some familiar songs, either old-time ballads or songs of religious nature. Finally we would all kneel down while Father offered the evening prayers. One distinct

Patron of the Theater

President Young once said that if he were charged with civilizing the people on a cannibal island, he would immediately build a theater for that purpose. In 1860 he began the building of such a theater in Salt Lake City, partly for the enjoyment and relaxation of the hardworking people and partly to civilize them. It took two years to build the impressive Salt Lake Theater, patterned after the famous Drury Lane in London. Considered by some to be one of the finest theaters in the United States, it had a parquet, dress circle, three balconies, and a seating capacity of 7,500 people. Though President Young was certainly interested in using the theater to help the Saints become better practitioners of their religion, considering the actors to be similar to missionaries in their service to the kingdom, he did not make this enterprise a vehicle for religious productions. Secular plays were produced that were considered valuable for the Salt Lake citizens, including multiple productions of *Hamlet, Macbeth, Richard III, Romeo and Juliet, Othello,* and *The Merchant of Venice.* In a time when few settlers of the American West could consider the theater anything more than a luxurious memory of days left behind in the East, President Young thought it crucial to the establishment of the Great Basin kingdom of God.[11]

Family members of Brigham and Mary Ann Angell Young.

settling the Great Basin was not a matter of simply occupying the land; he saw a paradise and had the determination to build it. "Let the people build good houses, plant good vineyards and orchards, make good roads," President Young taught his people, "build beautiful cities in which may be found magnificent edifices for the convenience of the public, handsome streets skirted with shade trees, fountains of water, crystal streams, and every tree, shrub and flower that will flourish in

phrase in his prayer I shall never forget it so impressed my childish mind was—'Bless the church and Thy people, the sick and the afflicted and comfort the hearts that mourn.'"[53]

In 1849, President Young convened a constitutional convention that created the State of Deseret—a vast area, comprising most of present-day Utah and Nevada and portions of Arizona, Oregon, Wyoming, Idaho, Colorado, New Mexico, and California. [54] He was elected governor of this provisional state and considered one of his most important goals to be getting Deseret admitted as a state in the United States. As a first response in 1850, the U.S. Congress changed the name from Deseret to Utah and established a territorial government for it rather than granting it statehood.[55] President Young would attempt to gain statehood for the territory several times, but Utah would not be granted such status until after his death.

President Young established the Perpetual Emigrating Fund Company in 1849 to help with the emigration of thousands of members of the Church to the area. His vision of

Advocate for Women

President Young appreciated the great role that girls and women had to play in the building up of the kingdom of God and encouraged them to develop their talents. He directed wards to form and sustain Relief Societies for the women "for the improvement of our manners, our dress, our habits, and our methods of living"[12] and "that the hearts of the widow and the orphan may be made glad by the blessings which are so abundantly and so freely poured out upon them."[13] For girls not yet old enough for the Relief Society he established the Young Ladies' Retrenchment Society. Beginning with his own daughters, he encouraged the girls to retrench ("reduce") the influence of worldly concerns in their lives. This program has experienced a number of name changes until it has become what is today the Young Women program for the Church.

this climate, to make our mountain home a paradise and our hearts wells of gratitude to the God of Joseph."[56]

In 1851, U.S. President Millard Fillmore appointed President Young as both governor and superintendent of Indian Affairs of Utah Territory. Though President Young certainly had the support of the people of Utah, he faced many problems working with the appointees who were assigned by the federal government. He did not see them as sympathetic to the Church or to the needs and interests of the people of the territory. Many of the individuals who had been appointed by the federal government in various capacities returned to the East with complaints about President Young and the Mormon people in general. In addition, the public announcement in 1852 about the practice of plural marriage caused even greater concern about the Saints among leaders in the United States. By 1857, Washington, DC, was filled with "rumors and allegations charging the Mormons with murder, destruction of legal records, religiously biased courts, and conspiracy with the native American Indians to promote conflict against non-Mormon immigrants."[57]

China belonging to Brigham Young personalized with the letter *Y*.

As a result of these allegations and rumors, U.S. President James Buchanan decided to replace President Young with a federally appointed governor and to send part of the U.S. Army to Utah to put down any Mormon rebellion. He did not inform President Young of the military action, so when soldiers were observed heading for the territory, President Young assumed the worst and told his people to prepare to defend their homes. "They never did anything against Joseph till they had ostensibly legalized a mob; and I shall treat every army and every armed company that attempts to come here as a mob," President Young told the members of the Church.[58] Before any battle became necessary, though, a peaceful solution was agreed upon and the Army occupied Camp Floyd, about forty miles from Salt Lake City. President Young was replaced as governor, and the Army left at the beginning of the Civil War in 1861.

President Young was first and foremost a disciple of Christ. He was a committed member of the kingdom and willing to serve faithfully and fully in whatsoever he was called upon to do. Above such titles as governor or such duties as organizer and colonizer, he was the President of The Church of Jesus Christ of Latter-day Saints. His organizational abilities and spiritual gifts were great blessings to the Saints. He divided the city into wards and appointed bishops, counseled with countless people, encouraged the Saints to develop their communities to be places of education and culture, and sent

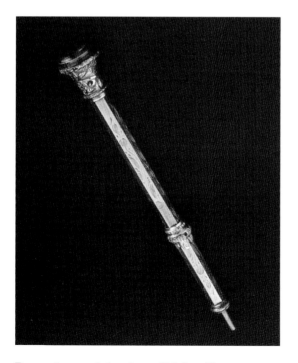

Decorative cane belonging to Brigham Young.

groups of missionaries to many countries. He gave hundreds of sermons in which he shared such things as his recollections of the Prophet Joseph, his commitment to the restored gospel, and his great views of the doctrines of the kingdom. Always searching for ways to bless the Saints, President Young encouraged the establishment of Relief Societies in each ward and opened the University of Deseret (later named the University of Utah) and Brigham Young Academy (later named Brigham Young University). And, though he would not live to see the completion of the Salt Lake Temple, he did dedicate the temple in St. George, Utah.

President Young taught his people the gospel with great enthusiasm and plainness. He believed in a practical gospel that could make a person's life not only better in the next life but in this one as well. "Life is for us, and it is for us to receive it to-day, and not wait for the millennium. Let us take a course to be saved to-day, and, when evening comes, review the acts of the day, repent of our sins, if we have any to repent of, and say our prayers; then we can lie down and sleep in peace until the morning, arise with gratitude to God, commence the labours of another day, and strive to live the whole day to God and nobody else."[59]

On August 29, 1877, a great period of Church history ended with the death of President Brigham Young. He had been suffering from what is now believed to be an infection caused by a ruptured appendix. As one of his daughters wrote, "When he was placed upon the bed in front of the window he seemed to partially revive, and opening his eyes, he gazed upward, exclaiming: 'Joseph! Joseph! Joseph!' and the divine look in his face seemed to indicate that he was communicating with his beloved friend, Joseph Smith, the Prophet. This name was the last word he uttered."[60]

Brigham Young was the man the Lord raised up for an especially difficult time to accomplish overwhelming tasks. And accomplish them he did. There is little wonder that he is known as the American Moses, the Lion of the Lord.

Various items relating to Brigham Young's life.

Salt Lake Temple under construction. Brigham Young never saw the temple completed.

St. George Temple. Brigham Young dedicated this edifice near the end of his life.

TEACHINGS OF PRESIDENT
BRIGHAM YOUNG

◆

Brigham Young served in Church leadership for most of his life and as prophet for thirty years. His many sermons were carefully recorded. His sermons knew few bounds for, to him, the gospel encompassed all truth. "I want to say to my friends that we believe in all good. If you can find a truth in heaven, earth or hell, it belongs to our doctrine. We believe it; it is ours; we claim it."[61] Before he was converted to the restored gospel, he was often frustrated with his study of other religions. They seemed to be lacking to him, talking of ethical behavior but not in complete harmony with the truth he found in the Bible. He was grateful to find the restored gospel, which he called "simply the truth. It is all said in this one expression— it embraces all truth, wherever found, in all the works of God and man that are visible or invisible to mortal eye."[62] President Young taught that the gospel includes "every system of true doctrine on the earth, whether it be ecclesiastical, moral, philosophical, or civil" and that it "incorporates all good laws that have been made from the days of Adam until now."[63]

Perhaps because of his conviction of what the gospel encompasses, President Young was not hesitant to offer counsel on just about any subject. He counseled the Saints, when tired and feeling the need for "spirituous liquor," to "take some bread and butter or bread and milk, and lie down and rest."[64] He instructed parents to give their children bread and milk in the morning, making certain that it was "not soft bread," but "hard-baked bread, that the Americans would call stale, but the English would not." He even explained how to bake the bread "with a slow heat" and not to make it "thicker than [his] two hands."[65] President Young's detailed counsel ranged topics as broad as the plains he led the Saints across, including politics, health practices, the arts, personal finance, education, the raising of children, husband and wife relationships, and the doctrines of the gospel.

His understanding of the gospel as comprising all truth should not be interpreted to mean that President Young simply thought that everything was part of the gospel and that there was no particular order or system to it. He saw the gospel as

Joseph Taught the Truth

"All that Joseph Smith did was to preach the truth—the Gospel as the Lord revealed it to him—and tell the people how to be saved, and the honest-in-heart ran together and gathered around him and loved him as they did their own lives. He could do no more than to preach true principles, and that will gather the Saints in the last days, even the honest-in-heart. All who believe and obey the Gospel of Jesus Christ are his witnesses to the truth of these statements."[14]

Politics

President Young gave hundreds of sermons and counseled with countless individuals and groups about a wide spectrum of topics. Though he respected the opinions and agency of others, he was willing to share what he had on his mind. One such example is politics. The Saints had had their share of troubles with government officials of the time, and President Young was not hesitant in voicing his thoughts on the matter. "Are we a political people? Yes, very political indeed. But what party do you belong to or would you vote for? I will tell you whom we will vote for: we will vote for the man who will sustain the principles of civil and religious liberty, the man who knows the most and who has the best heart and brain for a statesman; and we do not care a farthing whether he is a whig, a democrat, a barnburner, a republican, a new light or anything else. These are our politics."[15]

Be Compassionate

President Young was concerned about the way the Saints treated one another and often gave counsel on the subject. He was a man of high standards who strove to live them on a daily basis, but he also understood the need for compassion for others in their challenges. "Let all Latter-day Saints learn that the weaknesses of their brethren are not sins. When men or women undesignedly commit a wrong, do not attribute that to them as a sin. Let us learn to be compassionate one with another; let mercy and kindness soften every angry and fretful temper, that we may become long-suffering and beneficial in all our communications one with another."[16]

a "plan or system of laws and ordinances," and taught that God "has instituted laws and ordinances for the government and benefit of the children of men, to see if they would obey them, and prove themselves worthy of eternal life by the law of the celestial worlds."[66] This gospel system was not a mere set of beliefs, but a force that was to guide the daily lives of the Saints. "On reading carefully the Old and New Testaments we can discover that the majority of the revelations given to mankind anciently were in regard to their daily duties; we follow in the same path."[67] "We do not allow ourselves to go into a field to plough without taking our religion with us; we do not go into an office, behind the counter to deal out goods, into a counting house with the books, or anywhere to attend to or transact any business without taking our religion with us. If we are railroading or on a pleasure trip our God and our religion must be with us."[68] He saw the gospel as "full of good sense, judgment, discretion and intelligence"[69] and wanted his people to apply this good sense every day.

THE FIRST PRINCIPLES AND ORDINANCES OF THE GOSPEL

President Young taught that for people to correctly understand the first principles of the gospel, they "must have the wisdom that comes from above" and "be enlightened by the Holy Ghost." He continued by saying that our minds "must be in open vision" and that we must "enjoy the blessings of salvation . . . in order to impart them to others."[70] Though a

very practical man, he appreciated the spiritual nature of the gospel and the importance of the Spirit in teaching the truth. He also understood the need for ordinances, proclaiming that every "ordinance, every commandment and requirement is necessary for the salvation of the human family."[71]

Faith in Christ

President Young recognized faith in Christ as the first principle of the gospel. Quite simply, he taught that we need to believe that Christ is who "he is represented to be in the Holy Scriptures."[72] If we attempt to rely on human reason alone, we are "liable to error. But place a man in a situation where he is obliged or compelled, in order to sustain himself, to have faith in the name of Jesus Christ, and it brings him to a point where he will know for himself; and happy are those who pass through trials, if they maintain their integrity and their faith to their calling."[73] President Young taught as one who had been placed in such a situation many times. It is not difficult to believe that when he left his family to serve a mission in England, when he stood before the Church after the martyrdom to help determine who should lead the kingdom, and when he led the Saints across the challenging terrain and through the relentless weather, he knew what it meant to rely on his faith in Christ to sustain him.

Repentance

President Young saw repentance through his practical, no-nonsense eyes. It was a matter of the people needing to rely on the Atonement of Christ and change their ways. He taught that "Christ has died for all. He has paid the full debt, whether you receive the gift or not. But if we continue to sin, to lie, steal, bear false witness, we must repent of and forsake that sin to have the full efficacy of the blood of Christ. Without this it will be of no effect; repentance must come, in order that the atonement may prove a benefit to us. Let all who are doing wrong cease doing wrong; live no longer in transgression, no matter of what kind, but live every day of your lives according to the revelations given, and so that your examples may be worthy of imitation."[74] His approach to repentance was sensible. Dramatic proclamations of a changed life did not impress him, nor did enthusiasm void of action. "All I have ever asked for or contended for is a reformation in the life of this people; that the thief should stop stealing, the swearer his swearing, the liar his lying, the deceiver his deceiving, and the man who loves the world more than his God and his religion wean his affections from those objects and place them where they of right belong."[75]

Baptism

Acknowledging that he and his people "may not know the origin of the necessity of being baptized for the remission of sins," President Young taught that baptism "answers that portion of the law we are now under to teach the people in their ignorance that water is designed for purification, and to instruct them to be baptized therein for the remission of their sins."[76] He understood the importance of baptism even before he ever heard of the Restoration of the gospel, insisting to the leaders of the Methodist Church that he joined that he be baptized by immersion regardless of what their church taught.

The Need for the Spirit

"Do you know whether I am leading you right or not? Do you know whether I dictate you right or not? Do you know whether the wisdom and the mind of the Lord are dispensed to you correctly or not? These are questions which I will answer by quoting a little Scripture, and saying to the Latter-day Saints what was said to the Saints in former times, 'No man knoweth the things of God, but by the Spirit of God.' That was said in the days of the Savior and the Apostles, and it was no more true then than it is now, or than it was in the days of the Prophets, Moses, Abraham, Noah, Enoch, Adam, or in any and every age of the world. It requires the same manifestations in one age as in another, to enable men to understand the things of God. I have a request to make of each and every Latter-day Saint, or those who profess to be, to so live that the Spirit of the Lord will whisper to them and teach them the truth, and define to their understanding the difference between truth and error, light and darkness, the things of God and the things that are not of God. In this there is safety; without this there is danger, imminent danger; and my exhortation to the Latter-day Saints is—Live your religion."[17]

Gift of the Holy Ghost

President Young loved the truth of the gospel. His belief that the gospel included all truth excited him and caused him to rejoice at the limitless possibilities such a doctrine provides us. This love for the truth extended to the Holy Spirit, through whom we could learn the truth and change our lives for the better. "When true doctrines are advanced, though they may be new to the hearers, yet the principles contained therein are perfectly natural and easy to be understood, so much so that the hearers often imagine that they had always known them. This arises from the influence of the Spirit of Truth upon the [spirit] of intelligence that is within each person. The influence that comes from heaven is all the time teaching the children of men."[77]

President Young believed that a person could possess the Holy Ghost by living the teachings of Christ and that then the person would become "an expounder of truth." People who have the Holy Ghost in their lives "will know things that are, that will be, and that have been. They will understand things in heaven, things on the earth, and things under the earth, things of time, and things of eternity, according to their several callings and capacities."[78]

AGENCY

Brigham Young was always a strong individual, not one prone to follow others out of fear or convenience but only if he believed them to be leading him correctly. He treasured his agency as a gift from God and was very protective of it. "My independence is sacred to me—it is a portion of that same Deity that rules in the heavens," he taught. "There is not a being upon the face of the earth who is made in the image of God, who stands erect and is organized as God is, that would be deprived of the free exercise of his agency so far as he does not infringe upon other's rights, save by good advice and a good example."[79] Though he was ever firm in his conviction of the truthfulness of the gospel and completely convinced of its blessings for all humankind, he never believed it right to try to compel someone to join the Church or subscribe to its teachings. "The Lord does not compel any person to embrace the Gospel, and I do not think he will compel them to live it after they have embraced it."[80]

Even as there is today, there were those in President Young's time who twisted the concept of agency to support their unrighteous desires, proclaiming that because they could do whatever they choose to do, then whatever they choose to do is right. "Many are disposed through their own wickedness 'to do as I damned please,' " President Young observed, "and they are damned."[81] He taught his followers that being obedient to the Lord's commandments does not rob a man of his agency or freedom. "Does it follow that a man is deprived of his rights, because he lists in his heart to do the will of God? Must a man swear to prove that he has an agency? I contend there is no necessity for that, nor for stealing nor for doing any wrong. I can manifest to the heavens and to the inhabitants of the earth that I am free-born, and have my

liberty before God, angels and men, when I kneel down to pray, certainly as much as if I were to go out and swear. I have the right to call my family together at certain hours for prayer, and I believe that this course proves that I am a free agent, as much as if I were to steal, swear, lie, and get drunk."[82]

Though the Lord blessed His children with agency, President Young made it clear to the Saints that such a blessing did not mean they could choose the consequences of their actions as well as their actions. He understood that while the Lord "has given [people] the privilege of choosing for themselves, whether it be good or evil," the results of those choices were "still in his hand. All his children have the right of making a path for themselves of walking to the right or to the left, of telling the truth or that which is not true. This right God has given to all people who dwell on the earth, and they can legislate and act as they please; but God holds them in his hands, and he will bring forth the results of his glory, and for the benefit of those who love and serve him, and he will make the wrath of men to praise him. All of us are in the hands of that God."[83]

LEARNING

"The religion embraced by the Latter-day Saints, if only slightly understood, prompts them to search diligently after knowledge," President Young taught. "There is no other people in existence more eager to see, hear, learn, and understand truth."[84] He was a firm believer in learning by study and faith, guiding the Saints to read "good books, and extract from them wisdom and understanding as much as you possibly can, aided by the Spirit of God."[85] His commitment to the education of the youth is indicated not only by his sermons, but by his actions—establishing schools at every level as well as two institutions that have become the University of Utah and Brigham Young University. He wanted the Saints to "be a people of profound learning pertaining to the things of the world," to be "familiar with the various languages" and "understand the geography, habits, customs, and laws of nations and kingdoms."[86] "How gladly would we understand every principle pertaining to science and art, and become thoroughly acquainted with every intricate operation of nature, and with all the chemical changes that are constantly going on around us! How delightful this would be, and what a boundless field of truth and power is open for us to explore!"[87]

As we would expect of the greatly practical Brigham Young, he wanted his people to learn everything they could and apply that learning to living good and useful lives. "Learn to be good for something."[88] He saw education as a means of preparing people to serve the Lord, and was particularly concerned with missionaries learning what they could about the world and its people to help them be of better service in their callings. But his interest in learning was not just practical— he found value in education as a part of a well-rounded life. "Some think too much, and should labor more, others labor too much and should think more, and thus maintain an equilibrium between the mental and physical members of the individual; then you will enjoy health and vigor, will be active, and ready to discern truly, and judge quickly. Men who do much thinking, philosophers for instance, should apply their bodies to more manual labor in order to make their bodies more healthy and their minds more vigorous and active."[89] And his belief in the sacred importance of learning was not limited to this life. President Young believed that we would always learn, and he enthusiastically looked forward to the prospect. "I shall not cease learning while I live, nor when I arrive in the spirit-world; but shall there learn with greater facility; and when I again receive my body, I shall learn a thousand times more in a thousand times less time; and then I do not mean to cease learning, but shall still continue my researches."[90]

Not only did President Young teach the need to learn as much as we can in all the different fields of knowledge, but he also recognized the dangers of focusing so intensely on religious matters that a person begins to lose balance. If people are desirous to read nothing but the scriptures all the time, he noted, they are welcomed to do so, but he cautioned them that "when you [are] done, you may be nothing but a sectarian after all. It is your duty to study to know everything upon the face of the earth in addition to reading those books."[91] He mastered this balance between the spiritual knowledge we can gain through religious study and living and the secular knowledge available through education. In fact, it was less of a balance and more of an appreciation of the spiritual and temporal as one, with the gospel encompassing all truth and all truth coming from the same divine source. "There is no ingenious mind that has ever invented anything beneficial to the human family but what he obtained it from the one Source, whether he knows or believes it or not. There is only one Source whence men obtain wisdom, and that is God, the Fountain of all wisdom; and though men may claim to make their discoveries by their own wisdom, by meditation and reflection, they are indebted to our Father in Heaven for all."[92]

Knowledge

"Every art and science known and studied by the children of men is comprised within the Gospel. Where did the knowledge come from which has enabled man to accomplish such great achievements in science and mechanism within the last few years? We know that knowledge is from God, but why do they not acknowledge him? Because they are blind to their own interests, they do not see and understand things as they are. Who taught men to chain the lightning? Did man unaided of himself discover that? No, he received the knowledge from the Supreme Being. From him, too, has every art and science proceeded, although the credit is given to this individual, and that individual. But where did they get the knowledge from, have they it in and of themselves? No, they must acknowledge that, if they cannot make one spear of grass grow, nor one hair white or black without artificial aid, they are dependent upon the Supreme Being just the same as the poor and the ignorant. Where have we received the knowledge to construct the labor-saving machinery for which the present age is remarkable? From Heaven. Where have we received our knowledge of astronomy, or the power to make glasses to penetrate the immensity of space? We received it from the same Being that Moses, and those who were before him, received their knowledge from; the same Being who told Noah that the world should be drowned and its people destroyed. From him has every astronomer, artist and mechanician that ever lived on the earth obtained his knowledge. By him, too, has the power to receive from one another been bestowed, and to search into the deep things pertaining to this earth and every principle connected with it."[20]

ENJOYING LIFE

Though President Young was a man of tremendous spiritual and practical capacity, he also greatly valued the simple blessings of happiness. "To make ourselves happy is incorporated in the great design of man's existence."[93] He clearly taught that happiness is only realized through living the gospel. "We are all searching for happiness; we hope for it, we think we live for it, it is our aim in this life. But do we live so as to enjoy the happiness we so much desire? There is only one way for Latter-day Saints to be happy, which is simply to live their religion, or in other words believe the Gospel of Jesus Christ in every part, obeying the gospel of liberty with full purpose of heart, which sets us free indeed."[94] However, since he saw all truth and good as part of the gospel, he also recognized how the arts and recreation could greatly contribute to that happiness. He did not believe, as so many strict religious practitioners of his day did, that the spiritual aspects of this life had to make us so somber as to destroy the fun of living. "The Lord never commanded me to dance, yet I have danced: you all know it, for my life is before the world. Yet while the Lord has never commanded me to do it, he has permitted it. I do not know that he ever commanded the boys to go and play at ball, yet he permits it. I am not aware that he ever commanded us to build a theater, but he has permitted it, and I can give the reason why. Recreation and diversion are as necessary to our well-being as the more serious pursuits of life."[95]

President Young recognized the dangers of not living a life of variety, full of interests that keep us intelligent and well-rounded. "There is not a man in the world but what, if kept at any one branch of business or study, will become like a machine. Our pursuits should be so diversified as to develop every trait of character and diversity of talent. If you would develop every power and faculty possessed by your children, they must have the privilege of engaging in and enjoying a diversity of amusements and studies; to attain great excellence, however, they cannot all be kept to any one individual branch of study." He believed that the mind should be "kept active and [have] the opportunity of indulging in every exercise it can enjoy in order to attain to a full development of its powers."[96] President Young acknowledged that all of the good things of this life came from God and should be appreciated. "There is no music in hell, for all good music belongs to heaven," he said. "Sweet harmonious sounds give exquisite joy to human beings capable of appreciating music. I delight in hearing harmonious tones made by the human voice, by musical instruments, and by both combined. Every sweet musical sound that can be made belongs to the Saints and is for the Saints. Every flower, shrub and tree to beautify, and to gratify the taste and smell, and every sensation that gives to man joy and felicity are for the Saints who receive them from the Most High."[97]

WEALTH

Though President Young encouraged the Saints to enjoy the good things that life could provide, he never suggested that a good means of doing so was concentrating on the accumulation of possessions. He was gravely concerned about materialism and strongly warned his people of its trap. "How the Devil will play with a man who so worships gain!" President Young once said that he was "more afraid of covetousness in our Elders than . . . of the hordes of hell" and that "the things of this world called riches, are in reality not riches.

The Poor

Though President Young was successful in many different areas of his life and accumulated a good amount of worldly possessions, he never forgot the poor. He was a generous member of the Church and the community, willing to offer help to those less fortunate. "We need to learn, practice, study, know and understand how angels live with each other. When this community comes to the point to be perfectly honest and upright, you will never find a poor person; none will lack, all will have sufficient. Every man, woman, and child will have all they need just as soon as they all become honest. When the majority of the community are dishonest, it maketh the honest portion poor, for the dishonest serve and enrich themselves at their expense."[23]

We should find they are like mirages to the ignorant, mere phenomena to the inhabitants of the earth; to-day they are, to-morrow they are not; they were, but now they are gone, it is not known where."[98]

His concern for the dangers of materialism did not preclude an appreciation for how people devoted to the Lord could put wealth to good use. "A man or a woman who places the wealth of this world and the things of time in the scales against the things of God and the wisdom of eternity, has no eyes to see, no ears to hear, no heart to understand. What are riches for? For blessings, to do good. Then let us dispense that which the Lord gives us to the best possible use for the building up of his Kingdom, for the promotion of the truth on the earth, that we may see and enjoy the blessings of the Zion of God here upon this earth."[99] It is not wealth *per se* that can harm the possessor of it, but how he or she views it and makes use of it. The issue is not how much money we have or do not have—rather, it is how faithful we are. "If we are destroyed through the possession of wealth, it will be because we destroy ourselves. If we possessed hundreds of millions of coin and devoted that means to building up the Kingdom of God and doing good to his creatures, with an eye single to his glory, we would be as much blessed and as much entitled to salvation as the poor beggar that begs from door to door; the faithful rich man is as much entitled to the revelations of Jesus Christ as is the faithful poor man."[100]

Much of President Young's public teachings about wealth were rooted in his private philosophy and his attitude to his personal possessions. He considered everything he owned to belong to the Lord instead of to himself. "When a man wishes to give anything, let him give the best he has got. The Lord has given to me all I possess; I have nothing in reality, not a single dime of it is mine. . . . The coat I have on my back is not mine, and never was; the Lord put it in my possession honorably, and I wear it; but if he wishes for it, and all there is under it, he is welcome to the whole. I do not own a house, or a single farm of land, a horse, mule, carriage, or wagon, or wife, nor child, but what the Lord gave me, and if he wants them, he can take them at his pleasure, whether he speaks for them, or takes them without speaking."[101] He was a man prepared for the law of consecration, ready to give his all—spiritually and temporally—to the building of the Lord's kingdom.

Building Family Trust

"I will illustrate the method of establishing confidence in each other by taking, for example, the child of four or five years of age. The mother allows that child to own a small chest in which to keep his little trinkets, such as little bosom pins, ribbons, doll clothes, etc. This is considered by all the family the child's chest. Now let none go into that chest and take anything from it, without the consent of the child. This is a very small matter, some may think; but begin at as small a point as this to create confidence, and let it grow up from little to much. Wives, let your husband's stores alone, if they have not committed them to your charge. Husbands, commit that to your wives that belongs to them, and never search their boxes without their consent. I can boast of this. I have lived in the marriage relation nearly thirty years, and I never was the man to open my wife's chest, without her consent, except once, and that was to get out a likeness that I wanted on the instant, and she was not at home to get it for me. That was the first time I ever opened a trunk in my life, that belonged to my wife, or to my child. The child's little chest, with its contents, is as sacred to him, as mine is to me. If this principle were strictly carried out by every man, woman, and child among the Saints, it would make them a blessed people indeed."[24]

RAISING A HAPPY AND RIGHTEOUS FAMILY

While some of his counsel about families would not be considered as pertinent today as it was in his time (for example, "Let every man in the land over eighteen years of age take a wife"[102]), it is amazing how much of what President Young taught might be considered ahead of its time. Though he taught that the father should be "the head of the family" and "master of his own household," he went beyond the conventional wisdom of many of his time and instructed that the father should "treat [family members] as an angel would treat them."[103] "The father should be full of kindness, and endeavor to happify and cheer the mother," he taught, "that her heart may be comforted and her affections unimpaired in her earthly protector, that her love for God and righteousness may vibrate throughout her whole being, that she may bear and bring forth offspring impressed and endowed with all the qualities necessary to a being designed to reign king of kings and lord of lords."[104] As for mothers, he believed that they literally held the destiny of the world in their hands, calling them "the moving instruments in the hands of Providence to guide the destinies of nations. Let the mothers of any nation teach their children not to make war, the children would

Stewardship

"There is any amount of property, and gold and silver in the earth and on the earth, and the Lord gives to this one and that one—the wicked as well as the righteous—to see what they will do with it, but it all belongs to him. He has handed over a goodly portion to this people, and, through our faith, patience and industry, we have made us good, comfortable homes here, and there are many who are tolerably well off, and if they were in many parts of the world they would be called wealthy. But it is not ours, and all we have to do is to try and find out what the Lord wants us to do with what we have in our possession, and then go and do it. If we step beyond this, or to the right or to the left, we step into an illegitimate train of business. Our legitimate business is to do what the Lord wants us to do with that which he bestows upon us, and dispose of it just as he dictates, whether it is to give all, one-tenth, or the surplus."[25]

Being Good Examples for Children

"You see, hear and witness a good deal of contention among children—some of you do, if not all—and I will give you a few words with regard to your future lives, that you may have children that are not contentious, not quarrelsome. Always be good-natured yourselves, is the first step. Never allow yourselves to become out of temper and get fretful. Why, mother says, 'this is a very mischievous little boy or little girl.' What do you see? That amount of vitality in those little children that they cannot be still. If they cannot do anything else they will tip over the chairs, cut up and pull away at anything to raise a row. They are so full of life that they cannot contain themselves; and they are something like ourselves—boys. They have so much vitality in them that their bones fairly ache with strength. They have such an amount of vitality—life, strength and activity, that they must dispose of them; and the young ones will contend with each other. Do not be out of temper yourselves. Always sympathize with them and soothe them. Be mild and pleasant."[26]

grow up and never enter into it."[105] And while he taught that the husband was the head of his family and he expected wives to follow their husbands in righteousness, he "never counseled a woman to follow her husband to the Devil. If a man is determined to expose the lives of his friends, let that man go to the Devil and to destruction alone."[106]

Some of his most fascinating teachings regarding the family had to do with the raising of children. In an era of many preaching that "children should be seen and not heard" and that the woodshed had other uses than just storing wood, President Young recognized the divine in children and taught the Saints to raise them by loving example. He spoke of men who had "driven their children from them by using the wooden rod" and cautioned the Saints that where "there is severity there is no affection or filial feeling in the hearts of either party; the children would rather be away from father than be with him."[107] Instead of governing by the rod, President Young offered the alternatives of knowledge, kindness, truth, and holiness. "Parents should never drive their children, but lead them along, giving them knowledge as their minds are prepared to receive it. Chastening may be necessary betimes, but parents should govern their children by faith rather than by the rod, leading them kindly by good example into all truth and holiness."[108] He was concerned about overly strict parents who would not allow their children "recreation and amusement" but instead "bind them to the moral law, until duty becomes loathsome to them." President Young said that such children, "when they are freed by age from the rigorous training of their parents, . . . are more fit for companions to devils, than to be the children of such religious parents."[109]

JOSEPH SMITH

"I never saw any one, until I met Joseph Smith," President Young said, "who could tell me anything about the character, personality and dwelling-place of God, or anything satisfactory about angels, or the relationship of man to his Maker."[110] His loyalty and love for the Prophet Joseph were boundless. President Young was not a blind follower of the Prophet, nor was he unaware of the leader's imperfections, but he followed the Prophet with both eyes open—and a mind and heart open as well to what the Lord had to reveal to President Young through his leader. "What is the nature and beauty of Joseph's mission? . . . When I first heard him preach, he brought heaven and earth together; and all the priests of the day could not tell me anything correct about heaven, hell, God, angels, or devils; they were as blind as Egyptian darkness. When I saw Joseph Smith, he took heaven, figuratively

speaking, and brought it down to earth; and he took the earth, brought it up, and opened up, in plainness and simplicity, the things of God; and that is the beauty of his mission."[111]

President Young certainly recognized that Christ was the cornerstone of the Church, that He was the Son of God and unique among men. But he also realized that his appreciation for the Lord and his knowledge of the restored gospel had grown out of what the Prophet Joseph had taught him. "What I have received from the Lord, I have received by Joseph Smith; he was the instrument made use of. If I drop him, I must drop these principles; they have not been revealed, declared, or explained by any other man since the days of the Apostles. If I lay down the Book of Mormon, I shall have to deny that Joseph is a Prophet; and if I lay down the doctrine and cease to preach the gathering of Israel and the building up of Zion, I must lay down the Bible; and, consequently, I might as well go home as undertake to preach without these three items."[112]

Happiness and Righteousness

"I am happy; I am full of joy, comfort, and peace; all within me is light, for I desire nothing but to do the will of my Father in heaven. I delight not in unrighteousness, but in righteousness and truth. I seek to promote the good and happiness of myself and those with whom I am associated."[28]

Gratitude for Joseph Smith

One of the many constants in Brigham Young's life was his intense loyalty to the Prophet Joseph Smith. He never faltered in his devotion to the Prophet and was quick to defend him in any situation. "I feel like shouting Hallelujah, all the time, when I think that I ever knew Joseph Smith, the Prophet whom the Lord raised up and ordained, and to whom he gave keys and power to build up the Kingdom of God on earth and sustain it. These keys are committed to this people, and we have power to continue the work that Joseph commenced, until everything is prepared for the coming of the Son of Man. This is the business of the Latter-day Saints, and it is all the business we have on hand."[27]

GAINING A TESTIMONY

As powerful a man as Brigham Young was—governor, apostle, prophet, seer, revelator, President of the Church—he always knew that he was but a servant of the Lord. Though he was a great spiritual and temporal leader for thousands of people, he never asked those people to center their faith or obedience on him. He pointed them to the Lord and guided them to dedicating their lives to building up His kingdom upon the earth. President Young had received his testimony directly from the Lord and expected no one among the Saints to be satisfied with anything less. "I do not want men to come to me or my brethren for testimony as to the truth of this work; but let them take the Scriptures of divine truth, and there the path is pointed out to them as plainly as ever a guideboard indicated the right path to the weary traveler. There they are directed to go, not to Brothers Brigham, Heber, or Daniel, to any Apostle or Elder in Israel, but to the Father in the name of Jesus, and ask for the information they need. Can they who take this course in honesty and sincerity receive information? Will the Lord turn away from the honest heart seeking for truth? No, he will not; he will prove to them, by the revelations of his Spirit, the facts in the case. And when the mind is open to the revelations of the Lord it comprehends them quicker and keener than anything that is seen by the natural eye. It is not what we see with our eyes—they may be deceived—but what is revealed by the Lord from heaven that is sure and steadfast, and abides forever. We do not want the people to rely on human testimony, although that cannot be confuted and destroyed; still, there is a more sure word of prophecy that all may gain if they will seek it earnestly before the Lord."[113]

Never Made a Sacrifice

President Young loved his life and did not view anything that he experienced—even the trials—as an unfair burden to bear. "You hear many talk about having made sacrifices; if I had that word in my vocabulary I would blot it out. I have never yet made what I call sacrifices; in my experience I know nothing about making them."[29]

Charles Swift

Assistant Professor of Ancient Scripture, PhD
Brigham Young University.

NOTES

1. This table is adapted from Leonard J. Arrington, *Brigham Young: American Moses* (New York: Alfred A. Knopf, 1985), 413–17. His seminal biography of Brigham Young is invaluable to all who wish to learn about this great prophet of the last days. In the research for this chapter, I am indebted to him and his work.

2. Brigham Young, *JD*, 12:287.

3. Ibid., 4:112.

4. Eugene England, *Brother Brigham* (Salt Lake City: Bookcraft, 1980), 3.

5. *JD*, 10:360.

6. Richard Neitzel Holzapfel and R. Q. Shupe, *My Servant Brigham: Portrait of a Prophet* (Salt Lake City: Bookcraft, 1997), 57.

7. Ronald K. Esplin, "Conversion and Transformation: Brigham Young's New York Roots and the Search for Bible Religion," in *Lion of the Lord: Essays on the Life and Service of Brigham Young*, ed. Susan Easton Black and Larry C. Porter (Salt Lake City: Deseret Book, 1995), 23.

8. *JD*, 14:112.

9. Esplin, "Conversion and Transformation," 29.

10. *JD*, 3:91.

11. Arrington, *American Moses*, 30.

12. *JD*, 8:119.

13. Ibid., 1:313.

14. *Millennial Star* 25 (July 11, 1863): 439.

15. *JD*, 2:128.

16. Arrington, *American Moses*, 37.

17. Leonard J. Arrington, *The Presidents of the Church: Biographical Essays* (Salt Lake City: Deseret Book, 1986), 28.

18. *JD*, 10:20.

19. Arrington, *The Presidents of the Church*, 29.

20. Arrington, *American Moses*, 42–45.

21. Preston Nibley, *Brigham Young: The Man and His Work* (Salt Lake City: Deseret Book, 1965), 15.

22. *HC*, 2:181.

23. *JD*, 2:10.

24. Ibid., 10:20.

25. Arrington, *American Moses*, 48.

26. Ibid., 51–52.

27. Ronald K. Esplin, "Brigham Young and the Transformation of the 'First' Quorum of the Twelve," in *Lion of the Lord*, 62.

28. England, *Brother Brigham*, 31.

29. *JD*, 13:211.

30. James B. Allen, Ronald K. Esplin, and David J. Whittaker, *Men with a Mission, 1837–1841: The Quorum of the Twelve Apostles in the British Isles* (Salt Lake City: Deseret Book, 1992), 89.

31. Arrington, *American Moses*, 81.

32. Allen, Esplin, and Whitaker, *Men with a Mission*, 314.

33. Arrington, *American Moses*, 100–102.

34. *JD*, 3:266.

35. Arrington, *American Moses*, 102.

36. Milton V. Backman Jr., "The Keys Are Right Here: Succession in the Presidency," in *Lion of the Lord*, 109.

37. Arrington, *American Moses*, 109–110.

38. Backman, "The Keys," 107.

39. James B. Allen and Glen M. Leonard, *The Story of the Latter-day Saints*, 2nd ed. (Salt Lake City: Deseret Book, 1992), 216.

40. Lynne Watkins Jorgensen and *BYU Studies* staff, "The Mantle of the Prophet Joseph Passes to Brother Brigham: A Collective Spiritual Witness," *BYU Studies* 36, no. 4 (1997): 131, 125–204.

41. Benjamin F. Johnson, *My Life's Review* (Independence: Zion's Printing & Publishing Company, 1979), 103–4.

42. Brigham Young to Vilate Young, August 11, 1844, Brigham Young Papers, LDS Church Archives, Salt Lake City, as quoted in *My Servant Brigham*, 72.

43. Brigham Young, *Manuscript History of Brigham Young, 1846–1847*, ed. Elden J. Watson (Salt Lake City: 1971), 529.

44. Ibid., 142.

45. *HC*, 7:585.

46. Susan Easton Black, "The Mormon Battalion: Religious Authority Clashed with Military Leadership," in *Lion of the Lord*, 155.

47. Ibid., 167.

48. *JD*, 4:41.

49. Arrington, *American Moses*, 153.

50. *Millennial Star*, 439.

51. Charles Lowell Walker, *Diary of Charles Lowell Walker*, ed. A. Karl Larson and Katharine Miles Larson (Logan, UT: Utah State University Press, 1980), 1:422.

52. *JD*, 10:223.

53. Clarissa Young Spencer with Mabel Harmer, *Brigham Young at Home* (Salt Lake City: Deseret Book, 1968), 33.

54. Dale F. Beecher, "Colonizer of the West," in *Lion of the Lord*, 174.

55. Ibid., 175.

56. *JD*, 10:3–4.

57. Holzapfel and Shupe, *My Servant Brigham*, 16.

58. *JD*, 5:231.

59. Ibid., 8:124–25.

60. Susa Young Gates with Leah D. Widtsoe, *The Life Story of Brigham Young* (New York: The Macmillan Company, 1930), 362.

61. Brigham Young, *Discourses of Brigham Young*, comp. John A. Widtsoe (Salt Lake City: Deseret Book, 1954), 2.

62. Ibid.

63. Ibid., 4.

64. Ibid., 183.

65. Ibid., 192–93.

66. Ibid., 1.

67. Ibid., 12.

68. Ibid., 8.

69. Ibid., 9.

70. Ibid., 152.

71. Ibid.

72. Ibid., 153.

73. Ibid., 154.

74. Ibid., 156–57.

75. Ibid., 157–58.

76. Ibid., 159.

77. Ibid., 160

78. Ibid., 161.

79. Ibid., 62.

80. Ibid., 64.

81. Ibid., 65.

82. Ibid.

83. Ibid., 62.

84. Ibid., 247.

85. Ibid., 248.

86. Ibid., 254–55.

87. Ibid., 255.

88. Ibid.

89. Ibid., 261.

90. Ibid., 248.

91. Ibid., 256.

92. Ibid., 259–60.

93. Ibid., 236.

94. Ibid.

95. *JD*, 13:60–61.

96. Young, *Discourses of Brigham Young*, 238–39.

97. Ibid., 242–43.

98. Ibid., 306.

99. Ibid., 307.

100. Ibid., 314.

101. Ibid., 175.

102. Ibid., 194.

103. Ibid., 197–98.

104. Ibid., 199.

105. Ibid., 199–200.

106. Ibid., 201.

107. Ibid., 203.

108. Ibid., 208.

109. Ibid., 209.

110. Ibid., 458.

111. Ibid., 458–59.

112. Ibid., 458.

113. Ibid., 429–30.

SIDEBAR AND PHOTO NOTES

1. Esplin, "Conversion and Transformation," 30–31.

2. *JD*, 3:51.

3. *Deseret News* 25 (February 10, 1858): 386.

4. Orson F. Whitney, *Life of Heber C. Kimball* (Salt Lake City:

Kimball Family, 1888), 265–66.

5. Arrington, *American Moses*, 157–58.

6. *JD*, 10:106.

7. Arrington, *American Moses*, 172, 236, 283.

8. Arrington, *The Presidents of the Church*, 56.

9. Arrington, *American Moses*, 330–31.

10. *JD*, 11:117.

11. Arrington, *American Moses*, 288, 293.

12. *JD*, 19:68.

13. Ibid. 12:171.

14. Young, *Discourses of Brigham Young*, 463.

15. Ibid., 358.

16. Ibid., 273.

17. *JD*, 17:51.

18. Young, *Discourses of Brigham Young*, 330.

19. Ibid., 273–74.

20. Ibid., 246.

21. Ibid., 451.

22. Ibid., 305.

23. Ibid., 232.

24. Ibid., 204–5.

25. Ibid., 305.

26. Ibid., 209–10.

27. Ibid., 458.

28. Ibid., 451.

29. Ibid.

Chapter Three

JOHN TAYLOR

LIFE AND TIMES

1808	November 1	Born in Milnthorpe, Westmoreland County, England
1824		Joined the Methodist Church
1830		Immigrated to Canada
1833		Married Leonora Cannon
1836		Baptized by Parley P. Pratt
1838	December 19	Ordained an Apostle
1839–41		Served first mission to England
1842–46		Became editor of the *Times and Seasons*
1846–47		Served second mission to England
1849–52		Served mission to Europe
1855–57		Presided over Eastern States Mission
1857–76		Appointed member of Utah Territorial Legislature
1877		Elected territorial superintendent of schools; assumed leadership of Church as President of the Quorum of the Twelve Apostles
1878		Primary Association established
1880	October 10	Sustained as third President of the Church
1884		Dedicated the Logan Temple
1884		Moved into exile
1887	July 25	Died in Kaysville, Utah, at age seventy-eight

BIOGRAPHICAL HIGHLIGHTS

As a youth in England, John Taylor's interest in religion led him to join the Methodist Church. When his parents moved the family to Canada in 1830, John felt a call to preach the gospel. During this time he married Leonora Cannon.

After listening to Parley P. Pratt, John and Leonora accepted baptism in Toronto. In 1837 Joseph Smith called John as an Apostle, and soon John accepted a mission call to England. Upon his return he became editor of the *Times and Seasons* in Nauvoo. When the Prophet Joseph went to Carthage, John went with him and witnessed his death. Following this, John accepted a call to serve a second mission to England and a later mission to Europe.

With the death of Brigham Young, John assumed leadership of the Church as the President of the Quorum of the Twelve Apostles. Three years later in 1880, he was sustained as the third President of the Church. In 1885 persecution from federal officials forced President Taylor into hiding. His health began to fail, and on July 25, 1887, he died.

CONTRIBUTIONS

John Taylor's British heritage enabled him to participate in the first mission to Great Britain. In addition to his direct missionary work, he used his skill as an editor to publish the gospel message in newspapers and other publications such as the *Times and Seasons*, the *Nauvoo Neighbor*, and *The Mormon*.

As President, he reorganized and revitalized the priesthood quorums of the Church. He redefined the role of stake presidents and instituted quarterly conferences and a variety of priesthood leadership meetings.

At his funeral, he was heralded as a "Champion of Liberty." His twenty years in the territorial legislature are but a small part of his commitment to true political principles. His greater contribution lies in his staunch defense of the rights of Church members to practice their religious beliefs without government interference. Believing in the Constitution of the United States, he stood firm against federal attempts to deprive the Saints of their rights as citizens. For this cause, he finally gave his life.

TEACHINGS

The life and teachings of John Taylor reflect his creed, "The kingdom of God or nothing." As President he communicated his dedication with clarity and skill, thus encouraging others to follow his example.

Continuing the reorganization of the priesthood begun by Brigham Young, he redefined the Seventies quorum and revitalized the office of stake president by clearly teaching them their duties. He firmly believed that the progress of the Church depended on the purity and power of those who held the priesthood of God.

To celebrate the fiftieth anniversary of the Church, he taught the importance of being one both temporally and spiritually. He encouraged individuals and businesses to forgive loans and otherwise turn their attention to those in need.

When pressure from the federal government increased, President Taylor encouraged the Saints to stand firm. He helped them understand that the afflictions were part of the sanctification process of the Lord's people. Always his argument was not against his country, but against those who would use its power to abuse the rights of others. Certainly in word and deed, John Taylor is an example of a mortal life worth emulating.

LIFE OF
JOHN TAYLOR

◆

Brigham Young once remarked, "With regard to brother John Taylor, I will say that he has one of the strongest intellects of any man that can be found; he is a powerful man, he is a mighty man."[1] Anyone acquainted with the writings and sermons of John Taylor, the third President of the Church, knows that Brigham Young was not indulging in frivolous flattery of his friend and colleague. John Taylor's keen mind and rhetorical facility combined to produce a voice for the faith that he adopted as a young man. President Taylor's extraordinary ability to comprehend the essence of a topic, the significance of a set of circumstances, or the assumptions beneath a philosophical construct allowed him to quickly assess any given moment and turn the power of that moment toward the advancement of the kingdom of God. He did not quail or tremble, even in the face of great personal trial and tragedy, for he understood that the wisdom of God would prevail. He was possessed of the wisdom that comes of experience and a deep spiritual conviction that his life experiences had meaning beyond mortality.

In addition to his ability to reason and to judge, President Taylor was a goodly man who desired righteousness with all of his heart. Joseph F. Smith, the sixth President of the Church, said of President Taylor: "I bear my testimony to the integrity of John Taylor as one of the purest men I ever knew in my life, a man clean from head to foot, clean in body and clean in spirit, free from every vulgar thing, so common among the children of men. I know whereof I speak, for I was with him day and night, month after month, year after year, and I bear testimony of his integrity."[2]

To John Taylor, the mere intellectual awareness or acceptance of the principles of truth was not sufficient for any man called as a servant of God. Strict adherence to the will of God constituted the whole duty of mankind, for to do otherwise would be an insult to God and a denial of His love. John Taylor was prepared to invest his whole soul for the kingdom of God. He would be called upon to do so throughout the length of his life.

James and Agnus Taylor in 1886, parents of John Taylor.

YOUTH

The parents of John Taylor, James and Agnus Taylor, were modestly landed gentry, descendants of nobility, but children of younger brothers and sisters who received neither titles nor income from their family. Decades of war had created harsh economic conditions in England. Even those citizens fortunate to have an estate were often compelled to augment their income through outside employment. Thus, though James Taylor owned property in the village of Hale in the county of Westmoreland, England, he spent several years working for the British government. His employment with the excise board required him to move from place to place, including a five-year stay in the city of Liverpool. While living in Milnthorpe, Westmoreland County, Agnus gave birth to their second son, John, on November 1, 1808. In addition to their first two sons, the Taylors would bring two daughters and six other sons into the world.

Little is known of John Taylor's youth, but inasmuch as his parents were well educated, he likely received a gentleman's education. When the Taylors returned to Hale, John attended school at Beetham and learned skills associated with farming in the northwest of England. At age fourteen, typical of young men his age, he became an apprentice to learn a practical trade; he spent the first year as a cooper (a barrel maker) in Liverpool and then the next five years as a wood turner in Penrith, Cumberland County, near the border with Scotland. While at Penrith, John Taylor encountered the Methodist faith and soon found it far more acceptable than the cold rituals of the Church of England. By age seventeen, he was a lay minister for the Methodists in Cumberland. While serving in that capacity he was deeply impressed that he should change his missionary venue to North America. He would do so five years later when his family immigrated to Canada.

Influence of Poetry

In his adolescence, John Taylor was not only physically strong, but he was also gifted with a keen mind. Within a few short months he had become a capable hand at the lathe and was praised for an ability to work that was beyond his years. He also developed a love of reading classic authors and poets such as Shakespeare, Wordsworth, and Coleridge. Along with his expanding knowledge in literary works, his surroundings in England had an influential effect on him and allowed him to develop his talent in poetry. His use of poetry is revealed in many of his later lectures and writings.

The Church hymn entitled "Go, Ye Messengers of Glory" provides an example of John's skill as a poet. Two stanzas of that poem are given below.

Go, ye messengers of glory;
Run, ye legates of the skies.
Go and tell the pleasing story
That a glorious angel flies,
Great and mighty, great and mighty,
With a message from the skies.

Go to ev'ry tribe and nation;
Visit ev'ry land and clime.
Sound to all the proclamation;
Tell to all the truth sublime:
That the gospel, that the gospel
Does in ancient glory shine.

Bridge End Farm. Taylor home in Milnthorpe, Westmoreland County, England. Traditional birthplace of John Taylor.

Leonora Cannon Taylor.

A New Life in Canada

John Taylor settled in Toronto, Canada, in 1832, where he reestablished his wood turning business and continued to preach for the Methodist Church. During that time he met and courted Leonora Cannon, a fellow Methodist. They married on January 28, 1833.

Notwithstanding the fact that John was teaching the gospel of Christ in America, he was still somewhat unsure of his faith, and he confided to his young wife that a greater task awaited him. During this time, the Taylors associated themselves with a small group of intelligent and educated couples who were assiduous in their search for the truth. Though most

Baptism of John and Leonora Taylor

John Taylor hesitated to meet Parley P. Pratt, feeling that he would rather not associate with the Mormons. While he treated Parley curtly, he did listen to his message. John was delighted with Parley's teaching. He found that the restored gospel was an answer to his prayer to find truth in religion. He read the Book of Mormon and the Doctrine and Covenants and recorded and pondered all of Parley's addresses. After three weeks John and Leonora were baptized in Black Creek near Toronto, Ontario, Canada, by Parley P. Pratt.

Leonora Cannon Taylor
(1796–1868)

John met Leonora while preaching for the Methodist Church in Toronto. Also a native of England and a devout Methodist, Leonora had immigrated to Canada as the maid to the wife of Lord Aylmer, Governor General of Canada. She rejected John's first proposal of marriage, but a dream changed her mind. In her dream she saw herself happily married to John and felt impressed to then accept his proposal. They were married January 28, 1833.

Site of John Taylor's baptism. Black Creek in what is now North York, Ontario, Canada.

members of the group were of the Methodist persuasion, it was not long before they concluded that none of the existing religious organizations of the day could legitimately lay claim to being the true Church of Christ. When their notions came to the attention of the leadership of the Methodist Church in Canada, the church convened a conference to admonish the dissenters.

The group continued in their prayers and fasting, petitioning the Lord that they might know where to find the fulness of His truth on the earth. In answer to these fervent prayers, the Lord sent to them His servant Parley P. Pratt. John Taylor and his friends asked Parley to preach to them. The power and spirit that attended Elder Pratt's message impressed the group. For three weeks, John Taylor listened to the missionary and took copious notes of what he said in his sermons and exhortations. He afterward compared the doctrines taught with the writings of the ancient Apostles and prophets of the Bible. John and Leonora read the Book of Mormon and the Doctrine and Covenants, and they were convinced that God was once again laboring with His children. On May 9, 1836, Parley P. Pratt baptized both of them into the restored Church.

Parley P. Pratt (1807–1857), the missionary who baptized John Taylor and his wife.

John Taylor Chastises Parley P. Pratt

When John arrived in Kirtland, he found that his missionary friend, Parley, was doubting the Church. John's words to Parley helped him regain his faith and repent of his dissentient spirit.

"I am surprised to hear you speak so, Brother Parley. Before you left Canada you bore a strong testimony to Joseph Smith being a Prophet of God, and to the truth of the work he inaugurated; and you said that you knew these things by revelation, and the Gift of the Holy Ghost. You gave to me a strict charge to the effect that though you or an angel from heaven was to declare anything else I was not to believe it. Now Brother Parley, it is not man that I am following, but the Lord. The principles you taught me led me to Him, and now I have the same testimony that you then rejoiced in. If the work was true six months ago, it is true today; if Joseph Smith was then a prophet, he is now a prophet."[1]

THE BEGINNINGS OF JOHN TAYLOR'S MINISTRY

The work of spreading the gospel throughout Canada continued almost unimpeded, especially with the arrival of Elder Pratt's colleagues in the Quorum of the Twelve, Orson Hyde and Orson Pratt. In the fall of 1836, the three returned to Kirtland, Ohio, leaving newly ordained Elder John Taylor as the presiding officer of the Church in Canada. When Elder Taylor visited Kirtland in the spring of 1837, he found the Church suffering a degree of confusion and apostasy. Parley P. Pratt was somewhat negatively affected by a spirit of contention. However, with John Taylor's help, he realized his error and tearfully sought

Mission Preparations

In the midst of his family's bad health and poverty, John Taylor made preparations to join Wilford Woodruff and Zebedee Coltrin on a mission to England. Although he withstood the sickness and persecutions in Missouri and Nauvoo, as he journeyed eastward his health began to fail him. In Indiana, John "became suddenly and violently sick." He appeared to get sicker by the mile, and his companions decided that John was about to die and left his life in the hands of the Lord as they continued on their journey. John proclaimed, "The people in this neighborhood treated me with the greatest kindness, and as there was a chapel close to the inn where I stayed, at their request I preached to them, but I was so weak that I had to sit down and preach. After staying there about five weeks I was so far recovered as to be able to proceed."

Before leaving to join his companions in New York, John received a blessing from the people he had been preaching to in the neighborhood. Impressed with his character and willingness to preach to the neighborhood, a man offered to help pay for his medical and hotel bills. In reply to this man's charitable offer, John stated, "I preach without purse or scrip, leaving the Lord to manage those matters you speak of in His own way; and as you have been prompted by the Lord and your own generous impulses, I shall thankfully receive whatever assistance you are disposed to render me."[2]

forgiveness of the Prophet Joseph Smith. John Taylor was equally effective in strengthening the hearts and minds of others in Kirtland as the storms of oppression beat upon the Church.

John Taylor's tenure as the presiding officer of the Church in Canada was interrupted for a time by the presumption and arrogance of one Sampson Avard, who claimed presiding authority in Canada. When Joseph Smith and others of the leading councils of the Church arrived, they quickly resolved the matter. Elder Taylor learned from this experience the correct order of the priesthood and the rights of presidency. Before leaving Canada, Joseph Smith ordained John Taylor a high priest and reaffirmed his leadership of the Church in that region. As the presiding Church officer in Canada, John Taylor wrote a letter on behalf of Joseph Fielding, Orson Hyde, and Heber C. Kimball to Elder Fielding's brother,

James, a minister in Preston, England. The letter testified of the restoration of the gospel and of the Church of Christ. It had such a profound effect upon James Fielding that he allowed the missionaries to address his Methodist congregation in England.

CALL TO THE APOSTLESHIP

Elder Taylor's leadership was characterized by inspired counsel, direction, and compassion. The apostasy in Kirtland, Ohio, had, in part, been caused by an extreme financial crisis that had struck the nation in 1837. John Taylor's efforts to raise relief funds for the Saints in Kirtland did much to bind the hearts of the members together. In the fall of 1837, Elder Taylor learned that he had been selected to fill a vacancy in the Quorum of the Twelve Apostles. In his attempt to accept his appointment, John Taylor traveled to Kirtland to

Call to the Quorum of the Twelve

In 1837, the Prophet Joseph Smith sent a letter to John Taylor asking him to move to Far West, Missouri, and accept a position in the Quorum of the Twelve Apostles. At that time he was a missionary in Canada. After his mission he had hoped to return to live in Kirtland, Ohio, on a five-acre farm he had purchased near the temple. Obedient to the prophet's call, he loaded his possessions in a sleigh and several wagons and made the thirteen-hundred-mile trip to Missouri. Elder Taylor's call came at a difficult time in Church history. The failure of the Kirtland Safety Society had fanned the flames of apostasy in that city. Joseph was forced to flee for his life with the faithful members of the Church. John's call to the apostleship happened at this time because four of the original members of the group had left the Church, leaving vacancies in the quorum. Along with John Taylor, Wilford Woodruff, Willard Richards, and John Page received calls. They assumed leadership in a Church torn asunder by apostasy and mob persecution.

As a result, John's trip to locate the Prophet was difficult and fraught with danger. Finally he located the prophet in Far West, Missouri, where the faithful had gathered to begin, yet again, to build a temple to their God.

Times and Seasons Building in Nauvoo, Illinois.

Times and Seasons Building, Nauvoo, Illinois

The *Times and Seasons* newspaper moved to this site on Main Street in 1845. There John Taylor edited the *Times and Seasons* and the *Nauvoo Neighbor* newspapers. The Taylor family lived in the home attached to the printing shop. Today the renovated building features original presses of the period. The Times and Seasons Printing Complex was first built by James Ivins from 1842–44. John Taylor bought the buildings on behalf of the Church in 1845.

locate the Prophet. Finding the city deserted, he journeyed to Far West, Missouri, where the Saints had relocated. In the spirit of his new calling, the young Apostle preached the principles of the restored gospel of Christ as he made his way west. Shortly after John Taylor arrived in Missouri in the autumn of 1838, the state erupted in violence against the Latter-day Saints, resulting in the arrest of Joseph Smith, Sidney Rigdon, and other prominent leaders of the Church. Notwithstanding the turmoil and distress that enveloped the membership of the Church at that time, on December 19, 1838, Brigham Young and Heber C. Kimball laid their hands upon the head of John Taylor and ordained him an Apostle.

John Taylor then made his way to Liberty, Missouri, where he conferred with the Prophet Joseph regarding the affairs of the Church. With other members of the Twelve, Elder Taylor helped relocate the Saints to Illinois. He also participated in the dedication of the temple site at Far West, and after settling his family in Montrose, Iowa, he subsequently departed with Wilford Woodruff on a mission to the British Isles in August 1839. During that eighteen-month mission, Elder Taylor preached the gospel throughout England and introduced the restored Church to the people of Ireland and the Isle of Mann. He also used his editorial skills to publish the first edition of the Book of Mormon outside the United States, a hymn book, and several pamphlets. On July 1, 1841, he rejoined his friends and family in Nauvoo, Illinois.

NAUVOO

There was much in Nauvoo to challenge the faith of John Taylor. He returned to find his wife at the point of death, and only through the instrumentality of the priesthood of God was her life preserved. After learning of the doctrine of plural marriage, Elder Taylor struggled mightily until the Spirit of God distilled upon his soul and confirmed the truth of those teachings. Before leaving Nauvoo for the West, John Taylor was sealed to

Sister Taylor Was Quite Low

Upon returning to Nauvoo in July 1841, the missionaries could not have expected a better welcome than they received. Nearly three hundred Saints met them with greater love than they had ever known. All the missionaries found their families well, except "Sister Taylor who was quite low." Leonora was near dead in the one room home in Montrose, Iowa, where John left her two years before. "He sat beside the bed, holding her hand, while in a weak voice she poured out her travails. The old barrack was so dilapidated that a skunk came in every night. Twice she'd found a huge snake in the room. On a night when the children were sick, drunken Indians had come to the door, trying to get in. And in the months that he'd been away, not a single one of his relatives had put a nose in the door to offer help." These hardships had broken down her strength, and death was approaching rapidly. John called in twenty elders and gave her a blessing to regain her health. Soon after the blessing was given, "the Lord raised her up."[3]

three women for time and eternity by the holy priesthood of God. There would be no more articulate advocate of the principle of plural marriage than John Taylor, notwithstanding his early aversion to the precept.

During the time John Taylor dwelt in Illinois, he was actively engaged in a variety of pursuits. From 1842 to 1845, he served as the editor of the *Times and Seasons*, the *Wasp*, and the *Nauvoo Neighbor*, the latter two being local Nauvoo newspapers. In these publications, Elder Taylor ably defended the Saints, their Prophet, and the gospel principles of truth and justice. He served as a member of the Nauvoo City Council, as a regent for the University of Nauvoo, and as Judge Advocate in the Nauvoo Legion.

Upon learning of the arrest of Joseph Smith, he willingly accompanied the Prophet and his brother to Carthage Jail, where his two friends and colleagues were brutally murdered. During this experience, the attacking mob shot Elder Taylor five times. Had not Willard Richards acted to save Elder Taylor's life, he too would have died at Carthage. Section 135 of the Doctrine and Covenants contains much of Elder

Carthage Jail

On Monday, June 24, the Prophet Joseph Smith, his brother Hyrum, John Taylor, and others rode to Carthage. Charged and released on bail, John decided to remain with the Prophet and his brother who were placed in the Carthage Jail. On Wednesday night John was joined by Willard Richards, Dan Jones, and Stephen Markam. Early Thursday morning, Jones and Markam left the jail on errands. During the day the four remaining brethren read from the works of Josephus and the Book of Mormon. In the late afternoon Joseph asked John to sing. In response he sang all fourteen verses of "A Poor Wayfaring Man of Grief." Joseph asked him to sing it a second time, which he did. Then around 5:00 PM the mob rushed the jail, killing Joseph and Hyrum and wounding John. After the mob fled, Willard pulled John outside and gained the assistance of the town doctor, Thomas L. Barnes. Using a pen knife, the doctor extracted the ball lodged in John's hand. It was not until the next day that John's wound were cleaned and bandaged. He was then left in the Hamilton House hotel until he regained his strength for the return trip to Nauvoo.

Carthage Jail, Carthage, Illinois.

Taylor's recollection of the martyrdom. He describes Joseph and his brothers as "martyrs of religion" and reminds his readers that the Restoration had "cost the best blood of the nineteenth century" and that "glory is their eternal reward." He concludes by declaring that "their innocent blood . . . will cry unto the Lord of Hosts till he avenges that blood on the earth" (D&C 135).

EXODUS AND MISSION

With the death of Joseph and Hyrum, the leadership of the Church passed to Brigham Young and the Twelve. John Taylor joined with his colleagues in preparing the Saints for the move west, the completion of the Nauvoo Temple, and the administration of the endowment to worthy members of the Church. On February 16, 1846, Elder Taylor and his family crossed the Mississippi River with all of the supplies and possessions they could carry in eight wagons and a carriage. The Taylors left a fine two-story brick home, a brick store, a printing office, a barn, and another building lot in town. Additionally, he owned 186 acres of arable land and timber east of the city. For his property and improvements, he would receive little or no compensation.

Having helped the Saints settle upon the banks of the Missouri River at Council Bluffs, and having substantively aided in the organization of the Mormon Battalion, John Taylor, in company with Parley P. Pratt and Orson Hyde, left on his second mission to England, arriving in Liverpool on October 3, 1846. During the next five months, Elder Taylor, in conjunction with others of the Twelve, set in order the problems created by the defection of local priesthood leaders. He returned to Winter Quarters by way of New Orleans, bringing with him much needed scientific equipment, including sextants, barometers, several thermometers, and a telescope. Leaving Winter Quarters about June 21, 1847, John Taylor and Parley P. Pratt led a company of over 1,500 souls (more than half of them women and children), their cattle, and their belongings into the Salt Lake Valley.

Arriving on October 5, 1847, the Taylor/Pratt Company found the Saints anxiously preparing for their first winter in the Salt Lake Valley. During that winter, Elder Taylor labored

Letter from St. Louis

During the October 1849 conference in Salt Lake City, Brigham Young called John Taylor to serve a mission to Europe. He left his family on October 19 and began the journey east. Upon arriving in St. Louis, Elder Taylor wrote the following to his family in Utah.

"'But,' say you, 'do you not think of us and home? and do you never think of me, and of me?' This is what I have been wanting to get at for some time, and this long, tedious preface had become wearisome to me—let me tell my feelings if I can. Home! Home! Home! What shall I say? can I tell it? No, a thousand times no! Your forms, your countenances, your bodies and spirits are all portrayed before me as in living characters. You are with me in my imaginations, thoughts, dreams, feelings; true our bodies are separated, but there you live—you dwell in my bosom, in my heart and affections, and will remain together forever. Our covenants, our hopes, our joys are all eternal and will live when our bodies moulder in the dust. Oceans, seas, mountains, deserts and plains may separate us—but in my heart you dwell. . . . Our separations here tend to make us more appreciative of each other's society. A few more separations and trials, a few more tears, a few more afflictions, and the victory will be ours! We'll gain the kingdom, possess the crown, inherit eternal glory, associate with the Gods, soar amidst the intelligences of heaven; and with the noble, the great, the intellectual, the virtuous, the amiable, the holy, possess the reward held in reserve for the righteous, and live and love forever."[4]

in the sawpit manufacturing lumber. Evenings and Sabbath days were dedicated to strengthening the Saints by visiting families in their homes and seeing to their wants and needs. From time to time, the Saints held activities to break the monotony of wilderness life. John and Leonora enjoyed these social gatherings and sponsored the New Year's dance of 1848 in their home. Nearly seventy persons attended this event.

A SHORT RESPITE— THEN ANOTHER MISSION

For the next two years, John Taylor and his family made their new home as comfortable as possible in the midst of a lonely wilderness. Explorations of the valley continued as more immigrants arrived. To supplement their meager stores of food, Elder Taylor fished in Utah Lake and Sister Taylor wove the net he used. Elder Taylor helped the Saints build homes, fence pastures, and even erect a bridge over the Jordan River. His faith helped sustain the Saints through these challenging times with his optimism and love.

At the October conference of 1849, Elder Taylor once again accepted a call to leave his family in order to serve a mission to Europe. On October 19, he commenced his eastward trek across the plains to St. Louis, from thence to New York and Liverpool, arriving on May 27, 1850. After a short stay in England, Elder Taylor traveled to France, arriving in Boulogne-sur-Mer on June 18, 1850. While there, he dedicated France for the preaching of the gospel. He courageously refuted the false accusations and dubious logic of all those who would oppose the work that he had commenced among them. The Book of Mormon was painstakingly translated into French, and a local publication initiated *Etoile du Deseret* (*Star of Deseret*). The principles of the Restoration

were also introduced into Germany, including the translation and publishing of the Book of Mormon in German and the beginnings of *Zion's Panier* (*Zion's Banner*) as the Church's German periodical.

Throughout his European ministry, John Taylor took advantage of every opportunity to spread the gospel. During his mission, he wrote and published the masterful *Government of God*, a two-hundred-page text that demonstrates his literary ability and power as a moral philosopher. Elder Taylor also formed the Deseret Manufacturing Company, purchasing and shipping the machinery necessary to establish a sugar beet factory in the Salt Lake Valley. He arrived home on August 20, 1852, by way of Boston, Philadelphia, Washington, DC, and St. Louis, strengthening the Saints along the way and encouraging any friends of the Church.

POLITICAL AND MISSIONARY SERVICE

For the next twenty-five years, John Taylor's exertions on behalf of the kingdom of God were monumental. He twice served in the Territorial Legislature, for many years as the Speaker of the House. During the Utah War of 1857, he accompanied Lt. General Daniel H. Wells into the canyons to review the troops hedging the way before Johnston's Army. For three years he labored as Utah County's Probate Judge, and at the time he came to the Presidency of the Church, he was fulfilling the responsibilities devolving upon the Territorial Superintendent of Schools.

During the same period, he frequently dealt with developing circumstances adverse to the Church in the eastern parts of the United States. Together with George A. Smith, he was elected one of the delegates commissioned to petition the Congress of the United States for admission into the Union, ironically about the same time that Southern states were preparing to withdraw. From 1854 to 1856, he published in New York City a periodical entitled *The Mormon*, the masthead creed of which was "Mind Your Own Business." His compelling rhetoric swept away the argument of libelous detractors, great and small.

John Taylor in 1853.

THE MORMON

AND HE SAID LET THERE BE LIGHT AND THERE WAS LIGHT

YOUR OWN CREED, MIND YOUR OWN BUSINESS. Brigham Young.

GIVEN BY INSPIRATION OF GOD. Joseph Smith

UTAH

IT IS BETTER TO REPRESENT OURSELVES, THAN TO BE REPRESENTED BY OTHERS.

VOL. III.--NO. 3.   NEW-YORK, SATURDAY, MARCH 7, 1857.   PRICE FIVE CENTS.

Masthead of *The Mormon* newspaper published in New York City by John Taylor between 1855 and 1857. In the paper he defended the practice of plural marriage and other Church doctrines. This effort did little to stem the negative public opinion.

THE PRESIDENCY

On August 29, 1877, the great western colonizer Brigham Young died. For the next ten years, John led the Church, first as President of the Quorum of the Twelve Apostles and later as the President of the Church. Two of the major developments during his early administration were the establishment of the Primary Association in 1878 and the grand celebration of the Jubilee Year in 1880. In concert with the Old Testament tradition, during the fiftieth anniversary of the organization of the Church, he proposed to forgive half of the debt of the Perpetual Emigrating Fund and half of the delinquent tithing owed by the worthy poor. Provisions of cattle and grain were also given the worthy poor to help them extricate themselves from abject poverty.

At the October conference of 1880, President Taylor and his two counselors, George Q. Cannon and Joseph F. Smith, were sustained as the First Presidency of the Church. President Taylor's seemingly boundless literary energy brought forth his work on the atoning sacrifice of the Lord Jesus

A Prophet in Exile (1885–87)

For the last two years of his life, John Taylor lived in hiding to avoid arrest at the hands of federal officials. This was a most difficult challenge given his age and health. For much of that time he lived in the home of Thomas F. Rouche. He continued to communicate with the Church through written epistles. Through this period his health continued to decline. On July 25, 1887, President Taylor died in exile. Because of the circumstances of his death, he is considered to have died a martyr's death.

Christ in 1882, *The Mediation and Atonement*, a classic text that brings into sharp focus his powerful witness of the redemption of mankind. On May 17, 1884, President Taylor offered the dedicatory prayer for the Logan Temple.

Notwithstanding the intense persecution brought about by the passage of anti-Mormon legislation, President Taylor conducted the affairs of the Church, touring Arizona and California in order to assess the degree of distress experienced by the Saints in those areas because of a hostile press and government. On February 1, 1885, President Taylor delivered his last public sermon.

President Taylor essentially lived the remainder of his life in seclusion, meeting only rarely with other leaders and moving from place to place to avoid detection by federal authorities. Most of the business of the Church accomplished by President Taylor was conducted through correspondence with his counselor George Q. Cannon. Even general conference talks composed by John Taylor during this period had to be read in conference by other leaders since he was unable to personally attend such public gatherings of the Saints.[3]

This was a very difficult time in the life of the prophet. Long periods of administrative silence were only rarely interrupted by new directives. One such event occurred in 1886 when President Taylor called for the publication of a new Church hymnal, the first to include both lyrics and a musical score for each of the hymns.[4]

For the remaining days of his life, he lived in hiding to avoid the vexatious legal proceedings

Logan Temple dedicated by John Taylor on May 17, 1884.

Canadian pioneers in 1887: John A. Woolf, Henry L. Hinman, and Charles O. Card.

Mission to Canada

Charles O. Card, a stake president in Logan, Utah, asked President Taylor for permission to move his family to Mexico to escape persecution. President Taylor asked him to search out a place of refuge in Canada. He hoped that the Canadian government would be tolerant of the practice of plural marriage. While this proved to be a false hope, Charles Card did establish an LDS colony in Southern Alberta that thrived and became a major Church center in Canada.

Funeral of John Taylor, held on July 29, 1887 in the Tabernacle adjacent to the Salt Lake Temple, then under construction. Members of the Church waited in line for up to four hours to bid their prophet farewell.

brought against him by local and federal officers. On July 18, 1887, President Taylor and his counselors met together for the first time in three and a half years. That meeting would prove to be the last. Precisely one week later, on July 25, 1887, at 7:55 in the evening, John Taylor died in exile at the home of Thomas Roueché in Kaysville, Utah. At noon on July 29, 1887, funeral services were held in the Salt Lake Tabernacle, where he was eulogized by his friends, colleagues, and family. He was interred at the Salt Lake City Cemetery. Throughout his life, John Taylor lived true to his creed, "The kingdom of God or nothing."

TEACHINGS OF PRESIDENT
JOHN TAYLOR

The volume of material, the diversity of subjects, and the implications of the sermons and writings that appeared between August 1877 (the point where John Taylor's presidency begins) and April 1887 (the last recorded message from President Taylor to the members of the Church) are remarkable.

During that ten-year period, John Taylor, either as President of the Quorum of the Twelve or as the President of the Church, wrote a minimum of thirty-nine directives to various individuals and organizations in regulating the affairs of the Church. Those directives, together with the eighty-five major sermons published in the *Journal of Discourses* and the masterful *The Mediation and Atonement*, were published about the time when he went into exile (1882) and constitute a considerable body of work. What follows, then, is not comprehensive, but it will reflect the clarity with which President Taylor guided the course of the Church through a troubled time.

PRIESTHOOD MATTERS

During the last year of his life, President Brigham Young began a restructuring of the quorums of the priesthood within the Church. This began with a circular from the First Presidency dated July 11, 1877. It released Apostles from their assignments as stake presidents, together with other ancillary responsibilities, so that they might concentrate their energies toward their scripturally defined tasks.

During the summer of 1877, the First Presidency initiated the reformation of stake organization and related priesthood responsibilities. At the death of Brigham Young, John Taylor assumed leadership of the Church as the President of the Quorum of the Twelve Apostles. In this role he continued the work to clarify and refine the duties and conduct of

The Published Works of John Taylor

In 1943, G. Homer Durham, a young faculty member at Utah State Agricultural College (presently Utah State University) published *The Gospel Kingdom*, selections from the writings and sermons of President John Taylor. For that labor, Brother Durham had access to extensive collections held in libraries throughout Utah, including the personal libraries of his father-in-law, Elder John A. Widtsoe, and that of the Church historian. Elder Durham, subsequently of the Presidency of the Seventy, also collated material published by President Taylor while serving as the editor of *The Mormon* (published in New York City), the *Times and Seasons*, the *Wasp*, and the *Nauvoo Neighbor* (all Nauvoo publications). President Taylor's doctrinal volumes, *The Government of God* (1852) and *The Mediation and Atonement* (1882), together with additional smaller works ("Items on Priesthood," "On Marriage," "Three Nights' Public Discussion," and others) were correlated with the voluminous material to be found in the *Journal of Discourses*, the *Millennial Star*, the *Deseret News*, and the published and unpublished histories of the Church. The narrative of Elder Durham's text coalesced into six "books" or major divisions, entitled from first to last: "Some Latter-day Saint Philosophy," "The Gospel Message," "Priesthood: The Government of God," "The Kingdom of God," "The Kingdom of God and the Kingdoms of Men," and "Some Personal Reflections and Footnotes to History." Within those six headings, G. Homer Durham managed to doctrinally present the fifty-year ministry of the third President of the Church. It is a volume of more than four hundred pages, a daunting enterprise.

stake presidencies and the various priesthood quorums of the Church. Stake presidents received special counsel to measure up to their callings. President Taylor stressed that anyone called to serve as a presiding authority ought to be a gentleman, avoid self-aggrandizement, and be like a father to those for whom he had charge. He further instructed the stake presidents that while they wielded great authority, they must be subject to those whom the Lord called to preside over them. They would also be held accountable for any unworthy member of the Church who, through negligence or timidity, received permission to enter the temple. If the worthy poor suffered unnecessarily because of priesthood apathy, the quorum leaders and presidencies would be taken to task, both in time and in eternity. In all things, leaders must treat the Saints of God with kindness and tenderness befitting the Savior Himself.

In his efforts to reform the priesthood quorums and presidencies, he recognized that the quorum of the First Presidency remained unorganized. For a period of three years, John Taylor led the Church as the President of the Quorum of the Twelve. While he recognized that the Twelve had the authority to reorganize the First Presidency, he did not feel that the Lord had approved such action. He did not act until three years later when he felt it to be the Lord's will. During the afternoon session of the October conference in 1880, the membership of the Church sustained John Taylor as their new President with George Q. Cannon as First Counselor and Joseph F. Smith as Second Counselor. At that time, President Taylor expressed his personal feelings regarding the action that had taken place in sustaining him as the third President of the Church. For his part, he had been willing to allow the Twelve to continue as the presiding quorum, such was his own humility and meekness. Notwithstanding his reticence, President Taylor concluded:

"It is impossible for men acquainted with the order of the holy priesthood to ignore this quorum, as it is one of the principal councils of the church. While the Twelve stand as a bulwark ready to protect, defend and maintain, to step forward and carry out the order of God's kingdom in times of necessity, such as above referred to, yet when everything is adjusted and matters assume their normal condition, then it is proper that the quorum of the First Presidency, as well as all other quorums, should occupy the place assigned it by the Almighty. . . . It is for us holding the holy priesthood to see that all of the organizations of that priesthood are preserved intact and that everything in the church and kingdom of God is organized according to the plan, which he has revealed. Therefore we have taken the course, which you have been called upon to sanction by your votes today."[5]

During this time President Taylor also turned his attention to the Young Men's Mutual Improvement Association, first organized by Brigham Young in 1875. By the time John Taylor's tenure as President began, the young men of the Church had enthusiastically received the YMMIA organization. This resulted in the development of certain irregularities that concerned Church leaders. In May 1880, President Taylor counseled YMMIA leaders that they ought not to perceive themselves as pertaining to another "quorum" other than the one to which they had already been ordained, and that the activities of the YMMIA should not in any way interfere with the duties and responsibilities of the individual priesthood bearers. For example,

Development of Church Auxiliaries

Early in his administration, John Taylor gave special attention to the development of the Church auxiliary organizations. He directed efforts to strengthen the YMMIA by refining local and Church operations and appointing Apostle Wilford Woodruff as the new superintendent with Joseph F. Smith and Moses Thatcher as counselors.

Similar attention was given to the young women's auxiliary. Its name was changed from the Retrenchment Association to the Young Ladies' Mutual Improvement Association under the leadership of Eliza R. Snow. Upon completing this assignment, Elmina S. Taylor was called as president on the same day that Eliza R. Snow became general president of the Relief Society.

During the summer of 1878, Aurelia Spencer Rogers gained permission to organize the first Primary Association in the Church. While it started as a small organization, it soon spread throughout the Church. In 1880, President Taylor approved a Churchwide organization and appointed Louie B. Felt as president. President Taylor approved the calling of missionaries to encourage the development of the auxiliary organizations. Their responsibilities included the training of ward and stake leaders and to create interest among the members for participation. As the auxiliaries matured, the need for special missionaries decreased.

The First Presidency of the Church in 1880: George Q. Cannon, John Taylor, and Joseph F. Smith.

which they preside, and organize the Priesthood in their various Stakes according to my law, in all the various departments thereof, in the High Councils, in the Elders Quorums, and in the Bishops and their Councils, and in the Quorums of Priests, Teachers and Deacons; that every Quorum may be fully organized according to the order of my Church; and, then, let them inquire into the standing and fellowship of all that . . . Holy Priesthood in their several Stakes; and if they find those that are unworthy let them remove them, except they repent; for my Priesthood, whom I have called and whom I have sustained and honored, shall honor me and obey my laws, and the laws of my Holy Priesthood, or they shall not be considered worthy to hold my Priesthood, saith the Lord. And let my Priesthood humble themselves before me, and seek not their own will but my will; for if my Priesthood whom I have chosen, and called, and endowed with the spirit and gifts of their several callings, and with the powers thereof, do not acknowledge me I will not acknowledge them, saith the Lord; for I will be honored and obeyed by my Priesthood."[6]

THE YEAR OF THE JUBILEE

April 6, 1880, marked the fiftieth anniversary of the organization of the Church. In a spirit reminiscent of the Old Testament, President John Taylor declared a Jubilee Year among the Saints of the latter days. At the heart of the celebration was mercy and forgiveness.

For its part, the Church sought for temporal relief for the worthy poor and specifically called upon the bishops and upon the presidents of stakes to submit in writing the names of those in their congregations who would be best

in November 1885 the First Presidency cautioned the officers of the YMMIA that they ought not to think themselves authorized to select potential missionaries, but that that lot fell to the Quorum of the Twelve and others appointed to do so.

On October 13, 1882, the voice of the Lord again came through President Taylor. The counsel was strong: The Presidency and the Twelve were to be one, even as the Father and the Son are one; the high priests were to organize themselves and be prepared to receive and execute their divinely appointed responsibilities; and finally, the Church was to be cleansed every whit, that the blessings of God might be poured out upon them. The counsel given in 1882 is no less apt in this day and in this hour:

"And let the Presidents of Stakes also purify themselves, and the Priesthood and the people of the Stakes over

The Gardo House, Salt Lake City, Utah. This building served as the John Taylor home and Church Headquarters during much of the administration of John Taylor.

served by having past tithing indebtedness and loans from the Perpetual Emigration Fund forgiven. Nearly one million dollars of debt was forgiven as a result. Additionally, 1,000 milk cows and 5,000 sheep were appropriated for the relief of the Saints in need; 300 cows and 2,000 sheep were to come from the Church's general flocks and herds, the remainder to be donated by the various stakes. As part of the Jubilee Year, the Relief Societies agreed to provide wheat to their respective bishops in order that the priesthood might more effectively bring respite to the suffering poor.

As part of the effort to establish the Latter-day Saints as an economically independent community, the various settlements and small factories along the Wasatch Front specialized in producing goods of various kinds, including leather goods, carriages and agricultural equipment, and furniture. As these small companies grew, the Church created Zion's Cooperative Mercantile Institution (ZCMI) so that the products could be more easily distributed throughout the territory. Having first set the example, the Church called upon ZCMI and its affiliated cooperatives and businesses to "free the worthy debt-bound brother if you can"[7] and "Do [your] part honorably, justly, charitably."[8]

In conjunction with the Year of the Jubilee, President Taylor and his counselors encouraged the members of the Church to be far more cooperative with one another, to establish the spirit of Zion as taught in the scriptures. He asked them to forgive loans and mortgages and otherwise do all they could to lift the burden of the poor. In a letter to the Saints in the Bannock Stake, the First Presidency commended them for their willingness to establish public services such as irrigation systems, common grazing pastures, and the like. Presidents Taylor and Cannon suggested that much the same might be done with the timber, hay lands, and even the arable land in order to maintain equity among the settlers. The prophet emphasized repeatedly the importance of treating one another with kindness, gentleness, and equality as the members of the Church began their new community in Idaho. It was clear that every man was to conform to the laws requiring titles to individual property, but it was also important that everyone in the beginning was to have an equal opportunity to acquire farms of productive soil.

Three years later in the April 1887 conference, the First Presidency addressed a letter to the Saints gathered in Provo,

Utah, in which they taught: "Connected with our temporal labors there is probably no point of more importance than the providing of employment for our people."[9] The Presidency counseled those with means to look about themselves and establish industries that would not only enhance the economy, but would provide employment opportunities for the young men and women in the territory who were idling away their time. They also observed that many of those who were immigrating to the Intermountain West needed work to provide for their families. Therefore, in every ward and stake men were to be selected who could take direction of such potential investments and thus do away with idleness and poverty. Thus, the spirit of the Year of the Jubilee continued, providing a benchmark by which the Church could measure its progress toward establishing a society of one heart, one mind, dwelling in righteousness, and having no poor among them.

OBEDIENCE

What message could have been clearer in the teachings of John Taylor than that of the personal power and strength that springs directly from obedience to the voice of the Lord? During the October general conference of 1881, John Taylor taught the gathered Saints:

"We have learned this, that God lives; we have learned that when we call upon him he hears our prayers; we have learned that it is the height of human happiness to fear God and observe his laws and keep his commandments; we have learned that it is a duty devolving upon us to try and make all men happy and intelligent, which happiness and intelligence can only be obtained through obedience to the laws of God."[10]

Although President Taylor counseled the membership of the Church to adhere to the will of God in all things, particular emphasis was given to certain principles. In the

A Revelation to John Taylor

In October 1882 the voice of the Lord came to President Taylor. The resulting revelation directed those who held the priesthood to arise and magnify their callings. Members of the Church were to set their houses in order so that they might be free from sin. The revelation was submitted to the Twelve for their approval and then distributed for a vote of approval by the Seventy and the stake presidents of the Church.

B. H. Roberts says that President John Taylor submitted this revelation to the Twelve Apostles and that it was accepted by them and that afterward it was also submitted for a vote of the presidents of stakes, the First Council of Seventy, and others and accepted by them.[5]

"And, then, I call upon my Priesthood, and upon all of my people to repent of all their sins and shortcomings, of their covetousness and pride and self-will, and of all their iniquities wherein they sin against me; and to seek with all, humility to fulfill my law, as my Priesthood, my Saints, and my people; and I call upon heads of families to put their houses in order according to the law of God, and attend to the various duties and responsibilities associated therewith, and to purify themselves before me, and to purge out iniquity from their households. And I will bless and be with you, saith the Lord; and ye shall gather together in your holy places wherein ye assemble to call upon me, and ye shall ask for such things as are right, and I will hear your prayers, and my spirit and power shall be with you, and my blessings shall rest upon you, upon your families, your dwellings and your households, upon your flocks and herds and fields, your orchards and vineyards, and upon all that pertains to you; and you shall be my people and I will be your God; and your enemies shall not have dominion over you, for I will preserve you and confound them, saith the Lord, and they shall not have power nor dominion over you; for my word shall go forth, and my work shall be accomplished, and my Zion shall be established, and my rule and my power and my dominion shall prevail among my people, and all nations shall yet acknowledge me. Even so. Amen."[6]

Assembly Hall, Temple Square, Salt Lake City, Utah. The Assembly Hall was completed and used for the first time in April 1880 as part of the celebration of the fiftieth anniversary of the organization of the Church.

semiannual general conference held in Coalville, Utah, in October 1886, President Taylor wrote the Saints:

"Among the sins into which some who are called Saints have been betrayed is Sabbath-breaking and over indulgence in useless pleasure. . . . These commandments of the Lord do not admit of Sunday excursions to the lake or the canons or other places any more than manual labor. That day will be held sacred to the service and worship of God by every true Latter-day Saint. Those who desecrate it reject the word of the Lord and will not be held guiltless. We admonish all members of the Church to obey this commandment and the officers of the Church to see that it is not broken with impunity."[11]

The distress that President Taylor felt at watching the members of the Church conduct themselves contrary to the word of the Lord was expressed in print repeatedly, but hardly ever with more poignancy than in this article on the front page of the *Deseret News*:

"I sometimes see Elders of Israel bringing in loads of wood and loads of hay on the Sabbath Day. Why, it is a burning shame in the eyes of God, holy angels, and all other intelligent beings. . . . What do you think about a lying Elder, a swearing High Priest, a Sabbath-breaking Seventy, and a covetous Saint? The souls of such men ought to be inspired with the light of revelation, and they ought to be living witnesses, epistles known and read of all men! Do you think

you can live your religion, have the spirit of God and obtain eternal life, and follow after these things? I tell you nay."[12]

Together with the observance of the Sabbath, President Taylor cautioned against over indulgence in useless pleasure. In a letter previously cited, he clarified what he meant:

"The mania for recreations of various kinds which has seized upon many of the people is harmful in several ways. It unfits them for the regular duties of life. It renders them restless and impatient of proper restraint. It obstructs business. It tends to contract habits of dissipation. It throws our young folks into the company of persons whose society [should] be shunned. It cultivates worldliness. It conduces to many evils, and the spirit of purity, temperance, holiness and peace will not abide in resorts such as have been established for the purpose of enticing the Saints into folly. Many thousands of dollars have been worse than wasted during the past summer on excessive amusements and sometimes unseemly diversions. The influential men and women of the Church should discountenance this evil, and with all wisdom and prudence endeavor to check it and prevent its increase among the Saints."[13]

While the First Presidency was not adverse to proper amusement, they taught that it was the responsibility of the members of the Church to set the example before the world. "Our social parties," said they, "should be conducted in a manner to give gratification to all who attend them, however delicate and refined they may be in their feelings." Furthermore, "Rude and boisterous conduct and everything of an improper character should be forbidden at such assemblages."[14] Along with the satisfaction of having the Saints dwell in harmony with one another, observing the word of the Lord, President Taylor was concerned about worldly threats to the most intimate society, that of the family.

HONORING FAMILY LIFE

"The life of a saint is not simply a personal perfecting; it is also a factor in the entire scheme of earth's redemption." Thus began a major section of the Conference Epistle of October 1886 from the First Presidency. At the heart of their theme was the sacredness of the family.

"To a people who believe as we do, that true marriage was divinely instituted for the multiplication of mankind, and is not a union for time alone, but reaches into the eternities, the disruption of families by divorce is an evil of no ordinary character, not only bearing a harvest of sorrow and suffering in this life, but also having a far reaching influence into the world beyond the grave, and possibly involving others in ruin who had no voice in the separation or power to avert its occurrence. For this reason the Latter-day Saints of all people should be most loath to sunder sacred ties once formed, and most determinedly opposed to the severance of unions made in holy places in God's appointed way, for light and trivial causes. . . . Only when every kindly counsel and ministration fail should that last resort, a divorce, be permitted."[15]

In his counsel to avoid divorce and to prosper the marital relationship, John Taylor was quite clear as to the manner in which peace and harmony might be established.

"Husbands, do you love your wives and treat them right, or do you think that you yourselves are some great moguls who have a right to crowd upon them? They are given to you as a part of yourself, and you ought to treat them with all kindness, with mercy and long suffering, and not be harsh and bitter, or in any way desirous to display your authority. Then, you wives, treat your husbands right, and try to make them happy and comfortable. Endeavor to make your homes a little heaven, and try to cherish the good Spirit of God."[16]

EDUCATION

John Taylor took a keen interest in the formation of schools in the Utah Territory, and so closely was he identified with the development of public schooling that he was elected to the office of Territorial Superintendent of district schools in 1877. In his teachings, it is possible to perceive the delicate balance between the desire for academic awareness and the power and influence of the Spirit of God.

"We ought to foster education and intelligence of every kind; cultivate literary tastes, and men of literary and scientific talent should improve that talent; and all should magnify the gifts which God has given unto them. Educate your children, and seek for those to teach them who have faith in God and in his promises, as well as intelligence. . . . If there is anything good and praiseworthy in morals, religion, science, or anything calculated to exalt and ennoble man, we are after it. But with all our getting, we want to get understanding, and that understanding which flows from God."[17]

President Taylor was not only concerned about the academic preparation and the professional aptitude of those employed to teach the children of the Church, but he also maintained that the character of the teachers in Zion should match their learning. He taught that only in an atmosphere of purity and love could any man or woman truly motivate a

Educational Achievements of John Taylor

John Taylor received a letter of commendation from the Commissioner of Education of the United States for his service as the Utah Territorial Superintendent of district schools. His work to provide enhanced opportunities for public education earned him this recognition. Among his achievements was his effort to attract the best qualified teachers and to pay them a worthy wage. To those who opposed paying teachers he said, "You cannot afford not to employ them. We want our children to grow up intelligently, and to walk abreast with the peoples of any nation. God expects us to do it. . . . I have heard intelligent practical men say, it is quite as cheap to keep a good horse as a poor one, or to raise good stock as inferior animals. Is it not quite as cheap to raise good intelligent children as to rear children in ignorance?"[7]

student to adopt truth as the governing principle of life.

"There is no man living, and there never was a man living, who was capable of teaching the things of God only as he was taught, instructed and directed by the spirit of revelation proceeding from the Almighty. And then there are no people competent to receive true intelligence and to form a correct judgment in relation to the sacred principles of eternal life, unless they are under the influence of the same spirit, and hence speakers and hearers are all in the hands of the Almighty."[18]

In 1883, John Taylor counseled the Latter-day Saints regarding the responsibility that they had toward their children and their children's children:

Pioneer School yard. John Taylor's interest in education prompted him to support both the elementary school and the upper level academies in the territory.

"It is highly necessary that we should learn to read and write and speak our own language correctly; and where people are deficient themselves in education they should strive all the more to see that the deficiency be not perpetuated in their offspring. We ought to take more pains that we do in the training and education of our youth. All that we can possibly do by way of placing them in a position to become the equals, at least, of [mankind], we ought to take pleasure in doing; for in elevating them we bring honor to our own name, and glory to God the Father. To do this requires labor and means, and it also requires perseverance and determination on the part of all concerned."[19]

CHALLENGES FROM THE FEDERAL GOVERNMENT

During most of his administration, President Taylor faced attempts by the federal government to force an end to the practice of plural marriage. In the midst of this turmoil,

President John Taylor was clear in his condemnation of the various laws that had been proposed and enacted. Yet he spoke peace to the hearts of the Saints, helping them understand that the afflictions they were passing through would be a small moment of purification and sanctification of the people of God.

With the implementation of the Edmunds Act, a commission of five men was sent to the Territory of Utah to enforce the provisions of the new law. That commission arrived in Utah on August 18, 1882, and immediately imposed a test oath for every registered voter to the effect that the applicant was not in violation of the laws of the United States regarding bigamy or polygamy. President Taylor had some rather starchy remarks to make about the wording of the oath not being in conformity with the Edmunds Act, including the fact that it allowed licentiousness in the voter but proscribed honorable marriages of a virtuous man to more than one woman. To those who had in good conscience entered into plural marriage with an eye single to the glory of God, President Taylor wrote,

"In regard to our religion, or our eternal covenants, we have no compromise to make, nor principles to barter away; they emanate from God and are founded upon the rock of eternal ages; they will live and exist when empires, powers and nations shall crumble and decay; and with the help of the Almighty we will guard sacredly our covenants and maintain our interests and be true to our God, while time exists or eternity endures."[20]

John Taylor considered the Edmunds Act and others of that kind conceived in ignorance and begotten by prejudice. He felt that the commission and others subsequently appointed by them went far beyond the letter and the spirit of the law itself in an effort to "grind to powder" the Latter-day Saints and their institutions.[21] In a letter to the members of the Church dated October 6, 1885, President Taylor questioned once again the motives of those who were working their will against the kingdom of God:

"Satan never wrought greater ruin in Eden than these enemies of ours would work in our midst if we would listen to their blandishments or be frightened by their threats. And is all this havoc to be wrought because of our wickedness? No, ten thousand times, NO. Let those who are so loud in denouncing us, so active in persecuting us, look around them. Are there no people but the 'Mormons' to regenerate and purge from sin? Read the daily record of black crime which fills the journals of the land. If the correction of evil, the improvement of morals, the uprooting of vice, the repression of violence and crime were objects which animate those who seek to destroy society in these mountains, then we would say in the language of the Savior: 'Thou thyself beholdest not the beam that is in thy own eye. Thou hypocrite, first cast out the beam out of thine own eye; and then shalt thou see clearly to cast out the mote out of thy brother's eye.' "[22]

Because of the unrelenting and unjust prosecutions leveled at the leadership of the Church by the federal government, the First Presidency thought it wise to "go to ground" (underground or in hiding) for a time. Joseph F. Smith, President Taylor's Second Counselor, went into hiding during the whole of 1884, and in January 1885 he left for the Hawaiian Islands to supervise the missionary work there. President Smith came home in July 1887 when President Taylor was near death. Others of the Quorum of the Twelve Apostles left on missions rather than endanger their families with the continual harassment of federal officials. The First Presidency, while stressing the wisdom of avoiding unjust prosecutions, counseled the Saints to contend earnestly for their legal and constitutional rights. President Taylor cautioned the membership of the Church that only through their unity would they ultimately prevail. The federal prosecutors promised some of the brethren that if they would but plead guilty to the charges leveled at them, that they would merely be reprimanded and allowed to go free. The ploy, of course, was to establish a consensus based on the confessions extracted by those accused under the Edmunds Act. Wrote Presidents Taylor and Cannon:

"We do not think it advisable for brethren to go into court and plead guilty. We must not look at our own cases from individual standpoints, but in the light in which the whole people may be affected by our action, whatever it may be. Every case should be defended with all the zeal and energy possible. Let us contend for our rights, inch by inch, and not yield a particle to the demands of those who are assailing us.

Federal Anti-Polygamy Legislation

The U.S. House of Representatives passed the first bill designed to proscribe the practice of plural marriage on July 1, 1862. Standing in opposition to this effort to control religious doctrine, Church leaders agreed to a test case regarding the Morrill Act of 1862. George Reynolds, the private secretary to Brigham Young, surrendered himself to authorities. This began the legal process that would lead to a decision made by the Supreme Court of the United States. This body concluded on January 6, 1879, that the Anti-bigamy Law of 1862 was constitutional. Congress strengthened the Morrill Act with the Edmunds Act of 1882, which disenfranchised the Latter-day Saints. The Edmunds-Tucker Act of 1887 amplified the strictures placed upon the Church and its members. By 1890 over 1000 men had been convicted and imprisoned according to the dictates of the two bills. Then on June 30, 1887, the federal government began confiscating Church assets, attempting to take possession of all properties in excess of $50,000.

Some of the leaders of the Church imprisoned for religious beliefs. During the administration of John Taylor, federal officers persecuted Church leaders for practicing plural marriage. Those who were arrested and tried were sent to prison. George Q. Cannon, the First Counselor to President Taylor, is pictured sitting in front of the two men standing in the doorway.

We have rights under the Constitution, and however much these may be denied to us, it is still our bounden duty to contend for them, not only in behalf of ourselves, but for all our fellow citizens and for our posterity, and for humanity generally throughout the world. Were we to do less than this, we would fail in performing the mission assigned to us, and be recreant to the high trust which God has reposed in us."[23]

As might be surmised from the foregoing, President Taylor's argument was not against the peoples of the United States, but rather with those officials whose tyrannical conduct had brought misery and distress to thousands of American citizens among the Mormons. He asserted that the vast majority of the population had been deceived by religious bigots and political tricksters, and that if the world at large knew of the explicit details of the tribulation brought against the Saints, they would be as disgusted as the members of the Church at the outrageous crusade of oppression. In an epistle to the gathered membership of the Church in April 1886, President Taylor reminded the Saints:

"Persecution has raged, and hideous wrongs have been and are being perpetrated against us as a Church, but thus far our enemies have not been permitted to go to such length as the persecutors of the people of God did in the days of the first Alma, when they put tasks upon his people and put taskmasters over them, and put to death those whom they found calling upon God."[24]

He then pointed out that they need not recall such a distant past, but to merely remind themselves of the circumstances of their expulsion from Missouri and Illinois. President Taylor continued:

"However grievous the wrongs under which we suffer to-day, there is much yet to be thankful for. Our land is filled with plenty. . . . And with these blessings of good food, comfortable raiment and sufficient shelter, we have the inestimable blessing of the peace of God, which He gives to every faithful Saint—peace in our hearts, peace in our habitations, peace in our settlements—a peace which the world cannot give, and which, thank the Lord, it cannot take away. Let your hearts, therefore, brethren and sisters, be filled with thanksgiving and praise to our God for his goodness and mercy unto us as a people."[25]

President Taylor invariably perceived the positive aspects of affliction, even when he himself was the object of ridicule and derision. In his letter to the Latter-day Saints in April 1887 read at general conference, he declared, "Painful as they have been to very many, the day will come when they will be acknowledged as having been the means of bringing great benefits to Zion."[26]

Later in the same letter, President Taylor concluded with the same optimism frequently displayed by the servants of the Most High:

"The Church is passing through a period of transition, or evolution, as some might be pleased to term it. Such periods appear to be necessary in the progress and perfecting of all created things, as much so in the history of peoples and communities as of individuals. These periods of transition have most generally their pains, perplexities and sufferings. The present is no exception to the rule. But out of apparent evil, Providence will bring abundant good, and the lesson which the signs of the times should teach us is one of patience, endurance, and calm reliance on the Lord. The result will be that we shall be stronger, wiser, purer, happier, for the experience gained. . . . The final victory of the Saints is certain; after the trial comes the reward."[27]

John Taylor believed that fundamental to the plan of eternal progression were the opportunities that enable us to learn for ourselves who we are and the extent of our capabilities. We should have, as John Taylor clearly taught his brethren in January 1854, a witness of our true standing and position before God, having a comprehension of our strengths and weaknesses, our ignorance and intelligence, our wisdom and our follies, that we may know how to appreciate the principles of eternity. All this would combine to bring us to a point where we may treat all with due respect, that we not overvalue nor depreciate our own wisdom and that of others, that we might learn to be dependent upon the hand of God and put our trust in Him.

For his own part, President Taylor practiced the principles that he taught to his brethren. Throughout his life, he continually strove to increase in knowledge and understanding

that he might more fully be prepared to be a blessing to those around him. His discourses were powerful and clear. In a burst of ebullience, B. H. Roberts wrote of President John Taylor's rhetorical gift: "His eloquence was a majestic river full to the point of overflowing its banks, sweeping grandly through rich regions of thought."[28] Here, then, is an example of a mortal life worth emulating.

Paul Nolan Hyde

Retired Church Educational System instructor, PhD

NOTES

1. *JD*, 4:34.
2. Joseph F. Smith, *Gospel Doctrine* (Salt Lake City: Deseret Book, 1971), 170.
3. Matthew J. Haslam, *John Taylor: Messenger of Salvation* (American Fork, UT: Covenant Communications, 2002), 202–3.
4. Emerson R. West, *Latter-day Prophets: Their Lives, Teachings, and Testimonies* (American Fork, UT: Covenant Communications, 1999), 43.
5. John Taylor, *Gospel Kingdom: Selections from the Writings and Discourses of John Taylor, Third President of The Church of Jesus Christ of Latter-day Saints*, ed. G. Homer Durham, (Salt Lake City: Bookcraft, 1987), 141–42.
6. *MFP*, 2:348–49.
7. *HC*, 5:593–94.
8. *MFP*, 2:329.
9. Ibid., 3:113.
10. Taylor, *Gospel Kingdom*, 30.
11. *MFP*, 3:84–85.
12. *Deseret News*, March 20, 1877, 1.
13. *MFP*, 3:85.
14. Ibid., 3:121–22.
15. Ibid., 3:87–88.
16. Taylor, *Gospel Kingdom*, 284.
17. Ibid., 275.
18. Ibid.
19. *Deseret News*, June 12, 1883, 1; as quoted in *Teachings of the Presidents of the Church: John Taylor* (Salt Lake City: The Church of Jesus Christ of Latter-day Saints, 2003), 90.
20. *MFP*, 2:346–47.
21. Epistle to Saints in general conference, March 1886, as cited in *MFP*, 3:58.
22. Ibid., 3:38.

23. Ibid., 3:16.
24. Ibid., 3:46.
25. Ibid.
26. Ibid., 3:109.
27. Ibid.
28. B. H. Roberts, *The Life of John Taylor* (Salt Lake City: Deseret Book, 2002), 433.

SIDEBAR AND PHOTO NOTES

1. Roberts, *The Life of John Taylor*, 40.
2. Samuel W. Taylor, *The Kingdom of God or Nothing: The Life of John Taylor, Militant Mormon* (New York: Macmillan, 1976), 60–61.
3. Preston Nibley, *The Presidents of the Church* (Salt Lake City: Deseret Book, 74), 96.
4. Roberts, *The Life of John Taylor*, 207–9.
5. B. H. Roberts, *A Comprehensive History of the Church of Jesus Christ of Latter-day Saints*, 6 vols. (Provo, UT: Brigham Young University Press), 6:105.
6. *MFP*, 2:348–49.
7. Taylor, *Gospel Kingdom*, 273.

Chapter Four

WILFORD WOODRUFF

LIFE AND TIMES

1807	March 1	Born in Farmington, Hartford County, Connecticut
1832		Moved to Richland, New York, with his brother Azmon
1833	December 31	Baptized into the Church
1834		Met Joseph Smith and participated in Zion's Camp march to Missouri
1837	April 13	Married Phebe Carter in Kirtland, Ohio
1838		Received a letter advising him of his call to be an Apostle
1838		Raised his wife Phebe from the dead following a severe illness
1839	April 26	Ordained an Apostle in Far West, Missouri
1839–41		Served a mission to Great Britain
1844–46		Presided over the British Mission with his wife Phebe
1846		Left Nauvoo to settle in Winter Quarters at the Mt. Pisgah, Iowa, encampment
1847	July 24	Entered the Salt Lake Valley with Brigham Young
1851		Appointed to the Utah Territorial Legislature
1856		Appointed Assistant Church Historian
1857		Prepared and partially carried out a plan to move his families to Provo at the time of the "invasion" of Johnston's army
1858		Became president of the Deseret Agricultural and Manufacturing Society; conducted many farming and gardening experiments to improve Utah agriculture
1867		Participated in the reestablishment of the School of the Prophets in Salt Lake City
1876		Traveled to St. George for the dedication of the temple; called as temple president
1877		Provided temple blessing for signers of the Declaration of Independence, presidents of the United States, and other prominent men and women
1889	April 7	Sustained as President of the Church
1890		Issued the Manifesto concerning plural marriage
1896	April 6	Dedicated the Salt Lake Temple
1898	September 2	Died in San Francisco, California, at age ninety-one

BIOGRAPHICAL HIGHLIGHTS

Following the death of President John Taylor, Wilford Woodruff led the Church for two years as President of the Quorum of the Twelve. He was subsequently ordained in 1889 at the age of eighty-two to the office of prophet, seer, and revelator and became the fourth President of The Church of Jesus Christ of Latter-day Saints. He died in 1898 at the age of ninety-one. His decade as President was marked with many diplomatic and financial challenges for the Church and with dissention among some members and even a few of the Brethren over plural marriage and other issues. President Woodruff sought to bring harmony, peace, and reconciliation to the thriving community of Saints. He fought valiantly for the survival of the Church amidst the monetary, financial, and political upheavals of the time. He was stalwartly dedicated to preserving and prospering the Lord's latter-day kingdom on earth.

Converted to the Church in 1833 at the age of twenty-six, Wilford Woodruff's migrations paralleled those of the Latter-day Saints as he moved from New York to Kirtland, from Kirtland to Missouri, on to Nauvoo, and finally to the Salt Lake Valley. He served eight missions for the Church during a period of sixteen and a half years. He was ordained an Apostle on April 7, 1839. As one of the first missionaries to England, he and his fellow Apostles experienced phenomenal success, baptizing 1,800 people. Shortly after the Prophet Joseph Smith's death, Elder Woodruff was assigned to preside over the European Mission and is credited with keeping the Church together there during that trying time. Among the first party to enter the Salt Lake Valley, Elder Woodruff was a leading figure in the Saints' immigration to Utah and the establishment of the fledgling Zion in the Rocky Mountains.

CONTRIBUTIONS

President Woodruff labored tirelessly to integrate Utah into the larger community of the United States. After receiving revelations allowing him to suspend the practice of plural marriage, he issued the Manifesto of 1890, which declared that Utah would align itself with national law on this issue. He encouraged the Saints to join the prevailing political parties of the United States, and Utah became a state in 1893. In spite of growing financial debt in the Church, he spurred the completion of the Salt Lake Temple, which was a beacon of strength, harmony, and prosperity to the Saints. He was self-educated and widely traveled, which enabled him to make many friends for the Church wherever he went. Under his leadership, the Church began to emerge from a secluded and autonomous community to the worldwide organization it would soon become.

TEACHINGS

In his youth Wilford Woodruff wondered why there were no prophets or apostles on the earth. He was unsatisfied with what was preached in the churches of his day. When he heard the message of the Restoration, he was an instant convert and bore powerful testimony of the reestablishment of the kingdom of God on earth all the days of his life. He knew the Prophet Joseph Smith personally and testified boldly of the divinity of his mission. He was also profoundly affected by Joseph Smith's visions of eternity, especially the revelation of the degrees of glory. President Woodruff patiently taught the Saints the principles and practices of temple work for the living and the dead, and established the genealogical department of the Church. He also bore solemn witness of the principle of modern revelation and testified of the trust the members of the Church could have in the unfailing leadership of God's appointed prophet.

President Woodruff possessed a prophetic understanding of the unfolding events of the last days. He often taught about the Second Coming and the events and preparations leading up to the end of the world and the beginning of the Millennium. Because the era in which he lived was so fraught with economic and political turmoil, he often counseled the Saints in temporal matters as well as spiritual ones. He eschewed the acquisition of wealth as a priority. Politically, he led the Church into a workable relationship with the U.S. government and taught the importance of the separation of church and state. He also experienced and shared with the

Saints many remarkable spiritual manifestations where the veil between heaven and earth was parted for him. To the end of his long life, he was a powerful and beloved advocate of the restored gospel of Jesus Christ, leading the Saints through one of their most difficult decades in Church history.

LIFE OF
WILFORD WOODRUFF

◆

BIRTH, EARLY CHILDHOOD, AND HOME LIFE

Wilford Woodruff was born March 1, 1807, in the tiny Connecticut town of Avon (Farmington). His earthly sojourn ended September 2, 1898, three thousand miles to the west in San Francisco, California. His more than nine decades of life were filled with high adventure, both temporal and spiritual.

Wilford was the son of Aphek and Bulah Thompson Woodruff and the third of nine children born to Aphek. Wilford's mother died at age twenty-six when he was just fifteen months old. His father's second wife, Azubah Hart, lovingly raised Wilford and his two older brothers. Aphek and Azubah had six children born to them, but four of Azubah's own six children died before they became adults.[1] From an early age, Wilford labored long hours in the family flour mill beside his father and brothers, many times putting in eighteen-hour days.[2] He learned to enjoy physical labor and engaged in it throughout his long life. It was also in his childhood that he acquired a passion for fishing. Of his early love for fishing and the outdoors, he wrote: "My mind was rather more taken up upon these subjects in my boyhood than it was in learning my books at school."[3]

At age fourteen, while living with a neighboring farmer and attending school in the winter, Wilford read the scriptures and participated in Presbyterian prayer meetings, but Protestantism left him feeling empty. He later wrote, "The preaching . . . created darkness and not light, misery and not happiness and their teachings did not seem to enlighten my mind or do me good, although I laboured hard to obtain

A Marked Victim of the Adversary

In a separate chapter in his journal, Wilford Woodruff once recorded twenty-seven life-threatening incidents from which he had been miraculously spared.[1] One biographer summarizes them as follows: "At age 3 he fell into a cauldron of scalding water; once he fell from a beam inside a barn onto the bare floor; he fell down stairs and broke one of his arms; he very narrowly missed being gored by a bull; he was almost smothered by a full load of hay; he barely escaped drowning; he nearly froze to death; he was bitten by a mad dog; he was poisoned; he fell from a porch and broke his other arm; he was poisoned; he split the instep of his foot open with an ax; while climbing an elm tree he fell about 15 feet to the ground and was knocked unconscious; he fell from a horse and dislocated his ankles and broke his leg in two places."[2]

Other freak accidents included being kicked in the stomach by an ox, being in a wagon when it overturned, nearly being crushed by a water wheel, and on two occasions narrowly missing getting killed by gunfire. He came away unscathed from a train wreck and survived several life-threatening illnesses. Wilford wrote, "I have been a marked victim as an attack for the power of the destroyer from my infancy up to the present day. I have faced Accident, misfortune, and apparently death so many times and in so many shapes and forms from my childhood through life thus far that it has become a proverb with me to say that there has seemed to be two powers constantly watching me and at work with me one to kill and the other to save me."[3]

benefit from it."[4] As he grew older, he continued to have very strong religious feelings. Recalling a period of his young manhood, from 1827 to 1832, during which he was working at various flour mills near his home in Connecticut, he said, "I spent many a midnight hour in my mill and among the rocks, in the forests and in the fields . . . pouring out my soul to God . . . praying that I might live to behold a people on the earth who would teach (Bible) principles."[5] Wilford continued his education until he was eighteen years old. One biographer noted that this amount of formal education was uncommon for a nineteenth-century youth and made Wilford "one of the best educated of nineteenth-century Mormon leaders and better educated than any nineteenth-century LDS church president except Lorenzo Snow, who had attended Oberlin College."[6]

FRIENDSHIP WITH A PROPHET

In 1828, while Wilford was operating a mill owned by his aunt near East Avon, he became acquainted with a very religious old gentleman named Robert Mason, who had been seeking all his life to find the true church of God. Mr. Mason told Wilford about a revelatory dream he had experienced around the year 1800, which made clear to him that the true church did not exist on the earth but that the kingdom of God would be restored in the near future. Wilford Woodruff recorded in his journal Robert Mason's account of this dream as well as a prophecy the old gentleman made. Mr. Mason said that he himself would not become part of the restored kingdom in this life but that he would know of its establishment before his death. He then declared that Wilford would become a "conspicuous actor" in this great latter-day work.[7]

Immediately upon finding and joining the restored Church five years later, Wilford hastened to send Mr. Mason a letter informing him that the latter-day kingdom had indeed been reestablished on the earth. Rejoicing in this knowledge, Robert Mason died soon afterward. Years later in Nauvoo, Elder Woodruff, by then an Apostle, was able to provide a great blessing to his dear friend: "The first opportunity I had after the truth of baptism for the dead was

revealed, I went forth and was baptized for him in the temple font at Nauvoo."[8]

JOINING THE CHURCH

In 1832, while he was still working as a miller in Connecticut, Wilford first became acquainted with The Church of Jesus Christ of Latter-day Saints by reading a newspaper article ridiculing the foundling movement. He had a strong desire at that time to meet some Mormons. About a year later, after Wilford and his brother Azmon had moved to Richland, New York, two missionaries, Zera Pulsipher and Elijah Cheney, went to the home of Azmon and his wife, where Wilford was also living. The two Mormons extended an invitation to the family to attend a public meeting at the schoolhouse in Richland. At that first meeting Wilford received a powerful witness of the Spirit, and before the proceedings ended he was on his feet testifying to the audience that what the missionaries were preaching was true.[9] Later he wrote: "I wanted the Gospel of Christ; and the first sermon I ever heard preached in this Church I had a testimony for myself that it was the Gospel of Christ. . . . I had been looking, praying, hungering and thirsting to find some man on the face of the earth who had the Priesthood, and who could teach me the Gospel. When I heard this sermon, I knew the voice; I knew the shepherd; I knew it was true."[10] He was baptized shortly afterward at the age of twenty-six on December 31, 1833, in an icy stream. He described his baptism in these words: "The snow was about three feet deep, the day was cold, and the water was mixed with ice and snow, yet I did not feel the cold."[11]

MISSIONARY WORK

Ten of Wilford Woodruff's first fifteen years in the Church were spent almost exclusively serving missions.[12] Following his baptism, he traveled to Kirtland, Ohio, where he met the Prophet Joseph Smith. Soon after his arrival there, he responded to the Prophet's call for volunteers to join a military company called Zion's Camp and to make a nine-hundred-mile trek to Missouri to assist members of the Church who had been driven from their homes in Jackson County. The

Journal Keeping

Throughout his life, Wilford Woodruff kept a remarkable journal of more than seven thousand pages, providing primary documentation for much of the early history of the Church and detailing not only the trials and tribulations of the Church, but also the hand of the Lord in his own life. It contains scores of miraculous manifestations from revelatory dreams to visitations to the spirit world, to the raising of the dead. He wrote:

"I have had this spirit and calling upon me since I first entered this Church. I made a record from the first sermon I heard, and from that day until now I have kept a daily journal. Whenever I heard Joseph Smith preach, teach, or prophesy, I always felt it my duty to write it; I felt uneasy and could not eat, drink, or sleep until I did write; . . . I would go home and sit down and write the whole sermon, almost word for word and sentence by sentence as it was delivered, and when I had written it it was taken from me, I remembered it no more. This was a gift of God to me."[4]

"I have written more sacred history of the teaching of the prophets and Apostles and official acts of the Latter-day Saints than would make several testaments as large as the one handed down to us by the ancient Apostles. I have kept a journal of almost every day of my life since I have been a member of this Church."[5] His was often the only record of what took place. For example, of the sixteen discourses he recorded given by Joseph Smith, nine are found nowhere else except in his journals.[6]

President Wilford Woodruff's Bible and a sample of the style in which he wrote his letters and journals. He wrote in longhand or block print and often decorated the letters according to his mood.

A Sermon in the South

On March 27, 1835, while serving his first mission, Elder Woodruff arrived penniless, unkempt, and muddy at a tavern in Memphis, Tennessee. He asked if the innkeeper, Josiah Jackson, would allow him to stay the night, stating that he was a preacher of the gospel. Mr. Jackson was skeptical but agreed to accommodate Elder Woodruff if he would preach a sermon in the tavern that night. Delighted for the opportunity but feeling a little mischievous, Elder Woodruff played hard to get and "pleaded with him not to set me preaching. The more I pleaded to be excused the more determined Mr. Jackson was that I should preach." Before Elder Woodruff could finish his supper, a large crowd began to gather. He recorded:

"There were present some five hundred persons, who had come together, not to hear a gospel sermon, but to have some fun." Elder Woodruff invited the congregation to sing a hymn, but none of them would join him. He knelt down: "I prayed to the Lord to give me His spirit and to show me the hearts of the people. I promised the Lord, in my prayer, that I would deliver to that congregation whatever He would give to me. I arose and spoke one hour and a half, and it was one of the best sermons of my life. The lives of the congregation were open to the vision of my mind, and I told them of their wicked deeds. . . . The men who surrounded me dropped their heads. Three minutes after I closed, I was the only person in the room."[7]

From his bedroom that night, Elder Woodruff overheard some of the men discussing the sermon: "One man said he would like to know how that Mormon boy knew of their past lives. . . . In the morning . . . the landlord said if I came that way again to stop at his house, and stay as long as I might choose."[8]

Prophet hoped to reinstate these refugees to their usurped property. While this mission was unsuccessful in its stated goal, it was very effective in demonstrating the character and leadership of the men who made the trip. The Prophet Joseph Smith, who led the expedition, recognized greatness in the new convert from Richland, New York, and five years later Joseph received a revelation from God calling Wilford Woodruff to the Quorum of the Twelve Apostles.

In 1835, Wilford accepted a call to fill his first extensive mission for the Church to the southern states, where he served mostly in Kentucky and Tennessee. Reflecting on this mission, he declared that he "had traveled more than 8,000 miles and had baptized seventy people."[13] When he returned to Kirtland, he met and married Phebe Carter, a convert to the Church and a native of Maine.

His next mission, in 1836, was to the eastern states. He labored mostly on the Fox Islands just off the coast of Maine near his wife's family's home. It was while serving as a missionary in the Fox Islands that he received a letter informing him of his call to fill one of the vacancies in the Quorum of the Twelve. In a revelation given July 8, 1838, at Far West, Missouri, where the Saints had gathered, Joseph Smith received the following instruction from the Lord: "Let

my servant John Taylor, and also my servant John E. Page, and also my servant Wilford Woodruff, and also my servant Willard Richards, be appointed to fill the places of those who have fallen, and be officially notified of their appointment" (D&C 118:6). Shortly after notification of his call to the apostleship, he left the eastern states, leading about fifty of his converts from the New England area to gather with the Saints.

Even though his call to the Quorum of the Twelve Apostles had been announced publicly in the summer of 1838, Wilford was not ordained to the office until the spring of 1839. The setting for his ordination was unique. Earlier Joseph Smith had prophesied that the Twelve would leave on an important mission from Far West, Missouri. Now that violent mobs had driven the Saints from that area, leaving on their mission from that sacred site seemed not only inconvenient, but quite dangerous. The Twelve, however, were determined to see the prophecy fulfilled, and so without their enemies' knowledge, they slipped back into Missouri from their new location in Illinois. Early in the morning of April 16, 1839, they held a meeting at Far West on the abandoned lot where they had hoped to build a temple. While seated on a stone marker that had previously been placed at

Phebe Carter

"Phebe Carter was born on March 8, 1807, in Scarboro, Maine, seven days after Wilford's birth. . . . The daughter of Ezra Carter and Sarah Fabyan and named for her paternal grandmother, Phebe descended from Massachusetts and Maine-born English colonists. She had worked as a tailor and school teacher before joining the Mormon church, and continued the latter occupation after her conversion in 1834 and move to Kirtland."[9] In 1838, while accompanying her husband on a mission to the eastern states, Phebe gave birth to their first daughter, Sarah Emma, at Phebe's parents' home in Scarboro, Maine. Two years later, while Wilford was away on his first mission to England, their second child, Wilford Jr., arrived. Shortly after that, on July 17, 1840, their little daughter Sarah Emma died. Wilford did not learn of her death until three months after it occurred.[10] Two more daughters were born before his second mission to England in 1844—Phebe Amelia and Sarah Cornelia. Phebe was called to accompany her husband on this mission. They left Wilford Jr. and Phebe Amelia behind in Nauvoo with trusted family and friends but took Sarah Cornelia with them. In England, Phebe gave birth to a second son, Joseph. After returning to Nauvoo and joining the exodus to Iowa, their little son Joseph died in Winter Quarters; he was sixteen months old. Just a few days later, on November 20, 1846, their fifth child, Ezra, was born prematurely and only lived two days. In October of 1847, three months after reaching the Salt Lake Valley, another girl, Shuah Carter, was born. While the Woodruffs were traveling to another mission in the East, in 1848, Shuah died at the age of nine months. In 1851, Bulah Augusta was born, and in 1853 Phebe's last baby was born, a boy named after Wilford's father, Aphek, but he only lived a few hours. Of the nine children born to Phebe and Wilford, only four lived to become adults—Wilford Jr., Phebe Amelia, Sarah Cornelia, and Bulah Augusta. The other five died in their infancy. The loss of their children brought excruciating grief to both of them.[11]

In November of 1885, Wilford had returned to Salt Lake City temporarily from St. George, where he was living in exile to prevent arrest for plural marriage; he received news that Phoebe was dying and immediately risked making a visit to her. Unwell from an attack of chills, she had taken a fall and split open her scalp. She was unable to rally, and following a blessing he gave her, she died at the age of seventy-eight.[12]

the southeast corner of the temple site, Wilford Woodruff was ordained by Brigham Young to the sacred calling of an Apostle in the Lord's latter-day kingdom.

After returning to Illinois to arrange his affairs, Elder Woodruff, along with several of his fellow Apostles and under very adverse circumstances, departed to fulfill a ground-breaking mission to Great Britain. In England Elder Woodruff became the most productive missionary in this dispensation, baptizing or assisting to baptize over 1,800 converts in an eight-month period.

Phebe Carter Woodruff (1807–1885) married Wilford Woodruff in 1837 in Kirtland, Ohio.

John Benbow was among those converted and had title to a small stone building called the Gadfield Elm Chapel, where the Saints met.

A large number of these converts were members of a congregation of United Brethren, whom he baptized in a pond on the John Benbow farm in Herefordshire.

After nearly two years of remarkable service in England, Elder Woodruff returned to the United States. Under the dynamic leadership of the Prophet Joseph Smith, the Saints were building the beautiful, thriving city of Nauvoo, Illinois, which they eventually crowned with a stately temple. In Nauvoo, Elder Woodruff worked diligently at his calling as an Apostle and also served as business manager for the Church's newspaper, the *Times and Seasons*. His dedication prompted Joseph Smith to refer to him as "Wilford the Faithful," a title that remained with him for the rest of his life. During his sojourn in Nauvoo, he also labored with his own hands to construct a comfortable red brick home for his family. This stately edifice still stands today, a monument to his industry.

In 1843 and then again in 1844, Wilford accepted two more mission calls to the eastern states. During the second of these missions, while serving in Scarboro, Maine, he received the staggering news that his beloved leader and friend, the Prophet Joseph Smith, had been murdered with his brother Hyrum in Carthage Jail near Nauvoo. This devastating information came as a shock even though Joseph had given many indications and prophecies that his life would be cut short. Indeed this very mission to the East was an effort by the Prophet to get Elder Woodruff and other Apostles out of Nauvoo for their own safety. Joseph had told Wilford just prior to this mission, "I want you to go . . . and if you do not you will die."[14]

Elder Woodruff recorded a touching scene in his journal, describing how he and Brigham Young met in Boston after both of them had learned of the martyrdom of the Prophet and his brother: "Elder B. Young arived in Boston this morning. I walked with him to 57 Temple st. . . . Br Young took the bed and I the big Chair, and I here veiled my face and for the first time gave vent to my grief and mourning for the Prophet and Patriarch of the Church Joseph and Hiram Smith who were murdered by a gentile mob. After being bathed by a flood of tears I felt composed."[15]

PRESIDING OVER THE EUROPEAN MISSION

Following the death of the Prophet, Elder Woodruff returned to Nauvoo, but very soon his talents and leadership were sorely needed again in England. In August of that same year, only two months after the death of Joseph and Hyrum, Wilford and Phebe departed for the British Isles to preside over the European Mission headquartered in London. They took their one-year-old daughter with them but had to leave their other two children in the care of relatives and friends. Again, Elder Woodruff's presence was monumental in strengthening the Saints of the British Isles and in influencing many of them to gather to Zion, according to the counsel of Church leaders at that time. He provided a comforting and steadying leadership during the trying period that followed the Prophet's martyrdom.

SALT LAKE VALLEY

Upon his return from Great Britain nineteen months later on April 13, 1846, Elder Woodruff worked closely and tirelessly with Joseph Smith's successor, President Brigham Young, to accomplish the overwhelming task of moving thousands of Saints across the continent to the valley of the Great Salt Lake. In the spring of 1846, Wilford, along with many other refugees from Nauvoo, moved his family across the Mississippi River to Mount Pisgah, Iowa, and from there they traveled to Winter Quarters, Nebraska, where they remained for the winter. In the spring he traveled west with the advance pioneer company and was among the first of the Latter-day Saints to enter the Salt Lake Valley. In his journal he expressed his joy in beholding a "land of promise held in reserve by the hand of GOD for a resting place for the Saints upon which A portion of the Zion of GOD will be built."[16] A monument commemorating this event now stands at the mouth of Emigration Canyon. The three statues on

Raising His Wife from the Dead

While Wilford, Phebe, and their first baby, a daughter Sarah Emma, were en route from their mission field in Scarboro, Maine, attempting to help converts join with the body of the Saints in Nauvoo, Phebe became deathly ill. Wilford Woodruff's journal for 1838 records:

"December 3rd found my wife very low. I spent the day taking care of her and the following day I returned to Eaton to get some things for her. She seemed to be gradually sinking and in the evening, her spirit apparently left her body and she was dead. The sisters gathered around her body, weeping, while I stood looking at her in sorrow. The spirit and power of God began to rest upon me, until for the first time during her illness, faith filled my soul, although she lay before me as one dead. I had some oil. I took it and consecrated it before the Lord for anointing the sick. I then bowed before the Lord and prayed for the life of my companion and I anointed her with oil in the name of the Lord and I laid my hands upon her and in the name of Jesus Christ, I rebuked the power of death and the destroyer and commanded the same to depart from her and the spirit of life to enter her body. Her spirit returned to her body from that hour and she was made whole. We all felt to praise the name of God and to trust in Him and keep His commandments. While this experience was going on with me, my wife related afterwards that her spirit left her body and she saw her body lying upon the bed, and the sisters weeping. She looked at them and at me and upon the babe, and while gazing upon this scene, two personages came into the room carrying a coffin and told her they had come for her body. One of these messengers informed her that she could have her choice. She might go to rest in the spirit world or, on one condition, she could have the privilege of returning to her tabernacle and continuing in her body. The condition was if she felt she could stand by her husband and with him pass through all the cares, trials, tribulations and afflictions of life which he would be called to pass through for the Gospel's sake unto the end. When she looked at the situation of her husband and child, she said, 'Yes, I will do it.' At the moment that decision was made, the power of faith rested upon me and when I administered to her, her spirit entered her tabernacle and she saw the messengers carry the coffin out through the door."[13]

This Is the Place Monument.

other members of the Church from the relentless opposition and oppressive legislation imposed by the federal government to try to stop the practice of plural marriage. He saw civilization in the valley progress by leaps and bounds with the advent of the telegraph, railroad, and electricity, and he witnessed the remarkable colonization of hundreds of settlements throughout the West.

During the approximately forty years from his arrival in the Salt Lake Valley until he became President of the Church in 1889, Wilford engaged in a variety of pursuits. In order to support his numerous dependents, he undertook the arduous labor of moving several cabins he had built in the original small fort the Saints had erected in 1847 to property he owned southwest of Temple Square. He quarried stone from the canyons to build the foundations for the homes and cut poles from the nearby Oquirrh Mountains to fence his lots. His chief sources of income during this period of his life were raising cattle and farming. Although he engaged in a great deal of taxing physical labor, he still found time to try his hand at merchandizing. He was passionate about improving the level of education for himself and the Saints throughout the valley and participated in several organizations to advance learning. Among these were the Universal Scientific Society

the pinnacle of the historic marker represent Brigham Young, flanked by Heber C. Kimball and Wilford Woodruff.

Except for another call to preside over the Eastern States Mission (June 1848 to October 1850), Elder Woodruff was present in the Salt Lake Valley for all of the momentous events occurring in the new Zion in the West during the last half of the nineteenth century. These events included the history-making immigration of eighty thousand Saints to Utah, the threatened "invasion" by the United States Army into what the Saints had hoped would be a peaceful refuge, and the establishment of a territorial government in which Wilford Woodruff served as a legislator for many years. He suffered along with

Wilford the Counter

As part of his meticulous journal keeping, Elder Woodruff often gave totals of things he had counted. Some of these sums were unimportant, such as the number of bricks in his Nauvoo home or the number of letters received and written. Others were very significant, such as the following:

"In 1885 he compiled a fifty-year summary, observing that he had traveled 143,369 miles, held 4,191 meetings, and preached 3,250 discourses. Through his eight-month ministry in England, 1,800 people were added to the Church, of whom he personally baptized 1,043. He had organized 51 branches of the Church, confirmed 3,343 individuals, ordained 23 patriarchs, 93 high priests, 59 seventies, 23 bishops, and 667 elders, and assisted in ordaining 4,347 others. He had also ordained 446 priests, 66 teachers, and 15 deacons. He set apart and blessed 1,034 missionaries and assisted with 4,512 others, blessed 283 children, administered to 922 sick persons, worked in the Salt Lake Endowment House 603 days, spent 111 days supervising the digging of the Salt Lake Temple foundation, and collected $1,674 for the Nauvoo Temple."[14]

and the Polysophical Society, the latter designed to promote the theatre and other fine arts. His real passion, however, seemed to lie in improving the quality of crops in the new territory. He tirelessly studied scientific farming methods, led the way in Utah in importing seeds, grafts, and superior strains of plants from as far away as England, and established the Horticultural Society.[17] He was president of the Deseret Agricultural and Manufacturing Society for fourteen years and extended his expertise into promoting the improvement of animal breeds as well.[18]

His contributions to public life were not limited to agriculture. He also participated in many industrial pursuits and in the formation of numerous companies such as the Brigham Young Express and Carrying Company (the XY Company), which held the U.S. mail contract until it was cancelled due to the 1856 Utah War. During all of this secular activity, he continued to serve nobly as an Apostle of the Lord and kept meticulous records of Church-related matters, recording many sermons that Brigham Young and others gave throughout the territory. He supervised the "tithing hands," men who gave 10 percent of their time to work on the construction of the Salt Lake Temple. In 1856 he became Assistant Church Historian and made extensive collections and revisions of historical Church documents, continuing almost single-handedly to keep the Church records up to date.

In 1856, Elder Woodruff was a key figure in what was called the "reformation" of members of the Church and was often credited with lending a more fatherly edge to what some considered too harsh a call to repentance.[19] In October 1857, Elder Woodruff contributed an equipped wagon and a driver to the dramatic rescue of surviving members of the Willie and Martin Handcart companies, who had become stranded in freezing weather conditions in the mountains of Wyoming.[20]

Also in 1856, Wilford Woodruff and his families were part of the exodus from Salt Lake City during the threatened invasion by Johnston's army, moving themselves and many of their supplies to Provo with the idea that Salt Lake City would be burned if the army tried to take over. Wilford even moved many of the Church's precious records from the historian's office. The upset was so pervasive that it took him nearly a month to move back when a tenuous diplomacy averted the disaster in Salt Lake.[21] After the coming of the army and its numerous contractors and "camp followers," things were never really "normal" again for the Saints. In many ways the influx of outsiders into their peaceful valley home meant the end to their seclusion in Zion. The advent of the transcontinental railroad in 1869 also revolutionized life for all Utahns, including the Woodruffs. As economic complexities began to accelerate, Wilford became increasingly more active in Zion's Cooperative Mercantile Institute (ZCMI), which he had helped establish earlier, and in many other cooperative ventures. In 1874, he joined Brigham Young and other members of the Twelve in trying to promote the United Order in Utah, but most of these attempts died out within a matter of months.[22]

In 1876 and 1877, Wilford's life became focused on the completion of the first temple in the West in the Southern Utah settlement of St. George. Brigham Young asked him to offer its dedicatory prayer and serve as its first president. Wilford was an ardent promoter of temple work, officiating in hundreds of baptisms, endowments, and sealings, particularly in behalf of the dead, and urging his fellow Saints to do the same. Brigham Young's death on August 29, 1877, interrupted the great amount of attention Wilford devoted to this pursuit, and of necessity his involvement in temple work became more sporadic.

Following the death of Brigham Young, the Church entered a particularly turbulent era with John Taylor as President of the Twelve leading the Church until 1880 when the First Presidency was reorganized. The duties of the Apostles became absorbing and complex as they attempted to separate President Young's property from that of the Church. Increasing difficulties over polygamy, and even controversy centering around some financial dealings of George Q. Cannon, a member of the First Presidency, presented complicated challenges to Wilford Woodruff and his fellow Apostles. In 1885 raids and convictions of Utah polygamists forced Elder Woodruff into hiding. He spent much of his time in St. George until President Taylor's death in 1887. In spite of precedent, there was still some confusion over the procedure for succession to the presidency of the Church. An

President Woodruff (center) and his counselors, George Q. Cannon and Joseph F. Smith, on the day of the Salt Lake Temple dedication on April 6, 1893.

awkward period, called an interregnum, where the Twelve governed the Church for a few years between Presidents, occurred following the deaths of the first three Presidents of the Church, Joseph Smith, Brigham Young, and John Taylor. While it did not seem to serve any real purpose in Wilford Woodruff's case, this precedent was followed once again for two years from 1887 to 1889 when the First Presidency was finally reorganized. Foreseeing that his counselor Lorenzo Snow would outlive him and succeed him as President, he instructed Elder Snow to end the tradition of interregnums and proceed immediately upon his (President Woodruff's) death to reorganize the First Presidency. This practice has continued to the present.

PRESIDENT OF THE CHURCH

On April 7, 1889, after the two-year interregnum, Elder Woodruff assumed the role of President of the Church. He was eighty-two years old but still in vigorous health. His decade as President encompassed three remarkable developments in the kingdom. First, in 1890 he received the revelations that led to the issuing of the Manifesto, which ended the contracting of plural marriages. Second, in 1893 he oversaw the completion and dedication of the magnificent Salt Lake Temple. And third, in 1896, after nearly half a century of failed attempts, he was instrumental in helping Utah to finally attain statehood.

Wilford Woodruff's term as President of the Church cannot be properly understood without observing that there was a huge shift in viewpoint among members of the Church during his presidency. Originally the Latter-day Saints pictured themselves as creating an almost separate nation, or at the very least, a separate society from the rest of the United States. But the pervasive intrusion of the federal government into their affairs because of the practice of plural marriage soon made it apparent that the Saints would have to interact with the country in a much more integral way than they had envisioned or desired earlier. It was no longer possible to maintain their autonomy and their isolation from the rest of the United States.

MANIFESTO

When John Taylor died in 1887, the Saints were in the midst of severe persecutions as a result of congressional anti-polygamy legislation. The United Sates government became increasingly more aggressive in enforcing the Edmunds Act of 1882, which had established unlawful cohabitation as a crime and disenfranchised all practicing polygamists. Five years later, the Edmunds-Tucker Act of 1887 prohibited all Utah women from voting and made it legal to seize all Church holdings valued at more than $50,000. Many Mormon men, including a number of Church leaders, were forced into hiding to avoid being arrested or sent to prison.

Apostle Lorenzo Snow served a sentence of eleven months. Fear of arrest kept Elder Woodruff from attending President Taylor's funeral as it previously had the funeral of his first wife, Phebe Carter, who had died two years earlier in 1885. In 1889, two years after President Taylor's funeral, on the very day Wilford Woodruff was sustained in general conference as President of the Church, Wilford was still in danger of being captured. One biographer wrote, "He entered during the afternoon session to a thunder of applause from the people. He spoke only briefly before he had to leave early to avoid arrest for the practice of plural marriage."[23]

In addition to increased suffering on the part of individuals from the enforcement of anti-polygamy laws, the whole Church was dealt a staggering blow when the United States government actually confiscated millions of dollars' worth of Church property. At first, religious sanctuaries were considered exempt from being seized, but subsequently government officials began to threaten to seize meetinghouses and temples as well. President Woodruff and the other Apostles saw that they must take decisive action. In an attempt to stave off criticism and persecution, they issued several official pronouncements that proclaimed the Church's belief in the separation of church and state and promised Latter-day Saint conformity to United States law. These official documents reflected heavily the teachings and views of President Woodruff. One such statement was published in 1889 after the government accused the Church of conducting anti-American activities in the secret ceremonies of the temple and made vociferous allegations that leaders of the Church were exercising tyrannical control over the political activities of the members. In answer to these and other denunciations, the First Presidency issued the Official Declaration of December 12, 1889, which read in part, "We declare . . . that this Church, while offering advice for the welfare of its members in all conditions of life, does not claim or exercise a right to interfere with citizens in the free exercise of social or political rights and privileges. The ballot in this Territory is absolutely untrammeled and secret. . . . We declare that there is nothing in the ceremony of the endowment, or in any doctrine, tenet, obligation or injunction of this Church, either private or public, which is hostile or intended to be hostile, to the government of the United States. On the contrary, its members are under divine commandment to revere the Constitution as a heaven-inspired instrument and obey as supreme all laws made in pursuance of its provisions."[24]

Because of intolerable abuses against the Church, President Woodruff began as early as 1887 to advise members to cease contracting plural marriages, and he instructed the Brethren not to publicly preach the principle. But even though members were counseled to back off in this unofficial manner, it did little to eliminate the unbearable conditions imposed upon them. The government kept bombarding the Church with accusations, property confiscation, and imprisonment of its members. Public officials added another straw to the camel's back by refusing to grant naturalization to Utah immigrants. Idaho disenfranchised all Mormons whether or not they practiced or even believed in plural marriage.

For many agonizing months President Woodruff petitioned the Lord for a solution to the plight of the Church. Finally, the Lord answered his prayers through a series of revelations that opened up a sobering vision to him. He saw clearly how dire the future of the Church would be if the members continued to practice plural marriage. After receiving these pivotal revelations, President Woodruff made the wrenching decision to officially end the contracting of all plural marriages. Despite the intense unpopularity of this decision with many members of the Church and even with some members of the Twelve, the prophet fearlessly stood by it, defended it, and eventually convinced most Latter-day Saints of its validity. The official announcement of this monumental decision was called "The Manifesto of 1890" and

Four generation photograph. President Woodruff with a son, a grandson, and a great-grandson, all bearing the name Wilford.

Family

Wilford Woodruff married Phebe W. Carter in 1837 and added other wives during the years from 1846 to 1870. By 1890, Phebe and one of his other wives had died. Three wives remained—Emma Smith and Sarah Brown, who both married him on the same day in March 1853, and Sarah Delight Stocking, who married him in 1857. He lived with these three wives until 1898 when he died.[15] In all, Wilford Woodruff was the father of thirty-three children.

stated emphatically that no further plural marriages would be sanctioned or contracted by the Church. In his journal President Woodruff wrote, "[I have] arived at a point in the History of my life as the President of the Church of Jesus Christ of Latter Day Saints whare I am under the necessity of acting for the Temporal Salvation of the Church. The United State Government has taken a Stand & passed Laws to destroy the Latter day Saints upon the Subject of poligamy or Patriarchal order of Marriage. And after Praying to the Lord & feeling inspired by his spirit I have issued . . . [a] Proclamation which is sustained by my Councillors and the 12 Apostles."[25]

In explaining this declaration to the Church, he preached numerous times that he was acting under the direction of God and that he had seen what would happen to the

Church if the Lord's will was not followed. In one of the revelations, the Lord told President Woodruff to ask the people this question: "Which is the wisest course for the Latter-day Saints to pursue—to continue to attempt to practice plural marriage, with the laws of the nation against it and the opposition of sixty millions of people, and at the cost of the confiscation and loss of all the Temples, and the stopping of all the ordinances therein, both for the living and the dead, and the imprisonment of the First Presidency and Twelve and the heads of families in the Church, and the confiscation of personal property of the people (all of which of themselves would stop the practice); or, after doing and suffering what we have through our adherence to this principle to cease the practice and submit to the law, and through doing so leave the Prophets, Apostles and fathers at home, so that they can instruct the people and attend to the duties of the Church, and also leave the Temples in the hands of the Saints, so that they can attend to the ordinances of the Gospel, both for the Living and the dead? . . . This trouble would have come upon the whole Church, and we should have been compelled to stop the practice. Now, the question is, whether it should be stopped in this manner, or in the way the Lord has manifested to us, and leave our Prophets and Apostles and fathers free men, and the temples in the hands of the people, so that the dead may be redeemed."[26]

In his writings and sermons, President Woodruff described his revelatory experience and boldly affirmed that on his own, without the Lord's intervention, he would never have pronounced the end of plural marriage. He wrote, "The Lord showed me by vision and revelation exactly what would take place if we did not stop this practice. . . . All [temple] ordinances would be stopped throughout the land of Zion. Confusion would reign throughout Israel, and many men would be made prisoners. . . . But I want to say this: I should have let all the temples go out of our hands; I should have gone to prison myself, and let every other man go there, had not the God in heaven commanded me to do what I did do; and when the hour came that I was commanded to do that, it was all clear to me. I went before the Lord and I wrote what the Lord told me to write."[27]

Needless to say, as the leaders of the Church implemented the new policy, they encountered many serious complications and taxing problems. Some members ignored President Woodruff's revelation and continued to contract plural marriages. Those already involved in plural marriages struggled to maintain their families without incurring further persecution from the federal government. President Woodruff continued to support all of his families, but he appeared in public with only one of his wives (Emma) and advised all members of the Church to follow his example. But in spite of nearly insurmountable obstacles, the Manifesto did eventually bring about the end of plural marriage for law-abiding citizens in Utah and marked the beginning of realistic prospects for achieving statehood. It would be hard to overstate the vast ramifications of this revolutionary move on President Woodruff's part, but the Spirit bore witness to the faithful that, as difficult as it was, their courageous prophet had done exactly what the Lord wanted him to do.

COMPLETION OF THE SALT LAKE TEMPLE

During Wilford Woodruff's presidency, especially in the early part of the 1890s, the nation was suffering hard times as the result of an economic depression; for this and other reasons (chiefly the consequences of the government's pressure on the Church to end plural marriage), financial affairs were not going well for the Church either. President Woodruff faced serious debts incurred by the Church, which were exacerbated by a plummeting income due to reduced donations from members who were struggling financially themselves. In an attempt to avert financial disaster, President Woodruff initiated, among other enterprises, the establishment of the Utah Sugar Company. But instead of helping the Church's finances, this operation, along with numerous other complex ventures the Church was involved in, plunged the Church even deeper into monetary insolvency. Despite this bleak outlook (perhaps because of it), President Woodruff felt inspired to lay aside these weighty matters and make finishing the Salt Lake Temple a priority. It was a bold decision at such a perilous time. In the 1891 October conference, President

SALT LAKE TEMPLE
DEDICATION SERVICES.

AFTERNOON SESSION.

• • • ADMIT • ONE • • •

Thursday, April 13th, 1893.

W. Woodruff

Woodruff announced his determination to complete the temple and dedicate it on April 6, 1893, forty years to the day after the cornerstone was laid. He solicited the support of the Saints, both spiritually and financially. President Woodruff became very involved personally in seeing that the work went forward. One year before the scheduled dedication, he ascended to the top of the east center spire to have a look at the capstone, the ball, and the resplendent statue of Moroni, which were to be placed there.[28] President Woodruff appointed Joseph F. Smith, Lorenzo Snow, and Abraham H. Cannon to form a committee to speed the progress of the construction. He also sent five local artists to the Academie Julian in Paris to receive training on decorating the interior of the temple.[29] But the physical aspects of finishing the temple were dwarfed in comparison to the spiritual dimensions President Woodruff hoped to achieve by dedicating it at that time. He saw in its completion the opportunity to promote unity

in the Quorum of the Twelve where some dissention, particularly on the part of Moses Thatcher, had been plaguing the aged President. Members of the Church were also flagging in their commitment and unity. President Woodruff had faith that the temple dedication would bolster their spirituality and bring down upon all of them much-needed blessings from heaven. With the Saints putting forth a decidedly superhuman effort and with many blessings from the Lord, the temple was in fact finished and ready for dedication on April 6, 1893.

The forty-one dedicatory sessions, designed to accommodate nearly all who were worthy and able to enter the temple, continued over a two-week period. One sister who attended the first session, Lucy Flake from Snowflake, Arizona, recorded, "It had been predicted [that] the Devil would howl, and sure enough he did, for Salt Lake City had never witnessed such a storm, wind, rain, and snow.

The Salt Lake Temple.

Many houses and trees were blown over. . . . Hundreds of people stood in the snow for hours waiting for the Temple doors to open."[30] Many reported seeing a holy light surrounding the Brethren as they read the dedicatory prayer or conducted the sessions. Others heard heavenly music, some saw angels in their midst, and people outside the temple reported seeing a "glow of glorious light surround the Temple and circle about it as if it were an intelligible Presence."[31] In one of the sessions, President Woodruff said, "If the eyes of the congregation could be opened they would [have] seen Joseph and Hyrum, Brigham Young, John Taylor and all the good men who had lived in this dispensation assembled with us."[32] One member of the Quorum of the Twelve, Francis Lyman, attested to the fulfillment of President Woodruff's hopes that the temple dedication would bring the Apostles together in strength and unity. He said, "Never has there been so complete a union in the chief [councils] of the Priesthood."[33] Emmeline B. Wells reported a similar response among the members: "So exultant and enraptured were the saints in their rejoicing that their faces beamed with gladness, and the whole place seemed glorified and sanctified . . . on that never-to-be-forgotten occasion."[34] President Woodruff wrote, "The spirit & Power of God rested upon us. The spirit of Prophesy & Revelation was upon us & the Hearts of the People were Melted and many things [were] unfolded to us."[35]

Forty-six years earlier, just two days after their arrival in the Salt Lake Valley, Wilford Woodruff had stood with Brigham Young on the temple site. He saw the prophet put his cane into the ground and heard him declare, "I am going to build a temple here."[36] The prophecy was at last fulfilled, and the presence of the glorious temple blessed the Church with the strength the members needed to endure the many trials that still lay ahead.

STATEHOOD

Around 1861, following the failure of repeated attempts to attain statehood, Brigham Young and other General Authorities, now completely under the thumb of the non-member territorial officials appointed by the United States Government, set up a sort of "shadow" government. They reconstituted a group of priesthood holders, mostly Church leaders, and called it the Council of Fifty, the name by which a former governing body in Nauvoo was called. The First Presidency also reactivated the School of the Prophets, which was first held in Kirtland. These two organizations served as a means for Latter-day Saint leaders to maintain some influence over Church members in public matters. Wilford Woodruff played a prominent part in both of these groups.[37] In 1872, Utahns made another attempt to obtain statehood. This time, they drew upon the influence of non-Mormon friends of the Church such as former territorial appointees who had lived in Utah, but again the effort was unsuccessful. For many years after Brigham Young's death in 1877, the problems with anti-polygamy legislation completely dominated Utah politics and scuttled every attempt to achieve statehood. In a desperate effort to make some progress toward their goal, Church leaders began to "court" political leaders, especially Democrats who seemed sympathetic to the Mormon plight. Around 1887, they even urged missionaries to soften their proselytizing approach in order to lessen what Democratic supporters of the Church in Congress, especially Southerners, considered insults to them.[38]

The Church also sought to enlist the aid of friendly Republicans. In September of 1887, President Woodruff contacted two Californians, Alexander Badlam Jr. and Isaac Trumbo, both of whom had previously made investments with a major Utah mining company (The Bullion, Beck and Champion). He hoped to secure their help in forming favorable relationships with prominent California politicians.[39] A real turning point for President Woodruff personally, as well as for the pursuit of statehood, occurred in 1889 when he, with several other prominent Mormons, traveled to San Francisco to meet with Badlam and Trumbo, who successfully arranged meetings for them with Senator Leland Stanford, Judge Morris M. Estee, and other influential Californians.[40] Following the publication of the Manifesto of 1890, which signaled the official end of plural marriage, the goal of statehood became truly realistic.

At that time, nearly all members of the Church belonged to a political party called the People's Party. Nonmembers of the Church were by and large marshaled against them in what was called the Liberal Party. It was apparent to President Woodruff and other Utah leaders, both ecclesiastical and political, that Utahns needed to align themselves with the two prevalent parties of the United States, Democrats and Republicans. President Woodruff urged members of the Church to disband the People's Party and affiliate with either of the two established national parties. In fact, in some cases, Church leaders almost "assigned" Church members to one group or the other in order to form an equal division between the two. Accomplishing this revolutionary realignment was a major shift in Church policy and inevitably caused many points of contention over politics between members of the Church, which had not existed to this great an extent previously. But this radical change in Utah politics, along with the end of plural marriage and what proved to be the invaluable influence of their non-Mormon friends, including the Californians with whom they continued to have increasingly sanguine relationships, turned the tide of popular opinion in Utah's favor. Following the return to power of a Democratic congress in the elections of 1892, Joseph L. Rawlins, the newly elected delegate from Utah Territory, once again introduced the petition for Utah statehood to the House of Representatives. It passed on December 13, 1893, practically without opposition.[41]

Largely due to President Woodruff's efforts in settling the plural marriage issue, the stormy, half-century struggle to be freed at least in part from the oppressive rule of the federal government finally met with success. Consequently, an incredibly far-reaching change was wrought in the future of Utah and the Church.

LATER YEARS

As an extremely prominent member of Utah society, President Woodruff continued to direct a large number of business concerns for the Church as well as his own personal enterprises. As the scope of the Church

widened, President Woodruff traveled more and more. He made several trips to California to visit Isaac Trumbo and others with whom he had become acquainted during the quest for Utah's statehood, and with whom he now shared some business interests. One biographer reported, "In addition to trips to California, St. George, Bear Lake, and other places in the west, [President] Woodruff and entourage visited the World's Fair in Chicago in 1893."[42] This trip to the World's Fair was quite historic because he accompanied the Tabernacle Choir on their first national tour, attending their concerts en route as they performed in Denver, Independence, Kansas City, and St. Louis. He celebrated their success as they won second place in the competition at the fair.[43] Whenever he had a chance to get away from his overwhelming responsibilities, he still enjoyed fishing, gardening, and working on his farms; he read as much as he could, hosted important visitors to Salt Lake City, and continued to give personal attention to all of his families.

Wilford Woodruff's diligent efforts to bring reconciliation to many divergent opinions and factions within the Church and the state of Utah permeated his presidency. One of the last knotty issues he faced concerned General Authorities who neglected their priesthood duties in order to run for political

President Woodruff seated with his wife Emma and counselor George Q. Cannon during a trip to California.

Sportsman

President Woodruff was an avid fisherman, hunter, and lover of the great outdoors. When he was a missionary in Liverpool, England, he was introduced to the use of an artificial fly for catching trout. In 1847, on his journey to the Salt Lake Valley, he tried his skill with this innovation and wrote, "I went and flung my fly onto the [water]. And it being the first time that I ever tried the Artificial fly in America, or ever saw it tried, and I watched it as it floated upon the water with as much intens interest as Franklin did his kite when he tried to draw lightning from the skies."[16] It was a successful venture, ending in the acquisition of twelve fine fish. Evidence of his passion for fishing is seen in the fact that at age eighty-five he went on a ten-day camping trip to the headwaters of the Weber River in company with his wife Emma and one of his counselors, George Q. Cannon, and other friends. While in the mountains he composed a letter reviewing some of his sporting adventures and detailing information concerning wildlife and fish in Utah. The letter was sent to the editor of *Forest and Stream* magazine and was published in its September 22, 1892 issue.[17]

office and to accept time-consuming governmental positions in the East. In 1895, the First Presidency released what came to be known as the Political Manifesto, stating that those who held high Church offices must consult with Church authorities before accepting such political obligations. It was unclear how far down in the ecclesiastical chain this counsel extended, and once again, President Woodruff became embroiled in a pervasive controversy. His very nature rebelled against disunity and confrontation. He was a peacemaker at heart, and to encounter yet another crisis in a political matter at his age was a real hardship. The disagreements resulted in the disaffection of several prominent leaders, but the Political Manifesto and President Woodruff's fatherly guidance finally settled the matter and brought peace.

As an elderly man, President Woodruff saw clearly the far-reaching, eternal nature of family relationships and never abandoned his dedication to the salvation of his extended family, some of whom had joined the Church. Many times in his sermons and elsewhere President Woodruff emphasized the importance of family ties. To one of his daughters

he wrote: "We are all expecting to live together forever after death. I think we all as parents and children ought to take all the pains we can to make each other happy as long as we live that we may have nothing to regret."[44] Another distinguishing mark of his presidency consisted of doing away with the Church's traditional Thursday fast day observance. Practical considerations made it difficult if not impossible for members to hold the traditional fast meeting that day. Consequently, fasting was relegated to the present practice of being observed only once a month on the first Sunday. Also under President Woodruff's leadership, the Church began holding weekday religious instruction. Because of this small beginning, Wilford Woodruff is considered the father of the extensive Church Educational System, which enrolls nearly a million students today. He greatly expanded the worldwide missionary program of the Church and inaugurated the practice of allowing single sisters to serve full-time missions. He also organized the Church's Genealogical Society, forerunner of the family history program that exists today.

NINETIETH BIRTHDAY

On his ninetieth birthday, leaders of the Church and members organized a huge celebration in the Tabernacle for their aged President. They draped the speaker's stand with white and gold fabric and bedecked the organ with beautiful plants and flowers. They hung huge banners along the balconies emblazoned with such epithets as "Glory be to God," "Honor to His prophet," "We honor the man honored by God," and "1807—1847—1897," marking three significant years in President Woodruff's life: his birth, his entrance into the Salt Lake Valley, and his ninetieth birthday. Most of the nearly ten thousand attendees were young members of the Sunday School organization. These children were clothed all in white. He addressed them, saying: "The scene before me has been a fulfillment of all my prayers from my boyhood up to early manhood. Eighty years ago, I was a little boy attending school the same as you are here in the mountains of Israel. . . . Today, I stand in the midst of 10,000 young men and women of Israel—sons and daughters of prophets, patriarchs, and men of Israel."[45]

Of this memorable day, President Woodruff wrote: "This is my 90th birthday, and my wife Emma's 59th anniversary of her birthday. We met some 12,000 people in this big tabernacle who have met to celebrate our birthday, which congregation is composed of all parties, creeds and denominations. I delivered the first address to the assembly followed by G. Q. Cannon, L. Snow and others. I was almost covered up with flowers and roses. At the close of the service, myself and wife, Emma, took seats upon elevated chairs and shook hands with the congregation as they passed us, some 8,000 people. Of course our arms ached when we got through, but it was a great day."[46]

He later recalled: "The scene completely overpowered me. The events of my childhood and early manhood came to my mind. I remembered vividly how I prayed to the Lord that I might live to see a prophet or an apostle who would teach me the gospel of Christ. Here I stood in the great Tabernacle filled with ten thousand children, with Prophets, Apostles, and Saints. My head was a fountain of tears."[47]

DEATH

During his later years, President Woodruff was afflicted with poor health. Though not incapacitated, he suffered many bouts of illness. It was following one of these attacks that he sought rest in the favorable climate of California, a place he had grown to love. Arriving in San Francisco in August 1898, he underwent an extremely painful bladder operation. He appeared to be recuperating and participated in a number of civic activities with some of the many friends and acquaintances he had made in that state. One of his biographers wrote, "Then suddenly on September 1, he experienced complete kidney and bladder failure, and he rapidly lapsed into a coma. Doctors and those with him recognized that he could not survive such a crisis and he died at the Trumbo home at 6:40 AM on Friday, September 2."[48] He was ninety-one. His wife Emma and his faithful counselor in the First Presidency, George Q. Cannon, were at his bedside. At President Woodruff's funeral, President Cannon declared: "In the passing of President Woodruff, a man has gone from our midst whose character was probably as angelical as any person who has ever lived upon the earth. . . . He was of a sweet disposition and possessed a character so lovely as to draw unto him friends in every walk of life. . . . He was gentle as a woman and his purity was like unto that of the angels themselves. . . . He was a heavenly being. It was heaven to be in his company."[49] The man whom the Lord had preserved through so many accidents of childhood and trials of adulthood lived nearly a century and served the Lord valiantly, distinguishing himself as one of the great Presidents of The Church of Jesus Christ of Latter-day Saints.

TEACHINGS OF PRESIDENT
WILFORD WOODRUFF

THE DIVINITY OF THE CALLING OF THE PROPHET JOSEPH SMITH

Many years before he first heard the missionaries preach, young Wilford had felt great unrest with regard to religion. He had a keen sense that there was something missing from the Protestant churches that surrounded him. He stated several times that he wondered why there were no prophets and apostles in his day as there were formerly: "Before I ever heard of 'Mormonism,' when reading the Scriptures, I often wondered why it was that we had no Prophets, no Apostles, no gifts of graces, no healings by the power of God, no visions, no angels, no revelations, no voice of God. I often wondered why these things were not continued among the children of men, why they were not enjoyed by the different churches and denominations of the day, and in my conversation with theologians and divines, I often referred to these things, but they all told me that such supernatural manifestations were unnecessary in our day and age of the world . . . those things were given to establish the doctrine of Christ, and when it was once established they were no longer needed. This logic always appeared strange to me."[50]

Wilford had longed for many years to find such manifestations. When he finally found the restored gospel, he incessantly testified of the return of these glorious blessings to the earth: "He [Joseph Smith] received powers and keys from under the hands of Moses for gathering the house of Israel in the last days; he received under the hands of Elias the keys of sealing the hearts of the fathers to the children, and the hearts of the children to the fathers; he received under the hands of Peter, James and John, the Apostleship, and everything belonging thereto; he received under the hands of Moroni all the keys and powers required of the stick of Joseph in the hands of Ephraim; he received under the hand of John the Baptist the Aaronic Priesthood, with all its keys and powers, and every other key and power belonging to this dispensation, and I am not ashamed to say that he was a Prophet of God, and he laid the foundation of the greatest work and dispensation that has ever been established on the earth."[51]

President Woodruff in his advanced years.

111

President Woodruff had the distinction of being the last person living who served in the Quorum of the Twelve under the leadership of the Prophet Joseph Smith. In an early phonograph recording, he described the last meeting of the Twelve with Joseph before his martyrdom. It was at this time that the Prophet bestowed the keys of the kingdom upon the Apostles. Concerning the testimony Joseph bore on that occasion of the role of the Twelve in the government of the Church, Wilford Woodruff declared: "I am the only man now living in the flesh who heard that testimony from his mouth, and I know it is true by the power of God manifest through him."[52]

Many times during his life, he energetically reinforced the fact that the Prophet Joseph Smith had clearly delegated the priesthood keys to the Quorum of the Twelve. Those who wondered to whom the leadership of the Church belonged after Joseph's death could look to President Woodruff for an inspiring, unequivocal explanation of the true doctrine of succession of the presidency: "Joseph Smith was what he professed to be, a prophet of God, a seer and revelator. He laid the foundation of this Church and kingdom, and lived long enough to deliver the keys of the kingdom to the Elders of Israel, unto the Twelve Apostles. He spent the last winter of his life, some three or four months, with the Quorum of the Twelve, teaching them. It was not merely a few hours ministering to them the ordinances of the Gospel; but he spent day after day, week after week and month after month, teaching them and a few others the things of the kingdom of God."[53]

President Woodruff powerfully testified of the passing of the keys of the kingdom from the Prophet Joseph Smith down to himself: "When the Lord gave the keys of the kingdom of God, the keys of the Melchisedec Priesthood, of the apostleship, and sealed them upon the head of Joseph Smith, He sealed them upon his head to stay here upon the earth until the coming of the Son of Man. Well might Brigham Young say, 'The keys of the kingdom of God are here.' They were with him to the day of his death. They then rested upon the head of another man—President John Taylor. He held those keys to the hour of his death. They then fell by turn, or in the providence of God, upon Wilford Woodruff."[54]

Wilford Woodruff's teachings throughout his life resonated with the intimacy of his personal acquaintance with

Joseph Smith and his sure knowledge of the Prophet's divine mission. He knew the Prophet and carried the strength of that close association into the circle of the General Authorities until his death near the turn of the nineteenth century. He described his first meeting with Joseph and then testified, "This was my first acquaintance with the Prophet Joseph. And from that day until the present, with all the apostacies that we have had, and with all the difficulties and afflictions we have been called to pass through, I never saw a moment when I had any doubt with regard to this work. I have had no trial about this. While the people were apostatizing on the right hand and on the left, and while Apostles were urging me to turn against the Prophet Joseph, it was no temptation to me to doubt this work or to doubt that Joseph Smith was a Prophet of God."[55]

On numerous occasions Wilford Woodruff gave wonderful insights into the revelations and prophecies of Joseph. He said, "Joseph Smith was full of revelation. He could translate anything given to him of God. He could receive revelation without the Urim and Thummin. Many of the principal revelations contained in the Doctrine and Covenants were received without the use of the Urim and Thummim. They were given to him by the inspiration of Almighty God."[56] President Woodruff powerfully testified of two of Joseph's prophecies that he personally saw fulfilled: "I traveled thousands of miles with Joseph Smith. I knew his spirit. Many of the revelations given through him [have] been fulfilled. I myself wrote the revelation that was given through him concerning the war that would take place in this country between the north and south [D&C 87]. That revelation was published to the world for twenty years before the war. It broke out just as predicted, and I refer to it because it is one of the revelations that is fulfilled."[57]

Joseph Smith pronounced the second prophecy in the company of a small gathering of priesthood brethren close to the time of their Zion's Camp journey in 1834. In the last year of his life, President Woodruff recalled the occasion and reported: "Among other things, he [Joseph Smith] said, 'It [meaning the Church] will fill the Rocky Mountains. There will be tens of thousands of Latter-day Saints who will be gathered to the Rocky Mountains, and there they will open the door for the establishing of the Gospel among the Lamanites, who will receive the Gospel and their

Talking Machine Testimony

Shortly after his ninetieth birthday in March of 1897, President Woodruff made a recording of his voice on a clay cylinder made on an Edison-type gramophone. Having the sound of his voice preserved would have been enough of a blessing, but the testimony he bore is a remarkable historical and spiritual treasure.

"I bear my testimony that Joseph Smith was a true prophet of God, ordained of God to lay the foundation of his church and kingdom in the last dispensation and fullness of times. I bear my testimony that in the early spring of 1844 in Nauvoo, the Prophet Joseph Smith called the Twelve Apostles together, and he delivered unto them the ordinances of the church and kingdom of God; and all of the keys and powers that God had bestowed upon him, he sealed upon our heads. He told us we must round up our shoulders and bear off this kingdom or we would be damned. I am the only man now living in the flesh who heard that testimony from his mouth, and I know it is true by the power of God manifest through him. At that meeting he began to speak about three hours upon the subject of the kingdom. His face was covered with a power that I had never seen in the flesh before. In all his testimony to us, the power of God was visibly manifest in the Prophet Joseph.

"This is my testimony, spoken by myself into a talking machine on this the nineteenth day of March, 1897, in the ninety-first year of my age."[18]

endowments and the blessings of God. This people will go into the Rocky Mountains; they will there build temples to the Most High. They will raise up a posterity there.' . . . I name these things because I want to bear testimony before God, angels and men that mine eyes behold the day, and have beheld for the last fifty years of my life, the fulfillment of that prophecy. I never expected to see the Rocky Mountains when I listened to that man's voice, but I have, and do today."[58]

THE VISION OF ETERNITY

Another powerful aspect of President Woodruff's teachings emanated from his profound understanding of the realities of eternity and man's position in the vast panorama of the universe that the restored gospel illuminated so dramatically. He was deeply affected by Joseph Smith's vision of the three degrees of glory (D&C 76). Referring to that revelation, President Woodruff said, "Before I saw Joseph I said I did not care how old he was, or how young he was; I did not care how he looked—whether his hair was long or short; the man that advanced that revelation was a Prophet of God. I knew it for myself."[59] He judged this revelation to be the greatest of all time: "I consider that the Doctrine and Covenants, our Testament, contains a code of the most solemn, the most Godlike proclamations ever made to the human family. I will refer to the 'Vision' alone, as a revelation which gives more light, more truth, and more principle than any revelation contained in any other book we ever read. It makes plain to our understanding our present condition, where we came from, why we are here, and where we are going to. Any man may know through that revelation what his part and condition will be."[60]

His visionary understanding of eternity led him to be a dedicated promoter of temple work. He had great faith in the efficacy of the sacred ordinances and bore his testimony to this truth in many of his sermons and writings. In the early days of the Church, instead of being sealed to one's own ancestors, people were often sealed to a prominent Church leader. He firmly rejected this practice, urging members to seek out their own lineage and be sealed to their own progenitors: "There are men in this congregation who wish to be adopted to me. I say to them to-day, if they can hear me, Go and be adopted to your fathers, and save your fathers, and stand at the head of your father's house, as Saviors upon Mount Zion, and God will bless you in this. . . . Those of you who stand here—I do not care whether you are Apostles or what you are—by honoring your fathers you will not take any honor from your heads; you will hold the keys of the salvation of your father's house, as Joseph Smith does. You will lose nothing by honoring your fathers and redeeming your dead. It is a glorious work."[61]

Showing a remarkably clear comprehension of the work being done in the spirit world, he taught, "Joseph and Hyrum Smith, Father Smith, David Patten and the other Elders who have been called to the other side of the vail have fifty times as many people to preach to as we have on the earth. There they have all the spirits who have lived on the earth in seventeen centuries—fifty generations, fifty thousand millions of persons who lived and died here without having seen a Prophet or Apostle, and without having the word of the Lord sent unto them. They are shut up in prison, awaiting the message of the Elders of Israel. . . . Jesus himself preached to the antediluvian world, who had been in prison for thousands of years. So with Joseph Smith and the elders—they will have to preach to the inhabitants of the earth who have died during the last seventeen centuries; and when they hear the testimony of the Elders and accept it there should be somebody on the earth, as we have been told, to attend to the ordinances of the house of God for them."[62]

THE HOLY GHOST

Throughout his life President Woodruff had numerous spiritual experiences and manifestations that taught him the supreme importance of the Holy Ghost in the lives of the Latter-day Saints, both the leaders and the members. He taught, "Whenever the Lord requires any Prophet, Seer, Revelator, Apostle or leading man of the Church to speak, the Spirit of the Lord is with him to give counsel to the people from time to time as he is moved upon, and such the people ought to hear. But I want you to understand this one thing: The Holy Priesthood and power of God do not stop there; it does not stop with the . . . Twelve Apostles, it does not stop with our leading men of Israel; there is not a man on God's footstool that is sent forth into the world to preach the Gospel but ought to have the Spirit of the Lord upon him and the revelation of God to him. . . . There is no end to the Holy Ghost and the power of God and the revelations of God to man."[63]

But President Woodruff also emphasized that the proper channel for revelation to the Church as a whole was through the living prophet, seer, and revelator. He said, "There is an appointed way, however, by which revelation from the Lord for the government of His Church is received. There is but one man on the earth, at a time, who holds this power. But every individual member has the privilege of receiving revelation from the Lord for his guidance in his own affairs, and to testify to him concerning the correctness of public teachings and movements. . . . If there are any members of the Church who do not know by their own experience that this is true, they may be assured that they do not live up to their privileges."[64]

He also taught frequently that if the President of the Church were to depart from the revelations he received, the Lord would not suffer him to stand at the head of the Church. "The Lord would not permit me to occupy this position one

The Endowment House that stood on Temple Square, Salt Lake City, Utah.

I traveled with Joseph Smith quite a length of time. I traveled with Brigham Young forty years, at home and abroad. I traveled with him to this country. We came with the pioneers. Brigham Young, though he never wrote many revelations, had the revelations of God with him from the day that he embraced this work till the day of his death. I have often thought of the time when he was asked if he would not go on to California instead of stopping in this barren land. What was his answer? I was with him when he gave that answer. He said, 'No, I am going to stay right here. I am going to build a temple here. I am going to build a city here; I am going to build a country here.' Has it not been so? Yes, it has. Was it not by revelation? Certainly it was."[67]

THE LATTER DAYS

Throughout his life, President Woodruff was keenly aware of the teachings of ancient prophets concerning our day and age. He dwelt frequently on such doctrines as the restoration of the kingdom, the gathering of Israel, the return of the Jews to Israel, the destruction of the wicked, and the Second Coming of the Savior. Concerning the Jews, he preached: "They will gather to their own land, taking with them their gold and silver, and will re-build their city and temple, according to the prediction of Moses and the Prophets. When this time arrives, which is nigh, even at our doors, let the Gentile nations who reject the Gospel which is now sent to them, prepare to meet the judgments of an offended God! For when their cup is full even to the brim, the Lord will then remember the chastisements of the Jews, his favored people.... Woe unto the Gentiles, who have administered afflictions to the Jews for these many years! Woe unto them if they now reject this only means of salvation, for the awful calamities spoken of in these books, the Bible and the Book of Mormon, will certainly befall them."[68]

Of the restored latter-day kingdom, he proclaimed, "Now I want to say something with regard to the dispensation in which we live. The God of heaven has set his hand to fulfil

The First Presidency in April 1889. President Woodruff with George Q. Cannon (left) and Joseph F. Smith (right).

day of my life, unless I was susceptible to the Holy Spirit and to the revelations of God. It is too late in the day for this Church to stand without revelation."[65] And again, "I say to all Israel, the Lord will never permit me or any other man who stands as president of this Church to lead you astray. It is not in the programme. It is not in the mind of God. If I were to attempt that the Lord would remove me out of my place, and so He will any other man who attempts to lead the children of men astray from the oracles of God and from their duty."[66]

At times members of the Church would question whether the Presidents of the Church following Joseph Smith received revelations as the Prophet had. President Woodruff commented upon this issue, assuring the Saints that subsequent prophets just as surely received revelation to guide the Church: "I know the Lord is with this people. . . .

the volume of revelation which the Bible contains, to build up that kingdom that Daniel the Prophet saw in the interpretation of the dream of Nebuchadnezzar. The God of heaven has sent forth that angel which John the Revelator saw 'fly in the midst of heaven having the everlasting Gospel to preach to them that dwell on the earth, and to every nation, and kindred, and tongue, and people, saying with a loud voice, Fear God and give glory to him for the hour of his judgment is come' [Revelation 14:7]. That angel has delivered the Gospel to Joseph Smith, and I know it. I bear my record and testimony to this truth. It is the truth of the living God. He has set his hand, as I have said, to build up this kingdom."[69]

Of this last dispensation he further declared, "It is a day in which the Gospel is to be preached to every nation, tongue and people for a witness of what shall follow; a day in which the Israel of God who receive it in their dispersed and scattered condition are to gather together to the place appointed of God, the place where they will perform the 'marvelous work and wonder' spoken of by the ancients who, in vision, saw our day; and where they will begin to inherit the promises made to the fathers respecting their children. The work that is to be so marvelous in the eyes of men has already commenced, and is assuming shape and proportions; but they cannot see it. It will consist in preaching the Gospel to all the world, gathering the Saints from the midst of all those nations who reject it; building up the Zion of God; establishing permanently in the earth His kingdom; preparing for the work of the gathering of the Jews and the events that will follow their settlement in their own lands, and in preparing for ourselves holy places in which to stand when the judgments of God shall overtake the nations."[70]

On the subject of the Second Coming of the Savior, he reminded the Saints of the prophecies that must be fulfilled before that great and dreadful day: "I do not know that any people on the earth, except the Latter-day Saints, are looking for this great event. There may be exceptions. . . . But . . . he never will come until the revelations of God are fulfilled and a people are prepared for his coming. He will never come until the Jews are gathered home and have re-built their Temple and city, and the Gentiles have gone up there to battle against them. He will never come until his Saints have built up Zion, and have fulfilled the revelations which have been spoken concerning it. He will never come until the Gentiles throughout the whole Christian world have been warned by the inspired elders of Israel. They are called to thrust in the sickle and reap, for the harvest is ripe and the time has come, which is referred to in this revelation, when the Lord commands the Elders to go forth and warn the world for the last time, and call upon the inhabitants of the earth to repent."[71]

TEMPORAL MATTERS

As all of the prophets have done, President Woodruff gave the Saints sound, down-to-earth advice regarding their temporal affairs along with guidance in their spiritual concerns. He was an extremely practical man, believing that the building of the kingdom included a very real earthly kingdom as well as a spiritual one: "Strangers and the Christian world marvel at the 'Mormons' talking about temporal things. Bless your souls, two-thirds of all the revelations given in this world rest upon the accomplishment of this temporal work. We have it to do, we can't build up Zion sitting on a hemlock slab singing ourselves away to everlasting bliss; we

Wilford the Worker

Wilford was known throughout his life as a hard worker. At his funeral his counselor George Q. Cannon observed, "He did no man an injury, nor was he too proud, even is his Apostolic calling, to toil as other men toiled."[19] He labored on his farms well into his old age. Andrew Jenson, who succeeded Elder Woodruff as historian of the Church, wrote: "Much younger men than himself were not his equals in the performance of heavy labor. . . . He worked upon the threshing machine; he planted, irrigated, gathered and hauled from the farm . . . he planted vineyards, orchards, made ditches, watered, and pruned the trees and bushes of his orchard; he made roads, built bridges, hauled wood from the canyon, made adobes and did all forms of manual labor. . . . His industry was so conspicuous a part of his being that when, at the age of ninety years, one of his grandson excelled him a very little in hoeing some vegetables in the garden, he said with apparent humiliation: 'Well, it is the first time in my life that one of my children has ever outdone me in hoeing.'"[20]

Temple Work for Signers of the Declaration of Independence

Wilford Woodruff's entrance into the spirit world at the age of ninety-one must have been a very natural thing for him, for he had received visitors from that sphere on many occasions. Some of those visitors were Joseph and Hyrum Smith, Brigham Young, Heber C. Kimball, George A. Smith, and Jedediah M. Grant. Perhaps the most remarkable and well known of his spiritual experiences happened before he became President of the Church, while he was serving as the first president of the first completed temple in the West at St. George, Utah. George Washington and many other prominent men of the past sought the blessings of the temple at the hand of this spiritual servant of the Lord: "Two weeks before I left St. George, the spirits of the dead gathered around me, wanting to know why we did not redeem them. . . . These were the signers of the Declaration of Independence, and they waited on me for two days and two nights. . . . I straightway went into the baptismal font and called upon brother McCallister to baptize me for the signers of the Declaration of Independence, and fifty other eminent men, making one hundred in all, including John Wesley, Columbus, and others; I then baptized him [Brother McCallister] for every President of the United States, except three; and when their cause is just, somebody will do temple work for them."[21]

have to cultivate the earth, to take the rocks and elements out of the mountains and rear Temples to the Most High God; and this temporal work is demanded at our hands by the God of heaven. . . . This is the great dispensation in which the Zion of God must be built up, and we as Latter-day Saints have it to build. . . . We are obliged to build cities, town and villages, and we are obliged to gather the people from every nation under heaven to the Zion of God, that they may be taught in the ways of the Lord."[72]

However, while the physical kingdom was important, President Woodruff wanted the Saints to keep it in proper perspective: "The eternal destiny of every individual depends upon the manner in which the few short years of the life in the flesh are spent. I ask, in the name of the Lord, what is popularity to you or me? What is gold or silver, or this world's goods to any of us, any further than to enable us to obtain what we need to eat, drink, and wear, and to build up the kingdom of God. And for us to stop praying, and to become crazy after the riches of the world, is the very height of foolishness and folly."[73]

POLITICAL MATTERS

In October conference 1897, just a little under a year before he died, President Woodruff seemed to have a premonition of his imminent death. He said, "I do not know that I shall ever address you again; I cannot tell anything about this; but I feel strongly impressed to say a few words to you upon principle, although it is late." He went on to discuss a matter that

had been very much on his mind. When the First Presidency had encouraged the Saints to divide themselves into the two prevalent parties of the United States in order to obtain statehood, President Woodruff was concerned that their political differences were raising controversy, sometimes even enmity, among them. He spoke to the Saints of their duty as members of the Church to unite their efforts in choosing righteous men to lead them and not allow political extremism to divide them since they were fellow citizens in the Lord's kingdom. He said, "I want to say to you here, the day has come when God Almighty requires at your hands to unite together in your temporal business, and in your politics, so far as it is wisdom. I do not care whether a man is Republican or a Democrat, in that he is free; but it is your duty to unite in electing good men to govern and control your cities, your local affairs, and I will state that when you do not do this you are losers of the blessings of Almighty God. . . . Lay aside your extremes in democracy and republicanism, as far as is wise in that matter, and in other than local matters as Latter-day Saints unite together within your party lines and appoint good men. When you do that, God will bless you."[74]

MANIFESTATIONS FROM THE SPIRIT WORLD

President Woodruff had a remarkable gift for receiving spiritual manifestations. He often related these experiences to promote faith among the Latter-day Saints. One such experience occurred on his first mission to the southern states:

"Now, I will refer to a thing that took place with me in Tennessee . . . in the year 1835, and while at the house of Abraham O. Smoot, I received a letter from Brothers Joseph Smith and Oliver Cowdery, requesting me to stay there, and stating that I would lose no blessing by doing so. Of course, I was satisfied. I went into a little room and sat down upon a small sofa. I was all by myself and the room was dark; and while I rejoiced in this letter and the promise made to me, I became wrapped in vision. I was like Paul; I did not know whether I was in the body or out of the body. A personage appeared to me and showed me the great scenes that should take place in the last days. One scene after another passed before me. I saw the sun darkened; I saw the moon become as blood; I saw the stars fall from heaven; I saw seven golden lamps set in the heavens, representing the various dispensations of God to man—a sign that would appear before the coming of Christ. I saw the resurrection of the dead. In the first resurrection those that came forth from their graves seemed to be all dressed alike, but in the second resurrection they were a diverse in their dress as this congregation is before me to-day, and if I had been an artist I could have painted the whole scene as it was impressed upon my mind, more indelibly fixed than anything I had ever seen with the natural eye. What does this mean? It was a testimony of the resurrection of the dead. I had a testimony. I believe in the resurrection of the dead, and I know it is a true principle. Thus we may have dreams about things of great importance."[75]

During his second mission, this time to England, he received another manifestation from the Lord. He said, "When I was in the City of London on one occasion, with Brother George A. Smith, I dreamt that my wife came to me and told me that our first child had died. I believed my dream, and in the morning while at breakfast, I felt somewhat sad. Brother George A. noticed this and I told him my dream. Next morning's post brought me a letter from my wife, conveying the intelligence of the death of my child. It may be asked what use there was in such a thing. I don't know that there was much use in it except to prepare my mind for the news of the death of my child. . . . The Lord does communicate some things of importance to the children of men by means of visions and dreams as well as by the records of divine truth."[76]

While on this same mission, he experienced another frightening but faith-promoting incident, in which he was delivered by the administration of angels. President Woodruff related, "Brother Kimball, Brother George A. Smith and myself had . . . [an] experience in London, at a house where we were stopping. It seemed as if there were legions of spirits there. They sought our destruction; and on one occasion, after Brother Kimball had left us, these powers of darkness fell upon us to destroy our lives, and both Brother Smith and myself would have been killed, apparently, had not three holy messengers come into the room and filled the room with light. They were dressed in temple clothing. They laid their hands upon our heads and we were delivered, and that power was broken."[77]

For a number of years after his death, the Prophet Joseph appeared to President Woodruff from the spirit world. Describing some of these visitations, President Woodruff recounted:

"Joseph and Hyrum visited me, and the Prophet laid before me a great many things. Among other things he told me to get the Spirit of God; that all of us needed it. He also told me what the twelve apostles would be called to go through on the earth before the coming of the Son of Man, and what the reward of their labors would be; but all that was taken from me for some reason. Nevertheless it was most glorious, although much would be required at our hands.

"Joseph Smith continued visiting myself and others up to a certain time, and then it stopped. The last time I saw him was in heaven. In the night vision I saw him at the door of the temple in heaven. He came and spoke to me. He said he could not stop to talk with me because he was in a hurry . . .

"'Now,' said I, 'I want to know why you are in a hurry. I have been in a hurry all my life, but I expected my hurry would be over when I got into the kingdom of heaven, if I ever did.'

"Joseph said, 'I will tell you, Brother Woodruff. Every dispensation that has had the priesthood on the earth and has gone into the celestial kingdom has had a certain amount of work to do to prepare to go to the earth with the Savior when he goes to reign on the earth. Each dispensation has had ample time to do this work. We have not. We are the last dispensation, and so much work has to be done, and we need to be in a hurry in order to accomplish it.'

"Of course, that was satisfactory, but it was new doctrine to me."[78]

Throughout his long and inspiring ministry, President Woodruff blessed the Saints by sharing these and many other sacred spiritual manifestations with them. A twentieth-century Apostle and scholar, Elder John A. Widtsoe, paid fitting tribute to this great President of the Church in these words: "Withal he was a modest man, who, despite positions and honors, could cultivate his garden and live the simple life. He had a rich spiritual nature. His faith was profound and certain. He walked with the Lord all the days of his life. They who did not understand the power that accompanies true humility stood perplexed before him. The faithful, however, felt the living fire that made his career possible."[79] Indeed, "Wilford the Faithful" remained so all his life.

Lawrence R. Flake

Professor of Church History and Doctrine, PhD
Brigham Young University

Notes

1. Thomas G. Alexander, *Things in Heaven and Earth: The Life and Times of Wilford Woodruff, a Mormon Prophet* (Salt Lake City: Signature Books, 1991), 6.
2. Susan Arrington Madsen, *The Lord Needed a Prophet* (Salt Lake City: Deseret Book, 1990), 61.
3. Dean C. Jessee, "Wilford Woodruff," *The Presidents of the Church*, ed. Leonard J. Arrington (Salt Lake City: Deseret Book, 1986), 117.
4. Ibid., 118.
5. Golden A. Buchmiller, "President Wilford Woodruff," *Church News*, April 5, 1980, 12; originally in general conference address, April 7, 1887.
6. Alexander, *Things in Heaven and Earth*, 13–14.
7. Matthias F. Cowley, *Wilford Woodruff: History of His Life and Labors* (Salt Lake City: Bookcraft, 1964), 16.
8. Ibid., 18.
9. Madsen, *The Lord Needed a Prophet*, 63–64.
10. *Deseret Weekly News*, March 3, 1889.
11. Cowley, *Wilford Woodruff: History of His Life and Labors*, 35.
12. Lawrence R. Flake, *Prophets and Apostles of the Last Dispensation* (Provo, UT: Religious Studies Center, 2001), 44.
13. *Journal History of The Church of Jesus Christ of Latter-day Saints*, LDS Church Archives, November 25, 1836, as cited in Alexander, *Things in Heaven and Earth*, 42.
14. Arnold Irvin, "Moments with the Prophets," *Church News*, June 26, 1982, 16.
15. Scott G. Kenney, *Wilford Woodruff's Journal* (Midvale, UT: Signature Books, 1983), 2:423.
16. Wilford Woodruff's journal, July 24, 1847, 3:333–34, as cited in Alexander, *Things in Heaven and Earth*, 141.
17. Alexander, *Things in Heaven and Earth*, 170–73.
18. Ibid., 207–8.
19. Ibid., 184.
20. Ibid., 188.
21. Ibid., 197.
22. Ibid., 221.
23. Brian Smith, "Wilford Woodruff: 'Wilford the Faithful' Became God's Anointed," *Church News*, May 1, 1993, 10.
24. G. Homer Durham, comp., *The Discourses of Wilford Woodruff* (Salt Lake City: Bookcraft, 1998), 194; original in *Millennial Star*, 52:34–35, December 12, 1889.
25. Wilford Woodruff's journal, September 25, 1890, as cited in Alexander, *Things in Heaven and Earth*, 266–67.
26. *Deseret Weekly*, November 14, 1891; see also D&C, OD 1, 292–93.
27. Ibid; see also D&C, OD 1, 293.
28. Alexander, *Things in Heaven and Earth*, 290.
29. Ibid., 292.
30. Diary of Lucy Hanna White Flake, typescript, L. Tom Perry Special Collections, Harold B. Lee Library, Brigham Young University, Provo, UT, 168; as cited in LaRene Gaunt, "The Power of God Was with Us," *Ensign*, March 1993, 29.
31. Susa Young Gates, "More Than a Halo," *Juvenile Instructor*, November 15, 1907, 684; as cited in Gaunt, 31.
32. Gaunt, "The Power of God Was with Us," 29.
33. Francis M. Lyman journal, April 6, 1893, transcript; as cited in Richard N. Holzapfel, *Every Stone a Sermon* (Salt Lake City: Bookcraft, 1992); as cited in Gaunt, "The Power of God Was with Us," 29.
34. Gaunt, "The Power of God Was with Us," 30; original in Emmeline B. Wells, "Temple Dedication," *Women's Exponent*, April 15 and May 1, 1893, 156.
35. Wilford Woodruff's journal, April 9,1893, 9:246, as cited in Alexander, *Things in Heaven and Earth*, 296.
36. Durham, *The Discourses of Wilford Woodruff*, 322–23.
37. Alexander, *Things in Heaven and Earth*, 206–7.
38. Ibid., 248.
39. Ibid., 249.
40. Ibid., 252.

41. Ibid., 282.

42. Wilford Woodruff's journal, August 29–September 19, 1893, 9:259–64, as cited in Alexander, *Things in Heaven and Earth*, 298.

43. Alexander, *Things in Heaven and Earth*, 298–99.

44. Letter to Blanche Woodruff, September 16, 1894, as cited in Dean C. Jessee, "Wilford Woodruff," *Encyclopedia of Mormonism*, ed. Daniel H. Ludlow (New York: Macmillan, 1992), 4:1582.

45. *Church News*, September 15, 1973, 10.

46. *Church News* clipping in author's private collection.

47. Cowley, *Wilford Woodruff: History of His Life and Labors*, 615.

48. Wilford Woodruff's journal, September 1, 1898, 9:561, as cited in Alexander, *Things in Heaven and Earth*, 330.

49. Preston Nibley, *The Presidents of the Church* (Salt Lake City: Deseret Book, 1941), 168–70.

50. *JD*, 2:195–96.

51. Ibid., 16:267.

52. Transcript of gramophone recording, March 19, 1897, LDS Church Archives, Salt Lake City.

53. *JD*, December 12, 1869, 13:164.

54. *Millennial Star* (1889), 51:546–47.

55. *Millennial Star* (1891), 53:628.

56. *Millennial Star* (1891), 53:642.

57. *JD*, 24:242.

58. CR, April 1898, 57.

59. *Millennial Star* (1891), 53:627–28.

60. *JD*, 22:146–47.

61. *Millennial Star*, May 28, 1894, 56:339–401.

62. *JD*, 16:269.

63. CR, October 1897.

64. *Millennial Star* (April 6, 1888), 50:307–8.

65. *Millennial Star* (May 21, 1894), 56:324.

66. *Millennial Star* (1890), 52:741.

67. *Millennial Star*, 57:741–42.

68. *JD*, 18:220–21.

69. Ibid., 22:344.

70. Ibid., 24:51.

71. Ibid., September 12, 1875, 18:111.

72. Ibid., 16:268–69.

73. Ibid., 18:119–20.

74. CR, October 1897, 71.

75. *JD*, 22:332–33.

76. Ibid., 22:333.

77. *Deseret Weekly*, March 3, 1889, 38:389–90.

78. *Deseret Weekly*, October 19, 1896, 53:642–43.

79. Durham, *The Discourses of Wilford Woodruff*, x.

SIDEBAR AND PHOTO NOTES

1. Cowley, *Wilford Woodruff: History of His Life and Labors*, 5.

2. Brian Smith, "Wilford Woodruff," *Church News*, May 1, 1993, 8.

3. Kenney, *Wilford Woodruff's Journal*, 4:414.

4. Cowley, *Wilford Woodruff: History of His Life and Labors*, 476–77.

5. Dean C. Jessee, "Wilford Woodruff: A Man of Record," *Ensign*, July 1993, 29; original in Wilford Woodruff's journal, February 12, 1862.

6. Jessee, "Wilford Woodruff: A Man of Record," 29.

7. Cowley, *Wilford Woodruff: History of His Life and Labors*, 55.

8. Ibid., 56.

9. Ibid., 52.

10. Ibid., 99.

11. Ibid., summarized.

12. Ibid., 241.

13. Bryant S. Hinckley, *The Faith of Our Pioneer Fathers* (Salt Lake City: Deseret Book, 1956), 31–32.

14. Jessee, "Wilford Woodruff: A Man of Record," 30; original in Wilford Woodruff's journal, synopsis following the year 1885.

15. Alexander, *Things in Heaven and Earth*, xii.

16. Harold Schindler, "Publisher Prepares Wilford Woodruff Diaries," *The Salt Lake Tribune*, May 22, 1983, E3; original in Wilford Woodruff's journal, July 8, 1847.

17. James B. Allen and Herbert H. Frost, "Wilford Woodruff, Sportsman," *BYU Studies* 15, no. 1 (Winter 1974): 113–17.

18. Transcript of recording made March 19, 1897, Church Archives.

19. Nibley, *The Presidents of the Church*, 169.

20. Andrew Jenson, *LDS Biographical Encyclopedia* (Salt Lake City: Andrew Jenson History Company, 1901), 25–26.

21. Hinckley, *The Faith of Our Pioneer Fathers*, 41.

Chapter Five

LORENZO SNOW

LIFE AND TIMES

1814	April 3	Born in Mantua, Portage County, Ohio
1836		Attended Hebrew School in Kirtland
1836	June	Baptized a member of the Church
1837		Served a mission to Ohio
1838–39		Served missions to Missouri, Illinois, Kentucky, and Ohio
1840–43		Served a mission to Great Britain
1845 or 1846		Married Charlotte Merril Squires, Mary Adeline Goddard, Sarah Ann Prichard, and Harriet Amelia Squires
1849	February 12	Ordained an Apostle
1849–52		Served a mission to Italy
1852		Elected to the Utah Legislature
1853		Called to preside over the Saints in Box Elder County
1864		Served a mission to Hawaii
1872–73		Toured Europe and the Middle East; helped rededicate the Holy Land
1873		Organized the united order in Brigham City
1873–77		Served as one of seven counselors to Brigham Young
1885		Served a mission to American Indians in the Northwestern United States
1885		Served an eleven-month prison term for practicing plural marriage
1888	May 21	Publicly dedicated the Manti Temple
1889	April 7	Sustained as President of the Quorum of the Twelve Apostles
1893	May 19	Set apart as president of the Salt Lake Temple
1898	September 2	Visited by the Savior in the Salt Lake Temple
1898	September 13	Sustained as President of the Church
1899		Emphasized the law of tithing
1901	October 10	Died in Salt Lake City, Utah, at age eighty-seven

BIOGRAPHICAL HIGHLIGHTS

Lorenzo Snow served as President of the Church from 1898 to 1901. He was the last President who, as an adult, personally knew the Prophet Joseph Smith. President Snow was also the prophet who led the Church into the twentieth century. He gave dynamic leadership to the Church during times of financial crisis and inspired the Saints with a vision of their eternal potential.

Lorenzo was born on April 3, 1814, in Mantua, Ohio, to Oliver Snow and Rosetta Leonora Pettibone. He was the fifth of seven children and the oldest of three sons. When he was a young man, his sister Eliza invited him to go to Kirtland, Ohio, and take a Hebrew class that was sponsored by the Latter-day Saints. Lorenzo attended the class from January to March 1836 and then joined the Church in June of that year. In consequence of his new religious life, he served several missions for the Church during the next decade and made the trek to the Rocky Mountains with the Mormon pioneers.

CONTRIBUTIONS

Lorenzo accepted a call to be an Apostle on February 12, 1849. During the next half century, he served missions to such diverse places as Italy, Hawaii, and the Holy Land. He also served in the Utah Territorial Legislature and presided over the Saints in Box Elder County. In 1889 he was sustained as President of Quorum of the Twelve Apostles, and in 1893 he became the first president of the Salt Lake Temple. Lorenzo Snow was ordained and set apart as President of the Church on September 13, 1898.

TEACHINGS

President Snow will always be known as the prophet who reemphasized the principle of tithing, which ultimately helped lift the Church out of financial debt. He is also remembered as the leader who formulated the well-known couplet, "As man is, God once was; as God now is, man may be." In addition, President Snow is revered because of his extraordinary testimony of Jesus Christ. On September 2, 1898, soon after the death of Wilford Woodruff, the Savior appeared to President Snow in the Salt Lake Temple. This was certainly one of the most important experiences in the long life of this faithful servant of God.

LIFE OF
LORENZO SNOW

◆

"Great Men, taken up in any way, are profitable company," observed historian Thomas Carlyle. "We cannot look . . . upon a great man, without gaining something [from] him."[1] Lorenzo Snow, the fifth President of the Church, was certainly one of the great men of this dispensation. He was given a glimpse of his future greatness when he first met Joseph Smith Sr., the Prophet's father, in the spring of 1836 in Kirtland, Ohio. While Lorenzo was not yet a member of the Church, he decided to attend a "blessing meeting" in the Kirtland Temple. After observing Father Smith give patriarchal blessings to several people, Lorenzo met the Patriarch. During that first meeting, Father Smith prophesied that Lorenzo would soon be baptized, and then the patriarch made an extraordinary statement: "You will become as great as you can possibly wish—EVEN AS GREAT AS GOD, and you cannot wish to be greater."[2] This remarkable prophecy astonished Lorenzo, but history verifies that he went on to live a truly exceptional life. He gave dynamic leadership to the Saints during times of financial hardship and inspired them with a vision of their eternal potential.

YOUTH AND CONVERSION

Lorenzo Snow was born April 3, 1814, in Mantua, Ohio, to Oliver Snow and Rossetta Leonora Pettibone. Lorenzo was the fifth of seven children and the oldest of three sons.[3] He was especially close to his older sister Eliza, who would join the Church and remain faithful throughout her life. His father was born in Massachusetts, and his mother was a native of Connecticut. Both parents descended from Puritan ancestors who emigrated from England to America in search of religious freedom. Lorenzo's parents moved to Mantua,

Ohio, when they had only two small children. At the time, Mantua was a small farming town on the American frontier with a total population of only eleven families.[4]

Lorenzo's father was well respected in the region as a successful farmer. When he was away on business, he often left young Lorenzo, the oldest son, in charge of the farm. Lorenzo's sister Eliza claimed that even as a child, Lorenzo "exhibited the energy and decision of character which . . . marked his progress in subsequent life." She believed "an unseen hand" guided Lorenzo in his youth and prepared him for "the position in life he was destined to occupy."[5]

Even though Lorenzo was raised in a devout Baptist home, he did not seem to have a great deal of interest in religion in his youth. In this way he differed from Joseph Smith and many other early Latter-day Saint leaders who were

Eliza R. Snow

Eliza R. Snow (1804–1887) was the older sister of Lorenzo Snow. She had a special bond with her brother, which continued throughout her life. She became one of the most prominent women in the history of the Church. Eliza served as the first secretary of the Female Relief Society of Nauvoo, organized March 17, 1842. She then became the second general president of the Relief Society (1867–87) when it was reorganized in Utah. She also directed the founding of the Young Ladies' Mutual Improvement Association and the Primary Association. The Prophet Joseph Smith gave her the title of Zion's Poetess. She wrote lyrics to several LDS hymns, including "O My Father." She also wrote or edited nine books, including the *Biography and Family Record of Lorenzo Snow*. Eliza was sealed to Joseph Smith as a plural wife on June 29, 1842. After the Prophet was martyred, she was married "for time" to Brigham Young.[1]

especially concerned with finding the true church.[6] Lorenzo was an excellent student and had a fondness for books. He attended elementary school until he was twelve years old and thereafter took additional classes, primarily during the winter months. He also attended one term of high school in Ravenna, Ohio, about nine miles from his home.[7] Lorenzo enthusiastically pursued a military career, and as a young man progressed through the ranks. Even though his sister Eliza feared Lorenzo might someday lose his life in battle, she made him an impressive looking military uniform when he was twenty-one years old, which evidently pleased the ambitious young soldier.[8]

Thinking that a college education would benefit his military career, Lorenzo sold his portion of his inheritance and, in September 1835, enrolled in Oberlin College, which was located about fifty miles west of Mantua. Oberlin College was sponsored by the Presbyterian Church and was one of the most respected institutions of higher learning in the region.[9] While attending the college, Lorenzo became well acquainted with Presbyterianism. Even though he enjoyed the association he had with students and faculty, he became disillusioned with the teachings of the sponsoring church. Shortly before he left Oberlin, he wrote to his sister Eliza, lamenting, "If there is nothing better than is to be found here in Oberlin College, good bye to all religions."[10]

At this time, Eliza lived in Kirtland, Ohio. She had joined The Church of Jesus Christ of Latter-day Saints on April 5, 1835, and in December moved to Kirtland to be with the Saints.[11] Hoping to kindle Lorenzo's interest in her newfound religion, Eliza invited him to come to Kirtland and take a Hebrew class. Lorenzo accepted his sister's offer and soon found himself attending the Kirtland Hebrew School sponsored by the Latter-day Saints and attended by Church leaders, including the Prophet Joseph Smith and several Apostles.[12]

Early 1836 was a time of extraordinary religious excitement in Kirtland. This fervor was primarily associated with the construction and dedication of the Kirtland Temple. One historian observed, "During a fifteen-week period, extending from January 21 to May 1, 1836, probably more Latter-day Saints beheld visions and witnessed unusual spiritual manifestations than during any other era in the history of the Church. There were reports of Saints' beholding heavenly beings at ten different meetings held during that time . . . and at five of the services, individuals testified that Jesus, the Savior, appeared."[13]

In this pentecostal atmosphere Lorenzo soon converted to the Church. He was baptized in June 1836 by John Boynton, one of the original Twelve Apostles of this dispensation.[14] Two or three weeks after Lorenzo's baptism, he "began to feel very uneasy" that he had not yet received an actual testimony or spiritual witness of the truthfulness of the Church. He retired to a secluded grove of trees to pray. Lorenzo recalled, "I had no sooner opened my lips in an effort to pray, than I heard a

Kirtland Hebrew School

The Latter-day Saints sponsored the Kirtland Hebrew School, which lasted seven weeks, from January 26 to March 29, 1836.[2] The school served as an attempt to fulfill Joseph Smith's desire that the Lord would "speedily endow" the participants "with a knowledge of all languages" so that they would be better prepared to testify of the gospel.[3] The school met on the third floor in the west room of the Kirtland Temple to study the Hebrew language. Joshua Seixas, a member of one of the oldest Jewish families in America, taught the course. Seixas had previously taught Hebrew at Oberlin College, where Lorenzo Snow had been his student. The participants of the Kirtland Hebrew School used a text published specifically for the classes entitled *Supplement of J. Seixas' Manual Hebrew Grammar, for the Kirtland, Ohio, Theological Institution*. Originally Seixas taught classes Monday through Saturday at 10:00 AM and 2:00 PM. However, the course was so popular that additional classes were added. At least 115 students attended the school, including Joseph Smith and several Apostles. Eliza R. Snow invited her brother Lorenzo to come to Kirtland and attend the school even though he was not yet a member of the Church. Referring to Lorenzo's experience with the Hebrew school, Eliza wrote, "While he studied the dead language of the ancient Hebrews, his mind also drank in, and his heart became imbued with the living faith of the everlasting Gospel."[4] Lorenzo joined the Church a few months after the school concluded.

sound, just above my head, like the rustling of silken robes, and immediately the Spirit of God descended upon me, completely enveloping my whole person, filling me, from the crown of my head to the soles of my feet, and O, the joy and happiness I felt! . . . I then received a perfect knowledge that God lives, that Jesus Christ is the Son of God, and of the restoration of the holy Priesthood, and the fulness of the Gospel."[15] This was one of the first of many spiritual events that he recorded during his life.

Several months later, on December 15, 1836, Lorenzo had another experience that helped establish a new purpose and spiritual direction in his life. On this occasion Joseph Smith Sr., who had earlier prophesied of Lorenzo's destiny, now gave him an extraordinary patriarchal blessing. In part it said, "Thou hast a great work to perform. God has called thee to the ministry; thou must preach the gospel to the inhabitants of the earth. Thou shalt become a mighty man. . . . There shall not be a mightier man on earth than thou, thy faith shall increase and grow stronger till it shall become like Peter's."[16] The blessing also promised marvelous spiritual powers: "Thou shalt restore the sick. . . . The dead shall rise and come forth at thy bidding."[17] After receiving

The Kirtland Temple.

Kirtland Temple

The Kirtland Temple was the first temple built in this dispensation. The First Presidency—Joseph Smith, Sidney Rigdon, and Fredrick G. Williams—saw the temple in a vision before it was constructed. The Church appointed Artemus Millet to supervise the construction of the building, which was dedicated March 27, 1836. The Saints experienced a tremendous outpouring of spiritual manifestations for several weeks incident to the dedication of the temple. This Pentecostal season climaxed on April 3, 1836, when the Savior, Moses, Elias, and Elijah appeared to Joseph Smith and Oliver Cowdrey in the temple and committed unto them vitally important keys of this dispensation (D&C 110). The Church maintained control of the temple until about 1845, when it fell into the hands of dissident groups. The Reorganized Church of Jesus Christ of Latter Day Saints (now known as Community of Christ) obtained title to the building in 1880 and currently owns it.[5] Lorenzo Snow attended the Kirtland Hebrew School in the temple. He also received his patriarchal blessing from Joseph Smith Sr. in that building.

this blessing, Lorenzo gave up his ambition for a military career and dedicated himself to building the kingdom of God. During his noble life, he would see the fulfillment of these prophecies.

EARLY MISSIONS AND MARRIAGE

During the next few years, Lorenzo Snow served missions to Ohio, Missouri, Illinois, and Kentucky. Then in the spring of 1840, while living in Illinois, he received a call to serve a mission to Great Britain, where he labored for the next three years. This was a wonderful opportunity for him because he served under the direction of nine of the Twelve Apostles, who had experienced tremendous success as missionaries in Great Britain at the time. These Apostles included Brigham Young, Heber C. Kimball, Orson Hyde, Parley P. Pratt, Orson Pratt, John Taylor, Wilford Woodruff, George A. Smith, and Willard Richards.

On February 14, 1841, when Lorenzo was only twenty-six years old, Heber C. Kimball and Wilford Woodruff called him to serve as president of the London Conference (or district).[18] When Lorenzo assumed that office, there were fewer than one hundred members in the conference.[19] A little more than a year later, the number of members had increased to four hundred, living in ten different congregations.[20]

Then in October 1842, before departing for America, Elder Parley P. Pratt announced in the *Millennial Star* that he had called Thomas Ward to take his place as president "of the Church in Europe" and Lorenzo Snow to be Thomas's counselor.[21] While Lorenzo served in Great Britain, he had the distinction of presenting special bound copies of the Book of Mormon to Queen Victoria and Prince Albert.[22] Lorenzo also wrote a missionary pamphlet entitled *The Only Way to Be Saved* that was eventually published in several languages.[23] At the conclusion of his British mission, in January 1843, Lorenzo was given charge of 250 Saints emigrating to America.[24]

Soon after Lorenzo arrived in Nauvoo, he learned about the doctrine of plural marriage. Joseph Smith met privately with him on the banks of the Mississippi River and taught him the doctrine. Evidently, Lorenzo accepted the teaching with little difficulty.[25] Nevertheless, he remained a bachelor for about two more years. There is conflicting evidence as to the exact dates of Lorenzo's first marriages. However, it is clear that by the time he left Nauvoo in 1846 for the pioneer trek to the Rocky Mountains, he had married four wives: Charlotte Squires, Mary Adeline Goddard, Sarah Ann Prichard, and Harriet Amelia Squires.[26] Later in his life, Lorenzo would marry five more wives and would eventually become the father of forty-two children.[27]

It took the Snow family two years to make their trek across the plains because of sickness and also because Lorenzo was called to preside over the Saints at Mt. Pisgah, Iowa, one of the temporary settlements along the trail.[28] The family finally arrived in the Salt Lake Valley about September 1848.[29]

THE NEW APOSTLE OPENS MISSIONARY WORK IN ITALY

On February 12, 1849, Lorenzo Snow accepted a call to serve as a member of the Quorum of the Twelve Apostles. Three other brethren became Apostles on the same day: Charles C. Rich, Erastus Snow (a distant cousin), and Franklin D. Richards.[30]

During the October 1849 General Conference, the Church called four Apostles to serve missions in Europe. Franklin D. Richards was appointed to preside over the European Mission. The other three were called to open new fields of labor: John Taylor in France, Erastus Snow in Scandinavia, and Lorenzo Snow in Italy.[31] At the same conference, the Church appointed Joseph Toronto, an Italian convert, to serve as Lorenzo's companion in Italy.

Elders Snow and Toronto departed on their mission on October 19, 1849, with less than two weeks to prepare.[32] On their way to Italy, they stopped off in England, where Elder Snow called Thomas (T. B. H.) Stenhouse and Jabez Woodard to also serve in Italy.[33] Elders Snow, Toronto, and Stenhouse arrived at the Italian city-state of Genoa on June 25, 1850. (Elder Woodard would come three months later.) While in Genoa, Elder Snow read about the Waldensians (or Waldenses), a small French Protestant group that had settled in the Piedmont region of northern Italy at the foot of the Alps. When he pondered taking the gospel to the Waldensians, he said, "A flood of light seemed to burst upon [his] mind."[34] Soon thereafter the elders focused their efforts completely on the Waldensians.

During the months of July and August, Elder Snow wrote and compiled a tract entitled *The Voice of Joseph*, which he then had translated into French, the language of the Waldensians. In spite of such efforts the missionaries had little success. Then on September 6, something happened to change their fortunes. They came upon a three-year-old boy who was critically ill and near death: "His eyeballs turned upward—his eyelids fell and closed. . . . The cold perspiration of death covered his body as the principle of life was nearly exhausted." The boy's mother was in tears, and his father whispered to the missionaries, "He dies! He dies."[35] The following day Elders Snow and Stenhouse administered to the boy, and he made a miraculous recovery. Word of the healing spread rapidly through the community, and soon thereafter Elder Snow felt impressed to dedicate the land for preaching the gospel.

Elder Woodard arrived from England on September 18, and on the next day Elders Snow, Stenhouse, and Woodard (Toronto had left to visit his family in Sicily) climbed a nearby

Queen Victoria

Queen Victoria (1819–1901) was one of the most widely acclaimed rulers in the history of the English people. She was the queen of the United Kingdom of Great Britain and Ireland from 1837 to 1901. During this time, Great Britain reached its pinnacle of power and prestige. She was held in such high esteem that historians often refer to her era as the Victorian Age.[10] Lorenzo Snow presented a copy of the Book of Mormon to the queen when he was serving a mission in Great Britain from 1840 to 1843. On that occasion Queen Victoria autographed an album owned by Elder Snow. That autograph became a cherished possession that he treasured the rest of his life and ultimately handed down to his son LeRoi.[11] In commemoration of Lorenzo's visit with the queen, Eliza R. Snow wrote a poem entitled "Queen Victoria." Following are a few stanzas from that composition:

> Of all the monarchs of the earth,
> That wear the robes of royalty,
> She has inherited, by birth,
> The broadest wreath of majesty. . . .
> But still her sceptre is approved;
> All nations deck the wreath she wears;
> Yet, like the youth whom Jesus loved,
> One thing is lacking, even there.
>
> But lo! A prize possessing more
> Of worth than gem with honor rife—
> A herald of salvation bore
> To her the words of endless life. . . .
> O would she now her influence bend—
> The influence of royalty,
> Messiah's Kingdom to extend,
> And Zion's "nursing mother" be. . . .
> Though over millions called to reign—
> Herself a powerful nation's boast,
> 'Twould be her everlasting gain
> To serve the King, the Lord of Hosts. . . .
> The time—the time is near at hand
> To give a glorious period birth:
> The Son of God will take command,
> And rule the nations of the earth.[12]

mountain and formally organized the Church in Italy with Lorenzo Snow as its president.[36] Elder Woodard prophesied that the work of God would "go from this land, to other nations of the earth."[37] Elder Snow named the mountain where the dedication took place "Mount Brigham, and the rock upon which [they] stood the Rock of Prophecy."[38] About a month later, on October 27, they had their first baptism, Jean Bose.[39] By August 1, 1831, they had baptized thirty-one people.[40]

From Italy, the gospel did indeed spread to "other nations of the earth" just as Elder Woodard had prophesied on Mount Brigham. Before long, Elder Snow sent T. B. H. Stenhouse to open missionary work in Switzerland.[41] Lorenzo also called William Willes and Hugh Findlay to proselytize in far-off India.[42] In addition, Elder Snow assigned John D. Malan, a Waldensian convert who had been branch president, to preside over the Church in the Piedmont region, while Lorenzo and Jabez Woodard traveled to Malta to begin missionary work there.[43]

Elder Snow returned to Salt Lake City on July 30, 1852, after being gone for almost three years.[44] The *Millennial Star* summarized Lorenzo's historic mission with this tribute: "Elder Snow has accomplished a great work . . . of laying the foundation of the Church . . . in countries where gross darkness of superstition, and ignorance of the plan of salvation, reign in the minds of the people."[45]

COLONIZING BRIGHAM CITY

After returning to Salt Lake City, Elder Snow became deeply involved in domestic, Church, and community activities. He built a new home, energetically carried out his responsibilities as a member of the Quorum of the Twelve and, in 1852, was elected a member of the Utah Territorial Legislature. He would faithfully serve in that body for twenty-nine years, ten of those years as president of the legislative council.[46]

In the 1850s the Church often appointed Apostles to supervise colonizing efforts throughout the Intermountain West. During the October 1853 general conference, President Brigham Young called Lorenzo Snow to preside over a small

Waldensians

The Waldensians, a small French Protestant community, live in the Piedmont region of northern Italy, at the foot of the Alps. Peter Waldo (d. 1217) had founded their Church in Lyons, France, in the twelfth century. The group rejected the authority of the pope, who excommunicated them from the Catholic Church. The Catholics persecuted the Waldensians and forced them to flee France and find refuge in the valleys of the Piedmont in Italy. When Lorenzo Snow and his companions initiated missionary work in Italy, they concentrated their efforts on this group. From 1850 to 1867 approximately 180 Waldensians joined The Church of Jesus Christ of Latter-day Saints and about seventy of them migrated to Utah. The Malan, Beus, Cardon, Chatelain, Bertoch, and Pons families are some of the Waldensians that converted to the Church and made the trek to the Salt Lake Valley.[13]

struggling settlement in Box Elder County, about sixty miles north of Salt Lake City. He was also assigned to take fifty families with him to permanently settle the area. Elder Snow moved to Box Elder in 1854 and a year later renamed the community Brigham City in honor of the prophet.[47]

Over the next several years, Elder Snow took the lead in the early development and success of the settlement. In 1864 he established a prosperous cooperative store that led to the organization of the Brigham City Mercantile and Manufacturing Association in 1870.[48] This enterprise

Mount Brigham

Mount Brigham is the site where Lorenzo Snow dedicated the land of Italy for the preaching of the gospel on September 19, 1850. It is a prominent mountain near the city of La Tour (Torre Pellice), which is located in the Piedmont region at the base of the Italian Alps. Elder Snow offered the dedicatory prayer on a projecting rock near the top of the mountain. This rock was later named the Rock of Prophecy. During the dedication, Lorenzo prophesied that the Church would "increase and multiply, and continue its existence in Italy, till that portion of Israel, dwelling in these countries, shall have heard and received the fulness of the Gospel." Thomas (T. B. H.) Stenhouse and Jabez Woodard were with Elder Snow at the dedication. Elder Stenhouse also predicted that before the missionaries return to America, many people in Italy would "rejoice and bear testimony to the principles of Truth."[14]

Photo of Lorenzo Snow in 1867.

MISSION TO HAWAII

Elder Snow's work in Brigham City was suspended for a time in 1864 when the Church called him to serve a special short-term mission to the Sandwich Islands (Hawaii). The purpose of the mission was to help resolve problems caused by a man named Walter Murray Gibson, an unscrupulous missionary who had distorted the principles and practices of the Church. Gibson had been in Hawaii since 1861 and had given himself the title "Chief President of the Islands of the Sea, and of the Hawaiian Islands, for the Church of Latter-day Saints." He had ordained twelve Apostles, charging each of them $150 for their office. He had also sold other offices of the priesthood, including the position of archbishop.[53] When Brigham Young received word of Gibson's bizarre activities, he sent Elders Lorenzo Snow and Ezra T. Benson of the Quorum of the Twelve to the islands to put the Church in order. They were accompanied by Joseph F. Smith, Alma L. Smith, and William L. Cluff.

They safely crossed the ocean, but after they transferred onto a small boat off the coast of Hawaii, turbulent waves capsized their vessel. In the confusion, Elder Snow became separated from his friends. Eventually they discovered his stiff and apparently lifeless body underneath an overturned boat. They took him to shore and desperately tried to revive him using traditional methods, but to no avail. Ultimately his life was saved when his companions felt impressed to administer mouth-to-mouth resuscitation, a procedure that was unheard of in those days. It took about an hour before Elder Snow was revived.[54] Elder Snow always regarded this incident in his life as a true miracle. After this traumatic episode, the Brethren investigated Walter Gibson, found the charges against him to be true, and excommunicated him. Elders Benson and Snow assigned Joseph F. Smith to preside over the mission in Hawaii, and then the two Apostles returned to Utah.

REDEDICATION OF THE HOLY LAND

In 1872 Brigham Young called his Second Counselor, George A. Smith, to lead "an extensive tour" through Europe

functioned as a joint stock company (a business cooperative) that eventually had approximately four hundred shareholders from nearly every family in the community.[49] Within a few years the company branched out into forty departments, including a "woolen factory, dairy, butcher shop, sawmill, tailor shop, molasses mill, furniture and cabinet shop, blacksmith shop, rope factory, pottery shop, cooperage, tin shop, broom factory, and a shingle, lath, and picket mill."[50] These businesses did well even during the economic panic of 1873. Thereafter Brigham City was generally considered the most successful cooperative community in the Intermountain West.[51] On one occasion Brigham Young spoke in Box Elder County and gave the following tribute to the people and their leader: "I will say to the credit of the people here, they have done well. And brother Lorenzo Snow, who has had charge of you, has set the best example for the literal building up of the kingdom of God of any of our presiding Elders."[52]

Lorenzo Snow nearly drowned during his mission to the Sandwich Islands (Hawaii).

Lorenzo Snow in 1870 at about age fifty-five.

and the Middle East. The purpose of the trip was to explore possibilities "for the introduction of the gospel into the various countries" they were to visit and to dedicate the land of Palestine.[55] (This land had previously been dedicated by Elder Orson Hyde in 1841.) President Smith chose Elders Lorenzo Snow and Albert Carrington of the Quorum of the Twelve Apostles to go with him. They were accompanied by Feramorz Little, Paul A. Schettler, Thomas W. Jennings, Eliza R. Snow, and Clara Little. The trip lasted from October 1872 to July 1873 and took them to such diverse countries as England, Holland, Belgium, France, Italy, Egypt, Palestine, Syria, Lebanon, and Turkey.

They saw many of the same sites that a typical tourist might see, but they also visited with government officials. One of the highlights of the trip was their visit with Louis Thiers, president of the French Republic. Thiers and several members of his cabinet met with the entire Latter-day Saint delegation. President Smith said that his people sympathized with Thiers's attempt to establish a French Republic. Thiers treated the Mormons kindly and said he was "familiar with the history" of the Latter-day Saints.[56] At the conclusion of the meeting, George A. Smith said, "President Thiers, God bless you." This caught Thiers's attention, and he asked his interpreter to render

"a literal translation" of the statement. Lorenzo Snow maintained that the sincerity of the expression "excited pleasurable emotions" in Monsieur Thiers and his cabinet members.[57]

After their stay in France the tour group continued to the Holy Land by way of Italy and then Egypt. They spent several days visiting the sacred religious sites in Palestine. Then on Sunday, March 2, 1873, they participated in the most important event of the trip—the dedication of the Holy Land. Earlier that day President Smith had arranged for a "tent, table, seats and carpet" to be prepared for the occasion on top of the Mount of Olives. President Smith, Elders Snow and Carrington, and other members of the party rode horses

George A. Smith

George A. Smith (1817–75) was a first cousin to the Prophet Joseph Smith, and at age twenty-one George became the youngest man called to serve in the Quorum of the Twelve Apostles in this dispensation. He also served as Church historian and First Counselor to Brigham Young in the First Presidency. In 1872 Lorenzo Snow accompanied President Smith on an expedition to the Holy Land to rededicate the country as a gathering place for the descendants of Abraham.[15]

Louis Thiers

Louis Adolphe Thiers (1797–1877) was elected the first president of the Third Republic of France in 1871. He was also the author of the ten-volume *History of the French Revolution.*[16] In 1872, when President George A. Smith, Lorenzo Snow, and others were traveling through Europe on their way to the Holy Land, they met with President Thiers and some of his cabinet members. Thiers was familiar with the history of the Latter-day Saints and treated his Mormon guests kindly.

up the mount, visited the Church of the Ascension, and then entered their tent for the dedication. Lorenzo's sister Eliza R. Snow recounted: "President Smith [led] in humble, fervent supplication, dedicating the land of Palestine for the gathering of the Jews and the rebuilding of Jerusalem. . . . Other brethren led in turn, and we had a very interesting season." Eliza placed the event in perspective with these words, "To me it seemed the crowning point of the whole tour, realizing as I did that we were worshiping on the summit of the sacred Mount, once the frequent resort of the Prince of life."[58]

After their visit to the Holy Land, the group traveled to Syria, Lebanon, and Turkey and then made their way to Europe. During their stay in Vienna, Austria, Elder Snow received word that he had been called to serve "as one of seven counselors to Brigham Young," an office he would hold until President Young died in 1877.[59] Lorenzo Snow returned to Brigham City, Utah, from his mission on July 7, 1873.[60]

"Prisoner for Conscience' Sake"[61]

After his trip to the Holy Land, Elder Snow resumed his leadership role in religious and civic affairs. Unfortunately, he was soon arrested for violating the Edmunds Act of 1882, which prohibited the practice of plural marriage. A judge sentenced him to serve eighteen months in the federal penitentiary beginning in March 1886. Caleb C. West, the territorial governor of Utah, visited Elder Snow while he was in prison and promised him amnesty if the Apostle would "renounce the principle of plural marriage." To this Elder

Snow replied, "I thank you, Governor, but having adopted sacred and holy principles for which we have already sacrificed property, home and life on several occasions in their defense, we do not propose, at this late hour, to abandon them because of threatened danger."[62]

While he was in prison, Elder Snow again demonstrated his leadership skills. He received visits from people who occupied "important positions in high circles of society."[63] He also helped organize a school within the prison, which eventually had sixty-five inmate-students, many of whom could not read. Within three months, several prisoners learned to read, write, and do basic arithmetic.[64] Elder Snow served eleven months of his sentence and then received an early

Photo of Lorenzo Snow taken in the late 1860s.

release in February 1887 because of a ruling by the United States Supreme Court.[65]

THE PRESIDENT OF THE TWELVE PERFORMS A GREAT MIRACLE

Following his release from prison, Elder Snow energetically resumed his apostolic duties. Many of the leaders of the Church were in hiding because of federal laws against plural marriage, so the First Presidency asked Lorenzo Snow to take charge of the April 1887 general conference. In addition to Elder Snow there were only four Apostles in attendance: Franklin D. Richards, John Henry Smith, Heber J. Grant, and John W. Taylor.[66] A year later, on May 21–23, 1888, Elder Snow publicly dedicated the Manti Temple. President Wilford Woodruff had already privately dedicated the edifice on May 17 of that year.[67] Then on April 7, 1889, Elder Snow was sustained as President of the Quorum of the Twelve Apostles on the same day that Wilford Woodruff was sustained as President of the Church.[68]

While serving as President of the Quorum of the Twelve, Lorenzo Snow participated in one of the great miracles of this dispensation. On March 9, 1891, at about noon, while President Snow was speaking in the Brigham City Tabernacle, he was handed a note. The message informed him that his niece Ella Jensen had died about two hours earlier at 10:00. After reading the note, President Snow immediately stopped talking and asked to be excused. He requested that Rudger Clawson, president of the Box Elder Stake, accompany him to the Jensen home. After they arrived, they stood at the side of Ella's bed for a short time, and then to everyone's surprise, President Snow asked if there was some consecrated oil in the house. He asked President Clawson to anoint Ella, and then President Snow sealed the anointing. During the blessing he boldly proclaimed: "Dear Ella, I command you, in the name of the Lord, Jesus Christ, to come back and live, your mission is not yet ended. You shall yet live to perform a great mission."[69] After President Snow finished this remarkable blessing, he turned to Ella's parents and said, "Now do not mourn or grieve any more. It will be all right. Brother Clawson and I are busy and must go, we cannot stay, but you just be patient and wait." Ella lay in her bed lifeless for another hour, or about three hours from the time she was first pronounced dead. Then Ella opened her eyes, looked around the room, and asked, "Where is he? Where is he?" Her parents then asked, "Where is who?" To which Ella replied, "Why, Brother Snow. . . . He called me back."[70] This miraculous experience was actually a fulfillment of the prophetic utterance given in Lorenzo Snow's patriarchal blessing over a half century earlier: "The dead shall rise and come forth at thy bidding."[71]

PRESIDENT SNOW SEES THE SAVIOR

The Salt Lake Temple was dedicated on April 6, 1893. A month later, on May 19, President Woodruff set Lorenzo Snow apart as the first president of the temple. This responsibility was in addition to his calling as President of the Quorum of the Twelve. The Salt Lake Temple would provide the setting for one of the most remarkable spiritual experiences in the history of the Church. This took place on September 2, 1898, after President Snow received word that Wilford Woodruff, the President of the Church, had passed away.

Manti Temple. Lorenzo Snow offered the dedicatory prayer on May 1888.

Lorenzo Snow was then the senior Apostle and rightful successor to be the next President of the Church. Feeling the weight of this responsibility, President Snow found a quiet room in the Salt Lake Temple and knelt in prayer. He humbly presented himself to the Lord and asked for "guidance and instruction." President Snow expected a "special manifestation from the Lord," but nothing happened. Disappointed, he left the room and started back to his office. Then, while he was walking through the corridors of the temple, the Savior personally appeared to him. Years later President Snow recounted the experience to his granddaughter Allie while she was with him in the temple: "It was right here that the Lord Jesus Christ appeared to me. . . . He instructed me to go right ahead and reorganize the First Presidency of the Church at once and not wait as had been done after the death of the previous presidents, and that I was to succeed President Woodruff." President Snow then said, "He stood right here, about three feet above the floor. It looked as though He stood on a plate of solid gold."[72] Heber J. Grant and George Q. Cannon confirmed that President Snow was indeed "instructed of the Lord in the Temple the night after President Woodruff died."[73]

PROPHETIC LEADERSHIP DURING FINANCIAL CRISIS

President Snow humbly complied with the Lord's instructions and promptly called George Q. Cannon to serve as his First Counselor and Joseph F. Smith to be his Second Counselor. They were sustained as the new First Presidency of the Church on September 13, 1898.[74]

Perhaps the greatest challenge facing the Church at this time was financial indebtedness. In 1898 the Church was over 1.25 million dollars in debt.[75] Acting on the authority of the Edmunds-Tucker Law of 1887, the federal government had confiscated a great deal of Church property. Under these conditions, many members of the Church stopped paying tithing. Many rationalized, "Why turn tithing over to the church if the government [is] going to get it?"[76] This attitude prevailed for over a decade as the Church's financial woes became worse by the year.

President Snow wrestled with the problem for months without a clear answer. Then in the spring of 1899, after

Photo of Lorenzo Snow in 1892 at about age seventy-eight.

praying about the matter, the prophet felt impressed to take a trip to St. George in Southern Utah.[77] He also asked several General Authorities and their wives to accompany him. At the time he did not know exactly why he was traveling to St. George but felt strongly that he should go there nevertheless. They held a special conference in the St. George Tabernacle on May 17, 1899. While President Snow was speaking at this conference, he received a special revelation on tithing. In the middle of his talk, President Snow paused for some time and then spoke with great power. "He told them that he could see, as he had never realized before, how the law of tithing had been neglected by the people." He then promised the Saints that if they would pay a "full and honest tithing," the Church would be freed of its financial bondage. He also declared that the individual members of the Church would be blessed financially and "would become a prosperous people."[78] Then the prophet made this bold proclamation: "The word of the Lord is: The time has now come for every Latter-day Saint . . . to pay his tithing in full. That is the word of the Lord to you, and it will be the word of the Lord to every settlement throughout the land."[79] President Snow followed through on this statement. He stopped at several communities on his way back to Salt Lake City and preached tithing. During an eleven-day period, "he visited sixteen settlements, held twenty-four meetings, [and] delivered twenty-six addresses."[80] President Snow's reemphasis on tithing became a dominant theme of his administration. His energetic campaign paved the way for the Church to be completely relieved of its debt by 1907, six years after his death.

Another important theme in President Snow's administration was missionary work. On February 4, 1901, he called Elder Heber J. Grant of the Quorum of the Twelve and three others to begin missionary work in Japan.[81] Then on June 8, 1901, he reopened the missionary work in Mexico and set apart Ammon M. Tenney as president of the mission.[82] President Snow also counseled the Saints in foreign lands to stay in their own countries and build the Church there instead of immigrating to the Rocky Mountains.[83]

Lorenzo Snow literally wore himself out in the service of the Lord. He attended only one session of general conference in October 1901 because he was suffering from a severe cold. He spoke at the last session on Sunday afternoon, but his condition worsened. He passed away four days later on October 10, 1901.

A LIFE OF TRUE GREATNESS

During the Savior's mortal ministry, He gave a spiritual definition of greatness: "He that is greatest among you shall

A Verbal Picture of Lorenzo Snow

In 1898 the Reverend Dr. Prentis of North Carolina portrayed Lorenzo Snow as follows: "I had expected to find intellect, intellectuality, benevolence, dignity, composure and strength depicted upon the face of [President Snow]; but when I was introduced to [him] for a second I was startled to see the holiest face but one I had ever been privileged to look upon. His face was a poem of peace, his presence a benediction of peace. In the tranquil depths of his eyes were the 'home of silent prayer' and the abode of spiritual strength. As he talked . . . the strangest feeling stole over me, that I stood on holy ground. . . . The picture of that slight, venerable form hallowed with the aura of an ineffable peace will haunt my heart like the vision of a celestial picture."[17]

A Description of Lorenzo Snow by Frank G. Carpenter

"Mr. Snow is now 86 years of age but like many of the old men of his church he looks much younger. As he shook my hand I could hardly realize that he had passed his three-score and ten sixteen years ago. . . . President Snow does not weigh more than 125 pounds, but he is very active."[18]

A new First Presidency was organized in September 1898.

St. George Tabernacle

The St. George Tabernacle is one of the most prominent structures built by the Mormon pioneers. It was constructed between 1863 and 1869. During a special conference held in the tabernacle on May 17, 1899, Lorenzo Snow received a historic revelation on tithing.[19] The inspiration came while President Snow was giving a sermon. "All at once father paused in his discourse," his son LeRoi recorded. "Complete stillness filled the room. . . . When he commenced to speak again his voice strengthened and inspiration from God seemed to come over him, as well as over the entire assembly. His eyes seemed to brighten and his countenance to shine. He was filled with unusual power. Then he revealed to the Latter-day Saints the vision that was before him. . . . He told them that he could see . . . how the law of tithing had been neglected."[20]

be your servant" (Matthew 23:11). Lorenzo Snow spent his entire adult life diligently serving his fellow men and faithfully building the kingdom of God on earth.

He was a missionary, pioneer, colonizer, city builder, legislator, temple president, financier, apostle, and prophet. His ministry not only took him to many places in the United States but also to numerous countries in such diverse regions as the Middle East, Europe, and the islands of the Pacific. He associated with apostles and prophets in addition to world leaders such as the queen of England and the president of the French Republic. He opened missions, healed the sick, restored life to the dead, and gave inspired leadership to the

Church during a time of economic crisis. President Snow also had the extraordinary privilege of seeing the Savior.

Gazing into eternity. Photo taken late in the life of Lorenzo Snow.

A Tribute to Lorenzo Snow on the Occasion of His Funeral

President Rudger Clawson observed, "I was immediately associated with him in the Box Elder Stake when he was a resident Apostle of that stake. I had the advantage of his wisdom and experience and learned to know him, his integrity of heart and devotion to the cause of Christ. My confidence in him was made firm and strong, and I know that with him it was the kingdom of God which he sought above all else. I learned to know him while we were incarcerated in prison eleven months for conscience sake, and I wish to testify that he bore that trial with strength and fortitude. He was a man of refinement, culture, and learning, yet he met the trial with patience and his conduct was an inspiration to all who were sent there. We looked up to him in that trying position and learned to love him. To give an idea of his character I will speak of an incident which happened in that prison. President Snow called between thirty and forty of us together and said in substance to us: 'We have been sent to this place for conscience sake. We are associated in prison. I believe that if you all desire to do so, it is proper for us to express ourselves to God in a great and glorious shout. The shout to God which on more than one occasion has been given in the Temple and in the Tabernacle.' We all said that we desired to do so—to raise our voices in this manner, and we did offer up a great and mighty shout. I want to say that when that went out the foundation of the prison seemed to shake, and I firmly believe that that shout was acceptable in the celestial kingdom."[21]

TEACHINGS OF PRESIDENT
LORENZO SNOW

◆

If we work upon marble, it will perish; if we work upon brass, time will efface it; if we rear temples, they will crumble into dust," observed Daniel Webster, "but if we work upon immortal minds, if we imbue them with principles, with the just fear of God and love of our fellowmen, we engrave on these tablets something that will brighten to all eternity."[84] Lorenzo Snow understood the importance of inspiring the "immortal mind" with noble thoughts because he knew that if a person would act upon those ideas, he or she would, indeed, "brighten to all eternity." Even though President Snow presided over the Church for only three years, he taught several powerful truths that have greatly influenced the Latter-day Saints.

THE DIVINE POTENTIAL OF MAN

One of the teachings Lorenzo Snow is best remembered for is the doctrine that mortal beings have the capacity, in eternity, to become like God. This concept crystallized in Lorenzo's mind in the spring of 1840 before he left on his mission to England. At that time he was visiting in the home of a man named H. G. Sherwood who was living in Nauvoo. During the evening Sherwood attempted "to explain the parable of the Savior about the husbandman who sent forth servants at different hours of the day to labor in the vineyard." While listening to Sherwood's explanation, the "Spirit of the Lord rested mightily" upon Brother Snow. Lorenzo recorded, "The eyes of my understanding were opened, and I saw as clear as the sun at noon-day, with wonder and astonishment, the pathway of God and man. I formed the following couplet which expresses the revelation, as it was shown me, . . . As man now is, God once was: As God now is, man may be."[85]

To his credit, Lorenzo did not share this sacred experience with anybody except his sister Eliza because he had never heard any of the leaders of the Church teach the doctrine before. Then, when he was on a mission in England, Lorenzo privately discussed his spiritual experience with Brigham Young, President of the Quorum of the Twelve Apostles. President Young responded, "Brother Snow, that is a new doctrine; if true, it has been revealed to you for your own private information, and will be taught in due time by the Prophet to the Church; till then I advise you to lay it upon the shelf and say no more about it."[86] Elder Snow faithfully abided by President Young's counsel. Then, after Lorenzo returned to the United States, in 1843, he related his extraordinary manifestation to Joseph Smith. The Prophet replied, "Brother Snow, that is true gospel doctrine, and it is a revelation from God to you."[87]

About a year later, on April 7, 1844, Joseph Smith publicly taught the doctrine in what has become know as the King Follet Discourse. On that occasion the Prophet proclaimed: "God himself was once as we are now. And is an exalted Man."[88] President Snow's son LeRoi maintained that this "revealed truth impressed Lorenzo Snow more than perhaps all else; it sank so deeply into his soul that it became the inspiration of his life and gave him his broad vision of his own great future and mighty mission and work of the Church."[89] LeRoi also observed "that Lorenzo Snow was not only deeply impressed by this revelation in his youth, but . . . this impression remained fresh in his soul throughout his long life."[90]

When Lorenzo was seventy-seven years old, he wrote a poem entitled "Man's Destiny." It demonstrated the long-lasting influence this doctrine had on his life. The poem is written to the Apostle Paul and is meant to be a reply to what Paul wrote to the Philippians: "Let this mind be in you, which was also in Christ Jesus: who being in the form of God, thought it not robbery to be equal with God" (Philippians 2:5–6). Following are the first three stanzas of the poem:

Dear Brother:

Hast thou not been unwisely bold,
Man's destiny to thus unfold?
To raise, promote such high desire,
Such vast ambition thus inspire?

Still, 'tis no phantom that we trace
Man's ultimatum in life's race;
This royal path has long been trod
By righteous men, each now a God:

As Abra'm, Isaac, Jacob, too,
First babes, then men—to Gods they grew.
As man now is, our God once was;
As now God is, so man may be,—
Which doth unfold man's destiny.[91]

TITHING

Another inspired teaching that President Snow will always be remembered for is tithing. Perhaps the most pressing problem he faced during his presidency was the tremendous debt the Church incurred during the latter part of the nineteenth century. Much has been said through the years concerning the revelation Lorenzo received in St. George on May 17, 1899, that directed the prophet to preach the doctrine of tithing. However, many do not realize that the receiving of the revelation was only the beginning of a great episode in Church history. A major theme for the rest of Lorenzo Snow's life would be the emphasis on tithing.

On President Snow's trip from St. George to Salt Lake City, he stopped for a short time in Nephi, Utah. While he was in this settlement he called his traveling companions together in a unique meeting. On that occasion, "he commissioned every one present to be his special witness to the fact that the Lord had given this revelation [about tithing] to him." He also "put all the party under covenant and promise not only to obey the law of tithing themselves but also that

each would bear witness to this special manifestation and would spread the tithing message at every opportunity."[92]

President Snow returned to Salt Lake City on May 27, 1899. Three days later the Young Men's and Young Women's Mutual Improvement Associations began their annual conference. The prophet decided to use this gathering as a forum to get "the subject of tithing before the young people of the church." On May 30, President Snow spoke to the officers of the Young Men's Mutual Improvement Association on this subject. When the prophet concluded his remarks, members of the general board presented a formal resolution to those in attendance: "Resolved: That we accept the doctrine of tithing, as now presented by President Snow, as the present word and will of the Lord unto us, and we do accept it with all our hearts; we will ourselves observe it, and we will do all in our power to get the Latter-day Saints to do likewise." Those present unanimously accepted the resolution by "rising to their feet and shouting 'Aye.'" The prophet was noticeably moved by this expression of devotion. He rose and exclaimed: "Brethren, the God of our fathers, Abraham, Isaac and Jacob, bless you. Every man who is here, who has made this promise, will be saved in the celestial kingdom. God bless you. Amen."[93]

After the Young Men's and Young Women's Mutual Improvement Associations conference, President Snow felt impressed to call a special solemn assembly to be held in the Salt Lake Temple on July 2, 1899. According to President Snow's son, "the call for this assembly did not originate in [the prophet's] own mind, but was a command from the Lord who revealed it in vision." Every General Authority was present, as well as representatives from all forty stakes of the Church and 478 wards. The meeting lasted from 10:00 AM to 7:00 PM, and each of the eighteen speakers addressed the subject of tithing. "The spirit of the meeting was that of testimony and the promotion of faith, not one of temporal and business affairs."[94] Before long, the topic of tithing spread like fire throughout the Church. "Other speakers took up the theme," affirmed Orson Whitney, "and it was echoed and re-echoed until the whole region rang and resounded with it." Soon "tithes and offerings came pouring in with a promptness and plentitude unknown for years, and in every way, spiritually and temporally, the Church's condition improved and its prospects brightened."[95]

President Snow hoped the Church would be completely out of debt before he died, but this was not to be. Lorenzo Snow passed away in 1901; but six years later, on April 5, 1907, his successor, President Joseph F. Smith, announced: "Today The Church of Jesus Christ of Latter-day Saints owes not a dollar that it cannot pay at once. At last we are in a position that we can pay as we go."[96]

SENIORITY OF THE QUORUM OF THE TWELVE CLARIFIED

While President Snow was expending so much time and energy on matters pertaining to Church indebtedness, he was also required to resolve a pressing problem concerning seniority in the Quorum of the Twelve Apostles. When Franklin D. Richards, President of the Twelve, died on December 9, 1899, it brought to the forefront the question as to which Apostle was next in seniority. George Q. Cannon, Second Counselor in the First Presidency, was directly behind President Richards in seniority. However, the primary concern was who was next in seniority after President Cannon. Was it Brigham Young Jr. or Joseph F. Smith? Brigham Young Jr. had been ordained an additional Apostle in 1864 before there was a vacancy in the Quorum of the Twelve. Therefore, at the time, he was not sustained as a member of the Twelve. Two years later, in 1866, Joseph F. Smith received the same ordination, but like Elder Young, he did not become a member of the Twelve. Then, on October 8, 1867, Joseph F. Smith was called to fill a vacancy in the quorum. A year later, on October 9, 1868, Brigham Young Jr. was sustained to fill another vacancy in the Twelve. Thus Joseph F. Smith became a member of the Twelve before Brigham Young Jr., even though Elder Young had been ordained an Apostle first.[97]

On April 5, 1900, at a meeting of the First Presidency and Quorum of the Twelve, this matter of seniority was discussed. They "unanimously decided that the acceptance of a member into the council or quorum of the Twelve fixed his rank or position in the Apostleship." Furthermore, they determined that "according to seniority in the Apostleship of the Twelve; that ordination to the Apostleship under the hands of any Apostle other than to fill a vacancy in the

quorum, and authorized by the General Authorities of the Church did not count in precedence." In addition, they ruled "that if the First Presidency were dissolved by the death of the President, his counselors having been ordained Apostles in the Quorum of the Twelve would resume their places in the quorum, according to the seniority of their ordinations into that quorum."[98] Therefore, Joseph F. Smith was ahead of Brigham Young Jr. in seniority within the quorum. This decision was of vital importance. Because of his seniority, a year and a half later Joseph F. Smith became President of the Church.

GREETING TO THE WORLD

President Snow had the rare opportunity of presiding over the Church at the turn of a century. In anticipation of this event, he prepared an address entitled "Greeting to the World," which he delivered in the Salt Lake Tabernacle on January 1, 1901. The speech was then published in the *Deseret Evening News*. It was an optimistic message of conciliation and love.

The prophet looked forward to a new century of "peace, of greater progress, of the universal adoption of the golden rule. . . . War with its horrors should be but a memory. The aim of nations should be fraternity and mutual greatness." During his address, the President offered a challenge to the leaders of governments: "Awake, ye monarchs of the earth and rulers among nations. . . . The power is in your hands to pave the way for the coming King of Kings, whose dominion will be over the earth. Disband your armies; turn your weapons of strife into implements of industry."[99]

President Snow concluded his speech with a message of optimism: "I wish all a happy new year. I hope and look for grand events to occur in the twentieth century. At its auspicious dawn I lift my hands and invoke the blessing of heaven upon the inhabitants of the earth. May the sunshine from above smile upon you. . . . May the twentieth century prove the happiest as it will be the grandest of all the ages of time."[100]

In many ways the twentieth century turned out to be "the grandest of all the ages." One can only wonder how much better the century would have been if the rulers of the world would have followed Lorenzo Snow's admonition to disband their armies and turn their "weapons of strife into implements of industry."

MISSION OF THE TWELVE AND SEVENTY

During the last few weeks of President Snow's life he seemed to be preoccupied with the responsibilities of two specific groups of the General Authorities. According to Joseph F. Smith, at a council meeting held on August 22, 1901, President Snow declared that "he had been thinking of late whether we were justified in keeping at home the Apostles and Seventies. . . . They were really ministers to the nations of the earth."[101] A month later, on September 28, he declared, "Here are the apostles and the seventies, their business is to warn the nations of the earth and prepare the world for the coming of the Savior. . . . It looks to me that our minds ought to extend somewhat, and we get out of the beaten track, and a little change be made. For instance, we have started in this direction by sending Brother Grant over to Japan, but this is only a start."[102]

During President Snow's last public address, in general conference, given on October 6, 1901, he once again gave emphasis to this theme: "The apostles and seventies—it is their business, by the appointment of the Almighty, to look after the interests of the world. The seventies and the twelve apostles are special witnesses unto the nations of the earth." The prophet then went on to explain that it was the duty of the high priests, elders, and bishops to look after local matters concerning the stakes, wards, and auxiliaries. President Snow then affirmed: "I wanted to say this, and to speak it with energy in a way that you will not forget it, that you cannot forget it. It is a wonderful responsibility, and the Lord expects it of you."[103] Lorenzo Snow died four days later.

On November 1, 1901, Joseph F. Smith, the new President of the Church, responded to President Snow's last public address: "We accept what is contained therein on the duties of the Twelve, and presiding Priesthood, as the word of the Lord to us all. It is so plain and so convincing as to leave no room for doubt; and there remains but one thing for us to do, and that is to zealously and arduously labor to successfully accomplish all that is required at our hands."[104]

PREACHER OF RIGHTEOUSNESS

It is difficult to measure the influence of one man's teachings, especially a man who presided over a church with nearly three hundred thousand members. Nevertheless, after President Snow died, Emily H. Woodmansee wrote a poem in memory of President Snow wherein she attempted to summarize his far-reaching influence. Following are the first two stanzas of that poem:

> Another President has passed from earth,
> And left a host of loving friends behind;
> "A man of God" who prized Truth's wondrous worth,
> And sensed its import unto humankind.
>
> Like Apostolic men of olden times,
> Preachers of Righteousness unpraised, unpaid,
> He scattered light afar, in many climes,
> And many converts, by God's help he made.[105]

Arnold K. Garr

Professor of Church History and Doctrine,
Chair of the Department of Church History and Doctrine
Brigham Young University

NOTES

1. Thomas Carlyle, *Heroes and Hero Worship* (Chicago: Union School Furnishing Co., 1900), 4.
2. Eliza R. Snow Smith, *Biography and Family Record of Lorenzo Snow, One of the Twelve Apostles of The Church of Jesus Christ of Latter-day Saints* (Salt Lake City: Deseret News Company, Printers, 1884), 10.
3. Eliza R. Snow Smith, *Biography and Family Record*, 1–2.
4. Thomas C. Romney, *The Life of Lorenzo Snow* (Salt Lake City: Sugarhouse Press, 1955), 4–5.
5. Eliza R. Snow Smith, *Biography and Family Record*, 2–3.
6. *Presidents of the Church* (Salt Lake City: Department of

Seminaries and Institutes of Religion), 44.

7. Eliza R. Snow Smith, *Biography and Family Record*, 3.

8. Ibid.

9. Francis M. Gibbons, *Lorenzo Snow: Spiritual Giant, Prophet of God* (Salt Lake City: Desert Book, 1982), 2.

10. Eliza R. Snow Smith, *Biography and Family Record*, 5.

11. Jill Mulvay Derr, "Snow, Eliza R." in *Encyclopedia of Latter-day Saint History*, ed. Arnold K. Garr, et al. (Salt Lake City: Deseret Book, 2000), 1148.

12. D. Kelly Ogden, "The Kirtland Hebrew School (1835–36)," in *Regional Studies in Latter-day Saint Church History: Ohio*, ed. Milton V. Backman Jr. (Provo, UT: Department of Church History and Doctrine, Brigham Young University, 1990), 72.

13. Milton V. Backman Jr., *The Heavens Resound: A History of the Latter-day Saints in Ohio, 1830–1838* (Salt Lake City: Deseret Book, 1983), 285.

14. Eliza R. Snow Smith, *Biography and Family Record*, 7.

15. Ibid., 8.

16. LeRoi C. Snow, "Devotion to a Divine Inspiration," *Improvement Era* 22, no. 8 (June 1919): 655.

17. LeRoi C. Snow, "Raised from the Dead," *Improvement Era*, 32, no. 11 (September 1929): 881.

18. Eliza R. Snow Smith, *Biography and Family Record*, 52.

19. Ibid., 60.

20. Ibid., 65.

21. *Millennial Star*, 3, no. 6 (October 1842): 110.

22. Eliza R. Snow Smith, *Biography and Family Record*, 63.

23. Andrew Jenson, *Latter-day Saint Biographical Encyclopedia* (Salt Lake City: Andrew Jenson History Company, 1901), 1:28.

24. Romney, *The Life of Lorenzo Snow*, 47.

25. Eliza R. Snow Smith, *Biography and Family Record*, 68–69.

26. See Gibbons, *Lorenzo Snow*, 48; Eliza R. Snow Smith, *Biography and Family Record*, 84–85; see also Lyndon W. Cook, *The Revelations of the Prophet Joseph Smith: A Historical and Biographical Commentary of the Doctrine and Covenants* (Provo, UT: Seventy's Mission Bookstore, 1981), 352.

27. Cook, *Revelations of the Prophet Joseph Smith*, 352–53; see also Daniel H. Ludlow, ed., *Encyclopedia of Mormonism*, 5 vols. (New York: MacMillan, 1992), 4:1647.

28. Eliza R. Snow Smith, *Biography and Family Record*, 89–90.

29. Romney, *The Life of Lorenzo Snow*, 72.

30. *Deseret News 2003 Church Almanac* (Salt Lake City: *Deseret News*, 2002), 60, 70–71.

31. Gibbons, *Lorenzo Snow*, 60.

32. Eliza R. Snow Smith, *Biography and Family Record*, 109.

33. James A. Toronto, "Italy," in *Encyclopedia of Latter-day Saint History*, 556.

34. Eliza R. Snow Smith, *Biography and Family Record*, 122.

35. Ibid., 128–29.

36. Toronto, "Italy," 556–57; Eliza R. Snow Smith, *Biography and Family Record*, 130–32.

37. Eliza R. Snow Smith, *Biography and Family Record*, 132.

38. Ibid., 133.

39. Toronto, "Italy," 557.

40. Eliza R. Snow Smith, *Biography and Family Record*, 187.

41. Dale Z. Kirby, "Switzerland," in *Encyclopedia of Latter-day Saint History*, 1206.

42. R. Lanier Britsch, *From the East: The History of the Latter-day Saints in Asia, 1851–1996* (Salt Lake City: Deseret Book, 1998), 9.

43. JoAn Bitton, "Malta," in *Encyclopedia of Latter-day Saint History*, 697.

44. Eliza R. Snow Smith, *Biography and Family Record*, 232.

45. *Millennial Star*, 14 (July 3, 1852): 297.

46. Maureen Ursenbach Beecher and Paul Thomas Smith, "Snow, Lorenzo," in *Encyclopedia of Mormonism*, 3:1368; see also Gibbons, *Lorenzo Snow*, 73.

47. Scott R. Christensen, "Brigham City," in *Encyclopedia of Latter-day Saint History*, 132.

48. Ibid., 132.

49. James B. Allen and Glen M. Leonard, *The Story of the Latter-day Saints* (Salt Lake City: Deseret Book, 1992), 366.

50. Christensen, 132.

51. Allen and Leonard, *The Story of the Latter-day Saints*, 366; see also Beecher and Smith, "Snow, Lorenzo," 1368.

52. *JD*, 19:96.

53. Andrew Jenson, "Walter Murray Gibson," *Improvement Era* 4, no. 2 (December 1900): 87.

54. Romney, *The Life of Lorenzo Snow*, 185–86.

55. *HC*, 5:474.

56. Eliza R. Snow Smith, *Biography and Family Record*, 511.

57. Ibid.

58. Romney, *The Life of Lorenzo Snow*, 250.

59. Eliza R. Snow Smith, *Biography and Family Record*, 497.

60. Romney, *The Life of Lorenzo Snow*, 274.

61. This subtitle is also the title of a biography on George Reynolds; see Bruce A. Van Orden, *Prisoner for Conscience' Sake* (Salt Lake City: Deseret Book, 1992).

62. Romney, *The Life of Lorenzo Snow*, 361.

63. Ibid., 364.

64. Ibid., 362–63.

65. Ibid., 364.

66. Ibid., 371–72.

67. *2003 Church Almanac*, 503

68. Ibid., 60.

69. Snow, "Raised from the Dead," 884–85.

70. Ibid., 885–86.

71. Ibid., 881.

72. LeRoi C. Snow, "An Experience of My Father's," *Improvement Era* 36, no. 11 (September, 1933): 667.

73. Romney, *The Life of Lorenzo Snow*, 421–22.

74. *2003 Church Almanac*, 60–61, 63.

75. Leonard J. Arrington, *Great Basin Kingdom: An Economic History of the Latter-day Saints, 1830–1900* (Lincoln: University of Nebraska Press, 1966), 401.

76. Ibid., 400.

77. Romney, *The Life of Lorenzo Snow*, 426.

78. LeRoi C. Snow, "The Lord's Way out of Bondage Was Not the Way of Men," *Improvement Era* 41, no. 7 (July 1938): 439.

79. Ibid.

80. Ibid., 440.

81. R. Lanier Britsch, "Japan," *Encyclopedia of Latter-day Saint History*, 567.

82. *2003 Church Almanac*, 370.

83. See Beecher and Smith, "Snow, Lorenzo," 1370; see also Allen and Leonard, *The Story of the Latter-day Saints*, 426–27.

84. Paul H. Dunn, *You Too Can Teach* (Salt Lake City: Bookcraft, 1962), 14.

85. Snow, "Devotion to a Divine Inspiration," 656.

86. Romney, *The Life of Lorenzo Snow*, 35.

87. Snow, "Devotion to a Divine Inspiration," 656.

88. Ibid., 657.

89. Ibid., 656.

90. Ibid., 659.

91. Ibid., 660.

92. Snow, "The Lord's Way Out of Bondage," 440.

93. B. H. Roberts, *A Comprehensive History of the Church of Jesus Christ of Latter-day Saints*, 6 vols. (Provo, UT: Brigham Young University Press), 6:359.

94. Snow, "The Lord's Way Out of Bondage," 440.

95. Orson F. Whitney, "Lives of Our Leaders—The Apostles: Lorenzo Snow," *Juvenile Instructor*, 35, no. 1 (January 1, 1900): 7.

96. LeRoi C. Snow, "The Lord's Way out of Bondage," 441.

97. See *Church History in the Fulness of Times* (Salt Lake City: The Church of Jesus Christ of Latter-day Saints, 2000), 453.

98. Joseph Fielding Smith, *The Life of Joseph F. Smith: Sixth President of the Church of Jesus Christ of Latter Day Saints* (Salt Lake City: The Deseret News Press, 1938), 310–11.

99. *MFP*, 3:333–34.

100. Ibid., 335.

101. Joseph F. Smith, "The Last Days of President Snow," *Juvenile Instructor*, 36, no. 22, November 15, 1901, 689.

102. Roberts, *A Comprehensive History of the Church*, 6:377.

103. Ibid., 379.

104. Joseph F. Smith, "The Last Days of President Snow," 690.

105. Romney, *The Life of Lorenzo Snow*, 477.

Sidebar and Photo Notes

1. Beecher and Smith, "Snow, Eliza R.," 3:1364–66.

2. See Ogden, "The Kirtland Hebrew School," 63–87.

3. Joseph Smith Jr., *HC*, 2:376–77.

4. Eliza R. Snow Smith, *Biography and Family Record*, 6.

5. Elwin C. Robison, "Kirtland Temple," in *Encyclopedia of Latter-day Saint History*, 622–24.

6. Lawrence R. Flake, *Prophets and Apostles of the Last Dispensation* (Provo, Utah: Religious Studies Center, Brigham Young University, 2001), 375–76.

7. Flake, *Prophets and Apostles of the Last Dispensation*, 307–310.

8. Eliza R. Snow Smith, *Biography and Family Record*, 10.

9. Snow, "Devotion to a Divine Inspiration," *Improvement Era* 22, no. 8 (June 1919): 655.

10. James L. Godfrey, "Victoria," in *World Book Encyclopedia* (Chicago: Field Enterprises, 1965), 19:285.

11. Romney, *The Life of Lorenzo Snow*, 46.

12. Eliza R. Snow Smith, *Biography and Family Record*, 63–64.

13. James A. Toronto, "Waldensians" in *Encyclopedia of Latter-day Saint History*, 1303.

14. Eliza R. Snow Smith, *Biography and Family Record*, 132.

15. Craig K. Manscill, "Smith, George A." in *Encyclopedia of Latter-day Saint History*, 1114–15.

16. Frances J. Bowman, "Thiers, Louis Adolpe," in *World Book Encyclopedia*, 18:198.

17. Romney, *The Life of Lorenzo Snow*, 2–3.

18. Ibid., 3.

19. "Spotlight on Historic Sights: St. George Tabernacle," in *Church News*, 69, no. 28 (July 10, 1999), 2.

20. LeRoi C. Snow, "The Lord's Way Out of Bondage," 439.

21. Romney, *The Life of Lorenzo Snow*, 470–71.

Chapter Six

JOSEPH F. SMITH

LIFE AND TIMES

1838	November 13	Born in Far West, Missouri
1844	June 27	Father, Hyrum Smith, was martyred
1848		Drove a team of oxen across the plains from Winter Quarters to the Salt Lake Valley
1852	September 21	Mother, Mary Fielding Smith, died
1854		Served a mission to Sandwich Islands (Hawaii)
1859	April 5	Married Levira A. Smith, the first of six wives
1860–63		Served a mission to Great Britain
1864		Served a special mission to Sandwich Islands
1865–74		Elected member of the Territorial House of Representatives
1866	July 1	Ordained an Apostle and set apart as a counselor to President Brigham Young
1867	October 8	Became a member of the Quorum of the Twelve Apostles
1874–75		Served as president of the European Mission
1878		Served historical mission to the eastern United States
1880–87		Appointed counselor to President John Taylor
1889–98		Appointed counselor to President Wilford Woodruff
1898–1901		Appointed counselor to President Lorenzo Snow
1884–1991		Entered voluntary exile because of persecution for practicing plural marriage
1901	October 17	Ordained and set apart as President of the Church
1904	April 6	Issued the second manifesto on plural marriage
1906		Became first Church President to tour Europe
1909	November	First Presidency issued the doctrinal exposition "The Original Man"
1913	July 29	Dedicated the site of Alberta Temple
1915	June 1	Dedicated the site for the Hawaii Temple
1916	June 30	Issued doctrinal exposition "The Father and the Son"
1918	October 3	Received the vision of the redemption of the dead
1918	November 19	Died in Salt Lake City, Utah, at age eighty

BIOGRAPHICAL HIGHLIGHTS

Joseph F. Smith was the last President to personally know the Prophet Joseph Smith and the first President to be born in the Church. The son of Hyrum and Mary Fielding Smith, Joseph found that his life was closely connected to important events and people in the nineteenth-century Church. Orphaned by the murder of his father when Joseph was six and the untimely death of his mother when he was thirteen, he and his sister were left to suffer many hardships alone.

Joseph served five missions for the Church either as a missionary or mission president for a total of thirteen years. The first mission was to the Sandwich Islands (Hawaii) at age fifteen. He was the youngest President of the Church to serve a mission. Joseph F. married Levira A. Smith before leaving on his second mission to Great Britain in 1859. Over the next eighteen years, he married five other women under the law of plural marriage: Jalina Lambson, Sara Ellen Richards, Edna Lambson, Alice Ann Kimball, and Mary Taylor Schwartz. The father of forty-eight children, Joseph F. Smith knew the pains of sorrow, burying thirteen of his children during his lifetime.

In 1866, at the direction of Brigham Young, twenty-eight-year-old Joseph F. Smith was ordained an Apostle and called as a counselor in the First Presidency. From the death of Brigham Young in 1877 to the time Joseph F. Smith was sustained as President of the Church in 1901, he served continually in the First Presidency as a counselor for twenty-four years, serving Presidents John Taylor, Wilford Woodruff, and Lorenzo Snow. He labored fifty-two years as a General Authority in the service of his people, God, and church. He was ordained and set apart as the sixth President of the Church on October 17, 1901, serving the Church for seventeen years until his death on November 19, 1918. His service occurred at a time when Latter-day Saints' beliefs and practices were widely misunderstood. Many opponents waged harsh legal battles against the Church and its members. Through it all, however, Joseph F. Smith took the high road—setting an example of one who forgave and loved those who bitterly opposed him.

CONTRIBUTIONS

For more than half a century, President Joseph F. Smith served as a special witness of the Savior: as an Apostle, as a counselor in the First Presidency, and as President of the Church. While serving as President of the Church, he concurrently served from 1899 to 1911 as president of the Salt Lake Temple, general superintendent of the Sunday School, and general president of the Young Men's Mutual Improvement Association. During his administration as President of the Church, the Church was absolved from its debts. This new freedom allowed the Church to acquire historical sites and begin building visitors' centers, including the first information center on Temple Square. President Smith directed the construction of the new Church Administration Building and the Hotel Utah. He inaugurated the home evening program in 1915, created a committee that reformed and systematized priesthood work, instituted specific ages for Aaronic Priesthood ordinations, launched the seminary program in 1912, and admitted the program of the Boy Scouts of America into the Church. In addition he was a member of the Territorial Legislature of Utah from 1865 to 1874 and was the first President of the Church to tour the Church in Europe.

Blessed with a profound understanding of the gospel, he was able to lead his people in the principles of eternal truth and to steady the Church through attacks from opponents during the early years of the twentieth century. By the end of his administration, the hostilities had ended and members of the Church were accepted as loyal, law-abiding citizens.

TEACHINGS

Known as a powerful teacher of righteousness, President Smith studied the gospel assiduously and was appreciated for his scriptural understanding, his love of doctrine, and his powerful sermons. He wove various scriptural themes into his teaching throughout his ministry: the glory of God, the role of the Father and the Son, the divine origin of man and his dependence upon God, the importance of obedience, the necessity of chastity, the significance of the family unit, and the deportment of kindness to all are just a few of the many themes. His vision of the redemption of the dead, just six weeks before his death, is now canonized scripture. He could preach the gospel in its fulness in a single sermon, sometimes in a single sentence, ever focusing on the importance of knowing God the Father and His Son, Jesus Christ.

As a tribute to his gospel scholarship, President Smith's sermons and writings were gathered, classified, arranged, and printed in a volume known as *Gospel Doctrine*. This monumental book was the course of study for the Melchizedek Priesthood quorums of the Church from 1971 to 1972. Nineteen years later, in 2000 to 2001, the volume provided the basis for the compilation of the Melchizedek Priesthood and Relief Society courses of study.

LIFE OF
JOSEPH F. SMITH

A HERITAGE OF FAITH

Joseph F. Smith, the first child of Mary Fielding and Hyrum Smith, was born on November 13, 1838, in Far West, Caldwell County, Missouri, in the midst of the Missouri persecutions. Joseph Fielding Smith was named after two of his uncles, Joseph Smith Jr. and Joseph Fielding. Though given the name of Joseph Fielding Smith at his birth, President Smith is referred to as Joseph F. Smith, distinguishing him from his son Joseph Fielding Smith, tenth President of the Church. Being so close a relation to both Joseph Smith the Prophet and Hyrum Smith, Patriarch to the Church (his uncle and father, respectively), Joseph F.'s life was inescapably allied with significant events and people in nineteenth-century Church history. He said, "My childhood and youth were spent in wandering with the people of God, in suffering with them and in rejoicing with them. My whole life has been identified with this people."[1] He was acquainted

Here at Liberty Jail the infant Joseph F. Smith was given a name and blessing by his incarcerated father, Hyrum Smith.

with sorrow and suffering, violence and persecution, yet he was a peacemaker and a preacher of righteousness.

Two weeks before Joseph's birth, his father was taken prisoner by a mob and unjustly incarcerated in Liberty Jail. While Hyrum Smith, his brother the Prophet Joseph Smith, and others suffered privation in jail, Mary felt that her husband had been cruelly removed from her "at a time when [she] needed . . . the kindest care and attention of such a friend, instead of which, the care of a large family was suddenly and unexpectedly left upon [herself]." An immigrant from England who converted to the Church in Canada, she married Hyrum Smith following the death of his first wife, Jerusha, and was caring for the five Smith children at the time "my dear little Joseph F. was added to the number."[2]

With Mary bedridden because of illness and with Hyrum in jail, the Smith home was left defenseless. Members of the

Hyrum Smith, the father of Joseph F. Smith.

militia forced their way into many homes in the region on the pretext of searching for arms. The ruffians easily made their way into the Smith home, not caring for anyone's condition, which nearly resulted in the death of the infant Joseph F.

Joseph F. was still a babe in arms when his family escaped from Missouri, crossing the frozen Mississippi River and finding refuge in nearby Quincy, Illinois. His father was still in prison, and his mother—who was severely ill—had to be moved more than two hundred miles, chiefly on her bed.

Young Joseph F. spent most of his first eight years in Nauvoo, Illinois, the city the Saints built up on the banks of the Mississippi River. There, within the circle of the Smith family and the community of Saints, he was nurtured in the knowledge of the gospel of Jesus Christ. "I was instructed to believe in the divinity of the mission of Jesus Christ," he later recalled. "I was taught it from my father, from the Prophet Joseph Smith, through my mother . . . and all my boyhood days and all my years in the world I have clung to that belief." In addition, young Joseph was taught of the prophetic calling of his uncle Joseph Smith, that he "was a prophet of God; that he was inspired as no other man in his generation . . . to lay the foundations of God's Kingdom."[3]

Joseph F. was a mere five years old when his uncle Joseph and his father, Hyrum, were martyred for the kingdom of God. They were attacked and killed on June 27, 1844, by a vigilante mob. Throughout his life, Nauvoo evoked in him "sacred memories of the past, made doubly and at the same time Dear and dreadful, by the Sacred resting place of my Fathers Dust, and the Dreadful Scenes that once (and to my memory Clear as day) brought gloom and Horror upon the honest world and filled 10 thousand Hearts with grief and woe!"[4]

Hyrum's tragic death left Mary and her sister Mercy, who was also a widow, to care for a large family and to prepare to join the Saints in moving west. Their preparations were cut short in the fall of 1846, when threatening mobs compelled them to ferry "in an open flat boat, across the Mississippi river into Iowa, where we camped under the trees and listened to the bombardment of the city. We had left our comfortable home with all the furniture remaining in the house, together with all our earthly possessions, with no hope or thought of ever seeing them again."[5] His mother repeatedly assured her children, "The Lord will open the way,"[6] and the strength of her conviction nourished their own faith. "We were not far away when we heard the cannonade on the other side of the river," President Smith remembered, "but I felt just as certain in my mind then—as certain as a child could feel—that all was right, that the Lord's hand was in it, as I do today."[7]

Mary Fielding Smith (1801–1852), the mother of Joseph F. Smith.[4]

FROM NAUVOO TO SALT LAKE CITY

The westward journey for Joseph F. and his family was an adventure as well as a maturing experience. He observed his mother meet challenge after challenge with faith. When her company captain unkindly insisted that the widow would be a burden to the whole company, she let him know that she would do her part and make her way and even arrive in the valley before he did. And ultimately, she did. As the family's herd boy, Joseph F. was keenly aware of the importance of the family's precious cattle, so he never forgot how once through fervent prayer his mother located a lost team.

At the age of nine, Joseph F. drove one of the family's ox teams into the Salt Lake Valley on September 23, 1848. The Smiths settled on land south of Salt Lake City at Millcreek, and there young Joseph F. toiled as a teamster, herd boy, plow boy, irrigator, harvester, wood hauler, thresher, winnower,

A Mother's Faith

At a time when the Smith family gathered provisions for the trek from Winter Quarters to the Salt Lake Valley, Joseph saw the example of his mother's undaunted faith. One morning two of their best oxen were missing. To no avail, Joseph F. and his uncle did an extensive search for the missing yoke of oxen. He described the scene upon his return to camp: "I was the first to return to our wagons, and as I approached I saw my mother kneeling down in prayer. I halted for a moment and then drew gently near enough to hear her pleading with the Lord not to suffer us to be left in this helpless condition, but to lead us to recover our lost team, that we might continue our travels in safety. When she arose from her knees I was standing nearby. The first expression I caught upon her precious face was a lovely smile, which discouraged as I was, gave me renewed hope and an assurance I had not felt before."[5]

and general roustabout. The family lived, as did other early pioneers, in a small cabin. He learned to work hard and do his duty, to live without luxuries, to praise God, and to pay tithing on everything the family raised. Joseph F. recalls an important lesson on paying tithing:

"I recollect most vividly a circumstance that occurred in the days of my childhood. My mother was a widow, with a large family to provide for. One spring [between 1849 and 1852] when we opened our potato pits, she had her boys get a load of the best potatoes and she took them to the tithing office; potatoes were scarce that season. I was a little boy at the time, and drove the team. When we drove up to the steps of the tithing office, ready to unload the potatoes, one of the clerks came out and said to my mother, 'Widow Smith, it's a shame that you should have to pay tithing.' . . . He chided my mother for paying her tithing, called her anything but wise or prudent; and said there were others who were strong and able to work that were supported from the tithing office. My mother turned upon him and said: '. . . Would you deny me a blessing? If I did not pay my tithing, I should expect the Lord to withhold his blessings from me. I pay my tithing, not only because it is a law of God, but because I expect a blessing by doing it.' "[8]

Joseph F. Smith treasured his mother's matchless love and faith. He was overwhelmed when, following two months of illness, his mother died at age fifty-one. "After my mother's death there followed 18 months—from Sept. 21st, 1852 to April, 1854 of perilous times for me," he later wrote a childhood friend. "I was almost like a comet or fiery meteor, without attraction or gravitation to keep me balanced or guide me within reasonable bounds." Fatherless and motherless at age thirteen, he recalled that he was "not altogether friendless."[9] His well-beloved and remembered aunt, Mercy R. Thompson, continued to nurture him, and he never forgot the solicitude of Brigham Young, Heber C. Kimball, and George A. Smith, his father's cousin. These were men Joseph learned to love as he loved his father.

George A. Smith served as a surrogate father throughout Joseph F.'s life.

MISSIONARY SERVICE AND MARRIAGE

At the age of fifteen, Joseph F., orphaned and adrift, received a missionary call. When the First Presidency announced at the April 1854 general conference that Joseph F. was called to join a group of missionaries soon to depart, he exercised the faith he had garnered through his childhood and "cheerfully responded" to the call. He later gratefully reflected, "My four years mission to the Sandwich Islands restored my equilibrium, and fixed the laws and metes and bounds which have governed my subsequent life."[10]

Elder Joseph F. Smith arrived at Honolulu in the Sandwich Islands (Hawaii) on September 27, 1854, about six weeks before his sixteenth birthday. Assigned to the island of Maui, he was soon left alone at Kula to live among the people and learn their language and culture. The young elder sought earnestly the gift of tongues. Within a short time Elder Smith developed an extraordinary fluency in the language that enabled him to personally minister to the Hawaiian people.

Through the course of his mission, Elder Smith was appointed to preside first on the island of Maui, then at Hilo

Big Brother to the Rescue

Upon the death of his mother, Joseph F. cared for his sister, Martha Ann, his only full-blooded sibling, as a surrogate father. His deep feelings of commitment toward and love for his sister are demonstrated by the care that he put into tending to her needs and watching out for her welfare. To his friend Charles W. Nibley, Joseph F. related one particular instance of a time when Joseph and his sister attended school together. This incident gives a clear example of his watchful care over his sister. He here gives the following account of this event that caused the schoolteacher to leave his position because of shame, ended Joseph F.'s formal education, and indirectly opened the way for his first mission to the Hawaiian Islands:

"My little sister was called up . . . to be punished. I saw the schoolmaster bring out the leather strap, and he told the child to hold out her hand. I could not stand for that. I just spoke up loudly and said, 'Don't whip her with that,' and at that he came at me and was going to whip me, and instead of him whipping me, I licked him good and plenty."[6]

Joseph F. Smith's first mission was to the Sandwich Islands (Hawaii) in 1856. Sixty-one years later, as President of the Church, he dedicated the site for the Hawaii Temple.

on the island of Hawaii, and later on the island of Molokai. On Molokai, he contracted a severe fever and was seriously ill for three months. A fellow member of the Church, Ma Mahuhii, attended him as lovingly as though he were her own son. She never forgot him, nor he her, and they greeted one another with deep affection whenever they met in later years.

Proselytizing without purse or scrip often tried the faith and resourcefulness of Elder Smith. At one point, early in his mission, a fire destroyed most of his belongings, including "clothing, copies of the first edition (European) of the Book of Mormon, and the Doctrine and Covenants, which had been given as a present to his father, Hyrum Smith. In one of these books, Elder Joseph F. Smith had placed his elder's certificate. When the house was destroyed with its contents, Elder Smith's trunk, and every article in it, was reduced to ashes except his missionary certificate. In some remarkable manner it was preserved intact, except that it was scorched around the edges, but not one word was obliterated

even though the book in which it was contained was entirely consumed. Not only were the books destroyed but also Elder Smith's journals which he had faithfully kept."[11]

Out of this experience came an amusing incident that was a serious concern at the time. The clothing of the missionaries had been destroyed, so Joseph F. Smith and his companion for a short time had to share one suit between them. One elder stayed at home while the other wore the suit and went to meetings. Then the elders would switch roles along with the suit, the one staying at home while the next went out to the meetings. "Of course this did not continue but for a short time, but it was one amusing story that was frequently told in later years, when time had removed the suffering."[12]

Leaving Hawaii in October 1857, Joseph F. arrived home in Salt Lake City and accepted additional responsibilities given to him by President Brigham Young. He was called on a second mission to England from 1860 to 1863, serving nearly three years. It was during these years that a strong

Not yet nineteen years old, Joseph F. Smith returns home from his first mission, 1856–58.

bond formed between Elder Joseph F. Smith and President George Q. Cannon, who presided over the mission.

He had only been home a short time when, in the early spring of 1864, he was called to accompany Apostles Ezra Taft Benson and Lorenzo Snow on a third mission, again to Hawaii, to regulate the affairs of the Church.

After his return from Hawaii to Salt Lake City late in 1864, Joseph F. was employed in the Church historian's office, working under the guidance of Elder George A. Smith of the Quorum of the Twelve.

Between his first and second missions, Joseph F. Smith fell in love with his first cousin Levira A. Smith. She was one of the daughters of Samuel H. Smith, a younger brother to Hyrum. Levira was sixteen at the time of their marriage on April 5, 1859. While Joseph F. was away serving the Church in Great Britain and Hawaii, Levira lived at her home. It was a difficult separation from Levira. He noted, "I [am now] 5000 miles from what only a short time before was a peaceful lovely home, now broken up and its inmates scattered."[13]

His Family Was His Greatest Joy

Prior to leaving for his second mission to Great Britain, at age twenty-two Joseph F. Smith married his first wife, Levira Smith. During his mission he was comforted knowing someone was waiting for him on his return. This wife was later joined by five other wives (living in accordance with the practice of plural marriage).

April 5, 1859	Levira Smith, daughter of Samuel Smith
May 5, 1866	Julina Lambson, niece of George A. Smith
March 1, 1868	Sara Ellen Richards, daughter of Willard Richards
January 1, 1871	Edna Lambson, niece of George A. Smith
December 6, 1883	Alice Ann Kimball, daughter of Heber C. Kimball
January 13, 1884	Mary Taylor Schwartz, niece of John Taylor

Joseph was the father of forty-eight children. Two of his sons, Hyrum Mack Smith and Joseph Fielding Smith, served as Apostles, and Joseph Fielding became the tenth President of the Church.

Later his son Joseph Fielding Smith observed that his father's love for his family "was boundless in its magnitude and purity. The world did not know—could not possibly know—the depths of his love for them. The wicked and the depraved have ridiculed and maligned him; but the true condition of his family life and wonderful love for his family is beyond their comprehension. O how he prayed that his children would always be true—true to God, true to their fellow men; true to each other and true to him! . . . Let them, one and all, be true to him and true to the cause which he represented so faithfully for the period of his mortal life, and which was the dearest thing to him in all his life."[7]

THE QUORUM OF THE TWELVE AND THE FIRST PRESIDENCY

At age twenty-eight, Joseph F. Smith was serving as secretary to the Council of the First Presidency and Quorum of the Twelve Apostles. In a meeting on July 1, 1866, at the direction of President Young, twenty-eight-year-old Joseph F. Smith was ordained an Apostle and called as a counselor to the First Presidency. Joseph F. Smith desired with his whole soul to help move forward that great and glorious work. He taught, "You have embraced the gospel for yourselves, then go and do your whole duty, not by halves, or in part, but your full duty."[14] In addition to other responsibilities as a member

At the age of twenty-eight, Joseph F. Smith was called by President Brigham Young as an Apostle and as a counselor in the First Presidency.

President Joseph F. Smith and his family on his sixty-fifth birthday.

of the Quorum of the Twelve, he served two terms as president of the European Mission (1874–75; 1877). The call to the apostleship also brought with it the responsibility to teach the gospel. Although Joseph F. Smith's formal schooling was limited, he mastered a large vocabulary and learned to speak with power and persuasion. Elder Joseph F. Smith became widely known for the scope and power of his sermons.

For the next three decades, Joseph F. Smith labored continually to establish peace and goodwill and carry out his apostolic duties. During those years, John Taylor, Wilford Woodruff, and Lorenzo Snow each served as President of the Church, and Joseph F. Smith was called as a counselor in each successive First Presidency. During this period, Latter-day Saint beliefs and practices were widely misunderstood. Through the 1880s, opponents waged harsh legal battles against the Church and its members. "They do not want us to be, religiously or otherwise, a separate and distinct people from the rest of the world. They want us to become identified and mixed up with the rest of the world, to become like them, thereby thwarting the purposes of God," President Smith explained.[15] As difficult as these years were for Church leaders, it proved to be an important schooling experience for Joseph F. Smith.

Joseph F. Smith was blessed to be a part of the early building program of temples for the eternal union of families. His life and ministry were closely tied to temple work. His personal experiences began in Nauvoo in the winter of 1845–46 when his mother and her sister Mercy R. Thompson were much engaged in the work going on in the Nauvoo Temple. President Smith later said, "It was there that my father's children were sealed to their parents."[16] He was present at the laying of the cornerstone of the Salt Lake Temple in 1853 and at the dedication of the temple in 1893. In anticipation of the dedication, he said, "For forty years the hopes, desires, and anticipations of the entire Church have been centered upon the completion of this edifice. . . . Now that the great building is at last finished and ready to be used for divine purposes, need we say that we draw near an event whose consummation is to us as a people momentous in the highest degree?"[17] He served as president of the Salt Lake Temple from 1898 to 1911, nine of those years while he was President of the Church.

In 1913, President Smith dedicated the land in Cardston, Alberta, Canada, for the building of the sixth temple of the Church.

President Smith participated in the dedications of the St. George, Logan, and Manti Temples. In 1913 he dedicated the site in Cardston, Alberta, Canada, for the sixth temple of the Church; and in 1915 he dedicated the land in his beloved adopted homeland, Hawaii, for the first temple outside the continental North America. He recognized, however, that the Church was merely on the threshold of temple building: "I foresee the necessity arising for other temples . . . consecrated to the Lord for the performance of the ordinances of God's house, so that the people may have the benefits of the house of the Lord without having to travel hundreds of miles for that purpose."[18]

At the August 1907 dedication service of the Uintah Stake Tabernacle in Vernal, Utah, President Joseph F. Smith told the assembled Saints that he would not be surprised if a temple were built in their midst someday.[19] This prophetic utterance was fulfilled in November 1997 when the remodeled tabernacle in Vernal, Utah, was dedicated as the fifty-first temple of the Church.

Although very busy with his Church responsibilities, President Smith ever tended to the temporal and spiritual needs of his family, making his fatherly presence felt whether he was at home or away. In notes, letters, and poems, he

On November 10, 1901, Joseph F. Smith was sustained as President of the Church. He chose as his counselors John R. Winder from the Presiding Bishopric and Anthon H. Lund of the Twelve Apostles.

expressed his abiding affection for his loved ones. "My Dear Companion," he wrote to his wife on her thirty-ninth birthday, "I think better of you, prize you higher, you are nearer to me and I love you more today than I did . . . twenty years ago. Every hour, week, month and year, strengthens the bond of our union and each child cements it with an eternal seal."[20]

Although devoted to his family and Church callings, Joseph F. had his diversions. He was fond of music, especially Church hymns. He also enjoyed sports of all kinds, either as a spectator or participant. Given his choice, he would rather participate than watch. In the vigor of his youth he excelled at jumping, wrestling, and foot racing. In his mature years he took up golf.

PRESIDENT OF THE CHURCH

Observing the declining health of President Lorenzo Snow, Joseph F. Smith—being next in seniority in the Quorum of the Twelve Apostles—prepared himself for the inevitable greater responsibilities. On October 17, 1901, a week after the death of President Lorenzo Snow, the Quorum of the Twelve Apostles ordained and set apart Joseph F. Smith as the sixth President of The Church of Jesus Christ of Latter-day Saints. He would serve as President for seventeen years, from 1901 to 1918.

The opening decades of the twentieth century saw the Church move forward in several important ways. A period of prosperity enabled the Church to pursue an unparalleled building program of badly needed chapels and temples, while allowing the prophet to travel and bless the Saints in faraway lands. With an emphasis on supporting the family, significant progress was made to standardize curriculum in priesthood quorums, auxiliary classes, and Relief Society. Doctrinal clarifications and directing revelation helped buttress the Church's position against the radical philosophies and modernistic theories, which in correlation with world wars undermined the nation's moral fabric. In his first address to the Saints as Church President, he declared, "It is our privilege to live nearer to the Lord, if we will, than we have ever done, that we may enjoy a greater outpouring of His Spirit than we have ever enjoyed, and that we may advance faster, grow in

You Will Live to Be President of the Church

From the time that Joseph F. Smith was a young man, great men in the Church prophesied that he would one day become the President of the Church. In the April 1905 general conference of the Church, Elder Ben E. Rich spoke of President Joseph F. Smith, who was there presiding as the prophet: "I rejoice in this; . . . He occupies that position today in literal fulfillment of prophecies uttered by those who have occupied the same position before. I used to live in Ogden. Some of you brethren who live in Ogden may remember the time you sat in the Ogden tabernacle, many years ago, and listened to the voice of prophecy from the lips of President Wilford Woodruff, when he predicted in the name of God, and told the people to write it down and remember it, that Joseph F. Smith would be president of this church, and you know by the way in which it was spoken, that it came from God; and you know, too, that it has been fulfilled by the will of God the Eternal Father."[8]

President Snow said to Elder Joseph F. Smith, "You will live to be the President of the Church of Jesus Christ of Latter-day Saints, and when that time comes you should proceed at once and reorganize the Presidency of the Church."[9]

the knowledge of the truth more rapidly, and become more thoroughly established in the faith."[21]

Church membership during President Smith's ministry nearly doubled from 278,645 in 1901 to 495,962 in 1918. While the Church's membership was largely living in the western United States, President Smith felt a strong connection with members in many nations. He visited Europe in 1906, the first President of the Church to do so while in office, and returned there in 1910. Additionally, he made visits to the Saints in Canada and in the Hawaiian Islands. With international conflict overtaking the globe, he and his counselors in the First Presidency instructed members to be faithful and true in their allegiance to their governments, to be good citizens, and to remain in their native lands—forming congregations of a permanent character. At this time, members of the Church were no longer encouraged to move to Utah to gather with the then-predominate body of Saints.

For several decades Latter-day Saints had gathered to the tops of the mountains in Zion in order to forge unity and spiritual strength. With inspired direction, President Smith saw the necessity to direct Saints in the future to live

peaceably in their homelands while maintaining the legacy of unity and spiritual strength made possible through priesthood order, temple ordinances, and the sociality of the Saints. This proved to be significant counsel, resulting in bolstering numbers and the strengthening of the worldwide Church.

As one who understood the importance of the priesthood, President Smith spoke and wrote at great length about the incomparable power of the priesthood, and strove to help all members understand its significance. At the time Joseph F. Smith was sustained as President of the Church, the meeting schedules, lessons, and effectiveness of priesthood quorums varied from ward to ward. He desired to put the priesthood to work, thereby involving both the Aaronic and Melchizedek members to magnify their priesthood. For a long time President Smith wanted to do more to refine the quorums of the Aaronic Priesthood. Over the next few years, bishops provided young priesthood holders with important assignments, many of which are now standard practice. Both Aaronic and Melchizedek Priesthood quorums were strengthened as regular weekly, year-round priesthood

The Hotel Utah opened its doors in 1916. President Smith understood this building to be a fulfillment of D&C 124:23: "Houses that strangers could come from afar to lodge therein."

meetings were firmly established and as a central Church committee issued uniform courses of study for the quorums.

Furthermore, President Smith preached with continued emphasis on the payment of tithes and offerings, which his predecessors established. The Saints' faithful response enabled the Church to pay off all its debts by the end of 1906.

The Church's building program was reenergized during this era of prosperity, and many chapels and meetinghouses were constructed. One of the Church's largest investments was the new Hotel Utah, which opened its doors in 1911. The hotel would fill a function similar to the Nauvoo House—a place where "the weary traveler" could find rest and "contemplate the word of the Lord" (D&C 124:22–24). In addition, the Church Administration Building dedicated in 1917 provided the long-needed office space for the Church's administration, including space for the Church historian and genealogical society offices.

President Smith placed great emphasis on teaching the gospel in the home. To further strengthen the families of the Church, in 1915 he and his counselors in the First Presidency introduced a weekly home evening program, urging parents to use the time to instruct their children in the word of God. This home evening program represented President Smith's belief that a great and important duty placed upon parents was to teach their children, from the cradle until they became men and women, every principle of the gospel and endeavor to instill into their hearts a love of God.

Along with the changes and much-needed simplifications to the curriculum in this period of President Smith's

The Church Is at Last Out of Debt

The latter-day Church was in debt almost constantly from its inception until midway through the presidency of Joseph F. Smith. In pursuing the precedent set by his predecessors, President Joseph F. Smith continued to encourage the Saints to pay their tithes and offerings. Through the obedience and sacrifice of the Saints following the counsel of their prophet, the Church became financially solvent by the end of 1906. Joseph F. Smith's daughter Rachel had the privilege of being one of the first to hear the news:

"One afternoon in 1906, five years after he was sustained as President, his daughter Rachel saw him in the front hall as she was coming in from school. Grandpa had been all over the Beehive House looking for Grandmother.

"'Where is your mother?' he inquired.

"'I don't know.'

"'Where could she be?'

"'I don't know.'

"'When will she be here?'

"'I don't know, Papa. I don't know much. I just got home from school.'

"'Well, baby,' he said, 'I wanted your mother to be the first to know, but since you don't know anything I will tell you.' In his hand he held a piece of paper.

"'Do you see this paper?'

"'Yes, sir.'

"'It means the Church is at last out of debt.' He smiled. 'So now you really know something!' He then gave her the canceled bond to keep."[10]

A five-story granite building, the Church Administration Building has been the headquarters of the Church for the First Presidency and the Quorum of the Twelve Apostles since its completion in 1917.

leadership, there came significant advancement in the auxiliary organizations. The general boards of the Sunday School, the organizations for the young men and young women, and the Primary had begun publishing uniform courses of study. Also, to address the challenge of the increasing amount of leisure time of the youth, the Boy Scout program was adopted for young men, and a new Beehive program was developed for young women. The Relief Society, which since 1902 had encouraged stakes to write lessons for sisters, also began publishing uniform lessons in 1914, along with special messages for visiting teachers in 1916. These innovations became part of the new Relief Society magazine and better equipped Relief Society women to look after the spiritual, mental, and moral welfare of the mothers and daughters in Zion. For President Smith, it was vital that the auxiliaries work in harmony with their priesthood authorities to teach the gospel and strengthen bonds of fellowship among members.

Over the course of President Smith's ministry he witnessed persecution directed at the Church and its members. He was repeatedly at the center of the harassment by those who opposed the work of the Lord and His Church. Despite this abuse, he was intent on returning good for evil. He declared that efforts by detractors "have but been the means, indirectly, of forwarding the work in the world. They have called the attention of the world toward us, and that is just what we want. . . . We want the world to become acquainted with us. We want them to learn our doctrine, to understand our faith, our purposes, and the organization of The Church of Jesus Christ of Latter-day Saints."[22]

Often the persecution was the result of misunderstandings and inaccurate information. The President set things in motion to change that perception. In order to provide visitors to Salt Lake City with accurate information about Church beliefs and history, the Church established its first visitors' center on Temple Square grounds in 1902. During the first year of operation, the twenty-five volunteers at the Bureau of Information and Church Literature were overwhelmed with more than 150,000 visitors. As a result, by 1904 the bureau required additional workers and a larger building. In 1911 the Tabernacle Choir presented highly praised concerts in twenty-five cities throughout the eastern and midwestern United States, including a special concert at the White House for the president of the United States and his guests. Gradually, President Smith's hopes began to be realized, and the Church received greater respect in the United States and abroad.

President Smith continually exhorted the Latter-day Saints to become more deeply rooted in their own history and doctrine. President Smith initiated republication of Joseph Smith's *History of the Church* and supported the collection of pioneer diaries and manuscripts for the Church archives.

Reaching Out to a Friendless Girl

President Joseph F. Smith was both approachable and in tune with the Spirit. This combination of traits is demonstrated by a girl who was touched by the kindness of President Smith:

"In Salt Lake I got work as a maid in a hotel; but I did not like the place, and after staying there a short time I decided to leave. The morning I left the hotel I had only twenty-five cents. I was a stranger in the city, and did not know what to do nor where to go. I walked up the street until I came to the Eagle Gate. I stopped there, and stood looking at the people going to their work. How happy they all seemed! And Oh, how miserable I felt! No one spoke to me; in fact, no one seemed to notice me. How long I stood there I do not know.

"I was almost ready to cry, when the door of the Beehive House opened and President Smith came out. I knew him, but he did not know me. I had never spoken to him. He looked at me as he passed. He had gone but a few steps when he stopped, came back, and looking down into my face said, 'What is the matter, my girl? You seem to be in trouble.'

"He listened to me like my own father while I told him my story. Then he said, 'Well, daughter, come with me.' He took me to his home, and presenting me to his wife said, 'Here is a poor, friendless girl. Take care of her till she gets a good place to work.'

"I was taken into the house of the President, and was treated with much kindness. In a short time I found a good situation. . . . No, I shall never forget President Joseph F. Smith."[11]

The Apostle Reed Smoot experienced considerable opposition to his appointment as a U.S. senator. At the Smoot hearing, Joseph F. Smith testified in his behalf.

Bear No Malice

President Smith was often unjustly misaligned by the media, which resulted in persecution. His position was to return good for evil, and he was so determined to do good that if he learned he had offended another, he could not rest until the wounds were healed. Joseph F. Smith's daughter Edith Eleanor recalled a time from her youth: "The news media was really persecuting my father. Some of the people at school had in their possession false reports and lies about Father. I went home from school furious one day. As soon as Father came in that evening I said to him, 'Papa, why don't you do something? You're not doing one thing, and these mean men are taking advantage of you, printing all these lies, and you don't do one thing about it!' " Her father looked at her and smiled and said, "Baby, don't get upset. They are not hurting me one bit; they are only hurting themselves. Don't you know, Baby, that when someone tells a lie they are only hurting themselves more than anyone else?' "[12] In the face of persecution President Smith taught, "Our plain duty is to live in the spirit of forgiveness, in the spirit of humility before the Lord, in the love of truth more than the love of ourselves and our personal interests."[13]

The Reed Smoot Hearings

In 1902 Elder Read Smoot, an Apostle, was appointed by the Utah State legislature as a United States senator. Unfortunately, opposition to his appointment from both the state and national level drew public attention. Among other things, he was accused of being a polygamist. Although this was not true, he was required to appear in a hearing before the United States Senate. Despite these false charges, Elder Smoot was allowed to take his Senate seat while an investigation ran its course. The hearings lasted from 1904 to 1907, and for the first time a President of the Church was asked to appear before a governmental body in the nation's capital. The first witness was President Joseph F. Smith, who was interrogated for three days. His honesty and forthrightness in answering the questions won him the grudging respect of many of the senators. Other Church witnesses included James E. Talmage, who clarified points of doctrine; Francis M. Lyman, President of the Quorum of the Twelve Apostles; Andrew Jenson, assistant Church historian; B. H. Roberts; and Moses Thatcher, who had been dropped from the Quorum of the Twelve Apostles in 1896. Thatcher's testimony was particularly helpful in countering the charge that the Church leaders "controlled the lives of the Saints." On February 20, 1907, the proposal to remove Reed Smoot from his Senate seat was defeated. Elder Smoot served a distinguished and unprecedented thirty years as a senator. The hearings were an educational experience for President Smith. He learned that the general populace of the United States perceived Church leaders as trying to circumvent the law. This resulted in the issue of the second Manifesto, pronouncing that any officer of the Church who solemnized a plural marriage would be excommunicated—including those living outside of the United States.

He also authorized Church officials to purchase historic sites sacred to Latter-day Saints, including Carthage Jail in Illinois, where the Prophet Joseph Smith and his brother Hyrum were martyred in 1844 (1903); part of the temple site at Independence, Missouri (1904); the Vermont farm where Joseph Smith was born in 1805 (1905); and the farm of Joseph Smith Sr. in Manchester, New York, site of the grove where the Prophet beheld the Father and the Son (1907). President Smith testified, "There is something hallowed about those places, to me and to all, I think, who have accepted the divine mission of Joseph Smith, the Prophet."[23]

The Church Literature Building. The first visitors' center established on Temple Square in 1902 at the encouragement of Joseph F. Smith.

While traveling to Sharon, Vermont, in 1905, President Smith visited the Sacred Grove in Manchester, New York.

On November 10, 1918, the seventeenth anniversary of the day he was sustained as President of the Church, Joseph F. Smith gathered his family together and spoke of his life and what he had learned. All came to the occasion fasting and in the spirit of prayer. President Smith said, "If there is anything on earth I have tried to do as much as anything else, it is to keep my word, my promises, my integrity, to do what it was my duty to do."[24]

This was his last formal counsel. Nine days later, on November 19, 1918, President Joseph F. Smith died. An influenza epidemic prohibited a formal public funeral service. In tribute to this great leader, all public assemblies, entertainments, and official meetings were suspended. Theaters and many local businesses were closed. Thousands of citizens of Salt Lake City, both those who were members and those who were not members of the Church, thronged the streets to honor Joseph F. Smith as the funeral cortege made its way up South Temple to the Salt Lake City Cemetery. As the procession passed the Catholic Cathedral of the Madeleine, the bells in the cathedral tower tolled in tribute to this venerable leader who had influenced so many.

The passing of President Joseph F. Smith marked an epoch in the history of the Church. He was the last of the old school of veteran leaders. The patience with which he bore the arduous labors of this life—fully, bravely, and cheerfully—are an example to members of the Church. He guided the Church during most of the twentieth century's first two decades. His accomplishments and contributions positioned the Church to move forward and reach out to bless the lives of members of the Church and those with other beliefs worldwide in the decades to come.

TEACHINGS OF PRESIDENT
JOSEPH F. SMITH

A POWERFUL TEACHER OF RIGHTEOUSNESS

President Harold B. Lee said, "When I want to seek for a more clear definition of doctrinal subjects, I have usually turned to the writings and sermons of President Joseph F. Smith." President Smith left the Church a great heritage of gospel scholarship through his countless sermons and writings. He was blessed with a profound understanding of the gospel coupled with an awe-inspiring command of the language. Elder Wilford Woodruff observed, "Joseph F. Smith spoke an hour and fifteen minutes, and the power of God was upon him. He manifested the same spirit that was upon his uncle Joseph Smith, the Prophet, and upon his father, Hyrum Smith."[25]

Elder Heber J. Grant said, "I bear witness to you that from my early childhood days, when I could not thoroughly understand and comprehend the teachings of the gospel, that I have had my very being thrilled, and tears have rolled down my cheeks, under the inspiration of the living God, as I have listened to Joseph F. Smith when preaching the gospel. . . . I know that whenever I heard that Joseph F. Smith was going to speak in one of the wards, that time and time again as a young man I have left my own ward and gone to listen to him, because he always filled my being and lifted me up as I listened to him proclaim the gospel of Jesus Christ."[26]

As a public speaker, Joseph F.'s leading trait was his intense earnestness. He impressed his audiences with his message more from the sincerity and simplicity of its delivery and the honest earnestness of his manner than from any learned exhibition of logic or rhetorical powers.

For President Smith, the scriptures remained a constant source of spiritual wealth. He studied the gospel assiduously and was known for his scriptural understanding, his love of doctrine, and his powerful sermons. He wove the scriptures into his teaching throughout his ministry. The glory of God, the divine origin of man and his dependence upon God, the importance of obedience and holy ordinances, the need for loving gratitude, and the necessity of faithful devotion—these are the themes President Smith wove together again and again. Rarely did he address a single gospel principle in isolation from the whole plan of salvation. He could preach the gospel in its fulness in a single sermon, sometimes in a single sentence, ever focusing on the importance of knowing God the Father and His Son, Jesus Christ.

As a tribute to his gospel scholarship, Presidents Smith's sermons and writings were gathered, classified, arranged, and printed in a basal volume entitled *Gospel Doctrine*. This monumental volume was the course of study for the Melchizedek Priesthood quorums of the Church from 1971 to 1972. Nineteen years later, from 2000 to 2001, the volume provided the basis for the compilation of the Melchizedek Priesthood and Relief Society courses of study. The book is a classic and breathes the true spirit of the gospel. It stands firm through time as a doctrinal testimony of the Savior.

THE WORD OF WISDOM

President Smith taught that living the Word of Wisdom was a matter of obedience to the words of the prophets. It was more than a prohibition against tea, coffee, tobacco, and alcohol—it was a commandment. In addition, he emphasized that the Word of Wisdom contained practical counsel for good health and spiritual growth and that those Saints who obeyed it would draw nearer to the Lord and become more like Him. To remind the Saints of the importance of the Word of Wisdom, from time to time President Smith read section 89 of the Doctrine and Covenants in its entirety during a meeting. "Now, it may seem altogether unnecessary and out of place, perhaps, to many, for me to occupy the time of this vast congregation in reading this revelation," he once said. Still he read every word of it to emphasize the great value of the message.[27]

On another occasion President Smith taught:

"I recollect a circumstance that occurred three years ago in a party that I was traveling with. There were one or two who persisted in having their tea and coffee at every place they stopped. I preached the Word of Wisdom right along; but they said, 'What does it matter? Here is So-and-so, who drinks tea and coffee.' . . . I said at one time, 'Oh, yes, you say it is a good thing to drink a little tea or coffee, but the Lord says it is not. What shall I follow?' The Lord says that if we will observe the Word of Wisdom we shall have access to great treasures of knowledge, and hidden treasures; we shall run and not be weary, we shall walk and not faint; and the destroying angel shall pass us by, as he did the children of Israel, and not slay us. . . . I will pray for you and earnestly beseech you, my brethren and sisters, . . . to cease practicing these forbidden things, and observe the laws of God."[28]

EDUCATION

President Smith taught: "One of the greatest evils existing . . . is that of ignorance, coupled with indifference. I presume that if the ignorant were not so indifferent to these facts and to their condition they might be prompted to learn more than they do."[29] Even though President Joseph F. Smith had few opportunities for formal education, he was greatly influenced by the doctrine that the "glory of God is intelligence" (D&C 93:36), and he encouraged the Saints to obtain as much education as possible in both spiritual and temporal truths. President Smith continued to support the Church academies, which provided secondary school training and religious education for many Saints. He also laid the foundation for today's extensive Church Educational System by establishing the seminary program. The first seminary was opened in 1912, adjacent to Granite High School in Salt Lake City, Utah.

CHASTITY AND PURITY

President Joseph F. Smith was a great defender of virtue. He taught the Saints that sexual impurity was one of the great dangers the Saints would face. From his teachings comes an especially clear point of prophecy on this subject:

"There are at least three dangers that threaten the Church within, and the authorities need to awaken to the fact that people should be warned unceasingly against them. As I see these, they are flattery of prominent men in the world, false educational ideas, and sexual impurity. But the third subject mentioned—personal purity, is perhaps of greater importance than either of the other two. We believe in one standard of morality for men and women. If purity of life is neglected, all other dangers set in upon us like the rivers of waters when the flood gates are opened."[30]

President Smith expressed his gratefulness for the protecting guidance of the Lord's hand in helping him to remain true to his covenants. "O, how I thank my God for His protecting, watchful care, . . . preserving me from the deadly sins of the world, and many thousand times from my own weaknesses and proneness to err." He was determined to be the kind of person who could "look his fellows in the face, and with a clean conscience before God stand erect in honest pride of truth, morally and sexually pure." He rejoiced that he lived "in the pure unsullied love" of his family and said, "I would not abuse their love and confidence for all I have or am."[31] He lived the way of life he taught—one of purity and truth.

THE ORIGIN OF MAN

For several decades the world had been stepping up its pace in technological developments and advancing the theories of modern science. Prior to the turn of the century, intense discussions focused on theories of organic evolution and the origin of man. In the midst of these controversies the First Presidency asked Elder Orson F. Whitney of the Quorum of the Twelve Apostles to draft a statement that would convey the Church's official position on the origin of man. Elder Whitney's statement was subsequently approved and signed by the First Presidency and the Quorum of the Twelve Apostles and published in 1909 as an official declaration of the Church. This statement attests that:

"All men and women are in the similitude of the universal Father and Mother, and are literally the sons and daughters of Deity. . . .

"Man, as a spirit, was begotten and born of heavenly parents, and reared to maturity in the eternal mansions of the Father, prior to coming upon the earth in a temporal body to undergo an experience in mortality. . . .

"It is held by some that Adam was not the first man upon this earth, and that the original human being was a development from lower orders of the animal creation. These, however, are the theories of men. The word of the Lord declares that Adam was 'the first man of all men' (Moses 1:34), and we are therefore in duty bound to regard him as the primal parent of our race. . . . Man began life as a human being, in the likeness of our heavenly Father."[32]

Not discussed in the 1909 document was how Adam and Eve were created. Subsequently, President Smith responded in the April 1910 *Improvement Era* with a mention of several possibilities but a strong caution that these were questions not fully answered in the revealed word of God.

This crucial 1909 document has proven invaluable for many years in teaching the doctrine of the Church concerning man and his origin and purpose here upon the earth. This document entitled "The Origin of Man" is still being used today as the official document of the Church on the matter.

THE ROLES OF THE FATHER AND THE SON

While President of the Church, Joseph F. Smith sought to clarify the identity and roles of the Father and the Son, especially since some scripture passages designate Jesus Christ as "Father." Therefore, in an effort to help the Saints better understand certain scriptures concerning the Father and the Son, the First Presidency and the Quorum of the Twelve issued a doctrinal exposition on June 30, 1916, titled "The Father and the Son." This declaration affirmed the unity between God the Father and His Son, Jesus Christ, and clarified the distinct roles of each in the plan of salvation.

The exposition also explained the ways in which the term *Father* is applied in the scriptures to both our Father in Heaven and Jesus Christ: "The term 'Father' as applied to Deity occurs in sacred writ with plainly different meanings. Each of the four significations specified in the following treatment should be carefully segregated." First, the term *Father* is applied to God because He is our literal parent. Second, it is applied to Jesus Christ because He is the Creator of heaven and earth, or "the Father of heaven and earth" (Mosiah 3:8).

President Joseph F. Smith, left, at the dedication of the Hyrum Smith Monument in the Salt Lake City Cemetery.

Third, the term *Father* is applied to Jesus Christ because those who accept His gospel become His sons and daughters through spiritual rebirth. Finally, the term *Father* is applied to Jesus Christ by His divine investiture of authority, where He represents His Father "in power and authority."[33]

President Smith also answered a related question in connection with the Godhead. Although the terms Holy Ghost and Spirit of the Lord were often used interchangeably, he explained that "the Holy Ghost is a personage in the Godhead," while the Light of Christ, or the Spirit of the Lord, "is the Spirit of God which proceeds through Christ to the world, that enlightens every man that comes into the world, and that strives with the children of men, and will continue to strive with them, until it brings them to a knowledge of the truth and the possession of the greater light and testimony of the Holy Ghost."[34] These important doctrinal statements provide Church members with answers to critical questions and remain, to this day, the basis of LDS doctrine on these subjects.

FAMILY HOME EVENING

To President Joseph F. Smith, his family was precious, indeed priceless. He spoke often and eloquently of the "divinely ordained home" and said that "the very foundation of the kingdom of God, of righteousness, of progress, of development" is established in the home.[35]

In 1903 the Church steadily progressed as it developed curriculum and programs that would lead the members through the twentieth and into the twenty-first centuries. Even so, President Smith emphasized that these programs of the Church should be treated as "supplements to our teachings and training in the home."[36] He emphasized the importance of teaching the family in the home environment: "Not one child in a hundred would go astray, if the home environment, example, and training, were in harmony with the truth in the Gospel of Christ."[37]

In 1909 a weekly home evening program was begun in the Granite Stake in Salt Lake City, Utah. President Smith declared that the program was inspired. In 1915 the First Presidency consequently issued an official announcement that urged the Saints to begin a program that, if followed, would be a major contributor in the building of a happy and righteous family. An excerpt of this announcement is given here: "We advise and urge the inauguration of a 'Home Evening' throughout the Church, at which time fathers and mothers may gather their boys and girls about them in the home and teach them the word of the Lord. They may thus learn more fully the needs and requirements of their families."[38]

Additionally, the First Presidency gave suggestions on how the general program might be run from home to home. They instructed that "these gatherings will furnish opportunities for mutual confidence between parents and children, between brothers and sisters, as well as give opportunity for words of warning, counsel and advice by parents to their boys and girls. They will provide opportunity for the boys and girls to honor father and mother, and to show their appreciation of the blessings of home so that the promise of the Lord to them may be literally fulfilled and their lives be prolonged and made happy."[39]

This home evening program represented President Smith's fervent belief that a "great and important duty devolving upon this people is to teach their children, from their cradle until they become men and women, every principle of the gospel, and endeavor, as far as it lies in the power of the parents, to instill into their hearts a love for God, the truth, virtue, honesty, honor and integrity to everything that is good."[40]

In 1915 the First Presidency prophetically stated, "If the Saints obey this counsel, we promise that great blessings will result. Love at home and obedience to parents will increase. Faith will be developed in the hearts of the youth of Israel, and they will gain power to combat the evil influences and temptations which beset them."[41] Still, today the Church continues to emphasize many of the essential features of the original program instituted by President Joseph F. Smith.

REDEMPTION OF THE DEAD

As President Smith neared the end of his own mortal life, he faced a particularly heart-wrenching challenge. His son Hyrum M. Smith died on January 23, 1918. Hyrum was the eldest son of Joseph F. and also a member of the Quorum of

From 1901 to 1918, President Smith lived in the Lion House. It was here that he received the vision of the redemption of the dead on October 3, 1818.

the Twelve. President Smith loved Hyrum and mourned his death. The event caused President Smith to deeply reflect on the nature of life after death.

Eight months later, as President Smith sat meditating on the Atonement of Jesus Christ, he opened the Bible and read 1 Peter 3:18–20 and 4:6. As he did so, his mind was opened to a vision of the "hosts of the dead" who had gathered in the spirit world (D&C 138:11). He saw the Savior come among them after His mortal death, organizing missionary work among them, and was given to understand that since that time missionary work had been conducted continually in the spirit world and that faithful elders of the modern era who had died were participating in missionary work. Subsequently, President Smith presented the revelation to his counselors in the First Presidency, the Quorum of the Twelve, and the Patriarch to the Church, who all unanimously accepted it as revelation from the Lord. This vision gave new revelation about missionary work in the spirit world and the significance

of doing work for the dead in the temples of the Church. In 1976 this revelation was accepted by the Saints and was designated as canonized scripture. In 1981 it was added to the Doctrine and Covenants as section 138.

WORLD WAR I— TROUBLED TIMES

Near the end of President Smith's administration, the world was embroiled in war. Many Church members were drawn into the war on opposite sides, and hundreds lost their lives. Several of President Smith's own sons served in the armed forces, and one was wounded twice in action. During a Christmas message to the Saints, the First Presidency stated that "while rejoicing over the birth of the Incomparable One, the light of our gladness is overshadowed with the war clouds that have darkened the skies of Europe, and our songs and salutations of joy and good will are rendered sadly discordant by the thunders of artillery and the groans of the wounded and dying, echoing from afar, but harrowing to our souls as the awful tidings come sounding o'er the sea. Nations rising against nations, brothers against brothers, 'Christians' against 'Christians,' each invoking the aid of the God of love in their gory strife and claiming fellowship with the Prince of peace! What an awful spectacle is thus presented before the angelic host, a band of whom sang the immortal song of 'good will toward men' at the birth of the babe of Bethlehem!"[42] President Smith taught that peace begets peace: "There is only one thing that can bring peace into the world. It is the adoption of the gospel of Jesus Christ, rightly understood, obeyed and practiced by rulers and people alike. . . . For years it has been held that peace comes only by preparation for war; the present conflict [World War I] should prove that peace comes only by preparing for peace."[43]

President Smith lived to hear the news of the signing of the armistice that brought an end to hostilities and the destruction of life and property. The armistice was signed on November 11, 1918, just eight days before his death.

I KNOW MY REDEEMER LIVES

Joseph F. Smith's testimony—proclaimed from pulpits at home and in foreign lands, in the councils of the Church, and in the circle of his own family—evidenced a heart and soul committed to Jesus Christ and His glorious gospel. His words were eloquent; his message was clear: "I want to say as a servant of God, independent of the testimonies of all men and of every book that has been written, that I have received the witness of the Spirit in my own heart, and I testify before God, angels and men, without fear of the consequences, that I know that my Redeemer lives, and I shall see him face to face, and stand with him in my resurrected body upon this earth, if I am faithful; for God has revealed this unto me. I have received the witness, and I bear my testimony, and my testimony is true."[44]

He taught the doctrines of Jesus Christ with remarkable clarity and labored not only to preach righteousness by word but by example. His powerful witness of the Redeemer was the heart of his preaching and the center of his daily life.

At the close of his life, a special graveside funeral service was held in the Salt Lake City Cemetery, where members of the Tabernacle Choir sang in tribute one of his favorite hymns, "I Know That My Redeemer Lives." This phrase was to him the essence of his faith and the focus of his prophetic message: "I know that my Redeemer lives. I feel it in every fiber of my being. I am just as satisfied of it as I am of my own existence. I cannot feel more sure of my own being than I do that my Redeemer lives."[45]

From the age of fifteen until his death at age eighty, Joseph F. delivered hundreds of gospel sermons and discourses to help Saints understand and live the teachings of Jesus Christ. Speaking of his ability to instruct, Charles W. Nibley declared, "As a preacher of righteousness who could compare with him? He was the greatest that I ever heard—strong, powerful, clear, appealing. It was marvelous how the words of living light and fire flowed from him."[46]

Craig K. Manscill

Associate Professor of Church History and Doctrine, PhD
Brigham Young University

NOTES

1. *Deseret News: Semi-Weekly*, April 25, 1882, 1.
2. *Millennial Star*, June 1840, 40.
3. Joseph F. Smith, *Gospel Doctrine*, 3rd ed. (Salt Lake City: Deseret Book, 1986), 493–94.
4. Joseph F. Smith's journal, Leeds, April 13, 1861, holograph 5, LDS Church Archives.
5. *Deseret News: Semi-Weekly*, April 25, 1882, 1; spelling modernized.
6. Brian H. Stay, ed., *Collected Discourses* (Woodland Hills, UT: BHS Publishing, 1994), 2:348.
7. *Deseret News: Semi-Weekly*, July 10, 1883, 1.
8. Joseph F. Smith, *Gospel Doctrine*, 228–29.
9. Joseph F. Smith to Samuel L. Adams, May 11, 1888, *Truth and Courage: Joseph F. Smith Letters*, ed. Joseph Fielding McConkie (privately published by Joseph F. Smith Family Trustees and Officers, 1988), 2.
10. Joseph F. Smith to Samuel L. Adams, 2.
11. Joseph Fielding Smith, comp., *Life of Joseph F. Smith, Sixth*

President of The Church of Jesus Christ of Latter-day Saints (Salt Lake City: Deseret Book, 1969), 183–84.

12. Ibid.

13. Joseph F. Smith diary, November 13, 1860, Joseph F. Smith Paper, 1856–1918, LDS Church Archives; as cited in typescript extracts, Scott G. Kenney Collection, BYU.

14. *Collected Discourses*, 2:280.

15. *Deseret News: Semi-Weekly*, October 2, 1883, 1.

16. Joseph F. Smith, *Gospel Doctrine*, 197.

17. In *MFP*, 3:241–42.

18. CR, April 1901, 69.

19. Uintah Stake Historical Record: 1905–1909, Quarterly Conference, August 25, 1907, Historical Department Archives, The Church of Jesus Christ of Latter-day Saints, 246.

20. Joseph Fielding Smith, *Life of Joseph F. Smith*, 453.

21. CR, October 1901, 69–70.

22. CR, October 1908, 3.

23. CR, October 1906, 5.

24. Joseph Fielding Smith, *Life of Joseph F. Smith*, 107.

25. Wilford Woodruff journal, June 24, 1866.

26. *MFP*, 5:135.

27. Ibid., 4:180–81.

28. Joseph F. Smith, *Gospel Doctrine*, 366–67.

29. Ibid., 342–43.

30. Ibid., 312–13.

31. Joseph Fielding Smith, *Life of Joseph F. Smith* (1938), 450–51.

32. "The Origin of Man," *Improvement Era* (November 1909): 78, 80; *MFP*, 4:203, 205.

33. "The Father and the Son: A Doctrinal Exposition by the First Presidency and the Twelve," *Improvement Era* (August 1916): 934–40.

34. Joseph F. Smith, *Gospel Doctrine*.

35. "Editorial Thoughts," *Juvenile Instructor* (November 1916): 739.

36. Joseph F. Smith, "Worship in the Home," *Improvement Era* (December 1903): 138.

37. Ibid.

38. "Home Evening," *Improvement Era* (June 1915): 733–34.

39. Ibid.

40. Joseph F. Smith, *Gospel Doctrine*, 292.

41. "Home Evening," 733–34.

42. *MFP*, 4:319.

43. Joseph F. Smith, *Gospel Doctrine*, 421.

44. Ibid., 447.

45. Ibid., 69.

46. Ibid., 522.

SIDEBAR AND PHOTO NOTES

1. Joseph F. Smith, *Gospel Doctrine*, 493.

2. Francis M. Gibbons, *Joseph Fielding Smith: Gospel Scholar, Prophet of God* (Salt Lake City: Deseret Book, 1992), 26.

3. Preston Nibley, *The Presidents of the Church* (Salt Lake City: Deseret Book, 1974), 183.

4. Photograph courtesy of *Deseret News: Semi-Weekly*, January 5, 1892, 3.

5. Joseph Fielding Smith, *Life of Joseph F. Smith*, 132.

6. "Reminiscences of President Joseph F. Smith by Charles W. Nibley, Presiding Bishop of the Church," *Improvement Era* 22, no. 3 (January 1919).

7. Joseph Fielding Smith, *Life of Joseph F. Smith*, 4.

8. Elder Ben E. Rich, CR, April 1905, 97.

9. Joseph Fielding Smith, *Life of Joseph F. Smith*, 319.

10. *Ensign*, September 1993, 15.

11. *Improvement Era*, 31:1043.

12. Quoted in Norman S. Bosworth, "Remembering Joseph F. Smith, *Ensign*, June 1983, 22.

13. CR, April 1909, 4.

Author's note: The author of this chapter acknowledges that information in this chapter has been previously published in other Church writings of Joseph F. Smith of which the author was a contributor.

Chapter Seven

HEBER J. GRANT

LIFE AND TIMES

1856	**November 22**	Born in Salt Lake to Jedediah and Rachel Grant; father died nine days later
1877	**November 1**	Married Lucy Stringham, the first of three wives
1880		Called as president of the Tooele Utah Stake
1882		Ordained an Apostle by President George Q. Cannon of the First Presidency
1883–84		Served a mission among the American Indians
1884	**May**	Married Augusta Winters on May 26 and Emily Wells on May 27, second and third wives, respectively
1897		Served in the general presidency of YMMIA and as business manager of the *Improvement Era*
1901–03		Opened and presided over first Japanese mission
1904–06		Presided over British and European Missions
1916		Ordained President of the Quorum of the Twelve Apostles
1918	**November 23**	Ordained President of the Church
1919		Dedicated temple in Laie, Hawaii
1923		Dedicated temple in Cardston, Alberta, Canada
1924		First radio broadcast of general conference delivered
1926		First institute of religion established at University of Idaho
1927		Dedicated temple in Mesa, Arizona
1936		Established Church Security Plan (later renamed the Church Welfare Plan)
1937		Three-month tour of European missions
1945	**May 14**	Died in Salt Lake City, Utah, at age eighty-eight

BIOGRAPHICAL HIGHLIGHTS

Heber J. Grant was born in Salt Lake City on November 22, 1856, the son of Jedediah and Rachel Grant. He married three wives and was the father of twelve children. At the age of twenty-four, he was set apart as president of the Tooele Utah Stake. A year later, he was called as an Apostle by President John Taylor. He served for thirty-six years as a member of the Quorum of the Twelve, including two as its President. He was ordained as seventh President of the Church on November 23, 1918, at the age of sixty-two. His twenty-seven-year term as Church President was second in length only to Brigham Young. He died in Salt Lake City on May 14, 1945, at the age of eighty-eight.

CONTRIBUTIONS

President Grant was a capable and decisive administrator. Soon after his call as President, the First Presidency announced they would no longer serve as general Church auxiliary presidents, a policy extended in 1935 to include members of the Quorum of the Twelve. Two corporations were formed in 1922 to oversee the property of the Church: the Corporation of the President, which handled the administration of ecclesiastical, tax-free properties, and Zion's Securities Corporation, which managed investment and revenue-producing properties. Assistants to the Twelve were called for the first time in the April 1941 general conference.

During President Grant's administration, the Church began to be recognized as more than a Utah organization. Beginning with the creation of the Los Angeles Stake in 1923, the Church gradually expanded across the United States into other major metropolitan centers. Stakes were organized in San Francisco (1927), New York City (1934), Oahu (1935), Chicago (1936), Portland (1938), Seattle (1938), Denver (1940), and Washington, DC (1940). Overall, Church membership nearly doubled under President Grant, growing from 495,962 to 954,004 members and from 75 to 149 stakes. Temples were dedicated in Laie, Hawaii (1919), Cardston, Alberta, Canada (1923), and Mesa, Arizona (1927).

The Church celebrated numerous centennials under President Grant, including the one-hundredth anniversaries of the First Vision and of the organization of the Church. The Church Welfare Plan was developed and announced in 1936. President Grant ordained a dozen men to the apostleship, including future Church Presidents Harold B. Lee, Spencer W. Kimball, and Ezra Taft Benson.

TEACHINGS

President Grant presided over the Church during some of the most difficult times of the twentieth century—the aftermath of World War I, Prohibition and its repeal, the Depression, and World War II. He was close to the people. He understood the desires, the needs, and the challenges the Saints faced during the tempestuous decades of the 1920s, 1930s, and 1940s. His teachings centered on keeping the commandments, obeying the Word of Wisdom, paying tithing, and adhering to other principles of temporal welfare. These teachings reflected his keen understanding and deep spiritual nature. In 1943, under the direction of Elders John A. Widtsoe and Richard L. Evans of the Twelve, selections from the sermons and writings of President Grant were compiled by G. Homer Durham and entitled *Gospel Standards*.

First Address as President of the Church

"I stand here today in all humility, acknowledging my own weakness. . . . But . . . with the help of the Lord, I shall do the best that I can to fulfill every obligation that shall rest upon me . . . to the full extent of my ability. I will ask no man to be more liberal with his means than I am with mine, in proportion to what he possesses, for the advancement of God's kingdom. I will ask no man to observe the Word of Wisdom any more closely than I will observe it. I will ask no man to be more conscientious and prompt in the payment of his tithes and his offerings than I will be. I will ask no man to be more ready and willing to come early and to go late, and to labor with full power of mind and body, than I will."[1]

Book of Mormon Printed in Braille

The Book of Mormon was printed in braille for the first time in 1936. On that occasion, President Grant said, "I am very thankful that the Book of Mormon has been printed in Braille. . . . I am convinced that wonderful book, full of inspiration from Almighty God . . . will cause many a person to rejoice who has never been able to read the Book of Mormon heretofore."[2] On March 12, 1941, President Grant presented a copy of the Book of Mormon in braille to Helen Keller.

President Heber J. Grant presents a copy of the Book of Mormon in braille to Helen Keller, March 12, 1941.[3]

The Gospel Preached by Radio

1922   President Grant delivered the first gospel message by radio.

1924   General conference was broadcasted by radio.

1929   Tabernacle Choir began weekly broadcasts.

1930   *Music and the Spoken Word* began with Richard L. Evans as voice.

1935   The first of six *Church of the Air* programs was broadcast by more than seventy networks throughout the United States and Canada and by short wave to Europe and other countries.

1935   Church Radio, Publicity, and Mission Literature Committee was organized to prepare radio scripts and missionary tracts, with Gordon B. Hinckley, recently returned from the British Mission, appointed as executive secretary.

LIFE OF
HEBER J. GRANT

◆

A VALIANT HERITAGE

Heber was the son of Jedediah and Rachel Grant. Jedediah marched with Zion's Camp, served numerous missions, helped build the Kirtland Temple, was a major general in the Nauvoo Legion, led a group of Saints into the Salt Lake Valley, was the first mayor of Salt Lake City, and served as an Apostle and counselor in the First Presidency. He died at the age of forty, just nine days after Heber was born. Rachel provided for Heber as best she could by working as a seamstress and by housing boarders. "She lived in poverty. I sat on the floor at night until midnight and pumped the sewing machine to relieve her tired limbs."[1] Rachel taught Heber the values of self-reliance and hard work. Nearly deaf by age forty-six, she was deeply devoted to her religion, serving thirty-five years as president of the Salt Lake Thirteenth Ward Relief Society. Her example and love had a profound influence on Heber.

Jedediah Morgan Grant, father of Heber J. Grant.

Rachel Ivins, mother of Heber J. Grant.

The Profound Influence of His Mother

After being called as President of the Church, Heber paid tribute to his mother, saying: "I stand here today as one whose mother was all to him. She was both father and mother to me; she set an example of integrity, of devotion and love, of determination; and honor second to none. I stand here today as the President of the Church because I have followed the advice and counsel and the burning testimony of the divinity of the work of God, which came to me from my mother."[4] "It was [Rachel] who changed his timidity to courage; his self-depreciation to self-confidence; impetuousness to self-control; lack of initiative to perseverance."[5]

Rachel believed Heber would become a great leader in the Church. "My mother often said to me: 'Heber, behave yourself and you will someday be an Apostle.' I laughed. . . . Every mother thinks that her son will be the President of the United States, or something wonderful."[2] Others had similar feelings about Heber. Bishop Edwin Woolley had the impression, when blessing Heber as a baby, that he would become an Apostle.[3] When Heber was a toddler, general Relief Society president Eliza R. Snow prophesied that he would become a great man in the Church.[4] Years later, when Elder Heber C. Kimball was dining at the Grant home, he picked up Heber, set him on the table, and prophesied that he would become an Apostle and would "live to be a greater man in the Church than [his] father."[5] Shortly after his call as president of the Tooele Stake, Heber was blessed by Patriarch John Rowberry and was told he would become one of the leading men in the Church. Though he did not share his prompting at the time, Patriarch Rowberry felt sure that Heber would become President of the Church.[6]

LEGENDARY PERSISTENCE

A favorite motto of Heber J. Grant was that penned by Ralph Waldo Emerson: "That which we persist in doing becomes easier for us to do; not that the nature of the thing itself is changed, but that our power to do is increased."[7] The persistence of Heber J. Grant is legendary among members of the Church, as illustrated by his early experiences with baseball, penmanship, and singing.

As an only child, Heber was responsible for many household chores, including sweeping the floor and washing and drying the dishes. He had few opportunities to develop his athleticism. Desiring to fit in with other boys his age, he joined a baseball team but discovered that he had neither the arm strength to throw from one base to another, nor the physical aptitude to hit or run well. Still, Heber vowed he would become good enough to play for the territorial championship.

Immediately he went to work shining the shoes of his mother's boarders until he had enough money to buy a baseball. Then he went to Bishop Edwin Woolley and asked permission to use his barn for practice. He threw for hours at a time, and there were nights when his arm was so sore that he could not sleep until his mother tied his arm up with cold, wet rags to alleviate the pain. Eventually, his practice paid off. He made the team that not only won the Utah territorial championship but also beat the territorial champions from California, Colorado, and Wyoming.

When Heber was about twelve or thirteen, a friend drew his attention to a man coming out of Wells, Fargo and Company, who earned $150 a month as a bookkeeper. Astounded by the enormous salary, Heber dreamed of one day working for the bank and earning a similar income. He enrolled in a class to develop his penmanship. Fellow students teased him when they saw his handwriting. The comments hurt Heber's feelings, but they also aroused within him the determination to succeed—even to become expert enough to teach penmanship! Heber's hard work earned him a blue ribbon for the best penmanship in the territory and eventually qualified him for a position as an instructor of penmanship and bookkeeping at the University of Deseret.

At the age of ten, Heber, who was tone-deaf, joined a singing class and was told by his professor that he would never be able to sing. Another "expert" assured him that he could sing, but said he wanted to be at least forty miles away when he did. Once while practicing his singing in a room located next door to a dentist's office, a few of the waiting patients thought the noise was coming from some poor soul having his teeth pulled. Heber said, "I have had a great many of my friends come to me and beg me not to sing. Six months ago one of my fellow Apostles said to me, 'Come in, Heber, but don't sing'. . . . In our meetings in the Temple the brethren would say 'That is as impossible as it is for Brother Grant to carry a tune,' and that settled it; everybody acknowledged that was one of the impossibilities."[8]

Determined to succeed, Heber sought the help of Horace Ensign, a gifted musician. After four to five months practicing "O My Father" as many as 115 times a day, Heber felt confident enough to try singing the hymn at a meeting. "I only got as far as the 'O,' " he said, "and I did not [even] get that right."[9] Undeterred, Heber continued practicing until he

The Red Stockings, Utah territorial champions, August 1877.[6]

Heber J. Grant, Apostle of the Lord. Shown on the left is a handwritten copy of the revelation received by President John Taylor calling Heber to the Apostleship.[7]

could sing over two hundred songs and became good enough to join the Temple Choir. "I consider it one of the greatest accomplishments of my life," he said "that I have learned to sing."[10] His favorite hymn was "Come, Come, Ye Saints." In his later years, he found that singing helped him sleep. "A Poor Wayfaring Man of Grief" was a particular bedtime favorite. "Generally," he noted, "I can get to sleep by the time I have repeated four verses."[11]

SUCCESSFUL BUSINESSMAN

Influenced by English author Samuel Smiles's books on character, thrift, and self-help, and by the Wilson and National readers commonly used in elementary schools of the day, Heber grew up believing that financial success was the result of hard work and determination. At age fifteen, he secured his first job as a bookkeeper for H. R. Mann and Company. Four years later, he purchased the insurance company and built it into one of the most profitable in Utah. Besides the insurance business, Heber was a successful banker, established the largest wagon and implement dealer in Utah, owned the largest livery stable, oversaw the largest wholesale and retail business, and was the publisher of the *Herald*, an important Salt Lake City newspaper. One of the most successful and admired businessmen of his day, Heber could "walk into the offices of the executives and directors of the greatest financial and industrial institutions in America and be warmly and affectionately greeted by men who [were] proud to know him as a friend."[12]

APOSTLE OF THE LORD

In 1882 Heber was called to be an Apostle by President John Taylor. He said, "I arose to my feet to say it was beyond anything I was worthy of, and . . . the thought came to me, 'You know as you know that you live that John Taylor is a prophet of God, and to decline this office . . . is equivalent to repudiating the prophet.' I said, 'I will accept the office and do my best.' . . . There are two spirits striving with us always, one telling us to continue our labor for good, and one telling us that with the faults and failings of our nature we are unworthy."[13]

For four months Heber struggled with feelings of unworthiness. In addition, the Brethren had not been able to fill the two vacancies in the Quorum of the Twelve. Finally, in February 1883, while on assignment to the Navajo Indian

Reservation, the heaviness Heber felt drove him to his knees. He later testified that he saw what appeared to be a council in heaven. "In this council the Savior was present, my father was there, and the Prophet Joseph Smith was there. . . . The Prophet Joseph Smith and my father mentioned me and requested that I be called to that position. I sat there and wept for joy. It was given to me that I had done nothing to entitle me to that exalted position, except that I had lived a clean, sweet life. . . . It was because of their faithful labors that I was called. . . . It was also given to me that . . . from that day it depended upon me and upon me alone as to whether I made a success of my life or a failure." And he said that "from that day I have never been bothered, night or day, with the idea that I was not worthy to stand as an apostle."[14]

LOVE OF GOLF

Heber J. Grant was an avid golfer. His love for the game began as a result of an experience he had with President Joseph F. Smith. While serving as President of the Quorum of the Twelve, Heber often needed the signature of President Smith on important papers. At times, he found that President Smith had left the office and gone to the golf course. The following exchange between President Smith and Heber J. Grant was reported by Rulon Killian and demonstrates President's Smith love of the game and his consideration for Heber J. Grant.

"One particular day I had some very important papers that must be signed by Pres. Smith and mailed before closing time. I half ran to his office and to my disgust was told he was out on the golf course. I was mad when I got to him. He could see I was. He said, 'Heber, you are tense and overworked. You should learn to play this game. Many times I, myself, get overworked, weary and so tense I can accomplish but little. So I drop everything and come play golf. There is something about this game that relaxes me and causes me to forget my anxieties. When I get back to the office I can accomplish more in a few hours than I could in days when I am so tense.' I said to Pres. Smith, 'You will never catch me wasting my time playing that silly game. Now sign these papers and let me get back to work.' Pres. Smith said, 'No,

Heber J. Grant loved to golf.[8]

Heber, I will not sign a thing until you take my partner's club and finish out this round with me.' 'Not on your life' I retorted. 'I've got too much to do to fool away my time here.' 'Heber,' said he, 'I command you to take that club and play out this round with me.' 'Well,' I growled, 'If you are going to use your Priesthood on me I guess I'll have to, but you will have to show me how.' The caddy sat the ball on the little peg and I swung at it—I was very mad. I swung and knocked that ball a quarter of a mile down the fairway. Never since, in all my golf playing have I knocked a ball so far, and I have tried so hard and so many times to do it. After much persuasion by Pres. Smith and others, I took to playing golf and learned that Pres. Smith was right. Nothing I can do that relaxes me half as much as two hours on the golf course. I can return to the office and unravel problems that seemed unsolvable when I was tired and tense."[15]

MISSION TO JAPAN

On July 24, 1901, Heber and three companions (Horace Ensign, Louis Kelsch, and Alma Taylor) left Salt Lake to open the first mission in Japan. Sailing on the *Empress of India*, the quartet arrived in Yokohama Harbor on August 12. On Sunday, September 21, the missionaries climbed the hill of Ohmori. Forming a circle, they sang and prayed for the Spirit. Elder Grant offered the dedicatory prayer, "the greatest prayer of [his] life."[16] Alma O. Taylor said Elder Grant's "tongue was loosed and the Spirit rested mightily upon him; so much so that we felt the angels of God were near for our hearts burned within us. . . . I never experienced such a peaceful influence or heard such a powerful prayer before. Every word penetrated into my very bones and I could of wept for joy."[17]

The missionaries worked very hard to understand the culture and to master the language. The work was slow and difficult. When Heber was released in September 1903, he had baptized only two people. Though discouraged over the lack of success, he was buoyed by a spiritual witness that Japan would one day become "one of the most successful missions ever established in the Church," one that would "astonish the world in years to come."[18] The Japanese mission was closed in 1924 with only 174 converts in twenty-three years. The mission reopened in 1948. When President Gordon B. Hinckley visited Japan in 1996, there was a temple, over one hundred thousand members, twenty-five stakes, and nine missions. President Hinckley said, "If President Grant were here now,

Left to right: Goro Takahashi, who was a friend to the early missionaries in Japan, and Elders Louis A. Kelsch, Horace S. Ensign, Heber J. Grant, and Alma O. Taylor. Elder Grant served as president of the first mission in Japan from August 12, 1901, to September 8, 1903.[10]

he would weep with gratitude. . . . I see such strength I never dreamed of in this land."[19]

CENTENNIAL OF THE ORGANIZATION OF THE CHURCH

While there were many centennial celebrations of key restoration events during President Grant's administration, the most notable was the one hundredth anniversary of the organization of the Church at the Peter Whitmer farm in Fayette, New York. Held in the Tabernacle as part of the April 1930 general conference, the First Presidency prepared a special message, read by President Grant, in which members were exhorted to keep the commandments and to "rededicate their lives to the service of the Master and the establishment of his

An Address Given to the "Great and Progressive Nation of Japan"

Soon after arriving in Japan, President Grant published an address entitled "The Great and Progressive Nation of Japan." He declared, "As an Apostle and a Minister of the Most High God I salute and invite you to consider the important message which we bear. . . . Our mission is one of duty. We have been commanded of God to proclaim his word and will to the world. It is by divine authority that we act. . . . By this authority we turn the divine key, which opens the kingdom of heaven to the inhabitants of Japan."[9]

kingdom upon the earth."[20] The congregation was then led in the Hosanna Shout. A pageant, *The Message of the Ages*, was written for the occasion and was eventually seen by over 135,000 people. On this occasion, B. H. Roberts also presented to the Church his six-volume work, *A Comprehensive History of the Church*.

A Generous, Compassionate Spirit

When Heber was about twelve years old, a boarder by the name of Colossians Alex G. Hawes moved into their home. Hawes was the western manager of the New York Life Insurance Company and became one of Heber's closest friends. Twenty-five years later, when the nation was in economic upheaval, Heber was close to losing his business. Mr. Hawes learned of it and wanted to help. He went to every commercial bank in the city but was unsuccessful in securing a loan. Finally, he persuaded a savings bank to lend him money when he agreed to put up his own home as collateral. When Heber heard of the magnanimous gesture, he said, "I could not hold back the tears of gratitude that filled my eyes, to think that a man of the world would make such an offer as this to me in my time of distress."[21] Heber emulated that goodwill for the remainder of his life. It was common for Heber to pay off the mortgage or the taxes of a widow, to support a missionary, to employ the unemployed, to cover the medical expenses of the sick or those incurred by a young couple with the birth of a new baby, or to pay funeral expenses. Paintings and books, numbering well over 100,000 in his lifetime, were given as gifts.

Marriage and Family Relationships

Both members of the Salt Lake Thirteenth Ward, Heber and Lucy Stringham were longtime acquaintances. They frequently walked home from church together. Their friendship developed into love, and they were married in the St. George Temple on November 1, 1877. The trip from Utah County to St. George was difficult at that time and took several days each way. Despite the suggestion from many of his friends

Heber Made History While Commemorating It

President Grant had a deep love and appreciation for Church history. In 1926, the Church bought the Peter Whitmer farm in Fayette, New York, where the Church was organized. In 1928, a transaction was completed wherein 283 acres were acquired in Palmyra, including the Hill Cumorah and the Sacred Grove. A monument was dedicated at Hill Cumorah in 1935 and the annual Hill Cumorah pageant, *America's Witness for Christ*, began production in 1937. That same year, part of the Martin Harris farm, near Palmyra, was purchased and the Church began acquiring property in Nauvoo, including the former temple site. Liberty Jail was procured in 1939 and Spring Hill, Missouri, Adam-ondi-Ahman, was purchased in 1943. As William Mulder noted, "Heber J. Grant's administration has made history while commemorating it."[11]

that they not make the journey, Heber was determined to marry in the temple, no matter the sacrifice. Heber and Lucy were married for sixteen years and had six children: Susan (Rachel), Lucy (Lutie), Florence, Edith, Anna, and Heber, who died at age seven of a hip disease. For much of their marriage, Lucy struggled with her health. Heber responded with care and sensitivity. Daughter Lucy Cannon recalled, "For six months I was with my mother while she was receiving treatment in a California hospital, and as often as was possible he was with us. Flowers came at frequent intervals; fruit, dainties, new clothes—everything he could send her was hers. Almost every day a letter reached her. . . . I remember the Sister Superior (we were in a Catholic Hospital) saying . . . that in all her years of nursing she had never had any man treat his wife as considerately."[22] Despite his care, Lucy died on January 3, 1893, at age thirty-four.

On May 26, 1884, Heber married his second wife, Augusta Winters, and they had a daughter, Mary. Augusta traveled widely with Heber, and they shared many wonderful experiences together. One of the happiest periods of their marriage was the year Augusta and Mary spent with Heber as he presided over the mission in Japan. Augusta was well educated and a gifted writer. She was also loving and compassionate. She cared for the nine children left behind by the

Lucy Stringham, Heber's first wife.[12]

the British and European Missions. Emily and the four girls traveled extensively, enjoying the cultural, historical, and natural beauties of that part of the world. She died of cancer on May 25, 1908, at the age of fifty-one, seventeen months after returning from that mission.

To President Grant, the family was of utmost importance. There were many family outings—picnics, Church activities, dances, and drives through the city. Literature and culture were emphasized. There were weekly visits to the Salt Lake theater. There were daily family prayers, usually preceded by the singing of a hymn. The values and blessings of Church service were taught. "I am converted," he said, "to the thought that the way to peace and happiness in life is by giving service."[24] He also taught, "Every Latter-day Saint ought to be a lifter and not a leaner."[25] Each Thursday was temple night. Endowed family members went to dinner and then did ordinance work in the Salt Lake Temple. When away from home, Heber wrote letters to his family, literally thousands of them over the years, in which he shared experiences and impressions.

deaths of Lucy and Emily (Heber's third wife), treating them like her own. She served on the Young Women General Board. Her rule in life was to "like to do what I have to do, and . . . not want anything I cannot have."[23] She outlived Heber and ministered sweetly to him when his health failed. She died June 1, 1951, at the age of ninety-four.

The day after marrying Augusta, Heber married Emily Wells. They were blessed with four daughters, Martha "Dessie" Deseret, Grace, Emily, and Frances, and a son, Daniel, who died of pneumonia at age five. To avoid prosecution for plural marriage, Emily lived the first six years of their marriage in exile—first in England, where her father Daniel H. Wells served as mission president, and later in Manassa, Colorado. The difficulty of exile, for Emily, contrasted sharply with the happiness later experienced when she and the children accompanied Heber as he presided over

Huldah Augusta Winters, Heber's second wife.

Motherhood

"Motherhood is near to divinity. It is the highest, holiest service to be assumed by mankind. It places her who honors its holy calling and service next to the angels."[13]

"The mother in the family far more than the father is the one who instils in the hearts of the children a testimony, and love of the gospel."[14]

"Without the devotion and absolute testimony of the living God in the hearts of our mothers this Church would die."[15]

President Grant's legacy of service has been carried on by his posterity. Lucy Cannon served as the general president of the Young Women and Martha "Dessie" Deseret (Boyle) served in the general Primary presidency. Susan (Rachel), who married John H. Taylor, later of the First Council of the Seventy, served on the Young Women General Board, Frances Bennett served on the Primary General Board, and Mary (Judd) served on the Relief Society General Board. Edith married Clifford E. Young, later an Assistant to the Twelve, and Florence married Nicholas G. Smith, future Presiding Patriarch and Assistant to the Twelve. Emily married Axel

Madsen and became the mother of Truman G. Madsen, a well-known scholar, author, teacher, and Church leader.

DEATH OF PRESIDENT HEBER J. GRANT

Monday, May 14, 1945, marked the last day in mortality for Heber J. Grant. Businesses closed and capacity crowds filled the Tabernacle, the Assembly Hall, and the temple grounds to pay respects to their beloved leader, while thousands more listened to the funeral over KSL radio. President George Albert Smith presided and spoke along with J. Reuben Clark Jr. and David O. McKay, counselors to President Grant in the First Presidency. President Smith said Heber was a giant among men; a great missionary; deeply interested in youth; one who radiated hope, courage, and peace and was more determined, faithful, and anxious to make others happy than anyone he knew.[26] President J. Reuben Clark Jr. said President Grant was a "rare spirit"[27] and "was of the great ones of the earth."[28] President McKay described Heber as persevering, honest in all his dealings, uncompromising with evil, sympathetic with the unfortunate, magnanimous to the highest degree, faithful to every trust, considerate, and loyal to friends, to truth, and to God.[29]

Portrait taken in Liverpool, England, in 1905. Front row: Emily, Heber's daughter, and Heber J. Grant. Back row: Martha "Dessie" Deseret, Frances Marion, Emily Harris Wells (Heber's third wife), and Grace.

TEACHINGS OF PRESIDENT
HEBER J. GRANT

◆

KEEP THE COMMANDMENTS AND DO YOUR DUTY

O f reading the Book of Mormon as a young boy, Heber said, "I fell in love with Nephi, and more than any other character—of course excepting the Savior—his life, his example, his teachings have been the guiding stars of my life."[30] Nephi's example influenced the central theme of President Grant's administration: "There is but one path of safety for the Latter-day Saints, and that is the path of duty. It is not a testimony only . . . that will save you and me; but it is the keeping of the commandments of God. . . . I say to all Latter-day Saints: keep the commandments of God. That is my keynote—just these few words: keep the commandments of God!"[31]

One of President Grant's favorite hymns was "Do What Is Right." "There is no danger," he said, "of any man or woman losing his or her faith in this Church if he or she is humble and prayerful and obedient to duty."[32] "The devil is ready to

The Duty of Parents

"The Lord has told us that it is the duty of every husband and wife to . . . multiply and replenish the earth, so that the legions of choice spirits waiting for their tabernacles of flesh may come here and move forward under God's great design to become perfect souls. . . . By bringing these choice spirits to earth, each father and each mother assumes . . . an obligation of the most sacred kind, because the fate of that spirit in the eternities to come, the blessings or punishments which shall await it in the hereafter, depend, in great part, upon the care, the teachings, the training which the parents shall give to that spirit. . . . No loftier duty than this can be assumed by mortals."[16]

blind our eyes with the things of this world, and he would gladly rob us of eternal life. . . . But . . . no power will ever be given to him to overthrow any Latter-day Saint [who] is keeping the commandments of God [and] . . . doing [his] duty."[33] "As we keep the commandments of God . . . we become full of charity, long-suffering and love . . . and increase in all those things that go to make us noble and god-like. . . . It is by the performance of the plain, simple, everyday duties that devolve upon us that we grow in the spirit of God."[34]

THE WORD OF WISDOM

Heber J. Grant spoke more often and more adamantly about the Word of Wisdom than any other prophet. Elder Joseph B. Wirthlin said, "I believe the Lord inspired President Heber J. Grant to emphasize it frequently and forcefully to counter the media that was becoming increasingly sophisticated and persuasive during his time."[35] Some Church members wondered if he would ever speak on anything else. President Grant said, "There is seldom a conference when someone does not take it upon himself to tell us: 'Please do not speak on the Word of Wisdom. We hear it so much, we are sick and tired of it.' [But] . . . no . . . Latter-day Saint [who] is keeping the Word of Wisdom is ever sick and tired of hearing it. . . . I thank God nearly every day of my life for the Word of Wisdom."[36]

Part of his motivation for teaching the Word of Wisdom came from seeing the life of a friend, with whom he had played baseball, ruined because of tobacco and alcohol. The young man overcame smoking and served a faithful mission. Upon his release, however, he resumed the tobacco habit. His smoking led to alcohol abuse and to the eventual loss of his virtue. He was excommunicated from the Church and died at a young age. At his grave, Heber vowed he would

Heber's Life Spared by Obedience to the Word of Wisdom

Heber believed that, on several occasions, his life was spared because he lived the Word of Wisdom. One of those occasions was in May 1897 when Heber suffered a ruptured appendix and developed advanced peritonitis. Emergency surgery was scheduled. President Joseph F. Smith rushed to the hospital. President Grant said, "There were nine doctors present and eight said I had to die. The chief surgeon . . . turned to President Joseph F. Smith, and said, 'Mr. Smith you need not think . . . that this man shall live. . . . If he [did] it would be a miracle, and this is not the day of miracles.' . . . I asked [the doctor who believed I would pull through] why he disagreed with the other [doctors]. . . . He said: 'I have felt the pulse . . . of thousands of patients . . . in many hospitals, but I never felt a pulse just like yours. . . . Your heart never missed one single, solitary beat.' What kind of heart did I have? I had a heart that had pure blood in it, that was not contaminated by tea, coffee or liquor. That is why the poison in my system was overcome."[17]

do everything in his power to prevent the same thing from happening to others.[37]

In a general epistle to the Church on October 3, 1942, the First Presidency said:

"Drink brings cruelty into the home; it walks arm in arm with poverty; its companions are disease and plague; it puts chastity to flight; it knows neither honesty nor fair dealing; it is a total stranger to truth; it drowns conscience; it is the bodyguard of evil; it curses all who touch it.

"Drink has brought more woe and misery, broken more hearts, wrecked more homes, committed more crimes, filled more coffins, than all the wars the world has suffered. . . . We ask . . . every officer in every Church organization, strictly to keep the Word of Wisdom from this moment forward. If any feels too weak to do this, we must ask him to step aside. . . .

"We ask all Church presiding officers immediately to set their official houses in order."[38]

President Grant acknowledged that obedience to the Word of Wisdom would not prevent disappointment, trials, or illness in life, yet he unhesitatingly promised that the minds of the obedient would be clearer and able to advance farther and faster,[39] that they would become "one of the most wealthy people in the world," would have "increased vigor of body . . . [and] mind . . . would grow spiritually . . . [and] have a more direct line of communication with God,"[40] and would have greater power to resist the temptations associated with the law of chastity.[41]

PROHIBITION

President Grant's strong testimony of the Word of Wisdom was particularly evident during Prohibition. In 1918, concerned about the problems being created in American society by the consumption of alcohol, Congress submitted to the states the Eighteenth Amendment, which prohibited "the manufacture, sale, or transportation of intoxicating liquors." The amendment was ratified and the Prohibition era officially began at midnight on January 16, 1920. Immediately, efforts to repeal Prohibition began and gained widespread national support over the next decade. Meanwhile, the Word of Wisdom had come to be regarded as a binding commandment in the Church. Obedience was a prerequisite to Melchizedek Priesthood ordination and to receiving or officiating in the ordinances of the priesthood, including those of the temple.

As efforts intensified to repeal Prohibition, President Grant and other General Authorities pleaded with members to oppose the movement. In September 1932, the First Presidency stated the Church's position on Prohibition and asked members to uphold the law. In October 1933, President Grant said, "Let me promise you right here and now that if you vote for the repeal of the Eighteenth Amendment, there will be a great many more professing Latter-day Saints who will be drunkards. . . . I request each and every Latter-day Saint within the sound of my voice to . . . not vote for the repeal of the Eighteenth Amendment."[42] Despite the Prophet's importunings, Utah became the thirty-sixth (and deciding state) to vote for the repeal of Prohibition. In October 1934, President Grant said, "I have never felt so humiliated in my life over anything as that the State of Utah voted for the repeal of prohibition. . . . I could not help but feel humiliated when the

Latter-day Saints knew as well as they knew that they lived that [the Lord] wanted them to remain true to the Word of Wisdom and not vote for the repeal of Prohibition."[43] Years later, Elder George Albert Smith recalled, "From this very stand he pleaded with us not to repeal [Prohibition]. He didn't speak as Heber J. Grant, the man, he spoke as the President of the Church and the representative of our Heavenly Father. . . . Yet . . . there were enough Latter-day Saints . . . who paid no attention to what the Lord wanted, [and] ignored what He had said through his prophet. . . . [They] are [now] paying the penalty and will continue to do so until they turn away from their foolishness and desire with all their hearts to do what our Heavenly Father desires us to do."[44]

THE GREAT DEPRESSION AND THE CHURCH WELFARE PROGRAM

The 1920s were characterized by rapid economic expansion and a rising standard of living for most Americans. Machinery made it possible for many industries to produce goods faster and cheaper than ever before. Higher wages, decreased production costs, and the availability of credit made it easier for the average American to purchase items previously considered unaffordable, such as an automobile, a washing machine, or a refrigerator. Stock values nearly tripled from 1925 to 1929. Anticipating the trend would continue, many individuals, banks, and businesses invested large amounts of money in the stock market. On October 24, 1929, Black Thursday, stock prices plummeted. Stockholders, especially those who had acquired stock on credit, panicked and sold their shares at deflated prices. Individual fortunes were lost. Banks and businesses closed. At the same time, farm prices dropped nearly 40 percent. Many farmers defaulted on their loans, forcing hundreds of banks to close.

Even before these events occurred, the Church had already implemented a program, under the direction of the

Gordon B. Hinckley Was Inspired by President Grant

As a teenager, President Gordon B. Hinckley heard President Grant speak. He later recalled, "To me it was always impressive when this tall man stood to speak. Some kind of electricity passed through my boyish frame. His voice rang out in testimony of the Book of Mormon. When he said it was true, I knew it was true. He spoke with great power on the Word of Wisdom and, without hesitation, promised blessings to the people if they would observe it. I have often thought of the human misery, the pain that has resulted from the smoking of cigarettes, the poverty that has resulted from the drinking of liquor which might have been avoided had his prophetic counsel been followed."[18]

Presiding Bishopric and the Relief Society General Board, to help the needy. In 1933, at the height of the Depression, the First Presidency introduced the Church Security Plan and stressed the "necessity of living righteously, of avoiding extravagance, of cultivating habits of thrift, economy, and industry, of living strictly within their incomes, and of laying aside something . . . for the times of greater stress that may come to us."[45] As unemployment continued to rise and thousands of Church members were being supported by public relief funds, President Grant asked Harold B. Lee, president of the Pioneer Stake, to determine how to implement the welfare program Churchwide. The inspiration of Harold B. Lee enabled the First Presidency to announce the Church Welfare Program a year later in the October 1936 general conference.

The primary purpose of the Church Welfare Program was "to set up . . . a system under which the curse of idleness would be done away with, the evils of a dole abolished, and independence, industry, thrift and self respect be once more established amongst our people. The aim of the church is to help the people to help themselves. Work is to be re-enthroned as the ruling principle of the lives of our Church membership."[46] President Grant taught that "the law of success, here and hereafter, is to have a humble and a prayerful heart, and to work, WORK, WORK."[47] "Work is pleasing to the Lord" and "keeps people young."[48] "Let all of us be industrious and useful to the full extent of our strength and ability,"[49] and "let us hope that the spirit of independence that was with our pioneer fathers may be re-awakened in us, and that none who are Latter-day

Saints . . . will be guilty of being idle."[50] To jump-start the Church Welfare Program, President Grant donated a large dry farm he owned, valued at more than $80,000. Members were counseled to store a year's supply of food, clothing, and fuel, and to pay off the mortgages on their homes.[51] In 1938 the first Deseret Industries store was opened to provide low-cost goods and employment to the needy.

President Grant, who repeatedly taught members to live within their means and to avoid debt, said, "If there is any one thing that will bring peace and contentment into the human heart, and into the family, it is to live within our means. And if there is any one thing that is grinding and discouraging and disheartening, it is to have debts and obligations that one cannot meet."[52] He believed debt and speculation were the main reasons for the Depression and that if the Saints had listened to the advice of President Joseph F. Smith to not get into debt, the Saints would have been affected very little by the Depression.[53] President Grant admonished the Saints to not "mortgage their future" by purchasing "luxuries" or "even ordinary necessities of life" that they could not afford and warned that those who did were "laying burdens upon themselves that [would] come back with compound interest to cause them great trouble and humiliation."[54]

Tithing was a common theme. Elder Dallin H. Oaks said, "No prophet of the Lord in modern times has preached the law of tithing more fervently than Heber J. Grant."[55] President Grant said, "The law of financial prosperity . . . is to be an honest tithepayer. . . . And when I say prosperity I am not thinking of it in terms of dollars and cents alone, although as a rule the Latter-day Saints who are the best tithepayers are the most prosperous men, financially; but what I count as real prosperity . . . is the growth in a knowledge of God, and in a testimony, and in the power to live the gospel."[56] During the Depression, noted Elder Oaks, "some of our bishops observed that members who paid their tithing were able to support their families more effectively than those who did not. [They] tended to keep their employment, enjoy good health, and be free from the most devastating effects of economic and spiritual depression."[57]

Understanding how difficult the law of tithing was for many of the Saints, President Grant reassured them that "the harder it is for an individual to comply with requirements of the Lord in the payment of his tithing, the greater the benefit when he finally does pay it. The Lord loves a generous giver."[58] "I believe people are blessed in proportion to their liberality. I am not saying that they always make more dollars, perhaps, than the other man. But [they] . . . increase in the faith and in the testimony and the knowledge of the divinity of the work in which we are engaged. . . . They grow in capacity and ability more rapidly than those that are stingy."[59]

WORLD WAR II

President Grant consistently showed awareness and sensitivity to world events and how they affected the Saints and

Heber Gains a Testimony of Tithing

"In a fast meeting Heber attended as a boy, Bishop Edwin Woolley spoke on the subject of tithing and testified that the Lord would reward the faithful, fourfold. Heber had 50 dollars he intended to deposit in the bank, but upon hearing his bishop's testimony, he handed him the entire sum as tithing. Bishop Woolley took five dollars, placed it in a drawer and returned the rest to Heber, telling him that was his full share. Confidently, Heber asked, 'Didn't you preach here today that the Lord rewards fourfold? My mother is a widow, and she needs two hundred dollars.' Bishop Woolley replied: 'My boy, do you believe that if I take this other forty-five dollars you will get your two hundred dollars quicker?' 'Certainly,' Heber responded. Impressed by Heber's faith, Bishop Woolley took the money. Heber testified, "While walking from that fast meeting to the place where I worked, an idea popped into my head. I sent a telegram to a man asking him how many bonds of a certain kind he would buy at a specified price within forty-eight hours. . . . He was a man whom I did not know. I had never spoken to him in my life, but I had seen him a time or two on the streets of Salt Lake. He wired back that he wanted as many as I could get. My profit on that transaction was $218.50. Someone will say that it would have happened anyway. I do not think it would have happened. I do not think I would have got the idea."[19]

the worldwide mission of the Church. On August 24, 1939, when the outbreak of World War II seemed inevitable, the First Presidency sent word that all missionaries in Germany were to be evacuated and transferred to neutral countries. A few days later on September 3, Great Britain and France declared war on Germany. Within four days, all missionaries serving in Europe began to be withdrawn from their respective countries. In the October 1939 general conference, the First Presidency said:

"God is grieved by war and . . . He will hold subject to the eternal punishments of His will those who wage it unrighteously. . . . We call the unrighteous of the world to repentance. . . . We earnestly implore . . . all peoples whoever and wherever they are to banish hate from their lives, to fill their hearts with charity, patience, long-suffering, and forgiveness."[60]

On September 16, 1940, the Burke-Wadsworth Act was passed by Congress and signed by President Franklin D. Roosevelt, signifying the first time in American history that a draft had been instituted in peace time. The First Presidency immediately sent a letter to priesthood leaders regarding the calling of missionaries under the provisions of the act. The letter made it clear that the Church would not knowingly call anyone on a mission who was otherwise eligible for the draft.[61] In Berlin, on September 27, 1940, Japan signed a pact of alliance with the Axis powers. Knowing there were members of the Church on both sides of the conflict, in all participating countries, the First Presidency counseled all servicemen to support their respective governments and to pray "day and night that God [would] turn the hearts of their leaders towards peace, that the curse of war may end."[62] Mission presidents were advised that all missionaries were to register for military service.[63] Six months later, the First Presidency informed priesthood leaders that members who had registered under the Selective Service Act were not to be recommended for missionary service if they had received notification of induction into military service.[64]

The Japanese surprise attack on Pearl Harbor occurred December 7, 1941. The next day the United States declared war on Japan. On December 11, Germany and Italy declared war on the United States, and the United States declared war on the dictatorships of Europe. Two days later, the First Presidency gave their annual Christmas message and declared that the only way to attain lasting peace was by living the gospel and by ridding us, even in war, of "all cruelty, hate, and murder."[65] Mission calls were limited to the continental Americas and to the Hawaiian Islands.[66] In 1942, the first full year of World War II for the United States, the First Presidency released thirty-six messages, with nearly half of them concerned with the war or matters related to it, including the denunciation of communism, Nazism, and fascism,[67] and formal statements of the position of the Church on war.

President Grant ensured that LDS servicemen were not forgotten. In May 1941, Hugh B. Brown, who would later serve in the Quorum of the Twelve and in the First Presidency, was appointed as servicemen's coordinator for the Church. Seventeen months later, Elder Harold B. Lee of the Twelve was called as chairman of the newly organized Church Servicemen's Committee. By the end of the war, the committee had succeeded in securing the appointments of forty-six LDS chaplains, stationed at the larger military units, and approximately one thousand group leaders, who

Position of the Church on War

On April 6, 1942, the First Presidency stated the position of the Church on war: "The Church is and must be against war. . . . [but if] . . . constitutional law . . . calls the manhood of the Church into the armed service of any country to which they owe allegiance, their highest civic duty requires that they meet that call. If, hearkening to that call and obeying those in command over them, they shall take the lives of those who fight against them, that will not make of them murderers, nor subject them to the penalty that God has prescribed for those who kill. . . . To our young men who go into the service, no matter whom they serve or where, we say live clean, keep the commandments of the Lord, pray to Him constantly to preserve you in truth and righteousness. . . . The Lord will be always near you; He will comfort you; you will feel His presence in the hour of your greatest tribulation. He will guard and protect you to the full extent that accords with His all-wise purpose."[20]

were set apart to organize and preside over services at bases across the world. Upon entering military service, all LDS servicemen were given pocket-sized copies of the Book of Mormon, *Principles of the Gospel*, and a miniature version of the *Church News*.

President Grant also thought of the servicemen's families. He sought to comfort the mothers, wives, and children left at home to wait for the return of their loved ones. For example, as part of a First Presidency message of October 6, 1939, he prayed that "God [would] bring to all bereft and grieving mothers the sweet consolation of His Spirit, to the widow robbed of her helpmeet a faith that God [would] help her in her lonely struggle for a livelihood for her children, to those fatherless children a will to help their mother in her fight for their welfare and existence."[68]

Kent R. Brooks

Associate Professor of Church History and Doctrine, PhD
Brigham Young University

President Heber J. Grant in 1945, at age 88.[22]

Final Testimony of President Grant

"The most glorious thing that has ever happened in the history of the world since the Savior himself lived on earth, is that God himself saw fit to visit the earth with his beloved, only begotten Son, our Redeemer and Savior, and to appear to the boy Joseph. . . . I bear witness to you that I do know that God lives, that he hears and answers prayer; that Jesus is the Christ, the Redeemer of the world; that Joseph Smith was and is a prophet of the true and living God; and that Brigham Young and those who have succeeded him were, and are, likewise prophets of God. . . . Time and time again my heart has been melted, my eyes have wept tears of gratitude for the knowledge that he lives and that this gospel . . . is in very deed the plan of life and salvation . . . the Gospel of the Lord Jesus Christ."[21]

NOTES

1. Heber J. Grant, "Faith-Promoting Experiences," *Millennial Star*, November 19, 1931, 760.
2. Heber J. Grant, CR, April 1935, 13.
3. Preston W. Parkinson, comp. *The Utah Woolley Family* (Salt Lake City), 126.
4. Heber J. Grant, CR, October 1919, 32.
5. Heber J. Grant, CR, April 1935, 14.
6. Heber J. Grant, CR, October 1941, 12.
7. Heber J. Grant, *Gospel Standards*, comp. G. Homer Durham, 9th ed. (Salt Lake City: Deseret News Press, 1941), 355.
8. Heber J. Grant, CR, April 1901, 63–64.
9. Heber J. Grant, CR, April 1900, 61.

10. Joan Oviatt, "I Have Learned to Sing," *Ensign*, September 1948, 43.

11. Heber J. Grant, CR, April 1937, 11.

12. Heber M. Wells, "President Grant—The Business Man," *Improvement Era* (November 1936): 689.

13. Grant, *Gospel Standards*, 194.

14. Ibid., 195–96.

15. Rulon Killian, Missionary Journal typescript, LDS Church Archives, Salt Lake City, Utah. Information provided courtesy of Alexander L. Baugh, Department of Church History, Brigham Young University.

16. Susan Arrington Madsen, *The Lord Needed a Prophet* (Salt Lake City: Deseret Book, 1990), 113.

17. R. Lanier Britsch, *From the East: The History of the Latter-day Saints in Asia, 1851–1996* (Salt Lake City: Deseret Book, 1998), 50; see also Alma O. Taylor, Journal B, September 1, 1901, L. Tom Perry Special Collections, Harold B. Lee Library, Brigham Young University, Provo, UT.

18. Jerry P. Cahill, "News of the Church," *Ensign*, January 1981, 74.

19. "President Hinckley Visits Asian Saints, Dedicates Hong Kong Temple," *Ensign*, August 1996, 74.

20. Heber J. Grant, CR, April 1930, 3.

21. Heber J. Grant, CR, October 1919, 44.

22. Lucy Grant Cannon, "A Father Who Is Loved and Honored," *Improvement Era* (November 1936): 682.

23. Augusta Winters Grant, "A Tribute to Our Pioneer Martyrs," *Improvement Era*, November 1929, 17.

24. Grant, *Gospel Standards*, 187.

25. Heber J. Grant, "Settlement," *Improvement Era* (January 1941): 56.

26. "President Heber J. Grant," *Improvement Era* (June 1945): 332.

27. Ibid., 333.

28. Bryant S. Hinckley, *Heber J. Grant: Highlights in the Life of a Great Leader* (Salt Lake City: Deseret Book, 1951), 264.

29. "President Heber J. Grant," *Improvement Era* (June 1945): 334.

30. Heber J. Grant, CR, April 1934, 11.

31. Heber J. Grant, CR, April 1945, 9–10.

32. Heber J. Grant, CR, April 1934, 131.

33. Heber J. Grant, CR, April 1944, 10.

34. Heber J. Grant, CR, April 1900, 22.

35. Joseph B. Wirthlin, "Deep Roots," *Ensign*, November 1994, 77.

36. Heber J. Grant, CR, April 1937, 13.

37. Heber J. Grant, "Answering Tobacco's Challenge," *Improvement Era* (June 1931): 450.

38. Heber J. Grant, CR, October 1942, 8–9.

39. Heber J. Grant, CR, April 1925, 9–10.

40. Heber J. Grant, "Safeguard," *Improvement Era* (February 1941): 73.

41. Heber J. Grant,, CR, October 1944, 7–8.

42. Heber J. Grant, CR, October 1933, 6.

43. James H. Wallis, "President Grant—Defender of the Word of Wisdom," *Improvement Era* (November 1936): 698.

44. George Albert Smith, CR, October 1943, 47.

45. *MFP*, 5:333–34.

46. Heber J. Grant,, CR, October 1936, 3.

47. Heber J. Grant,, "Work, and Keep Your Promises," *Improvement Era* (January 1900): 195.

48. Heber J. Grant, CR, October 1938, 3, 15.

49. Heber J. Grant, CR, April 1945, 8.

50. Heber J. Grant, CR, October 1937, 10–11.

51. Heber J. Grant, CR, April 1937, 26.

52. Grant, *Gospel Standards*, 111.

53. *Relief Society Magazine*, May 1932, 299.

54. Heber J. Grant, CR, April 1926, 7.

55. Dallin H. Oaks, "Tithing," *Ensign*, May 1994, 33.

56. Heber J. Grant, CR, April 1925, 10.

57. Oaks, "Tithing," 33.

58. Grant, *Gospel Standards*, 62.

59. Ibid., 64.

60. *MFP*, 6:92.

61. Ibid., 6:119.

62. Ibid., 6:116.

63. Ibid., 6:144.

64. Ibid., 6:119–20.

65. Ibid., 6:141.

66. Ibid.

67. Heber J. Grant, CR, October 1942, 15.

68. *MFP*, 6:91.

SIDEBAR AND PHOTO NOTES

1. Heber J. Grant, CR, June 1, 1919, 4.

2. Heber J. Grant, CR, April 1936, 10–11.

3. Photograph found on page 49 of Robert C. Freeman et al., *On This Day in the Church: An Illustrated Almanac of the Latter-day Saints* (Salt Lake City: Deseret Book, 2002).

4. Heber J. Grant, CR, April 1934, 14.

5. *Improvement Era*, no. 6 (June 1945).

6. Photograph courtesy of Bertram T. and Jean C. Willis, part of CES Presidents of the Church slide set, J.

7. Photograph of revelation courtesy of Don O. Thorpe, part of CES Presidents of the Church slide set, J.

8. Photograph courtesy of Bob Freeman.

9. Bryant S. Hinckley, *Heber J. Grant: Highlights in the Life of a Great Leader*, 103–4.

10. Photograph from *Teachings of Presidents of the Church: Heber J. Grant* (Salt Lake City: The Church of Jesus Christ of Latter-day Saints, 2002), 82.

11. William Mulder, "Quarter Century," *Improvement Era* (November 1943).

12. Photograph from *Improvement Era* (1936).

13. "Message from the First Presidency," CR, October 1942, 12–13; read by President J. Reuben Clark Jr.

14. *Gospel Standards*, 150–51.

15. Heber J. Grant, CR, April 1930, 20.

16. "Message from the First Presidency," CR, October 1942, 12–13; read by President J. Reuben Clark Jr.

17. Heber J. Grant, CR, April 1933, 10–11.

18. Gordon B. Hinckley, "Believe His Prophets," *Ensign*, May 1992, 51.

19. Heber J. Grant, CR, August 1939, 457.

20. *MFP*, 6:148.

21. Heber J. Grant, CR, April 1945, 10.

22. Photograph from *Teachings of Presidents of the Church: HJG*, 210.

Chapter Eight
GEORGE ALBERT SMITH

LIFE AND TIMES

1870	April 4	Born in Salt Lake City, Utah
1875	September 1	Grandfather George A. Smith, for whom he was named, died
1880	October 27	Father, John Henry Smith, ordained an Apostle
1891		Served mission to Southern Utah settlements in behalf of the YMMIA
1892	May 25	Married Lucy Emily Woodruff in the Manti Temple
1892–94		Served full-time mission to the Southern States Mission
1898		Appointed receiver of the U.S. Land Office and disbursing agent for Utah
1903	October 8	Sustained member of the Quorum of the Twelve Apostles
1904		Wrote a personal creed to govern his life
1907	June 10	Purchased the Joseph Smith Sr. farm in Manchester, New York
1913		The Church inaugurated the Scouting program as a part of the YMMIA
1919–21		Served as president of the European Mission
1931		Elected member of the National Executive Board of the Boy Scouts of America
1937	November 5	Lucy, his wife of forty-five years, died
1943	July 1	Set apart as President of the Quorum of the Twelve Apostles
1945	May 21	Sustained as eighth President of The Church of Jesus Christ of Latter-day Saints
1945		Missionary work in Europe resumed following the end of World War II
1945	September 23	Dedicated Idaho Falls Temple; temple ordinances are provided in the Spanish language in the Mesa Arizona Temple
1945	November 3	Met U.S. President Harry S. Truman to obtain assistance to transport supplies for postwar Europe
1947	July	Led Churchwide celebration of the centennial of the arrival of Mormon pioneers in Utah
1947	December 1	Extensive microfilming of European genealogical records began
1947	December 31	The Church realized its first one million members
1949	October	First public television broadcast of general conference aired
1950	May–June	Dedicated monuments to Brigham Young in Whitingham, Vermont, and Washington, DC
1951	April 4	Died in Salt Lake City, Utah, at age eighty-one

BIOGRAPHICAL HIGHLIGHTS

Born within a block of Temple Square in Salt Lake City, Utah, George Albert Smith seemed to be destined for Church service. His father, grandfather, and great-grandfather before him had all served in the leading quorums of the Church, and an unusual blessing in his youth confirmed that he too would receive significant responsibility.

Never having robust health, George Albert learned to do the best he could with the energy he had. Several accidents and near-tragic experiences nearly prevented him from serving in future leadership opportunities. He served in the Southern States Mission during a time of intense bigotry but learned to love the people of the South and others throughout the world despite nationality, race, religion, or other perceived differences. George was called into the Quorum of the Twelve Apostles in 1903 and a year later wrote a personal creed that would be a guide for the remainder of his life.

Always willing to travel and teach the gospel wherever he went, Elder Smith became known as "the prophet of Christlike love." He was consistently kind to children, honored womanhood, and was solicitous to the less fortunate, including the impoverished, handicapped, sick, or injured, especially those without others to assist them. He served as President of the Church from 1945 at the death of President Heber J. Grant until April 1951, when he passed away peacefully during the annual general conference of the Church.

CONTRIBUTIONS

George Albert Smith's heritage seemed to direct his life and service. He was instrumental in obtaining a number of Church historical sites, including the Joseph Smith Sr. farm and the Sacred Grove; he negotiated for Hill Cumorah and encouraged the purchase of property in Harmony, Pennsylvania. He also participated in a reenactment of the pioneer trek. As a culmination of his efforts, he dedicated the This Is the Place Monument as part of the Church's pioneer centennial celebration in 1947. He dedicated the temple in Idaho Falls and resumed work on the Los Angeles Temple following World War II.

He is perhaps best known in the Church for his work with the Lamanites and his charitable assistance to survivors of World War II in Europe. He traveled extensively throughout the world but was the first Church President to visit the Saints in Mexico and American Indian reservations in the United States. He continually emphasized that we are all God's children, and through his personal example he encouraged members to treat others with kindness.

Always an advocate for the youth of the Church, Elder Smith promoted the new Scouting program for young men and was recognized for his leadership in that program by being awarded the highest honors of the Boy Scouts of America. He was further honored by numerous other groups throughout the nation. President Smith was highly visible as the international leader of the Church and was repeatedly featured by the national press, including interviews with presidents of the United States and congressmen. His personal creed continues to the present as an example of Christlike attributes and the vision of what is needed to heal the ills of society.

TEACHINGS

Repeatedly, as the President of the Church, President George Albert Smith memorialized the contributions of our predecessors in government and the Church. He encouraged Latter-day Saints to pray for and honor the leaders of their nation, irrespective of their country of origin, to be involved in the political process to elect principled representatives and to honor the legacy of their heritage and history.

A constant theme in his talks and his personal activities was to pay tribute to the Church's pioneers of the past. His efforts to do this encompassed many decades. His frequent travels around the nation were likewise an attempt to pay homage to those who laid the foundations we currently build upon.

President Smith championed the cause of the less fortunate in his public addresses and in his daily life. He honored Helen Keller and advocated assistance for the nation's sightless. He often fed the homeless and unemployed. He visited American Indians in their own homes and established programs to assist them spiritually and temporally. Likewise he visited the Saints in Mexico and called members of the Quorum of the Twelve Apostles to look after their needs, as well as their counterparts in other Latin American countries and in the Pacific Islands.

Honoring God's children throughout the world was a means of President Smith honoring the Lord himself. He offered poignant testimony of the Prophet Joseph Smith, of the Restoration of this latter-day work, and of the Savior Himself. He further reminded Church members to follow the counsel of their inspired leaders.

LIFE OF
GEORGE ALBERT SMITH

George Albert Smith came from one of the most prominent families in the Church, and his life stands as an exemplary witness to his family's long tradition of Latter-day Saint Church leadership. John Smith, George Albert's great-grandfather, was a brother of Joseph Smith Sr. and an early convert to the restored Church. John served as the Patriarch to the Church for several years (1849–54) and as an Assistant Counselor to the Prophet Joseph Smith (1837–44). He was a pivotal leader in five separate stakes ranging from Kirtland, Ohio, to Salt Lake City, Utah.

John's son George A. Smith served as one of the youngest members of Zion's Camp, where he endured the privations of that march along with his cousin Joseph Smith the Prophet. Following the martyrdom of the Prophet Joseph, George A. was called a member of the Quorum of the Twelve Apostles in 1839 at the age of twenty-one, and as such was the youngest man called to that Quorum in this dispensation. George

Joseph Smith's Heritage

Speaking of the Prophet Joseph Smith's heritage, President Brigham Young declared, "It was decreed in the counsels of eternity, long before the foundations of the earth were laid, that [Joseph Smith] should be the man, in the last dispensation of this world, to bring forth the word of God to the people, and receive the fulness of the keys and power of the Priesthood of the Son of God. The Lord had his eye upon him, and upon his father, and upon his father's father, and upon their progenitors clear back to Abraham, and from Abraham to the flood, from the flood to Enoch, and from Enoch to Adam. He has watched that family and that blood as it has circulated from its fountain to the birth of that man."[1] George Albert Smith took part in this great heritage as the grandson of George A. Smith, the Prophet's faithful cousin.

A. left Nauvoo with the refugee Saints and traveled west with the main body of the exiled pioneers. In 1868 Brigham Young selected him to be a counselor in the First Presidency, a position he retained until his death in 1875. His namesake son George Albert was killed in northern Arizona by the Navajo Indians in November 1862.[1] However, another son, John Henry Smith, had his life spared on a number of occasions and lived to be called to the Quorum of the Twelve Apostles in 1880 at age thirty-two. Following a distinguished career in that Quorum, he was called to serve in the First Presidency in 1910 as a counselor to his cousin, President Joseph F. Smith. He served in this position until his death in October 1911. John had served in the Quorum of the Twelve Apostles for twenty-three

The children of John Henry and Sarah Farr Smith. George Albert is on the far left side.

George Albert Smith as a child, about three and a half years of age.

years when his son George Albert Smith, namesake of John's father, was born in 1870.

CHILDHOOD

The second of eleven children, George Albert Smith was born April 4, 1870, to John Henry and Sarah Farr Smith. George was a responsible child, even in his tender years, and seemed to sense the significance of his heritage and potential. When his father was away serving as the European Mission president, George determined that he would plant a lawn. A lawn would have practical as well as aesthetic advantages. He financed the project himself and carried the water from the city creek to encourage its growth. When a heavy rain washed out the young, tender grass shoots, he reseeded the yard again with money he had earned and had been saving for school clothing.

Also evident in his youth were early indications of his marvelous sense of humor and an air of mischievousness. He was able to find humor and amusement in most every situation, even if it meant finding it through self-depreciation. On one occasion he took an egg, which he had borrowed from his grandmother's chicken coop, to a nearby store to trade for penny candy. The clerk gave him the candy, and as young George reached up to give him the egg, it exploded. The resulting smell drove the clerk and other customers outside. George hadn't known beforehand that the egg was old and rotten.[2] He found this experience amusing, especially in retrospect, and enjoyed sharing the experience with others.

George lived a fairly normal childhood, at least as normal as his heritage and the prominence of his family in the Church would allow, and he also showed attributes remarkable for his age and gender.

As a child he knew and was positively influenced by his grandfather and namesake, George A. Smith. George called him Grandpa Nuts because of the pine nuts that the Apostle would bring from his visits to the Church's Southern Utah settlements. Later in life, George was greatly impressed by the counsel and example of his grandfather.

George was baptized as a child in City Creek Canyon and attended the local Salt Lake City schools. In addition he had other opportunities for education that were not readily available to many of the children of Utah at that time. He spent a year in Provo at the Brigham Young Academy (BYA) in Provo and another year, 1887–88, at the University of Deseret in Salt Lake City. At the BYA his academic preparations were supervised by the venerable Karl G. Maeser. George's life was strongly influenced by Dr. Maeser, and he would often recall and quote specific statements first taught to him by his illustrious schoolmaster.

Among George's classmates at the academy were future General Authorities and statesmen with whom he would associate as an adult, including Apostle Francis M. Lyman, Senator and Apostle Reed Smoot, and George Sutherland, chief justice of the U.S. Supreme Court. These years of schooling and the associations he made because of them had a profound and lasting effect upon his future.

George Albert Smith at age sixteen.

As a result of being the second oldest in a large family, George also worked as a youth. At age thirteen he was employed by the Zion's Cooperative Mercantile Institution (ZCMI) in their clothing manufacturing operation, where he assisted in making overalls. Later, he also constructed boxes, where he excelled in his work and was given added responsibility due to his thoroughness. On one occasion, after being challenged, he made more boxes than any other employee had ever been able to make in a single day. His efficiency and hard work for ZCMI would lead to a more lucrative and prestigious job as a salesman (1888–91) for the company.

On January 16, 1884, while still thirteen years old, George Albert received a most unusual blessing. Patriarch Zebedee Coltrin, a close associate of the Prophet Joseph, went to the Smith home and announced to George's mother that he desired to bless her son and also pressed her into service as the scribe for the occasion. The blessing pronounced by Patriarch Coltrin upon the head of George Albert Smith was

as unusual in its content as it was in the way it came to him. George was told, "Thou shalt become a mighty prophet in the midst of the sons of Zion. . . . Thou are destined to become a mighty man before the Lord, for thou shalt become a mighty apostle in the Church and kingdom of God upon the earth, for none of thy father's family shall have more power with God than thou shalt have, for none shall excel thee."[3]

The blessing was prophetic, instructive, and most significant in the life of George Albert Smith. George Albert, if the blessing was to be literally fulfilled, was to represent the fourth consecutive generation of his family to serve in the leading councils of the Church. All three preceding generations had served as prophets, seers, and revelators: one as Patriarch to the Church and each of the others as senior members of the Quorum of the Twelve Apostles and as counselors

Impact of the Teachings of Karl G. Maeser

At a young age George Albert Smith attended the Brigham Young Academy in Provo, Utah, under the saintly influence of the revered Karl G. Maeser. Dr. Maeser, as he was known to many of the students, influenced the thinking and thereby the behavior of many students, including George. In later years Elder Smith paid the following tribute to Dr. Maeser.

"I love the memory of Brother Maeser. I think I have spoken of him more than any other man perhaps among those who have contributed to my education." One of the life-changing thoughts repeatedly taught by Brother Maeser that had a significant impact on young George Albert's mind was that individuals would be held accountable not only for the things that they did but also for their thoughts.

"A thirteen-year-old boy, whose thoughts galloped around as mine did, couldn't understand why I should be held accountable for my thoughts. I was sure Dr. Maeser was a truthful man, but I couldn't understand how I could be charged for my thoughts because I couldn't control my thoughts; and that worried me. . . . About two weeks after that an interpretation of what he meant came to me like a flash from the sky. It was this: of course, you will be held accountable for your thoughts. . . . Don't forget to care for these bodies of yours and keep them clean and sweet and pure, and you will do that if your thoughts are pure."[2]

in the First Presidency. George, moreover, served longer than any of his family members when he became the eighth President of the Church.

In 1891, at the age of twenty-one, George was sent by ZCMI as a traveling salesman to sell store goods in Juab, Millard, Beaver, and Parowan counties. Further, in an exhibition of unusual confidence by Church leaders, he was also called to serve a concurrent short-term mission to the stakes of Southern Utah to promote the interests of the Young Men's Mutual Improvement Association (YMMIA). He and his companion served for only about four months, but it is likely that this experience precipitated his lifelong love and work in behalf of the young men throughout the Church. While George was away, William L. Nuttle Allen, bishop of the Salt Lake Twenty-First Ward, predicted that George "would some day be an Apostle in the Church."[4] It is not apparent if George Albert ever knew of this prediction as he obviously knew of the earlier prophecy. At this time in his life, however, neither of these prophecies of his future were very important to him. He was busy focusing on other priorities in his life such as romance and the necessity of making a career for himself. Upon his return from a successful temporal and spiritual venture, he began to think seriously about marriage.

COURTSHIP AND MARRIAGE

About a year after George's return from Southern Utah, he married Lucy Emily Woodruff, daughter of Wilford Woodruff Jr. and Emily Smith, whom he had known most of his life. Lucy's grandparents were the Apostle Wilford and Phebe Whittemore Carter Woodruff and Elias and Lucy Brown Smith. Lucy's grandfathers were both distinguished Church and civic leaders. Wilford was a member of the Quorum of the Twelve and fourth President of the Church. Elias Smith was a judge in Salt Lake City and also a prominent churchman.

A Most Unusual Coincidence

In a most unusual coincidence, Elder George Albert Smith learned that the blessing given him by Elder Zebedee Coltrin at a young age was duplicated on at least one other occasion. This fact was learned when Elder Melvin J. Ballard was called to the Quorum of the Twelve Apostles and shared his own experience.

The irony of Patriarch Zebedee Coltrin's unannounced arrival at the Smith home to deliver such a significant blessing is increased when it is realized that this is not an isolated case. On January 7, 1919, Melvin J. Ballard was called to the apostleship and to serve in the Quorum of the Twelve Apostles. When he first met with others of his newly assigned quorum in the temple, he related his own experience of receiving a patriarchal blessing from Patriarch Coltrin in much the same way of that experienced by the youthful George Albert Smith. Elder Smith noted the coincidence of such an occurrence: "Such an announcement, to me was electrifying. Two great men [both just boys], living in different communities, near the same age, had each been promised [special blessings], by the same patriarch of the Church, that they would eventually become leaders in the Church, and each promise had been fulfilled to the very letter."[3]

Lucy had been living with her grandparents in Salt Lake City since the death of her mother, which brought her into close proximity with the John Henry Smith family. Although George and Lucy Emily had known each other most of their lives, it did not necessarily mean that they were always friends. George pestered Lucy Emily mercilessly by pulling her pigtails (one day he even tied her to a tree by her hair), chasing her, and teasing her—sometimes to tears. Demonstrating her own independent spirit, she reciprocated his mischievous treatment. These childhood exchanges, apparently, grew from their fondness for one another. As their friendship deepened, they made a childhood pact that they would marry each other. As adults, however, the earlier agreement appears to have been forgotten because in the meantime Lucy had attracted other interested suitors. Ultimately, George was successful in winning her love and her hand in marriage. They were married on May 25, 1892, in the Manti Temple. George's father, John Henry, performed the ceremony. Little did they know at that happy moment of the challenges that lay ahead.

An Unusual Romance

When George Albert Smith courted Lucy Emily Woodruff, he was courting a heritage nearly as unique as his own, in terms of Church leadership. Perhaps retaining the distinguished families ran in the bloodlines since Lucy's parents, Wilford Woodruff Jr. and Emily Jane Smith, had a very unusual courtship. Shared below is the account of a very unusual courtship that ultimately brought two unique personalities, George Albert Smith and Lucy Emily Woodruff, together. The story has passed into the family lore as follows:

Wilford Jr. went to his father, Apostle Wilford Woodruff, with what seemed to be an unsolvable problem.

"President Young has called me to the Muddy River colonization mission," he said, "and I must be married before I can go."

"That's fine," his father replied. "Whom are you going to marry?"

"I haven't any idea," the young man said. "I don't even know any girls."

"Surely you know some," his father remonstrated.

"Well," Wilford conceded, "I know of Emily Jane Smith, but I've never met her."

"How would you like to marry her?" the father pressed.

"I guess it would be all right," was the uncertain reply.

"Come on," the Apostle said.

They put on their hats and walked over to Judge Smith's home even though it was still early morning.

"Have you come to breakfast?" the surprised judge asked.

"No," said Wilford senior, "We've come on more serious business. Wilford here has been called on a colonizing mission to the Muddy. He can't go until he has a wife, so he would like to marry one of your daughters."

"Which one?" asked the startled judge.

"He doesn't know any of them," the father of the red-faced young man admitted, "but knows of Emily Jane."

Judge Smith summoned Emily Jane, then seventeen, and asked her if she knew Wilford Woodruff, Jr.

"I know who he is," the girl said demurely, "but I don't think we've ever been introduced."

Her father explained young Wilford's problem and added, "He thinks he would like to marry you. Are you willing?"

"Is that what you wish me to do?" the girl asked in meek submission.

"Yes, Emily. I think Wilford would make you a wonderful husband."

"All right, father, I'll do anything you wish."

They were married and left immediately for St. Thomas, Nevada, then believed to be in the territory of Utah. In this desolate spot they built a log cabin and Lucy Woodruff was born there on January 10, 1869.[4]

God's Protection at a Time of Terror

Elder Smith believed that as long as he was in the Lord's service, he had the promise of the Lord's protection. During one such event, which he later referred to as "one of the most horrible events" of his life, he experienced that protection. In this and other similar events he attributed his safety to the hand of a merciful providence, which protected him on numerous occasions.

While serving in the Central Tennessee Conference, George and several other missionaries accepted the hospitality of a poor local Latter-day Saint family. There was hardly room in the small house for the missionaries, or for their host family, let alone both, but somehow they managed to find a place for everyone and in time all retired to bed. "About midnight," George Albert recorded, "we were awakened with a terrible shouting and yelling from the outside. Foul language greeted our ears. . . . It was a bright moonlight night and we could see many people on the outside . . . ordering the Mormons to come out [and] that they were going to shoot them," an invitation the missionaries wisely refused. In a few moments the room was filled with shots. "Apparently the mob had divided itself into four groups and they were shooting into the corners of the house. Splinters were flying over our heads in every direction. There were a few moments of quiet, then another volley of shots was fired and more splinters flew." Throughout it all George Albert never even got out of bed. He believed that the Lord would protect him. "I felt absolutely no terror. I was very calm . . . [while] experiencing one of the most horrible events of my life, but I was sure that as long as I was preaching the word of God and following His teachings that the Lord would protect me, and He did!"[5]

SOUTHERN STATES MISSION

One of those challenges was that within less than a month after their marriage George was called by the First Presidency to serve a full-time mission to the Southern States with headquarters in Chattanooga, Tennessee. During the latter quarter of the nineteenth century, the South, and especially Tennessee, was "the scene of more persecution than any other LDS mission."[5] Into this hostile and dangerous arena, George, never particularly robust, was sent to proselyte. Despite his enthusiasm and his expectation that he would be called to serve, his resolve to leave his new bride and his safe environs in the West was severely challenged.

Harassment of Latter-day Saint members and missionaries gradually subsided in the South after several decades of intense persecution. George contributed to this change of attitude and intolerance through his love for the people and his desire to make friends for the Church. Mobs and persecutors, however, were not the only dangers missionaries faced. At times they also had to brave the elements. Once during a long walk to fulfill a teaching appointment, he and his companion were caught in a heavy rainstorm when darkness overtook them. Their route led them over a dangerous

Missionaries George Albert Smith and Henry Foster in the Southern States Mission, about 1892.

mountain pass, bordered on one side by a perilous cliff and on the other by a steep precipitous ledge. Being unfamiliar with the terrain, the missionaries groped their way along the ledge, picking their way very carefully. At one point, George let go of the ledge to follow what he thought was the trail. For a few shuffling steps, he moved in the darkness, when he abruptly stopped, following an acute impression that he was in immediate danger. He backed from the spot, until he again found the ledge, and then followed it as before until he arrived, some hours later, safely at his destination.

The next morning, with the aid of daylight, he retraced his route along the mountain path to retrieve some lost personal items, dropped the night before. Curiously he followed his footprints in the wet soil. "Erosion had opened a chasm in the precipice," and George found that he had walked to the very edge of it. "One more step," George determined, "and he would have plunged into the rocks and turbulent waters some twenty feet below." George realized his close call with disaster and believed that once again his life had been preserved by an act of divine intervention.[6] Divine intervention to preserve his life became a recurring theme of George Albert Smith's talks and life throughout his ministry as an Apostle and later as the President of the Church.[7]

After a few months of missionary service, his wife was permitted to join her husband and she too was set apart as a full-time missionary. They served together in the office, he as a counselor and assistant to the mission president, J. Golden Kimball, and Lucy Emily as a secretary. While in the mission field, they celebrated their first wedding anniversary together. In June 1894, after yet another year of missionary service, they were both released to return to Salt Lake, where seventeen months later they started their own family.

Near Drowning Experience

George Albert Smith's life was marked with sickness, misfortune, and accidents that severely threatened his life. He mentioned a number of these events in his public talks and writings in an effort to share examples of the Lord's mercies to preserve his life and thereby allow him to come to the leading place as President of the whole Church. This account was shared with the children of the Church in an effort to build and strengthen their faith and to express his own personal gratitude to a loving Heavenly Father.

"I was considered a very good swimmer and thoroughly enjoyed the sport. This particular day the tide was very high and very swift. As I left the shore and swam out into the ocean, I dived through the big breakers as they would crest and spray over me. My objective was the large swells beyond the breakers, where I could lie on my back and ride the big swells up and down. While engaging in this interesting sport, one very huge wave crested and broke before I could right myself following the dive through the previous one. The second one caught me and threw me to the floor of the ocean. I could feel myself being dragged out by the undertow. At this particular time many waves came in rapid succession and I was not able to right myself before I had to dive from one into another. I realized that my strength was rapidly leaving me, that it was going to be necessary for me to find some means of help. As I rode to the crest of one huge wave, I saw the under pilings of a pier close at hand, and I thought if with super-human effort I could reach the security of the pilings that I would be able to save my life. I silently asked my Heavenly Father to give me the strength to reach my objective. As I was washed into arm's length of the pier, I reached out and put my arms around one of the posts. They were covered with sharp dark blue barnacles, and as I wound my arms and legs around its security, they cut my chest, legs and thighs. I hung on as long as I could stand the pain and watched for a big friendly swell to come my way that I might throw myself on it and travel closer to shore. Each time with a prayer in my heart I would make the effort traveling from one pile to another with the aid of the rolling swell. Slowly but surely and with great difficulty, I made my way to the shore where the water was shallow enough for me to walk to the beach. When I reached the safety of the warm sand, I fell exhausted. I was so weak, and so nearly drowned I was unable to walk home until I had rested for some time. Lying on the sand with its warmth and security, I thought of the harrowing experience that I had just endured and my heart was filled with gratitude and humility that the Lord had again spared my life."[6]

HEALTH CONCERNS

George's health was never very good, which may have contributed to the decision to have him work for a time in the mission office. During his full-time missionary service and for much of the remainder of his life, George suffered from lupus erythematosus.[8] This condition caused chronic weakness in his body and as his system weakened, his body lost its ability to ward off disease. To complicate matters, for a brief period following his mission, George worked for the Denver and Rio Grande Railroad as a member of the surveying crew. "While he was working on the line to Green River, Utah," he endured the excessive heat over an extended period of time and the "sun glare damaged his eyesight."[9] It was, as it turned out, a permanent injury, and this coupled with general weakness and other illnesses severely endangered his health. In later life he had to recuperate, sometimes for months at a

Elder Smith at the time of his call to the Quorum of the Twelve Apostles, about 1903.

time, to regain his strength to a level that he could resume his labors.

In 1908, during one of these episodes, doctors grew concerned about his condition to the point of even despairing for George's life and suggested he move to Southern Utah to convalesce. In St. George, which was named after his grandfather, he lived in a tent out in the country and away from other people where he could benefit from the fresh air, sunshine, solitude, and freedom from the pressures and distractions that threatened his health. While in this condition, George experienced a vision of his grandfather. George loved and honored his grandfather.[10] The impact of this dream was forceful and affected George Albert Smith's future teachings as a Church leader.

APOSTOLIC CALLING AND SERVICE

Following his missionary experience, which lasted between 1892 and 1894, George went to work for the U.S. Government in 1898. Active in politics for a number of years, George accepted an appointment from U.S. President William McKinley as a receiver for federal monies in the United States Land Office and as a special disbursing agent for Utah. After McKinley's death, the appointment was renewed by President Theodore Roosevelt. Tuesday October 6, 1903, however was a day that changed his life forever. George Albert Smith had returned home in mid-afternoon from his office with plans to take his children to the state fair. The pressures of his business had kept him from attending the semiannual general conference of the Church.

Following the final session of the day, friends and neighbors gathered at his house to congratulate him on his call to the apostleship, which had been announced in the afternoon session. George, who was to succeed Elder Brigham Young Jr., had not been notified of the call, and he was therefore certain that a mistake had been made since his father, John Henry Smith, was currently serving in that Quorum. He was so certain that he had not been called, despite the blessing of his childhood, he convinced the visitors that it must be some other Smith who was called. When the visitors returned with

An Impressive Dream

After being called to the Quorum of the Twelve Apostles, Elder George Albert Smith collapsed due to overexertion. His heart itself was healthy, but its muscles had been strained and would lead to a serious attack if he did not rest them. His doctor prescribed at least one year of rest. Elder Smith followed the counsel of Church leaders and went first to Southern California and later to Southern Utah to convalesce. He was further instructed to sleep outside for the fresh air and ventilation. In the winter of 1909–1910, while in Southern Utah, sleeping in a tent near a home where his family stayed, Elder Smith had "a very vivid dream" of his grandfather, after whom he was named, and who had a great impact on the young Apostle's thinking, actions, and service. The following experience is quoted from Elder Smith's personal diary that he dictated to his wife.

"I lost consciousness of my surroundings and thought I had passed to the Other Side. I found myself standing with my back to a large and beautiful lake, facing a great forest of trees. There was no one in sight, and there was no boat upon the lake or any other visible means to indicate how I might have arrived there. I realized, or seemed to realize, that I had finished my work in mortality and had gone home. I began to look around, to see if I could not find someone. There was no evidence of anyone living there, just those great, beautiful trees in front of me and the wonderful lake behind me.

"I began to explore, and soon I found a trail through the woods which seemed to have been used very little, and which was almost obscured by grass. I followed this trail, and after I had walked for some time and had traveled a considerable distance through the forest, I saw a man coming towards me. I became aware that he was a very large man, and I hurried my steps to reach him, because I recognized him as my grandfather. In mortality he weighed over three hundred pounds, so you may know he was a large man. I remember how happy I was to see him coming. I had been given his name and had always been proud of it.

"When Grandfather came within a few feet of me, he stopped. His stopping was an invitation for me to stop. Then . . . he looked at me very earnestly and said:

"'I would like to know what you have done with my name.'

"Everything I had ever done passed before me as though it were a flying picture on a screen—everything I had done. Quickly this vivid retrospect came down to the very time I was standing there. My whole life had passed before me. I smiled and looked at my grandfather and said:

"'I have never done anything with your name of which you need be ashamed.'

"He stepped forward and took me in his arms, and as he did so, I became conscious again of my earthly surroundings. My pillow was as wet as though water had been poured on it—wet with tears of gratitude that I could answer unashamed."[7]

verification that he was indeed called to the Quorum of the Twelve, George Albert had already left home to take his children to the fair.

George Albert argued passionately against nepotism, especially as it related to Church leadership. When he learned that his name was announced as the newest member of the Quorum of the Twelve Apostles, George sought out his father, who was serving as a senior member of that Quorum. When the two men first met, his father's initial response was, "George, . . . I didn't have anything to do with it."[11] It had been President Joseph F. Smith who had nominated the new Apostle. Interestingly, John Henry Smith and George Albert Smith served in the Quorum of the Twelve Apostles for eight years and were the only father and son combination to serve in the Quorum together at the same time.[12] Elder Smith acknowledged that immediately following his call he was "oppressed with a sense of unworthiness," which kept him awake at nights. But before long, he said, "I got my confidence back . . . and I have never been afraid since."[13]

George quickly became immersed in his new responsibilities. With his call had also come an announcement that George would complete his government appointment in the U.S. Land Office. He was able to accomplish this assignment later that same year.

Assignments during his term as an Apostle included numerous trips across the nation, and a few even took him around the world. It was later reported of him that he had logged more than a million miles in the pursuit of his official

Personal Creed

Long a deep thinker regarding his relationship to Deity and his responsibility to Them, Elder George Albert Smith penned a list of Christlike attributes and traits that he wanted to emulate and standards he desired to achieve in his life. This list was written soon after his call to the Quorum of the Twelve Apostles. In retrospect, it can be seen from his life that he did live the standards that he had set for himself. In fact, he is known as the "prophet of Christlike love."

"I would be a friend to the friendless and find joy in ministering to the needs of the poor. I would visit the sick and the afflicted and inspire in them a desire for faith to be healed. I would teach the truth to the understanding and blessing of all mankind. I would seek out the erring one and try to win him back to a righteous and a happy life. I would not seek to force people to live up to my ideals, but rather love them into doing the thing that is right. I would live with the masses and help to solve their problems that their earth life may be happy. I would avoid the publicity of high positions and discourage the flattery of thoughtless friends. I would not knowingly wound the feelings of any, not even one who may have wronged me, but would seek to do him good and make him my friend. I would overcome the tendency to selfishness and jealousy and rejoice in the successes of all the children of my Heavenly Father. I would not be an enemy to any living soul. Knowing that the Redeemer of mankind has offered to the world the only plan that will fully develop us and make us really happy here and hereafter I feel it is not only a duty but also a blessed privilege to disseminate this truth."[8]

duties, more miles than any of his predecessors. During George Albert's lifetime, Church leaders served on the governing board of national railroad companies. As a result, Elder Smith received special consideration by the nation's railroads in his frequent travels across the nation. Further, he was sometimes invited to ride in the director's car, which was considerably more comfortable. As he rode, porters, conductors, and other railroad employees tried to make his trip more comfortable and convenient, and Elder Smith continuously tried to show his appreciation. He could not, however, remember all of their names, even when he recognized some of the workers he had seen before. Consequently, Elder Smith affectionately referred to all railroad employees as Bill and they in turn, endeared by his familiarity, attempted to return the kindness.

Soon after his call to the apostleship in 1904, George Albert Smith wrote what was later to be known as his personal creed. This creed, which became a trademark for his tenure as an Apostle and throughout his administration as prophet, was a series of goals and attributes he chose to live by. The success of his ministry and his endearment to Saints around the world are testament to his successfully disciplined life.

Another activity of his apostolic ministry was his interest in and involvement with the Church's historical sites. Whether the emphasis was due to his own familial interest or was a specific assignment is not certain, but it soon became one of his most noteworthy contributions. He attended, for example, the 1905 dedication of a monument to honor the Prophet Joseph Smith at his birthplace in Sharon, Vermont. Dozens of general Church leaders, including President Joseph F. Smith, attended this significant event, and afterward Elder George Albert wrote and spoke warmly of his experiences.

On his return trip west from the dedication, Elder George Albert Smith revisited the historic Smith farm in Manchester, New York. Over several years George had cultivated a friendship with its owner, William Avery Chapman, and in 1907 made arrangements with Chapman to purchase the farm. The purchase included nearly one hundred acres of the original Joseph Smith Sr. farm, including a part of the Sacred Grove and the frame home where the Prophet Joseph hid and translated the gold plates. While this property was initially purchased with his personal funds, George later deeded it to the Church for one dollar. Joseph F. Smith, the prophet at the time, shared George's interest in acquiring historic sites and otherwise preserving the Church's past. He encouraged George Albert's involvement in purchasing these sites and others.

The terms of the purchase of this historic site stipulated that Chapman be allowed to remain on the farm until he found other suitable living arrangements. It took an additional seven years before Chapman moved from the farm. When he did, Church leaders sent Willard and Rebecca Bean to New York to live on and be caretakers of the farm and to develop friendships for the Church. Because George Albert and Willard had served together as missionaries in the southern States, Elder Smith knew that Bean would be an ideal person to represent the Church as a missionary in upstate New York. The Beans were the first Latter-day Saints to return and live in the Palmyra area since the Saints had moved from New York and settled in Ohio in 1831.

George revered the Church's pioneers, among whom were his own ancestors, and he continued to honor them with similar acts of preservation the remainder of his life. In 1930, a century after the Church's initial organization, Elder Smith organized the Utah Pioneer Trails and Landmarks Association. This organization laid the foundation for other pioneer centennial celebrations in 1947 and symbolized his respect and became his tribute to the pioneers during his presidency.

George Albert Smith as an honored Scouting enthusiast.

Another long-term interest that highlighted his Church service was the Boy Scouting movement. Elder Smith had personally met Lord Baden Powell, who initially created the Scouting program in England. In 1912, Elder Smith served on a Church committee that reviewed Scouting for possible adoption as a program for the young men of the Church. He supported this proposal, and it was implemented as part of the YMMIA in 1913. Elder Smith proudly wore his Scouting uniform and encouraged the Church's youth to participate in the Scouting program. As a result of his continued interest and support, he was elected in 1931 as a member of the National Executive Board of the Boy Scouts of America and in 1932 and 1934 was awarded Scouting's highest honors: the Silver Beaver and the Silver Buffalo Awards.

Elder Smith's term as an Apostle lasted for forty-two years between 1903 and 1945. During this period he served under Presidents Joseph F. Smith and Heber J. Grant. During his tenure as a member of the Quorum of the Twelve Apostles, he traveled widely in the interest of improving the public image of the Church. As a result, the Church's national image improved dramatically during the early decades of the twentieth century.

This interest led to his involvement in several national organizations that contributed to the overall

Memorabilia, medals, and awards, including Republican political convention participant, government medals, recognition for participation in numerous agricultural conferences and Old Folks Day.

improvement of the Church's image. He was elected president of the International Irrigation Congress (1916) and of the International Dry Farm Congress (1917). He likewise served for decades as a delegate with the descendants of the Revolutionary War and was vice president of the National Society of the Sons of the American Revolution (1922).

After the death of President Joseph F. Smith (1918) and the end of World War I, George served for two years between 1919 and 1921 as the president of the European Mission. Upon his return from Europe in 1921, George, at the age of fifty-one, was appointed general superintendent of the YMMIA.

Elder George Albert Smith became the President of the Quorum of the Twelve Apostles in June 1943 upon the death of Elder Rudger Clawson. Nearly two years later, when he was notified by telegram of the death of President Heber J.

Grant on May 15, 1945, Elder Smith was en route to New York on one of his many cross-country trips. He got off his train in Chicago, sent a response to the telegram, and caught a return train that the railroad company delayed for him in order to expedite his return trip to Salt Lake City. He arrived in the city in time to assist in the funeral arrangements and to participate in the services for President Grant, held in the Salt Lake Tabernacle.

At the funeral services, George Albert Smith paid the warmest tribute to his predecessor: "He was a giant among men. . . . I know of none . . . who has been more determined, more faithful, more desirous of doing the thing that would enrich the lives of our Father's other children and bring happiness to them."[14]

Three days after the funeral, members of the Twelve Apostles met as a Quorum, and on May 21, 1945, George

Interview with U.S. President Harry S. Truman

In the waning months of World War II, the Church, under the direction and leadership of President George Albert Smith, felt the urgency to assist Latter-day Saints in war-torn Europe with food, clothing, and medical supplies. Church members donated their food and clothing, and Church stockpiles were used to meet the pressing need for supplies. Multiple shipments were sent by the Church, and Elder Ezra Taft Benson was assigned to oversee the distribution of supplies to the war-ravaged Saints in Europe. President Smith, in a conference address, tells of this involvement in behalf of the Church to get these supplies to those in need.

"Word comes from our people in Europe. In many cases they are still having difficult times, but they are faithful, in the main, to God and the Church, and the messages that they send us from time to time is expressing gratitude for food, clothing, and bedding we have sent them warm our hearts.

"It may be of interest to you to know that since World War II closed, more than seventy-five major [train] carloads of food and clothing and bedding have been shipped across the sea to those needy people over there, without any expense to them whatsoever.

"When the war was over, I went representing the Church, to see the president of the United States [President Harry S. Truman]. When I called on him, he received me very graciously—I had met him before—and I said, 'I have just come to ascertain from you, Mr. President, what your attitude will be if the Latter-day Saints are prepared to ship food and clothing and bedding to Europe.'

"He smiled and looked at me, and said: 'Well, what do you want to ship it over there for? Their money isn't any good.'

"I said: 'We don't want their money.' He looked at me and asked: 'You don't mean you are going to give it to them?'

"I said: 'Of course, we would give it to them. They are our brothers and sisters and are in distress. God has blessed us with a surplus, and we will be glad to send it if we can have the co-operation of the government.'

"He said: 'You are on the right track,' and added, 'we will be glad to help you in any way we can.'

"I have thought of that a good many times. After we had sat there a moment or two, he said again: 'How long will it take you to get this ready?'

"I said: 'It's all ready.'

"The government you remember had been destroying food and refusing to plant grain during the war, so I said to him: 'Mr. President, while the administration at Washington were advising the destroying of food, we were building elevators and filling them with grain, and increasing our flocks and our herds, and now what we need is the cars and the ships in order to send considerable food, clothing and bedding to the people of Europe who are in distress. We have an organization in the Church that has over two thousand homemade quilts ready.'

"The group that sang for you this morning, the Singing Mothers of the Relief Society, represent that organization. They had two thousand quilts made by their own hands ready to ship. The result was that many people received warm clothing and bedding and food without any delay. Just as fast as we could get cars and ships, we had what was necessary to send to Europe."[9]

Elder George Albert Smith.

Albert Smith was sustained as the eighth President of the Church in this dispensation. He selected Presidents J. Reuben Clark Jr. and David O. McKay as First and Second Counselors, respectively. Both of these men had served faithfully as counselors to his predecessor, President Heber J. Grant.

President Smith enjoyed air flight, despite some less than favorable early experiences that led to his threat that he would never fly again. He found that air travel allowed him to move faster and more comfortably around the country in fulfilling his many assignments. Further, he found that he could better focus his time and energies toward his ever-increasing responsibilities worldwide. He was the first Church President to take advantage of this technological advance in air transportation.

Areas of emphasis during his presidency included many of the same items that he had championed during his years in the Quorum of the Twelve. As an Apostle, for example, Elder Smith had received permission from President Grant to focus attention on the needs of the Lamanite people. As President of the Church, President Smith assigned the two newest members of the Twelve, Elders Spencer W. Kimball called in October 1943 and Matthew Cowley called in October 1945, and charged them to watch over the Lamanites.

Perhaps President Smith is best known for his work during his presidency to provide relief to Latter-day Saints and others in postwar Europe. In the October 1947 general conference, President Smith reported his negotiations with U.S. President Harry S. Truman for land and sea transportation for donated Church welfare relief supplies bound for Europe. Elder Ezra Taft Benson, another recent addition in 1943 to the Quorum of the Twelve Apostles, was called to travel to Europe and oversee the distribution of those supplies. Once when President Smith was shown the goods waiting to be sent, "tears ran down [his] face . . . he removed a new overcoat" and asked that it also be sent with the other supplies, although it was a cold day and he needed it.[15] His overcoat became a part of several massive shipments of food, clothing, tools, equipment, and medical supplies to be contributed by the Church for European relief, which included 140 rail carloads, estimated at nearly six thousand tons. Many thousands of Europeans were blessed and countless lives were saved in war-torn Europe as a result of President Smith's vision to bless his brothers and sisters in Europe.

In cooperative efforts, President Smith further encouraged the Saints from Holland to raise potatoes, the Canadian Saints to contribute wheat, and the Saints from the Scandinavian and other European countries to provide other aid for their previous international enemies in the continental conflict. The Swiss Saints adopted suffering children to nourish them back to health, and even the youth from the various countries providing relief participated by raising funds and other commodities.[16] A significant motivation, as recorded in his personal creed, was his determination to love all men, everywhere. This outpouring of love for his fellow man was motivated by his personal philosophy to love all men, and earned him the title among Saints throughout the world, as the "Prophet of Christlike Love."

Other activities that accentuated that theme of love included his work during his presidency with a group of disaffected Saints in Mexico, called the "Third Convention." Although seriously ill, feeble, and in pain, President Smith met with these Saints. He encouraged them, helped them to see their spiritual potential, and invited them to return to Church activity. Estimates of more than 1,200 individuals, consequently, returned to activity in the Church after nearly a decade of dissatisfaction. President Smith's love for these individuals reestablished a friendship with the people, but more important, established a foundation of future Church growth in Mexico.

President George Albert Smith presided over the Church for just less than six full years, and his administration yielded several "firsts" for the Church.

PRESIDENT—THE MAN AND HIS CONTRIBUTION TO THE CHURCH

George Albert Smith was a very mild-mannered man. President J. Reuben Clark noted that he had never seen him angry and that he was always in control of his emotions.[17] President Smith was six feet, one inch tall and weighed 160 pounds. He was a tall, slender man with a mustache, thick glasses, and a glowing personality. Usually, his concern was more for others than it was for himself. He loved people, but more important, he loved helping others. Not infrequently while on trips or as he moved about the city, he was willing to be inconvenienced in order to bless the lives of others.[18] He was personable but he was also practical and rarely wasted time. His favorite Church hymn was "Let Us Oft Speak Kind Words," and his favorite sayings were, "Always stay on the Lord's side of the line" and "Be compassionate."

President Smith was the first Church President to preside over the Church as a widower. His lifelong sweetheart, Lucy, had died on November 5, 1937, at the age of sixty-eight when her husband was still a member of the Quorum of the Twelve Apostles. President Smith was likewise the first Church President to appear on a television debut broadcast of general conference, and he frequently participated in radio broadcasts.

In September 1945 President Smith presided over the dedication of the Idaho Falls Temple and offered the dedicatory prayer. Other temples, including the Los Angeles Temple, were in varying stages of planning or production, but this is the only temple dedication that President Smith presided over. In 1946, he directed the reestablishment of missionary work in Europe and in 1947 reopened Japan for proselyting after decades of the Church's absence. It was also during President Smith's administration, in July 1947, that the Church celebrated the centennial of the arrival of the first Mormon pioneers into the Salt Lake Valley. As a part of these festivities, the Church sponsored numerous activities that reflected the achievements of its past. The pioneer centennial celebration included parties, pageants, art exhibitions, musicals, and the traditional Pioneer Day parade. In one of the most nationally acclaimed activities, the Church, with President Smith as its host, entertained the governors of

President Smith was the first Church President to participate in the televising of general conference.

Firsts for President George Albert Smith

President George Albert Smith distinguished himself as the President of the Church by instituting or participating in numerous significant activities. Following are a few of the "firsts" in his life, in the Church, and during his presidency.

- The first Church President to participate in air flight and to use it in the performance of his many worldwide responsibilities.

- The first Church President to preside over the Church as a widower.

- Presided over the dedication of the Idaho Falls Temple and offered the dedicatory prayer.

- Sought reunification of disaffected Latin members; President Smith visited Mexico in May 1946.

- Directed the reestablishment of missionary work in Europe after World War II.

- Reopened Japan for proselyting in 1947 after decades of the Church's absence from that country and continent.

- Led the celebration of the one hundredth anniversary of the arrival of the pioneers into the Salt Lake Valley in July 1947.

- Entertained the governors of forty-three states and several territories at a reception in Salt Lake City on July 15, 1947, to commemorate the contributions of the Latter-day Saints in the one hundred years since their arrival in the Salt Lake Valley.

- Dedicated the This Is the Place Monument at the mouth of Emigration Canyon on July 24, 1947, honoring the pioneers who entered the Salt Lake Valley one hundred years before.

- Presided over the Church when the plateau of its first one million members was reached.

- Featured on the cover of *Time* magazine, the first Church President to be so honored on a national scale.

- Assisted in the dedication of a hero-sized statue of President Brigham Young. It was placed in the rotunda of the nation's Capitol in Washington, DC, to honor the pioneer legacy of the Latter-day Saints.

- Helped the Church send immense shipments of relief supplies to war-torn Europe in 1947. He also encouraged Latter-day Saints in other countries to contribute to the temporal and spiritual needs of Saints in war-torn countries.

- Presided over the first general conference broadcast live over commercial television in 1948.

- Nominated three men to serve in the Quorum of the Twelve Apostles: Elders Matthew Cowley (1945), Henry Dinwoodey Moyle (1947) and Delbert Leon Stapley (1950).

forty-three states and three U.S. territories, who were guests at the Church's pioneer celebration on July 15, 1947. Many of the guests went away with a new awareness of the Church, its growth, and its programs. The parade held on July 24 was preceded by a reenactment of the transcontinental trek along the same route taken by the pioneers a hundred years before. A major difference between the two cross-country adventures was that participants in 1947 traveled in automobiles. President Smith participated in parts of the reenactment of the pioneer trek and arrived in time to participate in the grand dedication of the This Is the Place Monument, west of where the pioneers emerged from the mouth of Emigration Canyon.

During the same year the Church reached a monumental plateau as Church membership climbed to one million members. President Smith was featured on the cover of *Time* magazine in July 1947 in honor of the Church's achievements and of his own leadership. President Smith further attended,

spoke, and otherwise participated at the dedication of a hero-sized statue of President Brigham Young to memorialize his leadership to the Church and the colonization of the West. The statue was dedicated on June 1, 1950, 149 years after President Young's birth in Whitingham, Vermont. It was placed in the rotunda of the Capitol in Washington, DC.

In addition to these prominent activities, President Smith was even more active in lesser-known acts of service. When Elder Benson was away assisting with Church relief supplies in Europe, one of the Benson daughters was very ill. Sister Benson resisted notifying her husband so as not to distract him from his work, but President Smith went to the Benson home unannounced to express his concern and give Elder Benson's daughter a priesthood blessing.

President Smith constantly visited the sick, the widows, the bereaved, and others in need. Elder John A. Widtsoe, president of the University of Utah, was discouraged and had received serious criticism as a result of some of his decisions while presiding over the university. President Smith stopped by and said, "I am on the way home after my day's work. I thought of you and the problems that you are expected to solve. I came in to comfort you and to bless you." The two men talked for a while, after which President Smith gave the promised blessing to buoy Elder Widtsoe up and encourage him in his duties. Elder Widtsoe remembered, "That was the way of George Albert Smith. . . . Of course I appreciated that; I shall never forget it. . . . My heart was lifted. I was weary no longer."[19]

Frequently President Smith would interrupt his busy schedule to meet and shake the hands of the oppressed or to comfort and encourage all around him, especially children. He seemed to have an unfathomable depth of compassion for others, and he went out of his way to share and lighten their burden. In his talks President Smith would often attempt to fortify and encourage the youth of the Church. He spoke to them as a friend in an effort to help them avoid the temptations and pitfalls of the generation in which they lived. Two of the recurring themes of his ministry to these youth were to "give the Lord a chance" and to always stay on "the Lord's side of the line."

As a result of his tireless efforts, concern for the members, his own physical limitations, and continued efforts to

President George Albert Smith on the cover of *Time* magazine. The date for the publication was July 1947 in honor of the Church's pioneer centennial.

"The Lord's Side of the Line"

President George Albert Smith often spoke of the "Lord's side of the line," especially when speaking to the youth of the Church. He first learned of the principle from his grandfather, George A. Smith, but continued to add to it until it became more of his own theme than a borrowed insight.

"My grandfather used to say to his family, 'There is a line of demarkation, well defined, between the Lord's territory and the devil's. If you will stay on the Lord's side of the line you will be under his influence and will have no desire to do wrong; but if you cross to the devil's side of the line one inch, you are in the tempter's power, and if he is successful, you will not be able to think or even reason properly, because you will have lost the Spirit of the Lord.'"

"There are two influences in the world today, and have been from the beginning. One is an influence that is constructive, that radiates happiness and builds character. The other influence is one that destroys, turns men into demons, tears down and discourages. We are susceptible to both. The one comes from our Heavenly Father, and the other comes from the source of evil that has been in the world from the beginning, seeking to bring about the destruction of the human family. . . .

"When I have been tempted sometimes to do a certain thing, I have asked myself, 'which side of the line am I on.' If I determine to be on the safe side, the Lord's side, I would do the right thing every time. So when temptation comes, think prayerfully about your problem, and the influence of the spirit of the Lord will enable you to decide wisely. There is safety for us only on the Lord's side of the line."[10]

Give the Lord a Chance

A favorite theme of President George Albert Smith in his talks to motivate members, especially the youth, was to exercise faith and "give the Lord a chance." This advice had numerous applications. One application was that when he spoke to congregations of the Saints, he usually spoke without notes. He had a huge reservoir of personal experiences to draw upon. He loved people and learned a great deal by getting them into a conversation. He would draw upon these conversations and his vast personal experiences for his talks. Further, he counseled others to speak extemporaneously without the aid of a written text. Instead of memorizing the talk, he would counsel people to "give the Lord a chance" to speak through them, to magnify them and to inspire them with ideas, thoughts, and teachings of the Spirit.

Another application of giving the Lord a chance came when he counseled a young missionary in England. The missionary was anxious since he would be asking for permission to preach on the street corner. Elder Smith reminded him, "Now remember, give the Lord a chance. You are going to ask a favor. Give the Lord a chance. Ask him to open the way." The missionary went to see the mayor of the town, but the mayor was out, so instead he went to see the chief constable. Despite the fact that this was intimidating, the missionary followed counsel and determined to "give the Lord a chance."

The missionary's confidence seemed to disarm the constable, and when the elder asked if he could preach on the street corner, the constable asked him which corner he wanted. The young missionary admitted that he didn't know the city well but said that he didn't want to block traffic or pick an undesirable corner, so he asked the constable if he would go with him to choose a street corner. The constable agreed, and "in fifteen minutes they had one of the best corners in town, with permission to preach the gospel . . . where it had not been preached" and where it would most likely heard by the largest number of people.

If individuals have faith in their purpose, have confidence that God will assist them, and give the Lord a chance to direct them for good and make things happen, there is no end to the amount of good that can be accomplished.[11]

promote the gospel, his body grew weaker from the effects of age and disease. In December 1950, he gave his last public discourse. On Wednesday, April 4, 1951, during the annual general conference of the Church and on his eighty-first birthday, President Smith died from the effects of a respiratory infection.

His funeral was held in the Tabernacle, and speakers were predominantly taken from the General Authorities. Elder Matthew Cowley observed, "God attracts the Godly, and I am sure that the shortest journey this man of God ever made in all of his travels has been the journey which he has just taken." His counselors also spoke. President J. Reuben Clark Jr. noted, "Evil slunk away from him at all times. It could not abide the presence of his righteous [life]," and President McKay observed, "He lived as nearly as it is humanly possible for a man to live a Christlike life." The earthly remains of President George Albert Smith were interred in the Salt Lake City cemetery, where his tombstone stands today as a symbol of his life of faith in, devotion to, and love for his Father's children everywhere.

President George Albert Smith was a highly respected individual nationwide, but especially within the Church. He was very articulate but rarely wrote out a talk. At least one Apostle called under his presidency, Elder Matthew Cowley, was challenged to never write a talk but to speak from the heart, under the influence of the Spirit.

President Smith was entertaining and captivating as a speaker, not only because he was the President of the Church, but also because of the numerous personal experiences he shared. When he spoke, he talked quickly, and as he cited points of doctrine or emphasized his counsel to the Saints, his voice raised in volume. He was a congenial individual and could strike up a conversation with a complete stranger without an introduction. He stood tall and was gregarious and outgoing. Latter-day Saints and nonmembers alike were drawn to him because of his gentle appearance—an appearance that at once set him apart and commanded the respect of others. He rarely asked for favors for himself, but because of his stately appearance, individuals were drawn to serve and bless his life.

He was thirty-three years old when he was called to the Quorum of the Twelve Apostles; he was seventy-five when he succeeded President Heber J. Grant as the President of the Church.

Elder Smith's goal to be a friend to the friendless was realized. People revered him for his charitable acts, but few were aware of how much he was able to do. Elder Smith spoke softly, but people listened. He was charismatic but not overpowering; he accomplished much for the Church but remained very humble. He was among the great, but he never forgot the common and ordinary; in fact, he was as much at home with the unemployed, destitute laborer as he was with the heads of state or government leaders, and he didn't seem to esteem one above the other.

Major themes of President Smith's life include a love and gratitude of his own heritage, which included the Prophet Joseph Smith. George Albert Smith believed in following the living prophet all of his life, but he taught the principle as an Apostle and as the President of the Church This theme was strengthened by his personal efforts to preserve the locations and legacy of the pioneers of the past.

TEACHINGS OF PRESIDENT
GEORGE ALBERT SMITH

◆

President Smith constantly championed the less fortunate, the blind, the underprivileged, the homeless, and those in need. He gave freely to those who had less than he had himself. He was especially concerned with and became the self-appointed advocate for the Lamanites. He reinitiated missionary work and won a respect among the Americans Indians of North, Central, and South America. He not only sent Church representatives to watch over these people, the Polynesians, and the indigenous people of other lands, but he also went among these people himself. He was the first Church President to visit Mexico and the first to visit the American Indians on their own reservations.

Elder Smith also loved the music of the Church and saw in it the declaration of peace and the means of teaching the gospel. He often shared examples of how the hymns brought comfort, protection, and encouragement to Church members. He further encouraged the Latter-day Saints to be law-abiding citizens, to honor and obey the constitutional form of government under which they lived. He repeatedly bore his testimony of the principles of the Restoration, of the reality of Deity, and of his gratitude that he was a part of the great latter-day work.

LAMANITES

In 1951 at the funeral of President George Albert Smith, Elder Spencer W. Kimball disclosed President Smith's earlier involvement with the Lamanites. President Smith determined it was time to do something constructive for these Indian people who had fallen into misfortune. "He went to [President] Heber J Grant . . . and asked him for permission to do work among the Indian people which was granted."

President Smith noted, "I have been intensely interested in doing something for the American Indians. . . . I have seen the need of something more being done."[20]

President Smith called Elders Kimball and Cowley to watch over the Lamanites. The Lamanites responded to their love and concern and made a significant contribution among their own people as it pertains to Church matters but also in temporal, day-to-day affairs. President Smith invited Lamanite people representing different tribes and people to visit Salt Lake City. In one case, Elder Smith had the chief of the Catawba Indian tribe of South Carolina speak in general conference.

The Catawba Tribe was one of the American Indian tribes that may have helped to stimulate Elder Smith's interest in the Lamanites. Chief Samuel Blue was a prominent Church leader and a tribal chief. He was an elder and had gone west to receive temple blessings for his family and himself. President Smith reported in conference that 97 percent of the members of the Catawba Tribe were members of the Church and represented a legacy of faithful service in the Church and elsewhere.[21]

Another American Indian who won President Smith's respect was Washakie. A close personal friend of President Brigham Young, Washakie not only joined the Church but influenced others to do so. This great warrior, chief, and friend to the Latter-day Saints was a significant influence for good among his own people and was memorialized on the This Is the Place Monument.

In August 1954, less than four years after President Smith's death, the Church instituted the Indian Student Placement Program. No doubt a part of the realization of President Smith's hopes for the Lamanites, the purpose of this program was what the prophet had envisioned for them.

Role of the Living Prophet

Among his many duties, President George Albert Smith also served as a member of the board of directors for Western Airlines, much the same as he had done for the railroad companies and other business corporations. As the President of the Church, George Albert Smith rarely traveled alone; usually he was accompanied by his personal secretary, D. Arthur Haycock. One day, however, Brother Haycock did not go, and President Smith flew to and from California alone. Upon his return he related the following experience to Brother Haycock, who shared it in the words of President Smith:

"I had an interesting experience flying home last night. It was foggy in Los Angeles when we took off. I thought we'd get above it, but we didn't and I was concerned. I knew we had some high mountains to get over; I just didn't know if we could.

"Being an officer of the company, I went up to the front to talk to the pilot, and I asked him, 'How do you know where you are going? How high are we? You have all these instruments, but how do you know you are on the right direction for Salt Lake?'

"The pilot told me that he wore his earphones to receive a signal that he would follow. He said that if he got off course to the right, he would hear dot-dot-dot. If he got off course to the left, he would hear dash-dash-dash. If he heard a steady signal, he knew he was right on course."

"President Smith asked the pilot, 'Are you sure your altimeter is all right?'

"The pilot nodded, 'Yes.'

"In a few minutes, the pilot set the plane down without a bump at the Salt Lake City airport."

Then President Smith noted, "I've been thinking about that experience. I've likened that plane to the Church. The passengers are the members, and the pilot is the president. That pilot had earphones on, and he could hear the signals, but I couldn't hear anything. I could have gotten a parachute and jumped out over Nevada and landed on a cactus in the desert, but I decided to stay with the plane. I've concluded that if the people of the Church, the passengers, will stay with the plane and have confidence in the pilot, the prophet, who has on the earphones, who gets the messages and knows where they come from, they'll land safely as well." President Smith summed up the experience: "The prophet of the Church hears the message, and he knows the source."[12]

Its stated purpose was "to make possible educational, spiritual, social and cultural opportunities for Latter-day Saint Indian children."[22]

CHURCH MUSIC

President Smith posed a significant question to members of the Church. "I wonder sometimes if we realize the importance of music," he said. "I wonder if we know that the Lord himself is concerned about it." He then instructed the Saints, "Heavenly Father has given a revelation teaching us that it was our privilege [and] blessing, to sing and that our songs should be sung in righteousness."[23] Two missionaries in the South, President Smith noted, were working in an area where serious threats had been made against the elders. Unknown to the missionaries, they were watched by a mob as they arrived to visit a family who had befriended them. The mob's intent was to drive the missionaries from the area, but the missionaries decided to sing for their friends some of the songs of Zion. The missionaries chose the hymn "Do What Is Right." The mob, preparing to make good on their earlier threats, also heard the hymn and were touched by the spirit of the message it bore. "The leader," it was later learned, "was so impressed with what he heard the missionaries sing that he said to his associates: 'We made a mistake. These are not the kind of men, we thought they were. . . . These men sing like angels. They must be servants of the Lord."[24] The result of this experience was that the mob leader was converted and after a short time was baptized. President Smith concluded, "I never hear that hymn sung but I think of that very unusual experience when two missionaries, under the influence of the spirit of God, turned the arms of the adversary away from them and brought repentance into the mind of those who had come to destroy them."[25]

President Smith further witnessed, "I am grateful for a Church that teaches the joy and encourages the sweet influences that come from music. So important are the hymns of the Church that our Heavenly Father appointed the Prophet's wife Emma to select hymns that were appropriate for sacred services."[26] President Smith noted further "that even our Primary children, beginning in their tender years, are taught . . . to sing the praises of our Heavenly Father and to give thanksgiving in the music that is prepared. What a comforting, uplifting influence there is in music."[27] Repeatedly, President Smith also referred to the quality of the music furnished by the Mormon Tabernacle Choir and other choirs in the Church. The President told of a young man, a soldier injured in war, who listened to the Tabernacle Choir and believed that he was healed by the influence of the good music they performed. President Smith even listed, for his conference listeners, some of the hymns that had made the greatest impact upon his own life. "I was not a very good singer," he noted, "but I enjoyed music, and I remember some of the hymns that influenced my life." Among those that had affected him personally was "Haste to the Sunday School." Of this hymn he noted, "I think that was the way I got my idea of punctuality, because when I was a boy we dared not go into a class late." President Smith listed nearly twenty other hymns that had influenced his life for good and commented on a few of them. He concluded one such address by saying, "I feel that the hymns that have been taught the sons and daughters of the Latter-day Saints . . . are a continuous sermon of righteousness. I am sure they have inspired many of us to do the things that the Lord would like us to do."[28]

A DEFENSE OF AMERICA AND THE U.S. CONSTITUTION

Another theme frequently shared with the Saints was the inspired nature of the U.S. Constitution. Probably because of his heritage and the teachings of his parents, but also as a result of his own government service, President George Albert Smith loved freedom and America. "The government of the United States," he observed, "was begun under the direction of our Father in Heaven . . . to be an example unto the nations of the earth."[29]

President Smith taught that the freedoms and liberties we have came with a price, and that price is to support what God provided for us. "It is your duty and mine to remember in our prayers the President of the United States of America, to remember the men who represent us in the Congress. . . . the executives of the states of the nation, and to pray for them that they may have divine aid."[30]

While his motivation for the foregoing may have been due to the involvement of the United States in World War II, this was a recurring theme throughout his ministry. The same thoughts were expressed in the aftermath of World War I and between the two great wars. For example, in 1935, Elder Smith taught, "Sustain the constitution of the United Sates. The Lord himself has said that he raised up the very men who prepared it to the end that it might be an example to all the world. Do you believe it? If you do then sustain it and don't let your voice be among those that shall deride and break down the things that are so important for us."[31]

He further provided a more fundamental application of the individual's responsibility by saying, "From time to time we are arrayed against each other in political campaigns. . . . I regret that men are sometimes led to say and do things that are unworthy of a Latter-day Saint. The great political parties are necessary. It is important that our liberties be preserved and all should be interested." His counsel to Latter-day Saints was to be concerned first and foremost "in the welfare of the nation, and sustain good and great men . . . in order that we may continue to enjoy freedom. Some of our brethren have become so wrapped up in their political ambitions that they place them in advance of their faith in God." His caution then was poignant, "Whenever your politics cause you to speak unkindly of your brethren, know this, that you are upon dangerous ground. . . . After the great political nations of this world have crumbled, . . . the Church . . . will be in existence, and the Master Himself will continue to be its head."[32]

Near the conclusion of his life, President Smith boldly stated, "Our Heavenly Father raised up the very men that framed the Constitution. . . . To me the Constitution of the United States of America is just as much from my Heavenly Father as the Ten Commandments."[33] He noted too that if a man believed this to be true, then he would act a little differently toward laws and governments that affected him.

President Smith repeatedly shared his experiences and bore testimony of the inspired nature of Church organization, its programs, and its activities. He shared his witness of sacred, basic truths that were a part of his very soul. "I know that God lives. I know that Jesus is the Christ. I know that Joseph Smith was a prophet of the living God, as I know that I stand here and talk to you. . . . I know that the Church . . . possesses divine authority and is guided by the Father of us all."[34] In a later conference he testified in addition to the foregoing, "If we will observe the advice that has been given to us, if we will honor him, who is the Author of our being, not only we but our children and children's children will also be among those whom God will bless throughout eternity."[35]

In the final public discourse that President Smith gave in the Tabernacle, it was almost like he knew he had a final chance to bear his witness of Jesus Christ to the Church and to the world. He spoke at length about the life, mission, and ministry of the Lord Jesus Christ. This final testimony was not so different in content from other testimonies that he had given through the years, but the aged prophet did spend more time talking about his faith in and the reality of the mission of Jesus Christ. He likewise emphasized the reality of the Restoration of the gospel, including the coming forth of the Book of Mormon. He reminded the Saints to be obedient to counsel, wherein lay lasting happiness. In conclusion, as before, he bore his testimony "that God lives, that Jesus is the Christ, that Joseph Smith was a prophet of the Living God." In conclusion, he reiterated, "I know that as well as I know that I live, and I bear that witness to you in humility, and realizing the seriousness of such a statement if it were not true, I still bear this testimony to you."[36]

David F. Boone

Associate Professor of Church History and Doctrine, EdD
Brigham Young University

NOTES

1. A narrative of the death of George A. Smith Jr. is given in Pearson H. Corbett, *Jacob Hamblin: The Peacemaker* (Salt Lake City: Deseret Book, 1952), 182–96.
2. Lynda Cory Hardy, *Boys Who Became Prophets* (Salt Lake City: Deseret Book, 1982), 47.
3. Joseph Fielding Smith, "Latter-day Prophets Receive Revelation Today," *Instructor*, November 1963, 383.
4. George A. Smith, "The New Apostle," *Deseret Evening News*, October 7, 1903.
5. Andrew Jenson, "Southern States Mission," *Encyclopedic History of The Church of Jesus Christ of Latter-day Saints* (Salt Lake City: Deseret News Publishing Company, 1941), 821.
6. George Albert Smith, CR, October 1945, 116; Merlo J. Pusey, *Builders of the Kingdom: George A. Smith, John Henry Smith, George Albert Smith* (Provo, UT: Brigham Young University Press, 1981), 218–19.
7. See sidebar on page 201, Near Drowning Experience. George Albert Smith, *A Story to Tell, for Teachers, Parents and Children*, comp. the Primary Association General Board and the Deseret Sunday School Union Board (Salt Lake City: Deseret Book, 1959), 158–59.
8. Systemic Lypus Erythematosus (SLE) is the name by which

the disease is known today. It is one of several inflammatory, autoimmune diseases that may adversely affect the body's systems, including skin, joints, and internal organs. This disease is characterized outwardly by red scaly patches of skin all over the body. It is further accompanied by any or all of the following symptoms: fever, fatigue, malaise, weight loss, sensitivity to sunlight, swelling and pain in the joints, arthritis, swollen glands, aching muscles, extreme nausea, violent vomiting, chest pains, and even seizures. Side effects may include abdominal pain, hair loss, and severe mouth sores. Even today, there is no known cure for this disease. George Albert Smith suffered from many of these problems. Whether they were all caused by SLE is not specifically known.

9. Joy N. Hulme, *The Illustrated Story of President George Albert Smith: Great Leaders of The Church of Jesus Christ of Latter-day Saints* (Provo, UT: Eagle Systems International, 1982), 31.

10. Glen R. Stubbs, "A Biography of George Albert Smith, 1870–1951," dissertation, Brigham Young University, 1974, 106–7.

11. Pusey, *Builders of the Kingdom*, 225.

12. Francis M. Gibbons, *George Albert Smith: Kind and Caring Christian, Prophet of God* (Salt Lake City: Deseret Book, 1990), 45. While there were other father and son combinations who served as General Authorities (including Brigham Young and Brigham Young Jr., John Taylor and John W. Taylor, Wilford Woodruff and Abraham O. Woodruff, and Joseph F. Smith and Joseph Fielding Smith), these men did not serve concurrently in the Quorum of the Twelve.

13. "The Passing of a Saint," *Time*, April 16, 1951, 65.

14. Pusey, *Builders of the Kingdom*, 313.

15. Glen L. Rudd, *Pure Religion: The Story of Church Welfare since 1930* (Salt Lake City: The Church of Jesus Christ of Latter-day Saints, 1995), 248–50.

16. Frederick W. Babbel, "Dutch Saints Ship Potatoes to Germany," *Improvement Era* (December 1947): 824.

17. J. Reuben Clark Jr., "No Man Had Greater Love for Humanity than He," *Deseret News*, April 11, 1951, 10.

18. Thomas S. Monson, address given at Brigham Young University Devotional, Provo, UT, October 10, 1989.

19. Alan K. Parrish, *John A. Widtsoe: A Biography* (Salt Lake City: Deseret Book), 232.

20. Spencer W. Kimball, "Elder Kimball Tells of Pres. Smith's Concern for His Lamanite Brethren," *Deseret News*, April 11, 1951, 11.

21. George Albert Smith, CR, April 1950, 143–44.

22. *Church News*, September 4, 1965, 8–9.

23. George Albert Smith, *Deseret News*, February 16, 1946, 6.

24. George Albert Smith, CR, October 1945, 116.

25. Ibid.

26. George Albert Smith, CR, April 1935, 47.

27. Ibid.

28. George Albert Smith, "Tribute to Richard Ballantyne," *Instructor*, November 1946.

29. George Albert Smith, *Sharing the Gospel with Others: Excerpts from the Sermons of President [George Albert] Smith*, comp. Preston Nibley (Salt Lake City: Deseret Book, 1948), 169.

30. George Albert Smith, CR, October 1945, 174.

31. George Albert Smith, CR, October 1935, 122.

32. George Albert Smith, CR, April 1914, 11–12.

33. George Albert Smith, CR, April 1948, 182.

34. George Albert Smith, CR, October 1945, 175.

35. George Albert Smith, CR, October 1947, 167.

36. George Albert Smith, CR, October 1950, 160.

SIDEBAR AND PHOTO NOTES

1. Brigham Young, *JD*, 7:289–90.

2. Quoted in Stubbs, "A Biography of George Albert Smith," 20–21.

3. *Deseret Evening News*, October 7, 1903; see also, Melvin R. Ballard, *Melvin J. Ballard: Crusader for Righteousness* (Salt Lake City: Bookcraft, 1966), 63.

4. Pusey, *Builders of the Kingdom*, 205–6.

5. George Albert Smith, *A Story to Tell*, 156.

6. Ibid., 158–59.

7. Quoted in Stubbs, "A Biography of George Albert Smith," 106–7.

8. George Albert Smith, "My Personal Creed," *Improvement Era* (March 1932): 295.

9. George Albert Smith, CR, October 1947, 5–6.

10. Quoted in Nibley, *Sharing the Gospel with Others*, 42–43.

11. Gibbons, *George Albert Smith: Kind and Caring Christian, Prophet of God*, 26; see also Nibley, *Sharing the Gospel with Others*, 14–15.

12. D. Arthur Haycock, "George Albert Smith," *In the Company of Prophets* (Salt Lake City: Deseret Book, 1993), 27–28.

Chapter Nine

DAVID O. MCKAY

LIFE AND TIMES

1873	September 8	Born in Huntsville, Utah, to David McKay and Jennette Evans McKay
1897		Graduated from University of Utah with a Normal (teaching) Certificate
1897–99		Served a mission to British Isles
1899–1902		Became a teacher in the Weber Stake Academy
1901	January 2	Married Emma Ray Riggs
1902–06		Became principal of the Weber Stake Academy
1906		Ordained an Apostle
1908		Became Chairman of the General Priesthood Committee
1918		Became Superintendent of the Deseret Sunday School Union
1919		Served as Church Commissioner of Education
1920		Embarked on world tour of Church missions and schools
1921	January 9	Dedicated land of China for preaching of the gospel
1922–24		Served as president of the European Mission
1934–51		Served as counselor to Presidents Heber J. Grant and George Albert Smith
1947		Dedicated Pioneer Memorial Monument
1951	April 9	Sustained as President of The Church of Jesus Christ of Latter-day Saints
1951		Toured South Africa, South America, Central America, and Mexico
1955		Became first prophet to tour with Tabernacle Choir in Europe; Swiss Temple is dedicated
1956		Los Angeles Temple is dedicated
1958		Dedicated Church College of Hawaii
1959		New Zealand and London Temples are dedicated
1963		Dedicated remodeled Salt Lake Temple
1970	January 18	Died in Salt Lake City, Utah, at age ninety-six

BIOGRAPHICAL HIGHLIGHTS

President David Oman McKay was ordained and set apart as the ninth President of the Church on April 12, 1951, after serving forty-five years as an Apostle, including seventeen years as a counselor in the First Presidency. He remained the President for nineteen years. In total, President McKay served as a General Authority for nearly sixty-four years—longer than any previous man—and his service extended over much of the twentieth century. Recognition of the Church as a worldwide organization, phenomenal growth, and development of modern new programs marked this prophet's administration.

After growing up in the small, rural town of Huntsville, Utah, David Oman McKay went from second counselor in a stake Sunday School presidency to member of the Quorum of the Twelve Apostles at the young age of thirty-two. Before his appointment as an Apostle, President McKay had served a mission to Great Britain. At the age of seventy-seven he was set apart and sustained as the prophet of The Church of Jesus Christ of Latter-day Saints. Standing over six feet tall, with a full head of snow-white hair, David O. McKay was an imposing figure who many said looked like a prophet. He was active into his ninety-sixth year.

CONTRIBUTIONS

President McKay stated that his greatest accomplishment was making the Church a worldwide organization.[1] Active in missionary labors, he traveled the world in support of missions. His efforts are reflected in the fact that Church membership doubled during his tenure. The Church grew from a small intermountain sect to a worldwide organization with astonishing growth outside of the United States, including Europe, Latin America, New Zealand, and the isles of the Pacific. President McKay visited every mission outside the United States and met with leaders of foreign nations, ambassadors, U.S. presidents, and other government officials.

TEACHINGS

President McKay often discussed the sanctity of marriage and the home; he declared that family was the source of happiness and the surest defense against trials and temptations. The maxim "No other success can compensate for failure in the home" became his motto as he called on parents to spend more time with their children and teach them about character and integrity. He encouraged members to "accept [the gospel] and cherish its ideals and apply them in their daily lives."[2] His sermons on the subjects of the Savior, agency, and self-mastery were embraced by Church members, and President McKay was seen as a powerful force in their lives.

LIFE OF
DAVID O. MCKAY

A HERITAGE OF HIGH IDEALS

David Oman McKay's Scotch and Welsh background had direct impact on his views about life. He frequently mentioned his heredity and believed that many of his personality characteristics, such as his dry sense of humor, came directly from his ancestry. His paternal grandparents, William and Ellen Oman McKay, were among those in the British Isles to convert to the Church in 1850. Though persecuted for his new religion, Grandfather William offered this advice to his family: "When that cold snowy wind is blowing, and you are out in it, you can't do anything about it. You just turn up your coat collar and let her blow."[3] David O. McKay may have received his missionary zeal from his grandmother, Ellen Oman McKay. Wanting to share her newfound faith with her family, she gave LDS tracts and books to her ten siblings. William, Ellen, and their five children came to the United States in 1856; they sold all their possessions to finance the trip. After reaching the LDS settlements in Iowa ... [they] walked a thousand miles across the plains to Ogden, Utah Territory.[4]

President McKay's maternal forebears, Thomas Evans and Margaret Powell, were from South Wales. After marrying in 1837, they settled in Cofen Coed, near Merthyr Tydfil, Glamorganshire.

David and Jennette McKay and their children.

Thomas, Margaret, and their children were also baptized members of the Church in 1850. Coincidentally, both the McKay and the Evans families arrived in Ogden during August 1859. Although both families settled there, William's son and Thomas's daughter did not meet until 1865.[5]

THE INFLUENCE OF NOBLE PARENTS

It was in Ogden, Utah, where fifteen-year-old David McKay Sr. first saw his future wife, Jennette Evans. Peeking underneath a pink sunbonnet, nine-year-old Jennette was sitting on the tongue of a wagon when David Sr. first looked into her big, brown eyes. He was mesmerized, and the two later fell in love. David convinced Jennette's parents to let her marry before the age of eighteen, and the couple was married on

April 9, 1867, by Apostle Wilford Woodruff.[6] They made the small settlement of Huntsville, Utah, their home.

The union was soon blessed with two daughters, Margaret and Ellen, named after their two grandmothers. The McKays' first son, David Oman McKay, was born on September 8, 1873. President McKay credited his boyhood home with being the dominant component in molding his life. He remarked, "My home life from babyhood to the present time has been the greatest factor in giving me moral and spiritual standards and in shaping the course of my life."[7]

Though President McKay met with LDS leaders, royalty, American presidents, and celebrities, when asked to name the greatest man he had ever met, he replied without hesitation, "My father."[8] At the tender age of twelve, President McKay's father left his family to be employed by a doctor, at fifteen he crossed the plains, and at eighteen he enlisted in the Utah militia. Despite a lack of formal education, David McKay Sr. taught himself the necessary skills to be elected to the Utah Territorial Legislature and served three terms in the Utah Senate. He was also the bishop of the Eden and Huntsville wards from 1885 to 1905.[9] Being the bishop's son carried a weight of responsibility and duty for David O. McKay. At a young age, he expressed this sense of accountability to his younger brother, Thomas, as they walked home from church, passed a park, and saw some boys playing baseball. Thomas said, "'Come on, David! Let's play ball.' David replied, 'Tommy, it's the Sabbath and our father is the bishop. We're going home.' "[10] David McKay Sr. also shared his testimony with his young son and taught him about the commandments. President McKay remembered, "As a boy, I sat and heard that testimony from one whom I treasured and honored as you know I treasured no other man in the world, and that assurance was instilled in my youthful soul."[11]

Jennette Evans McKay was as an equally strong influence in David O. McKay's formative years. Before her marriage, Jennette Evans taught school. Her training as a teacher aided in her experiences as a mother. As an adult, President McKay recalled, "My mother once told me that she considered Robert E. Lee a great general because he tried to protect the lives of his soldiers. This childhood impression made by my Angel Mother many years ago has remained with me through life,

and I am still deeply impressed with the fact that true generalship consists in saving men, not in slaughtering them."[12]

Jennette had lofty goals for her firstborn son. When David was a baby, one of his uncles visited the home and directed a teasing remark toward the young boy. Jennette corrected this relative and quickly said, "Don't talk like that to him. . . . You do not know, he may be an apostle some day!"[13] From his mother's teachings and example, David O. learned to value such ideals as respect for life, confidence, and discipline.

EARLY EXPERIENCES

David O. McKay was a very energetic little boy. As an aunt observed early on, Jennette had her hands full. One of the biggest jobs for frontier wives was to feed the threshers when they came to help with a harvest. During one harvest, Jennette asked her sister to watch David O. while she took care of this task. After a few hours, his aunt offered to trade jobs. She had decided that cooking for all the threshers would be an easier task than watching David O.[14]

As a little boy going up to bed, David O. was frightened because he heard noises. One night when he was about six years old, he became afraid. He got up and said a prayer to feel better. When he got up, he heard a voice saying, "Don't be afraid. Nothing will hurt you."[15] Such early experiences left a firm impression of the blessings of sincere prayer.

When David O. was just seven years old, he lost both of his older sisters. Margaret died of rheumatic fever, and Elena, the second daughter, developed pneumonia and died on the day of her older sister's funeral, April 1, 1880. That same year his father received a letter from "Box B" at Church headquarters, calling him to serve a mission in the British Isles. Before leaving, David Sr. asked his oldest son, then seven years old, to take care of his mama and to become the man of the house. Thus, David O. assumed responsibilities that far surpassed his years of experience.[16]

YOUTH

The McKays provided a secure home environment for their growing family, giving encouragement and guidance to their children. These teachings helped to form the character of this future prophet. Many of these messages later found their way into President McKay's sermons. One such sermon, which President McKay often repeated, had to do with the principle of sacrifice. One day the McKay boys were out collecting hay. The tenth load was to be given as a tithing offering to the Church. Father McKay told the boys to get the tenth load from a better spot than they had been gathering: "That is the tenth load, and the best is none too good for God." President McKay later said that this was the "best sermon on tithing I ever heard in my life."[17]

David O. McKay was enrolled in a Sunday School program at an early age. There he was given experience speaking in front of groups. The Huntsville ward minutes records David bearing his testimony and delivering talks.[18] At the age of twelve, he was called to his first priesthood responsibility as the second counselor of his deacons quorum. As the newly installed counselor, David told the group that he "felt his inability to fill his position when he could see others that were more capable to occupy it than himself," but "he felt to press on with the help of the Lord."[19] He led the boys in fulfilling responsibilities such as "keeping the chapel clean, seeing that chopped wood was always available for the chapel's stoves, and . . . for the widows of the ward."[20] A responsible and diligent leader, he attended 100 percent of his Church meetings in 1889.[21]

Eliza R. Snow, former general Relief Society president, attended one Huntsville meeting. As she looked down at the audience, she prophesied, "I can see in that group of boys bishops of wards, presidents of Stakes, Apostles, and some of you will live to see the Savior."[22] Another prophecy of David O. McKay's future was made when he was thirteen years old and playing marbles. Church Patriarch John Smith, who was visiting the McKay home, placed his hands on David's shoulders, looked into his eyes, and declared, "My boy, you have something to do besides playing marbles." He then gave David O. his patriarchal blessing, which included the following: "The eye of the Lord is upon thee. . . . The Lord has a work for thee to do, in which thou shalt see much of the world, assist in gathering scattered Israel and also labor in the ministry. It shall be thy lot to sit in council with thy brethren and preside among the people and exhort the Saints

David at age five.

Lifelong Love of Horses

President McKay loved to train horses. He often repeated a story about a horse named Dandy who resented restraint and would nibble at the tie-rope until he was free. One day Dandy got free and ate a sack of grain that was poisoned with bait for rodents and died a painful death. President McKay would relate the following comparison: "How like Dandy are many of our youth! They are not bad; they do not even intend to do wrong, but they are impulsive, full of life, full of curiosity, and long to do something. They, too, are restive under restraint, but if kept busy, guided carefully and rightly, they prove to be responsive and capable; but if left to wander unguided, they all too frequently find themselves in the environment of temptation and too often are entangled in the snares of evil."[1]

As a student at the Weber Stake Academy.

University of Utah graduating class of 1897.

President David O. McKay and the University of Utah football team, 1896.

to faithfulness." David O. went into the kitchen and said to his mother, "If he thinks I'm going to stop playing marbles, he is mistaken."[23]

As a youth, David O. was more concerned with having fun than with worrying about such things as a "responsible position" and "the ministry." Along with playing marbles, he enjoyed dancing, playing the piano with the town's dance orchestra, acting in home dramatics, debating, and singing in the glee club; and in all these activities he was seen as an enthusiastic leader. Other pursuits included reading English classics, writing poetry, riding and training horses, and working on the farm.[24]

Athletics were also part of David O.'s youth. Along with playing baseball, he would jump head first into a swimming hole after others had put their toes in and decided it was too cold.[25] Young David O. had a mind of his own; later in life he confessed to being a "roguish" and "doubting" boy.[26] President McKay often talked of an experience he had in trying to gain a testimony of the Church. One day, while taking a horseback ride, he got down from the horse and asked for a testimony. He left the experience quite disappointed when a spiritual witness did not come. Later he conceded, "I had in mind that there would be some manifestation, that I should receive some transformation that would leave me without doubt."[27]

EDUCATION

In 1889 at the age of sixteen, David finished his course work at the Huntsville public school. Most of his peers in Huntsville, Utah, and America as a whole discontinued their formal education with primary school. David, wanting more education, enrolled in Weber Stake Academy.[28]

David found a wider academic curriculum at the academy than that offered at the Huntsville school. He especially liked studying English classics and enjoyed reading them at home while performing chores or herding cattle. It was during these times that he learned to love Robert Burns and William Shakespeare and memorized passages that remained in his memory for the rest of his life. After completing his studies at Weber, he taught at Huntsville Primary School from 1893 to 1894, serving as the principal, though he was barely twenty years old.[29]

About this time, David's grandmother Margaret Evans made a financial gift of $2,500 to each of her living children. Money was tight for the McKay family, and Jennette's brother and sister suggested that she put the money in stocks. When Jennette was asked what she wanted to do with the money, she replied, "Every cent of this goes into the education of our children."[30] David, along with his brother and two sisters, journeyed to Salt Lake City by wagon to attend the University of Utah.

David became a tackle and guard on the first official University of Utah football team, which won high honors. He was a popular piano player at dances and became class president. As a student in the "normal education department," his emphasis was English literature. In 1897, David O. McKay received his teaching certificate, graduating as valedictorian from the University of Utah Normal Department.

David was offered a teaching job in Salt Lake County and made arrangements to begin teaching in the fall.[31] He was greatly perturbed, however, when he received a letter in July from the First Presidency requesting that he accept a call to be a missionary. His first response was to reject the call, but after thinking it over, he realized that no member of his family had "ever

President McKay was a lifelong student of great authors.

Principal of Weber Stake Academy.

refused a call to work in any capacity in the Church." Making a decision that would affect the remainder of his life, he changed his plans and prepared to follow his father's footsteps to the British mission, which included Scotland and Wales.[32]

MISSION

On August 1, 1897, David O. McKay was set apart as a missionary. He spent the first part of his mission in Stirling, Scotland, where he became acquainted with James L. McMurrin, a member of the European Mission presidency. President McMurrin had confidence in Elder McKay and placed him in leadership positions. In 1898, he was called to be a member of the presidency of the Scottish Conference (or district). Elder McKay wrote the following in his diary about the experience: "Realizing to some extent what a responsibility this is, I seemed to be seized with a feeling of gloom and fear, lest in accepting I should prove incompetent. I walked to a secret spot in the wood, just below [William] Wallace's monument, and there dedicated my services to the Lord and implored him for his divine assistance."[33]

A poignant experience took place on May 29, 1899, just three months before he came home. During a memorable priesthood meeting, Elder McKay felt he was given an answer to the prayer he had offered as a lad in Huntsville years before in regard to a testimony. President McKay recounted, "I remember, as if it were yesterday, the intensity of the inspiration of that occasion. Everybody felt the rich outpouring of the spirit of the Lord. . . . Never before had I experienced such an emotion. It was a manifestation for which, as a doubting youth, I had secretly prayed. . . . It was an assurance to me that sincere prayer is answered 'sometime, somewhere.'

"During the progress of the meeting, an elder on his own initiative arose and said, 'Brethren, there are angels in this room.' Strange as it may seem, the announcement was not startling, indeed, it seemed wholly proper, though it had not occurred to me that there were divine beings present. I only

President David O. McKay's missionary picture in 1897.

Whate'er Thou Art

President McKay tells of an incident that took place during his mission:

"I remember as a missionary in Scotland . . . I saw an unfinished building standing back from the sidewalk several yards. Over the front door was a stone arch, something unusual in a residence, and what was still more unusual, I could see from the sidewalk that there was an inscription chiseled in that arch.

"I said to my companion: 'That's unusual! I am going to see what the inscription is.' When I approached near enough, this message came to me, not only in stone, but as if it came from One in whose service we were engaged: 'Whate'er Thou Art, Act Well Thy Part.'[2]

As the prophet of the Church he shared this motto with the Church membership. The original stone and inscription is now located at the LDS Church History Museum of Art.

A group of missionaries attended conference in Glasgow, Scotland, in 1899. It was at this conference that President James McMurrin uttered prophecy concerning President David O. McKay.

knew that I was overflowing with gratitude for the presence of the Holy Spirit. . . . Such was the setting in which James McMurrin gave what has since proved to be a prophesy. . . . He said, 'Let me say unto you, Brother David, Satan hath desired you, that he may sift you as wheat, but God is mindful of you. . . . If you will keep the faith, you will yet sit in the leading councils of the Church.' "[34]

Before he reached the United States in September 1899, he received an appointment to teach at his alma mater, the Weber Stake Academy, and was later called to be a member of the Weber Stake Sunday School Board.[35]

COURTSHIP

During David O. McKay's second year at the University of Utah, he and his siblings had made arrangements with Emma Louisa Riggs to rent a cottage in the back of her house. Mrs. Riggs and her daughter Emma Ray were watching out the window as the McKay boys and their mother walked up on the first day. Mrs. Riggs observed, "There are two young men who will make some lucky girls good husbands. See how considerate they are."

Emma Ray replied, "I like the dark one [David]."[36]

A few days later while walking behind Emma Ray on campus, David said to a companion, "I am going to marry a girl just like her some day." When Emma Ray first met David, she was engaged to another young man. One day she passed a room at the university and heard the familiar voice of her tenant speaking at a Normal Society meeting. She said she had never heard someone talk with such sincerity and power. She thought to herself, "He is going to amount to something some-day." Some months later she decided she wasn't in love with her fiancé and broke off the engagement. David and Emma Ray's first date took place at his missionary farewell. Their real romance came with letters sent back and forth between Salt Lake and Scotland. At first the letters were formal, but gradually they became "warmer and warmer."[37]

Emma Ray continued her schooling while David was on his mission. She graduated in 1898 with a bachelor of arts in education. That same year, her mother died, so Emma Ray moved to Cincinnati to live with her father and study piano at the Cincinnati College of Music.[38] Upon returning to Salt Lake less than a year later, she was offered two teaching positions, one in Salt Lake City and the other at Madison School in Ogden. "Her home, family, and friends were in Salt Lake City, and there was every reason but one to stay there."[39] Her "reason" for teaching in Ogden came home in August 1899.

That fall, David O. began teaching at Weber Academy, and Emma started teaching sixth grade at Madison School. During that school year, Emma Ray and David O. often met in a park between their schools. It was there that David O. asked Emma Ray to marry him. She replied, "Are you sure you want me?" "Yes, I am very sure," he said. On January 2, 1901, Emma Ray Riggs and David Oman McKay became one of the first couples in the twentieth century to be married in the Salt Lake Temple.[40]

MARRIAGE AND FAMILY

Many have viewed the McKays' union as an ideal marriage. Sister McKay related that early in their marriage, President McKay wanted her to "go everywhere with him." She recalled, "I would pack my baby in a heavy shawl and we would go with our horses and buggy before automobile

Heart Petals

In general conference, President McKay often shared poems he wrote to his wife, Emma Ray Riggs McKay. He called these poems heart petals. On his ninetieth birthday he wrote:

Family cares came heavy but not a complaint
Forty-four children now crown her as saint;
Companion, counselor, advisor alway
My wife for eternity, my own Emma Ray.
You insist that I'm ninety?
My limbs say you are right,
As I hobble along a pitiable sight;
But I shall always feel young
With the gospel that's true,
With loved ones around me, and friends like you.[3]

David O. McKay with his wife, Emma Ray Riggs McKay.

days and ride through the heat, through mud, rain, and often through the snow, to these country towns," while President McKay served in the Sunday School.[41] Sister McKay added, "I knew that my husband was inspired of God in everything he did. In the morning, many a time, he has told of what would happen down in the office in some important thing before he would go down there, and when he would come back, I would say, 'Well, did it happen as [you] said it would?' 'Just exactly.' "[42]

Seven children were born to David O. McKay and Emma Ray Riggs in Ogden, Utah. Sadly, only six of their children lived to adulthood. Their fourth child, and third son, Royle, died at the age of three. Of their surviving children, they had four boys and two girls. David Lawrence McKay was born in 1901; three years later, another son, Llewellyn, joined the family; and Louise, often called Lou Jean, was their third child. Their second daughter, Emma Rae, was given her mother's name, with a slight variation on the spelling. Then came two more boys, Edward, known as Ned; and Robert, known as Bobbie. David Lawrence McKay wrote: "Our parents' expectations provided the path for us to follow, and our love for them provided an irresistible motivation for us to walk that path. We learned to love them because they first dearly loved each other and us."[43] As a father, President

Emma Ray Riggs

When their only daughter was born on June 23, 1877, Obadiah and Emma decided to name her Emma Ray, for a ray of sunshine. As the only daughter, she played marbles and ball games and became better at them than her five brothers. As a little girl, Emma Ray learned homemaking skills from her mother and grandmother. Filling the lamp oil and doing the weekly washing and ironing were some of her chores. In her spare time she had two hobbies. One was reading. Like her future husband, "in her girlhood, she was an avid reader of Dickens, Scott, and Shakespeare." She once said that as a child she was "never lonely" because she "always had the companionship of good books." Her other hobby was playing the piano. At the age of seventeen she had her first Sunday School assignment where she directed approximately ninety children. Before her marriage she also served as her ward's Primary president.[4]

Wit of a Prophet

President McKay loved humor and frequently infused his addresses with anecdotes. The following are examples of his wonderful wit:

"How do you know when your youth has been spent? When your get up and go has got up and went!"[5]

During the October 1962 general conference, two of the young Presidents of the Seventy had just concluded giving outstanding conference addresses. President Hugh B. Brown nudged President McKay and said, "President McKay, I believe this Church is going to carry on after you and I are gone." President McKay turned to President Brown with the comment, "Gone where? I am not going any place. . . . Where are you going?"[6]

"You wonder why one child is so different in disposition from another. . . . The first babe had no brothers to tease him; the tenth babe perhaps had nine."[7]

"The problem of choosing a proper, congenial mate is very vital. In regard to this I suggest in general that you follow the advice of Sandy, the Scotchman, but not his example. His friend MacDonald came to Sandy and said, 'I'm verra much worried, Sandy. I dinna ken [I don't know] whether to marry a rich widow whom I do not love, or marry a puir lass [poor lass] of whom I'm verra fond.'
"And Sandy said, 'You'd better follow the promptins o' yer [of your] heart, MacDonald.'
"'All right,' said MacDonald, 'I'll do it. I'll marry the puir lass.'
"'In that case,' said Sandy, 'would you mind giving me the address of the widow?'"[8]

McKay "gave off an air of command that called implicitly for obedience. 'Never give an order that's not obeyed, or cannot be obeyed,' he once told his children, 'and if you give an order, be certain that it's followed through.' His general manner, however, was more genial than stern, his smile more ready than his frown."[44]

PROFESSIONAL EDUCATOR

In the fall of 1899, David O. McKay joined the Weber Stake Academy faculty as school registrar and instructor of teacher education and literature. Three years later, at the age of twenty-nine, he became Weber's principal, serving in this capacity until June 1908, when he became a full-time member of the Quorum of the Twelve Apostles. He did continue, however, to serve as president of the Weber Board of Trustees. Even as a principal, David O. McKay was a favorite among students.

He believed that education was for everyone. Serving as a principal in an era when very few women received a secondary education, he set out to change this at Weber, and female student enrollment greatly increased during his tenure. The seven McKay years at Weber were marked by phenomenal growth. However, it was not his experiences as a professional educator that gained the attention of Church leadership.

FROM STAKE CALLING TO APOSTLE OF THE LORD

In 1899, David O. McKay was called as the second assistant to the stake superintendent of Weber Sunday Schools and received the responsibility to direct class work. Up until this time, there had been little direction for the Sunday School organization from the general leadership of the LDS Church. In this calling, Brother McKay developed (1) a collection of uniform lessons, (2) a program for dividing students by age, (3) a definite course of study for each age group, and (4) an adequate teaching force in each ward, with corresponding supervisors for every department of the stake board.[45] News spread quickly of the great success the Weber Stake Sunday School was experiencing. Eventually, this success was noticed by the general leadership of the Church, including Church President Joseph F. Smith. In 1905, when Brother McKay organized and directed a parents' convention, President Smith attended, noting the progress of the Sunday School and David's influence.

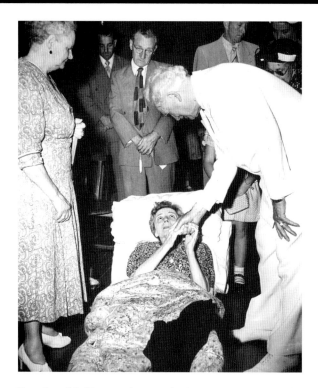

President McKay was known for his compassion and for wearing a white suit.

David O. McKay was called to be an Apostle of the Lord in 1906.

A Terrible Accident

In 1916, Elder McKay was in a terrible automobile accident; his neck was wrenched, lips lacerated, upper jaw fractured, and all of his teeth except five knocked out or loosened. He was told he would be disfigured for life. In a blessing, President Heber J. Grant promised him that he would not be permanently disabled, disfigured, or scarred. Elder McKay was free from pain after the blessing. The following October, at a banquet given to the General Authorities, he sat at a table near where President Grant was sitting. Elder McKay noticed that President Grant was looking at him somewhat intently, and then President Grant said, "David, from where I am sitting I cannot see a scar on your face!" Elder McKay answered, "No, President Grant, there are no scars—your blessing was realized completely."[9]

APOSTLE

On April 8, 1906, at the young age of thirty-two, David O. McKay was called to be an Apostle of the Lord. His success in the Sunday School program of the Weber Stake had brought him to the forefront of Church leadership. He was also called be the second assistant to President Joseph F. Smith in the general superintendency of the Sunday Schools. (During this time the President of the Church also served as the Sunday School superintendent.) In this position Elder McKay immediately organized a Churchwide convention for all stake Sunday School superintendents and boards. In 1918 he became the General Sunday School superintendent, a position he served in for the next sixteen years. As superintendent he introduced ideas that became standard practices throughout the Church, such as Gospel Doctrine class and a progressive course of study that covered all ages. During this time he also wrote the book *Ancient Apostles*, which was used as one of the first official Sunday School manuals.

In 1919, a new Church Commission of Education was created to assume the responsibility of the administration of Church education, which the First Presidency had directed previously. David O. McKay was appointed as the first Church Commissioner of Education. Part of his responsibility included a worldwide tour of the missions and schools of the Church. The objective of the tour was to obtain firsthand information regarding members of the Church throughout the world.[46]

Leaving Utah in December 1920, he made his way to the West Coast and boarded the *Empress Japan*, where he spent most of the time below deck. While on tour, Elder McKay dedicated the land of China for the gospel. He found that each culture possessed unique characteristics. In Japan he found courtesy and consideration; in Korea, interest and picturesque scenery; in China, wonder and inspiration; and in the Polynesian islands, people with a depth of love he had not before experienced. While visiting the peoples of Hawaii, Tahiti, and New Zealand, Elder McKay made a profound commitment to provide educational opportunities for the Pacific Saints. Much of the force behind this commitment stemmed from an experience he had on the island of Oahu at a Church-owned elementary school in the small town of Laie. While participating in a flag raising ceremony on February 7, 1921, he was impressed with the many nationalities all pledging allegiance to their new country. At that time Elder McKay envisioned the same scene being duplicated on a large scale, picturing the community of Laie as the intellectual center of the Pacific. This dream came to fruition thirty-four years later with the dedication of the Church College of Hawaii.

Elder McKay had spiritual experiences in the Pacific that had a profound impact on him. During one prayer, he was made aware of the presence of Joseph F. Smith and George Q. Cannon, who had introduced the gospel to the islands over seventy years before. On another occasion, he was impressed to get off a lookout ledge just before it crumbled into the molten lava of the Kilauea volcano crater below.[47] His experiences in the Pacific crystallized in his mind the idea of providing opportunities for the Polynesian people. Elder McKay and his companion, Hugh Cannon, persevered around the globe, traveling more than 62,000 miles, enough miles to circumnavigate the globe twice, visiting all the LDS schools and missions except for the South African mission.[48] Elder McKay returned to Salt Lake City on Christmas Eve, 1921.

The McKay family during the period of President McKay's service as president of the European Mission.

EUROPEAN MISSION PRESIDENT

Elder McKay's stay in Salt Lake was short-lived. He was appointed president of the European Mission, headquartered in Liverpool, England, on November 3, 1922. The *Millennial Star* declared that he was a veritable genius in leadership—as he reorganized the missionaries into groups, with several acting as traveling elders to spread better teaching methods. By the end of his two-year stay, he knew over five hundred missionaries in Europe by name.[49] It was during this service that he first used his motto, "Every Member a

The Gift of Tongues

President McKay enjoyed the gift of tongues on several occasions. He shares one such memory:

"One of the most important events on my world tour of the missions of the Church was the gift of interpretation of the English tongue given to the Saints of New Zealand at a session of their conference. . . . When I looked over that vast assemblage and contemplated the great expectations that filled the hearts of all who had met together, I realized how inadequately I might satisfy the ardent desire of their souls, and I yearned, most earnestly, for the gift of tongues that I might be able to speak to them in their native language.

"Until that moment, I had not given much serious thought to the gift of tongues, but on that occasion, I wished with all my heart that I might be worthy of that divine power. . . .

"From the depth of my soul, I prayed for divine assistance.

"When I arose to give my address, I said to Brother Steward Meha, our interpreter, that I would speak without his translating, sentence by sentence, what I said, and then to the audience I continued: 'I wish, oh, how I wish I had the power to speak to you in your own tongue, that I might tell you what is in my heart; but since I have not the gift, I pray, and I ask you to pray, that you might have the spirit of interpretation, of discernment, that you may understand at least the spirit, and then you will get the words and the thought when Brother Meha interprets.'

"My sermon lasted 40 minutes, and I have never addressed a more attentive, more respectful audience. My listeners were in perfect rapport—this I knew when I saw tears in their eyes. Some of them at least, perhaps most of them, who did not understand English, had the gift of interpretation. . . .

"Brother Meha gave a synopsis of the speech in Maori.

"During the translation, some of the Maoris corrected him on some points, showing that they had a clear conception of what had been said in English."[10]

Missionary." He would issue this directive to all Church members in 1959. Upon his return to Church headquarters in 1924, he resumed his duties as a member of the Quorum of the Twelve Apostles.

COUNSELOR IN THE FIRST PRESIDENCY

In 1934, President Heber J. Grant chose J. Rueben Clark and David O. McKay as his counselors; Presidents McKay and Clark served in the longest consecutive First Presidency association in Latter-day Saint history, lasting twenty-seven years until J. Rueben Clark's death in 1961.[50] President McKay was a member of the highest governing quorum of the Church during the turbulent 1930s and 1940s; he helped to guide Church members through the Great Depression and World War II. When President George Albert Smith was sustained as the prophet on May 21, 1945, President Smith also chose President McKay and President Clark to serve as his counselors.

PROPHET, SEER, AND REVELATOR

On April 9, 1951, at the age of seventy-seven, David Oman McKay became the ninth President of The Church of Jesus Christ of Latter-day Saints. The Church population nearly tripled during President McKay's administration; two-thirds of the Church knew no other prophet. The Church's spiritual growth was strengthened during President McKay's service. President McKay developed an organized curriculum and revolutionized teaching methods. He defined Church principles and, under his administration, attendance in meetings increased, indicating more activity and enlarged commitment by Church members. During the chaotic 1960s, he was forced to deal with media critical of the Church's position regarding the restriction of the priesthood from blacks. President McKay also helped develop an extensive network of radio and television stations, including a globe-circling shortwave radio station. Old "bureaus of information" were transformed into more effective visitors' centers. Extensive

Pacific Saints with David O. McKay.

David O. McKay and Hugh Cannon on a world tour in 1921.

programs were developed for world fairs and national and local exhibits. These were supplemented by tours throughout the United States, Canada, and Mexico by the Tabernacle Choir—the choir's records went on to become best-sellers.[51]

Among the developments in Church government during the McKay administration was the ordination of members of the First Council of the Seventy as high priests. This allowed General Authorities to fully carry out various assignments. Also, beginning in 1968, a body of priesthood leaders known as the regional representatives of the Twelve began to conduct leadership training of stake officers and ward bishoprics.[52]

In 1951, there was only one stake located outside of North America. With the advent of jet travel, President McKay felt that organizing stakes on foreign soil was possible. The first overseas stake was formed in New Zealand in 1958, the first European stake in Manchester, England, the first non-English speaking stake in Holland, and the first Latin American stake in Mexico City. He was also the first prophet to visit South Africa.

As the leader of a world religion, President McKay met with other world leaders, leading the Church during both the Korean Conflict and the Vietnam War. During the Korean Conflict of the 1950s, missionary service was curtailed by the draft, decreasing the missionary force. Subsequently, President McKay called stake seventies quorums to provide an additional thousand missionaries. Many of these men left wives, children, and careers behind to follow the prophet.[53]

Sea Sick

During his 1921 world tour, President McKay experienced much seasickness. He once related the following experience about an attempt to come above deck: "I reached only the top of the stairs, when that intense yearning to be alone drove me back to my cabin. Good-bye last night's dinner! Good-bye yesterday's Rotary luncheon! And during the next sixty hours, good-bye everything I had ever eaten since I was a babe on mother's knee. I'm not sure I didn't even cross the threshold into the pre-existent state."[11]

NEW PROGRAMS

Among the extraordinary and far-reaching developments during President McKay's administration was the creation of the Church correlation program in 1961. Correlated

curriculum for the priesthood and auxiliary organizations helped to avoid duplication and to provide a systematic schedule of teaching throughout the Church. On the ward level, a priesthood executive committee (PEC) and a ward correlation council (ward council) were formed in 1964. In addition, in 1965, the family home evening program was enhanced, with structured programs, lessons, and activities.[54]

CHURCH EDUCATION

Under President McKay's guidance, growth in Church education was significant. In the first ten years of his administration, student enrollment in institute and seminary classes increased from 67,000 to 162,000. Originally, seminaries had operated in local schools on a released-time basis, meaning a building was constructed near high schools and students were released during the regular school day to attend. As Latter-day Saints spread outside of the Intermountain West, released-time seminary was not possible, so early morning and home study seminary programs were established.[55]

Church schools, including Brigham Young University, the Church College of Hawaii (now BYU—Hawaii), Ricks

The McKay home in Salt Lake City, 1037 East South Temple Street.

Greeting Saints.

College in Idaho (now BYU—Idaho), and the Church College of New Zealand (a high school) grew in enrollment and physical size under President McKay's direction. He also established elementary and high schools in Tahiti, Samoa, Tonga, Chile, South America, and Mexico.[56]

THE MISSIONARY PRESIDENT

Many Latter-day Saints characterized President McKay as "the missionary President." In his first decade as prophet, the number of missionaries quadrupled. The number of annual converts rose from 12,000 to 180,000, with conversions greatly accelerated in Latin America and the South Seas as a result of an expanded missionary program.[57] This program found its impetus in President McKay's admonition to the Church: "Every member a missionary." He emphasized that investigators be taught in members' homes. The first proselyting plan for use by all missionaries worldwide appeared in 1952. This plan, entitled "A Systematic Program for Teaching the Gospel," grouped information into six discussions. In 1961, the first worldwide mission presidents' seminar was scheduled. The seminar allowed these leaders to share their experiences with one another. As part of the missionary program, three language training schools were also developed at Brigham Young University, Ricks College, and the Church College of Hawaii at Laie.

President McKay was active into his tenth decade. On January 18, 1970, David O. McKay, at the age of ninety-six, died of acute congestion of the heart. On the day he died, the five hundredth stake of the Church was formed. Until the last week of his life he received official guests and conducted Church affairs. United States President Richard M. Nixon issued the following statement when he heard of President McKay's death: "Today the Mormon Church has been deprived of a distinguished and great leader. And America has lost a foremost citizen and human being."[58] One obituary read, "The warmth and humanity of the personality and the breadth of his approach to religion. He captured the esteem and [affection] not only of his own people, but also of people of other faiths."[59]

Visiting with President Eisenhower.

Greeting President Lyndon B. Johnson.

Farming

President McKay maintained the farm in Huntsville, Utah, until his death. Farm life "shaped his early years, gave him a lasting interest in horsemanship . . . and outdoor life, and was the place he retired to meditate from time to time."[13]

President McKay on the farm in Huntsville, Utah.

TEACHINGS OF PRESIDENT
DAVID O. MCKAY

A PERSONAL CHRIST

In 1951, when David Oman McKay was sustained as the prophet, he gave Latter-day Saints reassuring counsel:

"No one can preside over this Church without first being in tune with the head of the Church, our Lord and Savior, Jesus Christ. He is our head. This is his Church. Without his divine guidance and constant inspiration, we cannot succeed. With his guidance, with his inspiration, we cannot fail. . . . I pledge to you that I shall do my best so to live as to merit the companionship of the Holy Spirit, and pray here in your presence that my counselors and I may indeed be 'partakers of the divine spirit.' "[60]

As illustrated by the passage above, President McKay's teachings over six decades centered on the Savior. He instructed: "What you sincerely in your heart think of Christ will determine what you are, will largely determine what your acts will be. No person can study this divine personality, can accept His teachings without becoming conscious of an uplifting and refining influence within himself."[61] Elder McKay described the ultimate result of a living, personal Christ as a delightful, beautiful, and glorious life. He often spoke of the "abundant life," that was "obtained not only from spiritual exultation, but also by the [daily] application . . . of the principles that Jesus taught."[62] President McKay guaranteed that following the gospel brought individuals joy, happiness, and supreme satisfaction.

Many Church members saw President McKay as an example of how to live a happy life. Though his life spanned almost a century of turbulence, he personified happiness and contentment for Church members. Helping to guide the Church during both world wars, President McKay saw the answer to both personal peace and national security in the principles of The Church of Jesus Christ of Latter-day Saints. President McKay taught, "The solution of the great world problems is here in the Church of Christ. Ample provision is made not only for the needs of individuals, but for the nation and groups of nations."[63]

COUNSEL ON WAR

When Church members were called to serve in the armed forces, President McKay became a voice of comfort and reason. At the beginning of World War II he counselled, "The Saints on either side [of a war] have no course open to them but to support that government to which they owe allegiance. But their prayers should go up day and night that God will turn the hearts of their leaders towards peace, that the curse of war may end."[64] As a member of the First Presidency, he succinctly described the justification for war:

many occasions he insisted that agency was God's greatest gift to man and absolutely necessary for progress.[67] For President McKay, the principle of agency was coupled with the principle of responsibility. He directed that "man's responsibility is correspondingly operative with his free agency. . . . [A] responsibility correlated and even coexistent with free agency, which is too infrequently emphasized, and that is the effect not only of a person's actions but also of his thoughts upon others. Man radiates what he is, and that radiation affects to a greater or less[er] degree every person who comes within that radiation."[68]

"There are . . . two conditions which may justify a truly Christian man to enter—mind you, I say enter, not begin—a war: (1) an attempt [by others] to dominate and to deprive another of his free agency, and (2) loyalty to his country. Possibly there is a third, viz., defense of a weak nation that is being unjustly crushed by a strong, ruthless one.

"Paramount among these reasons, of course, is the defense of man's freedom. An attempt to rob man of his free agency caused dissension even in heaven."[65]

"In times of war and peace, one tenet President McKay taught was his insistence that each individual's agency be protected."[66]

AGENCY, SELF-MASTERY, AND SPIRITUALITY

For President McKay, agency was a fundamental principle of the gospel. It was essential to man's salvation, man's greatest endowment, and a "measuring rod by which the actions of men, of organizations, of nations may be judged." On

President McKay asked Church members to be introspective and cleanse the inner vessel; he expected them to achieve self-mastery. Instructing members on how to obtain self-mastery, President McKay shared, "In self-mastery, there is no one great thing which a man may do to obtain it; but there are many little things by observing which self-control may be achieved; and a subjecting of the appetite to the will, and a refusal to satisfy desire are two of these little things."[69]

Mastery of self was to be highly valued. On one occasion President McKay stated, "The hardest battles of life are fought within the chambers of the soul. A victory on the inside of a man's heart is of far more worth in character building than a dozen conquests in the everyday battle of business, political, and social life."[70] For President McKay spirituality was "the consciousness of victory over self and of communion with the Infinite. Spirituality impels one to conquer difficulties and acquire more and more strength. To feel one's faculties unfolding and truth expanding in the soul is one of life's sublimest experiences."[71] Thoughts were important to President McKay; he encouraged members of

Personal Influence

President McKay believed that each person radiated a certain influence. Many who met him felt his influence. The quote below shares his ideas about the radiation of personality:

"Personality is a very important factor in removing prejudice and in bringing investigators. However, that personality must be such that we radiate confidence; and unless our actions are in harmony with our pretensions, our personality will produce a disappointment instead of confidence. This means, therefore, that you . . . carry the responsibility of preaching the gospel by your actions even more than by your words.

"There is one responsibility that no man can evade. That is the responsibility of personal influence. The effect of your words and acts is tremendous in this world. Every moment of life you are changing to a degree the life of the whole world. Every man has an atmosphere or a radiation that is affecting every person in the world. You cannot escape it. Into the hands of every individual is given a marvelous power for good or for evil. It is simply the constant radiation of what a man really is. Every man by his mere living is radiating positive or negative qualities. Life is a state of radiation. To exist is to be the radiation of our feelings, natures, doubts, schemes, or to be the recipient of those things from somebody else. You cannot escape it. Man cannot escape for one moment the radiation of his character. You will select the qualities that you will permit to be radiated."[14]

the Church to have high ideals running through their minds continually, because spirituality was highly connected to their thoughts.

HIGH IDEALS

President McKay stressed that leaders should have and be an example of high ideals. He wrote, "If every man born into the world would have as the beacon of his life . . . ideals, how much sweeter and happier life would be! With such an aim, everyone would seek all that is pure, just, honorable, virtuous, and true—all that leads to perfection; for these virtues he would glorify whoever seeks to glorify God. He would eschew that which is impure, dishonorable, or vile."[72]

President McKay followed the admonition he gave Primary workers in 1932 to give each child aspirations: "What is aspiration? A yearning for something high and good, an exalted desire. . . . Let us make our children aspire for the good, the true, and the beautiful, and let us use the best means possible."[73] For President McKay, aspirations came from the "great minds [of] all ages." Though he always made it clear that "the highest of all ideals are the teachings and particularly the life of Jesus of Nazareth," he also conceded that "history is replete with men, who, as Wordsworth expresses it, 'By the vision splendid, were on their way attended.' "[74]

A Formidable Work Day

President McKay put in a formidable work day. Usually he was awake at 4:00 AM, and in his sparely furnished office on the first floor of the grey granite Church headquarters building by 5:30. He sat in a plain leather swivel chair; his desk was an oblong glass-covered table, at which he received visitors. With an interruption for lunch (his preference was a beef steak, rare) and a short nap, he dispatched religious and temporal business until early evening. He then would dine with his wife and some Church official or member of his family and retire early.

Never a Cross Word

Claire Middlemiss, who served as President McKay's secretary for thirty years, remembered, "From the moment I started working for President McKay, I could see that he was a great man. I never heard a cross word from President McKay in all the years I worked for him. . . . I never heard him speak a cross word even to the Brethren when they were in meeting, when there were many things that came up that probably could have caused a little irritation. So I said to him one day, 'President McKay, how do you do it?' I said, 'I can't be that way.' He said, 'Sister, you must learn to control your feelings.' He said, 'I learned many years ago, when I felt a surge of anger or retort coming over me, to put my tongue way back in my mouth and clamp my teeth down on it, and not to say an unkind and hurtful thing, . . . every time that I did that, I found that it was easier the next time to control my feelings.' . . . This great man went about his business and you never knew that he had the problems weighing upon him, because he always had a smile on his face."[15]

President McKay's sermons were buttressed by scripture and quotations that reflected his great love for classical literature and poetry. Being well acquainted with the words of great authors, he frequently used passages he memorized as a boy in his conference addresses. Finding duplicate ideals in great literature that reinforced hallmarks of the gospel of Jesus Christ was a common practice of President McKay. For instance, he told Church members,

"Wordsworth's heart leaped up when he beheld a rainbow in the sky. Burns' heart wept when his plowshare overturned a daisy. Tennyson could pluck the flower from the 'crannied wall,' and see, if he could read in it the mystery, 'all that God and man is.' All these, and other great men, have shown to us, in the works of nature, the handiwork of God."[75]

Another way he illustrated high ideals and aspirations was to use his own life experiences. President McKay used his parents' relationship with each other—and his relationship with his parents—as examples of what a great marriage, home, and family should be like.

NO SUCCESS CAN COMPENSATE FOR FAILURE IN THE HOME

President McKay addressed family principles more than any other topic. His talks often dealt with courtship, marriage, family, home, and parenting. He often spoke of his parents, family, upbringing, and beginnings in a small rural town as an ideal way of life and frequently held up his mother as an example worthy of emulation. He said,

"I cannot think of a womanly virtue that my mother did not possess. . . . To her children, and all others who knew her well, she was beautiful and dignified. Though high spirited she was even-tempered and self-possessed. Her dark brown eyes immediately expressed any rising emotion which, however, she always held under perfect control. . . . In tenderness, watchful care, loving patience, loyalty to home and to right, she seemed to me in boyhood, and she seems to me now after these years, to have been supreme."[76]

As the lines above illustrate, President McKay portrayed Jennette Evans McKay as the ideal image of a wife and mother. He esteemed all woman from his experiences with his own mother and instructed, "The true gentleman is he who is as courteous and considerate to his mothers and sisters as he is to the most estimable lady he meets. His actions at home are just as refined as his manners in society."[77] As a Church leader, President McKay was known for his gentlemanly manners. Even after he was confined to a wheelchair, he still tried to rise when a woman entered a room. Ideals such as these, learned from his family and through his own obedience, helped him to lead the Church by example.

Following the traditions of his own upbringing, President McKay advised, "The best time for the child to learn [the] rules of conformity is between the ages of three and five. If the parents do not get control of the child during those ages, they will find great difficulty in getting control later."[78]

Along with using his upbringing as a pattern to follow, he also identified his own marriage as exemplary. He often spoke about the love he felt for his children and for his wife, Emma Ray. His marriage of over sixty years became the model union for future generations of Church members. He admonished, "Let us teach youth that the marriage relation is one of the most sacred obligations known to man, or that man can make."[79] Many thought he was a "great example of the way you should treat [your] wife."[80] He explained that a good husband was also a "true gentlemen," and that a true gentlemen was "open, loyal, true . . . honorable," and faithful to himself, others, and God.[81]

More than any other prophet, President McKay talked about courtship and dating. In a wonderful statement, he advised, "During courtship keep your eyes wide open; but after marriage, keep them half shut."[82] In his teachings, President McKay answered questions that many young people continue to ask such as, "How do I know when I am in love?" President McKay gave the following counsel:

"If you meet a girl in whose presence you feel a desire to achieve, who inspires you to do your best, and to make the most of yourself, such a young woman is worthy of your love and is awakening love in your heart.

"I submit that, young men, as a true guide. In the presence of the girl you truly love you do not feel to grovel; in her presence you do not attempt to take advantage of her; in her presence you feel that you would like to be everything that a Master Man should become, for she will inspire you to that ideal. And I ask you young women to cherish that same guide. What does he inspire in you?"[83]

President McKay directed couples to court continuously after marriage. Speaking from experience he taught, "I know of no other place than home where more happiness can be found in this life. It is possible to make home a bit of

heaven; indeed, I picture heaven to be a continuation of the ideal home."[84] His counsel about marriage is timeless and continues to bless lives. The quotation below is typical of President McKay's teachings on how to have a happy, fulfilled union: "Young people, marriage is a relationship that cannot survive selfishness, impatience, domineering, inequality, and lack of respect. Marriage is a relationship that thrives on acceptance, equality, sharing, giving, helping, doing one's part, learning, and laughing together."[85]

In speaking of marriage, President McKay taught that the home should become the center of Latter-day Saint life: "Mothers, fathers, treasure sacredly and sense keenly your responsibility to the child during those first five plastic years of its life."[86] His sermons often discussed the sanctity of marriage and the home. The axiom "No other success can compensate for failure in the home" became a call to parents to spend more time with their children and to teach them about character and integrity.[87] He promised that "pure hearts in a pure home are always in whispering distance of heaven."[88] He called the home the "cell-unit of society," and declared that "parenthood is next to Godhood."[89] Emphasizing family

President McKay with his family.

home evening, he prophesied: "The strength of a nation, especially of a republican nation, is in the intelligent and well-ordered homes of the people. If and when the time comes that parents shift to others or to the state the responsibility of rearing their children, the stability of the nation will be undermined and its impairment and disintegration will have begun."[90]

President McKay loved children and felt that a nation's greatest asset was its children. In addition, he observed that "next to eternal life, the most precious gift that our father in heaven can bestow upon man is his children."[91] His background as an educator came into play as he shared his expertise and prophetic vision with parents. On one occasion he reminded parents, "In teaching children, it should ever be kept in mind that 'Behavior is caught, not taught.' Example is more potent than precept. Parents have the duty to be what they would have their children become in regard to courtesy, sincerity, temperance, and courage to do right at all times."[92]

Prophetically, President McKay knew that an attack on the family was imminent and prepared members of the Church for the future. He warned, "When family life disintegrates, the foundation and bulwark of human society is undermined."[93] While divorces became more prevalent during the 1960s and 1970s, he defined the Church's stand on divorce as follows:

"Except in cases of infidelity or other extreme conditions, the church frowns upon divorce. . . . A man who has entered into a sacred covenant in the House of the Lord to remain true to the marriage vow is a traitor to that covenant if he separates himself from his wife and family just because he has permitted himself to become infatuated with the pretty face and comely form of some young girl who flattered him with a smile. Even though a loose interpretation of the law

President David O. McKay with the missionaries in San Jose, California, and his son Llewelyn on his lap in 1909.

of the land would grant such a man a bill of divorcement, I think he is unworthy of a recommend to consummate his second marriage in the temple."[94]

As seen previously, President McKay had clear behavioral requirements for the husbands of the Church. He had a great respect for manhood and the priesthood, and he often directed his sermons specifically to the Church's young men. He believed in Goethe's words and quoted them often: "The destiny of any nation at any given time depends upon the opinions of the young men under five and twenty."[95] He instructed, "There is nothing in life so admirable as true manhood" and a country's greatest asset is its manhood.[96]

EVERY MEMBER A MISSIONARY

Another axiom that President McKay embedded in the minds of Church members was "Every Member a Missionary." President McKay encouraged Church members not to wait for "some special opportunity" to "proclaim the gospel of Jesus Christ." He emphasized that Latter-day Saints could proclaim the gospel in their acts, social circles, politics, businesses, and everywhere they mingled. He felt that each member could reach others with the power of his or her personality. In 1969 he taught, "There is no power so potent, no power so effective in influencing the lives of others, as Personality. It is not just an influence, but many times is an inspiration. . . . *Each of us can become an inspiration to others.*"[97]

ETERNAL LIFE

Ultimately, President McKay desired that each Church member receive the blessing of eternal life. He described a wonderful vision he had of that ultimate ideal:

"I then fell asleep, and beheld in vision something infinitely sublime. In the distance I beheld a beautiful white city. Though it was far away, yet I seemed to realize that trees with luscious fruit, shrubbery with gorgeously tinted leaves, and flowers in perfect bloom abounded everywhere. The clear sky above seemed to reflect these beautiful shades of color. I then saw a great concourse of people approaching the city. Each one wore a white flowing robe and a white headdress. Instantly my attention seemed centered upon their leader, and though I could see only the profile of his features and his body, I recognized him at once as my Savior! The tint and radiance of his countenance were glorious to behold. There was a peace about him which seemed sublime—it was divine!

"The city, I understood, was his. It was the City Eternal; and the people following him were to abide there in peace and eternal happiness.

"But who were they?

"As if the Savior read my thoughts, he answered by pointing to a semicircle that then appeared above them, and on which were written in gold the words:

President David O. McKay surrounded by his daughter Emma Rae McKay Ashton and grandchildren.

He Is Not Dead

President McKay and his wife had a close-knit family. In 1912, President McKay recorded in his journal the experience of losing his three-year-old son Royle:

"Royle was too weak and the complications of diseases too many. He battled bravely all day, taking the little stimulant given him at intervals as willingly as a grown person would. At 9:30 pm Papa, Thomas E. and I again administered to him. Emma Ray felt very hopeful, and lay down on the cot beside him for a little rest. Soon his little pulse weakened, and we knew that our baby would soon leave us. 'Mama' was the last word on his precious lips. Just before the end came, he stretched out his little hands, and as I stooped to caress him, he encircled my neck, and gave me the last of many of the most loving caresses ever a father received from a darling child. It seemed he realized he was going, and wanted to say, 'Goodbye, Papa,' but his little voice was already stilled. . . . I am sure he recognized his Mama a moment later. She had rested only a few minutes; and noticing that the nurses were somewhat agitated she was bending over her darling baby in a second and did not leave him until we gently led her from the room from which Death had taken our baby boy.

The end came at 1:50 am without even a twitch of a muscle. 'He is not dead but sleepeth' was never more applicable to any soul, for he truly went to sleep. He did not die."[16]

"These Are They Who Have Overcome the World Who Have Truly Been Born Again!"[98]

Mary Jane Woodger

Associate Professor of Church History and Doctrine, EdD
Brigham Young University

NOTES

1. Alden Whitman, "Missionary President," *David O. McKay Scrapbooks 110*, LDS Church Archives, Salt Lake City.

2. Henry A Smith, "President McKay 79 Next Monday," *Church News*, September 6, 1952, 3.

3. David B. Haight oral history interview by Mary Jane Woodger for the Brigham Young University, College of Education, McKay Research Project, August 20, 1996, Salt Lake City, transcription of taped interview in author's possession.

4. Jeanette McKay Morrell, *Highlights in the Life of President David O. McKay* (Salt Lake City: Deseret Book, 1966), 4, 6, 8–9.

5. Ibid., 8–9; David O. McKay, synopsis of an address delivered at cornerstone-laying ceremonies of Ogden Tabernacle, Ogden, Utah, July 16, 1954, *David O. McKay Scrapbooks 29*.

6. Morrell, *Highlights*, 10.

7. Jeanette McKay Morrell, "Boyhood of President David O. McKay," *Relief Society Magazine* 40, no. 10 (October 1953): 656; Richard O. Cowan, *The Latter-day Saint Century* (Salt Lake City: Bookcraft, 1999), 158; Terry W. Call, "David O. McKay," *Church News*, September 25, 1993, 10.

8. Call, "David O. McKay," 10.

9. International Society of the Daughters of the Utah Pioneers, David McKay file (1955); Francis M. Gibbons, *David O. McKay: Apostle to the World, Prophet of God* (Salt Lake City: Deseret Book, 1986), 15; Richard L. Evans, "David O. McKay: Portrait of a President," *Improvement Era* 54 (June 1951): 401.

10. Gunn McKay oral history interview by Mary Jane Woodger for the Brigham Young University, College of Education, McKay Research Project, June 28, 1995, Huntsville, Utah, transcription of taped interview in author's possession.

11. David O. McKay, "Peace Through the Gospel of Christ," *Improvement Era* (March 1921): 405–6.

12. Leonard J. Arrington and Susan Arrington Madsen, *Mothers of the Prophets* (Salt Lake City, Deseret Book, 1987), 143; David O. McKay to Anthony W. Ivins, August 12, 1912, in David O. McKay Papers 1897–1983, Mss 668, microfilm copy of holograph, reel 1, no. 107, University of Utah Marriott Library, Special Collections, Western Americana Collection.

13. Marie F. Felt, "David, a Boy of Promise," *Instructor* (September 1969): 329.

14. Ernest L. Wilkinson, "David O. McKay Building Dedication," in *Speeches of the Year*, Brigham Young University (Provo, UT: Brigham Young University, 1954), 2.

15. Emma Ray McKay, Dedicatory Services of the Saleneatu Chapel in Samoa, January 15, 1955, *David O. McKay Scrapbooks 143*.

16. Morrell, "Boyhood of President David O. McKay," 656–57; Gibbons, *David O. McKay: Apostle to the World, Prophet of God*, 10.

17. David O. McKay, "The Temple Ceremony," address given at the Salt Lake Temple Annex, September 25, 1941, 4.

18. Richard N. Armstrong, *The Rhetoric of David O. McKay: Mormon Prophet* (New York: Peter Lang, 1993), 4.

19. Leland H. Monson, "David O. McKay was a Deacon, Too," *Instructor* (September 1962): 298–99.

20. Morrell, *Highlights*, 28.

21. "David O. McKay file," (1955), International Society of the Daughters of Utah Pioneers reading room, Salt Lake City.

22. John C. Peterson to President McKay, *David O. McKay Scrapbooks 188*.

23. Morrell, *Highlights*, 26.

24. Ibid., 26, 28.

25. Thomas E. McKay, "Standards for LDS Youth," in *Address to the Brigham Young University Student Body* (Provo, UT: The BYU Extension Division and Delta Phi, 1953), 2.

26. Morrell, *Highlights*, 29, 38.

27. David O. McKay, "A Personal Testimony," *Improvement Era* (September 1962): 628.

28. Keith Terry, *David O. McKay: Prophet of Love* (Santa Barbara: Butterfly Publishing Inc., 1980), 30.

29. Armstrong, *The Rhetoric of David O. McKay*, 4; Department of Seminaries and Institutes of Religion, comp., "David O. McKay," *Presidents of the Church* (Salt Lake City: The Church of Jesus Christ of Latter-day Saints), 98.

30. Morrell, *Highlights*, 31.

31. Gibbons, *David O. McKay: Apostle to the World, Prophet of God*, 35.

32. Morrell, "Boyhood of President David O. McKay," 662.

33. Jeanette McKay Morrell, "Life of President David O. McKay: A Few Highlights of a Busy Life," *The Relief Society Magazine* (November 1953): 730.

34. Preston Nibley, *The Presidents of the Church* (Salt Lake City: Deseret Book, 1971), 314–15.

35. The Utah State Historical Society, *Utah, a Centennial History* (New York: Lewis Historical Publishing Company, 1949), 416; Richard W. Sadler and Richard C. Roberts, *History of Weber State College* (Salt Lake City: Publisher's Press, 1988), 23.

36. David Lawrence McKay, *My Father, David O. McKay* (Salt Lake City: Deseret Book, 1993), 1–2.

37. International Society of the Daughters of Utah Pioneers, "Tribute to Emma Ray McKay," (Salt Lake City: International Society of the Daughters of Utah Pioneers); La Rue Sneff, "Mrs. McKay is 'Ray of Sunshine,'" *Deseret News Church Section* (January 22, 1950): 6; Edward and Lottie McKay oral history interview by Mary Jane Woodger for Brigham Young University, College of Education, McKay Research Project, June 30, 1995, Salt Lake City, transcription of taped interview in author's possession.

38. Emma Rae McKay Ashton, "Emma Ray Riggs McKay," *The Relief Society Magazine* 47, no.6 (June 1960): 351; University of Utah, Emma Ray Riggs Transcripts; Llewellyn R. McKay, *Home Memories of President David O. McKay* (Salt Lake City: Deseret Book, 1956), 171; International Society of the Daughters of Utah Pioneers, "Emma Ray McKay," (Salt Lake City: International Society of the Daughters of Utah Pioneers).

39. David Lawrence McKay, "Remembering Father and Mother: President David O. McKay and Sister Emma Ray Riggs McKay," *Ensign*, August 1984, 36.

40. International Society of the Daughters of Utah Pioneers, "Tribute to Emma Ray McKay."

41. Remarks of Sister Emma Ray Riggs McKay, wife of President David O. McKay, September 8, 1957, Wells Stake Conference, Granite Stake Tabernacle, Salt Lake City, *David O. McKay Scrapbooks 39*.

42. Ibid.

43. David Lawrence McKay, *My Father, David O. McKay*, 99.

44. Whitman, "Missionary President."

45. Morrell, "Life of President David O. McKay," 732.

46. W. Dee Halverson, *Stephen L Richards, 1879–1959* (Salt Lake City: Heritage Press Ltd., 1994), 127.

47. Richard O. Cowan, *The Church in the Twentieth Century* (Salt Lake City: Bookcraft, 1985), 235.

48. International Society of the Daughters of Utah Pioneers, "David O. McKay," (Salt Lake City: International Society of the Daughters of Utah Pioneers).

49. International Society of the Daughters of Utah Pioneers, "Tribute to Emma Ray McKay"; Terry, *David O. McKay: Prophet of Love*, 93.

50. D. Michael Quinn, *J. Reuben Clark: The Church Years* (Provo, UT: Brigham Young University Press, 1983), 29–30, 113–14.

51. "President Assisted Expansion," *Deseret News*, January 18, 1970, M3, *David O. McKay Scrapbooks 110*, 1–3.

52. Ibid.

53. Ibid.

54. Ibid.

55. Ibid.

56. Ibid.

57. Whitman, "Missionary President," 4, 8.

58. "David O. McKay, Mormon Leader, Is Dead at Ninety-six," *New York Times, David O. McKay's Scrapbooks 110*, 3.

59. Whitman, "Missionary President," 3.

60. David O. McKay, CR, April 1951, 157.

61. Ibid., 93.

62. David O. McKay, *Gospel Ideals* (Salt Lake City: Deseret Sunday School Union Board, 1957), 151.

63. David O. McKay, CR, April 1920, 118.

64. David O. McKay, CR, October 1940, 6.

65. David O. McKay, CR, April 1944, 72.

66. Ibid., 72–73.

67. David O. McKay, CR, October 1965, 7; David O. McKay, CR, April 1950, 32–33.

68. Ibid., 33–34.

69. David O. McKay, "On Fasting," *Improvement Era* 66 (March 1963): 156.

70. David O. McKay "Sylvester Q. Cannon," *Improvement Era* 46 (August 1943): 465.

71. David O. McKay, CR, October 1969, 8.

72. David O. McKay, "Peace and Goodwill," *Improvement Era* 58 (December 1955): 893–894.

73. General Session of Thirtieth Annual Convention of Primary Association Officers in Barrett Hall, University of Utah, Salt Lake City, June 10, 1932, as found in *David O. McKay Scrapbooks 2*, 3.

74. David O. McKay, CR, April 1951, 93.

75. David O. McKay, CR, October 1908, 108.

76. Bryant S. Hinckley, "Greatness in Men: David O. McKay," *Improvement Era* 35 (May 1932): 391.

77. David O. McKay, "The Religion Class Workers of Weber and Ogden Stakes," *Thoughts* (Ogden, Utah: 1912).

78. David O. McKay, "Home . . . and the Strength of Youth," *Improvement Era* 62 (August 1959): 583.

79. David O. McKay, *Pathways to Happiness*, comp. Llewelyn R. McKay (Salt Lake City: Bookcraft, 1967), 113.

80. Hartman Rector Jr., interview by Mary Jane Woodger for Brigham Young University, College of Education, McKay Research Project, October 10, 1996, Salt Lake City, transcription of taped interview in author's possession.

81. Kentucky Conference minutes, November 29, 1926, David O. McKay papers 1897–1983, Mss 668, microfilm copy of holography, reel 8, no. 498, University of Utah Marriott Library, Special Collections, Western Americana Collection.

82. David O. McKay, "Ideals for 'Courtship and Marriage,'" *Improvement Era* 63 (February 1960): 110.

83. David O. McKay, "As Youth Contemplates an Eternal Partnership," *Improvement Era* 41 (March 1938), 139.

84. McKay, *Gospel Ideals*, 490.

85. McKay, "Ideals for 'Courtship and Marriage,'" 110.

86. McKay, *Pathways to Happiness*, 115.

87. James Edward McCulloch, *Home: The Savior of Civilization*

(Washington, DC: The Southern Co-operative League, 1924), 42; see David O. McKay, CR, April 1935, 115–16.

88. Harold B. Lee, *Stand Ye in Holy Places* (Salt Lake City: Deseret Book, 1974), 176.

89. McKay, *Pathways to Happiness*, 117.

90. Ibid., 3.

91. David O. McKay, "Utah White House Conference on Child Health and Protection," April 7, 1931, as found in *David O. McKay Scrapbooks 2*, 2; "General Sunday School Conference," October 2, 1949, as found in *David O. McKay Scrapbooks 14*, 17–18.

92. David O. McKay, CR, April 1935, 114.

93. David O. McKay, CR, October 1947, 119.

94. David O. McKay, "The Home Front," *Improvement Era* 46 (November 1943): 657.

95. David O. McKay, "A Message for LDS College Youth," *BYU Speeches of the Year* (Provo, UT: BYU Press, October 10, 1952), 4.

96. David O. McKay, CR, October 1908, 108; David O. McKay, "Parental Responsibility," *Relief Society Magazine* 49 (December 1962): 878.

97. David O. McKay, CR, April 1910, 107, and David O. McKay, "The Radiation and Influence of a Powerful Personality," *The Instructor* (August 1969): 265.

98. David O. McKay, *Cherished Experiences from the Writings of President David O. McKay*, comp. Clare Middlemiss (Salt Lake City: Deseret Book, 1976), 59–60.

SIDEBAR AND PHOTO NOTES

1. McKay, "Home . . . And the Strength of Youth," 582–83.

2. McKay, *Cherished Experiences*, 160; David O. McKay, CR, October 1954, 83.

3. Lee, *Stand Ye in Holy Places*, 178.

4. Ashton, "Emma Ray Riggs McKay," 351; Sneff, "Mrs. McKay is 'Ray of Sunshine,' "6.

5. Boyd K. Packer, "David O. McKay Symposium," October 9, 1996, Brigham Young University, 2.

6. Hugh B. Brown, "Dedicatory Program: Clark Library, Smoot Administration Building, Physical Plant Building," October 10, 1962, *BYU Speeches of the Year*, 13.

7. David O. McKay, "Relief Society Conference," *Relief Society Magazine* 18 (1931): 349.

8. David O. McKay, "Temple Marriage," *Deseret News Church Section* (February 27, 1952): 3.

9. McKay, *Cherished Experiences*, 140.

10. "Testimony of President McKay: Illustrated lecture on his world tour of the missions," December 25, 1934, as found in *David O. McKay Scrapbooks 107*.

11. Terry, *David O. McKay: Prophet of Love*, 65.

12. David O. McKay, "Report given regarding his trip to his native town, Huntsville, Utah, to participate in the dedication of the New Church Edifice," March 31, 1959, as found in *David O. McKay Scrapbooks 44*.

13. Whitman, "Missionary President."

14. David O. McKay, CR, October 1969, 87.

15. Interview with KSXX radio station, broadcast January 20, 1970, Clare Middlemiss, as found in *David O. McKay Scrapbooks 110*.

16. David Lawrence McKay, *My Father, David O. McKay*, 84–85.

Chapter Ten

JOSEPH FIELDING SMITH

LIFE AND TIMES

1876	July 19	Born in Salt Lake City, Utah
1898		Married Louie Shurtliff
1899		Served a mission to Great Britain
1901		Employed as a clerk in the Church historian's office
1906		Sustained as assistant Church historian
1908		Louie died; marries Ethel Georgina Reynolds
1910	April 7	Ordained Apostle
1921–70		Served as Church historian
1934–64		Served as president of the Genealogical Society
1937		Ethel died
1938		Married Jessie Evans
1945		Served as president of the Salt Lake Temple
1950		Became Acting President of the Quorum of the Twelve Apostles
1951		Became President of the Quorum of the Twelve Apostles
1951		Awarded an honorary Doctor of Letters degree from BYU
1965		Called as a counselor to President David O. McKay
1970	January 23	Set apart as President of the Church
1970		Published *Seek Ye Earnestly*
1971		Presided over first area conference of the Church in Manchester, England; Jessie died
1972	July 2	Died in Salt Lake City, Utah, at age ninety-five

BIOGRAPHICAL HIGHLIGHTS

President Joseph Fielding Smith was set apart as the tenth President of the Church on January 23, 1970. At that time he had served just over four years as a counselor in the First Presidency and sixty years as an Apostle. He was a kind and soft-spoken man who was compassionate, caring, and merciful. His capacity to teach and write about the principles and doctrines of the gospel was a defining element of his presidency.

Joseph Fielding Smith grew to manhood under the tutelage of his father, Joseph F. Smith, Apostle and then President of the Church. He served a mission to Great Britain and thereafter worked for the Church in the historian's office. At age thirty-three he was ordained an Apostle and for the next sixty-two years served in the presiding quorums of the Church. At the time of his death his family consisted of eleven children, fifty-nine grandchildren, and ninety-nine great-grandchildren. Even though he became President of the Church, Joseph Fielding Smith's first and foremost priority was helping his own family live upright and honorable lives.

CONTRIBUTIONS

Though he was President of the Church for only two and a half years, Joseph Fielding Smith is known for instituting at least three significant changes within the Church. He consolidated Church magazines into three publications (*Ensign*, *New Era*, *Friend*), established Monday night as the uniform time for family home evening, and created Church Social Services.

TEACHINGS

The ministry of Joseph Fielding Smith was ever focused on three things: the love of Jesus Christ and our absolute need to return to Him through repentance, the Restoration of the gospel of Jesus Christ in the latter-days through the Prophet Joseph Smith, and the central role of the family in God's plan of happiness.

LIFE OF
JOSEPH FIELDING SMITH

The life of Joseph Fielding Smith stands as a bridge between the Latter-day Saint pioneers of the nineteenth-century frontier and the modern, respected, and international body of Saints of the twentieth and twenty-first centuries. At his birth in 1876, the Church had been in the Salt Lake Valley just less than thirty years, the president of the United States was Civil War hero Ulysses S. Grant, and the Salt Lake Temple would not be completed for more than ten years. In fact, the first temple to be completed in Utah was the St. George Temple. It was dedicated in 1877 by Brigham Young when Joseph was only one year old, and Joseph Fielding Smith was in attendance with his father Joseph F. Smith.

Trained Up by a Prophet

"My father, Joseph F. Smith, the sixth President of the Church . . . was the most tenderhearted man I ever knew. His sympathy was perpetually drawn out toward the downtrodden and oppressed. . . . He was a preacher of righteousness, and the sincerity of his words penetrated the souls of men. . . . Among my fondest memories are the hours I spent by his side discussing principles of the gospel and receiving instruction as only he could give it. In this way the foundation of my own knowledge was laid in truth, so that I, too, can say I know my Redeemer lives and that Joseph Smith was a prophet of the living God."[1]

He later joked, "My first church assignment . . . was to accompany Brigham Young to the dedication of the St. George Temple. Of course, I don't remember that assignment too well, for I was just one year old then."[1] He grew up surrounded by pioneers who had crossed the plains in handcarts and wagons.

Joseph Fielding Smith and his father, Joseph F. Smith.

In contrast to his pioneers' origins, Joseph Fielding Smith came to embrace the modern era. Characteristic of his progressive vision was his supervision of the construction of a thirty-one-story skyscraper to serve as Church headquarters for the approximately three million Latter-day Saints throughout the world at the time. His personal life also reflected his interest in things modern. At age eighty he developed a love for flying in fighter jets. He flew frequently with pilots from the Utah Air National Guard and received an honorary commission to the rank of brigadier general. An acquaintance fondly remembers paying a visit to President Smith's office only to learn that he was not in at the moment. His secretary, Rubie Egbert then said, "Step to the window here and maybe you can see him." The acquaintance walked to the window but could see nothing but a jet streaking through the sky high above the Great Salt Lake. "You mean he's in that plane?" he asked in shocked tones. "Oh yes, that's him all right. He's very fond of flying."[2] President Smith was a man who was comfortable at the reins of a horse-drawn carriage or in the cockpit of a fighter jet. He had successfully bridged two centuries.

Joseph Fielding Smith in the cockpit of a fighter jet.

A Ninety-Year Old "Fighter Pilot"

Joseph took his maiden flight in the cockpit of a fighter jet in 1956 to celebrate his eightieth birthday. He was hooked! He flew in fighters so frequently that at age ninety-two he was awarded the honorary rank of brigadier general in the National Guard. Joseph's secretary recalled, "A friend in the National Guard calls him up and says, 'How about a relaxing?' and up they go. Once they get in the air he often takes over the controls. Flew down to Grand Canyon and back last week, 400 miles an hour!"[2] Of flying President Smith would exclaim, "That's about as close to heaven as I can get just now."[3]

CHILDHOOD

Joseph Fielding Smith was born on July 19, 1876, in the family home at 333 West First North in Salt Lake City. His father, Joseph F. Smith, was the son of Hyrum Smith, who was martyred with his younger brother Joseph Smith at Carthage, Illinois, on June 27, 1844. His mother was Julina Lambson Smith who was the second of six plural wives of Joseph F. Smith. He was preceded in the family by nine brothers and sisters and was followed by thirty-three more by birth and five by adoption.

Joseph learned the responsibilities associated with work at an early age. From the time he was eight until he was fifteen, his father lived in exile because of the persecution Latter-day Saints faced over plural marriage. Therefore, young Joseph quickly matured doing work usually reserved for men. The family owned a farm in Taylorsville where he worked tirelessly. By the time he was ten he served as his mother's assistant in her midwifery practice. Regardless of the time, day or night, when the call came for his mother's services it was Joseph's duty to hitch up the mare "Old Meg" and drive his mother to the home of the expectant mother. Joseph would then wait in the wagon until his mother was finished. This sometimes took hours, which was tolerable in the summer months but was nearly unbearable in the dead of winter. Joseph marveled that so many babies were born in the middle of the night and jokingly wished that the mothers of these new babies timed their deliveries better.

EDUCATION AND BOOKS

As his mother's oldest son, and with his father so frequently in hiding or engaged in Church business, the financial burdens of maintaining the household fell, in part, on the shoulders of Joseph. Hence, his formal education came to an end following two years of study at the Latter-day Saint College in his late teens. He then went to work full-time to help support the family.

Birthplace of Joseph Fielding Smith.

The Name Joseph

Joseph Fielding Smith carried the name of his father, Joseph F. Smith; his great-uncle, the Prophet Joseph Smith Jr.; and his great-grandfather, Joseph Smith Sr. We learn from the Book of Mormon that Joseph (who was sold into Egypt) was granted a revelation concerning Joseph Smith's family in the last days. The revelation states: "And thus prophesied Joseph, saying: Behold, that seer [Joseph Smith Jr.] will the Lord bless . . . and his name shall be called after me; and it shall be after the name of his father [Joseph Smith Sr.]. And he shall be like unto me; for the thing, which the Lord shall bring forth by his hand, by the power of the Lord shall bring my people unto salvation" (2 Nephi 3:14–15).

In its Hebrew form, the name Joseph means "to add upon." In the Smith family, the name Joseph was held as an honored title that should never be shortened to Joe. Like his father before him, Joseph Fielding Smith developed a reverential awe for the sacredness of his name. And, like his father before him, Joseph Fielding Smith lived up to the meaning of his name—he added to the richness of the kingdom of God in a variety of ways.

Read, Read, Read!

Joseph read constantly and was anxious to see his eleven children do the same. He encouraged them to read from the scriptures and other good books every chance they could. Joseph's son, Joseph Jr., remembers that his father "was always encouraging us to read the scriptures and to study. I remember as a boy of approximately 13 years, I received five dollars which was offered for reading the Book of Mormon."[4] With eleven children reading, the financial commitment was significant. Nevertheless, Joseph felt it was worth the investment and the sacrifice.

Nevertheless, his desire to learn never waned. He earnestly studied throughout his life and became a noteworthy scholar and author of twenty-five books.

Joseph Fielding Smith maintained a lifelong love affair with books. Of his favorite books he said, "From my earliest recollection, from the time I first could read, I have received more pleasure and greater satisfaction out of the study of the scriptures, and reading of the Lord Jesus Christ, and of the Prophet Joseph Smith, and the work that has been accomplished for the salvation of men, than from anything else in all the world."[3]

Joseph was quiet and reserved as a young man. He loved to study from books in his father's library and would hurry through

Joseph Fielding Smith, You Can Bank on Him!

Shortly after he was sustained as the tenth President of the Church in 1970, Joseph received recognition for maintaining the oldest active bank account at Zion's Bank. His account was opened by his father, Joseph F. Smith, the year he was born in 1876. At that time the bank was only three years old. This account remained open until Joseph Fielding Smith's death in 1972. The principles of thrift that he learned at a young age allowed him to prosper temporally during times of financial boom or bust in greater economic circles. His active bank account spanning almost one full century stood as an emblem of how actively he embraced thrift as an important value in his life.[5]

his chores not so he could join the other boys in playing, hunting, or fishing, but so he could spend his leisure time reading.

A library was one luxury that he afforded himself in his own home. Joseph's children fondly recall his love for reading. They reported that frequently, when it was time to do homework, their textbooks would be missing. Finding them was rather simple, however, because if they could find their father they could find their book. He had simply slipped away to read.

MARRIAGE, MISSION, AND CAREER

Late in the summer of 1894, Joseph met a beautiful young woman from Ogden named Louie Shurtliff. The Smith family had invited her to stay with them while she attended the University of Utah because her father was a close friend of Joseph F. Smith. A romance ensued between Joseph and

Joseph Fielding Smith reviewing an old Zion's bank signature book.

Louie Shurtliff.

Joseph Fielding Smith reading to his grandchildren.

Louie almost from the day they met. Joseph would bring her small sacks of candy from ZCMI that they would eat as they studied together. They attended church, plays, and other social affairs in the city. Following her graduation from the University of Utah she returned to Ogden to teach. Joseph traveled to Ogden as often as possible to see her. On at least one occasion when he could not afford a train ticket north he rode his bicycle from Salt Lake to Ogden to be near Louie. They were married on April 26, 1898, by Joseph F. Smith in the Salt Lake Temple.

On March 17, 1899, after less than one year of marriage, Joseph was called by President Lorenzo Snow to serve a mission. The call was not entirely unexpected as Joseph had received a preliminary interview by Elder Franklin D.

Richards (President of the Quorum of the Twelve Apostles). During their conversation, President Richards asked Joseph where he'd prefer to serve. Joseph responded by telling President Richards that he would serve wherever the Brethren sent him. President Richards then remarked that there must be a place he would prefer to serve. With this coaxing Joseph conceded that he would very much like to serve in Germany. "So," Joseph wrote jokingly, "they sent me to England."[4]

Joseph departed Salt Lake City on May 13, 1899. His passport described him as having a light complexion, brown hair, bluish-gray eyes, and standing five feet nine inches tall. The day prior to his departure he was ordained a seventy by his father.

Joseph arrived in Liverpool on April 3, 1899, and was assigned to the Nottingham region. There he learned firsthand the taxing nature of missionary service. Sixty years earlier thousands of people had joined the Church in Great Britain. But Joseph Fielding Smith now found the people of England apathetic toward religion in general and even less interested in the Latter-day restoration. In his letters to Louie, Joseph described the challenges of mission life, his homesickness for her, and the honor of serving the Lord whether the people gave heed to his message or not. Initially, he found proselytizing to be very challenging. He was reserved and quiet by nature and preaching at street meetings in England tested him. However, over time these experiences proved to deepen his convictions and promote a confidence in his manner that would strengthen him for the rest of his life.

Missionary success was so limited that Joseph and his companions eventually formed a musical quartet known as

Joseph Fielding Smith as a young missionary in England.

The Sagebrush Singers claiming that once people heard the elders sing they were glad to hear them talk! Joseph's diligence in the mission caught the eye of the mission president who called him to serve as the clerk of the Nottingham conference. This trusted position included the tasks of maintaining accurate records of mission finances, conducting correspondence for the president, and distributing Church literature such as the *Millennial Star* to the members of the Church in the region. Joseph was highly respected and his work ethic was acknowledged by his fellow missionaries. Even so, at the time of his departure from England on June 20, 1901, he had not baptized one person during his two years of service, yet his mission experience proved invaluable. In fact, Joseph's conference president in the mission (Stephen W. Walker) wrote home that Joseph would undoubtedly leave his mark upon the world.[5] In many respects, the trials he faced as a missionary tempered him for the leadership roles in the Church that he would assume just a few years after his return from England.

Joseph arrived at his home in Salt Lake City on July 9, 1901. He was thrilled to be reunited with Louie, and they immediately turned their hopes toward starting a family. This desire sent Joseph in search of a job that would enable him to support a wife and children.

On October 1 of that year, Joseph accepted a position as a clerk in the Church historian's office. At the time of Joseph's appointment, the Church was undergoing a barrage of anti-Mormon attacks in the media. Many of these maintained an anti-polygamy perspective and therefore were constantly aimed at Joseph's father (who became President of the Church on October 17, 1901) and other beloved men in his life. Joseph mounted a defense that resulted in his second publication *Blood Atonement and the Origin of Plural Marriage* (1905). From his earliest days in the Church historian's office, Joseph was known as a staunch and able defender of the faith. This characteristic made him a valuable and respected member of the historian's staff and in 1906, Joseph was sustained as assistant Church historian replacing Elder Orson F. Whitney of the Quorum of the Twelve Apostles. He held this position until 1921 when he was named Church historian. He served as Church historian until he became President of the Church in 1970 when Howard W. Hunter was appointed to the position.

Joseph Fielding Smith (center) as Church Historian with his assistants Andrew Jenson (left) and A. William Lund (right).

he prayed for direction. His father, and President of the Church, counseled him to promptly seek a wife and a mother for his daughters. Joseph was thirty-one years old at the time.

He was soon blessed with the companionship of Ethel Georgina Reynolds. She was eighteen years old and worked in the Church historian's office where they had become acquainted. After courtship, which included several outings with his young daughters, Joseph proposed and the two were married in the Salt Lake Temple on November 8, 1908. Together they had five sons and four daughters. Throughout her years of young motherhood Ethel served as a member of the Relief Society General Board for a combined total of fifteen years. In 1933 she became ill, and her condition continued to

A WIDOWER

Tragedy struck the Smith family on March 30, 1908, when Louie passed away due to complications associated with pregnancy. She had been the center of Joseph's world for ten years. Her death was almost unbearable for him. They had two young daughters, Julina and Josephine, who cried themselves to sleep night after night. As a family, they were broken without their matriarch. Joseph moved his small family into the Beehive House with his parents and was helped by the collective family with his grieving and that of his daughters. Knowing that his little girls needed a mother, yet hesitant to search for a new companion so soon after Louie's death,

Joseph Fielding Smith searching in the archives.

The Joseph Fielding Smith family in 1938. Front row left to right: Lewis (inset, serving a mission), Reynolds, Joseph Fielding Smith, Jessie Evans Smith, Joseph Fielding Jr., Milton. Back row left to right: Emily, Naomi, Lois, Josephine, Julina, Amelia, Douglas.

worsen until she died of a cerebral hemorrhage on August 26, 1937. She was only forty-seven years old.

On April 12, 1938, Joseph Fielding Smith was sealed to Jessie Ella Evans in the Salt Lake Temple. She was a renowned vocalist with the Mormon Tabernacle Choir. Joseph was sixty-two years old and Jessie was thirty-six and had never been married. Of Joseph's eleven children only three sons still lived at home. Jessie's personality was bright and vivacious and brought Joseph's playful side to the surface. After thirty-three years of marriage, Jessie died on August 3, 1971, just eleven months prior to the death of her husband.

CHURCH SERVICE

Joseph Fielding Smith received his patriarchal blessing at the age of twenty from John Smith, Patriarch to the Church. Portions of that blessing clearly expounded Joseph's future role

Ethel Smith.

as a servant-leader in the Church. In it he was told: "It is thy privilege to live to a good old age and the will of the Lord that you should become a mighty man in Israel. . . . It shall be thy duty to sit in counsel with thy brethren and to preside among the people. It shall be thy duty also to travel much at home and abroad, by land and water, laboring in the ministry, and I say unto thee, hold up thy head, lift up thy voice without fear or favor as the Spirit of the Lord shall direct, and the blessing of the Lord shall rest upon thee. His Spirit shall direct thy mind and give the word and sentiment that thou shalt confound the wisdom of the wicked and set at nought the councils of the unjust."[6]

The prophesy that Joseph would become a "mighty man in Israel" and one who would "preside among the people" finds part of its fulfillment in the fact that following his mission, he held very few positions in the Church that were not general Church assignments. Some of his local Church service would include the following: In 1901, he began a nine-year period of service as a missionary in the Salt Lake Stake. In 1903, he was called to serve as the President of the Twenty-fourth Quorum of the Seventy. Then in 1904 he was called to serve on the high council of the Salt Lake Stake, at which time he was ordained a high priest by his older brother Hyrum Mack Smith, who was an Apostle.

Joseph's first calling to a general Church position came in 1903 when he was appointed to serve on the general board of the Young Men's Mutual Improvement Association. He held this position until 1919. However, on April 7, 1910, at the age of thirty-three, he was called to serve in the Quorum of the Twelve Apostles. His Church service for the next sixty years was wide and varied but all emanated first, and foremost, from his role as an Apostle of the Lord Jesus Christ.

Jessie in flower garden.

Joseph Fielding Smith and Jessie surrounded by their children and grandchildren.

"Genealogy, I am Doing It"

Joseph was a pioneer in genealogical research in the Church. He was the first editor in chief of the Utah Genealogical and Historical Magazine, a publication he started from scratch. This magazine served the needs of genealogical researchers for thirty years until it was discontinued in 1940. He also served as the president of the Genealogical Society from 1934–1964. Under his direction the Church's genealogical library grew from about 1400 volumes to the largest library of its kind in the world.[6]

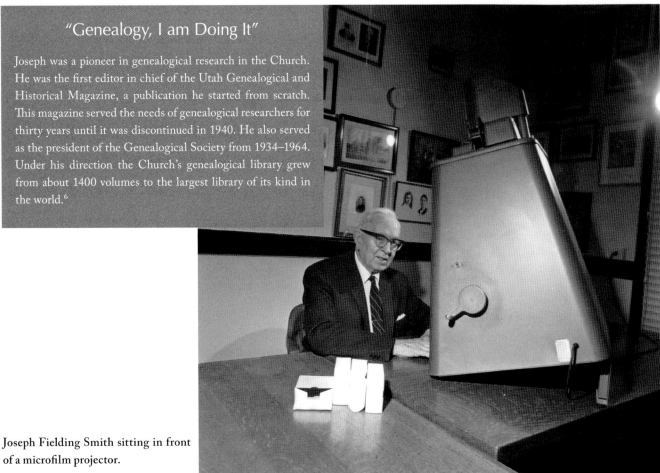

Joseph Fielding Smith sitting in front of a microfilm projector.

THE APOSTLESHIP AND FIRST PRESIDENCY

John R. Winder, First Counselor to President Joseph F. Smith, had died on March 27, 1910. As Joseph entered the tabernacle for general conference on April 6, 1910, he had no idea that he had been selected to fill the vacancy in the Quorum of the Twelve Apostles. It was not the practice of Church leaders to notify a person in advance. A person first heard of his appointment over the pulpit. Joseph was certain that he would not be called. His father was the President of the Church and his older brother Hyrum had been a member of the Quorum of the Twelve since 1901.

As assistant Church historian, Joseph had a reserved seat on the bottom row of the stand of the tabernacle. As he entered the building the doorkeeper asked Joseph who would serve as the new Apostle. Joseph responded, "I don't know. But it won't be you and it won't be me."[7] When Heber J. Grant read Joseph's name as the newest Apostle, Joseph was stunned. He later recalled that "I was so startled and dumbfounded I could hardly speak."[8] The next morning he was ordained by his father, Joseph F. Smith.

As an Apostle, Joseph's service immediately became far reaching. He was named a member of the board of trustees for Brigham Young University in 1912 and five years later was appointed to serve as a member of the Church Board of Education. In 1915 he was called to serve as a counselor in the presidency of the Salt Lake Temple. He served in this capacity under two different presidents until 1935. Ten years later he was called to be the president of the Salt Lake Temple. At that time he held the following positions simultaneously: Apostle, president of the Genealogical

Society, Church historian, chairman of the General Church Melchizedek Priesthood Committee, member of the Church Board of Education, and chairman of the Church committee on publications. In August 1950, he was also called to serve as the Acting President of the Quorum of the Twelve. He became President of that Quorum eight months later when David O. McKay became Church President following the death of George Albert Smith. Lastly, Joseph was called to be a counselor to President McKay in the First Presidency in October 1965.

Over his six decades in the Quorum of the Twelve and First Presidency, Joseph was distinguished as a great doctrinal scholar and teacher. The fruits of his gospel scholarship are evident in his widely published writings. No other Church President to date has published more books and articles than Joseph Fielding Smith. His contribution to the base of Latter-day Saint literature was acknowledged on June 4, 1951, when he was awarded an honorary Doctor of

Joseph Fielding Smith receiving an honorary doctorate in spiritual scholarship.

Letters degree for spiritual scholarship from Brigham Young University.

THE PRESIDENCY

President David O. McKay died on January 18, 1970, and on January 23, 1970, Joseph Fielding Smith was sustained by his Brethren as the tenth President of the Church. He was sustained by the body of the Church in a solemn assembly, which convened in the Tabernacle on April 6, 1970. He was ninety-three years old and had been in the presence of every prophet of God in this dispensation excepting Joseph Smith.

Despite the depth of his writings and the intensity of his teachings, President Smith was friendly, compassionate, and even playful. An example of his friendly nature occurred on the day he was sustained in a solemn assembly to be the President of the Church in April 1970. Following this session of general conference a large crowd gathered at the door of the Tabernacle to greet or get a glimpse of the prophet. One young girl squeezed her way through the crowd of adults and

Joseph Fielding Smith at the time of his ordination to the apostleship.

approached President Smith. He reached down, swept her off her feet, and gave her a big hug. A *Deseret News* photographer captured the hug on film, and the little girl disappeared back into the crowd as quickly as she came. The picture was so engaging that it appeared in the next edition of the *Church News* with the following caption: "Unidentified little girl meets President Joseph Fielding Smith after a session."[9]

Milo Hobbs of Preston, Idaho, read the *Church News* and recognized the little girl as her granddaughter. She wrote a letter to President Smith explaining that the little girl's name was Venus Hobbs of Torrence, California. She explained that Venus was three years old and would turn four later that month on April 17. President and Sister Smith were in California on that day and surprised young Venus with a telephone call wherein they sang happy birthday and wished her all possible happiness. During this phone conversation President and Sister Smith were also given the details behind Venus' charming yet mysterious appearance and disappearance outside the doors of the Tabernacle on Temple Square.

Joseph Fielding Smith as President of the Twelve.

Venus had attended the conference with two of her aunts. Following the session she slipped out of sight and the two women searched frantically for her with no success. After a short time, Venus emerged from the crowds and was reunited with her aunts. They quickly asked, "How did you get lost?" "I wasn't lost," Venus explained. "Who found you?" queried the aunts to whom Venus replied, "I was in the arms of the Prophet."[10]

An example of Joseph Fielding Smith's compassionate disposition is evident in the counsel he would frequently give to new bishops prior to setting them apart. Regarding the wayward, he would encourage them to always err on the side of mercy in their judgments. Throughout his life he was a kind and gentle judge.

Joseph Fielding Smith with his two counselors in the First Presidency.

Joseph Fielding Smith in the Quorum of the Twelve.

Venus Hobbs being held by Joseph Fielding Smith.

His playful side can be found in his willingness to sing with his wife Jessie. When they spoke together, she would frequently sing a song as a conclusion to her comments. As she finished her remarks she would often say in hushed and urgent tones, "I think I can persuade the President to sing a duet with me. Would you like to hear it?" The crowd would always respond with enthusiasm and Jessie would say something like, "President, they want us" and signal Joseph to rise and move toward the piano with her. Walking toward the piano he would often stop at the microphone and say, with feigned agitation in his voice, "This isn't a duet—it's a do it!" Then, to the delight of the audience, they would go to the piano and sing.

Joseph Fielding Smith was President of the Church for just two and a half years. Nevertheless, during his tenure as President significant strides were made in three major areas. First, certain organizations of the Church were adjusted and revamped to more effectively accommodate the needs of a growing Church. In some cases, his efforts to reorganize led to several men being called or appointed to significant positions of trust who later became presiding authorities in the Church. Second, an aggressive building program was carried out. Third, instruction to Church members by presiding priesthood authorities became more common throughout the world. President Smith established a pattern of sending presiding authorities to nearby and distant lands to be among the Saints in person.

ORGANIZATION

Organizationally, President Smith felt moved to modify certain organizations to suit the needs of an expanding Church. In some instances, this required expanding programs and personnel and in others it required reduced services. For example, there had not been a commissioner of the Church Educational System (CES) for about twenty-five years when President Smith felt the need to reorganize CES

Joseph Fielding Smith with Jessie, singing at the piano.

and reinstitute the commissioner position. He appointed University of Utah administrator Neal A. Maxwell to the job. Under Brother Maxwell's leadership Dallin H. Oaks was appointed to serve as president of Brigham Young University and Henry B. Eyring was appointed president of Ricks College. All three were eventually called to serve in the Quorum of the Twelve Apostles.

President Smith made additional changes to the Deseret Sunday School Union. At that time, a superintendent directed the organization through a fairly extensive board. He reorganized the "union" and renamed it the Sunday School of The Church of Jesus Christ of Latter-day Saints. The office of the superintendency was dropped and a presidency appointed. A prominent heart surgeon named Russell M. Nelson received the call to serve as the first Sunday School general president. Several years later he too was called to serve in the Quorum of the Twelve Apostles. Elders Maxwell, Oaks, Eyring, and Nelson were directly guided and tutored by Joseph Fielding Smith. Decades after his death, President Smith's influence was still a factor in shaping the destiny of the Church through these four men and many others.

Finally, his father Joseph F. Smith had instituted a program in 1912 that came to be known as family home evening. Several decades later, President Joseph Fielding Smith formalized Monday as the day to be set aside for family home evening for Latter-day Saint families throughout the earth. Of course, this seemed like a rather simple organizational adjustment at the time, but decades later the significance of President Smith's formalizing this inspired program cannot be overstated.

BUILDING

The building program carried out during Joseph Fielding Smith's presidency was an indication of the hearty growth of the Church throughout the world. He oversaw the construction of the thirty-one-story Church Office Building in downtown Salt Lake City. This building made it possible for most auxiliaries and service departments of the Church to be located in one center. The Church had grown so rapidly that the administration of the Church was being conducted from thirteen different buildings. Not only did the construction of the Church Office Building solve this problem, it became a defining element of the vitality of downtown Salt Lake City and a prominent feature of its skyline.

President Smith also directed the construction of two temples during his presidency. Both of them were in Utah. The first was in Ogden and the second in Provo. The laying of the cornerstone in Ogden took place on September 7, 1970. This is significant because prior to the Ogden Temple, the most recent cornerstone-laying ceremony for a temple in Utah had been in Manti in 1879.

Finally, President Smith presided at the dedication of a new visitors' center in Independence, Missouri, on May 31, 1971. The dedication was held outdoors, and the weather quickly turned unpleasant as rain-laden clouds billowed overhead. As he spoke lightning flashed, and thunder clapped. He paused in his comments just long enough to say, "I hardly expected to have to fight the devil here today!"[11]

THE INTERNATIONALIZATION OF THE CHURCH

Six months into his presidency and one week before his ninety-fourth birthday, President Smith stood before thousands of Latter-day Saints in Mexico City. It was his first trip outside the United States as the President of the Church. He was the first President of the Church to visit Mexico in twenty-five years.

A legacy of Joseph Fielding Smith's presidency that is felt keenly in the Church today is how he promoted face-to-face contact between Church leaders and members throughout the world. President Smith and his counselors in the First Presidency initiated area general conferences. The intent of these

The *Ensign, New Era,* and *Friend*

Beginning in January 1971, Church publications such as the *Improvement Era,* the *Relief Society Magazine,* the *Instructor,* and the *Millennial Star* which had served the Church for many decades were consolidated into three new publications: the *Ensign* (for adults), *New Era* (for youth), and *Friend* (for children). President Smith and his Brethren mandated that these new publications be "pledged to use the best talents in the Church to produce quality products—magazines that will be worthy of the great mission assigned them: strengthening the faith of Church members, promulgating the truths of the gospel, and keeping members abreast of vital and current Church policies and happenings."[7]

Up to the year 1971, there were a surprising number of periodicals published by the Church. President Smith felt strongly that as the Church grew domestically and abroad that one clear voice should ring out through Church publications. These new magazines did much to guarantee clear and unified instruction throughout the world. The *Ensign, New Era,* and *Friend* came under the direct charge of the First Presidency and Quorum of the Twelve Apostles and they were correlated with all other Church publications. Thus, more than any publications of the Church before, these new magazines constitute the official Church organs and serve to bring a worldwide Church closer to a unity of faith.

The last Era (December 1970) and the first *Ensign* (January 1971).

conferences was to emphasize the international character of the Church and encourage Saints in different parts of the world to build up the Church in their respective nations instead of moving to Utah. It was decided to hold the first area general conference in England since that was where the first international missionary effort of the Church was conducted beginning in 1837.

The three-day conference was held from August 27 to 29, 1971. President Smith traveled to Manchester, England, with thirteen other General Authorities and five auxiliary leaders.

Very, Very Tall Buildings

In 1899, Joseph was called to serve a mission to Great Britain. His travels to the field took him to New York City where he saw the tallest building in the city standing thirty stories. Never in his wildest dreams could young Joseph have imagined that he would one day oversee the construction of a skyscraper that equaled the height of that building.

When Joseph served in England there were approximately four hundred thousand members of the Church. By 1960, Church membership had swelled to nearly three million and the First Presidency announced that a new Church administration building would be constructed. In 1969, they commissioned architect George Cannon to design a building that could accommodate the growing administrative needs of the Church. He designed a thirty-one-story high rise that was scheduled to be finished in July 1972. Therefore, the lion's share of the construction took place under President Smith's watchful eye.

Keeping in mind that when Joseph was born, the automobile had not been invented it is astonishing to consider that the parking garage of the Church Office Building could accommodate 1300 cars. At the time of its completion, the building maintained twenty-five floors of office space and a cafeteria to seat 750. Furthermore, two four-story wings were constructed on the east and on the west of the high-rise tower. The east wing housed the Church historian's offices, a reference library, and a 350-seat auditorium. The west wing housed the Genealogical Society. It was modern, utilitarian, and represented the largest construction project in the Church up to that time. Today it stands as a reminder of Joseph Fielding Smith's life and presidency.

Joseph Fielding Smith at the dedication of the cornerstone for the Ogden Temple on September 7, 1970.

Leadership, general, and youth sessions were held during the conference. President Smith spoke five times. In many ways, this conference was the beginning of a significant movement in the Church wherein the prophets came to the people. It was also a precursor to the worldwide training and instruction provided by Church leaders today.

THE DEATH OF JESSIE SMITH AND THE PASSING OF THE PROPHET

Just over one month before the Manchester conference Jessie began to have health problems and was hospitalized. She was only sixty-nine years old and had experienced good health up to that time. Joseph spent his ninety-fifth birthday at Jessie's side. While her sickness raised concerns, Joseph had no reason to believe that her illness was terminal. Nevertheless, she quietly passed away on August 3, 1971. Her funeral was held on August 5 in the Tabernacle. For the third time in his life, Joseph was a widower. His grief was almost overwhelming. Although he did not want to travel, the anticipation of the English Saints moved him to fly to England and participate in the Manchester conference. Returning to his mission field and interacting with the Saints in England served as a needed balm for his aching heart. It turned out to be his last trip abroad.

The shock of Jessie's death and the rigors of his ongoing responsibilities began to weigh upon President Smith toward the end of 1971. In December he fell, breaking his hip and three ribs. Disinterested in interrupting his schedule, Joseph hobbled in pain for ten days before finally agreeing to consult a physician. Upon viewing the X-rays, the doctor prescribed treatment and recommended that President Smith use a wheelchair while his body healed. Impatient with the way the wheelchair interrupted his routine, he only used it for two or three days.

As his ninety-sixth birthday approached in July 1972, President Smith was living with his daughter Amelia and her husband Elder Bruce R. McConkie, who was then one of the seven Presidents of the Seventy. President Smith still worked in his office almost every day, meeting with the Brethren to direct the Church, and speaking in a wide variety of meetings. On the evening of July 2nd, Amelia was visiting with her

Joseph Fielding Smith in a rose garden in Manchester, England.

father and writing a letter. At about 9:20 PM she left the room to search for an address. President Smith was sleeping calmly in an easy chair. When she returned, she discovered that he had slipped away from this mortal life. Elder McConkie later explained, "His passing was as sweet and easy, as calm and as peaceful as though he had fallen asleep, which in fact he had. . . . Truly when the Lord took his prophet, there was no sting. President Smith did not taste of death."[12]

Soon after President Smith's death, Elder McConkie wrote: "Perhaps no man in this dispensation has traveled more miles, attended more meetings, preached more sermons, performed more ordinances, or written more voluminously in proclaiming the truths of salvation than he has. For years to come his voice will speak from the dust as generations yet unborn learn the doctrines of the gospel from his writings."[13] Decades after his death, the words of Elder McConkie regarding President Joseph Fielding Smith stand fulfilled.

Joseph Fielding Smith preaching during general conference.

Joseph Fielding Smith and Jessie wearing flowers in Hawaii.

TEACHINGS OF PRESIDENT
JOSEPH FIELDING SMITH

◆

Joseph Fielding Smith's six decades of apostolic service resulted in extensive contributions to the literature of the Church. He boldly proclaimed the veracity of the principles and doctrines of the gospel. The most impressive endorsement of President Smith's apostolic teachings came from his own declaration at the October 1970 general conference. As President of the Church, he reflected on his writings and teachings over the previous sixty years and concluded, "What I have taught and written in the past I would teach and write again under the same circumstances."[14]

President Joseph Fielding Smith presided at six general conferences of the Church. Six themes emerge from his sermons at these worldwide conferences: (1) maintaining doctrinal purity in the Church; (2) repentance; (3) pure worship over ritual performance; (4) defining the role of priesthood; (5) the family; and (6) Joseph Smith and the Latter-day Restoration.

Apostolic Companions for Six Decades

It would be difficult to find in all the world a brotherhood more bound together in loyalty and love than the associations found in the Quorum of the Twelve Apostles of the Church. Joseph Fielding Smith and David O. McKay enjoyed this association for many decades. Speaking of this dear friend, President Smith explained:

"For 60 years I sat by his side in the presiding councils of the Church. . . . I came to know him intimately and well, and I loved him as a man and honored him as a prophet. . . . In the early days of his ministry the Brethren used to go out on assignments two by two. Often President McKay and I went together. We would travel as far as we could by train and then the local brethren would meet us with a white top or a wagon. Sometimes we continued on horses or mules or by ox team. Many times we slept out under the stars or in such houses or cabins as were available.

"In all his travels President McKay was a perfect gentleman—always kind and considerate, more interested in my comfort than in his own."[8]

Joseph Fielding Smith and David O. McKay.

A Prolific Writer

Over the course of his ministry, Joseph Fielding Smith authored twenty-five books and pamphlets. Most of these books were published as a response to the nonstop flow of gospel questions that flooded his office week in and week out. The following is a list of the books written by him and the year of publication:

Essentials in Church History, 1922

The Way to Perfection, 1931

The Progress of Man, 1936

The Life of Joseph F. Smith, 1938

Teachings of the Prophet Joseph Smith, 1938

Principles of the Restored Gospel, 1942

The Signs of the Times, 1942

The Restoration of all Things, 1944

Church History and Modern Revelation, I, 1953

Church History and Modern Revelation, II, 1953

Man, His Origin and Destiny, 1954

Doctrines of Salvation, I, 1954

Doctrines of Salvation, II, 1955

Doctrines of Salvation, III, 1956

Answers to Gospel Questions, I, 1954

Elijah the Prophet and His Mission and Salvation Universal, 1957

Answers to Gospel Questions, II, 1958

Answers to Gospel Questions, III, 1960

Answers to Gospel Questions, IV, 1963

Answers to Gospel Questions, V, 1966

Take Heed to Yourselves!, 1966

Seek Ye Earnestly . . ., 1970

Pamphlets authored by Joseph Fielding Smith:

Asahel Smith of Topsfield, Massachusetts, with Some Account of the Smith Family, 1903

Blood Atonement and the Origin of Plural Marriage, 1905

Origin of the Reorganized Church and the Question of Succession, 1907

Joseph Fielding Smith holding a copy of *Take Heed to Yourselves!*

MAINTAINING DOCTRINAL PURITY IN THE CHURCH

As stated earlier Joseph Fielding Smith stands as a bridge between the Latter-day Saint pioneers and the Church in the modern era. Without question, he presided over the Church at a time when prevalent philosophical stances and false educational ideas may have brought some members to conclude that the revelations granted to Joseph Smith in the nineteenth century were outdated and could therefore be minimized or ignored altogether. In this light, President Smith was very concerned about maintaining doctrinal purity in the Church—especially in Church instruction. Concerning the responsibility of those who speak and teach in Church, President Smith said, "All my days I have studied the scriptures and have sought the guidance of the Spirit of the Lord in coming to an understanding of their true meaning. . . . We are not called or authorized to teach the philosophies of the world or the speculative theories of our scientific age. Our mission is to preach the doctrines of salvation in *plainness* and simplicity as they are revealed and recorded in the scriptures."[15]

President Smith's concern that Church members might drift away from eternal principles upon which the Restoration was founded led him to state and restate these principles with great fervency. The following is one of many such warnings: "We are engaged in the Lord's work; this is his church; he is the author of the plan of salvation; it is his gospel which we have received by the opening of the heavens in this day; and our desire and whole purpose in life should be to believe the truths he has revealed and to conform our lives to them. No person in or out of the Church should believe any doctrine, advocate any practice, or support any cause that is not in harmony with the divine will. Our sole objective where the truths of salvation are concerned should be to find out what the Lord has revealed and then to believe and act accordingly."[16]

REPENTANCE

President Smith spent the last decade of his life witnessing the counterculture revolution of the 1960s. Promiscuity, drug abuse, and defiance of authority were embraced as mediums through which attempts at happiness were made. These were days of spiritual crisis in the world, and the voice of Joseph Fielding Smith rang out clear and strong. He called for change. In fact, few have taught the doctrine of repentance with more clarity than President Smith. The following statement captures the tender and yet direct way in which President Smith urged the Saints to repent and be strictly obedient. He said,

"Now may I say to all those who forsake the world and join the Church, and to all the members of the Church, that Church membership alone will not assure us of the full blessings of the gospel or guarantee us an entrance into the celestial kingdom. After baptism we must keep the commandments and endure to the end. . . .

"There is no more important thing that anyone in the world can do than to receive the gospel and inherit its glorious blessings.

"And there is no more important counsel that can be given to any member of the Church than to keep the commandments after baptism. The Lord offers us salvation on condition of repentance and faithfulness to his laws.

"I plead with the world to repent and believe the truth, to let the light of Christ shine in their lives, to keep every good and true principle they have, and to add to these the further light and knowledge that has come by revelation in this day. . . . I plead with the members of the Church

to do the works of righteousness to keep the commandments, to seek the Spirit, to love the Lord, to put first in their lives the things of God's kingdom, and thereby work out their salvation with fear and trembling before the Lord."[17]

President Smith maintained this theme of his ministry at a later general conference of the Church when he taught: "I call upon the Church and all its members to forsake the evils of the world. We must shun unchastity and every form of immorality as we would a plague. . . . No member of the Church can be accepted as in good standing whose way of life is one of rebellion against the established order of decency and obedience to law. We cannot be in rebellion against the law and be in harmony with the Lord."[18]

At a time when rebellion and other social ills were accorded a certain level of acceptance in society, President Smith taught, "And there is no cure for the ills of the world except the gospel of the Lord Jesus Christ. Our hope for peace, for temporal and spiritual prosperity, and for an eventual inheritance in the kingdom of God is found only in and through the restored gospel. There is no work that any of us can engage in that is as important as preaching the gospel and building the Church and kingdom of God on earth.

I Was So Excited I Had a Heart Attack!

When a woman in Canoas, Brazil, who had recently joined the Church learned that Joseph Fielding Smith would soon visit nearby Porto Alegre, Brazil, she got so excited that she had a heart attack and was rushed to the hospital. When President Smith arrived he was informed of the situation and of the woman's deep disappointment over not being able to meet the President of the Church. President Smith decided to visit the woman in her hospital room.

Upon his arrival she exclaimed, "Now that he has come, I'm sure to get well!" President Smith gave her a priesthood blessing wherein he commanded the sickness to depart from her. From that moment forward she had no further symptoms of the heart attack. She explained that when the prophet put his hands upon her head and began to speak that the pain immediately subsided. The physicians were baffled by her immediate recovery. She was released from the hospital and went on to bear many testimonies of the truthfulness of the gospel and the power of God's priesthood.[11]

Thou Shalt Not Kill

Joseph was troubled by wanton and bloodthirsty killing of animals. His teachings on the subject are harmonious with those of his father. In fact, Joseph would quote a couplet that he learned from his father: "Take not way the life you cannot give, For all things have an equal right to live."

Subsequently, Joseph taught: "There is no inference in the scriptures that it is the privilege of men to slay birds or beasts or to catch fish wantonly. The Lord gave life to every creature, both the birds in the heavens, beasts on the earth, and the fishes in the streams or seas. They also were commanded to be fruitful and multiply and fill the earth. It was intended that all creatures should be happy in their several elements. Therefore to take the life of these creatures wantonly is a sin before the Lord."[12]

Joseph lived by these teachings. As a young father he would occasionally fish with his boys, but later in life he would not even take the life of a fish.

"And so we invite all our Father's children, everywhere, to believe in Christ, to receive him as he is revealed by living prophets, and to join The Church of Jesus Christ of Latter-day Saints. We call upon the world to repent, to worship that God who made them, and to believe the words of those whom he hath sent in this day to proclaim his gospel."[19]

PURE WORSHIP ORIGINATES IN THE HEART

Linked to the doctrine of repentance is the critical aspect of faith, that religion should be a deep matter of the heart. President Smith taught that the gospel of Jesus Christ must be planted firmly within us because ultimately, true religion has little to do with outward ritual, position, or callings in the Church. He shared this principle with the brethren of the priesthood in the following way:

"I do not care what office you hold in the Church—you may be an apostle, you may be a patriarch, a high priest, or anything else—but you cannot receive the fulness of the priesthood and the fulness of eternal reward unless you receive the ordinances of the house of the Lord; and when you receive these ordinances, the door is then open so you can obtain all the blessings which any man can gain. Do not think because someone has a higher office in the Church

than you have that you are barred from receiving the fullness of the Lord's blessings. You can have them sealed upon you as an elder, if you are faithful; and when you receive them, and live faithfully and keep these covenants, you then have all that any man can get."[20]

To the general body of the Church he further explained, "We believe that worship is far more than prayer and preaching and gospel performance. The supreme act of worship is to keep the commandments, to follow in the footsteps of the Son of God, to do ever those things that please him. It is one thing to give lip service to the Lord; it is quite another to respect and honor his will by following the example he has set for us. Our Savior, Jesus Christ, is the great Exemplar. Our mission is to pattern our lives after him and do the things he wants us to do."[21]

DEFINING THE ROLE OF THE PRIESTHOOD

Not a single conference presided over by President Smith passed without his defining the priesthood in brief and simple terms. Joseph Fielding Smith employed the language that his father, Joseph F. Smith, used during his presidency and we still use this simple and forthright definition today. President Smith taught that the priesthood "is the power and authority of God delegated to man on earth to act in all things for the salvation of men."[22]

Concerning those chosen to hold the holy priesthood President Smith taught,

"As the Lord's agents we are bound by his law to do what he wants us to do regardless of personal feelings or worldly enticements. Of ourselves we have no message of salvation, no doctrine that must be accepted, no power to baptize or ordain or marry for eternity. All these things come from the Lord, and anything we do with reference to them is the result of delegated authority.

"When we join the Church and receive the priesthood, we are expected to forsake many of the ways of the world and live as becometh saints. We are no longer to dress or speak or act or even think as others too often do. Many in the world use tea, coffee, tobacco, and liquor, and are involved in the use of drugs. Many profane and are vulgar and indecent, immoral and unclean in their lives, but all these things should be foreign to us. We are the saints of the Most High. We hold the holy priesthood."[23]

To the women in the Church, President Smith taught that while men hold the priesthood, the blessings of the priesthood are not gender specific. He explained: "I think we all know that the blessings of the priesthood are not confined to men alone. These blessings are also poured out upon our wives and daughters and upon all the faithful women of the Church. These good sisters can prepare themselves by keeping the commandments and by serving in the Church, for the blessings of the house of the Lord. The Lord offers to his daughters every spiritual gift and blessing that can be obtained by his sons, for neither is the man without the woman, nor the woman without the man in the Lord."[24]

THE FAMILY

President Smith felt deeply and passionately about the importance of the family. At a time when the family was under constant barrage from the world, he taught that the greatest blessings of the Lord are bestowed within family units. He explained: "To all the families in Israel we say: The family is the most important organization in time or in eternity. Our purpose in life is to create for ourselves eternal family units. There is nothing that will ever come into your family life that is as important as the sealing blessings of the temple and then keeping the covenants made in connection with this order of celestial marriage."[25]

To youth within families President Smith taught: "The Lord bless you and keep you, which most assuredly will be so as you learn his laws and live in harmony with them. Be true to every trust. Honor thy father and thy mother. Dwell

The Man I Know: Joseph Fielding Smith as a Husband and Father

Ethel Georgina Smith was Joseph's second wife and mother of nine of his eleven children. In an interview she provided the following touching tribute to her husband:

"You ask me to tell you of the man I know, I have often thought when he is gone people will say, 'He is a very good man, sincere, orthodox, etc.' They will speak of him as the public knows him; but the man they have in mind is very different from the man I know. The man I know is a kind, loving husband and father whose greatest ambition in life is to make his family happy, entirely forgetful of self in his efforts to do this. He is the man that lulls to sleep the fretful child, who tells bedtime stories to the little ones, who is never too tired or too busy to sit up late at night or to get up early in the morning to help the older children solve perplexing school problems. When illness comes, the man I know watches tenderly over the afflicted one and waits upon him. It is their father for whom they cry, feeling his presence a panacea for all ills. It is his hands that bind up the wounds, his arms that give courage to the sufferer, his voice that remonstrates with them gently when they err, until it becomes their happiness to do the thing that will make him happy.

"The man I know is most gentle, and if he feels that he has been unjust to anyone the distance is never too far for him to go and, with loving words or kind deeds, erase the hurt. He welcomes gladly the young people to his home and is never happier than when discussing with them topics of the day—sports or whatever interests them most. He enjoys a good story and is quick to see the humor of a situation, to laugh and to be laughed at, always willing to join in any wholesome activity.

"The man I know is unselfish, uncomplaining, considerate, thoughtful, sympathetic, doing everything within his power to make life a supreme joy for his loved ones. That is the man I know."[13]

together in love and conformity. Be modest in your dress. Overcome the world, and do not be led astray by the fashions and practices of those whose interests are centered upon the things of this world.

"Marry in the temple and live joyous and happy lives. . . . Remember also that our hope for the future and the destiny of the Church and the cause of righteousness rest in your hands."[26]

JOSEPH SMITH AND THE LATTER-DAY RESTORATION

Concerning his own family roots, President Smith was quick to teach, write, and testify of the veracity of the mission of his great uncle the Prophet Joseph Smith and the Restoration of the gospel in the latter-days. The following testimony reveals his deep convictions in this regard:

"I have a perfect knowledge that the Father and the Son appeared to Joseph Smith in the spring of 1820 and gave him commandments to usher in the dispensation of the fulness of times.

A portrait of Joseph Fielding Smith and Jessie in their later years.

Joseph Fielding Smith holding a baby and cooing.

You Make My Tired Ache!
Gentle Discipline

Amelia Smith McConkie recalls that Joseph "was kind yet firm [and] he never resorted to physical punishment for any misbehavior on our part, but would put his hands on our shoulders and say in a very hurt tone, 'I wish my kiddies would be good.' That was the most effective punishment he could give us and was far worse than any spanking could have been, simply the thought that we had hurt him."[14]

Douglas (second to youngest son) reported that discipline from his father usually consisted of "a gentle lecture [usually followed by] . . . a hug and an expression of love. [Although] on rare occasions he would give what was more of a pat than a kick with the side of his foot to the seat of your pants."[15]

Finally, Joseph did have one favorite line that he used for scolding. It was a statement of nonsense but communicated his frustration in a gentle and fun-loving way. He would look his errant child carefully in the eye and say, "You make my tired ache!"[16]

Of the central and essential role of Joseph Smith in moving the work of the Lord forward in the last days President Smith taught, "In every age when the gospel is on earth, it must be revealed to the Lord's prophets, and they must be called to stand as legal administrators to perform and to direct the performance of the ordinances of salvation for their fellowmen.

"Joseph Smith is the prophet whom the Lord called in this day to restore the truths of salvation and to receive the keys and powers to administer these saving truths. . . . Thus we link the names of Jesus Christ and of Joseph Smith. Christ is the Lord; he worked out the atoning sacrifice; he is the resurrection and the life; through him all men are raised in immortality, while those who believe and obey his laws shall also gain eternal life.

"Joseph Smith was a prophet, called in these last days to receive by revelation the saving truths of the

"I know that Joseph Smith translated the Book of Mormon by the gift and power of God, and that it has come forth 'to the convincing of the Jew and Gentile that Jesus is the Christ, the Eternal God, manifesting himself unto all nations.'

"I know that The Church of Jesus Christ of Latter-day Saints is the kingdom of God on earth, and that as now constituted and officered it has the Lord's approval and is moving in the course so directed.

"Let all men know assuredly that this is the Lord's Church and he is directing its affairs. What a privilege it is to have membership in such a divine institution!

"And I pray that the gospel cause shall spread, and that the honest in heart in every nation shall be brought to a knowledge of the Lord Jesus Christ."[27]

Joseph Fielding Smith greeting the youth of the Church.

He Was Not an Austere Man

Elder Bruce R. McConkie was Joseph Fielding Smith's son-in-law. Given the fact that he was in constant contact with President Smith as he mingled within the intimate circles of both the Smith family and the General Authorities of the Church, his perspective is unique and trustworthy. Shortly after the death of President Smith, Elder McConkie wrote,

"If I may now express myself by the power of the Holy Ghost, and if you may be enlightened by that same power, I shall try and give a true feeling relative to the tender, gracious, and gentle personality of President Smith—the feeling for him which is had by his family, his close friends, and the General Authorities.

"He was not an austere man, as he was long ago described in a published article, but rather one of the most kind and considerate of our Father's children. He had tender feelings and an instinctive sympathy and solicitude for the weak, the weary, and the wanting. In judgment he was temperate and reserved, and as President Spencer W. Kimball said at his passing, 'Many times we have said that since the Twelve will be judges of Israel, any of us would be happy to fall into his hands, for his judgment would be kind, merciful, just, and holy.' "[17]

Joseph Fielding Smith embracing a young girl outside a meetinghouse.

gospel and to stand as a legal administrator, having power from on high, to administer the ordinances of the gospel. . . . The ends of the earth are now beginning to inquire after the name of Joseph Smith, and many people in many nations are rejoicing in the gospel restored through his instrumentality."[28]

FINAL PRAYER AND TESTIMONY

The final testimony uttered by President Smith in a general conference address evolved into a heartfelt prayer of faith, hope, and love for the Saints. This testimony and prayer captures his deep sensitivities and serves as a fitting capstone for his many teachings. He prayed: "O God our Heavenly and Eternal Father, look down in love and in mercy upon this thy church and upon the members of the church who keep thy commandments. Let thy Spirit dwell in our hearts forever; and when the trials and woes of this life are over, may we return to thy presence, with our loved ones, and dwell in thy house forever, I humbly pray, in the name of Jesus Christ. Amen."[29]

Blair G. Van Dyke

Church Educational System instructor, EdD
Brigham Young University

NOTES

1. Joseph Fielding Smith Jr. and John J. Stewart, *The Life of Joseph Fielding Smith Tenth President of The Church of Jesus Christ of Latter-day Saints* (Salt Lake City: Deseret Book, 1972), 49; see also, Joseph F. McConkie, *True and Faithful: The Life Story of Joseph Fielding Smith* (Salt Lake City: Bookcraft, 1971), 74.

2. Smith and Stewart, *Life of Joseph Fielding Smith*, 1–2.

3. Joseph Fielding Smith, CR, April 1930, 91.

4. Francis M. Gibbons, *Joseph Fielding Smith: Gospel Scholar, Prophet of God* (Salt Lake City: Deseret Book, 1992), 60.

5. Ibid., 111.

6. A. William Lund, "Elder Joseph Fielding Smith: Forty Years an Apostle," *Improvement Era* (April 1950): 315.

7. Gibbons, *Joseph Fielding Smith*, 145.

8. Smith and Stewart, *Life of Joseph Fielding Smith*, 176.

9. *Church News*, week ending April 11, 1970, 9; see also J. M. Heslop and Dell R. Van Orden, *Joseph Fielding Smith: A Prophet among the People* (Salt Lake City: Deseret Book, 1971), 6.

10. Heslop and Van Orden, *Joseph Fielding Smith: A Prophet among the People*, 6–7.

11. Smith and Stewart, *Life of Joseph Fielding Smith*, 363; see also Heslop and Van Orden, *Joseph Fielding Smith: A Prophet among the People*, 93.

12. Ibid., 377.

13. Bruce R. McConkie, "Joseph Fielding Smith: Apostle, Prophet, Father in Israel," *Ensign*, August 1972, 27.

14. Joseph Fielding Smith, "That the Fulness of My Gospel Might Be Proclaimed," *Improvement Era* (December 1970): 2.

15. Ibid.; italics in original.

16. Joseph Fielding Smith, "Out of the Darkness," *Ensign*, June 1971, 2.

17. Smith, "That the Fulness of My Gospel," 4.

18. Joseph Fielding Smith, "Our Responsibilities as Priesthood Holders," *Ensign*, June 1971, 50.

19. Joseph Fielding Smith, "Counsel to the Saints and to the World," *Ensign*, July 1972, 27.

20. Joseph Fielding Smith, "Magnifying Our Callings in the Priesthood," *Improvement Era* (June 1970): 65–66.

21. Joseph Fielding Smith, "I Know That My Redeemer Liveth," *Ensign*, December 1971, 27.

22. Smith, "Magnifying Our Callings," 65.

23. Smith, "Our Responsibilities," 49.

24. Smith, "Magnifying Our Callings," 66.

25. Smith, "Counsel to the Saints," 27.

26. Ibid., 28.

27. Smith, "That the Fulness of My Gospel," 4.

28. Ibid., 3.

29. Joseph Fielding Smith, "A Prophet's Blessing," *Ensign*, July 1972, 130.

SIDEBAR AND PHOTO NOTES

1. *Era*, November 1970, 11.

2. Smith and Stewart, *Life of Joseph Fielding Smith*, 2.

3. Ibid.

4. Ibid., 221.

5. Ibid.

6. Ibid., 192–194; see also Gibbons, *Joseph Fielding Smith*, 140–42).

7. Doyle L. Green, "The Church and Its Magazines," *Ensign*, January 1971, 12.

8. Joseph Fielding Smith, "One Who Loved His Fellowmen," *Era*, February 1970, 87–88.

9. Heslop and Van Orden, *Joseph Fielding Smith: A Prophet among the People*, 151.

10. *Hymns of The Church of Jesus Christ of Latter-day Saints* (Salt Lake City: The Church of Jesus Christ of Latter-day Saints, 1985) no. 127.

11. Smith and Stewart, *Life of Joseph Fielding Smith*, 316–17.

12. Joseph Fielding Smith, *Answers to Gospel Questions* (Salt Lake City: Deseret Book, 1963), 4:43–44.

13. Bryant S. Hinckley, "Joseph Fielding Smith," *Improvement Era* (June 1932): 459.

14. Gibbons, *Joseph Fielding Smith: Gospel Scholar, Prophet of God* (Salt Lake City: Deseret Book, 1992), 228.

15. Ibid.

16. Smith and Stewart, *Life of Joseph Fielding Smith*, 15.

17. Bruce R. McConkie, *Ensign*, August 1972, 28.

Chapter Eleven

HAROLD B. LEE

LIFE AND TIMES

1899	March 28	Born in Clifton, Idaho, to Samuel M. Lee and Louisa Bingham Lee
1912–16		Enrolled in Oneida Stake Academy
1916		Received first teaching job near Weston, Idaho
1917		Became school principal in Oxford, Idaho
1920–22		Served mission to western states
1922–23		Attended University of Utah; completes degree later by correspondence
1923	November 14	Married Fern Lucinda Tanner
1923–28		Became principal in the Granite School District
1930–37		Sustained as president of the Pioneer Stake
1932		Served as Salt Lake City Commissioner; established Pioneer Stake welfare program
1937		Served as Managing Director of Churchwide Welfare Program
1941	April 10	Ordained an Apostle
1941–45		Served as Chairman of Serviceman's Committee during World War II
1945		Published *Youth and the Church*
1958		Toured South Africa Mission and the Holy Land
1960		Organized first stake in England
1961		Became chairman of the Church's new correlation program
1962		Wife, Fern L. Tanner, died
1963		Married Freda Joan Jensen
1970		Sustained as First Counselor in the First Presidency
1971		Spoke at first area general conference held in Manchester, England
1972		Dedicated Provo Temple
1972	July 7	Ordained and set apart as eleventh President of the Church
1972		Organized Jerusalem Branch in Israel
1973		Organized first stake on mainland Asian in Korea
1973	December 26	Died in Salt Lake City, Utah, at age seventy-four

BIOGRAPHICAL HIGHLIGHTS

President Harold B. Lee was ordained President of The Church of Jesus Christ of Latter-day Saints on July 7, 1972, following two and a half years as a counselor to President Joseph Fielding Smith and over thirty-one years as an Apostle. He served the second shortest term as the President, yet his overall influence on the kingdom has been one of the most profound.

From an obscure beginning in Clifton, Idaho, Harold B. Lee rose quickly to become a school principal at age eighteen and later served a faithful mission to the western states. He would thereafter serve as a Sunday School superintendent, then a counselor in the stake presidency, and, at age thirty-one, as a stake president. During his tenure as stake president, he served as a Salt Lake City commissioner, and he and his counselors established a security program that would become the model for a Churchwide welfare program. At age thirty-eight he became managing director of the Church Security program and four years later was called to the apostleship. From his six-month radio program to the youth in 1945 to his introduction of the correlation program to the Church in the early 1960s, his service as an Apostle was significant. President Lee's spiritual and ecclesiastical experience prepared him well in the three years he served as a counselor in the First Presidency and as the President of the Church. Not since the days of Joseph Smith was a prophet's death more unexpected than the passing of Harold B. Lee in December 1973.

CONTRIBUTIONS

Elder Lee is most noted for his premonition and insight to begin the work on what would eventually become the Church Welfare Program. Moreover, Elder Lee's gospel insight led President David O. McKay to select Elder Lee to head up the important work of the new Church Correlation Program. Under his direction, the effort to more fully standardize and harmonize the Church curriculum went forward. Priesthood leader training was strengthened, and the role of the scriptures in the home and in Church curriculum took on a renewed importance.

TEACHINGS

President Lee is remembered as a forthright and powerful teacher. It was his firm conviction that "you must teach the doctrines of the Church so plainly that no one can misunderstand."[1] He often taught the youth of the Church to stand firm in their beliefs and values, even inviting them to lean on his testimony until they had one of their own. President Lee repeatedly sounded a warning voice against spurious revelations and false doctrines, while continually encouraging the Saints to follow the Brethren. His lifelong involvement in the welfare program also influenced his teachings. However, he is best remembered for his counsel on marriage and the family. Perhaps few statements are more often repeated than his timeless counsel: "The most important of the Lord's work you will ever do will be within the walls of your own homes."[2]

LIFE OF
HAROLD B. LEE

◆

The eighteen-month tenure of President Harold B. Lee was unexpectedly short. Since he was the youngest prophet in forty years, it was believed that he would serve for many years. However, as will be seen, perhaps more than any other prophet to this day, his influence on the kingdom was felt in significant ways long before his call as President of the Church. The counsel, teachings, and spiritual foresight of President Lee profoundly impacted the Church for decades.

A NOBLE HERITAGE

The great-grandparents of Harold B. Lee, Francis and Jane Lee, experienced the infamous extermination order in Missouri and eventually went west with the Saints, arriving in the Salt Lake Valley in 1850. They were sent by Brigham Young to colonize Meadow Valley in what would become southeastern Nevada. Their life was difficult, and problems with Indians were frequent. Two sons of this brave couple married the McMurrin sisters. Samuel Lee married Margaret and Francis Lee married Mary. In these primitive conditions, without the aid of delivery rooms and doctors, Margaret was pregnant eleven times and, in each case, the child did not survive. Finally, after her twelfth pregnancy,

Margaret paid the ultimate price. She gave her life, but the premature baby, Samuel Jr., survived. The hand of the Lord must surely have been manifest in the preservation of young Samuel. Little could his parents know what was yet ahead through this, their only posterity.

Margaret's sister Mary nursed the young baby along for a time until her health required that the baby be taken to Grandmother McMurrin in Salt Lake City. Samuel lived with his grandmother McMurrin until she died when he was seventeen. At that time, he went to live with an aunt in Clifton, Idaho, where he worked on a farm and later met Louisa Bingham, whom he married in the Logan Temple in 1895.

Young Harold B. Lee at five years of age.

Preservation from Childhood Accidents

President Lee experienced each of the following incidents as a young boy:

• He slipped and fell, seriously gashing his hand on a broken bottle. His mother was impressed to use ashes to help heal the hand and prevent blood poisoning.

• He narrowly missed being struck by lightning because his mother had an impression to forcefully push him out of the doorway of their home.

• He nearly lost a finger that became caught in a milk separating machine.

• A tub of caustic lye water was accidentally spilled over his head and arms. His mother used vinegar to save him from being seriously scarred.

• He inadvertently drank lye water that he thought was fruit juice. His mother used olive oil to save him from serious injury.

CHILDHOOD—THE LORD'S PRESERVING HAND

Samuel and Louisa Lee became the parents of six children. The second of these six children, Harold Bingham Lee, was born on March 28, 1899, in Clifton, Idaho. Farm life for the Lee family was difficult. Quite often, there was little income to show for their hard work. Harold characterized his childhood well when he said, "We had everything that money could not buy."[3] Harold was an unusually bright young boy and was invited by the schoolteacher to begin school a year early.

Like Wilford Woodruff, Harold B. Lee's youth was filled with a number of accidents and incidents that could have ended tragically. The preserving hand of the Lord seemed to be upon him throughout his childhood. Perhaps the best known of Harold's childhood incidents was one he referred to as "my first intimate touch with divinity." He recounts, "As a young boy I was out on a farm, waiting for my father to finish his day's work, playing about, manufacturing things to while away the time, when I saw over the fence into the neighbor's yard some broken-down buildings with the sheds caving in and with rotting timbers. I imagined as a young

boy that that might be a castle that I should explore, so I went over to the fence and started to climb through; then I heard a voice as distinctly as you are hearing mine: 'Harold, don't go over there.' I looked in every direction to see where the speaker was. I wondered if it was my father, but he couldn't see me. There was no one in sight. I realized that someone was warning me of an unseen danger—whether a nest of rattlesnakes, whether the rotting timbers would fall on me and crush me, I don't know. But from that time on, I accepted without question the fact that there were processes not known to man by which we can hear voices from the unseen world, by which we can have brought to us the visions of eternity."[4]

YOUTH—A DIVERSITY OF TALENTS

One of the prized possessions in the Lee home was the piano, and young Harold seemed particularly adept. This early exposure would develop in Harold a lifelong love for music. Besides playing the piano, he also learned to play the organ, mandolin, baritone horn, and the trombone. Harold's experience with and love for music would serve him well later in his life when, as an Apostle, he would serve as the chairman of the Church Music Committee.

At Oneida Academy, he first met a schoolmate named Ezra Taft Benson. Though they were a year apart in school, they became friends and sang together in the school choir. It is remarkable that these two future prophets were associated together at such a young age. Little could they know what lay ahead for them both.

Harold excelled in debate. On one occasion he had traveled out of town on a high school debate meet, which he and his companion won. He came to understand more deeply the love of his mother; he recounted, "I . . . called mother on the telephone only to have her say: 'Never mind, Son. I know all about it. I will tell you when you come home at the end of the week.' When I came home she took me aside and said:

Harold with his Oneida Stake Academy debate partner, Sparrel Huff. They were on the first team from their school to defeat Fielding Academy in a tournament, 1915–16.

'When I knew it was just time for this performance to start I went out among the willows by the creek side, and there, all by myself, I remembered you and prayed God you would not fail.' "[5]

Harold's favorite sport was basketball. He was elected as the school's athletic manager and, thus, traveled with all the teams and took care of the finances and trips. Harold also played basketball on the senior team that won the class championship. Later he would use his basketball skills to help him earn the respect of his students when he became a school principal.

YOUNG ADULT—A FULL LIFE

Harold earned his teaching certificate from Albion State Normal School at age seventeen and received a teaching position at the one-room Silver Star School near Clifton. The next year, he was named as the principal of the Oxford School, which was about four miles from Clifton.

With his musical talents and athletic abilities, he kept himself involved in community activities. During this time, he added the trombone to his musical repertoire in order to play for a local dance orchestra. This provided Harold with needed additional income so he could assist with his family's finances, since his father had been paying for his

Harold B. Lee accompanies Mark E. Petersen, Matthew Cowley, Spencer W. Kimball, and Ezra Taft Benson of the Twelve.

education. In addition to his responsibilities as a principal and member of the dance band, he organized and directed a young women's chorus, which sang at school and church events.

It was also at this time that Harold was called as elders quorum president. This was a significant responsibility for such a young man to assume prior to his mission. It does illustrate the confidence the local leaders had in this capable young man. He undoubtedly learned much from this experience that would help him as a future missionary. Following his mission, the stake leaders again called him to serve as president of the elders quorum.

At age twenty-one, Harold received a call from President Heber J. Grant to serve in the Western States Mission. Just three days into the mission field, he met in the mission office Fern Tanner, a sister missionary with whom he was deeply impressed. Little did he know then that she would one day become his eternal companion.

Elder Lee and his first missionary companion often used their musical talents of playing piano and cello to touch the hearts of those whose homes they entered. Harold soon rose to leadership in the mission field as his diligence and faithfulness caught the attention of his mission president. He served much of his mission as president of the Denver conference, or district, presiding over several missionaries and the members in that area. His mission president came to trust him implicitly. He baptized over forty people during his mission.

One of his most memorable experiences occurred one day as they came to the door of a woman who belonged to a faction that had fallen away after the death of Joseph Smith. After a lengthy and spirited discussion, the conversation turned to this woman's son, who had been stricken

Harold B. Lee (back row, far right) was active in athletics. He was elected as student manager of athletics and developed a reputation as a good basketball player.

Young Harold with the enviable role of young women's chorus director in about 1919, before his mission.

Missionary Service

Elder Lee served in the Western States Mission from 1920–22. His mission president, John M. Knight, sent this report to the First Presidency at the conclusion of Elder Lee's mission: "Qualifications—As a speaker, 'Very Good.' As a presiding officer, 'Good.' Has he a good knowledge of the Gospel? 'Very Good.' Has he been energetic? 'Very.' Is he discreet and does he carry a good influence? 'Yes.' Remarks: 'Elder Lee presided over the Denver Conference with marked distinction from August 8th 1921 to December 18th 1922. An exceptional missionary."[2]

Harold B. Lee as a young missionary.

Harold was principal of the Oxford School in Idaho. He had previously taught at Silver Star School but transferred at a 50 percent increase in salary, which allowed him to send more money home to his parents to help with the family finances.

Oxford, Idaho, district school where Harold B. Lee became principal at age eighteen, 1917–18.

with an incurable disease and died before he could be baptized. The woman expressed her belief that a child should be baptized at eight years of age, but because of his illness he was unable to be baptized and died at about age nine. "She asked, 'What do you think we ought to do for our child?' Elder Lee said, 'Oh, that is easy. Have him baptized for [the dead] in the temple. That is what temples are for.' 'But,' she said, 'we have no temple.' . . . As I thought about her plight, I realized that the gates of hell had prevailed against her church because the keys and the power to reveal knowledge from heaven were not to be found in that church."[6]

YOUNG MARRIED LIFE— EXPERIENCE AND GROWTH

On his way home from the mission field, Harold stopped in Salt Lake City to report his mission to the Brethren and then to renew his acquaintance with the young sister missionary he had met in the mission field. Fern Lucinda Tanner was a beautiful, spiritual young woman.

Their courtship, which had begun via letters, continued in the same manner for a few months until Harold moved to Salt Lake City to pursue his schooling. On November 14, 1923, they married in the Salt Lake Temple about eleven

Eternal Companion

Harold B. Lee and Fern Tanner were married November 14, 1923, in the Salt Lake Temple on Fern's twenty-seventh birthday. Fern was small of stature, yet was a spiritual woman and a successful missionary. As a young woman she managed the office of a drug store and later worked for the Utah State Legislature and as a stenographer for the office of the Utah Secretary of State. She was an exemplary homemaker and mother, teaching her two daughters all the homemaking skills she had refined. She was an exceptional cook and a gracious hostess. She was known to all the neighborhood children as "Aunt Fern." Her daughter Helen recalled how complimentary her father was of her mother. "All during my growing-up years, whatever Mother did, whether it was arranging furniture or flowers, making a bed or ironing a shirt, Daddy would always say to us, 'Now, girls, when you can do that just like your mother, you'll be the best there is.' "[3] She was a source of inspiration to her husband and influenced him in many positive ways.

Fern Lucinda Tanner, first wife of Harold B. Lee.

Harold and his wife, Fern Tanner, in front of their first home located on 1538 West 800 South in Salt Lake City. They moved into the home following their marriage in November 1923.

Harold B. Lee in the mid-1930s, while serving as both Salt Lake City commissioner and president of the Pioneer Stake.

months after his mission ended. The couple was blessed with two beautiful daughters, Helen and Maurine. It was on the west side of Salt Lake City that they purchased their first home. Finances were tight, and they learned how to make do with little. This time in his life would help Harold appreciate more keenly the plight of the poor when he later served as a stake president. The Granite School District hired Harold as a principal. However, because the wages were low, he had

to supplement his income each summer by working various jobs. Over those early years, he sold meat, produce, books, and cars; worked at a grocery store and service station; served as a watchman; and worked for the Salt Lake City Street Department checking out equipment. Even with the long hours of work, the Lee home was full of love and devotion to spiritual matters such as family prayer.

Many opportunities also came to Harold to serve in the Church. He served on the high council, as a counselor in the stake presidency, and then, at the young age of thirty-one, as the stake president of the Pioneer Stake. He was the youngest stake president in the Church at that time. During the time of his service as stake president, he was also appointed and then later elected to the City Commission.

Perhaps the greatest challenges President Lee faced as stake president were the problems associated with the Great Depression that had fallen upon the nation and the world. For example, more than half of his stake members were unemployed. Counseling with other leaders in the stake, they began to put together a carefully planned program to assist the many needy in their boundaries. Harold instituted on a much larger scale what he had seen his father do as bishop in Idaho, namely a bishop's storehouse, which provided both work and goods for the needy.

The undertaking was impressive, as people were put to work in building, planting, harvesting, canning, sewing,

Harold B. Lee seated at a table at the Salt Lake City Commission. At age thirty-four, Harold was appointed to fill the vacancy created by the death of Commissioner Joseph H. Lake. He was elected to the post a year later and served until January 11, 1937, when he resigned at the request of the First Presidency to serve as managing director of the Church Welfare Program.

The Great Depression

During the spring of 1932, the Great Depression was raging, and Harold B. Lee was serving as president of the Salt Lake Pioneer Stake. With an unemployment rate of about 50 percent, the stake organized and sent members to assist farmers in harvesting crops for a share of the harvest. An old, dirty warehouse at 333 Pierpont Avenue was restored to a bright, cheerful place and the surplus crops were brought there to be put up by the sisters. The next year there was a bumper crop of onions, which were stored over the winter and sold in the spring, which gave them capital to fund their endeavors. Elder Lee said, "In those days we learned a bitter lesson, but not as soon as we should. When a man is starving there is no opportunity to feed him spiritually. Only when a man has been fed and clothed and his temporal wants have been satisfied, and only then, can you begin to spiritualize that man."[4]

Putting the Welfare Program to Work

In the midst of the Great Depression, Stake President Lee felt that recreation would help unite the Saints and lift their spirits in an otherwise discouraging time. He formulated a plan to build a recreation center, which provided work for many unemployed members as well as recreation. Each ward was assessed three hundred dollars. It took from ten to twelve calls at some homes to gather the entire amount. Only two of the eleven wards were successful in turning in their full assessment.

Nevertheless materials were salvaged from business buildings that had been demolished in downtown Salt Lake City. The only major purchase was for steel girders and few other essentials. The furnace and the gym equipment was purchased with funds raised by the YMMIA. All labor was donated and the project was completed in 1933 at a cost of only fifteen thousand dollars. In honor of President Lee, the Pioneer Stake gymnasium was renamed in 1954 to Harold B. Lee Hall.

Pioneer and Salt Lake Stakes Bishops' Storehouse, one of the first bishops' storehouses.

Pioneer Stake Gymnasium, now called Harold B. Lee Hall.

reconditioning, repairing, and gathering up goods and supplies that were being donated. It was termed "job relief without charity."[7] One of the most remarkable projects that was undertaken was to employ many laborers in taking the materials from an old business building that was being demolished and using them to build a stake gymnasium to provide a place for the stake social and recreational activities. This building stands today as a reminder of the significant effort of these people.

ROAD TO THE APOSTLESHIP

As others noticed the efforts of the Pioneer Stake, some neighboring stakes began to implement similar programs. In 1936, President Heber J. Grant launched what was called the Church Security program, now known as the Church Welfare Program. One year prior to this announcement, the First Presidency asked President Lee to meet with them on a Saturday morning. After a lengthy discussion of the welfare

The Lee Family in 1941. Harold and Fern with their two daughters, Helen (standing) and Maurine.

The Lee Family

Because of frail health and complications with her first two pregnancies, Sister Lee was unable to bear more children. The Lees were extremely grateful for the daughters the Lord had blessed them with. Their family was close-knit. The principle of positive reinforcement was the pattern used in the Lee home. Music played an important role in their home, and the girls learned to love music because of their parents' appreciation for good music. The scriptures were an important part of the spiritual development of the Lee family. Helen and Maurine knew how important it was for them set a proper example. One of the most remembered lessons they had from their father was a line he wrote in one of their scriptures: "The sermons of your father will be no better than the lives of his daughters."[5]

Perhaps the two most difficult trials of President Lee's life were losing his beloved wife in 1962 and, three years later, losing his youngest daughter, Maurine. In later years, President Lee spoke of the lessons he had learned: "I speak from personal experience when I say to you who mourn, do not try to live too many days ahead. The all-important thing is not that tragedies and sorrows come into our lives, but what we do with them. Death of a loved one is the most severe test that you will ever face, and if you can rise above your griefs and if you will trust in God, then you will be able to surmount any other difficulty with which you may be faced."[6]

needs of the membership of the Church, the First Presidency requested that Harold resign his position as a city commissioner and they would release him as stake president in order that he might head up the Church's efforts to take care of their needy. He said of this experience, "There I was just a young man in my thirties. My experience had been limited. I was born in a little country town in Idaho. I had hardly been outside the boundaries of the states of Utah and Idaho. And now to put me in a position where I was to reach out to the entire membership of the Church, worldwide, was one of the most staggering contemplations that I could imagine. How could I do it with my limited understanding?"[8] As he left the First Presidency's office, he determined to drive up City Creek Canyon to a secluded place where he could petition the Lord in prayer. In his journal, he wrote the following of this experience:

"As I knelt down, my petition was: 'What kind of an organization should be set up in order to accomplish what the Presidency has assigned?' . . . There came to me on that glorious spring afternoon one of the most heavenly realizations of the power of the priesthood of God. . . . It was as though something were saying to me: "There is no new organization necessary to take care of the needs of this people. All that is necessary is to put the priesthood of God to work. There is nothing else that you need as a substitute, and if you use it, the temporal welfare of the Latter-day Saints will be safeguarded."[9]

During the challenging years that Harold served as the managing director of the Church Welfare Department, he was tutored by President J. Rueben Clark with whom he developed a special relationship. Harold gained a deep appreciation for the challenges the Church leadership faced and for the opposition that sometimes came as the work moved forward. Little did he know that his involvement with the leaders of the Church and his travels with some of the Twelve would prepare him for even greater responsibilities.

As general conference approached in April 1941, the usual meetings and appointments filled his schedule. However, early Saturday morning on April 5, he awoke to a definite impression that he would be named a member of the Quorum of the Twelve. His premonition was fulfilled that very night when President Grant called him to the apostleship following the priesthood session of conference. Humbled by the call, this man of faith knew he needed the strength of the Lord to sustain him in this high responsibility. Shortly after his ordination as an Apostle, he had a significant experience that affirmed the divinity of his call. In his own words, Elder Lee recounted the event: "One of the Twelve came to me and said, 'Now we would like you to be the speaker at the Sunday night service. It is for Easter Sunday. As an ordained Apostle,

Council of the Twelve at the installation of Harold B. Lee, 1941.

The Quorum of the Twelve

John A Widtsoe said of Harold B. Lee, "He is full of faith in the Lord; abundant in his love of his fellow man, loyal to the Church and State, self-forgetful in his devotion to the Gospel; endowed with intelligence, energy, and initiative; and gifted with eloquent power to teach the word and will of God. The Lord to whom he goes for help will make him a mighty instrument in carrying forward the eternal plan of human salvation. . . . He will be given strength beyond any yet known to him, as the prayers of the people ascend to the Lord in his behalf."[7]

Reading to grandsons David and Hal. President Lee loved to spend time with his grandchildren.

you are to be a special witness of the mission and resurrection of the Lord and Savior Jesus Christ.' That, I think, was the most startling, the most overwhelming contemplation of all that had happened.

"I locked myself in one of the rooms of the Church Office Building and took out the Bible. I read in the four Gospels, particularly the scriptures pertaining to the death, crucifixion, and resurrection of the Lord, and as I read, I suddenly became aware that something strange was happening. It wasn't just a story I was reading, for it seemed as though the events I was reading about were very real as though I were actually living those experiences. On Sunday night I delivered my humble message and said, 'And now, I, one of the least of the Apostles here on the earth today, bear you witness that I too know with all my soul that Jesus is the Savior of the world and that He lived and died and was resurrected for us.' I knew because of a special kind of witness that had come to me the preceding week."[10]

MINISTRY AS AN APOSTLE

Elder Lee became known for his love of young people. As a young Apostle in 1945, he gave a series of twenty-four fireside talks presented over KSL radio from January 1 until June 24. This proved to be both a challenge and an opportunity. Because of the necessary preparation, Elder Lee was relieved for a time from some conference assignments so he could prepare each week for the radio addresses. This meant he could

Treated like Royalty

"Anyone who came into his home was a prince or a princess. He treated them like royalty. He was a most gracious host. It was difficult ever to see him standing while he was with a group, because he would be kneeling down talking to a child or bent over giving comfort to an elderly person. Everyone meant something to [him]. He loved people—all people."[8]

Elder Lee was known for his efforts to strengthen the youth of the Church.

Harold B. Lee visiting servicemen.

spend more time with his family, which became a welcome blessing. He sought input and advice from his daughters and received valuable help. The radio addresses were soon published throughout the Church under the title *Youth and the Church*. The book would later be expanded and published as *Decisions for Successful Living*. He continued to speak often to youth and young adult groups throughout the Church.

Among Elder Lee's other assignments was that of chairman of the Church Servicemen's Committee. This provided opportunities for him to travel and visit the servicemen during World War II, the Korean War, and the Vietnam War. In

1954, Elder Lee taught a doctrinal course to seminary and institute teachers during their summer session at Brigham Young University. All of these and many other opportunities provided him with invaluable experiences.

In 1962, President Lee faced what he considered the greatest challenge of his life. The death of his beloved Fern proved a soul-wrenching experience. There were many dark days as he struggled in the Spirit with the loss of his beloved companion of nearly forty years. The weight of this loss eventually softened when, in July 1963, he married Freda Joan Jensen, a friend of the Lees for many years. A wonderful,

Visiting Servicemen

In 1942, Elder Lee was assigned to accompany Elder Albert E. Bowen and others to visit servicemen on the West Coast and determine what the Church might do to better help meet the needs of its members in the armed services. From those visits it was determined that the needs were regular correspondence from home, Church-sponsored social activities where possible, and the spiritual sustenance gained from personal prayer, scripture study, and worship services. Thus, the Church, under Elder Lee's direction as chairman of the serviceman's committee, began serious efforts to promote each of these needs. Later, the Church developed pocket-sized editions of the scriptures for servicemen to carry. Elder Lee served as chairman of the Servicemen's Committee during the latter part of World War II, the Korean War, and the Vietnam War. He was called by President McKay to visit servicemen and members of the Church in Japan, Okinawa, Korea, the Philippines, Guam, and other regions in Asia. This visit was the first time a General Authority had visited Korea. While there were at the time only three members of record in Pusan, over 200 people attended: 100 soldiers who were, for the most part, members, and 103 Koreans, nearly all of whom were investigators. This visit, along with proselyting efforts of the soldiers, began the growth of the Church in Korea. In reporting of his visit to the Far East among the servicemen, Elder Lee reported to President McKay, "I have gone now under your appointment to the Far East. We have seen the miracles of God's divine intervention. We have seen how the gospel has been preached, to the poor as an evidence of its divinity. God grant that . . . those [worthy] shall be free to receive in fullness the gospel of Jesus Christ, for I am convinced that there are hundreds of thousands of souls who are begging for the truth."[9]

Elder Lee and his wife, Fern, relished the limited time they could spend together at home.

A New Companion

Some months following the death of President Lee's first wife Fern, he renewed a friendship with Sister Freda Joan Jensen, who had been a friend of the Lees for many years. Sister Jensen was born July 2, 1897, in Provo, Utah. After graduating from BYU, she pursued graduate studies at the University of Utah, University of California, and Columbia University. She taught elementary school for some years before becoming the supervisor of primary education in the Jordan School District. During this time, she also served on the Primary and Young Women General Boards and was also a member of the Church Music Committee. Joan played the piano and loved music. She met the three characteristics that Elder Lee had set in his mind: she was someone near his age, she had known and admired his first wife, Fern, and she had never been married before. After obtaining the approval and encouragement of his two daughters, he moved ahead with plans to marry Sister Jensen. They were married June 17, 1963, by President David O. McKay in the Salt Lake Temple. Her life was one of whole-hearted devotion to the gospel.

loving companion, she made the burdens of Elder Lee's responsibility much easier to bear. Three years later, tragedy again struck his life when his daughter Maurine died suddenly, leaving four children. Gordon B. Hinckley, a close associate of Elder Lee, wrote of these trying times, "These searing experiences, difficult to bear, served to increase his sensitivity to the burdens of others. Those who have sustained similar losses have found in him an understanding friend and one whose own tested faith has become a source of strength to them."[11]

Under the direction of President David O. McKay, the Church Correlation Committee was established in the early 1960s and Elder Lee was called upon to chair the committee. His vast experience with the Church administration and programs and his keen understanding of the doctrine made him a natural for this responsibility. Elder Lee worked tirelessly to bring the curriculum, programs, and efforts of the Church into harmony and to redefine their focus. Ward teaching became home teaching, new Church magazines presented a changed format and focus, family home evening received new

President Lee and his second wife, Freda Joan Jensen.

Committee Correlation

The ideas concerning correlation of Church programs and curriculum were first introduced to Harold B. Lee by President J. Reuben Clark in 1941. It would not be until the 1960s that these ideas really began to see fulfillment. In 1960, a comprehensive study of the Churchwide curriculum was formally begun. In April 1963, Elder Lee was asked by President David O. McKay to make a major presentation at the general priesthood meeting of the Church concerning the four new priesthood committees over welfare, genealogy (family history), missionary work, and home teaching. In the priesthood session of October 1967, he was again called upon to present the progress of the correlation of curriculum for adults, youth, and children. He also explained the newly announced regional representatives of the Church and their functions in assisting the Quorum of the Twelve. The impact of Elder Lee's efforts with the correlation committee of the Church is still being felt significantly today. The major emphasis on the home and family as the institution around which all efforts are centered was critical then and continues to be so today.

Churchwide Service

"The vast effort made under his direction has resulted in a correlated curriculum designed to impart knowledge of every phase of Church activity and doctrine and to build spirituality in the membership. The strength of his leadership has been evident in this undertaking. His hand has been firm, his objectives clearly defined. The entire Church is the beneficiary of his service."[12]

Missionary Temple Meetings

For many years as an Apostle and then as the President of the Church, he met nearly weekly in the upper assembly room of the Salt Lake Temple with the newly departing missionaries after their first endowment session. This question and answer session was the highlight of the week for the young elders. Concerning those special meetings President Lee explained, "We always say to them repeatedly as we have finished, 'I want you to notice that all the answers I have given have been given from out of the scriptures. I wouldn't dare attempt to make an answer to your questions anywhere else but from the scriptures or from the statements of a President of the Church, which, to us, as they give inspired utterances, are scripture.' "[10]

Speaking of these sacred meetings, Joseph Anderson, former secretary for the First Presidency, wrote, "I hope the missionaries fully appreciate this sacred privilege of an intimate appearance before them of God's chosen servant and the inspired wisdom of his timely advice and counsel."[11]

emphasis, each family member owning their own scriptures was stressed, and scripture study was encouraged. These and many more efforts were refined or put in place. In addition, during this time efforts to increase the effectiveness of the Church leadership improved with the calling of regional representatives of the Twelve. This would be the precursor to later changes in the Quorums of the Seventy and eventually the Area Presidencies.

While working tirelessly on these and other assignments, Elder Lee found time almost every week to meet with the newly called missionaries in the upper room of the Salt Lake Temple for a question and answer session. The impressive thing to those who attended those meetings was Elder Lee's constant reference to the scriptures to answer the questions. During these years, appointments came for Elder Lee to serve on the board of directors of several business and civic organizations, which added to the demands on his time.

At this time of tremendous responsibility, a remarkable experience occurred in 1967 that demonstrated the Lord's hand in preserving his life for further service in the kingdom. Elder Lee related the experience as follows:

which, had they occurred while we were in flight, I wouldn't be here today talking about it. I know that there are powers divine that reach out when all other help is not available."[12]

SERVING IN THE FIRST PRESIDENCY

It was not long before it became apparent why Elder Lee's life had been spared. In January of 1970 President David O McKay died. Joseph Fielding Smith was ordained as the next prophet, and he selected Elder Lee as his First Counselor. During his short time as a counselor in the First Presidency, several significant events occurred, not the least of which was the first Area Conference of the Church, which was held in England. In an effort to take the leadership of the Church closer to the members, the Area Conference became a welcome event. President Lee attended two more Area Conferences during his time as President of the Church—one in Mexico City and the other in Munich, Germany. The Saints in these areas responded favorably to an opportunity to personally meet many of the leaders of the Church.

Time away from his work in the ministry was limited, but when he did find time, President Lee enjoyed working around the home or, as on this occasion, deep-sea fishing.

"On the way across the country, we were sitting in the forward section of the airplane. Some of our Church members were in the next section. As we approached a certain point en route, someone laid his hand upon my head. I looked up; I could see no one. That happened again before we arrived home, again with the same experience. Who it was, by what means or what medium, I may never know, except I knew that I was receiving a blessing that I came a few hours later to know I needed most desperately.

As soon as we arrived home, my wife very anxiously called the doctor. It was now about eleven o'clock at night. He called me to come to the telephone, and he asked me how I was; and I said, 'Well, I am very tired. I think I will be all right.' But shortly thereafter, there came massive hemorrhages

First Presidency from 1970 to 1972: President Joseph Fielding Smith, Harold B. Lee, N. Eldon Tanner. Harold B. Lee's energy and experience were a great help to President Tanner, who had been carrying most of the administrative load at that time.

The construction of the Provo and Ogden Temples was completed, and President Lee gave the dedicatory prayer at the Provo Temple. He was also involved in other decisions that helped to advance temple work in foreign lands. With the ever-increasing profile of the Church, it was felt that a Public Relations Department should be organized to help respond to the questions and issues that involved the Church. This decision proved to have long-term benefits for the Church.

PROPHET, SEER, AND REVELATOR

On July 2, 1972, President Joseph Fielding Smith passed away peacefully at home. The weight of the calling as President of the Church now rested squarely upon the shoulders of President Harold B. Lee. He was ordained the eleventh President of the Church on July 7, 1972. He selected as his counselors N. Eldon Tanner and long-time associate Marion G. Romney.

A few weeks after his call as President of the Church, President Lee shared the following with the members of the Church in attendance at the Mexico City Area Conference: "I want to tell you a little sacred experience I had following the call to be the president of the Church. On the early morning thereafter with my wife I kneeled in humble prayer, and suddenly it seemed as though my mind and heart went out to over three million people in all the world. I seemed to have a love for every one of them no matter where they lived nor what their color was, whether they were rich or poor, whether they were humble or great, or educated or not. Suddenly I felt as though they all belonged to me, as though they were all my own brothers and sisters."[13] This statement came to reflect the feeling and spirit conveyed by President Lee in his ministry.

Much was done in the year and a half he was President to improve and streamline efforts in the Sunday School organization, the missionary department, the youth and young adult

Voting in the Solemn Assembly, October 6, 1972, when Harold B. Lee was sustained as President of the Church.

The First Presidency as it was organized in 1972. President N. Eldon Tanner was the First Counselor and President Marion G. Romney was the Second Counselor.

programs, teacher development, and leadership training for bishops. In May 1973, President Lee put forward an initiative to begin building smaller, "stake center sized" temples to help bring the temples closer to more of the people. Concerning his work with the other members of the First Presidency and the Twelve he wrote, "It was a most delightful experience to review the unity which had developed a warm, spiritual feeling of brotherhood to bind us together with bonds more sacred than blood relationships, as we together had sought the blessings of the Lord upon his work."[14]

President Lee was constantly on the move to be out and among the people, holding firesides, conferences, and meetings. The demands were great but the blessings of seeing the people respond with such warmth, gratitude, and faith sustained him in these demanding times. To one of his grandsons he confided, "I know the Lord will sustain me as long as he wants me to be here, but I can't rest."[15] It was also during his short administration that press conferences and interviews became fairly common events as the Church became more prominent in the nation and the world. He became the first President of the Church to visit the Holy Land, and while there, he established the first branch of the Church in Jerusalem. In reflecting back upon the life and ministry of President Lee, President Marion G. Romney declared, "All the programs of the Church operative during the nearly thirty-three years he served as one of the General Authorities bear the mark of his prophetic genius. . . . He was one of the most powerful men in modern Israel."[16]

In what would be President Lee's last general conference address, he spoke of the signs of the Second Coming that were becoming more apparent. He then invoked upon the Saints a blessing of peace, not through legislation but "by overcoming all the things of the world."[17] It was his great desire to see people find the peace that comes by following the Savior. Truly his ministry had come to reflect the counsel and instruction he had received in a vision so many years before: "If you want to love God, you have to learn to love and serve the people. That is the way you show your love for God."[18] It was the way that Harold B. Lee fulfilled his ministry.

He died suddenly and unexpectedly from heart and lung failure on December 26, 1973.

President Lee became a progressive user of electronic media, giving television and newspaper interviews.

A Giant of a Man

"A giant of a man he was. A man endowed with a rare native intelligence, he recalls a thousand experiences over the terrain of time, a unique gift to quickly get the heart of matters under consideration and quickened by a capacity to discard extraneous information, thus freeing the mind for decisive action. . . . A master teacher, who much like the Savior, took the ordinary experiences of today to teach the will of the Lord. Yes, among our generations has walked one of God's most noble, powerful, committed, and foreordained giant redwoods—President Harold B. Lee."[13]

President Lee is remembered as a powerful speaker who was always forthright in all he taught. He delivered his last conference address in October 1973.

TEACHINGS OF PRESIDENT
HAROLD B. LEE

◆

On the morning of July 7, 1972, the fourteen members of the Quorum of the Twelve met in the upper room of the Salt Lake Temple to reorganize the First Presidency of the Church. Following this meeting when Harold B. Lee was ordained the eleventh President of the Church, a press conference was held in the Church Administration Building. When asked what his first message as President would be, he responded, "The greatest message that one in this position could give to the membership of the Church is to keep the commandments of God, for therein lies the safety of the Church and the safety of the individual. Keep the commandments. There could be nothing that I could say that would be a more powerful or important message today."[19] This statement was an effective summary of the teachings of President Lee before and during his administration in the Church's highest office.

In the face of so much civil unrest in the United States of America, the uncertainty about communism and the outcome of the Vietnam War, and the general decline of moral standards, President Lee declared to a group of young adults, "There are two things that, if fully applied, would save the world. The first is to put the full might of the priesthood of the kingdom of God to work, and second, the powerful teachings of the gospel of Jesus Christ."[20] These two principles would be the underpinning of all his efforts as President of the Church.

President Lee loved to read the scriptures.

Love of the Scriptures

A lifelong student of the scriptures, President Lee always drew deeply from their inspired doctrines. On one occasion, he asked leaders of the Church, "Do you have a daily habit of reading the scriptures? If we're not reading the scriptures daily, our testimonies are growing thinner, our spirituality isn't increasing in depth."[14] Elder Joseph Anderson, who served as a secretary to the First Presidency for many years, wrote, "President Lee is a thorough student of the scriptures. He has a great knowledge and understanding of them, and his memory pertaining thereto is unusually remarkable and reliable."[15] President Lee was noted for his in-depth understanding of the doctrine of the Church. Much of this understanding had come as a direct result of his continued reliance on the scriptures.

Using the Scriptures as Our Guide

During his lifetime, President Lee came to learn first-hand the importance and power of scripture study. He constantly relied on the scriptures in his work in the kingdom. During the 1960s the world became full of young and old alike who began to question the old standard of right and wrong. The mottos of "Free Love" and "God Is Dead" captured the headlines and represented the attitude of many of the rising generation. The belief that values were relative became a fashionable philosophy. President Lee's teachings countered such attitudes. "Except for the standard Church works, there is no accurate guide as to what is right and what is wrong on the earth," he affirmed.[21] With this principle in mind, he voiced the following concern:

"I say that we need to teach our people to find their answers in the scriptures. If only each of us would be wise enough to say that we aren't able to answer any question unless we can find a doctrinal answer in the scriptures! And if we hear someone teaching something that is contrary to what is in the scriptures, each of us may know whether the things spoken are false—it is as simple as that. But the unfortunate thing is that so many of us are not reading the scriptures. We do not know what is in them, and therefore we speculate about the things that we ought to have found in the scriptures themselves. I think that therein is one of our biggest dangers of today."[22]

In the foregoing statement, President Lee voiced a general concern that was felt among the Brethren. It was for this reason that the Church's Sunday School curriculum was changed to studying each of the standard works on a rotating basis, so as to encourage and help the members become more familiar with the scriptures. Their concern was not just the need to answer questions from the scriptures, but also the need to be conversant enough to know whether a question was answered in the scriptures. This emphasis on scripture-based courses has continued to this day in the Sunday School, seminary, and institute curricula. It has led to the rising generation in the Church being much more conversant with the scriptures than previous generations.

On another occasion, President Lee counseled Church leaders on teaching doctrine, saying, "With respect to doctrines and meanings of scriptures, let me give you a safe counsel. It is usually not well to use a single passage of scripture in proof of a point of doctrine unless it is confirmed by modern revelation or by the Book of Mormon. I want you to think of that, brethren. To single out a passage of scripture to prove a point, unless it is confirmed also by revelation or by the Book of Mormon, is always a hazardous thing. Be careful in quoting comments from writers about a certain scriptural matter as though it was authoritative unless you, likewise, have tested their expression by the Book of Mormon and the revelations."[23] Many a person could have saved himself from making a serious error in judgment or in doctrine if he had applied the above rule. This principle is particularly important for those called to teach the gospel.

Warning about Spurious Writings

In the Book of Mormon, one reads over and over how the people were deceived because they were not conversant with the scriptures. In the latter days, the same problem has plagued many Latter-day Saints. Doomsayers, false teachers, and false prophets continue to put forth their doctrinal interpretations, time lines, and predictions. These conditions led President Lee to voice the following concern, "One of the amazing phenomena of today among our people is their gullibility to seize upon rumors without identifying the source."[24] Given his continuing concern about the Saints being led astray concerning the signs of the times, he gave the following helpful guidelines:

"There are among us many loose writings predicting the calamities which are about to overtake us. Some of these have been publicized as though they were necessary to wake up the world to the horrors about to overtake us. Many of these are from sources upon which there cannot be unquestioned reliance. . . . Brethren, these [JST Matthew 1; D&C 38, 45, 101, 133] are some of the writings with which you should concern yourselves, rather than commentaries that may come from those whose information may not be the most reliable and whose motives may be subject to question. And may I say, parenthetically, most of such writers are not handicapped by having any authentic information on their writings."[25]

As the time of the Savior's Second Coming approaches, the more important it is that people heed the cautions President Lee gave. There is a great need to avoid speculation and delving into mysteries that God has not chosen to reveal to men. One of the major purposes of the correlation program of the Church was to standardize the doctrine and teachings in the curriculum of the Church and to keep members from going off on teaching tangents that were often confusing, misleading, or divisive. Focusing on fundamental doctrines ultimately leads to strength in individuals and families who believe and follow them. This is why President Lee was so focused on teaching about the need to use the scriptures and to follow the teachings of living prophets.

FOLLOW THE PROPHET

Because of the tendency for unauthorized individuals to step forward and presume authority or power to direct the Lord's work, President Lee addressed this issue in the Munich Area Conference in August 1973: "If anyone, regardless of his position in the Church, were to advance a doctrine that is not substantiated by the standard Church works, meaning the [scriptures], you may know that his statement is merely his private opinion. The only one authorized to bring forth any new doctrine is the President of the Church, who, when he does, will declare it as a revelation from God, and it will be so accepted by the Council of the Twelve and sustained by the body of the Church."[26]

President Lee spoke of "tight places" the Church and individuals would have to pass through before the Lord comes. The power of Satan is increasing in the world, as can be observed on every side. Because of the increasing acceptance of wickedness, President Lee gave this solemn warning:

"The only safety we have as members of this church is to do exactly what the Lord said to the Church in that day when the Church was organized. We must learn to give heed to the words and commandments that the Lord shall give through His prophet, 'as he receiveth them, walking in all holiness before me; . . . as if from mine own mouth, in all patience and faith' (D&C 21:4–5). There will be some things that take patience and faith. You may not like what comes from the authority of the Church. It may contradict your political views. It may contradict your social views. It may interfere with some of your social life. But if you listen to these things, as if from the mouth of the Lord Himself, with patience and faith, the promise is that 'the gates of hell shall not prevail against you; yea, and the Lord God will disperse the powers of darkness from before you, and cause the heavens to shake for your good, and his name's glory' (D&C 21:6)."[27]

This promise and council to follow the living prophet is as vital for the members of the Church today as it was in the day it was given by President Lee. Perhaps one of the tests or challenges many will face is to have an issue in the world where our view differs from the position taken by the Church. President Lee's counsel to follow the living prophets can save us from a lifetime of frustration and an eternity of regret.

COUNCIL TO YOUTH: LOYAL TO THE ROYAL WITHIN

Love and concern for the youth of the Church was a trademark of Harold B. Lee's life. He knew something of the ever increasing challenges they faced. As President, he counseled young people to "go to your parents, they who are concerned about you and love you dearly, and put your arms around them now and tell them about what you've learned here [at youth conference]. Thank them for what they've done. Be true to your Heavenly Father's guardians, your parents, and help them to be better parents. Strive to be a better son or daughter and there will be great joy in your home."[28]

President Lee had great compassion for the youth of the Church. His teachings demonstrated his deep concern for them and their future. His expressions of love for them were frequent. "The Lord loves you; I love you; and I want you to know that there isn't anything in the world that I would not do, as I am directed by the Lord, to help you be guided on your way. This is His work. This is the plan of salvation. This is the only plan that will save the world.

"You are on the right course, you wonderful young people. As the President of the Church, I bless you and hope you will remain in the purity of your lives. Keep yourselves pure and sweet and clean. If you have made mistakes, don't repeat them. Walk humbly from now on. Prepare yourselves to go to the house of the Lord. Prepare yourselves for wifehood and motherhood, you girls; and you young men, prepare yourselves to be the sweethearts and companions and husbands and fathers of the children yet unborn."[29]

President Lee believed that the youth born in the latter days are among some of the most noble of our Heavenly Father's children. He knew they had been reserved to come to earth at a critical time:

"I say to you, youth of the noble birthright, in your veins there runs the purest blood there is upon this earth today. . . . You have been raised up for this time, the choicest that have lived on the earth, to build up the Church and to prepare for the coming of the Lord, which may not be far away, maybe closer than any of us know. Youth of the noble birthright, I say to you, 'Be loyal to the royal within you!'

I leave you my blessing. I love you young people. I pray to God that you, as the parents of tomorrow's youth, will prepare yourselves now. Keep yourselves worthy to be the fathers and mothers of the children yet to come upon the earth. Give them clean bodies. Keep yourselves worthy to receive the Spirit of the Lord, I humbly pray."[30]

Through these words, one can sense the love our Heavenly Father has for each of His children. President Lee was a champion of youth and desired so much for them to be prepared to meet and fulfill their foreordained missions.

The Most Important Work

With the rapid changes in the world, the ever increasing demands upon the time of parents, and the decline in moral standards, President Lee was keenly aware of the significant challenges facing families. He had been assigned as an Apostle to oversee new efforts to strengthen the family, including renewed and increased emphasis on family home evenings. Recognizing that significantly more families were

being confronted with children who were straying from the path, he said, "I pray that our families in the Church can have many opportunities together, to stay together, pray together, work together, so that strong bonds will be formed. Then, if the children should stray away temporarily from the path of truth and duty, the strongest bond that can be forged in their minds will be their fear of losing their place in the eternal family circle."[31] To those who had experienced a wayward child, he offered this encouragement: "I would like to say to you mothers: Don't give up on that [wayward] boy or girl; one day he may, like the Prodigal Son, return to the home from which he came, as a ship in a storm returns to a safe harbor. . . . Let yours be that kind of a home where they can come and you have to take them in no matter what they have done."[32] On another occasion he added, "No home is a failure unless it quits trying to help."[33]

President Lee reaffirmed that "we believe that the home is the greatest institution there is in all the world, and the best the Church can do is to help to strengthen the home. But we must urge our parents to do all they can to help themselves to teach their children."[34] He understood that there is a danger that parents may abdicate from their duties to teach, train, and provide nurturing love for their children. Explaining this concern, he wrote the following:

"It is becoming increasingly clear that the home and family are the key to the future of the Church. An unloved child, a child who has not known discipline, work, or responsibility, will often yield to satanic substitutes for happiness—drugs, sexual experimentation, and rebellion, whether it is intellectual or behavioral. Our intensified efforts around family home evening, which we have not only urged our members to hold, but concerning which we have supplied more and more help, hold much promise if we will but use these opportunities.

"There is no better place than in the home to teach and learn about marriage, love, and sex as these can properly combine in a sanctified temple marriage. There is no better place to deal with the doubts of our young than where there is love—at home. Love can free our youth to listen to those whom they know they can trust. Our curricula, quorums, and classes should *supplement* the home, and where homes are seriously defective, we will have to compensate as best we can."[35]

President Lee came to the office of President of the Church as one of the most trusted and respected among the General Authorities. His knowledge and understanding of the inner workings of the kingdom was unsurpassed. This is one of the last portraits taken of President Lee.

This principle, that the Church exists to supplement the home, is even more critical today. The tendency is to allow the Church to shoulder the responsibility for teaching, training, and instilling faith in our youth. President Lee clearly understood the danger such an attitude would present to the forward movement of the Church.

As our lives become increasingly busy and demands for our time press at us from every side, it becomes even more important to keep an eternal perspective while making important choices in our lives. No statement by President Lee is better recognized than one he repeated at Brigham Young University just three months before his death. He declared, "I have frequently counseled, and I repeat it to you again, to all of you here: 'The most important of the Lord's work you will ever do will be within the walls of your own homes.' We must never forget that."[36] This statement merits continual repetition in a society where we are constantly being pressed with various ways to spend our time and energy. President Lee repeated this message on several occasions and used it as a warning to some who excused themselves from neglecting their families because of their Church callings.

MAINTAINING A TESTIMONY

Over his lifetime, President Lee saw many who either failed to obtain a testimony or failed to maintain the testimony they had. This became a frequent topic he addressed during his short tenure as the Prophet. While visiting sacred sites pertaining to the restoration of the Church in upstate New York he counseled, "One may have a testimony as of today, but when he stoops to do things that contradict the laws of God, it is because he has lost his testimony and he has to fight to regain it again. Testimony isn't something that you have today and you keep always. Testimony is either going to grow and grow to the brightness of certainty, or it is going to diminish to nothingness, depending upon what we do about it."[37] As to what one must do to maintain their testimony, President Lee gave the following instruction:

"Testimony is as elusive as a moonbeam; it's as fragile as an orchid; you have to recapture it every morning of your life. You have to hold on by study, and by faith, and by prayer. If you allow yourself to be angry, if you allow yourself to get into the wrong kind of company, you listen to the wrong kind of stories, you are studying the wrong kind of subjects, you are engaging in sinful practices, there is nothing that will be more deadening as to take away the Spirit of the Lord from you until it will be as though you had walked from a lighted room when you go out of this building, as though you had gone out into a darkness."[38]

President Lee had the ability to strike to the very core of the issue of obtaining or maintaining a testimony. He recognized the ever-increasing cynicism in the world toward spiritual matters. His counsel clearly addressed both how to obtain a testimony and how to avoid losing what we have gained.

In addition to one's responsibility to gain and maintain a testimony, President Lee also spoke profoundly of our responsibility to lift and build testimonies in others. "You cannot lift another soul until you are standing on higher ground than he is. You must be sure, if you would rescue the man, that you yourself are setting the example of what you would have him be. You cannot light a fire in another soul unless it is burning in your own soul. You teachers, the testimony that you bear, the spirit with which you teach and with which you lead, is one of the most important assets that you can have, as you help to strengthen those who need so much, wherein you have so much to give."[39]

President Lee understood the impact of a powerful testimony. He knew how it would enhance one's capacity to make correct choices and to find peace in a troubled world. With all his heart, he desired to help instill testimonies in those he taught. On several occasions, he lovingly invited those he taught to lean on his testimony until they could gain one of their own. In his teaching over the years, President Lee bore powerful testimony of the work of the kingdom and the reality of Jesus Christ who stands at its head. His sure witness of the life and mission of the Savior added additional power to his teachings. At the close of one particularly profound spiritual meeting, President Lee bore this powerful witness:

"I want to close by bearing you my witness . . . of the Lord and Savior, Jesus Christ. I didn't know what it was to have the more sure word of prophecy until a call came that required it. When I saw and knew and was brought to the realization of the reality of the mission of the Lord, that gave me the right to bear witness more certainly and more surely than if I had seen and had been there in person to have accompanied the Master on his journey. I know that he lives. If there are any of you who don't have a full and complete testimony, will you cling to my testimony until you develop one for yourselves? I know that he lives. I have been near enough to him to know his influence. As I see some of the pictures that artists try to paint, no one yet has caught the reality of what I know to be what the Master looks like. You, too, can know because you have all that is necessary for you to know and to understand and to have that same kind of a witness that will keep you sure and steadfast in the midst of all the difficulties that are confronting you in this day. . . . God bless you, keep you always, humble, prayerful, so that the Lord can take you by the hand as it were and give you answer to all your prayers."[40]

The remarkable thing about the teachings of Harold B. Lee is how timeless and consistently relevant they are. His concerns about the family, the youth, the use of the scriptures, and the gaining and maintaining of a testimony are still the core issues we face today. The teachings of Harold B. Lee are a living witness of his prophetic vision and foresight.

Clyde J. Williams

Professor of Ancient Scripture, EdD
Brigham Young University

NOTES

1. Harold B. Lee, *The Teachings of Harold B. Lee*, ed. Clyde J. Williams (Salt Lake City: Bookcraft, 1996), 459.
2. Ibid., 280.
3. Leonard J. Arrington, *The Presidents of the Church: Biographical Essays* (Salt Lake City: Deseret Book, 1986), 347.
4. Harold B. Lee, "The Way to Eternal Life," *Ensign*, November 1971, 17.
5. Harold B. Lee, CR, April 1941, 120.
6. Harold B. Lee, *Stand Ye in Holy Places* (Salt Lake City: Deseret

An Impressive Man

"As I have thus listened to and observed President Lee over the years he has impressed me as being a man of great physical and moral courage. He has always had the courage of his convictions and is not fearful of expressing them. He has always demonstrated great faith in the gospel of Jesus Christ and in the leadership of the Church. He has a remarkable memory. His retention of things that have happened in the past, of actions taken, expression made by the brethren is almost uncanny."[16]

Book, 1974), 128.

7. Arrington, *The Presidents of the Church*, 356.

8. Lee, *The Teachings of Harold B. Lee*, 300–301.

9. L. Brent Goates, *Harold B. Lee: Prophet and Seer* (Salt Lake City: Bookcraft, 1985), 142–43.

10. Lee, *The Teachings of Harold B. Lee*, 638–39.

11. Gordon B. Hinckley, "President Harold B. Lee, an Appreciation," *Ensign*, November 1972, 10.

12. Lee, *The Teachings of Harold B. Lee*, 491.

13. Lee, Mexico and Central America Area Conference Report, August 1972, 151.

14. Goates, *Harold B. Lee: Prophet and Seer*, 530.

15. Ibid., 565.

16. Marion G. Romney, "He Was Most Like the Prophet Joseph," in L. Brent Goates, ed., *He Changed My Life* (Salt Lake City: Bookcraft, 1988), 23.

17. Harold B. Lee, CR, October 1973, 171.

18. Ibid., April 1973, 180.

19. Harold B. Lee, *Ensign*, August 1972, back cover.

20. Lee, *The Teachings of Harold B. Lee*, 389.

21. Ibid., 149.

22. Ibid., 153.

23. Ibid., 157.

24. Ibid., 401.

25. Ibid., 399.

26. Ibid., 543–44.

27. Ibid., 525–26.

28. Ibid., 627.

29. Ibid., 626–27.

30. Ibid., 625–26.

31. Ibid., 273.

32. Ibid., 279.

33. Ibid., 278.

34. Ibid., 267.

35. Ibid., 264; emphasis added.

36. Ibid., 280.

37. Ibid., 139.

38. Ibid.

39. Ibid., 462.

40. Harold B. Lee, Laurelife Leadership Conference (transcript), August 23, 1970, 6–7.

SIDEBAR AND PHOTO NOTES

1. As cited in Goates, *He Changed My Life*, 24–25.

2. Hinckley, "President Harold B. Lee, an Appreciation," 5–6.

3. Goates, *Harold B. Lee: Prophet and Seer*, 133.

4. Harold B. Lee, address to Pioneer Regional bimonthly welfare meeting, March 17, 1959, 3.

5. Goates, *Harold B. Lee: Prophet and Seer*, 123.

6. Lee, *The Teachings of Harold B. Lee*, 53.

7. John A. Widtsoe, *Improvement Era*, May 1941, 288.

8. Verda Lee Ross, President Lee's Sister, personal interview, *Presidents of the Church Student Manual* (The Church of Jesus Christ of Latter-day Saints, 1979), 265.

9. Harold B. Lee, CR, October 1954, 131.

10. Lee, *The Teachings of Harold B. Lee*, 153–54.

11. Joseph Anderson, *Prophets I Have Known* (Salt Lake City: Deseret Book, 1973), 187.

12. Hinckley, "President Harold B. Lee, an Appreciation," 11.

13. Spencer W. Kimball, "A Giant of a Man," *Ensign*, February 1974, 86–87.

14. Lee, *The Teachings of Harold B. Lee*, 152.

15. Anderson, *Prophets I Have Known*, 184.

16. Ibid.

SUGGESTED READING

Francis M. Gibbons, *Harold B. Lee: Man of Vision, Prophet of God* (Salt Lake City: Deseret Book, 1993).

L. Brent Goates, *Harold B. Lee: Prophet and Seer* (Salt Lake City: Bookcraft, 1985).

L. Brent Goates, ed., *He Changed My Life* (Salt Lake City: Bookcraft, 1988).

L. Brent Goates, *Modern-Day Miracles: From the Files of President Harold B. Lee* (American Fork: Covenant Communications, 1996).

Harold B. Lee, *Youth and the Church* (Salt Lake City: Deseret Book, 1970).

Harold B. Lee, *Decisions for Successful Living* (Salt Lake City: Deseret Book, 1973).

Harold B. Lee, *Stand Ye in Holy Places* (Salt Lake City: Deseret Book, 1974).

Harold B. Lee, *Ye are the Light of the World* (Salt Lake City: Deseret Book, 1974).

Harold B. Lee, *The Teachings of Harold B. Lee*, ed. Clyde J. Williams (Salt Lake City: Bookcraft, 1996).

Teachings of the Presidents of the Church: Harold B. Lee (Salt Lake City: The Church of Jesus Christ of Latter-day Saints, 2000).

Chapter Twelve

SPENCER W. KIMBALL

LIFE AND TIMES

1895	March 28	Born in Salt Lake City
1897		Family moved to Thatcher, Arizona
1903		Baptized on eighth birthday
1906		Mother died
1914–16		Served mission to the central states
1917	November 16	Married Camilla Eyring
1927		Established the Kimball-Greenhalgh Agency
1938		Called as president of the Mount Graham Arizona Stake
1943	July 8	Called as an Apostle
1957		Throat surgery performed
1969		Published *The Miracle of Forgiveness*
1972		Underwent open heart surgery and became President of the Quorum of the Twelve Apostles
1973	December 29	Ordained President of The Church of Jesus Christ of Latter-day Saints
1978	June 7	Received revelation on priesthood
1980		New edition of LDS scriptures is published
1985	November 5	Died in Salt Lake City, Utah, at age ninety

BIOGRAPHICAL HIGHLIGHTS

As a boy, Spencer Kimball learned the value of hard work as he labored on the family farm in Thatcher, Arizona. He enjoyed sports of all kinds and was a talented musician. Following a mission to the central states, Spencer married Camilla Eyring in 1917, and they had four children. In his professional life he worked as a bank clerk and later as an insurance agent. At the time of his call to the apostleship, he was serving as president of the Mount Graham Arizona Stake. During his forty-two years as a General Authority, Elder Kimball suffered from severe health ailments, including throat cancer, heart failure, boils, and deafness. His patience, compassion, and enthusiasm for the work inspired members around the globe.

CONTRIBUTIONS

President Spencer W. Kimball served as President of The Church of Jesus Christ of Latter-day Saints for twelve years between 1973 and 1985. During his presidency the missionary force doubled in response to his call for every worthy young man to serve a mission. Over two million converts joined the Church under his leadership. President Kimball motivated the Church with his passionate appeal to the members to "lengthen your stride" and "do it!"

President Kimball spoke with prophetic power against the ills of modern society. His book *The Miracle of Forgiveness* has helped generations of members through the repentance process. Under his direction, a new edition of the scriptures was published in 1980. In 1978 he issued Official Declaration 2, which extended the priesthood to all worthy males. The number of temples more than doubled during President Kimball's presidency, and so did the number of actual endowments performed per member of the Church (from .75 endowments a year per member in 1974 to 1.5 a year per member in 1985). His presidency witnessed the Church grow into a truly international organization.

TEACHINGS

For more than forty years, Spencer W. Kimball taught as a prophet, seer, and revelator. Although he was unable to teach publicly due to health issues in the years preceding his death, the depth and breadth of his previous teachings provided sufficient instruction, correction, counsel, and inspiration to enlighten the Saints. In many ways, the teachings of President Spencer W. Kimball continue in the same vein today. His comprehensive teaching on repentance and forgiveness, for example, was published as *The Miracle of Forgiveness*, which is still considered as the outstanding treatise on the subject today. Some of his cherished sermons dealing with faith, revelation, death, self-restraint, testimony, preparedness, and the future of the Lamanites were published in *Faith Precedes the Miracle.*

President Kimball was open, honest, and refused to dilute his message on sensitive subjects in hopes of making them more palatable during difficult times. At the same time, his approach exuded with humility, sincerity, genuine affection and compassion, and a unique personable charisma that allowed his teachings and counsel to be considered and embraced by the Church. His teachings dealing with young men serving missions, provident living, the priesthood, the role and responsibility of women, the need for the youth to embrace modesty and chastity, and the importance of nurturing and safeguarding marriage and family were all delivered during tumultuous times and circumstances when traditional social and moral codes were criticized. President Kimball's unique approach laid both a doctrinal foundation and a practical application to living the gospel. As such, the power of his teachings has extended beyond his tenure as President of The Church of Jesus Christ of Latter-day Saints and continues to inspire and guide the Saints today.

LIFE OF
SPENCER W. KIMBALL

"LIKE GOLD SEVEN TIMES TRIED IN FIRE"

Daniel prophesied that the kingdom of God would roll forth as a stone cut without hands until it had filled the whole earth (Daniel 2:34–35). Spencer W. Kimball dedicated his life to pushing that stone toward its glorious destiny. He believed every push helped, and he longed for the day when the Saints would unite in building "a Latter-day Zion, a Zion characterized by love, harmony, and peace—a Zion in which the Lord's children are as one. . . . This day will come; it is our destiny to help bring it about!"[1] His vision of the kingdom of God inspired members young and old to "do it!"

Spencer Kimball's stride far exceeded what one might expect from a man five-foot and six-inches tall. Unlike Nephi of old, Spencer Kimball was small of stature—but as a man of God, he was a giant among men. President Kimball's spiritual stature grew from his dependence upon the Lord, whom he humbly acknowledged as his "perfect leader."[2] Two of President Kimball's favorite scriptures reflect his faith in the Lord: "For with God nothing shall be impossible" (Luke 1:37) and "Is anything too hard for the Lord?" (Genesis 18:14). For Spencer Kimball, the Lord always came first. As Elder Neal A. Maxwell said, "President Kimball was the Lord's man and nobody else's."[3]

The path to prophethood was filled with many challenges. Spencer Kimball endured financial hardship, physical suffering, and spiritual struggles with Job-like patience and faith. His life echoed the words of his predecessor, Joseph Smith, who said, "I know that . . . the Saints will come forth like gold seven times tried in fire, being made perfect through sufferings and temptations, and that the blessing of

President Kimball in December 1973 at the time he became the twelfth prophet of The Church of Jesus Christ of Latter-day Saints.

heaven and earth will be multiplied upon their heads; which may God grant for Christ's sake."[4] President Kimball emerged from the refiner's fire with a deepened love for the Lord and his fellowmen.

BOYHOOD

Spencer Woolley Kimball was born a robust nine-pound baby on March 28, 1895, the sixth child of Andrew and Olive Kimball. Olive's patriarchal blessing had promised her, "Thy sons shall be stars of the first magnitude in thy crown and shall be healthy, strong, and vigorous in helping to direct the purposes of God in this last dispensation."[5] When Spencer was three, the First Presidency called his father to serve as

Picture of the Kimball family.

Milking Cows

To help pass the time, Spencer often memorized hymns and scriptures while performing his chores on the farm. One day, while Spencer was singing a hymn to himself as he milked the cow, his father and a neighbor watched him from a distance. His father told the neighbor, "That boy, Spencer, is an exceptional boy. He always tries to mind me, whatever I ask him to do. I have dedicated him to be one of the mouthpieces of the Lord—the Lord willing. You will see him some day as a great leader. I have dedicated him to the service of God, and he will become a mighty man in the Church."[1] Even at that young age, Spencer was preparing for a great work.

president of the St. Joseph Stake in Arizona. Andrew and Olive accepted the call in faith, moving their family of eight from their comfortable home in Salt Lake City to Thatcher, Arizona. At the time, Thatcher was a Mormon town located in the fertile Gila Valley, an environment that became an important force in shaping Spencer's character and childhood. The land taught him responsibility, provided hard work, nurtured his humility, and instilled within him a sense of community.

The Kimballs settled on ten acres of land purchased for them by the stake. Spencer participated in the family chores, including feeding hogs, milking cows, hauling hay, and irrigating crops. Andrew required the very best from his sons,

First Miracle

Spencer witnessed his first miracle when he was six years old. He had accompanied his father to the Cluff home, where three-year-old Leo was dangerously near death. The young Cluff boy had been gored by a cow, ripping his stomach open and exposing his internal organs to infection. The doctor arrived nine hours after the accident and washed the wound; then he sewed the stomach shut. Despite his best effort, the doctor believed the boy was beyond help, but the Cluffs asked Spencer's father, Andrew, to give their boy a blessing in hopes of divine intervention. Andrew administered to Leo, promising him by the power of the priesthood that he would be healed. Leo's miraculous recovery impressed Spencer with a reverence for the priesthood of God. Years later, Spencer told Leo, "I prayed for you, and I knew you were going to get well."[2] Even at six, Spencer knew something of the efficacy of prayer and the power of faith.

Young Spencer was raised in Thatcher, Arizona.

teaching Spencer to always do his finest work. Spencer admired his father, who he believed was the most important man in Arizona. He consciously tried to emulate his father by developing traits such as faith, frugality, integrity, and industry.

The Kimball home was filled with reminders of faith. When Spencer was five, the family fasted and prayed for rain for their parched crops, teaching Spencer about their dependence upon the Lord. When Spencer was seven, he had a near-death experience while swimming in a pond with his family. When no one was watching him, he slipped below the water, and his lungs filled with liquid, preventing him from calling for help. As he floundered, his father rescued him just in time from drowning. He later became afflicted with Bell's palsy, which paralyzed the muscles in his face. His family petitioned the Lord for his healing, and he recovered completely. Several years later, Spencer contracted typhoid fever. He convalesced for seven weeks before regaining his health. During these boyhood illnesses, Spencer felt the providence of God watching over him.

Grief filled his young heart when his sister Fannie died on his ninth birthday. The family experienced another severe trial when his mother passed away two years later when Spencer was only eleven. The family had fasted and prayed for their mother's health, but Spencer learned that the Lord does not always answer our prayers in the way we wish. Spencer cried and cried, his heart bursting with sorrow. Those tearful days taught him that one can endure almost anything.

The Kimball home felt empty without their mother. Spencer's thirteen-year-old sister, Ruth, dropped out of school so she could tend the house and young children full-time. Spencer called her their "angel-mother." Before passing, Olive had encouraged Andrew to remarry, giving her blessing to a family friend, Josephine Cluff. Several weeks following their mother's funeral, Andrew asked each child for their permission to wed Josephine, and all consented. While Andrew and Josephine traveled to Salt Lake to be sealed in the temple, Spencer's two-year-old sister Rachel became critically ill of diphtheria. The children called the doctor, but he was helpless to save her. Rachel's death brought Andrew and Josephine back immediately from their honeymoon. These trials of the Kimball family reinforced Spencer's faith, who learned to pray, "Thy will be done."

YOUTH

Spencer was very active in his ward. He served as deacon's quorum president and Sunday School chorister and gained a reputation for his near-perfect attendance at Church meetings. Spencer loved singing the hymns and was gifted with a beautiful baritone voice. His father encouraged the children to learn to play the piano by allowing them to stop work in the hot afternoons and sit in the cool parlor and practice. Spencer jumped at the chance. He learned to play by ear and, by the time he was fourteen, joined a band that played for a little money on the weekends. Spencer was always the life of the party. He delighted his friends with his quick wit and good nature.

Spencer attended high school at the Gila Academy. Each year he was elected president of his school class. His school record reflected his determination to excel, showing straight A's during his four years, except for one B in chemistry. When he was not studying or doing chores, Spencer loved to play sports. He enjoyed tennis and baseball but excelled in basketball—playing as the star forward on the St. Joseph's stake basketball team.

Reading the Bible as a Boy

One Sunday in church, Spencer was impressed by a talk he heard by one of Brigham Young's daughters, Susa Gates. In her talk, Sister Gates asked how many in the congregation had read the Bible cover to cover. Only a few hands went up. Spencer returned home determined to read the Bible from start to finish. That very night, he climbed into the attic and started to read Genesis by the light of an old coal-oil lamp. He finished all 1,519 pages in one year, completing the entire book by the time he was fourteen years old. He said of his experience, "I had a glowing satisfaction that I had made a goal and that I had achieved it."[3] Elder Kimball later used this story to encourage youth to set righteous goals and then pursue those goals with determined faith and hard work.

Spencer (center) when about ten, with brothers Andrew Gordon (left) and Delbert (right).

Spencer served as class president all four years in high school.

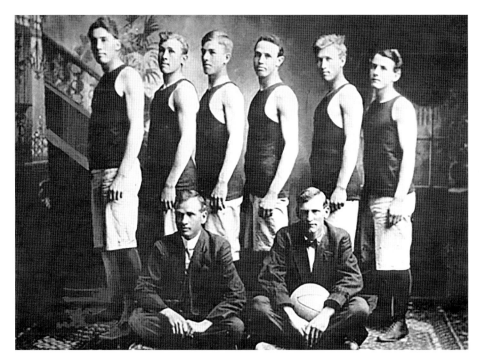

Although short, Spencer won a spot on the St. Joseph's Stake basketball team through hard work.

At his high school graduation ceremony, Spencer received a shock as he listened to his father announce to those in the audience that he would be serving a mission instead of starting college. Spencer could not conceal his surprise—that was the first he had heard of it! However, Spencer accepted this assignment in faith like any other, just as he had learned from the example of his own father.

MISSION

To pay for his mission, Spencer took a job at a dairy. He saved most of his money after tithing and sold his horse for $175 (enough to support him for six-months in the field). He had originally been called to the Swiss-German Mission, but because of World War I, he was reassigned to the Central States Mission. He served for the first month without a companion while building a new chapel in Independence,

April Fool's Day Prank

When Spencer was a senior in high school, Principal Peterson of Gila Academy sternly told the students that he would not tolerate any pranks on April Fool's Day that might disturb class. Despite the warning, Spencer and his friends convinced most of the boys in school to join them for hayrides rather than show up for class on April Fool's Day. When school started with hardly a boy in sight, the principal was furious. At an assembly, he told the mostly female audience that all the boys who had skipped class were expelled and would not be allowed to graduate. He also told the students that he would not allow any of them back on school grounds unless they apologized. True to his word, the following day none of the pranksters were allowed to enter the school. The senior girls stood by the boys, telling the school administration that if the boys could not graduate, then the girls would not either.

The young men congregated at the Kimball home to decide what to do. Spencer, as class president, persuaded the group to return to the school and apologize. The next day the boys asked forgiveness at an assembly, promising never to repeat the offense. Later in life, Spencer remembered the incident and felt that the school had overreacted, though he conceded the prank was "to my shame, I suppose."[4]

Spencer (middle center) at his high school graduation.

Missouri. He learned to adapt to the challenges of missionary work, including bed bugs, indifferent people, and lazy companions.

His spirits were buoyed by letters from home. His father quipped to him in one letter, "Your girls are O.K. so far as I

Spencer worked at the Globe Dairy to earn money for his mission.

know. I am doing my best to keep at least one for you."[6] But not all news from home was welcome. Spencer was not prepared the day he received a telegram from his father, saying, "Your sister Ruth died here last night."[7] In disbelief, Spencer realized he would never see his "angel-mother" again in this life.

As difficult as it was to be away from home at such times, Spencer found comfort in hard work and service. He noted that during a six month period he had contacted 3,844 non-members. Hard work led to his appointment as president of the East Missouri Conference, providing him with valuable leadership experience. After two long years, Spencer returned home having served an honorable mission and having performed five baptisms.

CAMILLA

When Spencer returned home from his mission, he planned to pursue an education and become a teacher. Shortly before leaving for Brigham Young University in Provo, Utah,

Mission

One day on his mission, Spencer was going door-to-door in hopes of finding someone who might be interested in the message of the restored gospel. At one home, a woman told him she was not interested and began to close the door. Spencer, not easily dissuaded, called out, "You have a nice-looking piano." The woman paused, and replied tentatively, "We just bought it." Spencer continued, "It's a Kimball, isn't it? That's my name, too. I could play a song on it for you that you might like to hear." The woman ushered him in, and Spencer sat down to the piano and played for the woman "O, My Father," touching her with his lovely voice and the spirit of its message.[5] Elder Kimball never learned whether the woman joined the Church, but his experiences as a missionary taught him to share the restored gospel without fear.

Elder Kimball as a young missionary.

Elder Kimball as a missionary in the Central States Mission.

Elder Kimball presided over the East Missouri Conference in 1915. Spencer is in the middle row, third from left.

Spencer began dating a young teacher at the Gila Academy named Camilla Eyring. Spencer had seen her picture in the local paper and told a friend, "That's the girl I'm going to marry." He arranged to ride the same bus that Camilla took to school, where he introduced himself and asked if he could call on her. She said yes but was not prepared the next night when Spencer arrived unannounced. Camilla awkwardly told him that she already had a date that night, but Spencer said he would be happy to join them. Much to Camilla's surprise, he stayed and made a threesome of the date.[8]

The young couple dated until the time Spencer left for BYU. From Provo, Spencer wrote Camilla, "I have been lonesome today. . . . Two weeks tomorrow since I left, does it seem that long to you? It seems like two years or months to me. . . . Please write soon. I love to hear from you."[9] He didn't have to wait long for a reunion, because the First World War draft called him home just four weeks after he had left. Spencer immediately began preparing to enter military service.

While Spencer waited for his unit to be called into active duty, he and Camilla began to court in earnest. Each day he picked her up after school and drove her home, spending time together well into the evenings. Spencer became a common fixture in the Eyring home, where he was welcomed with enthusiasm. Their whirlwind courtship finally culminated when Spencer proposed marriage to Camilla. It was probably the most important decision of his life—a decision that blossomed into a beautiful sixty-eight-year marriage.

Because Spencer was bound by the draft and could depart any day for the war waging in Europe, the young couple could not travel to Salt Lake to be sealed. They decided to marry civilly until they could make the trip to the temple. On November 16, 1917, they were married in Camilla's living room by the bishop, in a quiet ceremony with only the young couple's parents and older siblings for guests. President Kimball recalled the event years later, "When Sister Kimball and I were married, we had no ring nor costly reception. Eight years later I bought her a small diamond. She was content to wait until then."[10]

The young couple shortly after their wedding.

FAMILY

Since the newlyweds had only ten dollars to their name, they moved into Spencer's parents' home and later into his sister Alice's home, where their living quarters were partitioned off with a flannel sheet. Spencer began hiring himself out doing odd jobs until he found employment as a bank clerk. In 1918, the world celebrated the end of the war, and Camilla and Spencer were relieved to have the uncertainty removed from their future. They used their savings to travel to Salt Lake, where they were sealed in the temple.

Those early married years were difficult. Camilla was often sick and Spencer worked himself to exhaustion. Not only was he working at the bank, but he was also keeping the books for several companies in town. In addition to his other responsibilities, his father called him to serve as stake clerk, which was one of the most time-consuming callings in the

Camilla Eyring Kimball was an unfailing support to her husband and the heart of the Kimball home.

Camilla (1894–1987)

Camilla served beside her husband for sixty-eight years. She was born Camilla Eyring in Colonia Juarez, Mexico. When Camilla was eighteen, her family was forced from their home during the Mexican Revolution of 1912. The Eyrings relocated to Arizona, but Camilla continued on to Utah, where she attended the BYU Academy between 1912 and 1914. She pursued higher education at the University of California in 1915, and completed her degree at the Utah State Agriculture College in 1917.

Camilla was a skilled homemaker. She enjoyed cooking, bottling fruit, sewing, and gardening. She had many interests, including painting, public speaking, music, and reading. Throughout her life she nurtured a love of learning and serving. She traveled extensively with her husband, who often remarked how she added to his peace and well-being. Camilla was Spencer's anchor, caring for him during his many illnesses and operations.

Camilla volunteered at the hospital, library, and PTA, and she always sought to magnify her Church callings. She counseled the women of the Church to continually seek for self-improvement. "A woman needs to be concerned with church, school and community. If she buries herself inside four walls, she does not reach her potential."[6] For her untiring service to family, church, and community, the University of Utah awarded her an honorary doctorate and BYU established the Camilla Eyring Kimball Chair of Home and Family Life. But her greatest honor was the love of her husband, children, and grandchildren.

Elder Neal A. Maxwell said of Camilla, "Ever at [President Kimball's] side has been his elect lady, Camilla, caring for him, encouraging him, adding her own strong testimony throughout her own ministry. She has been, and is, a model for Latter-day Saint women. It was she who encouraged anxious Spencer at the time of his call to the Twelve, saying, 'Spencer, you can do it.' It was she who has been at his bedside in hospitals and in performing the many duties of recuperation. It was she who once refused a hospital bed, sleeping on a mattress on the floor in order to be at his side during a lengthy hospital stay."[7] Camilla's selfless example and devotion to her husband inspired women throughout the Church.

Church at that time. Spencer gave everything 100 percent—he didn't know any other way.

The couple was overjoyed at the birth of their firstborn, Spencer LeVan. But their hearts broke when they miscarried their second child. Another child, Olive Beth, arrived two years later. The family eventually grew to four children with the later births of Andrew and Edward. Spencer was promoted at the bank and served on the city council in Thatcher. Their prospects appeared rosy and the young family moved into their first home. But their fortunes soured when Spencer's bank abruptly shut down. Spencer not only lost his job, but also all of the family's savings that were in the bank, leaving them destitute almost overnight. Fortunately, Spencer was able to find employment at another bank. Shortly afterward, Spencer grieved the death of his father, who had been his childhood hero and anchor. Andrew Kimball's death was mourned by all of Arizona, where he had served as stake president for twenty-six years. Spencer, now twenty-nine years old, was called as second counselor in the reorganized stake presidency.

A major step in Spencer's life came when he left the security of his bank job to go into business for himself. He joined Joseph Greenhalgh to form an insurance company that also handled investments and real estate. Spencer was determined to make the Kimball-Greenhalgh Agency a success. He had always been a hard worker, but

President and Sister Kimball served side by side for sixty-eight years.

as his own boss he could see the direct results of his labor. He often remarked that after being in business for himself, he would never go back to working for another.

In 1933, at the height of the Great Depression, Spencer and Camilla's three-year-old son, Eddie, was diagnosed with polio. He was treated in Los Angeles for two and a half months, where Camilla stayed with Eddie while Spencer returned home to tend the other children and be at the office. He wrote Camilla almost every day. Over the next eight years, Eddie recovered gradually and slowly learned to walk again. During this time, the family vacationed in California where Eddie received regular check-ups. The children earned

President Kimball playing a game of Mahjongg.

Family

Spencer and Camilla had four children, each four years apart: Spencer LeVan, Olive Beth, Andrew, and Edward. Spencer's duties at the office and at church required him to be away from home much of the time. When he was home, the family enjoyed playing Rook (a popular card game) and Mahjongg, reading together, doing chores, or working on school projects. The Kimballs also enjoyed the cinema and had a monthly pass to the town theatre. On the weekend, Spencer took Camilla square dancing for their weekly date and often invited friends over for parties and get-togethers.

Spencer and Camilla believed that the children should have as much freedom as possible, but also that they should bear the responsibility for their choices. On one occasion, Ed went to the state fair on Sunday. Camilla had counseled him not to, but told him that he could make his own choice. The entire time at the fair he felt guilty and regretted having gone, teaching him a valuable lesson about keeping the Sabbath holy that he never forgot. On another occasion, the boys were playing ping-pong on the Sabbath. A girl who was visiting asked Elder Kimball, "How come they play on Sunday?" He replied, "I don't do it, but they must decide for themselves."[8] Spencer and Camilla taught their children true principles and respected their children's ability to make correct choices.

The Kimball family at the time of Spencer's call to the Twelve. In front: Camilla, Spencer, and Olive Beth; in back: Edward, Spencer LeVan, and Andrew.

Spencer W. Kimball.

Spencer replied he would rather be clerk and was released from the presidency. It was only two years later when the St. Joseph Stake was divided in two, and Spencer was called as president of the newly created Mount Graham Stake. At first Spencer felt inadequate to his task. He wrote Camilla, "I find I am weak and too small and too lazy and too inefficient. Maybe they will release me after a year or two. I really hope so."[11] Despite his wish, he continued to serve faithfully until his call to the apostleship.

In 1940, the family designed and built their dream home—six rooms and one and a half baths—in a distinctive pueblo-style architecture. Two years later Camilla and Spencer celebrated their silver wedding anniversary in that home, inviting over six hundred friends to join them in commemorating their twenty-five years together. Spencer and Camilla were in their mid-forties and felt secure in life. Spencer was a successful businessman and stake president, they had a maturing family, and they were settled in their new home. They felt like things would go on much in the same way. But they soon learned that the Lord had other plans in store.

money for their vacations by doing chores and selling magazines door to door. They were also paid five cents for memorizing the Articles of Faith or verses of scripture.

Spencer was active in the community. He served as Rotary Club president and later as a prestigious Rotary district governor. He also started a local radio station, served on the Safford city council, the board of the Chamber of Commerce, the board of the Gila College (formerly the Academy), the board of the Red Cross, the Arizona Teachers Retirement Board, and as director of the Arizona Association of Insurance Agents.

Although Spencer was second counselor in the stake presidency, he continued to serve as stake clerk. When the demands of two callings became overwhelming, the stake president asked Spencer which calling he would prefer.

CALL TO THE APOSTLESHIP

The General Authorities in Salt Lake knew Spencer well from his family connections and service as stake president. On July 8, 1943, Spencer had just arrived home for lunch when the phone rang. Ed answered the phone and called to his dad, "Salt Lake City is calling." Spencer took the receiver and answered, "Hello?" He recognized the voice of President J. Reuben Clark Jr. on the other end. "Spencer, this is Brother Clark. Do you have a chair handy?" He was not prepared for what followed: "The Brethren have just chosen you to fill one of the vacancies in the Quorum." In a daze, Spencer replied, "Oh, Brother Clark! It seems so impossible. I am so weak and small and limited and incapable. Of course, there could be only one answer to any call from the Brethren but—" There was a long pause. President Clark asked, "Are you there?" "Yes, Brother Clark, but you've taken my breath. I am all in a sweat." After asking several questions, Spencer hung up the phone. He turned to find Camilla, Andrew, and Ed standing there, all staring at him. He simply told them, "They have called me to become an Apostle." The family returned confused expressions. "Are you sure that you were to be an Apostle?" Camilla asked. "No, I am not sure now," Spencer admitted. He was bewildered. The family ate lunch in semi-silence. Afterward, Spencer lay down on the floor as he often did to nap. But he couldn't rest. He began to cry. "I wept and wept. . . . My wife was sitting by me on the floor, stroking my hair, trying to quiet me."[12]

He wrestled for many weeks with the weight of his new assignment. "There was one great desire, to get a testimony of my calling. . . . How I prayed! How I suffered! How I wept! How I struggled!" Finally, he felt the oppressive doubts leave him. "My soul was at peace. A calm feeling of assurance came over me, doubt and questionings subdued. It was as though a great burden had been lifted. . . . I felt nearer my Lord than ever at any time in my life."[13]

On Friday, October 1, 1943, Spencer was sustained in general conference. In his first year as an Apostle, Elder Kimball attended thirty-one stake conferences and toured two missions. The pace of his schedule made him frequently absent from home. During one four-month period, he slept in his own bed only two nights. Despite the pressures of his new responsibilities, he wanted to remain close to his family. He wrote in his journal, "I am trying hard to keep close to my boys and keep their love and respect and palship!"[14]

Elder Kimball approached his new calling with his characteristic humor, hard work, and

Spencer and Camilla celebrated their silver wedding anniversary in 1942—a year before his call to the Twelve.

spirit. He identified with the Saints wherever he went. He played softball with the Japanese Saints; he milked a stake president's cow; he waded into chest-deep water to help pull in a net at a hukelau in Hawaii; in Peru he played jacks with some young girls; at a prison, he listened to an inmate weep. The breadth of Elder Kimball's travels permitted him to see into the common heart of all people, regardless of gender, race, or faith.

LAMANITES

In 1946, President George Albert Smith gave Elder Kimball a special assignment. He said, "I want you to look after the

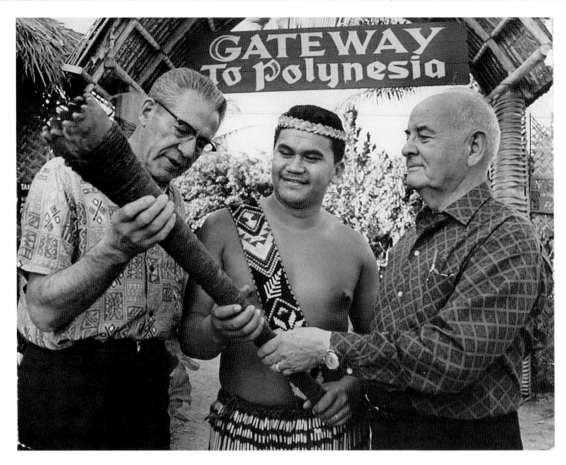

Presidents Kimball and Tanner touring the Polynesian Cultural Center.

Indians—they are neglected. Take charge and watch after the Indians in all the world."[15] At the age of nine, Elder Kimball had received a patriarchal blessing that promised, "You will preach the gospel to many people, but more especially to the Lamanites, for the Lord will bless you with the gift of language and power to portray before that people, the gospel in great plainness."[16] Elder Kimball envisioned the day when "the Lamanites shall blossom as the rose" (D&C 49:24). He traveled across North and South America visiting "his people," discouraged that their future was trapped between dirt and ignorance. Because he believed education would unlock the door of opportunity, Elder Kimball established Church schools on the reservations and later initiated the Indian Student Placement Program.

His work among the Lamanites was tireless. Harold B. Lee called him "the great Indian defender."[17] He plead with the Saints in general conference, "How I wish you could go with me through the Indian reservations . . . and see the poverty, want, and wretchedness. . . . Think of these things, my people, and then weep for the Indian, and with your tears, pray; then work for him."[18] His service endeared him to the Indians, who honored him with the name "Washte-Ho-Wamblee," which means "he who flies across the world lifting his voice to bring good tidings of truth."[19]

COUNSELOR

Elder Kimball spent thousands of hours counseling members. He cared deeply for individuals. At times he would join the transgressor in fasting for strength. He prayed daily for those he counseled. The mail usually brought him letters from members who needed help or encouragement, and he

Elder Kimball at a Navajo tribal council with President George Albert Smith and Elder Matthew Cowley.

always responded with his characteristic compassion. After more than twenty-five years of conducting tearful interviews as a General Authority, Elder Kimball wrote his masterpiece, *The Miracle of Forgiveness*. The book took nine years to write, but it reflected a lifetime of lessons.

HEALTH

Elder Kimball was a modern Job, struggling his entire life with severe health problems. He would not allow his health to slow him down, and he disregarded much of the advice he received from doctors. When he suffered a heart attack while on a Church assignment, he would not end his tour early. But further pain, ulcers, and boils could not all be dismissed.

The Brethren encouraged Elder Kimball to lighten his load, but that only embarrassed him. He always felt like he was the smallest and weakest of the Twelve and fought to make up for it by working twice as hard.

Elder Kimball ignored the warning signs of failing health and soon experienced a second heart attack. He and Camilla prepared for the worst by talking over the family finances and possible funeral arrangements. President

Elder Kimball at an Indian Placement meeting.

George Albert Smith gave him a blessing and charged him to rest. But, after two months in bed, Elder Kimball was restless. He decided to convalesce with the Indians whom he loved so much. After two weeks on the Navajo Reservation, he felt rejuvenated. But when he returned to the office, he soon exhausted himself again. Under strict doctor's orders, he and Camilla retreated to a little apartment in Long Beach, California, where Elder Kimball tried to regain his strength. After he returned from his enforced vacation, he met with President Smith, who reassured him that he was still appreciated and needed. Elder Kimball was deeply touched when the President "came near me and said they all loved me and the Church loved me and he drew me to him, put his arms about my shoulders and kissed my forehead."[20]

President Kimball's good nature and humor won many friends to the Church.

Humor

Elder Kimball used his warm wit to put others at ease. Once a slightly agitated nonmember husband came to see President Kimball. As the man burst into President Kimball's office, he said, "President Kimball, my wife's a member, but I am not!" Deflecting the man's forcefulness, President Kimball lovingly put his arm around the man, and replied, "There's a little bit of room left in the Church, if you'd like to join!"[9]

One fast Sunday at church, President Kimball was seated on the stand next to the bishop. He mentioned to the bishop that he would like to bear his testimony, but before he could, Sister Kimball arose and bore her testimony of the scriptures. Following her remarks, President Kimball leaned over to the bishop and said, "One Kimball a meeting is enough." The bishop encouraged President Kimball to go ahead and bear his testimony anyway. When he stood before the congregation, he told them, "The bishop has given me permission to say a few words."[10]

Elder Kimball used humor to help him through his physical suffering. Following his throat surgery in New York, he and Camilla relocated to the Eastern States Mission home to convalesce. The couple decided to eat out rather than take their meals with the mission president's family, because, as he explained on a note pad, he did not want to be "a pain in the neck."[11] During his painful recovery, he wrote his children of his condition: "Insomnia is my trouble," he told them. "Why, I couldn't even doze in Sacrament meeting yesterday."[12]

But despite the outpouring of love and well-wishes from friends and family, Elder Kimball became discouraged over his poor health. His heart pains prevented him from putting in full days at the office. He felt like he was getting behind in his duties and felt miserable that he could not carry his full load among the Twelve. His fragile health received a crushing blow in 1950 when his throat became extremely sore and sensitive. He had it treated, but the problems recurred in 1956. Elder Kimball sought out the best physicians in New York City, who feared he had throat cancer. Following a biopsy, they ordered him to thirty days of complete silence, lest he aggravate the problem by overtaxing his voice. As the months passed, Spencer learned to whisper softly when he spoke. He contemplated the consequences of undergoing surgery, but he knew that surgery might deprive him of his voice, which he felt was essential in fulfilling his duties as an Apostle. How would he interview, counsel, and preach without a voice?

The surgeons eventually removed one vocal cord and part of the other, but left the larynx. The operation was followed by five months of silence, forcing Elder Kimball to write out his words whenever he wished to communicate. Finally, after nearly half a year of unbearable silence, the doctors freed him to begin using his voice again. He returned to his dear Gila Valley to make his maiden speech. His voice was weak, like a raspy whisper. He knew the sounds he made were unpleasant to hear, but he had faith that his Arizona friends would be patient with him. He arose to the pulpit and told the congregation that he had been back East, where he had fallen among cutthroats and thieves who had stolen his voice. The laughs in the congregation gave him courage and he continued. He learned in time to control his voice, though it never regained its original strength.

By 1971, President Kimball's health was again rapidly declining. His voice sounded hoarse, and the doctors concluded he again had throat cancer. He underwent painful radiation treatments that devastated what remained of his voice. He could barely whisper. Following several priesthood blessings, the doctors declared the cancer cured. After his throat treatments, President Kimball began wearing a voice box that amplified his weak voice for listeners. His signature voice box endeared him to Saints around the globe.

While grateful for his miraculous cure, President Kimball was troubled over recurring pain in his heart. His physician diagnosed a blocked coronary artery. His condition was severe enough to require open-heart surgery, but at seventy-seven years of age, he was dangerously old to have such an operation. He decided to undergo the surgery with Dr. Russell M. Nelson performing the delicate bypass.

President Kimball's recovery was blessed again by the administration of the priesthood. "Spencer lives from blessing to blessing," his close friend Harold B. Lee said.[21] During his recuperation, President Kimball's face became partially paralyzed by an attack of Bell's palsy, which impaired his hearing for the rest of his life. It was during these trying ordeals that he learned of President Joseph Fielding Smith's death, making him the President of the Council of the Twelve Apostles in 1972.

Because of throat cancer, President Kimball's voice was a hoarse whisper, requiring him to wear a voice box to amplify his voice when speaking to large audiences.

President and Sister Kimball served as equally yoked companions during their long, happy marriage.

PROPHET

With thirty years experience as an Apostle of the Lord Jesus Christ, President Kimball became the twelfth President of The Church of Jesus Christ of Latter-day Saints on December 29, 1973, following the death of President Harold B. Lee. President Kimball was as surprised as anyone, assuming his poor health would prevent him from surviving the younger President Lee. President Kimball felt a heavy burden fall on his shoulders. Camilla described his feelings when she said, "There's no place for him to go except to the Lord."[22]

As the prophet of the Church, President Kimball lost no time in moving the kingdom forward at his quick pace. He rallied the Church with his cry for more missionaries to fill the earth with the gospel message. After President Kimball shared his vision of missionary work with the General Authorities, President Ezra Taft Benson declared, "Surely there is no doubt, my brethren, after this message this morning that there is in very deed a prophet in Israel."[23] Church leaders were awed by his prophetic voice. "None of us can ever be quite the same after that," Elder Gordon B. Hinckley said.[24]

President Kimball's challenge to "lengthen your stride" resounded with the growing Church membership. Under his leadership, the missionary force doubled and fifty-one new missions were created. The number of stakes more than doubled, accommodating more than two million converts during his presidency. President Kimball set an unprecedented rate of temple growth, expanding the Church's fifteen temples in 1974 to thirty-seven by 1985—a 250 percent increase. He conducted area conferences around the world, held fifty-eight solemn assemblies, directed the publishing of a new edition of scriptures, and organized the First Quorum of the Seventy.

President Kimball's worldwide vision gained new meaning in 1978 when the priesthood was extended to all worthy males. The prophet had wrestled over this question for many years. On June 7, 1978, the Brethren met in the temple and received the direction for which they had fasted and prayed. After each member of the First Presidency and Twelve had spoken, they united in formal prayer with President Kimball acting as voice. Elder Bruce R. McConkie wrote of the experience, "It was during this prayer that the revelation came. . . . From the midst of eternity, the voice of God, conveyed by the power of the Spirit, spoke to his prophet. . . . He heard the voice and we heard the same voice. All doubt and uncertainty fled. He knew the answer and we knew the answer."[25] The revelation brought the Church closer to President Kimball's goal of having the gospel taught to all the world.

Spencer W. Kimball served as President of the Church for twelve years. During the last years, his health failed as he underwent three more operations. At the age of ninety, he died peacefully on November 5, 1985.

CONCLUSION

Spencer W. Kimball lived ahead of his time. He viewed the future with the eyes of a seer and revelator, warning a teetering world against the ills of divorce, immorality, selfishness, and disobedience. He spoke "with the trump of God, with a voice to shake the earth, and [cried] repentance unto every people" (Alma 29:1). President Kimball's voice, though weak, carried a powerful message. While it is ironic that the mouthpiece of God should need a voice box, his life echoed the Lord's promise, "For unto this end have I raised you up, that I might show forth my wisdom through the weak things of the earth" (D&C 124:1).

The fruit of Spencer Kimball's suffering became the seed of his greatness. These words he spoke could well serve as his own eulogy: "One must do what [Jesus] did in boldly denouncing evil,

bravely advancing righteous works, courageously meeting every problem, becoming the master of himself and the situations about him and being near oblivious to personal credit."[26] Thus, Spencer Kimball went from a young boy slopping hogs to the great prophet pleading for the prodigal. For him, doing the Healer's work was all in a day's work.

It was once said that the prepared sermons of Spencer W. Kimball prior to becoming the President of The Church of Jesus Christ of Latter-day Saints were contained in binders that occupied four and a half feet of shelf space. It would be hard to imagine the amount of shelf space required for all of President Kimball's teachings. Besides his formal published addresses, Spencer W. Kimball wrote books and countless letters and spoke extemporaneously at funerals, conferences of every sort, firesides, and devotionals. Whatever the form of his sermons, the topics were often crafted from experiences dealing with his Church assignments. For example, Elder Kimball often spoke about the Lamanites while he was serving as the head of the Church Indian Committee. It was his experience as a stake president and as an Apostle dealing with countless individuals seeking the solace of forgiveness that prompted Elder Kimball to write *The Miracle of Forgiveness.*

A sign of rapid Church growth, the number of temples more than doubled under the leadership of President Kimball.

Finally, in his calling as a General Authority, Elder Kimball taught countless sermons throughout the world. Many of these carefully constructed sermons were compiled and published in *Faith Precedes the Miracle*, his second book.

As President of The Church of Jesus Christ of Latter-day Saints, President Kimball's teachings were, once again, an outgrowth of his stewardship and the current events during his service. As President of the Church, it was typical for President Kimball to speak five times during general conference. Thus, rather than focusing on a singular topic in depth, President Kimball was more prone to speak on a wide range of both Church and gospel-related issues, current affairs, and to give general counsel, inspiration, and encouragement to the Saints. His stewardship as the shepherd of the Church clearly laid the foundation for his ministry. In his maiden address as President of the Church in 1974, he taught, "We shall serve you, our people, and love you and do our utmost to guide you to your righteous, glorious destiny, with our hearts overflowing with love and appreciation for you."[27]

Love of the Prophet

Once a Latter-day Saint artist asked President Kimball, "If you were going to hang a painting of the Savior in your office, what would you want that picture to be like?" President Kimball responded after some reflection, "I love people; that's my gift. I truly love people. Can you see anything in my eyes that tells you that I love people? In that picture, I would like to see in the Savior's eyes that he truly loves people. It is not affected; it is not his job. He truly loves all people."[13] President Kimball's eyes, his embrace, and his brotherly kiss all testified that he was a true follower of Christ. "By this shall all men know that ye are my disciples, if ye have love one to another" (John 13:35).

President Kimball had a gift of loving others with Christlike compassion.

TEACHINGS OF PRESIDENT
SPENCER W. KIMBALL

LENGTHEN OUR STRIDE

President Kimball not only believed that members of the Church had a glorious destiny, but he fully intended to help the Church realize that destiny. It became clear that in order to fulfill this destiny, the Church and its membership could no longer be complacent. In October 1974, President Kimball taught, "So much depends upon our willingness to make up our minds, collectively and individually, that present levels of performance are not acceptable, either to ourselves or to the Lord. In saying that, I am not calling for flashy, temporary differences in our performance levels, but a quiet resolve . . . to do a better job, to lengthen our stride."[28] Besides the call to new heights, the phrase "lengthen our stride" became a favorite of the members—a motto of sorts. Sensing this, President Kimball later elaborated:

"When I think of the concept of 'lengthening our stride,' I, of course, apply it to myself as well as urging it upon the

President Kimball's clear counsel guided the Church during a time of shifting values and uncertainty.

Church. The 'lengthening of our stride' suggests urgency instead of hesitancy, 'now,' instead of tomorrow; it suggests not only an acceleration, but efficiency. It suggests, too, that the whole body of the Church move forward in unison with a quickened pace and pulse, doing our duty with all our heart, instead of halfheartedly. It means, therefore, mobilizing and stretching all our muscles and drawing on all our resources. It suggests also that we stride with pride and with a sense of anticipation as we meet the challenges facing the kingdom. Out of all this will come a momentum that will be sobering and exhilarating at the same time."[29] The Church membership was primed to take action.

MISSIONARY LABOR

President Kimball's attention often focused on missionary work. He taught, "If there were no converts, the Church would shrivel and die on the vine. But perhaps the greatest

President Kimball provided timely counsel to a growing Church.

reason for missionary work is to give the world its chance to hear and accept the gospel. The scriptures are replete with commands and promises and calls and rewards for teaching the gospel. I use the word command deliberately, for it seems to be an insistent directive from which we, singly and collectively, cannot escape."[30] It was evident that President Kimball was ready to move missionary work to a new plateau. "Today we have 18,600 missionaries," he taught in 1974. "We can send more. Many more! We need more young men and we need a great many more of our mature couples."[31] President Kimball's vision of missionary labors was in terms of "an army of missionaries."[32]

With only a fraction of young men choosing to serve a mission, President Kimball spoke in certain terms of a young man's responsibility to serve a mission. "So let us make that the rule—that every boy ought to go on a mission. There may be some who can't, but they ought to go on a mission."[33] When this responsibility was questioned, President Kimball responded, "The question is frequently asked: Should every young man fill a mission? And the answer has been given by the Lord. It is 'Yes.'"[34]

President Kimball was able to connect with Saints around the globe.

President Kimball's missionary zeal was not solely to increase the number of missionaries alone. "When I ask for

Love for the People

Spencer Kimball had a special gift for loving others. Even though he was very busy, he found time to express his concern and love for the Saints. Once he met with a married couple who had come to his office to confess a serious sin. President Kimball listened carefully and then asked them, "Do you mind if I come over and kneel and have a prayer with you?" As they knelt in his office, President Kimball pled before the Lord in behalf of the couple. Following the prayer, the husband put his arms around President Kimball and sobbed. The wife took President Kimball's hands and kissed him on the cheek. President Kimball gently told them that the Lord had forgiven them of their sin. He said, "I don't ever want you to mention it again. It's closed."[14]

On another occasion, Elder Kimball visited two BYU students from Mexico. It was the middle of winter and the two young men were renting a room with no heat other than a little gas stove. Because they were not accustomed to snow, they had neglected to bring any winter clothing with them from their home. They spoke little English and had hardly any money left over after purchasing their books for school. The only food they had was some chocolate milk that had frozen during the night. As they discussed how they could defrost the milk, they heard a knock at the door. They opened the door and found Elder Kimball on their doorstep. "Hi, boys. I am on my way to stake conference in Sanpete County and I thought I would stop and say hello and see how you were getting along." The boys were stunned to find an Apostle calling on them. With dozens of thoughts passing through their minds in Spanish, one of them managed to say, "Come in, Brother Kimball."

Elder Kimball asked them how they were doing and put them at ease with his loving manner. He didn't stay long, but long enough to lift the young men's spirits. As he left, he shook hands with them and left a twenty-dollar bill in their grip. "God bless you," he told them. "Let me know how you get along." After their visitor had gone, the two young men looked at each other in disbelief, staring at the twenty-dollar bill. "I wonder how he knew," one of them said. The other replied, "He is a prophet of the Lord, and he knows."[15]

more missionaries," President Kimball taught, "I am asking that we start earlier and train our missionaries better in every branch and every ward in the world. That is another challenge—that the young people will understand that it is a great privilege to go on a mission and that they must be physically well, mentally well, spiritually well, and that 'the Lord cannot look upon sin with the least degree of allowance.' "[35] Throughout his ministry, President Kimball encouraged young men to prepare early, "so that each anticipates his mission with great joy."[36] President Kimball's vision of preparation also included financial preparation. At a conference in London, President Kimball gave a twelve-year-old boy a shilling and said, "Here is a shilling to start you on your mission. Now you go back to your seat and tell your father and mother back there that you are going on a mission."[37] In a larger context, President Kimball counseled, "Every time money comes into your hands, through gifts or earnings, set at least a part of it away in a savings account to be used for your mission. Every boy would like to be independent and furnish his own funds for his mission, rather than to ask his parents to do that for him. Every boy in every country in all the world who has been baptized and received the Holy Ghost will have the responsibility of bearing the message of the gospel to the people of the world. And this is also your opportunity, and it will contribute greatly toward your greatness."[38]

President Kimball felt that the Lord would open the doors of the nations if the Saints were better prepared. "I believe the Lord can do anything he sets his mind to do. But I can see no good reason why the Lord would open doors that we are not prepared to enter. Why should he break down the Iron Curtain or the Bamboo Curtain or any other curtain if we are still unprepared to enter?"[39] President Kimball urged the Saints to make missionary work a regular part of their prayers. "I'm hoping that, beginning now, the prayers of the Saints will be greatly increased from what they have been in the past, that we will never think of praying except we pray for the Lord to establish his program and make it possible that we can carry the gospel to his people as he has commanded. It is my deep interest and great prayer to you that this will be accomplished."[40]

Missionary Work

Elder Kimball was known for his relentless push to have every worthy young man serve a mission. When he visited stakes around the world, he would ask the boys in the congregation to stand up, and then asked them, "What will you be doing when you are nineteen?" He would then pass out dollar bills or coins to the boys, telling them to use it to start their own missionary fund. Spencer once noted how he and Camilla "save pennies to give away thousands."[16]

Elder Kimball appreciated the importance of saving for missions. He himself had paid his own way years before while serving as a missionary in the central states. At one time during his mission, he and his companion were without money. They had used their last quarter to pay for heat in their apartment. Not knowing what to do, the missionaries prayed to the Lord for aid, and in response a letter arrived for Spencer that contained two dollars. The relieved missionary said it was the "most welcome two dollars I have ever seen in my life."[17]

Elder Kimball washing his feet on his mission.

The success of the missionary labors during President Kimball's administration not only opened the doors of nations to missionary work but also opened new opportunities to members of the Church in an unsuspected way. In 1978, N. Eldon Tanner read from a letter signed by President Kimball and his counselors: "As we have witnessed the expansion of the work of the Lord over the earth, we have been grateful that people of many nations have responded to the message of the restored gospel, and have joined the Church in ever-increasing numbers. This, in turn, has inspired us with a desire to extend to every worthy member of the Church all of the privileges and blessings which the gospel affords." President Kimball's great desire to share the gospel and allow every worthy member to fully embrace the fulness led to "extended meditation and prayer in the sacred rooms of the holy temple." The resultant revelation was formally announced and sustained in the October 1978 general conference. "He has heard our prayers, and by revelation has confirmed that the long-promised day has come when every faithful, worthy man in the Church may receive the holy priesthood, with power to exercise its divine authority, and enjoy with his loved ones every blessing that flows therefrom, including the blessings of the temple. Accordingly, all worthy male members of the Church may be ordained to the priesthood without regard for race or color."[41]

MARRIAGE

Another topic that President Kimball heavily emphasized was the importance of marriage. "Marriage is perhaps the most vital of all decisions and has the most far-reaching effects, for it has to do not only with immediate happiness, but also with eternal joys. It affects not only the two people involved, but also their families, particularly their children and their children's children, down through the latest generations."[42] Once again, preparation and righteous living became the emphasis of President Kimball's approach to marriage. To prepare the youth for marriage, President Kimball counseled, "I suggest again the following standard. Any dating or pairing off in social contacts should be postponed until at least the age of 16 or older, and even then there should still be much judgment used in selections and in the seriousness. Young people should still limit the close contacts for several years, since the boy will be going on his mission when he is 19 years old."[43] President Kimball promised, "One can have all the blessings if he is in control and takes the experiences in proper turn: first some limited social get-acquainted contacts, then his mission, then his courting, then his temple marriage." He then warned, "In any other sequence he could run into difficulty."[44]

President Kimball taught that the Saints' approach to marriage was the key to a successful marriage. "First, there must be the proper approach toward marriage, which contemplates the selection of a spouse who reaches as nearly as possible the pinnacle of perfection in all the matters which are of importance to the individuals. And then those two parties must come to the altar in the temple realizing that they must work hard toward this successful joint living." While the selection

President Kimball waves to the Saints during general conference.

of a spouse is critical, President Kimball also taught the Saints that "'soul mates' are fiction and an illusion; and while every young man and young woman will seek with all diligence and prayerfulness to find a mate with whom life can be most compatible and beautiful, yet it is certain that almost any good man and any good woman can have happiness and a successful marriage if both are willing to pay the price."[45]

President Kimball taught that "a great unselfishness, forgetting self and directing all of the family life and all pertaining thereunto to the good of the family, subjugating self" was vital to a successful and happy marriage.[46] While President Kimball left ample counsel dealing with marriage, his teachings were always founded upon the teaching that for happy marriages to exist, "there must be a complete living of the commandments of the Lord as defined in the gospel of Jesus Christ."[47]

President Kimball maintained that "home life, home teaching, parental guidance, father in leadership—these are the panacea for the ailments of the world, a cure for spiritual and emotional diseases, a remedy for problems."[48] It was of little surprise, then, that family home evening was reemphasized under President Kimball's leadership and that the Saints were admonished to "give preference in time and energy . . . and observe properly and conscientiously the family home evening."[49] In 1980, the Church announced the consolidated meeting plan to which President Kimball linked the changes to families. He taught, "The new consolidated schedule permits you, if you plan well, to hold all the meetings in the consolidated schedule along with the necessary administrative meetings and still have several hours with your family every Sunday. Please see to it that this is done, so that you priesthood brethren do not neglect your own families and so that our wonderful stake presidents, bishops, branch and quorum presidents, and others can do likewise."[50]

TEMPLES

For President Kimball, his urgent emphasis on missionary work was also related to temple work. "I hope to see us

President and Sister Kimball enjoyed a lasting courtship during their marriage. They were frequent travel companions and inspired the Saints around the world with their love.

Love Letters

During the seventy years that Spencer and Camilla were together, they wrote one another frequently—often daily—when separated from each other. Their first separation occurred when Spencer left for BYU following their brief courtship. Camilla sent him her picture for a keepsake. Spencer wrote back, "The picture came to me here in Salt Lake last night and I laughed as you requested HaHa. It was fine. I promptly cut off the head (ugh!!) and pasted it in my [pocket] watch as I demonstrated for you 'That Last Night.' My cousins actually accuse me of keeping too strict watch of the time since."[18]

On their sixteenth wedding anniversary, Camilla wrote Spencer, "I wanted to tell you again as I perhaps do too often how much I love and appreciate you. Every year increases my love and respect. . . . The fact that never once in the time of our acquaintance have I found cause to doubt or mistrust is I consider one the foundation stones upon which real happiness and contentment in marriage is built. . . . How I long for you and the strength received from your beautiful character. There is no other so fine and so true. Your devoted wife, Camilla."[19]

dissolve the artificial boundary line we so often place between missionary work and temple and genealogical work, because it is the same great redemptive work!"[51] As a result, temple building became an important part of President Kimball's administration. "There now begins the most intensive period of temple building in the history of the Church," President Kimball taught. He continued, "We look to the day when the sacred ordinances of the Church, performed in the temples, will be available to all members of the Church in convenient locations around the globe."[52] The same zeal President Kimball demonstrated for missionary work was also expressed for temples: "We feel an urgency for this great work to be accomplished and wish to encourage the Saints to accept their responsibility of performing temple ordinances, writing their personal and family history, participating in the name extraction program when called to do so, completing their four-generation research, and then continuing their family research to ensure the redemption of their kindred dead."[53]

MORAL STANDARD

In a time of moral shifting, President Kimball's teachings dealing with moral conduct served to firmly anchor the Church's standards. "That the Church's stand on morality may be understood, we declare firmly and unalterably, it is not an outworn garment, faded, old-fashioned, and threadbare. God is the same yesterday, today, and forever, and his covenants and doctrines are immutable; and when the sun grows cold and the stars no longer shine, the law of chastity will still be basic in God's world and in the Lord's Church. Old values are upheld by the Church not because they are old, but rather because through the ages they have proved right. It will always be the rule."[54] President Kimball taught against moral turpitude with boldness and clarity. He felt it necessary to speak both frankly and boldly against the sins of the day (pornography, petting, adultery, homosexuality, masturbation, and lust). His boldness was designed to warn the Saints because of the turbulent and deceitful times. "This is a most unpleasant subject to dwell upon, but I am pressed to speak of it boldly so that no youth in the Church will ever have any question in his mind as to the illicit and diabolical nature of this perverse program. Again, Lucifer deceives and prompts logic and rationalization which will destroy men and make them servants of Satan forever."[55]

PROVIDENT LIVING

Throughout his ministry, President Kimball stressed a model of provident living for the Saints. "As you know, in the recent past we have placed considerable emphasis on personal and family preparedness. I hope that each member of the Church is responding appropriately to this direction. I also hope that we are understanding and accentuating the positive and not the negative."[56] Such preparation included having a "year's supply of commodities,"[57] planting and eating from a garden,[58] keeping a personal journal,[59] and even cleaning up homes and farms.[60]

President Kimball frequently counseled the youth of the Church to remain true to the faith and to marry in the temple.

WOMANHOOD

During President Kimball's administration, a divisive debate concerning women's roles in society arose. As a result, President Kimball often addressed the role and importance of womanhood. He taught, "How special it is for Latter-day Saint women to be given the lofty assignments they have been given by our Father in Heaven, especially those of you who have been privileged to be born in this part of this last dispensation. Let other women pursue heedlessly what they perceive as their selfish interests. You can be a much needed force for love and truth and righteousness on this planet. Let others selfishly pursue false values, but God has given to you the tremendous tasks of nurturing families, friends, and neighbors, just as men are to provide. But both husband and wife are to be parents!"[61] It is evident that President Kimball was also concerned about the effect changing roles might have upon the family and society. For example, President Kimball said, "We worry, therefore, conversely over these trends which would reduce the mother's love in our world. God has placed women at the very headwaters of the human stream. So much of what our men and our institutions seek to do downstream in the lives of erring individuals is done to compensate for early failures. Likewise, so much of life's later rejoicing is a reflection of a woman's work well done at the headwaters of the home."[62]

PROCLAMATION TO THE WORLD

In 1980, under the direction of President Kimball, a proclamation to the world was issued from the Peter Whitmer Sr. home in Fayette, New York. President Kimball introduced the proclamation by saying, "Now, my brothers and sisters, with

Music

President Kimball used music to uplift, instruct, and inspire. As a young couple, Spencer and Camilla took evening classes at the Gila Academy for self-improvement. During Spencer's music class, he formed a quartet with three friends. They called themselves the Conquistadores. For more than a decade, the group sang at community functions, funerals, and in musicals.

Once, during his convalescence on the Navajo Reservation, a little girl taught Elder Kimball to sing in Navajo. To the Navajos' delight, Elder Kimball tied a ribbon around his forehead and sang the song for a gathered group. Elder Kimball also used music among the missionaries. While touring one mission, he rewrote the words to the song "Happy Days Are Here Again" and sang it to the missionaries, hoping it would motivate them to work harder.

Elder Kimball lived in the same ward as President Marion Romney and Elder Delbert Stapley. At one ward reunion, the three men sang "I'll Serve the Lord While I Am Young." The audience applauded the men—all in their seventies. As an Apostle, he recruited several of his colleagues (Elders Benson, Peterson, and Cowley) to join him in a quartet to sing at a social for the General Authorities. Elder Lee accompanied them on the piano as they sang "Teach Me to Pray." That song was followed by a lighter number about a cure for baldness. While the quartet sang, Elders LeGrand Richards and Milton Hunter (both bald) sat on stage with their heads wrapped in a towel. At the end of the song they undid the towels, revealing bushy red hair atop Elder Richards and an English barrister's wig on Elder Hunter, much to the amusement of the audience.

For many years, Spencer sang in a quartet called the Conquistadores.

President Kimball presided over the sesquicentennial of the Church in 1980 at the Peter Whitmer farm in New York.

The prophet pondering during general conference.

the future before us, and sensing deeply the responsibilities and divine mission of the restored Church on this sacred occasion, the First Presidency and the Quorum of the Twelve Apostles declare to the world a proclamation. We have felt it appropriate to issue this statement from here, where the Church began."[63] In official fashion, the proclamation affirmed, among other things, the reality of the Restoration of the gospel of Jesus Christ, the truthfulness of the Book of Mormon, the importance of temple work, and that the family is of divine creation.

DO IT!

As the Church tried to lengthen its stride, President Kimball's sense of urgency was cleverly conveyed as he admonished the Saints to "quicken your pace." He took his stewardship seriously and expected the Saints to embrace the Lord's vision for them. "As important as it is to have this vision in mind," President Kimball taught, "defining and describing Zion will not bring it about." He then clarified, "That can only be done through consistent and concerted daily effort by every single member of the Church. No matter what the cost in toil or

sacrifice, we must 'do it.' That is one of my favorite phrases: 'Do it.' "[64] Needless, to say, the Church embraced President Kimball's saying of "do it" as a rallying point.

TESTIMONY

In his last address at general conference, President Kimball bore his familiar testimony. He testified, "For the past

Prayer of a Prophet

On one occasion, after conducting a solemn assembly in Canada, President Kimball retired to his hotel room, where the other members of the First Presidency and Elder M. Russell Ballard joined him in prayer. Elder Ballard had not heard the prophet pray before and was profoundly moved as he listened to President Kimball communicate with his Father in Heaven. Elder Ballard said, "I was overwhelmed. I have to tell you that tears welled up in my eyes as we knelt down around that bed. . . . I felt the Spirit as I never had before—you can understand it—for when a prophet talks to God, it is close friends speaking."[20]

century and a half since the Restoration, beginning with the Prophet Joseph Smith, the latter-day prophets of God have raised their voices in clarity and with authority and truth as they have borne their testimonies of the divinity of this great latter-day work and the redemptive power of the gospel of Jesus Christ.

"To the testimonies of these mighty men I add my testimony. I know that Jesus Christ is the Son of the living God and that He was crucified for the sins of the world. He is my friend, my Savior, my Lord and my God. With all my heart I pray that the Saints may keep His commandments, have His Spirit to be with them, and gain an eternal inheritance with Him in celestial glory.

"As we begin this conference let us wait upon the Lord for His blessing and His divine approbation. I pray the Lord to bless you; and as His servant, I bless you."[65]

What Others Have Said about President Kimball

Leo Cluff (childhood friend):

"If Spencer Kimball knew you, if he was your friend, he was always your friend, no matter where you met him or under what circumstances. If you weren't his friend, and you came into contact with him, he soon made you his friend. He didn't know anyone but friends; everyone was a friend to him. And he had a friendly greeting. He'd put his arm around you and give you a handshake. He remembered faces, people, and names."[21]

Carmen Smith (stenographer for the Kimball-Greenhalgh Insurance and Realty Company):

"I think one of his outstanding characteristics was his kindness. He just never tried to put anyone down. He never criticized or said an unkind word to anyone. Do you know, I never heard one word of contention the whole time I was employed by the company? No contention with his partner, nor with employees, nor with any customer who came to do business with him."[22]

Elder Neal A. Maxwell:

"Church members will be nourished and encouraged by the eloquence of the example of this seer in overcoming (or coexisting with) adversity after adversity. His resilience was exemplary. His deft humor occupied the place which might have so easily been commandeered by self-pity. His selfless dedication, time and again, caused him to be up and about his Father's business

(sometimes even before he was well). The examples are legendary and will be recounted for many years!"[23]

Elder Marvin J. Ashton:

"After one of our lengthy temple meetings, when I had been a member of the Twelve for only a short time, President Kimball took hold of my arm and said, 'Will you wait just a few minutes? I want to talk to you.' Of course I waited. When we were alone he said, 'I don't want the First Presidency or the other members of the Twelve to know, but I don't feel very good today. Will you please give me a blessing?' . . . Why do I love this great man? In his hour of need he was exhibiting love for and confidence in me. He has learned the art of making people feel good about themselves. By his actions we know he loves us."[24]

Elder Russell M. Nelson (President Kimball's private physician):

"As I watched him face his own trials, I witnessed the reality of his love. When his beloved Camilla developed severe illness, I sensed the intensity of his love for her. I witnessed the depth of his love for others as he frequently disappeared from his own hospital bed to bless the sick, even strangers. Whether their problems involved fever, cancer, or the heart, he could say in sympathy, 'I know how you feel.' "[25]

Matthew O. Richardson

*Professor of Church History and Doctrine, EdD
Brigham Young University*

Timothy Merrill

*Adjunct Instructor Religious Education, JD
Brigham Young University*

NOTES

1. Spencer W. Kimball, "Becoming the Pure in Heart," *Ensign*, May 1978, 80.
2. Spencer W. Kimball, "Jesus: The Perfect Leader," *Ensign*, August 1979, 5.
3. Neal A. Maxwell, "Spencer, the Beloved: Leader-Servant," *Ensign*, December 1985, 15.
4. *HC*, 2:353.
5. Ezra Taft Benson, "Spencer W. Kimball: A Star of the First Magnitude," *Ensign*, December 1985, 33.
6. Edward L. Kimball and Andrew E. Kimball Jr., *Spencer W. Kimball: Twelfth President of The Church of Jesus Christ of Latter-day Saints* (Salt Lake City: Bookcraft, 1977), 76.
7. Ibid., 77.
8. "President Spencer W. Kimball: On the Occasion of His 80th Birthday," *Ensign*, March 1975, 8.
9. Kimball and Kimball, *Spencer W. Kimball*, 87.
10. Spencer W. Kimball, "The Marriage Decision," *Ensign*, February 1975, 4.
11. Kimball and Kimball, *Spencer W. Kimball*, 173.
12. Ibid., 188–91.
13. Ibid., 195.
14. Ibid., 223.
15. Ibid., 237.
16. Benson, "Spencer W. Kimball: A Star of the First Magnitude," 34.
17. Kimball and Kimball, *Spencer W. Kimball*, 342.
18. Spencer W. Kimball, CR, April 1947, 151.
19. Boyd K. Packer, "President Spencer W. Kimball: No Ordinary Man," *Ensign*, March 1974, 13.
20. Kimball and Kimball, *Spencer W. Kimball*, 255.
21. Ibid., 401.
22. Ibid., 411.
23. Maxwell, "Spencer, the Beloved," 10.
24. Kimball and Kimball, *Spencer W. Kimball*, 416.

25. Bruce R. McConkie, "Priesthood: The New Revelation on Priesthood," in *Priesthood*, comp. Spencer W. Kimball (Salt Lake City: Deseret Book, 1981), 128.
26. Spencer W. Kimball, "Humility," *BYU Speeches of the Year*, January 16, 1963, 2.
27. Spencer W. Kimball, "What Do We Hear?" *Ensign*, May 1974, 47.
28. Spencer W. Kimball, Regional Representative's Seminar, October 3, 1974, cited in "The Words of a Prophet," *Ensign*, December 1985, 26.
29. Edward L. Kimball, ed., *Teachings of Spencer W. Kimball: Twelfth President of The Church of Jesus Christ of Latter-day Saints* (Salt Lake City: Bookcraft, 1982): 174–75.
30. Spencer W. Kimball, "When the World Will Be Converted," *Ensign*, October 1974, 4.
31. Spencer W. Kimball, "First Presidency Message: When the World Will Be Converted," *Ensign*, April 1984, 3.
32. Ibid.
33. Edward L. Kimball, *Teachings of Spencer W. Kimball*, 551.
34. Spencer W. Kimball, "When the World Will Be Converted," *Ensign*, October 1974, 8.
35. Ibid., 7.
36. Ibid., 3.
37. Edward L. Kimball, *Teachings of Spencer W. Kimball*, 557.
38. Spencer W. Kimball, "The Davids and the Goliaths," *Ensign*, November 1974, 83.
39. Spencer W. Kimball, "When the World Will Be Converted," 3.
40. Spencer W. Kimball, "Fundamental Principles to Ponder and Live," *Ensign*, November 1978, 43.
41. N. Eldon Tanner, "Revelation on Priesthood Accepted, Church Officers Sustained," *Ensign*, November 1978, 16.
42. Spencer W. Kimball, "The Importance of Celestial Marriage," *Ensign*, October 1979, 3.
43. Spencer W. Kimball, "President Kimball Speaks Out on Morality," *New Era*, November 1980, 39.
44. Spencer W. Kimball, "The Marriage Decision," 2.
45. Spencer W. Kimball, "Oneness in Marriage," *Ensign*, March 1977, 3.
46. Ibid.
47. Ibid.
48. Spencer W. Kimball, "Train up a Child," *Ensign*, April 1978, 2.
49. Spencer W. Kimball, "A Report and a Challenge," *Ensign*, November 1976, 4.
50. Spencer W. Kimball, "Ministering to the Needs of Members," *Ensign*, November 1980, 45.
51. Spencer W. Kimball, "The Things of Eternity—Stand We in Jeopardy?" *Ensign*, January 1977, 3.
52. Spencer W. Kimball, "We Feel an Urgency," *Ensign*, August 1980, 2.

53. Ibid.

54. Spencer W. Kimball, "President Kimball Speaks Out on Morality," 39.

55. Ibid.

56. Spencer W. Kimball, "Welfare Services: The Gospel in Action," *Ensign*, November 1977, 76.

57. Spencer W. Kimball, "God Will Not Be Mocked," *Ensign*, November 1974, 6.

58. Spencer W. Kimball, "The True Way of Life and Salvation," *Ensign*, May 1978, 4.

59. Spencer W. Kimball, "Let Us Move Forward and Upward," *Ensign*, May 1979, 84.

60. Spencer W. Kimball, "God Will Not Be Mocked," 4.

61. Spencer W. Kimball, "The Role of Righteous Women," *Ensign*, November 1979, 102.

62. Spencer W. Kimball, "The True Way of Life and Salvation," 4.

63. Spencer W. Kimball, "Introduction to the Proclamation," *Ensign*, May 1980, 51.

64. Spencer W. Kimball, "Becoming the Pure in Heart," 79.

65. Spencer W. Kimball, "The Lord Expects Righteousness," *Ensign*, November 1982, 4.

SIDEBAR AND PHOTO NOTES

1. CR, October 1943, 17.

2. "President Spencer W. Kimball: On the Occasion of His 80th Birthday," 6.

3. CR, April 1974, 127.

4. Kimball and Kimball, *Spencer W. Kimball*, 67.

5. Ibid., 79–80.

6. Emerson Roy West, *Latter-day Prophets: Their Lives, Teachings, and Testimonies, with Profiles of Their Wives* (American Fork: Covenant Communications, Inc., 1997), 130.

7. Maxwell, "Spencer, the Beloved," 12.

8. Kimball and Kimball, *Spencer W. Kimball*, 151.

9. Maxwell, "Spencer, the Beloved," 13.

10. "President Spencer W. Kimball: On the Occasion of His 80th Birthday," 11.

11. Kimball and Kimball, *Spencer W. Kimball*, 308.

12. Ibid., 309.

13. James C. Christensen, "That's Not My Jesus: An Artist's Personal Perspective on Images of Christ," *BYU Studies* 39, no. 3 (2000), 11–12.

14. Vaughn J. Featherstone, *BYU Speeches of the Year*, August 1, 1976, 382–83.

15. "President Spencer W. Kimball: On the Occasion of His 80th Birthday," 12.

16. Kimball and Kimball, *Spencer W. Kimball*, 331.

17. Ibid., 80.

18. Ibid., 85.

19. Ibid., 140–41.

20. M. Russell Ballard, "You—the Leaders in 1988," *Ensign*, March 1979, 71–72.

21. "President Spencer W. Kimball: On the Occasion of His 80th Birthday," 8–9.

22. Ibid., 9.

23. Maxwell, "Spencer, the Beloved," 8.

24. Marvin J. Ashton, "Spencer W. Kimball: A True Disciple of Christ," *Ensign*, May 1985, 43–44.

25. Russell M. Nelson, "Spencer W. Kimball: Man of Faith," *Ensign*, December 1985, 40–41.

Chapter Thirteen

EZRA TAFT BENSON

LIFE AND TIMES

1899	August 4	Born in Whitney, Idaho
1914		Attended Oneida Academy; became captain of the basketball team
1920	Fall	Met his future wife, Flora Amussen
1921		Attended Utah Agricultural College
1921	July	Served mission to Great Britain
1926		Graduated from BYU
1926	September	Sealed in the Salt Lake Temple
1929		Appointed Franklin County agricultural agent
1930		Appointed agricultural economist with University of Idaho Extension Division in Boise
1938		Called as president of the Boise Stake
1939		Appointed executive secretary, National Council of Farmer Cooperatives
1940		Called as the first president of the Washington DC Stake
1943	July 26	Called to the Quorum of the Twelve Apostles
1946	January	Set apart as European Mission president to provide aid and reorganize the Church following World War II
1953	January 13	Appointed 15th Secretary of Agriculture in U.S. President Eisenhower's Cabinet
1973	December 30	Set apart as President of the Quorum of the Twelve Apostles
1985	November 10	Ordained and set apart as President of the Church
1994	May 30	Died in Salt Lake City at the age of ninety-four

BIOGRAPHICAL HIGHLIGHTS

President Ezra Taft Benson was the thirteenth President of the Church. Ordained and set apart on November 10, 1985, he served for eight and a half years until his death on May 30, 1994, of heart failure. President Benson championed the Book of Mormon as the heart of proclaiming the gospel and perfecting the Saints. He gave personalized messages to members in their different roles in life and invited all to beware of pride.

Born on his father's farm in the small community of Whitney, Idaho, Ezra grew to maturity, hoping to be a farmer like his father and grandfather before him. He met his wife, Flora Amussen, in Logan, Utah, where he studied agriculture at Utah Agricultural College. Immediately following their marriage in the Salt Lake Temple, they left for Iowa State University where he completed a master's degree in agriculture. He became the national secretary of a large farmer's organization in Washington, DC. In 1943, he was called as an Apostle. He traveled to Europe in 1946 to reorganize the Church and help suffering Saints following World War II. A few years later, Ezra was named Secretary of Agriculture by U.S. President Dwight D. Eisenhower. He became President of the Quorum of the Twelve in 1975 and President of the Church in 1984.

President Benson may have been the best-known Church President among Americans, generally. As Secretary of Agriculture during the Eisenhower administration, his name was a household word in the United States during the 1950s and early '60s. He was already serving as an Apostle when approached by President Eisenhower. As the former executive secretary of the National Council of Farmer Cooperatives, he had come to the attention of political leaders. When Dwight D. Eisenhower assumed office, he appointed Elder Benson as Secretary of Agriculture and kept him through the full eight years of his presidency. Known for his no-nonsense approach to the economics of farming, President Benson stuck to his independent, free-enterprise feelings about less government interference in the agricultural community. His stance made him controversial at times, but no one doubted his commitment to God and country. Later, as President of the Church, he would approach difficult issues such as mothers employed outside the home and marriage-reticent men head on. He also championed the Book of Mormon as the agent for spiritual sustenance for mankind.

CONTRIBUTIONS

President Benson was a writer. All of his books were written after his call as an Apostle. By the time *The Teachings of Ezra Taft Benson* (Bookcraft, 1988) was published, he had already written twelve books. Some were aimed at a general audience and addressed farming and political issues. Typical of these were *Farmers at the Crossroads* (Devin-Adair, 1956) and *Crossfire: The Eight Years with Eisenhower* (Doubleday, 1962). Others were written to Church members and referred to spiritual issues affecting church and state. Two of these were *God, Family, Country: Our Three Great Loyalties* (Deseret Book, 1974) and *The Constitution: A Heavenly Banner* (Deseret Book, 1986).

TEACHINGS

President Benson loved the Book of Mormon and drew attention to the great spiritual power inherent in studying it. He initiated a publishing campaign to "flood the earth" with the Book of Mormon, which resulted in many times the number of books being produced and placed in homes, libraries, and offices around the globe. He left no doubt where he stood on important social, moral, and spiritual issues such as pride, God-given freedoms, and a host of themes in between. His clear and bold warning voice lit the way for millions of members to humble themselves and come unto Christ.

LIFE OF
EZRA TAFT BENSON

◆

GREAT-GRANDFATHER EZRA T. BENSON

Later photograph of Ezra T. Benson in Utah.

President Benson was the great-grandson of Ezra T. Benson, who was ordained an Apostle at Council Bluffs during the exodus of the Latter-day Saints from Nauvoo. Ezra T. moved to Nauvoo in 1841 and filled responsible Church positions there. When the Saints began their westward trek, Ezra received a letter from Brigham Young, who was out ahead on the trail, asking that he fill the vacancy in the Quorum of the Twelve vacated by

A young picture of early Apostle Ezra T. Benson, Ezra Taft Benson's great-grandfather, who joined the Church during the Nauvoo period of Church history.[1]

John E. Page. He traveled westward and was ordained an Apostle on July 16, 1846, at Council Bluffs.

He and his growing family were also assigned by President Brigham Young to preside over the Church in the Cache Valley of Northern Utah. The Benson family would reside here for several generations. Ezra's oldest son, George Taft Benson (who had been born in Garden Grove, Iowa, during the flight from Nauvoo), grew up in Logan and would later marry Louisa Ballif on December 20, 1867, in Salt Lake City. Together they had thirteen children. Louisa served for several years as the president of the far-flung Oneida Stake Relief Society. George was bishop of the Whitney Ward for twenty years.

"Mean Trick"

While speaking in Logan, Utah, near the Benson homestead, President Ezra Taft Benson recounted how President Heber J. Grant told an interesting story about his grandfather, Ezra T. Benson, and how the Benson family ended up in Cache Valley:

"Your great-grandfather built the finest home in Salt Lake City on that corner, with the exception of Brigham Young's home (which, of course, was the Lion House). He had it all finished. It was a beautiful home—two stories with a porch at both levels on both sides of the house. It had a white picket fence around it with fruit trees and ornamental trees and with a little stream running through the yard. He was all ready to move his families in from their log cabins when President Young called him into the office one day. 'Brother Benson,' he said, 'we would like you to go to Cache Valley and pioneer that area and preside over the Saints. We suggest you sell your home to Daniel H. Wells.'

"'Now,' President Grant said, 'Daniel H. Wells was Brigham Young's counselor. Wasn't that a mean trick?'

"In all the years that I had attended the Benson reunions I had never heard that story. So I had it verified by the Church Historical Department, and they assured me that the facts were as President Grant related them. They told me they had a tintype picture of the old home.

"Since that time, I have been most grateful for the so-called 'mean trick' of President Young, because were it not for that, the Bensons would not have their roots in Cache Valley."[2]

Young Scoutmaster Ezra Taft Benson (center) and his assistants shaved their heads prior to a ten-day hike to fulfill a promise made when their Scouts won a singing competition.

Unusual Birth

President Benson was born on August 4, 1899. Dr. Allan Cutler assisted with the birth in the bedroom of the Benson farm home. Both grandmothers, Louisa Benson and Margaret Dunkley, were there. The delivery was long and undoubtedly hard, but a large, eleven and three quarter-pounds boy eventually came forth.

The doctor couldn't get him to breathe. Soon, he laid him on the bed and pronounced, "'There's no hope for the child, but I believe we can save the mother.'" While Dr. Cutler feverishly attended to Sarah, the grandmothers rushed to the kitchen, praying silently as they worked, and returned shortly with two pans of water—one cold, the other warm. Alternately, they dipped the baby first in cold and then in warm water, until finally they heard a cry. The 11¾ pound boy was alive! Later both grandmothers bore testimony that the Lord had spared the child. George and Sarah named him Ezra Taft Benson."[3]

RUNNING THE FARM

The second son (and fourth child) of George and Louisa Benson was born June 24, 1875, and named after his father. George T. Benson Jr. loved the gospel and was always active in the Church. He married Sarah Dunkley on October 19, 1898, in the Logan Temple. The oldest of their eleven children was named after his great-grandfather, Ezra Taft Benson. George was an excellent farmer and passed the love of the land on to his oldest son, Ezra Taft Benson, who became known to friends and family simply as "T."

Due to his father's call as a missionary when Ezra was only twelve years old, he became intimately acquainted with farm operations. While much of the farm was rented out during George T. Benson's 1912–1914 Northern States Mission, Ezra took care of the dairy herd and managed the pasture and hay fields not rented out.

His father was pleased with the way his son stepped up to attend to farm duties, and things were managed so well that upon his return from missionary labors, George was actually able to expand his farming operations. Several years later, Ezra and his brother Orval purchased their father's farm in Whitney for $17,000. On this land they tried some of the methods they learned while studying agriculture at Utah State and BYU.

FLORA AMUSSEN

Ezra attended Oneida Academy, a Church school, in Preston, Idaho, before entering Utah Agricultural College (now Utah State University) in Logan, Utah. He saw his future wife, Flora Smith Amussen, drive by in a red Ford convertible during a campus visit before his mission. She was a popular co-ed, active in student leadership, tennis, and college dramas, and able to play the piano well by ear. He told a cousin standing by him on the corner that he would date her when he returned to attend school.

Flora lived in Logan with her widowed mother, Barbara Smith Amussen. Her father, Carl Christian Amussen, had died when she was a baby. Carl was a wealthy jeweler and a dentist who had been born and raised in Denmark and had

traveled and worked in Russia, Europe, Australia, and New Zealand. His family name was Asmussen, but he dropped the first S after arriving in Utah. He had found a copy of Parley P. Pratt's *Voice of Warning* pamphlet on a street in New Zealand and was so moved that he traveled and sought out the Church in Liverpool, England, at the address given on the back of the pamphlet.

Because he had accumulated significant assets as a jeweler, Carl was able to gather with the Saints in the Salt Lake Valley, establishing a business with hired hands and materials he brought with him. He sought the business counsel of President Brigham Young upon his arrival in Utah and was surprised to be invited to consider plural marriage as one who could well afford the expenses of more than one family. He married Barbara Smith as his third wife in 1885. She was over forty years his junior and together they had eight children. Flora was their youngest.

Flora was living alone with her mother when "T," as she would also call Ezra throughout their married life, came to call on her in early 1921. He was always touched by Flora's close and kindly relationship with her mother.

Ezra served a mission to Britain from July 1921 through 1923 and returned to discover that Flora wished to serve a mission also. She was called to Hawaii and loved it. She was delighted to serve her final six months with her mother, who went to Hawaii to serve a short-term mission. She and Ezra wrote through her mission, and both were anxious to meet again when she returned.

Flora and Ezra were married in the Salt Lake Temple September 10, 1926, by Orson F. Whitney, Ezra's first mission president. (David O. McKay was his second.) Following a wedding breakfast, they left immediately for Iowa State, camping out along the way. While Flora was serving her mission, Ezra had completed his bachelor's degree in agriculture. Together, they determined he should go on to graduate school, and he finished his master's degree in agriculture with honors in just one year. He was a hardworking student and received an offer to stay at Iowa State and teach. He turned down the offer, returning to Whitney, Idaho, where he farmed with his brother Orval until Orval went on a mission. Then Ezra farmed until he was offered a job as the extension agricultural agent for Franklin County in March 1929. His two sons, Reed and Mark, were born exactly sixteen months apart during this time. A year and a half later, he was appointed agricultural economist with the University of Idaho Extension Division in Boise. It was during this time that their daughters Barbara and Beverley were born.

CALLED TO SERVE

Ezra was called as president of the Boise Stake in November 1938. This would be a short assignment, since almost immediately his name was put forward as candidate for the appointment of executive secretary to the National Council of Farmer Cooperatives. This meant a move to Washington,

DC, where, on March 30, 1940, daughter Bonnie Amussen Benson was born. Each child had been given the name Amussen in honor of Flora's father.

Church leaders approved of the move from Boise to the East, and on June 30, 1940, Ezra Taft Benson was sustained as president of the newly organized Washington Stake. His tireless efforts on behalf of American Farmers, as well as his strong personal leadership of the Washington Stake, did not go unnoticed. In July of 1943, Ezra Taft Benson was called as a member of the Quorum of the Twelve Apostles. The call came as a complete surprise to him. He was in Salt Lake City following a business trip through citrus farms in California. He had taken his oldest son, Reed, on this trip, and they stopped to visit with his second mission president,

A Powerhouse in Her Own Right: Sister Flora Benson

Being married to a Church President would seem to eclipse a woman, but like many wives of other Church leaders, Sister Benson was an outstanding individual and a strong example. President Benson was attracted to her even more deeply when he saw how kind and loving she was to her widowed mother, Barbara Amussen, when he picked Flora up for their first date. As they left her home, Flora tenderly kissed her mother good-bye in a way that deeply touched the young man.

Even though she was well known and active socially while attending college, she was unaffected and forthright as a young woman. She had been elected as vice president of the student body at what is now Utah State University in Logan, Utah, as well as president of the Women's Athletic Club on campus. (She would later, to his great surprise, "whip" her husband in a tennis match he suggested shortly after their marriage.)

Flora also loved the stage and played the lead in Shakespeare's *Twelfth Night*. This resulted in her election to an honorary dramatic fraternity. She also loved to play the piano. Her natural ability to play popular songs after listening to them put her in demand at parties and socials.

Perhaps her greatest talents shone through as a wife and mother. During her husband's frequent absences, she maintained a close relationship with her children and made them a "model" family featured in magazines and television while President Benson was Secretary of Agriculture during the Eisenhower years.

In 1955 she was elected Homemaker of the Year by the National Home Fashions League. She was deeply touched by the honor. Ezra joined her for the presentation that was made October 26, 1955. It was another opportunity to put her religion, interwoven with her many talents, on display.

In her later years, while traveling with her prophet-husband, she would enchant Church members by reciting, with great inflection, Edgar Guest's well-known poem, "Home":

It takes a heap o' livin' in a house t' make it home
A heap o' sun an' shadder an' ye sometimes have t' roam
Afore ye really 'preciate the things ye lef' behind,
An' hunger for 'em somehow, with 'em allus on yer mind.
Ye've got t' sing an' dance fer years, ye've got t' romp an' play,
An' learn t' love the things ye have by usin' 'em each day.[4]

President Heber J. Grant called Ezra Taft Benson to be a member of the Quorum of the Twelve Apostles.[5]

Elder Benson and family in 1955 during his days in the Eisenhower administration.

David O. McKay. Following the visit, they made a short trip up to Whitney, where friends and relatives were delighted to see them. On returning to Salt Lake City, July 26, 1953, he discovered President McKay's office staff had been trying to locate him. They indicated President Heber J. Grant wished to see him at his cabin at the mouth of Emigration Canyon. Worried about catching his train on time, Ezra quickly sped to the cabin and was invited directly into the President's bedroom where he was resting. The President took his right hand and lovingly issued the call to serve as a member of the Quorum of the Twelve. Ezra was flabbergasted and completely humbled at the invitation to join this group of men he had honored and revered his entire life.

The following October, Ezra went to general conference, where he was officially sustained as the sixty-third Apostle called since the restoration of The Church of Jesus Christ of Latter-day Saints. His resignation from the National Council of Farmer Cooperatives brought congratulations from men who had little understanding of the nature of his new appointment. But great friendships had been made that would ultimately influence the future course of his apostleship and his public service. A short time after their move to

Utah, the Benson's youngest daughter, Flora Beth Benson, was born in Salt Lake City.

SPECIAL POST— WWII ASSIGNMENT

The armistice signed at the end of World War II brought a welcomed peace to Europeans, who had endured over five years of danger and strife. Included among them were Latter-day Saints in several missions who were destitute and hungry. Church leaders felt that a coordinated effort to bring relief was necessary, and the First Presidency designated the youngest Apostle, Ezra Taft Benson, to spearhead the effort as European Mission president. This would allow him to work with several mission presidents, some of whom were indigenous "acting" mission presidents quickly assigned when war broke out and their American Church leaders were called home. The assignment would mean, however, that President Benson would go into Europe alone, without the presence of Flora and the children. Ezra would stay there for almost a year, traveling throughout Europe and the British Isles, organizing relief efforts and arranging for food, clothing, and other supplies to be shipped from Welfare Square at Church headquarters. His heart was deeply touched as he encountered many members who had lost everything but whose hearts seemed revitalized by the presence of an Apostle. Time after time, travel arrangements that had seemed impossible due to inherent military restrictions were made possible at the last moment.

President Benson and his traveling associates pushed on and brought comfort and assurance to thousands of Latter-day Saints impacted by the war. The depth of the suffering of the Saints caught in the war deeply touched the young Apostle. In his journal President Benson noted,

"Later I faced in a cold half-wrecked third floor auditorium off a bombed street 480 cold half-starved but faithful Latter-day Saints in a conference meeting. It was an inspiration to see the light of faith and hear their harrowing experiences, including murder, rape, and starvation of their loved ones. Yet there was no bitterness or anger but a sweet reciprocation and expression of faith in the gospel. We were together in a partly bombed building for three-and-a-half hours. Not a single member registered any complaint about their circumstances in spite of the fact that some were in the last stages of starvation right before our very eyes.

"In Berlin alone we were told that there are well over one hundred suicides daily due to the mental attitude of the people who have no hope in view of the ravages of war. Our Saints, on the other hand, are full of hope, courage, and faith, and everywhere they look cheerfully forward with expressions of deepest faith for the gospel and for their membership in the Church. It was one of the greatest demonstrations we

The Spirit Moves

President Benson's life was marked with profound spiritual direction. One experience illustrates the kind of divine intervention that seemed to prevail during Ezra's term as European Mission president:

"Our first interview with General [Joseph T.] McNarney, the top general in the American forces, was in the I. G. Farben Building in Frankfurt, which had been spared by 'pin bombing' because the Americans expected it would be their headquarters when the war was over, and it was.

"We had driven our little jeep up to the building, parked it, and gone in to see if we could get an appointment with the general. We wanted to get permission from him to make distribution of our welfare supplies to our own people through our own channels. Everything was being distributed through the military.

"We were told by the colonel at the desk that we couldn't get an appointment for three days. The general was very busy with important delegations coming to see him.

"We returned to our car and had a prayer together, then we went back in.

"In the meantime the secretary at the desk had been changed, and in less than fifteen minutes we were in the presence of General McNarney.

"Then I saw the Spirit operate on that man. I heard him say, 'Under no conditions can you have permission to distribute your own supplies to your own people. They must come through the military.'

"Of course we recognized immediately that if we had to go through the military, our Saints wouldn't get much of the supplies, and so we started telling him about the program of the Church.

"When he saw we were somewhat determined, he said, 'Well, you go ahead and collect your supplies, and probably by the time you get them collected the policy will be changed.'

"I said, 'General, they are already collected; they are always collected. We have ninety warehouses full of supplies. Within twenty-four hours from the time I wire our First Presidency in Salt Lake City, carloads of food, bedding, clothing, and medical supplies will be moving toward Germany.'

"When I said this, he said, 'I never heard of people with such vision.'

"And before we left him we had written authorization to make our own distribution to our own people through our own channels, and from that moment on we had wonderful cooperation."[6]

have ever seen of the real fruits of the gospel in the lives of men and women.

"Our travels during the day to the various meetings took us through mile after mile of unspeakable destruction and desolation. Words cannot begin to describe the ruin that has been heaped upon this city. Only one small portion of the front wall of the former East German Mission home remains standing. Across the street where the once beautiful Tiergarten stood is nothing but a yawning wilderness of splintered tree stumps and an occasional badly shattered lifeless tree. Many streets are still impassable, piled high with rubble.

"Hardly a day passes that skeletonized buildings do not crash into the street below, often burying passersby. Most bridges are entirely blown up, and the large mass of unsupported, shell-ridden walls presents a constant menace as they continue to crumble and cave in. Traveling amid such surroundings leaves one with a feeling so appalling that it must be experienced to be understood."[1]

Great distances were covered as President Benson presided over the European Mission during this time of recovery from the ravages of war. Sometimes sleeping with refugees in damaged buildings, the President did his best to try to assure the people of the love and interest of Church leaders. Always highlighting the spiritual condition of the people in his talks, his descriptions show his deep concern for these members whose lives had been turned upside down and inside out.

Elder Benson stands on a corner in London where he had been "mobbed" as a missionary years earlier.

> ### The K-Ration Quartet
>
> Some missionary work was also accomplished during this time. Ezra recorded the following in the *European Mission History*, dated Saturday, March 30, 1946:
>
> "From here we went to Stuttgart, where announcements were made over the radio of our meeting with the Saints this evening. We were gratified to see 275 persons in attendance of which at least 100 were investigators and 16 were servicemen.
>
> "In this meeting President Max Zimmer, Chaplain Howard C. Badger, Brother Frederick W. Babbel, and I sang "Let the Lower Lights Be Burning," to the delight of the entire audience. On our trip we have often sung the songs of Zion together and decided to make a public appearance before becoming separated. We named our quartet 'The K-Ration Quartet.' "[7]

But with the spiritual food, he was always trying to arrange for the delivery of physical nourishment that saved the lives of all but those in the last stages of starvation.

Saints back in America were aware of his difficult mission, and many Church leaders as well as ward members tried to do what they could to ease the burdens of Flora and the children during Ezra's absence. Baby Flora Beth became seriously ill during his absence, and Ezra was unaware until the crisis had passed. A letter that arrived two weeks after the incident shocked him and caused him to immediately make a phone call home. He felt the call was miraculous in itself, as phone communication was difficult and sometimes took hours or even days to arrange. But within fifteen minutes, he was talking with his wife over a clear connection. She was able to assure him of the baby's recovery, and they talked about the visit of President George Albert Smith, the new Church President, and his blessing to baby Flora Beth.[2]

In July of 1946 the First Presidency assigned Elder Alma Sonne, an Assistant to the Twelve, to replace President Benson in Europe. President Benson would not become aware of the change until several days later, when he returned to Berlin from Warsaw and visited the home of Eugene Merrill, who was the head of communications for the U.S. military there. Merrill, a Church member, was living in the beautiful home of a former "chocolate magnate" in Germany.

"Brother Merrill informed me he had just received a letter from home containing a clipping to the effect Brother Alma Sonne has been appointed to preside over the

Elder Benson (second from the right) with his father and six brothers. He loved working with boys and helped further organize LDS Scouts in England after the war; he was always an avid supporter of Boy Scouts. He was the recipient of the Bronze Wolf Award—the highest possible from the World Scout Committee.

European Mission and that he will come as soon as he can make arrangements. Although it is a surprise, if true—and I had expected to continue for at least another four to six months—I will be pleased to turn over to him the pleasant responsibility of directing affairs in Europe for the Church."[3]

"When President Sonne finally arrived, Ezra reviewed conditions among the Saints in the missions of Europe:

"Spent the afternoon and evening going over mission matters with President Sonne, who seemed astonished at the humble accomplishments of the past nine-and-a-half months. Truly as I, of necessity, reviewed them with President Sonne, even I was amazed at the manner in which the Lord has opened the way before us in this glorious mission."[4]

They visited missions together, and Elder Benson did all he could to introduce President Sonne to military and

government dignitaries whose influence could facilitate travel, delivery of supplies, and further establishment of the Church and its programs.

BACK HOME AGAIN

His arrival home following a transatlantic flight was sweet after an eleven-month absence. Flora and the children were so excited to have "Daddy" return home. They had bravely carried on as normally as possible while he was gone, but doctors had told Flora she needed an operation as a result of difficulties brought on during childbirth. Shortly after his arriving home, she went into the hospital and endured the successful medical procedure. Elder Benson was greatly relieved and felt that prayers had been answered.

What followed were several years of intense and busy apostolic and civic activities that included heading the Church's Melchizedek Priesthood Committee, being the senior advisor to the YMMIA and YWMIA programs, serving on the Boy Scouts of America National Executive Board, and speaking at major Church, university, and farming events. Republican presidential candidate Thomas Dewey even approached Elder Benson about a cabinet position should he be elected. His sons, Reed and Mark, served missions, and the girls grew into beautiful young women. Constant stake conference visits and mission tours were mingled with family vacations, but growing Church responsibilities kept Elder Benson away from home and family more than he wanted to be.

SECRETARY OF AGRICULTURE

On November 20, 1952, a phone call from Utah Senator Arthur V. Watkins came as a bombshell. Ezra was informed that President-elect Dwight D. Eisenhower was considering him for the cabinet post of Secretary of Agriculture. Consulting with Church President David O. McKay, Ezra was told to accept the post if it came in the right spirit. The following Monday Ezra flew to New York, where President Eisenhower asked him to accept the position. Ezra laid all of his reservations on the table. He raised concerns about his political leanings as well as his Church leadership role. But

Ezra Taft Benson is sworn in as Secretary of Agriculture as President Eisenhower looks on.

Eisenhower was unmoved by any of them. Ezra accepted. Within minutes the appointment was announced to the press. He would become the fifteenth U.S. Secretary of Agriculture and the first member of the Church to hold such an executive office in the federal government.

His would be a principle-based administration. Alarmed at the level of subsidies farmers were receiving at the time, Ezra spoke often about the free market system and farmers' desire to be independent. The Department of Agriculture had previously amassed vast storage of excess food supplies that threatened to play havoc with world markets if dumped cheaply. He wrestled with how to deal with such a situation. Ezra frequently visited with leaders of farm organizations and traveled the nation to talk to farmers themselves about these issues. As he presented his views on the principles of good agricultural economics, farmers listened, but the media mocked and politicians howled. Over time, however, his views gained favor with a majority of farmers and respect for the Secretary grew. People felt he was honest and said what needed to be said, as plainly as he knew how to say it. Political strategists winced, but Elder Benson did not flinch.

Ezra Taft Benson as Secretary of Agriculture during the eight years of the Dwight D. Eisenhower administration, May 26, 1950.

The Love of the Land

President Benson had farming in his blood, as did his father. He studied agriculture in school and planned to return to the farm when he graduated. In fact, the same day he was married, he and Flora left for Iowa State University so he could complete a master's degree in agriculture, making him a rather highly educated "farmer" in his day. He returned to the farm, until his local county commissioners approached him about being the county agricultural agent. His acceptance of the offer gave him a broad view of farming conditions and practices in that area of southeastern Idaho. He also became an avid 4-H club booster and promoted the program extensively.

His performance was highly recognized and resulted in an invitation to move to Boise, Idaho (the state capital) where he became an Agricultural Economist with the University of Idaho Extension Division. Ezra was analytical about farming problems and saw the big picture when it came to the future of farming. His studied approach made him an attractive candidate as executive secretary to the National Council of Farmer Cooperatives in Washington, DC. When he was ultimately named to the post, he took his no-nonsense, practical approach on the road nationally and won the attention of elected leaders as well as farmers. His ability to work hard for long hours kept him abreast of legislative issues that involved agriculture and the cooperative movement in America. He was soon appearing before congressional committees, answering hard questions, and lobbying for the American farmer and the cooperatives that gave a strong voice to the "little man." His ability to be bold without being contentious helped ingratiate him in the eyes of prominent national leaders. It was also while he served in this important agricultural capacity that he was made president of the Washington Stake in 1940, and later, in 1943, called as an Apostle.

His experience in crisscrossing the country, meeting with local cooperative leaders and at the same time becoming acquainted with national political leaders, prepared him well for the ultimate roll he would play in farming. In 1953, Ezra Taft Benson, with the blessing of Church President David O. McKay, became the Secretary of Agriculture in the cabinet of Dwight D. Eisenhower. Suddenly, his conservative and religious views on freedom, responsibility, and what was right for America were simultaneously being applauded and castigated in the general public. His opinions were strong and his vision determined, and many in the media as well as the general public did not like it. On the other hand, many people (including many American farmers) appreciated his straightforward manner and strong, clear voice that did not seem to be easily affected by political pressures. His views and recommendations for farming were fodder for the public press, and at times he wearied of having to deal with reporters, not to mention senators and representatives who wished to drag him before multiple committees to explain his policies and account for his actions as Secretary. His ability to demonstrate good common sense and to face tough questions without a show of anger or disgust won the hearts of many Americans. It became clear to many that he was interested in what was good and right for agriculture and the farmer, not what was good for politics or his own image. Again, in his role as Secretary of Agriculture, he spent much time on the road, visiting farmers in meetings and on their farms. He wanted to know what they really needed and what they really thought. And when they talked to him, they knew they were talking to someone who understood agriculture and loved farming.[8]

The Secretary would often stop and talk to farmers, whether on the street or in the field. Some previously opposed to his agriculture programs were convinced otherwise once they had met and visited with him. He was down-to-earth and spoke plainly with people.

Sister Benson and the children similarly put off ostentation and showy behavior. On one occasion, the wives of cabinet members were invited to the Benson home, where homemade dishes graced the menu and were served by the Benson daughters. This was in stark contrast to the elaborate, catered dinners that were the norm at such functions.

Ezra's popularity rose and fell with regularity. Sometimes praised and sometimes roasted, the Secretary became used to having his policies praised and panned. He even offered to step down on one occasion, but President Eisenhower insisted he stay to "the bitter end." They then joked about whether the end would be bitter or not. The two drew closer over time as bills passed by a Democratic congress would be vetoed by the President with the strong encouragement of the Secretary of Agriculture.

President Eisenhower suggested that Elder Benson travel abroad from time to time. These diplomatic efforts put

The Benson family visits with President Eisenhower.

As U.S. Secretary of Agriculture, Ezra Taft Benson appeared on the cover of *Time* magazine twice. He also was featured on the covers of *US News* and *World Report*, *Newsweek*, and *Business Week*.

him in contact with many world leaders. His international reputation would later do much good for the Church as well as the country. In later years, dignitaries would often be invited to Church meetings and special events when Elder Benson visited other nations while on Church business.

Soviet Premier Nikita Khrushchev visited the United States in 1959. During his visit, Ezra hosted the Russian leader through a tour of several farms. The Soviets returned the favor and invited Elder Benson to Moscow. There, he became painfully aware of the inefficiencies of the Soviet system and the restrictions placed on the Russian people. At the end of his tour, the American entourage visited the Central Baptist Church in Moscow. Filled mostly with elderly people whose faith predated the communist take-over, the congregation warmly received the group. Elder Benson spoke to the group and tenderly testified of Heavenly Father, Jesus Christ, and the power of love, peace, and prayer. The deeply felt response of the people caused virtually everyone in the American entourage to weep over the experience. Media members would comment later about the spirituality of the event and the powerful feeling they experienced in the old church that day. It was clear that Ezra Taft Benson had a deep testimony of the Savior and wore his religion comfortably and sincerely, and that he was unafraid to open his heart when occasion permitted.

Ezra Taft Benson and J. Willard Marriott, founder of the Marriott corporation of well-known restaurants and hotels, became close friends and served in Church leadership together in the Washington, DC, area.

The Benson family often enjoyed visiting the Marriott ranch for recreation.

BACK TO THE QUORUM

At the end of his two terms as Secretary of Agriculture, President David O. McKay called Ezra to once again assume the presidency of the European Mission, which included four stakes and twelve missions. His notoriety as former U.S. Secretary of Agriculture meant that the press followed his arrival and subsequent activities with significant interest. Elder Benson used this opportunity to create a public relations organization in the mission that would enhance the visibility of the Church in Europe for the twenty-one months of his presidency. He also continued to speak on themes related to freedom. Some listeners equated his talks on freedom as being overdone, prompting Elder Benson to counsel with President McKay. The President only encouraged him to continue to speak his mind.

Some Americans wished Elder Benson would run for president of the United States. In the mid-1960s a committee was formed to encourage his candidacy. President McKay suggested that he neither encourage nor discourage such a movement and, over time, the interest dwindled.

When President McKay died on January 18, 1970, Ezra lost his beloved mission president. They had remained close throughout their lives, and Ezra was asked to offer the benediction at the funeral. On Friday, January 23, 1970, ninety-three-year-old Joseph Fielding Smith became the President of the Church. Two and a half years later, his death would result in Ezra's high school friend, Harold B. Lee, becoming President. Church members were shocked when President Lee soon died. This resulted in Ezra's thirty-year colleague in the Quorum of the Twelve, Spencer W. Kimball, becoming President of the Church. At that time Ezra would become the President of the Quorum of the Twelve.

PRESIDENT OF THE QUORUM

President Benson had felt for some time that it would be best if the Twelve could be relieved of their many administrative duties in order to focus on the spiritual affairs of the kingdom. He began by streamlining assignments within the Quorum. He also made sure meetings started and ended on time. Quorum members always felt they could speak freely about important items, but he was very effective in turning open discussions into united decisions—in the right way, at the right time, with the right feeling. His humility and openness impressed each quorum member to speak his mind without regard to seniority.

His diplomatic status as a former Secretary of Agriculture, combined with his affable manner in greeting and meeting with government officials, opened many doors for the Church and its missionaries throughout the world.

Given President Kimball's prophetic and electrifying vision of the spread of missionary work throughout the world, it was an advantage to have someone with President Benson's experience with diplomacy and government serving as President of the Quorum of the Twelve.

President Benson was intimately involved in several momentous events as quorum president. In 1976, the First Quorum of the Seventy was organized as a body of General Authorities. A year later, the Assistants to the Quorum of the Twelve were all added to that quorum. Later, in June of 1978, the revelation on priesthood extended the priesthood to all worthy males.

A personal challenge arose a month later, when he was knocked down by a horse that reared unexpectedly, and he broke his hip. The recuperation time was slow, but by September he was able to attend his quorum meetings and take care of regular Church business.

"No Empty Chairs"

President and Sister Benson were famous for their wonderful family life. An early television talk show, hosted by Edward R. Murrow called "Person to Person," featured a Benson family home evening. Millions of viewers watched the family talk and sing and answer questions from the host. Fan mail and comments from Mr. Murrow indicated that the episode was a hit and that many were touched by the evening with the Benson family. As the family grew and the Benson children married and had their own families, they got together often as an extended family. President Benson challenged his children to teach their children well, saying, "Let there be no empty chairs in our heavenly home." Another familiar quote to family members, repeated often by Sister Benson and attributed to her Scottish grandfather was, "The Lord bless ya and the devil miss ya!"

A virtual litany of "sayings" designed to remind children and grandchildren of the importance of living good lives and practicing good principles became familiar to the family through constant repetition:

"Prayer keeps you from sin and sin keeps you from prayer."

"It is better to prepare and prevent than to repair and repent."

"Never make a joke at someone's expense, especially to a spouse or child."

"Choose your love and love your choice."

"Don't major on the minor things."

"You are loved by many important people."

"The job is never done until they're safely dead." (Speaking of raising children.)

"Like a good game of tennis, to succeed you first must serve."

"If you can't stand for something you'll fall for anything."

"Crying children, like good resolutions, should be carried out."

"Don't be on time, be early."

"If you snooze, you lose."

Daughter Barbara Benson Walker says, "Mom and Dad used these little sayings all the time. We grew up with them and passed them on to our children."[9]

President Benson at a news conference the day after being named
President of the Church on November 10, 1985.

THE PRESIDENT

The last few years of President Spencer W. Kimball's life were fraught with poor health and diminished strength. When the phone call came announcing the death of the venerable prophet, President Ezra Taft Benson was stricken with grief and reverence for the ominous task that now fell to him. On the Sunday following the death of President Kimball, November 10, 1985, the Quorum of the Twelve met in the Salt Lake Temple at 3:00 PM. This most solemn of assemblies saw President Benson ask Gordon B. Hinckley and Thomas S. Monson to serve as his counselors. President Howard W. Hunter, next in seniority, pronounced Ezra Taft Benson's ordination and setting apart as President of The Church of Jesus Christ of Latter-day Saints. That evening the Bensons attended the previously scheduled Young Women fireside, broadcast by satellite from the Tabernacle on Temple Square.

The next morning, the traditional news conference announcing a new Church President was held in the foyer of the Church Administration Building.

President Benson vowed to continue the threefold mission emphasis (proclaim the gospel, perfect the Saints, redeem the dead) of the Church as outlined by President Kimball, and answered question from members of the press.

Several developments occurred under the new presidency. For instance, they announced that faithful member spouses of nonmembers could be endowed in the temple. Another action was to reach out in their Christmas message to alienated members and invite them to return to Church activity. A new set of missionary discussions was released in July 1986. They were designed to allow missionaries to teach more in their own words than previous discussions.

Important Events of President Benson's Presidency

- A new set of missionary discussions was published in July 1986 that focused less on memorization.

- The first stake in West Africa was organized as the Aba Nigeria Stake, May 15, 1988.

- The Church received legal recognition in Hungary and missionaries were allowed to serve to and from East Germany, both previously behind the "Iron Curtain" in June and November 1988, respectively. In 1990, missions were organized in the former Soviet Block countries of Czechoslovakia, Hungary, and Poland.

- Several countries gave the Church official legal recognition during President Benson's service as President. These included the African nations of Kenya, Ivory Coast, Zambia, Tanzania, and Ethiopia; Russia, Italy, Mexico, Madagascar, Cameroon, Mongolia, and Cambodia also granted official status to the Church.

- Nine temples were dedicated and 112 missions were created during President Benson's administration.

- Church records were completely digitized in 1991.

- Macmillan Publishing Company of New York produced the five-volume *Encyclopedia of Mormonism*.

- TempleReady, a computer program to clear ancestor names for temple ordinances, was unveiled in 1993.

- Church membership grew by approximately 2.6 million, and the overall missionary force grew by 18,000 during this time to a total of 47,311 by the end of 1994.[10]

Church growth featured the first stake organized in West Africa as well as the legal recognition of the Church in Hungary. In November of 1988 an agreement with the GDR (German Democratic Republic) allowed missionaries to serve there. Young men were also allowed to serve missions throughout the world from that country. These negotiations foretold the impending collapse of the Soviet Union.

Missionary work everywhere continued to flourish. Twenty-nine new missions were created in 1990 alone, and the equalization of mission costs for U.S. and Canadian missionaries, which made all monthly payments by parents the same for all missions, blessed the expansion of missionary work across the globe. In fact, over three hundred stakes were organized during President Benson's presidency. The Church grew from almost 6 million members to almost 9 million under his leadership. Nine new temples were dedicated and three rededicated after being refurbished. The Jerusalem Center was also completed and dedicated on May 16, 1989,

by then President of the Quorum of the Twelve Howard W. Hunter. A decision was made to close the old Hotel Utah in Salt Lake City. It was completely renovated to later reappear as the Joseph Smith Memorial Building.

New technological advances made possible the rollout of FamilySearch (a suite of computer programs designed to enhance and simplify family history work) and TempleReady (a software program that streamlined the clearance of names for temple work).

Perhaps it was only fitting that the Berlin Wall came down during President Benson's administration. No one better understood the importance of this symbolic fall of the Iron Curtain installed by the old Union of Soviet Socialist Republics. Communist nations in Europe were transformed during President Ezra Taft Benson's service as Church President. His strong admonitions on the evils of communism and the importance of freedom for Americans and all mankind seemed to be vindicated by these major world events.

President Benson waves as the First Presidency prepares for general conference.

Members grew to love President Benson. One thing the President did that endeared him to many, especially to children and their parents, was to sing in some regional conferences, a capella, the old children's song "I am a Mormon Boy." Sister Benson also delighted audiences from time to time by reciting from memory the lengthy Edgar A. Guest poem "Home."

As long as they could, President and Sister Benson attended the temple every Friday morning. Temple patrons were delighted to find themselves in an endowment session with the President of the Church and his wife. It elevated the importance of temple attendance in the eyes of many.

As President Benson aged, like President Kimball, he faced health concerns incident to old age. At age eighty-nine he had a mild heart attack that slowed him somewhat. Over time, he needed help getting around, and he began to attend general conference in a wheelchair. Then, on August 14, 1992, his beloved wife, Flora, died. They had been married for sixty-six years and Ezra was now alone. His health continued to decline until May 30, 1994—Memorial Day—when he died of heart failure at age ninety-four.

President and Sister Benson steal a kiss at the wedding breakfast of their granddaughter, Holly Walker, and her new husband, Karl Tilleman.[11]

TEACHINGS OF PRESIDENT
EZRA TAFT BENSON

———◆———

One month prior to the death of President Kimball, Elder Benson talked about the nature of God and the nature of men. He called on Church members to remember the greater purposes of God and how He works with His children. In the October 1985 general conference, Elder Benson said,

"The Lord works from the inside out. The world works from the outside in. The world would take people out of the slums. Christ takes the slums out of people, and then they take themselves out of the slums. The world would mold men by changing their environment. Christ changes men, who then change their environment. The world would shape human behavior, but Christ can change human nature."[5]

Within a month of saying this, President Kimball had passed away and this talk would be Ezra Taft Benson's first published talk while he was Church President. Surely the Lord had taken Ezra Taft Benson from the backwoods of Idaho and put him into positions where he could change his environment.

THE BOOK OF MORMON

"There are three ways in which the Book of Mormon is the keystone of our religion. It is the keystone in our witness of Christ. It is the keystone of our doctrine. It is the keystone of testimony."[12]

Early in his presidency, President Benson urged members to read and study the Book of Mormon, promising greater power in their lives as a result. He asked the General Authorities to read the book again before the April 1986 general conference where the Book of Mormon became the theme of his first talk. While he had spoken about the Book of Mormon many times before, his stature as President of the Church carried the message deep into the hearts of his listeners. He said,

"My beloved brethren and sisters, today I would like to speak about one of the most significant gifts given to the world in modern times. The gift I am thinking of is more important than any of the inventions that have come out of the industrial and technological revolutions. This is a gift of greater value to mankind than even the many wonderful advances we have seen in modern medicine. It is of greater worth to mankind than the development of flight or space travel. I speak of the gift of the Book of Mormon, given to mankind 156 years ago."[6]

He then referred to a "condemnation" spoken of by the Lord in Doctrine and Covenants 84:54–57, and related the warning to members in modern times.

"If the early Saints were rebuked for treating the Book of Mormon lightly, are we under any less condemnation if we do the same? The Lord Himself bears testimony that it is of eternal significance. Can a small number of us bring the whole Church under condemnation because we trifle with sacred things? What will we say at the Judgment when we stand before Him and meet His probing gaze if we are among those described as forgetting the new covenant?"[7]

"The Book of Mormon is the keystone of our religion, and the Doctrine and Covenants is the capstone, with continuing latter-day revelation."[13]

He urged members to read from its pages daily, and the Church membership responded with faith and enthusiasm— writing letters and sending cards to show their support and desire to come out from any possible "condemnation" of themselves or the Church. A general upsurge in spirituality seemed to follow his admonitions about reading the Book of Mormon. His 1988 book, *A Witness and a Warning: A Modern-Day Prophet Testifies of the Book of Mormon*, further made available his thoughts and talks about the Book of Mormon and its place in gospel living. As members immersed themselves in the Book of Mormon and more and more families made sure they had some kind of scripture study out of the Book of Mormon, spiritual commitment rose along with Church attendance. He wanted the earth "flooded" with the Book of Mormon, and missionary use of it in proselyting increased, as well as its placement in the homes of the friends and neighbors of Church members. It became the hallmark of his presidency—read and study the Book of Mormon.

> "What's best for the kingdom?"[14]

SPECIFIC COUNSEL

> "I have often said that one of the greatest secrets of missionary work is work! If a missionary works, he will get the Spirit; if he gets the Spirit, he will teach by the Spirit; and if he teaches by the Spirit, he will touch the hearts of the people and he will be happy. Work, work, work—there is no satisfactory substitute, especially in missionary work."[15]

The President delivered several general conference and special fireside talks to members in their various Church and family roles. He began by addressing remarks specifically to the Young Men of the Church in his April 1986 talk in the general priesthood meeting. He said:

"Young men, look forward to full-time missionary service. Show your love and commitment to the Lord by responding to His call to serve. Know that the real purpose in going into the mission field is to bring souls unto Christ, to teach and baptize our Heavenly Father's children so that you may rejoice with them in the kingdom of our Father. (See D&C 18:15.)"[8]

> "The revelation to produce and store food may be as essential to our temporal welfare today as boarding the ark was to the people in the days of Noah."[16]

He spoke "To the Mothers in Zion" in a February 1987 fireside and "To the Fathers in Israel" later the same year.[9] President Benson felt strongly that mothers should be at home raising their children rather than unnecessarily taking positions in the workplace. The Church later produced both talks in pamphlet form. He addressed the young women of the Church, and would go on to specifically address the children, single adult men, and single adult women in a similar format.[10] His counsel to returned missionaries and other young adult men to "arise from the dust . . . and be men" (2 Nephi 1:21) by faithfully seeking marriage, flew in the face of so-called modern ideas of waiting until one's late twenties or even thirties to marry. These talks, later made into pamphlets, were distributed throughout the Church. Bishops found them useful in encouraging members with the personalized information provided by President Benson. Faced with a changing society that reduced emphasis on the traditional family, President Benson's counsel sounded a clear call for righteousness and dedication as a counterpoint to other voices drawing attention to worldly solutions that caused confusion for some members.

> "If there is one message I have repeated to my brethren of the Twelve it is that it's the Spirit that counts. It is the Spirit that matters. I do not know how often I have said this, but I never tire of saying it—it is the Spirit that matters most."[17]

THE AMERICAN CONSTITUTION

In the October 1987 general conference he reflected on the bicentennial celebrations of the United States in 1976 and reminded his listeners of the inspired nature of the U.S. Constitution: "The Constitution of the United States has served as a model for many nations and is the oldest constitution in use today."[11] His experience at the heart of government as

Secretary of Agriculture no doubt gave him unique insight and deeper spiritual perspective regarding the Constitution. He felt strongly the need for Americans to cherish their freedom and the laws and practices that kept freedom intact. His ideas were expressed in strong words that did not allow people to misunderstand what he believed. He was bold and confident in his declarations about freedom and the nature of good government.

PRIDE

Perhaps President Benson's most powerful address was his last. Although he was unable to speak to conference attendees personally (President Hinckley read his speech), his admonitions in "Beware of Pride" seemed to strike a chord of truth within all who heard it. He wrote,

"The central feature of pride is enmity—enmity toward God and enmity toward our fellowmen. *Enmity* means 'hatred toward, hostility to, or a state of opposition.' It is the power by which Satan wishes to reign over us."

The idea that pride was based on hatred was moving to those who heard his words. Identifying pride as Satan's power carried an almost shocking impact as listeners awoke to the counsel they were receiving from one they held to be a prophet. He was not just referring to the wickedness found outside the Church, he was talking about members who could relate to the kind of pride he was referring to. He noted that when he said,

"Pride is essentially competitive in nature. We pit our will against God's. When we direct our pride toward God, it is in the spirit of 'my will and not thine be done.' As Paul said, they 'seek their own, not the things which are Jesus Christ's.' (Philippians 2:21.)

"Our will in competition to God's will allows desires, appetites, and passions to go unbridled. (See Alma 38:12; 3 Ne. 12:30.)"[12]

His words seemed to prick the collective conscience of all devout members of the Church. It caused them to reflect on how they could overcome the tendency to prideful selfishness and the problems and pain it produces. Generations of members have studied the talk with compelling interest as they sought to overcome their natural tendency to pride so typical of human nature.

President Benson would not speak in a general conference again prior to his death on Memorial Day, May 30, 1994. But his teachings persist as upcoming generations of young Latter-day Saints discover his words anew. To them he speaks with power and clear, convincing testimony of the importance of living the gospel with selfless enthusiasm and determination. He expressed his concerns in words that could not be ignored by those who heard them. The teachings of President Ezra Taft Benson clearly drew lines in the spiritual sand. Church members knew the danger of crossing those lines because their prophet had told them succinctly of the perils that lay in their path.

John P. Livingstone

Associate Professor of Church History and Doctrine, EdD
Brigham Young University

NOTES

1. Ezra Taft Benson, *A Labor of Love: The 1946 European Mission of Ezra Taft Benson* (Salt Lake City: Deseret Book, 1989), 65–66.
2. Ibid., 75–76.
3. Ibid., 169–70.
4. Ibid., 216.
5. Ezra Taft Benson, "Born of God," *Ensign*, November 1985, 65.
6. Ezra Taft Benson, "The Book of Mormon—Keystone of our Religion," CR, October 1986, 4.
7. Ibid, 4–5.
8. Ezra Taft Benson, "To the 'Youth of the Noble Birthright,'" *Ensign*, May 1986, 44.
9. Ezra Taft Benson, "To the Fathers in Israel," *Ensign*, November 1987, 48.
10. See Ezra Taft Benson, "To the Single Adult Brethren of the Church," *Ensign*, May 1988, 51; "To the Children of the Church," *Ensign*, May 1989, 81; "To 'the Rising Generation,'" *New Era*, June 1986, 4; "To the Single Adult Sisters of the Church," *Ensign*, November 1988, 96; "To the Home Teachers of the Church," *Ensign*, May 1987, 48; "To the 'Youth of the Noble Birthright,'" 43; "To the Young Women of the Church," *Ensign*, November 1986, 81.

11. Ezra Taft Benson, "Our Divine Constitution," *Ensign*, November 1987, 4.

12. Ezra Taft Benson, "Beware of Pride," *Ensign*, May 1989, 4.

SIDEBAR AND PHOTO NOTES

1. Photo courtesy of HBLL digital library.

2. Ezra Taft Benson, "What I Hope You Will Teach Your Children about the Temple," *Ensign*, August 1985, 6.

3. Sheri Dew, *Ezra Taft Benson: A Biography* (Salt Lake City: Deseret Book, 1987), 13–14.

4. *Collected Verse of Edgar A. Guest* (Chicago: Reilly and Lee Co., 1934), 12; Derin Head Rodriguez, "Flora Amussen Benson: Handmaiden of the Lord, Helpmeet of a Prophet, Mother in Zion," *Ensign*, March 1987, 14.

5. Photo courtesy of HBLL digital library.

6. Ezra Taft Benson, *A Labor of Love: The 1946 European Mission of Ezra Taft Benson* (Salt Lake City: Deseret Book, 1989), 47–49.

7. Benson, *A Labor of Love*, 74.

8. See Dew, *Ezra Taft Benson*, 15–303.

9. Barbara Benson Walker, interview by author, January 19, 2004; interview notes in author's possession.

10. See *Deseret News 1999–2000 Church Almanac* (Salt Lake City: Deseret News, 1998), 554.

11. Photo courtesy of Ferrel A. Massey.

12. Benson, "The Book of Mormon—Keystone of our Religion," 3–7.

13. Ezra Taft Benson, "The Book of Mormon and the Doctrine and Covenants," *Ensign*, May 1987, 83.

14. Ezra Taft Benson, quoted by Boyd K. Packer, "We Honor Now His Journey," *Ensign*, July 1994, 32.

15. Ezra Taft Benson, "Keys to Successful Member-Missionary Work," *Ensign*, September 1990, 2.

16. Benson, "To the Fathers in Israel," 48.

17. Ezra Taft Benson, address at mission presidents' seminar, April 3, 1985, cited in *Missionary Guide: Training for Missionaries* (1988), 73.

Chapter Fourteen

HOWARD W. HUNTER

LIFE AND TIMES

1907	November 14	Born in Boise, Idaho, to John William Hunter and Nellie Marie Rasmussen Hunter
1920	April 4	Howard and sister, Dorothy, are baptized in indoor swimming pool in Boise, Idaho
1923	May 11	Earned rank of Eagle Scout, the second Eagle in the state of Idaho
1924		Organized Hunter's Croonaders dance band
1927	January 5	Set sail on *SS President Jackson* with Hunter's Croonaders for a two-month cruise of the Orient
1927	February 6	Father, Will Hunter, baptized a member of the Church
1928	March 13	Moved to Los Angeles, California
1930		Hired as a junior officer at First Exchange State Bank in Inglewood, California
1931	June 10	Married Claire Jeffs in the Salt Lake Temple; they have three sons: Howard William (Billy) Hunter Jr., who dies at age six months; John Jacob Hunter, and Richard Allen Hunter
1934	January	Worked in title department of Los Angeles County Flood Control District
1939	June 8	Graduated *cum laude*, third in his class, from Southwestern University School of Law; in October, he passed the California Bar Exam
1940	April	Began law practice after being admitted to California Bar
1940	August 27	Called as bishop of newly organized El Sereno Ward, Pasadena Stake
1950	February 25	Called as stake president of the Pasadena Stake in California
1959	October 15	Ordained an Apostle by President David O. McKay
1961	April	Moved from California to Salt Lake City
1972		Claire's health began to deteriorate
1980	July 23	Suffered his first heart attack
1983	October 9	Claire died
1986	October 12	Had coronary bypass surgery
1990	April 10	Married Inis Bernice Egan in the Salt Lake Temple
1994	June 5	Ordained fourteenth President of The Church of Jesus Christ of Latter-day Saints
1995	March 3	Died at home in Salt Lake City, Utah, at age eighty-seven

BIOGRAPHICAL HIGHLIGHTS

Growing up in Boise, Idaho, Howard W. Hunter was involved in the little branch of the Church there, attending church with his mother and younger sister. His father was not a member of the Church until after Howard was grown, but he was supportive of the family's church activities. As a young man, President Hunter performed in his own dance band, Hunter's Croonaders, which performed on a cruise ship through the Orient. He then moved to California where he met his wife, Claire Jeffs. He supported himself and his family as he went through law school and became an attorney in California.

His church service included Scoutmaster, bishop, high priest group leader, and stake president before he was called as a member of the Quorum of the Twelve Apostles, where he served for thirty-four years, including ten years as the Acting President or President of the Quorum of the Twelve. President Howard W. Hunter was ordained and set apart as the fourteenth President of the Church on June 5, 1994. He served as the President of the Church for only nine months, the shortest period a President has served in the history of the Church.

CONTRIBUTIONS AND TEACHINGS

Although his tenure as the President of the Church was a brief nine months, he made a significant contribution to the direction of the Church. President Hunter's presidency is characterized by a focus on Christlike living and temple worthiness.

He desired Church members to give more attention to studying the life of Christ and to following the example of love, compassion, kindness, and forgiveness that Christ set for us. He called out to Church members who had been hurt or disaffected from the Church to come back and partake of the blessings of the Church again. President Hunter also asked that all adult Church members be worthy of and carry a temple recommend. He suggested that we should see the temple as a symbol of our membership in the Church, to focus our efforts to become temple worthy, and to teach our children the importance of temple covenants and ordinances. During President Hunter's time as President, Church members made a greater effort to utilize the temple and to maintain their temple recommends.

LIFE OF
HOWARD W. HUNTER

◆

Although his tenure as the President of The Church of Jesus Christ of Latter-day Saints lasted only nine months (June 5, 1994–March 3, 1995), President Howard W. Hunter made important contributions to the Church throughout his life. President Hunter's life was centered on the gospel and on Christlike service. During the years leading up to his call as the prophet, Howard W. Hunter emphasized in his teachings that we should be focused on becoming more like Christ. At the time of his call as the prophet, he invited all Church members to "establish the temple of the Lord as the great symbol of their membership."[1] Both his life and his teachings show that his presidency continued laying the foundation upon which the future of the Church could be built.

FAMILY BACKGROUND

Howard William Hunter was born in Boise, Idaho, on November 14, 1907, to Nellie Marie Rasmussen and John William Hunter. His sister, Dorothy, was born two years later. Although several of his progenitors had joined the Church, Howard's father, Will, was not baptized a member of The Church of Jesus Christ of Latter-day Saints until February 6, 1927. His Hunter ancestors had joined the Church in Scotland and had come to Utah in 1860, only to become disaffected from the Church soon after their arrival. Will's mother's ancestors had also been Church members a generation before, but his mother's family had become inactive, some of them marrying out of the Church. The Hunter family continued to have some ties with friends and family who were Church members, but Will Hunter was not reared as a member of the Church. He lived much of his early life in Boise, Idaho.[2]

Portrait of parents: Nellie R. and Will Hunter.

Nellie Rasmussen came from a family of pioneer ancestors, many of whom were among the earliest Church members in Scandinavia, immigrating to Utah by the end of the 1850s. They settled in Mount Pleasant, Sanpete County, Utah. Nellie's mother passed away when Nellie was two years old, and she grew up in several homes of different relatives, until her aunt and uncle invited her to live with them in Boise, Idaho. Nellie was nineteen years of age, and, after arriving in Boise, she met Will Hunter.[3] Nellie and Will courted and corresponded through letters while Will was working away from town, and by 1906, Will proposed marriage to Nellie. She was unsure whether she should marry a man who was not a member of the Church, so she traveled to visit relatives in Colorado and Mount Pleasant to think about the proposal. After some time, Will followed Nellie to Mount Pleasant, and by December 3, 1906, they were married in Mount Pleasant. The next day, they took the train back to Boise, where they made their home.[4]

Howard W. Hunter at eight months.

Howard W. Hunter at about one year of age.

CHILDHOOD AND EARLY FAMILY LIFE

Nellie gave birth to their son, Howard William Hunter, on November 14, 1907, and his sister, Dorothy Elaine, was born two years later on November 1, 1909. Although growing up in what might be termed a "part-member" family, Howard W. Hunter and his younger sister Dorothy were taught the truths of the gospel at an early age. Their mother was a faithful Latter-day Saint, ensuring that her children participated fully in Church meetings and teaching her children the gospel at home. Although he was not a member of the Church, Will was supportive of the Church activity of his wife and children throughout the early years. He occasionally attended Church when his work schedule permitted.

From his earliest childhood, Howard had a testimony of the gospel. He knew that God lived. He remembered, "My mother had taught me to pray and to thank Heavenly

Portrait of young Howard W. Hunter.

Portrait of Howard W. Hunter at about age five.

Father for all the things I enjoyed. . . . I also learned to ask Him for the things that I wanted or needed."[5] Although he had a testimony, Howard was not baptized at age eight. His father wanted him to wait to be baptized until he was old enough to decide for himself which church he should join. When he turned twelve and saw his friends ordained deacons and passing the sacrament, Howard again requested that his father give him permission to be baptized. Finally, nearly five months after his twelfth birthday, on April 4, 1920, both Howard and Dorothy were baptized at the Natatorium, an indoor swimming complex in Boise.

When Howard turned twelve, his father allowed him to participate in the Church-sponsored Boy Scout troop in Boise. He worked hard at earning merit badges and enjoyed participating in Scout camps. He received his Eagle Scout award in May 1923, having earned a total of thirty-two merit badges. He was the second boy to reach the rank of Eagle in all of Idaho.[6]

Howard W. Hunter in his Boy Scout uniform.

Howard and Dorothy with their dog at the irrigation ditch in Boise, Idaho.

Youth in Boise

While growing up in Boise, Howard W. Hunter was an ambitious individual. In high school, he performed well both academically and socially, focusing on many interests. In addition to his schoolwork, he had several jobs throughout his early years, including caddying, serving ice cream sodas, writing advertising copy for a newspaper, and working at a local hotel doing maintenance and as a bellboy.[7]

Music was an important part of Howard's youth. As a child, he took piano and violin lessons. After winning a marimba from a local music store, he taught himself to play it. He also performed on the drums, saxophone, clarinet, and trumpet.[8] He played music for dances most weekends all through high school, sometimes traveling many miles from home.[9] After high school he formed his own band, Hunter's Croonaders, which performed on weekends throughout Idaho. The Hunter's Croonaders band was invited by the Admiral Oriental Line to become the onboard dance band as the ship sailed throughout Asia.[10] They spent two months on a cruise that ended in February 1927, seeing many sights and experiencing things that would not have been typical for a boy from Idaho.

When he arrived home from the cruise, he found out that his father had been baptized a member of the Church while he was away. For the first time, his whole family was involved in the Church in Boise. The baptism of his father was a great joy and blessing for Howard.

After his experience in the Orient, Howard ambitiously tried several different business ventures: selling shoes, performing with his band, and marketing transportation and postal schedules.[11] When these activities did not go as well as he had hoped, he went to Los Angeles to visit a friend who had traveled with the Croonaders. During that trip, he stayed with his father's aunt and uncle. He enjoyed a few weeks of vacation and relaxation and then decided that if he found a good job, he would like to live in California.[12]

California Life and Courtship

With his friend, Bill Salisbury, Howard worked in the Sunkist packing house for a few days and as a shoe salesman in Huntington Park on weekends, but he soon decided that he would rather work at a bank. He applied and was immediately hired at the main office for the Bank of Italy in downtown Los Angeles, learning to use adding and bookkeeping machines and to process deposits. At the same time, Howard enrolled in evening classes to work toward a college degree. In addition to his work and classes, he performed with dance bands on many weekends and evenings. While living in Huntington Park with his uncle and aunt, Edward and Lyde Nowell, he became a member of the Huntington

Howard Hunter (center, holding saxophone) and his band,
Hunter's Croonaders.

Park Ward, and was involved in many church activities.[13] On
June 8, 1928, at an M-Men and Gleaner dance sponsored
by the Mutual Improvement Association, Howard met his
future wife, Clara May (Claire) Jeffs. The first night he met
her, she was his friend's date. He said that the next time his
group of friends went out, "I took Claire."[14]

In the fall of 1928, Howard's parents and his sister,
Dorothy, arrived in California, where they decided to live
after Will Hunter's job in Boise was no longer available. After
his family found an apartment, Howard moved in with them.
He became an active member of the Adams Ward, serving in
the elders quorum presidency and as Scoutmaster.[15] In addition to his church assignments, he was busy with his work
at the Bank of Italy, performing at dances, taking banking
classes at night, and maintaining a busy social life. In early
1931, Claire and Howard were considering marriage, but
Howard still had a desire to serve a mission. Claire was willing to wait for him, working and supporting him financially

Young Howard the musician, with his saxophone.

Clara May Jeffs as a teenager.

Howard W. Hunter as a young man.

Claire and Howard close to the time they married.

while he was gone, but he did not feel right about that idea. They decided instead to marry and serve a mission together later in their lives.

The decision to marry in the Salt Lake Temple led to other influential decisions in Howard's life. During the temple recommend interview in preparation for his marriage, the bishop asked Howard how he could support his wife on such a low income. The bishop had seen how much tithing he paid and surmised that his income was small. Howard realized that because he had grown up in a part-member home, he had not been taught the importance of tithing, and so had not been a full tithe-payer. He and Claire resolved to live the law of tithing throughout their marriage.

Howard made another major decision before his marriage regarding his musical activities. He recognized that, in spite of his enjoyment of music, he did not want to have a musician's life which sometimes led to association with others with lower moral standards. On June 6, 1931, four days before his wedding, Howard played his last engagement, then packed up his instruments and put them away, not playing them again except in the company of close family and friends.[16]

CAREER AND FAMILY LIFE

At the marriage sealing in the Salt Lake Temple, Elder Richard R. Lyman of the Quorum of the Twelve Apostles had advised Howard and Claire not to go into debt, being sure to live within their means. They were careful in buying the necessities of life, even if they did not have everything they wanted.[17] Although the effects of the stock market crash in October 1929 were felt by his family, Howard's employment at the First Exchange State Bank continued until 1932 when the bank was finally forced to close. Because they had been careful about not getting into debt, the young couple was not in the great financial difficulty that others around them experienced. Howard worked at a variety of jobs over the next two years, making just enough money to survive. When it became too hard to make ends meet, Howard and Claire moved into Claire's parents' home in Los Angeles, where they stayed the next three years. Howard worked for a time for his father-in-law, Jacob Jeffs, painting bridges over a new highway.[18]

LAW SCHOOL

Howard's interest in the law was piqued when, in January 1934, he began to work in the title department of the Los Angeles County Flood Control District. This job involved working with many legal matters, including examining titles, writing legal documents, and helping attorneys prepare cases involving property and flood control. He decided to enroll in Southwestern University's law school because it had a night program. Prior to beginning his law studies, however, he had to take many prerequisite classes because he did not have an undergraduate degree. He was very busy working full-time during the day and taking a full load of courses in the evening. For the next five years as he pursued his degree he kept up this schedule, usually not arriving home in the evening until 10:00 PM, and spending many hours while at home studying and preparing for his classes.[19]

On March 20, 1934, Howard and Claire became the parents of their first son, Howard William Hunter Jr. During the summer of that year, they noticed that Billy seemed lethargic. Because of the doctor's diagnosis of anemia, Howard donated blood for the baby. Billy still did not thrive and was finally admitted to the hospital in early September for additional tests. Doctors found a problem with his intestine that was causing blood loss, and scheduled surgery. During the operation, Howard again gave blood for the baby. After the surgery, little Billy was still critically ill, and his parents stayed with him constantly for the next seventy-two hours. On the evening of the third day, they returned home to have some rest. Howard wrote, "We had not been home long when a call came asking us to return to the hospital because there had been a turn for the worse. Later that night, October 11, 1934, he slipped quietly away as we sat by his bed. We were grief-stricken and numb as we left the hospital into the night."[20]

In June 1939, Howard W. Hunter finished his law school examinations and graduated third in his class, with *cum laude* recognition. In October, he took the California Bar Examination and was relieved in December to learn that he passed. On April 1, 1940, he began his own law practice in rented offices in downtown Los Angeles, while continuing to work part-time for the Los Angeles County Flood Control District for five more years.[21] During Howard's law school years, Claire gave birth to two more sons: John Jacob Hunter, born May 4, 1936, and Richard Allen Hunter, born June 29, 1938.

FATHERHOOD

While his sons grew, Howard was busy with his law practice and his Church assignments as a bishop and later as stake president. In spite of his heavy responsibilities, his children remember that both their parents were involved in their lives. Even before the Church had formally adopted Monday as the night for family home evening, the Hunters met together regularly as a family to share gospel lessons, have fun, or go on special outings. Howard and Claire spent time teaching their children the gospel and helping them with their schoolwork or other activities. The boys attended music lessons, and their father helped them in practicing their musical instruments. After a couple of years, Howard decided that their interest in music was not as high as his own, and allowed them to stop their lessons. Although Howard no longer played music professionally, when among family members and friends, he sometimes performed on the piano or clarinet to accompany the singing of hymns, songs, or favorite dance tunes from his youth.

When John and Richard were old enough to participate in Scouting, their father and mother helped them with their merit badges, often spending nights camping and going on river trips.[22] Both John and Richard served missions to Australia, and Howard and Claire received permission from the Church's missionary committee to take Richard to his mission field at the time they went to pick up John from his mission in 1958. On the way to Australia, they visited Hawaii, Fiji, and New Zealand. After being reunited with John and saying farewell to Richard, the family continued to travel around the world for two months, visiting more than twenty countries in the Orient, Middle East, and Europe.[23]

As Howard's law practice grew in the 1940s and 1950s, he specialized in corporate and business law, along with probate issues. His legal work with businesses and corporations led to his being appointed to the boards of many of the companies he represented. He was known as an honest and kind counselor and friend to the people with whom he worked. His ability to determine the essential elements of legal problems and to communicate well with others led to great respect from his clients, colleagues, and even by attorneys on the opposing sides of his legal cases.[24] At times, when his clients were unable to pay, he did not charge them for the legal advice he had given.[25]

CHURCH SERVICE IN CALIFORNIA

In addition to working and studying full-time during the early years of marriage, Howard and his wife, Claire, were involved in the Alhambra Ward's MIA program. They also chaired the financial committee for the building fund because the ward was meeting in a rented hall. This experience was helpful to his future callings when as a bishop he gathered funds to buy a lot for a chapel for his new ward. Again as a stake president, he was involved in raising the money for a Pasadena Stake Center and the construction of the Los Angeles Temple.[26]

In August 1940, the Hunters learned that their Alhambra Ward was going to be divided and they would be part of the newly formed El Sereno Ward. Howard was surprised to be called to serve as bishop of the new ward. With two children and his law practice underway, Howard and Claire purchased a new home with a little more room. They found one that had a room he could convert into an office where he could meet with ward members. He served as the bishop for six years. In 1948,

The Hunter family in California: Richard, Claire, John, and Howard.

the Hunters again moved to a new home in Arcadia, becoming members of the Las Flores Ward. As Southern California continued to grow in population, the Church membership also grew. The Pasadena Stake was divided on February 25, 1950, and Howard W. Hunter was called by Elders Stephen L Richards and Harold B. Lee of the Quorum of the Twelve Apostles as the new stake president.

During his tenure as stake president, he was also called as chairman of the Southern California regional council of stake presidents, where he was involved in several developments, including the building of the Los Angeles Temple. While he presided over the Pasadena Stake, he noted the importance of family home evening in his own family. Although the Church had suggested that families make an effort to be together one night a week, it was not a Churchwide program. The Pasadena Stake, under the direction of President Hunter, adopted Monday nights for family home evening as a stake-wide program. The Pasadena Stake and other surrounding stakes of the Los Angeles area were asked to pioneer a new early-morning seminary program for high school students. Howard was appointed as the chairman of the committee to study the feasibility of such a program, and then to implement early-morning seminary for three high schools in the area. The response from the young students was so positive that early-morning seminary later became a Churchwide program.[27]

One memorable experience occurred on his forty-sixth birthday in 1953. The Pasadena Stake had an excursion to the Mesa Arizona Temple, where he spoke at a special meeting in the chapel of the temple. Without his knowledge, his parents, Will and Nellie Hunter, had prepared themselves to go to the temple for their own ordinances. As he spoke to his stake members, he looked up to see his parents enter the chapel both dressed in white. They received their endowments and sealing that day, and Howard was also sealed to them.[28]

SERVICE IN THE QUORUM OF TWELVE APOSTLES

On October 9, 1959, Howard W. Hunter traveled to Salt Lake City for the general conference of the Church. After the first session, one of his stake counselors saw Howard and

Teaching as a Bishop

As a young bishop in the El Sereno Ward in Los Angeles, California, Howard W. Hunter knew the importance of loving and teaching the young women and young men. According to the memories of one of the young women in the ward, the teenagers were constantly invited to participate in activities with their bishop leading the way. The group of teenagers was hard for their Sunday School teachers to manage, so Bishop Hunter often taught the class. "The bishop never used a lesson manual or read a lesson. He just sort of chatted with us. . . . It didn't seem to be a formal lesson, but an informal discussion that was always interesting enough to keep everyone's attention. . . . I remember thinking that the bishop really knew a lot of stuff."[1]

said that President David O. McKay wanted to speak with him. He assumed that the purpose for the visit was to report on an issue the First Presidency had asked him to consider. His journal states that President McKay invited him in, and directly stated, "The Lord has spoken. You are called to be one of his special witnesses, and tomorrow you will be sustained as a member of the Council of the Twelve." Howard's feelings at that time were multi-faceted. He wrote, "Tears came to my eyes and I could not speak. I have never felt so completely humbled as when I sat in the presence of this great, sweet, kindly man—the prophet of the Lord. . . . The interview lasted only a few minutes, and as I left I told him I loved the Church, that I sustained him and the other members of the First Presidency and the Council of the Twelve, and I would gladly give my time, my life, and all that I possessed to this service."[29]

The calling to the Quorum of the Twelve changed Howard's life dramatically. He felt the weight of the charge to bear testimony to the world and to spend all his efforts and energies in building up the kingdom of God. Prior to his call, he and Claire had become grandparents for the first time as their son John and his wife, Louine, had a son, Robert. Now, with a calling as an Apostle, gone were the thoughts that he could spend the rest of his days in a leisurely manner, enjoying retirement with his friends and family in California. Instead, he immediately began his work as a special witness of Jesus Christ, while still working as an attorney in California.

A year and a half passed before Howard was able to completely transfer his legal work to his law partner. At the same time, he was serving as a member of the Quorum of the Twelve. During those many months of commuting from California, Howard would spend the early part of the week at his office in Los Angeles, then board a train or an airplane on Tuesday or Wednesday for a trip to Salt Lake City, where he would arrive in time for the Thursday morning meetings of the Quorum of the Twelve and the First Presidency. He would then spend the next few days taking care of the business and Church matters at his office in the Church Administration Building. In addition, he frequently traveled to stake conferences on the weekends, arriving home in California late on Sundays or early Monday mornings in time to return to his law office for a new week. Elder and Sister Hunter finally sold their home in California and moved to Salt Lake City in April 1961.[30]

ASSIGNMENTS AND TRAVELS

As a member of the Quorum of the Twelve Apostles, Howard kept up his usual hectic pace, as he had done from his youth. He had many opportunities to travel on assignment to meet with members of the Church throughout the world. In the summer of 1960, their son Richard was released as a missionary in Australia, and Howard and Claire had planned to take

him on a two-month world tour as they had done with John. After his call to the Twelve, Howard was reluctant to take so much time away from his responsibilities, but President McKay encouraged him to go ahead, since he could spend some of his travel time meeting with Church members and conducting official visits. This tour was the beginning of travels he made throughout the United States and to many countries of the world, which led President Thomas S. Monson to call him the "most-traveled General Authority" at his funeral in March 1995.[31]

Several important assignments that Elder Hunter received while he was a member of the Quorum of the Twelve

Major Assignments and Events from 1961–1994, While He Was in the Quorum of the Twelve

1961	January	Appointed as chair of the advisory board for New World Archaeological Foundation, based at Brigham Young University
1964	January	Assigned as president of the Genealogical Society of Utah
1965	January	Appointed as president and chairman of the board of Polynesian Cultural Center in Hawaii
1966	June	Oversaw dedication of Granite Mountain Record Vault, where the Church stores genealogical microfilms
1969	August	Coordinated first Church-sponsored World Conference on Records and the concurrent World Convention and Seminar on Genealogy in Salt Lake City
1970		Called as Church historian and recorder
1974		Appointed to oversee funding and building of Orson Hyde Memorial Garden in Jerusalem. The dedication occurred on October 24, 1979
1979	April	First Presidency authorized him to negotiate purchase of property for BYU's Jerusalem Center for Near Eastern Studies
1985	November 10	Set apart as Acting President of the Quorum of the Twelve due to President Marion G. Romney's ill health
1988	June 2	Set apart as President of the Quorum of the Twelve
1989	May	Dedicated BYU Jerusalem Center
1993	February 7	Unharmed when an intruder threatened him during a speech at Brigham Young University's Marriott Center

had an impact on his life and teachings. Among these were his role in the development of the Church's presence in the Holy Land and his involvement in genealogy and Church history. His other major assignments included serving as the chair of the advisory board for Brigham Young University's New World Archaeological Foundation (appointed in January 1961) and as president of the board of the Polynesian Cultural Center in Laie, Hawaii (appointed in January 1965). Both of these assignments led to numerous trips to Mexico, Central America, and Hawaii. In addition to travels associated with these appointments, Elder Hunter also spent many weeks throughout his service as a General Authority meeting with Latter-day Saints all over the world in stake conferences and other assignments.

THE HOLY LAND

One of the early trips Elder Hunter made as a newly ordained Apostle was a tour to Israel, Egypt, and the Middle East during Christmas 1961. He and Claire traveled with Elder Spencer and Sister Camilla Kimball as they traced the steps of Abraham, Moses, Mary and Joseph, and Jesus during His mortal ministry. In a letter Elder Hunter and Elder Kimball sent to the other members of their quorum, they said, "We believe these travels will have made us more aware of the realness of the past; the relationship of the past to the present; and our debt to our Lord whose life and death and sacrifice seem even more real."[32] Elder Hunter had many more opportunities to visit the Holy Land on official Church business because of his assignment to oversee the development and building of both the Orson Hyde Memorial Garden in Jerusalem and the Brigham Young University Jerusalem Center for Near Eastern Studies.

The Orson Hyde Memorial Garden was created to honor Elder Orson Hyde's visit to Jerusalem in 1841 when he offered a prayer of dedication on the Mount of Olives. The Church desired to place a monument commemorating the prayer of Orson Hyde. On one of his trips to Jerusalem, Elder Hunter met with government officials and looked for a possible site for the monument. The City of Jerusalem was interested in creating a greenbelt area on the Mount of

A portrait of the Hunters when he was in the Quorum of the Twelve.

Olives, and Elder Hunter was able to negotiate for a sizeable area to be developed as the memorial. The First Presidency then assigned Elder Hunter and Elder LeGrand Richards to oversee the entire project, including raising the funds for its development. Five years after the initial proposal and negotiations, Elder Hunter was in attendance at the dedication of the garden. During the many experiences in the Holy Land, Howard Hunter became a very good and trusted friend with long-time mayor of Jerusalem, Teddy Kollek. Elder Hunter received the Medal of the city of Jerusalem at the same time as the dedication of the Orson Hyde Memorial Garden.[33] Their friendship would last throughout their lives, as evidenced by Mr. Kollek's expression of condolence at the time of President Hunter's passing in 1995.[34]

The second major assignment in Jerusalem for Elder Hunter was the building of BYU's Jerusalem Center for Near Eastern Studies. This particular responsibility was given to him at the time the garden was nearing completion.

Upon finding a suitable site for the center on the Mount of Olives, the Church and its representatives began making negotiations with the city for approval both of the concept for the center and the architectural design. The process of gaining authorization for the center was only one of the difficulties. There were many local people, both Israelis and Palestinians, who were opposed to the Church's having any permanent presence there, even in the form of an educational center. After the lease for the land was signed in 1984, many people were angry and asked that the government rescind their permission for the project. Elder Hunter's negotiation skills, able legal mind, and sensitivity to others were essential in retaining the center's position. The problem was resolved after Elder Hunter worked with all the parties and provided the government with the Church's agreement not to use the center as a proselyting tool. The United States Congress also wrote a letter in

BYU Jerusalem Center for Near Eastern Studies

Howard W. Hunter was a key figure in the building of the BYU Jerusalem Center as the Church's representative and negotiator for the Center. About his leadership on the project, James E. Faust stated, "During the building of the BYU Jerusalem Center, President Hunter and I went to the Holy Land on a regular basis. President Hunter had the assignment under the First Presidency to make all the arrangements for building the center. That included finding a site to lease land for building the center, and to work with the architects and move forward with the building. . . . Whenever we would run into difficulties, which would seem insurmountable, President Hunter always would say, 'I think we should just go ahead.' . . . He didn't get upset. He was able to keep his balance and his moorings all the time. He would just be his gracious, cordial, friendly personality with everybody he met."[2]

Similarly, Jeffrey R. Holland, who at the time was the president of BYU, remarked, "It goes without saying that without President Howard W. Hunter . . . there would have been no BYU Jerusalem Center. He was the constant thread and the loving watchman on the tower over that project from the time it was only a dream, and from the time the Orson Hyde Memorial Garden was being planned. . . . He was visionary and solid as a rock. He was always absolute, a valiant defender of the principles in which he believed and of the truths he loved."[3]

Dedication of Orson Hyde Memorial Gardens in Jerusalem on October 29, 1979. Pictured are Spencer W. Kimball, Camilla E. Kimball, Dorothy H. Rasmussen (Howard's sister), Howard W. Hunter, Jerusalem Mayor Teddy Kolleck, Ezra Taft Benson, and Flora A. Benson.

At the Garden Tomb in 1985 with the Fausts and the Hollands.

support of the center. In May 1989, as a member of BYU's Board of Trustees and President of the Quorum of the Twelve Apostles, Howard W. Hunter gave the dedicatory prayer for BYU's Jerusalem Center for Near Eastern Studies.[35]

GENEALOGY AND CHURCH HISTORY

In 1964, Howard W. Hunter became president of the Genealogical Society of Utah, currently called the Family and Church History Department of the Church. The Society directed all the genealogical work of the Church, including microfilming records throughout the world, developing the world's largest genealogical library in Salt Lake City, and providing teaching tools to help people in their own family history research. Previous to his appointment as president of

the society, he had served for three years as a member of the board of directors. After his release as president eight years later, he continued to serve on the board for three more years until 1975.[36]

During the time Elder Hunter was heavily involved in the Genealogical Society of Utah, the society implemented new developments and policies that had a far-reaching effect on the genealogical activity of the Church and its members. For example, the Church constructed the Granite Mountain Records Vault in 1966, which houses millions of microfilms of genealogical records. Under Elder Hunter's direction, the Church sponsored the 1969 World Conference on Records and the concurrent World Convention and Seminar on Genealogy in Salt Lake City, bringing together world-renown archivists, government officials, and genealogists to discuss the importance of record-keeping, preservation, and dissemination. Before he was released from that assignment in 1972, Elder Hunter had guided the society to begin utilizing computers in the processes of recording data and preparing names for temple work.[37]

Elder Hunter was appointed as the Church Historian and Recorder in 1970, replacing Joseph Fielding Smith who had become the President of the Church. The Historian's Office included not only a large staff, but also many thousands of volumes of records, histories, and documents relating to the history of the Church. The responsibility of the historian was to keep a "record of all things that transpire in Zion" (D&C 85:1). Not only was his office in charge of the historical documents of the Church, but it also had to make decisions regarding preservation and microfilming of records.

PRESIDENT OF THE QUORUM OF THE TWELVE

At the death of President Spencer W. Kimball in November 1985, Marion G. Romney became the President of the Quorum of the Twelve. Because of his ill health, however, he was unable to carry out the duties of that calling, and Howard W. Hunter was sustained as Acting President of the Quorum. He continued in this position until after the death of President Romney. President Hunter was set apart on June 2, 1988, to be the President of the Quorum of the Twelve. As the senior member of the Council of the Twelve, his responsibilities included overseeing a number of the Church's general departments and committees. He continued to travel extensively and to participate in stake and regional conferences, despite the fact that his health began to deteriorate, and for some time he was in a wheelchair.[38]

Howard W. Hunter as the Church Historian examines the records in the Historian's office, 1970.

Genealogy

Important developments in family history and genealogical research during Howard W. Hunter's involvement with the Genealogical Society of Utah in the 1960s and 1970s:

- Dedication of the Granite Mountain Records Vault to house genealogical microfilms, June 1966

- World Conference on Records and the concurrent World Convention and Seminar on Genealogy in Salt Lake City, August 3–8, 1969.

- Establishment of Branch Genealogical Libraries, eventually housing them in stake centers throughout the Church.

- Development of the Four-Generation Program, asking all Church members to compile their own records and ensure temple work was completed for at least four generations back.

- Use of computer systems for data collection, storage, and analysis.

Teachings about Adversity

Howard W. Hunter experienced much adversity in life, including his own health problems, the deteriorating health and death of his wife, Claire, and the death of his baby son, Billy. He taught about adversity as one who had experience:

"I have observed that life—every life—has a full share of ups and downs. Indeed, we see many joys and sorrows in the world, many changed plans and new directions, many blessings that do not always look or feel like blessings, and much that humbles us and improves our patience and our faith. We have all had those experiences from time to time, and I suppose we always will."[4]

"Doors close regularly in our lives, and some of those closings cause genuine pain and heartache. But I do believe that where one such door closes, another opens (and perhaps more than one), with hope and blessings in other areas of our lives that we might not have discovered otherwise."[5]

"I acknowledge that I have faced a few [personal difficulties], and you will undoubtedly face some of your own now and later in your life. When these experiences humble us and refine us and teach us and bless us, they can be powerful instruments in the hands of God to make us better people, to make us more grateful and more loving, to make us more considerate of other people in their own times of difficulty."[6]

"Adversity touches many, many lives. What makes the difference is how we accept it. It's important to know it's all within the purposes of the Lord, whatever they are for us. If we can submit ourselves to that, we can go forward in faith and understanding."[7]

PERSONAL LIFE WHILE SERVING IN THE QUORUM OF THE TWELVE

The years of serving in the Council of the Twelve in the late 1970s and the 1980s, although very fulfilling, were also somewhat difficult for Elder Hunter in his personal life. His wife, Claire, suffered from ill health for more than a decade. Her health difficulties included headaches, loss of memory, cerebral hemorrhages, and other problems. During this time period, in spite of his heavy schedule of travel and work at the office, Elder Hunter spent many hours each day and night caring for Claire. In 1981, she suffered another cerebral hemorrhage that left her without the ability to walk or communicate, but Elder Hunter insisted on caring for her at home with the help of a nurse. Eighteen months before her death in 1983, she was moved to a care center, and Elder Hunter visited her daily. He showed her much love and affection throughout this period of trial, although she was in a coma and could not respond to him.[39]

Two of his fellow members of the Twelve commented on Elder Hunter's care for Claire. Elder James E. Faust wrote, "In 1983 his beloved wife, Clara Jeffs Hunter, passed away. She had suffered a devastating stroke several years before that had left her very much diminished. President Hunter tended to her needs,

providing loving care with respect and an uncommon devotion for many years, with a complete disregard for his own health. But there was a reward, for as diminished as she was, Claire would smile and respond only to him. . . . We have never seen such an example of devotion of a husband to his wife. Theirs was a many-splendored love affair. Love is service."[40] President Gordon B. Hinckley, in speaking at the funeral for President Hunter, said the following: "Claire suffered much in the later years of her life. President Hunter carried that burden locked in his heart. We sensed something of the depth of his quiet suffering, but he seldom spoke of it. Though her illness had been long and difficult, when she passed away it was a crushing blow to him."[41]

In addition to being a loving and caring husband to his wife throughout her long illness, Howard W. Hunter was a concerned and loving father and grandfather to his sons and daughters-in-law and his eighteen grandchildren. Despite his active schedule in serving in the Church, his sons recounted that he always made time for his children and grandchildren.[42] His daughters-in-law recalled that while he loved staying with their families, he did not like sitting around with nothing to do. They found that he enjoyed his visits more if he could work on home repairs or build toys for the children. "We would sometimes make a list of things that needed to be done around the house. He was a great fix-it man. . . . His knowledge about carpentry, appliances, electronics, plumbing and everything else around the house was just amazing."[43]

HEALTH DIFFICULTIES

Not only was Howard W. Hunter involved in caring for his wife during her health problems, he had his share of difficulties with his own health. He suffered a heart attack in July 1980, for which he was hospitalized. In order to regain his strength and to combat any further heart problems, he began walking through his neighborhood. Not wanting to waste time while walking, he listened to the scriptures or general conference talks on tape. Although he wrote in his journal, "I don't become enthusiastic about walking," he continued to do so every morning before going to the office, "not because I enjoy it but because the doctors insist."[44]

That same determination to continue his work despite health difficulties was seen throughout the rest of Howard W. Hunter's life. After the first heart attack, he lived through coronary bypass surgery, surgery for a bleeding ulcer, kidney failure, excruciating lower back pain from deteriorating disks, and back surgery, all of which were painful and difficult for him. After his back surgery in June 1987, his back healed, but his legs were weakened from nerve damage. Walking became an increasingly difficult thing to do, and after a short time, he began using a wheelchair. At October general conference 1987, he spoke from

An Example of Resilience

M. Russell Ballard said about President Hunter's health, "He had more problems than anybody I know of, just one thing after another. . . . He was in a wheelchair for a considerable time after surgery he had on his back. Then one day he came in on a walker into the Quorum of the Twelve meeting and announced that 'This is my present to the Quorum of the Twelve,' that he could walk."[8]

After a year and a half of being wheelchair-bound, in April 1989 general conference President Hunter stood at the pulpit to give his address. During the talk he lost his balance and fell back into the flower arrangement. He was immediately helped to stand up, and he continued his talk as if nothing had happened. Afterward, tests showed that he had broken three ribs in the fall.[9]

a sitting position, with a specially made pulpit in front of his chair. He began his talk with his usual good humor: "Forgive me if I remain seated while I present these few remarks. It is not by choice that I speak from a wheelchair. I notice that the rest of you seem to enjoy the conference sitting down, so I will follow your example."[45] Through months of painful therapy and continual effort on his part, Howard W. Hunter worked to recover the use of his legs. Over a year later, in December 1988, he walked with a walker from his office in the Church Administration Building to the meeting with the Quorum of the Twelve in the

"Life has a fair number of challenges"

On Sunday, February 7, 1993, President Howard W. Hunter spoke at the Marriott Center on Brigham Young University's campus for a Church Education System Young Adult Fireside. Just after he was introduced and began his speech, a man rushed onto the stage, shouting, "Stop right there!" He claimed he had a bomb in his briefcase and a detonator in his hand, and demanded that President Hunter read a prepared statement. President Hunter stood calmly and refused to read the statement that called for the release of the First Presidency and Council of the Twelve, stating that the man was to be the prophet. In the tumult, the audience, at first stunned and upset, began to sing, "We Thank Thee, O God, for a Prophet" and "I Am a Child of God."[10]

The assailant was sprayed by a can of mace, and then security officers and other students were able to wrestle him to the ground. Security officers and others helped President Hunter lie down on the floor. After the intruder was escorted away, the so-called bomb and detonator were found to be a briefcase of books and a radio, and a telephone receiver wrapped in black tape. President Hunter rested for a few minutes, then again went to the microphone where he continued his prepared speech is if nothing had happened.[11]

The next words he read were, "Life has a fair number of challenges in it." Looking at the audience he added, "As demonstrated." His talk continued to teach the young people that they should not fear the challenges around them, "if [their] faith and hope is anchored in Christ."[12]

Salt Lake Temple.[46] The following general conference in April 1989, Church members were happy to see him again stand at the pulpit to speak, as he did for the rest of his life.

MARRIAGE TO INIS STANTON

Many lonely years passed for Elder Hunter after the death of his wife Claire in 1983. These were also years of physical suffering for him. However, he continued his work in building up the Church, traveling to many countries and carrying out the work in his office. One spring day in 1990, at the end of the weekly Thursday morning meeting in the Temple with the Twelve, President Hunter announced that he was going to be married that afternoon to Inis Egan Stanton, a woman he had known from his days as a bishop in the El Sereno Ward in California. President Gordon B. Hinckley officiated at the sealing in the temple. At President Hunter's funeral, President Hinckley stated, "He was wonderfully bright and happy and full of smiles and buoyant talk on that day. She has been a great blessing to him. Together they have traveled far and wide under assignment in the Church. She added a dimension to his life."[47] Elder James E. Faust gave a similar tribute to Inis Hunter when he said, "Together they have shared so many happy memories and experiences. We are grateful beyond expression to you, Inis, for your companionship and your loving and devoted care of him. You brought a sparkle to his eye and joy to him in the crowning years of his life and his ministry."[48]

FOURTEENTH PRESIDENT OF THE CHURCH

Ezra Taft Benson passed away on May 30, 1994, after many years of ill health. Howard W. Hunter was set apart as the

Enduring Health Problems

At the funeral for President Hunter, President Boyd K. Packer said that he had "endured to the very end," referring to the many health problems that President Hunter had during the last two decades of his life. President Packer said, "I once asked President Hunter if he had a doctor's book, and if so I wanted to borrow it. He asked why. I said, 'I want to keep it. It seems to me you read through it looking for some major affliction you haven't had, wonder what it would be like, and decide to try it.'"[13]

Some of the major health difficulties President Hunter endured as a General Authority include:

- Mumps, contracted while in Mexico organizing new stakes

- Heart attack in 1980

- Coronary bypass surgery in 1986

- Surgery for a bleeding ulcer, requiring a transfusion of nine pints of blood

- Deteriorating disks and back problems, finally leading to surgery in June 1987

- Being wheelchair-bound for many months. Through much effort, he learned to walk again and could stand to deliver his talks

- Pneumonia

- Gall bladder surgery, after which he was in a coma-like sleep for twenty days

- Prostate cancer first diagnosed in 1980, finally taking his life in 1995

fourteenth prophet, seer, and revelator of the Church on the following Sunday, June 5, 1994. At the press conference the following day, President Hunter announced that the counselors in the First Presidency were Gordon B. Hinckley and Thomas S. Monson, with Boyd K. Packer as Acting President of the Quorum of the Twelve. He also read a statement expressing his desire to serve the Lord and the Church: "My greatest strength through these past hours and recent days has been my abiding testimony that this is the work of God and not men, that Jesus Christ is the authorized and living head of this church and He leads it in word and deed. I pledge my life, my strength, and the full measure of my soul to serving Him fully."[49]

In addition, at that time he issued two invitations to the Church which set the tone for his presidency over the following nine months:

"First of all, I would invite all members of the Church to live with ever more attention to the life and example of the Lord Jesus Christ, especially the love and hope and compassion He displayed. . . .

"Secondly, and in that same spirit, I also invite the members of the Church to establish the temple of the Lord as the great symbol of their membership and the supernal setting for their most sacred covenants."[50]

President Hunter wrote or spoke on these two themes of following the Savior and looking to the temple as a symbol of membership in the Church throughout his presidency. After President Hunter's death, Elder W. Eugene Hansen, then a member of the Presidency of the Seventy and executive director of the Temple Department, stated that in response to President Hunter's invitation for people to go to the temple, there was "a marked increase in participation in temple work in many of the temples throughout the world. There has also been a clear indication of increased effort by members to become more temple worthy and to qualify for and carry a current temple recommend."[51] President Hunter's counsel regarding the temple appears to have influenced Church members worldwide.

Many in the world wondered at President Hunter's becoming a prophet when he was not well, but Church members saw him gain in strength and stamina over the next few months as he continued to travel to meet with Church members and as he spoke with authority at general conference. After he was called by President Hunter on June 23, 1994 to become a member of the Quorum of the Twelve, Jeffrey R. Holland said in general conference that he saw a miracle in President Hunter's ability to carry out the work of the prophet. Elder Holland described that on the day he was called, President Hunter interviewed him, set him apart, and conducted meetings with the First Presidency and Quorum of the Twelve, "and through it all he was strong and fixed and powerful. Indeed, it seemed to me he got stronger and more powerful as the day progressed."[52]

Portrait of Inis and Howard Hunter.

Events During Howard W. Hunter's Presidency
(June 5, 1994–March 3, 1995)

1994	June 32	Ordained Jeffrey R. Holland an Apostle and Member of the Quorum of the Twelve
1994	June 26	Spoke in Nauvoo and Carthage, Illinois, commemorating the 150th anniversary of the martyrdom of Joseph and Hyrum Smith
1994	August 8–16	Traveled to Switzerland for conferences and visits
1994	September 13	Spoke at Provo MTC during missionary training satellite broadcast
1994	September 18	Spoke at Tucson, Arizona, biregional conference
1994	September 23	Spoke at general Relief Society meeting
1994	October 1	Sustained as prophet, seer, revelator, and President of the Church in a solemn assembly during the 164th Semiannual General Conference
1994	October 9	Dedicated Orlando Florida Temple
1994	October 15–16	Attended fifty-eighth anniversary of the Pasadena California Stake and spoke at stake conference
1994	November 13	Spoke in Salt Lake Tabernacle for the one hundredth anniversary of the Genealogical Society of Utah
1994	November 14	Eighty-seventh birthday
1994	November 18	Presided over inauguration of Eric B. Shumway as president of BYU—Hawaii
1994	December 4	Spoke at annual First Presidency Christmas Devotional
1994	December 11	Presided over creation of the Church's 2,000th stake: Mexico City Mexico Contreras Stake
1995	January 8–14	Dedicated Bountiful Utah Temple
1995	January 12	Hospitalized for exhaustion. Doctors found that prostate cancer had recurred and spread to the bones.
1995	January 16	Released from hospital to return home
1995	Mid-January and February	Continued work of the Presidency from his home, with visits from his counselors, other General Authorities, and his secretary
1995	March 3	Passed away at home

The First Presidency at a press conference June 5, 1994.

ACCOMPLISHMENTS AND TRAVELS

President Hunter continued to show that strength in his activities over the next few months. In addition to carrying out the work of the presidency and the administrative details of the Church, he traveled to a number of places. In June, he traveled to Nauvoo for the commemoration of the 150th anniversary of the martyrdom of Joseph and Hyrum Smith, speaking at the Nauvoo Ward sacrament meeting, again at the unveiling of a Nauvoo Temple sunstone display at the temple site, and later that day, he spoke for a satellite broadcast at Carthage. His travels also took him to Switzerland, Arizona, and California, where he participated in stake and regional conferences and spoke at numerous other meetings. He visited Hawaii, where he presided over the inauguration of Eric B. Shumway as president of BYU—Hawaii, and also traveled to Mexico where he created the Church's 2,000th stake in Mexico City in December. He also dedicated two temples during his administration: the Orlando Florida

Temple, dedicated in October 1994, and the Bountiful Utah Temple, dedicated in January 1995.[53]

In addition to his travels, President Hunter gave several major public addresses at home in Utah, including speaking at the general Relief Society meeting and three times during the 164th Semi-Annual General Conference in October 1994. He spoke in September at the Provo MTC for a missionary training satellite broadcast. November found him presiding and speaking in a fireside in the Salt Lake Tabernacle commemorating the one hundredth anniversary of the Genealogical Society of Utah. In December, he spoke again in the Tabernacle for the First Presidency's Christmas Devotional, broadcast via satellite to the Church. Along with these public talks, President Hunter also wrote messages that were published in the *Ensign* and the *Church News*.

ILLNESS AND DEATH

The last public appearance Howard W. Hunter made was at the dedication of the Bountiful Utah Temple January 8–14, 1995. He attended six sessions and spoke at four of them

Howard W. Hunter at the inauguration for the President of BYU—Hawaii.

before he became fatigued. He was admitted into the hospital on January 12, 1995, and treated for exhaustion. Upon examination, doctors found that the prostate cancer for which he had undergone surgery in 1980 had recurred and spread to his bones. From that time until his death on March 3, 1995, President Hunter stayed either in the hospital or at his home, where he was cared for by his wife, family, and medical personnel. Although he was not publicly involved in the workings of the Church, his counselors, the members of the Twelve, and others closely connected to him, visited and conferred with him many times during that period.

At the funeral, President Gordon B. Hinckley talked of his suffering: "I believe that it went on longer and was more sharp and deep than any of us really knew. He developed a high tolerance for pain and did not complain about it. That he lived so long is a miracle in and of itself. His suffering has comforted and mitigated the pain of many others who suffer. They know that he understood the heaviness of their

burdens."[54] After several weeks of enduring the pain of cancer, on Friday, March 3 1995, Howard W. Hunter said "'thank you,' to those about him; his spirit left his pain-racked body and stepped across that threshold into a better world."[55]

Although Howard W. Hunter's life as the President of the Church was short, his Christlike example, his testimony, and his teachings left an impression on the Church and endeared him to Church members and others throughout the world. After he had passed away, a *Church News* article stated, "President Hunter lived in total harmony with what he taught. . . . He became more and more like the Savior through his life, and that was more important to him than any other thing."[56] James E. Faust also explained the impact he left on members of the Church in his funeral address for the prophet: "They have seen in him the personification of the attributes of the Savior himself. They have responded in a remarkable way to his prophetic messages of making our lives more Christlike and of making our temples the center of our worship."[57]

The First Presidency at the dedication of the Bountiful Temple in January 1995.[14]

Gordon B. Hinckley, Howard W. Hunter, and Thomas S. Monson as the First Presidency.

TEACHINGS OF PRESIDENT
HOWARD W. HUNTER

◆

During his period of service in the Quorum of the Twelve Apostles, President Hunter talked on a variety of subjects, including the basic principles of the gospel, the plan of salvation, building strong marriages and family relations, dealing with adversity, temple and family history work, sharing the gospel, living the gospel, and following Christ more fully. Similar topics were treated in the few months he led the Church as

Howard W. Hunter at the pulpit during October 1975 general conference.

President, but there was an especial focus on two main subjects. At the first media conference when Howard W. Hunter was introduced as the prophet and President of The Church of Jesus Christ of Latter-day Saints, he issued two invitations to Church members worldwide. These two invitations were reiterated throughout the remainder of his presidency:

"There are two invitations I would like to leave with the members of the Church as we strive to keep the commandments of God and receive the full measure of His blessings. First of all, I would invite all members of the Church to live with ever more attention to the life and example of the Lord Jesus Christ, especially the love and hope and compassion He displayed.

"I pray that we might treat each other with more kindness, more courtesy, more humility and patience and forgiveness. . . .

"Secondly, and in that same spirit, I also invite the members of the Church to establish the temple of the Lord as the great symbol of their membership and the supernal setting for their most sacred covenants. It would be the deepest desire of my heart to have every member of the Church be temple worthy. I would hope that every adult member would be worthy of—and carry—a current temple recommend, even if proximity to a temple does not allow immediate or frequent use of it.

"Let us be a temple-attending and a temple-loving people. Let us hasten to the temple as frequently as time and means and personal circumstances allow. Let us go not only for our kindred dead, but let us also go for the personal blessing of temple worship, for the sanctity and safety which is provided within those hallowed and consecrated walls. The temple is a place of beauty, it is a place of revelation, it is a place of peace. It is the house of the Lord. It is holy unto the Lord. It should be holy unto us."[58]

President Hunter spoke or wrote on the two themes of becoming more Christlike and focusing on temple work throughout his short administration. In addition to talking of Christ and the temple, President Hunter taught about family life, missionary service, and Joseph Smith's life and testimony.

FOLLOWING THE EXAMPLE OF JESUS CHRIST

President Hunter's desire for all Church members to follow Christ's example was reiterated several times during his nine months as the prophet. He taught that Christ has given each one of us a personal invitation to follow Him. Indeed, he said that each one of God's children would at some time have to answer the question that Christ asked His disciples: "Whom say ye that I am?" (Matthew 16:15). He went on to say, "Our personal salvation depends on our answer to that question and our commitment to that answer. . . . Our challenge is to answer correctly and live accordingly before it is everlastingly too late."[59]

President Hunter invited all members of the Church, even those who had been offended or were struggling with transgressions, to come back to the Church and follow Christ.[60] Furthermore, he taught that following Christ is a matter of thinking more on holy things and acting as the Savior would expect His disciples to act. He suggested that we strive to build a personal testimony of Jesus Christ and His Atonement through studying Jesus' life and teachings. As we come to understand and gain a testimony of the Savior, we will desire to live more like Him.[61] As President Hunter taught, "We must know Christ better than we know him; we must remember him more often than we remember him; we must serve him more valiantly than we serve him. Then will we drink water springing up unto eternal life and will eat the bread of life."[62]

In addition to asking Church members to learn from Christ's example, President Hunter also gave some practical suggestions as to how we can live more like the Savior in our daily lives. At the First Presidency's Christmas Devotional in 1994, he suggested: "This Christmas, mend a quarrel. Seek out a forgotten friend. Dismiss suspicion and replace it with trust. Write a letter. Give a soft answer. Encourage youth. Manifest your loyalty in word and deed. Keep a promise. Forgo a grudge. Forgive an enemy. Apologize. Try to understand. Examine your demands on others. Think first of someone else. Be kind. Be gentle. Laugh a little more. Express your gratitude. Welcome a stranger. Gladden the heart of a child. Take pleasure in the beauty and wonder of the earth. Speak your love and then speak it again."[63]

TEMPLES

As the second major emphasis in his tenure, President Hunter encouraged the Saints to make the temple the symbol of their Church membership by teaching their children about the temple, keeping a picture of the temple in their homes, being worthy of the temple by maintaining a temple recommend, and then attending the temple as frequently as their circumstances allow. He recognized that temples were not accessible for all Church members to attend frequently, but he asked that members have the desire to participate in temple work as often as was feasible for them. He taught that being temple worthy helps us to follow Christ: "We must live worthy to enter the temple. We must keep the commandments of our Lord. If we can pattern our life after the Master, and take His teaching and example as the supreme pattern for our own, we will not find it difficult to be temple worthy, to be consistent and loyal in every walk of life, for we will be committed to a single, sacred standard of conduct and belief."[64]

President Hunter taught that ultimately, the three dimensions of the mission of the Church revolve around the temple: "All of our efforts in proclaiming the gospel, perfecting the Saints, and redeeming the dead lead to the holy temple. This is because the temple ordinances are absolutely crucial; we cannot return to God's presence without them."[65] Because President Hunter knew the significance of the ordinances found only in the temple to provide salvation for ourselves and our kindred dead, he taught that the temple should be central to our religious life. He invited those adults who had not received their temple blessings to work toward the day when they could enter the temple.[66] He also taught that not only are there blessings from serving in the temple for our ancestors, but we personally gain strength from being there:

"We should go not only for our kindred dead but also for the personal blessing of temple worship, for the sanctity and safety that are within those hallowed and consecrated walls. As we attend the temple, we learn more richly and deeply the purpose of life and the significance of the atoning sacrifice of the Lord Jesus Christ. Let us make the temple, with temple worship and temple covenants and temple marriage, our ultimate earthly goal and the supreme mortal experience."[67]

President Hunter's emphasis on temple worthiness and on temple attendance was a significant contribution to the Church throughout the world. As a result, many members in remote areas of the world endeavored to keep a current temple recommend, even when they could not see a time in the near future when they would be able use it. They recognized in the prophetic counsel that being temple worthy was a symbol of their faith in God's plan.[68]

FAMILY

In the only general conference over which President Hunter presided, he spoke to the brethren in the general priesthood session regarding the importance of being a righteous and worthy husband and father. While he spoke to the men and young men attending the conference, his advice and direction is important for all family members. He used the scriptures to teach that the relationship between men and women in marriage was ordained of God (Moses 2:28) and that men were to love their wives "as Christ loved the Church and gave himself for it (see Ephesians 5:25–31).

"Tenderness and respect—never selfishness—must be the guiding principles in the intimate relationship between husband and wife. Each partner must be considerate and sensitive to the other's needs and desires. Any domineering, indecent, or uncontrolled behavior in the intimate relationship between husband and wife is condemned by the Lord."[69]

In his message, President Hunter also warned against anyone who would abuse or demean his spouse physically or spiritually. He taught that such behavior is wrong and that any man who was abusive was "guilty of grievous sin and in need of sincere and serious repentance."[70] Instead of having

domineering behavior, a priesthood holder should view his wife as an equal partner in the leadership of the home and family. President Hunter taught that this partnership included a full participation in decision-making in all family matters and that a man who makes decisions without regard to his wife's counsel is exercising unrighteous dominion. He reminded Church members, "The Lord intended that the wife be a helpmeet for man (*meet* means equal)—that is, a companion equal and necessary in full partnership."[71] In order to lead a family in righteousness, parents must get their own "spiritual life in order through regular scriptural study and daily prayer" along with honoring the covenants made in the temple.[72]

President Hunter also told fathers that their own expressions of love and affection toward their children are as important as the expressions that mothers often give. Children need to recognize that their fathers love them. They will respect and have confidence in their fathers as they see him participate "in their social, educational, and spiritual activities and responsibilities."[73]

Finally, President Hunter taught that the family is important both to society and to the Church. He recognized that the society in which the Church exists sometimes does not promote family life, so he taught that the Church's program for family home evening is an inspired program to help develop faith, love, and obedience in the home.[74] His own life had reflected the importance of that program, as he had weekly lessons and outings with his children, even before the Church made it an official policy. President Hunter also taught that "the Church has the responsibility—and the authority—to preserve and protect the family as the foundation of society. The pattern for family life, instituted from before the foundation of the world, provides for children to be born to and nurtured by a father and mother who are husband and wife, lawfully married. Parenthood is a sacred obligation and privilege, with children welcomed as a 'heritage of the Lord' (Ps. 127:3).

"A worried society now begins to see that the disintegration of the family brings upon the world the calamities foretold by the prophets."[75]

Although "The Family: A Proclamation to the World" was not issued until the September after he had passed away, these words shared by President Hunter indicate that many of the issues about families and society that were later addressed in the Proclamation may have been in the minds of President Hunter and earlier Church leaders.

FAMILY HISTORY

President Hunter's experience and involvement with the Genealogical Society of Utah led to his continued interest in family history work. He recognized the importance of that work to the salvation of all human beings so that temple work for the dead could go forward. He taught that temple work was even more fulfilling when we also pursue the genealogical research that makes it possible to perform ordinances for our own kindred dead. One of his suggestions to Church members was that, if they could not attend the temple with frequency because of the distance, expense, and time involved, they should focus on family history research and send the names to the temple so ordinances could be performed by others. He also warned that members who only did temple work while neglecting their own ancestors might "lose a blessing by not seeking their own kindred dead as divinely directed by latter-day prophets." He continued,

"I have learned that those who engage in family history research and then perform the temple ordinance work for those whose names they have found will know the additional joy of receiving both halves of the blessing.

"Furthermore, the dead are anxiously waiting for the Latter-day Saints to search out their names and then go into the temples to officiate in their behalf, that they may be liberated from their prison house in the spirit world. All of us should find joy in this magnificent labor of love."[76]

One of the few public speeches that President Hunter made as Church President was at the celebration of the Genealogical Society of Utah's one hundredth anniversary. At that time, he said that his main message about family history and temple work was that it must hasten because there are so many of our ancestors needing the ordinances of the temple. That hastening of the work has occurred since his lifetime is evidenced in the current use of technology in family history research. President Hunter prophetically stated,

"The role of technology in this work has been accelerated by the Lord himself, who has had a guiding hand in its development and will continue to do so. However, we stand only on the threshold of what we can do with these tools. I feel that our most enthusiastic projections can capture only a tiny glimpse of how these tools can help us—and of the eternal consequences of these efforts."[77]

Since the above statement was made, the Internet has grown and is now developed and used extensively as a family history tool. With digital imaging and other available technology, online searching for ancestors in original records is now possible. These searching techniques were not even imagined in 1994 when President Hunter prophetically recognized the potential applications of technology to family history.

MISSIONARY WORK

President Hunter taught missionaries serving throughout the world in a satellite broadcast originating at the Mission Training Center at Provo, Utah. He counseled them that they could not be "a part of worldly things and also carry out [their] role as a representative of the Lord. The two are not compatible." He reminded them that Satan will always try to hinder the work they do, but as they work together in their companionships to live in faith and be prayerful, they can "be an awesome force in the work of the Lord."[78]

In addition to reminding the missionaries of the importance of sharing the gospel, President Hunter suggested that every faithful member of the Church has a responsibility to share the gospel. He taught, "A great indicator of your personal conversion to the gospel of Jesus Christ is the desire to share it with others. . . . Each of us present today has a duty to bear faithful testimony of our Lord and Savior and His restored gospel."[79]

JOSEPH SMITH AND THE RESTORATION OF THE GOSPEL

In June 1994, President Hunter participated in a commemoration of the 150-year anniversary of the martyrdom of Joseph Smith by traveling to Nauvoo and Carthage, Illinois, where

What Others Have Said about President Hunter

Gordon B. Hinckley:

"I believe that President Hunter's life was preserved over this long period, and that during these years he was polished and refined, that he was disciplined and trained and taught under the plan of the Almighty to stand at this season as prophet to the nations and revelator to the people."[15]

James E. Faust:

"President Hunter is one of the most loving, Christlike men we have ever known. His spiritual depth is so profound as to be unfathomable. . . . He has an inner peace, tranquility, and nobility of soul that is unique among the children of God. His intense suffering on so many occasions has been as a 'refiner's fire,' permitting him to become God's pure vessel and prophet on the earth in this day and time."[16]

Boyd K. Packer:

"The administration of President Howard W. Hunter, though very brief, has been a historic one. Things have transpired during those few months of his leadership, some of them as yet unannounced, which will bless this church for generations to come."[17]

L. Tom Perry:

"[President Hunter's] life's story is filled with accounts of determination, accomplishment, faith, and true Christian love. He is an inspiration to all of us. He is our prophet. We sit at his feet ready to feast on the wisdom of this true and faithful servant-leader. We stand ready to heed his voice because we know he speaks for the Lord."[18]

David B. Haight:

"President Hunter understands compassion, thankfulness, graciousness, charity, and gratitude towards individuals and towards mankind, and he has the saintly bearing of a prophet of God. He, in my estimation, is truly Christlike."[19]

M. Russell Ballard:

"[President Hunter's] contribution to the church was that he put great emphasis on temple attendance and the blessings that would come from temple worship. He also was an advocate that everybody ought to hold a temple recommend. Even if they had no opportunity to use it, they should be worthy. . . . He was a really great man. . . . He was a gentle giant."[20]

Jeffrey R. Holland:

"I testify that God has worked his will on Howard William Hunter. He has touched his lips and spread the prophetic mantle of ordained leadership upon his shoulders. President Hunter is a miracle—one who has been fashioned, molded, refined, and sustained for the service he now renders. He is a most remarkable blend of velvet and steel. Like every prophet before him—including Joseph Smith, Jr.—and every prophet who will succeed him, President Hunter was called and foreordained in the grand councils of heaven before this world was."[21]

he spoke at a satellite broadcast. In that broadcast, President Hunter pointed out that the Prophet Joseph Smith's greatness came from the fact that he actually "saw the Father and the Son and that he responded to the reality of the divine revelation."[80] President Hunter called that vision the "first pillar of our faith" because it is the foundation upon which the Restoration of the gospel is placed. He then described the Book of Mormon as the second pillar of our faith: "It is through reading and studying the Book of Mormon, and prayerfully seeking confirmation of its contents, that we receive a testimony that Joseph Smith was a prophet of God and that the Church of Jesus Christ has been restored to the earth."[81]

President Hunter continued, saying that the third pillar of our faith is the restoration of the holy priesthood. "Without the holy priesthood, exaltation would not be possible inasmuch as the necessary ordinances and covenants come through the use of that sacred power." President Hunter then identified the fourth pillar of faith as being related to the salvation for the dead. Although the Nauvoo Temple was not completed during Joseph Smith's lifetime, "the groundwork laid by the Prophet and the keys and authority given to the Twelve, including instruction regarding the ordinances of the temple, laid the foundation for the numerous temples which now dot the whole earth."[82] President Hunter taught that these pillars of faith were what strengthened the early Saints of this dispensation to devote their lives for the cause of truth, and will similarly strengthen the Saints of today to continue upholding the gospel and stay true to the Church.

CONCLUSION

President Howard W. Hunter was able to teach members of the Church the importance of following the Savior's example more closely in our relationships with one another, of being worthy of and attending the temple, and of having faith to share the gospel with our friends and loved ones. His own life was an example of one whose only desire was to follow Christ and build His kingdom. His willingness to serve in the Church and his gentle way of interacting with people of all faiths endeared him to people throughout the Church and the world.

Cynthia Doxey

Associate Professor of Church History and Doctrine, PhD Brigham Young University

NOTES

1. Howard W. Hunter, "The Great Symbol of Our Membership," *Ensign*, October 1994, 2.
2. Eleanor Knowles, *Howard W. Hunter* (Salt Lake City: Deseret Book, 1994), 2–6.
3. Ibid., 12–14.
4. Ibid., 14–15.
5. Kellene Ricks, "Friend to Friend," *Friend*, April 1990, 6.
6. Knowles, *Howard W. Hunter*, 39–41.
7. "President Howard W. Hunter: The Lord's 'Good and Faithful Servant,' " *Ensign*, April 1995, 9–10.
8. Ibid., 10.
9. Knowles, *Howard W. Hunter*, 46.
10. "President Howard W. Hunter: The Lord's 'Good and Faithful Servant," 10.
11. Ibid.
12. Ibid.
13. Knowles, *Howard W. Hunter*, 63–64.
14. Ibid., 65.
15. Ibid., 72.
16. Ibid., 69–71.
17. Ibid., 80–81.
18. Ibid., 82–83.
19. Ibid., 84–85.
20. Ibid., 85–86.
21. Ibid., 88.
22. Ibid., 92–93.
23. Ibid., 112–13.
24. Ibid., 141–42.
25. Ibid., 117–19.
26. "President Howard W. Hunter: The Lord's 'Good and Faithful Servant,' " 12.
27. Knowles, *Howard W. Hunter*, 126–27.
28. Ibid., 131–32.
29. "President Howard W. Hunter: The Lord's 'Good and Faithful Servant,' " 12.
30. Journal of Howard W. Hunter, as quoted in Knowles, *Howard W. Hunter*, 144.

31. Knowles, *Howard W. Hunter*, 151.

32. Thomas S. Monson, "President Howard W. Hunter: A Man for All Seasons," *Ensign*, April 1995, 31.

33. Letter from Spencer W. Kimball and Howard W. Hunter cited in "As We See It," *Church News*, January 20, 1962, 5.

34. Knowles, *Howard W. Hunter*, 212–15; see also "President Howard W. Hunter: The Lord's 'Good and Faithful Servant,'" 14.

35. George H. Niederauer, "Civic, religious leaders send condolences," *Church News*, March 11, 1995, 14.

36. Knowles, *Howard W. Hunter*, 216–25; see also "President Howard W. Hunter: The Lord's 'Good and Faithful Servant,'" 15.

37. James B. Allen, Jessie L. Embry, and Kahlile B. Mehr, *Hearts Turned to the Fathers: A History of the Genealogical Society of Utah, 1894–1994* (Provo, UT: *BYU Studies*, Brigham Young University, 1995), 174.

38. Knowles, *Howard W. Hunter*, 189; "President Howard W. Hunter: The Lord's 'Good and Faithful Servant,'" 14–15.

39. Knowles, *Howard W. Hunter*, 287–89.

40. "President Howard W. Hunter: The Lord's 'Good and Faithful Servant,'" 15; see also Mike Cannon, "He was a caring husband, father, grandfather," *Church News*, March 11, 1995, 16.

41. James E. Faust, "The Way of an Eagle," *Ensign*, August 1994, 10.

42. Gordon B. Hinckley, "A Prophet Polished and Refined," *Ensign*, April 1995, 34.

43. Cannon, "He was a caring husband, father, grandfather," 15.

44. "Daughters-in-law Share Memories of 'Dad,'" *Church News*, March 11, 1995, 16.

45. Knowles, *Howard W. Hunter*, 273–74.

46. Howard W. Hunter, "The Opening and Closing of Doors," *Ensign*, November 1987, 54.

47. Knowles, *Howard W. Hunter*, 284.

48. Hinckley, "A Prophet Polished and Refined," 34.

49. James E. Faust, "Howard W. Hunter: Man of God," *Ensign*, April 1995, 28.

50. Jay M. Todd, "President Howard W. Hunter: Fourteenth President of the Church," *Ensign*, July 1994, 4.

51. Ibid., 4–5.

52. Dell Van Orden, "Gentle, Compassionate Leader," *Church News*, March 11, 1995, 14.

53. Jeffrey R. Holland, "Miracles of the Restoration," *Ensign*, November 1994, 32.

54. "Nine busy months for 14th president," *Church News*, March 11, 1995, 8.

55. Hinckley, "A Prophet Polished and Refined," 33.

56. Ibid., 35.

57. Van Orden, "Gentle, Compassionate Leader," 14.

58. Faust, "Howard W. Hunter: Man of God," 26.

59. Todd, "President Howard W. Hunter: Fourteenth President of the Church," 4–5.

60. Howard W. Hunter, "He Invites Us to Follow Him," *Ensign*, September 1994, 2.

61. Todd, "President Howard W. Hunter: Fourteenth President of the Church," 4–5; see also Howard W. Hunter, "This Is My Gospel," Tuscan Regional Conference, Tuscan, Arizona, September 18, 1994; excerpts in *Church News*, September 24, 1994, 4.

62. Hunter, "He Invites Us to Follow Him," 5.

63. Hunter, "The Gifts of Christmas," First Presidency Christmas Devotional, Salt Lake Tabernacle, December 4, 1994 (adapted from an unknown author); excerpts from *Church News*, December 10, 1994, 3.

64. Howard W. Hunter, "The Great Symbol of Our Membership," *Ensign*, October 1994, 5.

65. Howard W. Hunter, "Follow the Son of God," *Ensign*, November 1994, 88.

66. Hunter, "This Is My Gospel."

67. Hunter, "A Temple-Motivated People," *Ensign*, February 1995, 5.

68. See Anne C. Pingree, "Seeing the Promises Afar Off," *Ensign*, November 2003, 13.

69. Howard W. Hunter, "Being a Righteous Husband and Father," *Ensign*, November 1994, 51.

70. Ibid.

71. Ibid.

72. Ibid.

73. Ibid.

74. Hunter, "This Is My Gospel." The First Presidency had also issued a letter, dated August 30, 1994, that counseled members to hold regular family home evenings.

75. Howard W. Hunter, "Exceeding Great and Precious Promises," *Ensign*, November 1994, 9.

76. Hunter, "A Temple-Motivated People," 4–5.

77. Howard W. Hunter, "We Have a Work to Do," *Ensign*, March 1995, 65.

78. Howard W. Hunter, "The Standard of Truth," Missionary Training Center Satellite Broadcast, Provo, Utah, September 13, 1994, as cited in Clyde J. Williams, ed., *The Teachings of Howard W. Hunter* (Salt Lake City: Bookcraft), 251–52.

79. Hunter, "The Standard of Truth," as cited in "President Hunter's Speeches Covered Variety of Topics," *Church News*, March 11, 1995, 7.

80. Howard W. Hunter, "Come to the God of All Truth," *Ensign*, September 1994, 72.

81. Hunter, "'The Pillars of Our Faith,'" *Ensign*, September 1994, 54.

82. Ibid.

SIDEBAR AND PHOTO NOTES

1. Barbara Willard Larson, *Barbara Willard Larson's Memories of President Howard W. Hunter* (self-published, 1995), 7.

2. Gerry Avant, "He wanted to visit the Holy Land 'just one more time,'" *Church News*, March 11, 1995, 9.

3. Ibid., 9.

4. Hunter, "The Opening and Closing of Doors," 54.

5. Ibid., 59.

6. Howard W. Hunter, "An Anchor to the Souls of Men," in *BYU 1992–93 Devotional and Fireside Speeches* (Provo, UT: BYU Press, 1993), 69.

7. Howard W. Hunter, *Church News* interview, June 25, 1988, reported in *Church News*, March 11, 1995, 13.

8. M. Russell Ballard, personal interview with Cynthia Doxey, October 12, 2003.

9. "President Howard W. Hunter: The Lord's 'Good and Faithful Servant,'" 16.

10. Sheridan R. Sheffield, "Fireside disrupted with threat of bomb," *Church News*, February 13, 1993.

11. Ken Myers, "Terrorist interrupts fireside," *The Daily Universe* 46, no. 96, February 8, 1993.

12. Hunter, "An Anchor to the Souls of Men," 67.

13. Boyd K. Packer, "President Howard W. Hunter—He Endured to the End," *Ensign*, April 1995, 28.

14. Photo by Gerry Avant.

15. Hinckley, "A Prophet Polished and Refined," 35.

16. Faust, "The Way of an Eagle," 13.

17. Packer, "President Howard W. Hunter—He Endured to the End," 30.

18. L. Tom Perry, "Heed the Prophet's Voice," *Ensign*, November 1994, 19.

19. David B. Haight, "Solemn Assemblies," *Ensign*, November 1994, 16.

20. M. Russell Ballard, personal interview with Cynthia Doxey, October 12, 2003.

21. Jeffrey R. Holland, "Miracles of the Restoration," 32.

LIFE AND TIMES

1910	June 23	Born to Bryant Stringham Hinckley and Ada Bitner Hinckley
1919		Baptized by his father
1932	June 4	Graduated from University of Utah
1933–35		Served as missionary in the European Mission, headquartered in London, England
1935		Became executive secretary of Church Radio, Publicity, and Mission Literature Committee
1937	April 29	Married Marjorie Pay in the Salt Lake Temple
1937–46		Served on Sunday School General Board
1951		Called by President Stephen L Richards to serve as executive secretary of the General Missionary Committee
1953		Asked by President David O. McKay to help with preparation of temple instruction to be presented in different languages in Swiss Temple
1956	October 28	Called as president of East Millcreek Stake by Elders Harold B. Lee and George Q. Morris
1958	April 6	Called as Assistant to the Quorum of the Twelve
1961	October 5	Sustained as member of the Quorum of the Twelve
1981	July 23	Called by President Kimball to serve as counselor in the First Presidency
1995	March 12	Became President of the Church
1995	September 23	Read "The Family: A Proclamation to the World" from the First Presidency and the Quorum of the Twelve at the general Relief Society meeting
1999	April 4	Announced the reconstruction of the historic Nauvoo Temple
2000		Published *Standing for Something: 10 Virtues That Will Heal Our Hearts and Homes*
2000	October 8	Dedicated the new Church Conference Center in Salt Lake City, Utah
2000	November 12	Addressed the youth of the Church about six "ways to be" at a special fireside
2002	June 27	Dedicated the reconstructed Nauvoo Temple
2002		Published *Way to Be!: 9 Ways to Be Happy and Make Something of Your Life*
2004	April 6	Marjorie Pay Hinckley died in Salt Lake City
2004	June 23	Awarded the Presidential Medal of Freedom by President George W. Bush
2005		Traveled nearly twenty-five thousand miles on a tour to Taiwan, Russia, South Korea, China, India, and Africa
2008	January 27	Died in Salt Lake City, Utah, at age ninety-seven, as the longest-lived President of the Church

BIOGRAPHICAL HIGHLIGHTS

President Gordon B. Hinckley was ordained and set apart as the fifteenth President of the Church on March 12, 1995, after serving since 1981 as a counselor in the First Presidency and since 1961 in the Quorum of the Twelve Apostles. His ministry was characterized by a desire to be out among the people and to provide temples for Church members everywhere. In a remarkable way, he lived his motto to "go forward with faith."

President Hinckley grew up in Salt Lake City and spent his summers in East Millcreek, where his parents owned a home and several acres of land. During the economic depression of the 1930s, Gordon served a mission to England. This experience augmented his growth in the gospel and strengthened his testimony and leadership abilities, as well as provided opportunities to develop his writing and speaking skills.

In 1937 he married Marjorie Pay, who had lived across the street from him during their childhood. President and Sister Hinckley were the parents of five children: three daughters and two sons, and more than three score grandchildren and great-grandchildren. He passed away at the age of ninety-seven in Salt Lake City on January 27, 2008.

CONTRIBUTIONS

The Lord prepared and placed a prophet to lead the Church into the twenty-first century who both understood and appreciated the past but stepped boldly into the future. President Hinckley had an inexhaustible ability to work, a quick wit and a keen mind, and an uncompromising testimony of restored truth. No one in the history of the Church has worked for more years in more assignments at Church headquarters than Gordon B. Hinckley.

President Hinckley will always be remembered as the temple builder. Since he was called to the First Presidency in 1981, he has dedicated or rededicated 95 of the 124 operating temples. He was involved in the construction and dedication of more temples over a longer period of time than any other person in this dispensation. Two major milestones were reached under his leadership: the Church reached 12 million members and, since the organization of the Church in 1830, an estimated 1 million missionaries have served throughout the world. About 400,000 of those missionaries, or 40 percent of all missionaries who have served, entered the mission field since he became President of the Church in 1995.

No President of the Church traveled more miles to more lands over more years than President Hinckley. He met with the Saints in every corner of the world, traveling to more than sixty countries after becoming President. He met with leaders, media, and ordinary people around the globe. One of the hallmarks of President Hinckley's presidency was his desire to reach out in love to others not of our faith and to extend a hand of friendship.

TEACHINGS

President Hinckley was known for his strong doctrinal messages that proclaimed the risen Lord, the Restoration of the gospel through the Prophet Joseph Smith, and the fundamental principles and practices of the latter-day Saints of God. For nearly fifty years he addressed audiences at general conference, as well as congregations of the faithful around the world. Always he admonished faith in the Lord, service to others, and dedication to truth and righteousness. Over the years he repeatedly denounced arrogance and self-righteousness among Church members. President Hinckley was beloved for his positive, hopeful outlook on life and for his messages of simple eloquence and uncommon wisdom.

LIFE OF
GORDON B. HINCKLEY

◆

Only two Presidents of The Church of Jesus Christ of Latter-day Saints have led the Church into a new century. Lorenzo Snow ushered in the twentieth century, and Gordon B. Hinckley the twenty-first. While the world and its people certainly changed in those ten decades, one thing remained the same: the Lord prepared and placed a man to lead the Church who both understood and appreciated the past but stepped boldly into the future. Like all his predecessors, President Hinckley had prophetic vision. He also had an inexhaustible ability to work, a keen mind and a quick wit, and an uncompromising testimony of restored truth. To bridge the twentieth and twenty-first centuries, the Lord chose a remarkable leader for His kingdom on earth. Gordon Bitner Hinckley was no more than a man but no less than a prophet of God.

Gordon B. Hinckley as a baby.

EARLY YEARS

"There was for me an underlying foundation of love that came from great parents and a good family, a wonderful bishop, devoted and faithful teachers, and the scriptures to read and ponder. Although in my youth I had trouble understanding many things, there was in my heart something of a love for God and his great work that carried me above any doubts and fears. I loved the Lord and I loved good and honorable friends. From such love I drew great strength."[1]

Gordon B. Hinckley came into the world at the end of the first decade of the twentieth century, June 23, 1910. He was a "spindly, frail boy susceptible to earaches and other illnesses" and a "constant worry to his mother."[2] He was the son and grandson of faithful members of the Church, stalwarts in building the cause of Zion. His grandfather, Ira Nathaniel Hinckley, was sent by Brigham Young to build Cove Fort in Millard County, Utah, after which he and his family moved to Fillmore where he served as stake president for twenty-five years and then as stake patriarch. Ira's son Bryant Stringham Hinckley was a prominent Church leader himself, serving as a stake president in Salt Lake City, as a member of the YMMIA General Board, and as mission president over the Northern States Mission. He was also widely known as an

Bryant and Ada Hinckley, the parents of Gordon.

The Hinckley family (Gordon is second from the left on the back row).

educator, businessman, eloquent speaker, and exceptional writer. Bryant's first wife and the mother of their ten children (two died in infancy) died in 1908.

Thirteen months later, Bryant married Ada Bitner, a faculty member of LDS Business College, where he had been serving as principal. Together they had five children; the oldest, Gordon, was given his mother's maiden name for his middle name. Years later, Gordon would say about his early years, "I look back at myself as a shy and bashful boy—freckle-faced and awkward. But, I was blessed with a great father, a man of many gifts, literary gifts, business acumen and a tremendous capacity to accomplish. He was a man of steady faith and a great teacher."[3]

His parents' patriarchal blessings foreshadow the fruit of their loins. In part, Bryant's reads: "You shall not only become great yourself but your posterity will become great, from your loins shall come forth statesmen, prophets, priests and Kings to the most High God. The Priesthood will never depart from your family, no never. To your posterity there

The Lord's Name in Vain

"When I was a small boy in the first grade, I experienced what I thought was a rather tough day at school. I came home, walked in the house, threw my books on the kitchen table, and let forth an expletive that included the name of the Lord.

"My mother was shocked. She told me quietly, but firmly, how wrong I was. She told me that I could not have words of that kind coming out of my mouth. She led me by the hand into the bathroom, where she took from the shelf a clean washcloth, put it under the faucet, and then generously coated it with soap. She said, 'We'll have to wash out your mouth.' She told me to open it, and I did so reluctantly. Then she rubbed the soapy washcloth around my tongue and teeth. I sputtered and fumed and felt like swearing again, but I didn't. I rinsed and rinsed my mouth, but it was a long while before the soapy taste was gone. In fact, whenever I think of that experience, I can still taste the soap. The lesson was worthwhile. I think I can say I have tried to avoid using the name of the Lord in vain since that day. I am grateful for that lesson."[2]

The Hinckley farm cottage in East Millcreek.

Gordon as a young boy.

name shall be perpetuated and live in the memory of the Saints."[5]

Bryant and Ada's first child, Gordon, was sickly with allergies, asthma, hay fever, and whooping cough, aggravated by the smoke of Salt Lake City's coal-burning stoves. Upon their doctor's recommendation, the Hinckleys purchased several acres of farmland in East Millcreek, where they lived during the summer and where Gordon could breathe fresh air. The summer home was a place of work and outdoor adventure. It was a place to tend animals, plant trees, and explore. Some nights were spent lying in the grass sleeping under the stars.

The city home had a library with a thousand volumes. It was a place for Gordon to follow the habits of his parents in reading and pondering good books. These two places of Gordon B. Hinckley's childhood and young adulthood exemplify twin characteristics that were so much a part of him. He loved the outdoors and always spent time planting trees and flowers; he enjoyed home repairs and projects, and he didn't mind getting his hands dirty. But he was also a man of letters and language, a person who loved to read and was well acquainted with good literature.

shall be no end . . . and the name of Hinckley shall be honored in every nation under heaven."[4] Ada's patriarchal blessing also tells of her great mission in preparing her posterity for service to the Lord: "The eye of the Lord has been upon thee from thy birth and a decree of the Father has gone forth that thou shalt have a mission to fill, a work to do. . . . Thy

Testimony of the Prophet

Shortly after Gordon was ordained a deacon, he attended a stake priesthood meeting with his father. Bryant sat on the stand, Gordon on the back row. Priesthood brethren filled the chapel as the meeting began with the congregation standing to sing the opening song "Praise to the Man." He later recalled that experience, "It touched my heart. It gave me a feeling that was difficult to describe. I'd never had it previously in terms of any Church experience. There came into my heart a conviction that the man of whom they sang was really a prophet of God. I'm grateful to be able to say that that conviction, which came I believe by the power of the Holy Spirit never left me."[3]

The Hamilton School, where Gordon attended.

University of Utah graduate, 1932.

we didn't like it, because it was hard work. Yet we did learn something from it: You can determine the kind of fruit crop that you will have in September by the way you prune the trees in February. That was a great lesson, and it applies to people as well. You can pretty much determine the kind of adults you will have by the way you care for them as children."[6]

Gordon's first two decades overflowed with the happy, ordinary experiences of a joyful boyhood. He was obviously gifted in many ways, yet also a typical boy: full of adventure and mischief. He was earnest, but fun-loving. He grew in wisdom and testimony in a home filled with stability, love, and contentment. Years later Gordon remembered, "We didn't openly speak about love for one another very much in those days. We didn't have to. We felt that security, that peace, that quiet strength which comes to families who pray together, work together, and help one another."[7]

The happiness of his first two decades was shaken by family heartache in 1930 when his beloved mother, Ada, died of cancer at age fifty. Even in death, his mother's influence on her son was profound and lasting. Whenever Gordon faced challenges, he often thought of his courageous, faithful mother, who was a constant influence for good in his life. On occasion he felt her influence sustaining him in difficulty.

He was a mix of city and country. He could meet with heads of state, kings and queens from around the globe, but he could also get his work clothes on, fix a toaster, plant a tree, weed a garden, and enjoy the beauty of God's creations. He said of his childhood, "I learned to live around animals and learned the lessons of nature—the beauty that is there and the penalties that come when nature in abused. We had large fruit orchards, and we learned how to prune trees. . . . In January, February, and March we pruned the trees, but

Honorary Doctorates

President Hinckley received ten honorary doctorates. In the most recent he was extolled as a "tremendous leader in faith, education, and higher ideals, affecting people around the world," and as a man who has made "endless contributions toward humanitarian causes."[4]

"I tried then, as I have tried since, to so conduct my life and perform my duty as to bring honor to her name. The thought of living beneath my mother's expectations has been painful, and has afforded a discipline that otherwise might have been lacking."[8]

Gordon was an excellent student from his early grades at Hamilton School, through Roosevelt Junior High School and LDS High School, and through college at the University of Utah, where he graduated in 1932 with a major in English and a minor in ancient languages. Years later he would be honored with the University of Utah Distinguished Alumnus Award and an honorary doctorate. In 2003 the Gordon B. Hinckley Endowment for British Studies was established at the University of Utah because of his affinity and connection to Great Britain, along with his lifelong advocacy for the humanities and literature.

In 1932, his future was bright. At twenty-two years of age, Gordon wanted to attend Columbia University in New York City to study journalism—but the Lord had other plans for him in England.

Elder Hinckley served in the European Mission from 1933–35.

MISSION

"I came to know that if we put our faith in the Lord and go forward in trust, he will open the way."[9]

Gordon's educational aspirations changed when he was called to preach the gospel in the European Mission, with headquarters in London. The Great Depression had wreaked havoc on the financial assets of the country and of Gordon B. Hinckley, who had lost nearly all his savings in a bank that failed. A mission seemed impossible. But his father and brother offered to help, and it was discovered that his dear mother had set aside a small savings account with the coins she received in change when buying groceries that she had earmarked for her sons' missionary service. Gordon considered his mission funds sacred and determined not to squander those consecrated monies.

As Gordon stepped on the train, nervous and uncertain for his trip across the ocean to England, his dear father handed him a card on which he had written five words,

Elder Hinckley's missionary passport photo.

"Be not afraid, only believe" (Mark 5:36). Years later, as prophet, he would speak at a Church Educational System fireside for young adults and deliver an address with the same title: "There may be some lean days ahead for some of you. There may be troubles. None of us can avoid them all. Do not despair. Do not give up. Look for the sunlight through the clouds. Opportunities will eventually open to you. . . . No matter the circumstances, I encourage you to go forward with faith and prayer, calling on the Lord."[10]

His first weeks of missionary work were discouraging and difficult. Suffering with hay fever and homesickness, he wrote home to his father that he felt he was wasting his time and his father's money and that perhaps he should just return home. His father responded as both dad and stake president: "Dear Gordon, I have your recent letter. I have only one suggestion: forget yourself and go to work." The next morning as he studied Mark 8:35 with his companion, Elder Hinckley had a change of heart. He later said, "That July day in 1933 was my day of decision. A new light came into my life and a new joy into my heart. The fog of England seemed to lift, and I saw the sunlight. Everything good that has happened to me since then I can trace back to the decision I made that day in Preston."[11] He put his shoulder to the wheel and never looked back. He served as assistant to the mission president (Elder Joseph Merrill of the Quorum of the Twelve) and had many experiences that augmented his growth in the gospel and strengthened his testimony and leadership abilities, as well as provided opportunities to develop his writing and speaking skills.

In 1935 he returned home, weary and weighing only 126 pounds, saying he had no desire ever to travel again. Considering that no Church leader traveled more miles over more years, that sentiment was one of the great ironic miscalculations of his life!

PROFESSION

"This is the Lord's work. I feel I will make my best contribution in life by continuing to do my humble part to further the cause."[12]

Upon returning from the mission field, his mission president had arranged for Elder Hinckley to report to the First Presidency on missionary work in the European Mission. He met with President Heber J. Grant and his counselors,

Elder Hinckley conducting a street meeting as a missionary in England.

From 1935 to 1958, with the exception of two years, Gordon worked in the headquarters of the Church.

J. Reuben Clark and David O. McKay, in the Church Administration Building (the same building where, sixty years later, Gordon B. Hinckley would himself preside over the Church). President Grant told Elder Hinckley that he had fifteen minutes. Elder Hinckley left the room an hour and fifteen minutes later after responding to questions. Impressed with this newly returned missionary, a few days later President McKay offered him the position of executive secretary of the Church's Radio, Publicity, and Mission Literature Committee of the Church.

Supervised production of the Church exhibit at San Francisco World's Fair on Treasure Island in 1939.

With a camera.

A radio broadcast with Richard L. Evans and J. Reuben Clark.

Became executive secretary of the Church Radio, Publicity, and Mission Literature Committee in 1935.

Except for a brief two-year interlude during World War II (when he worked for the Denver & Rio Grande Railroad), Gordon B. Hinckley spent more than seventy years in staff assignments and General Authority callings at the headquarters of the Church. No one in the history of the Church has worked for more years in more assignments at Church headquarters than he did. And, considering his nickname during those years was "the Slave," perhaps no one has worked harder. Gordon was known for his intelligence and diligence, his responsiveness and creativity, his complete commitment to the gospel and the work of the Lord. He wrote hundreds of radio scripts, filmstrips, missionary pamphlets, public relations materials, and books for use in the mission field. Later he was asked by President McKay to find a way to present the temple ceremonies in various languages. This led to producing the temple ceremonies in fourteen languages, using film. He personally carried the completed film to Switzerland, where it was first used in the Swiss Temple following its dedication in September 1955. From that time on, President Hinckley had an unequaled involvement in the dedication or rededication of temples around the world.[13]

MARRIAGE AND FAMILY

"I don't know how anyone could have been more richly blessed than we have been. We've had problems. We've lived through all the things that parents go through—sickness with their children, things of that kind. But really, when all is said and done, if you can live with a good woman through your life and see your children grow to maturity as happy, able individuals who are making a contribution, then you can count your life a success. It isn't how many cars you own, the size of your house, or things of that kind. It is the quality of life that you've lived that makes a difference."[14]

President Hinckley has shown over many years the outstanding attributes of an effective and decisive leader. "But," according to President Boyd K. Packer, then Acting President of the Quorum of the Twelve Apostles, "The greatest judgment he has ever shown in his entire life is the judgment he showed in marrying Marjorie Pay. You cannot know him unless you know her—the tender, guiding, patient influence she has been in his life and in that of their children."[15]

How They Met

Gordon and Marjorie lived across the street from each other in Salt Lake City. They were members of the First Ward, where Marjorie was known for the impressive readings she gave in Church meetings and other activities. It was one of those youthful readings she gave that first caught Gordon's notice: "I saw her first in Primary. She gave a reading. I don't know what it did to me, but I never forgot it. Then she grew older into a beautiful young woman, and I had the good sense to marry her."[5]

Marjorie Pay in 1937.

They associated over the years of adolescence and young adulthood, dated a little, and became good friends. Marjorie fully supported Gordon's decision to serve a mission. They wrote occasionally during his mission, drew closer, and observed a mutual and growing spiritual maturity. They had been attracted to each other's sense of humor, innate optimism, love of life, and commitment to the restored gospel. They began to seriously date when Elder Hinckley returned from Great Britain and began a career with the Church. Marjorie said, "As we got closer to marriage, I felt completely

The young Hinckley family.

confident that Gordon loved me. But I also knew somehow that I would never come first with him. I knew I was going to be second in his life and that the Lord was going to be first. And that was okay."[16]

Gordon Bitner Hinckley and Marjorie Pay were married April 29, 1937, by Elder Stephen L Richards of the Quorum of the Twelve in the Salt Lake Temple. With little money to spare for traditional wedding fanfare, and Gordon's father away serving as mission president in the Northern States,

they did without a reception. Their honeymoon was a trip to the solitude and privacy of Southern Utah's beautiful state parks.[17]

President and Sister Hinckley were the parents of five children: three daughters and two sons, and more than sixty grandchildren and great-grandchildren. They were a close-knit extended family, unfailingly supportive of one another. Each of their children is accomplished in his or her own right. Their two sons have both become the fourth generation of Hinckleys to serve as stake presidents. The children love their parents, Gordon and Marjorie, and speak highly of them. A daughter, Virginia, said of her mother, "She's really tough and independent. But it's not a selfish independence. She was always willing to make herself available to Dad. She's been remarkably adaptive. And she thinks my dad is remarkable—in a non-adulation way. She knows him inside and out and doesn't think he's perfect. They're a great team. They're very funny together. The humor has been a lifesaver. It has allowed Dad not to take himself too seriously."[18] Another daughter, Kathleen, said of her parents: "What you see is what you get. There is nothing behind closed doors that is any different than their public persona. It's really a gift. They just know who they are, and they are comfortable with who they are."[19]

A Happy Home

Marjorie Hinckley: "I have been thinking back—way back to 1937. We were married during the Depression—'the bottom of the Depression,' as my husband always says. Money was scarce, but we were full of hope and optimism. Those early days were not all blissful, but they were filled with determination and a great desire to establish a happy home. We loved each other, there was no doubt about that. But we also had to get used to each other. I think every couple has to get used to each other.

Early on I realized it would be better if we worked harder at getting accustomed to one another than constantly trying to change each other—which I discovered was impossible. Try not to be too demanding of one another. There must be a little give and take, and a great deal of flexibility, to make a happy home."[6]

A picnic with Grandpa and Grandma Hinckley.

President Hinckley's eightieth birthday celebration.

Marjorie frequently accompanied Gordon on his trips around the globe.

After nearly seven decades of marriage, they had traveled to the far corners of the world together; they walked side by side the pathway of life—ever faithful, loving, and supportive. Sister Hinckley passed away on April 6, 2004, just three weeks short of their sixty-seventh wedding anniversary. President Hinckley said, "Through all of these years we have been blessed in marvelous and remarkable ways. I feel only a great sense of gratitude. I thank the Lord for my beloved companion, for her loyalty, her love, her encouragement, her companionship. I thank the Lord every day for her, for our children and

Tomatoes for Sale

Sister Hinckley: "During World War II, we were encouraged to plant gardens, not only by the Church but by the government. My husband dug 3,000 holes in the property to the south of our home and planted 3,000 tomato plants. He hoed them and weeded them and irrigated them at 4:30 every Monday morning. When the tomatoes were ripe, I spent my days picking them. Baskets full, boxes full. We put up a sign: 'Tomatoes for Sale.' Toward the end of the crop, we couldn't give them away. My back ached. I could have said, 'Is this what I was born to do?' But the tomatoes went on people's food shelves, and the money we were paid for them paid the taxes that year, the taxes on our house that gave us shelter and was a home for our children. The whole project gave my husband and me a sense of 'togetherness.' The wife does not walk in front of or behind her husband, but at his side. And what is a blessing for him is a blessing for her. I have never felt to apologize to anyone for my supporting role as a wife and mother."[7]

Well Prepared

President James E. Faust said of President Hinckley: "I don't know of any single man who has come to the presidency of this Church who has been so well prepared. He has been taught by all of the great leaders of our time, one-on-one."

Elder David B. Haight commented: "President Hinckley has been prepared in a marvelous way. He has been schooled and carefully honed for this wonderful, marvelous call to be God's prophet on the earth."[8]

our posterity. I think of how empty my life would have been without her. I think we have experienced the problems that most people experience. But somehow, with the blessings of the Lord, we have made it to this station along the road of immortality and eternal life. All in all, it has been a wonderful journey."[20]

CHURCH SERVICE

"We ought to recognize something of the breadth and depth and height—grand and wonderful, large and all-encompassing—of the program of the Lord, and then work with diligence to meet our responsibility for our assigned portion of that program. Each of us has a small field to cultivate. While so doing, we must never lose sight of the greater picture, the large composite of the divine destiny of this work."[21]

In 1936 Gordon B. Hinckley was called as Sunday School superintendent of the Liberty Stake. From 1937 to 1946 he served on the Sunday School General Board. As part of this assignment he wrote a manual for the study of the Book of Mormon that was used in Sunday Schools throughout the Church for two decades. In 1946, he was called as second counselor in the East

Presenting President McKay with a copy of the Book of Mormon in Chinese.

Millcreek Stake presidency. Two years later, he was called as first counselor, and eight years after that he was called to stake president—becoming the third generation of Hinckleys to serve as a stake president. As a stake leader he was known for his efficiency, diligence, wisdom, and wonderful sense of humor.

Loyalty and Unity

"There is unity in the First Presidency of the Church. There is unity between the Presidency and the Twelve, perfect unity. There is unity among the members of the First Quorum of the Seventy and the Presiding Bishopric. I am somewhat familiar with the history of the Church, and I do not hesitate to say that there had never been greater unity in its councils and the relationships of those councils one to another, than there is today. I love my brethren. To a man they are loyal. They are supportive. Without hesitation they respond to every call regardless of personal convenience. They are true disciples of the Lord Jesus Christ."[9]

Total Unanimity

"It is important, my brethren, that there be no doubts or concerns about the governance of the Church and the exercise of the prophetic gifts, including the right to inspiration and revelation in administering the affairs and programs of the Church, when the President may be ill or is not able to function fully. The First Presidency and the Council of the Twelve Apostles, called and ordained to hold the keys of the priesthood, have the authority and responsibility to govern the Church, to administer its ordinances, to expound its doctrine, and to establish and maintain its practices. Each man who is ordained an Apostle and sustained a member of the Council of the Twelve is sustained as a prophet, seer, and revelator . . . Counselors [in the First Presidency are] drawn from the Council of the Twelve. Therefore, all incumbent members of the Quorum of the First Presidency and of the Council of the Twelve have been the recipients of the keys, rights, and authority pertaining to the holy apostleship. . . . When the President is ill or not able to function fully in all of the duties of his office, his two Counselors . . . carry on with the day-to-day work of the Presidency. . . . Major questions of policy, procedures, programs, or doctrine are considered deliberately and prayerfully by the First Presidency and the Twelve together. . . . No decision emanates from the deliberations of the First Presidency and the Twelve without total unanimity among all concerned."[10]

On April 6, 1958, he was called by President McKay to full-time Church service as Assistant to the Quorum of the Twelve. Two and a half years later, at the October 1961 general conference, he was sustained as a member of the Quorum of the Twelve Apostles (just three months after the passing of his beloved father). Elder Hinckley was respected at Church headquarters and among the Saints for his devoted service and leadership, his writing and speaking abilities, and for his good nature and kindly disposition. In two decades of service in the Twelve he traveled tens of thousands of miles as a special witness of the Lord in all the world. He supervised missions in Asia and in South America and filled innumerable headquarters assignments and committee responsibilities. As an Apostle, he helped organize and obtain land for temples and chapels; he divided missions and stakes, trained mission presidents and local leaders, and dedicated countries for the preaching of the gospel.

An example of the scope of his duties is reflected in the history of the Mormon Tabernacle Choir. Upon the death of Elder Richard L. Evans of the Twelve, the First Presidency assigned Elder Hinckley to supervise the Mormon Tabernacle Choir as its advisor. Even as President of the Church, he retained that responsibility and met regularly with the choir president and music director. His love and support for the choir was well-known and appreciated.

The next two decades would bring new callings and additional responsibilities. In July 1981 he was called by President Spencer W. Kimball to serve as an additional counselor in the

Elder Hinckley visiting with sailors of the *USS Kittyhawk*.

Called as an Assistant to the Quorum of the Twelve on April 6, 1958.

Not Forgotten

In October 1966, as part of a tour throughout Asia, Elder Hinckley, escorted by Major Allen C. Rozsa (advisor to South Vietnam's Air Force Photographic Reconnaissance Squadron) on a Vietnamese C-47, embarked on a forty-eight-hour tour of war-torn Vietnam. He visited Da Nang, Nha Trang, and Saigon. At Da Nang, LDS servicemen gathered for a meeting with Elder Hinckley. Stacking their M-16 rifles on the back few rows and with pistols and knives at their sides, they began with a memorial service to honor and remember the LDS soldiers who had recently died in combat and ended with a testimony meeting. Major Rozsa recalled, "Elder Hinckley made us feel that we weren't forgotten. His visit boosted our morale in a phenomenal way. He made us feel that we were good, honest men, and that what we were doing was honorable."[11]

First Presidency. In December 1982, upon the passing of Nathan Eldon Tanner, Gordon B. Hinckley was called as Second Counselor in the First Presidency. In November 1985, upon the dissolving of the First Presidency with the death of President Kimball, he was called as a First Counselor to new Church President Ezra Taft Benson. Nine years later, upon President Benson's death, he was set apart as First Counselor to Howard W. Hunter on June 5, 1994. As each of the three Presidents with whom he served as counselor experienced age-related illnesses, President Hinckley carried much of the day-to-day responsibility for the

A tender moment with President Spencer W. Kimball.

administration of the Church. He said, "That was a very heavy and overwhelming responsibility. It was an almost terrifying load at times. Of course, I consulted with our brethren of the Twelve. I recall on one particular occasion getting on my knees before the Lord and asking for help in the midst of that very difficult situation. And there came into my mind those reassuring words, 'Be still and know that I am God' (D&C 101:16). I knew again that this was His work, that He would not let it fail, that all I had to do was work at it and do our very best, and that the work would move forward without let or hindrance of any kind."[22] President Hinckley deeply loved the brethren with whom he served; he had worked side by side with them over many decades of consecrated service, and with the loss of these beloved colleagues came more responsibility.

On March 13, 1995, President Gordon B. Hinckley, accompanied by his newly called counselors and the members of the Twelve, spoke from the lobby of the beautiful Joseph Smith Memorial Building to a room of media. He made a brief statement and took questions. The day before, Sunday March 12, 1995, he had been sustained by the Quorum of the Twelve and ordained and set apart as the fifteenth President of The Church

Gordon B. Hinckley was called as an additional counselor in the First Presidency in 1981.

of Jesus Christ of Latter-day Saints (President Hunter had died a week earlier after nine months as President). A reporter asked him about his focus, the theme of his administration. Without hesitation he answered, "Carry on! Our theme will be to carry on the great work which has been furthered by our predecessors."[23] This would foreshadow a hallmark of his presidency as he was interviewed by media outlets, large and small, around the world. He was comfortable with journalists, not afraid to be interviewed, and welcomed the opportunity to present the Church and its beliefs to the world.

To the Saints, his face was familiar and comforting. People knew him, they trusted him. They had come to know that this most remarkable man could be relied upon to lead the Church and do the Lord's will. With his theme of carrying on this great latter-day work, he followed his predecessors in expanding and accelerating the growth and mission of the Church in unique and important ways. Some of the

The First Presidency.

milestones and hallmarks of his presidency include: temple building, "The Family: A Proclamation to the World," construction of the Conference Center, the Perpetual Education Fund, the establishment of additional Quorums of the Seventy, world travel, interaction with the media, interfaith outreach and tolerance, and Church growth.

TEMPLES

Generations yet unborn will, among many things, remember and acknowledge Gordon B. Hinckley as the temple builder. He was involved in the construction and dedications of more temples over a longer period of time than any other person in this dispensation.

Smaller Temples: At the conclusion of the April 1998 general conference, President Hinckley announced a "tremendous undertaking," a program to begin immediately to construct smaller temples across the earth that would bring the blessings and ordinances of the Lord's house to more people. President Hinckley said, "Nothing even approaching

Leading by Example

"President Gordon B. Hinckley was named one of 2002's 'Most Caring People in America' November 18 in Washington, DC.

"The designation was given by the Caring Institute, and organization founded in 1985 to honor and promote the values of caring, integrity and public service. . . . President Hinckley was chosen for his example and leadership of the Church, which responds to world tragedies and natural disasters by sending food, medicine and supplies, and providing tens of millions of dollars annually in relief worldwide. . . .

"President Hinckley did not attend the Monday night awards ceremony, reportedly opting instead to stay home and observe family home evening."[12]

Since he was called to the First Presidency in 1981, he dedicated or rededicated 95 of the 124 operating temples.

A Temple Building Prophet

No other Church leader has been directly involved with the construction and dedication of more temples than President Hinckley. Joseph Smith, Joseph Young, Daniel H. Wells, John Taylor, George Albert Smith, Marion G. Romney, and Boyd K. Packer each dedicated one temple; Wilford Woodruff, Joseph Fielding Smith, Ezra Taft Benson, and Howard W. Hunter each dedicated two temples; Heber J. Grant dedicated three temples; Spencer W. Kimball dedicated four temples; David O. McKay dedicated five temples; Thomas S. Monson and James E. Faust have each dedicated seven temples. Gordon B. Hinckley dedicated an unprecedented ninety-five temples in locations all over the globe.[13]

it has ever been tried before."[24] Six months later, in the October 1998 general conference, he added, "I speak of these temples as smaller temples. Actually, they do not look small, they look large. They are beautiful. They are built of the best materials and in the best fashion of which we know. Each will be a house of the Lord dedicated to His holy purposes."[25] His prophetic leadership has increased the number of temples worldwide from 51 in 1998 to 124 today.

Nauvoo Temple: President Hinckley made a surprise announcement in the closing session of general conference on April 4, 1999: "I feel impressed to announce that among all of the temples we are constructing, we plan to rebuild the Nauvoo Temple. . . . The new building will stand as a memorial to those who built the first such structure there on the banks of the Mississippi."[26] Three years later—a day never to be forgotten—the Nauvoo Temple was dedicated June 27, 2002, at 5 PM, the very hour and day that Joseph and Hyrum Smith were martyred in Carthage Jail 158 years before. The dedicatory services were carried to some 3.5 million Church members in 72 countries, making it the largest meeting in the history of the Church. It was a particularly emotional and joyous time for President Hinckley, whose father presided over the Northern States Mission headquartered in Chicago in 1939 and had suggested a rebuilding of the Nauvoo Temple to mark the one hundredth anniversary of the establishment of Nauvoo. The Church did not have the financial resources to do so then, but President Hinckley was able to fulfill his father's desire sixty years later.

THE FAMILY: A PROCLAMATION TO THE WORLD

President Hinckley read "The Family: A Proclamation to the World" in the general Relief Society meeting of the Church on September 23, 1995. To underscore its importance, this is only the fifth proclamation issued by the First Presidency and the Quorum of the Twelve Apostles in this dispensation. The proclamation sets forth fundamental gospel doctrine about marriage, family, gender, Heavenly Father's plan of happiness, the sacred responsibilities of spouses and parents, and

Preserving the Family: 10 Specific Things

- Accept responsibility for our role as parents and fulfill our obligations to our children
- Get married and stay married
- Put the father back at the head of the home
- Recognize and value the supreme importance of mothers
- Celebrate and treat children as our most priceless treasures
- Discipline and train children with love
- Teach values to children
- Teach children to work
- Read to and with children
- Pray together[14]

A Magnificent Pulpit

"President Hinckley planted trees every spring, except for only two or three years that he was away from the city. In the spring of 1964 he planted a black walnut tree, which grew straight and tall but then died in 1999. Knowing that walnut is used to make furniture, President Hinckley called on Brother Ben Banks, who was in the business of hardwood lumber before his call as a Seventy. One of Elder Banks' sons had an idea. President Hinckley recalled, "One of them suggested that it would make a pulpit for [the Conference Center]. The idea excited me. The tree was cut down and then cut into two heavy logs. Then followed the long process of drying, first naturally and then kiln drying. The logs were cut into boards at a sawmill in Salem, Utah. The boards were then taken to Fetzer's woodworking plant, where expert craftsmen designed and built this magnificent pulpit. . . . The end product is beautiful. I wish all of you could examine it closely. It represents superb workmanship, and here I am speaking to you from the tree I grew in my backyard, where my children played and also grew. It is an emotional thing for me. . . . I offer my profound thanks for making it possible to have a small touch of mine in this great hall where the voices of prophets will go out to all the world in testimony of the Redeemer of mankind."[15]

principles of successful marriage and family. It also provides a solemn warning that the disintegration of the family would undermine society. President Hinckley declared, "We commend to all a careful, thoughtful, and prayerful reading of this proclamation. The strength of any nation is rooted within the walls of its homes. We urge our people everywhere to strengthen their families in conformity with these time-honored values."[27]

CONFERENCE CENTER

Because the Church had outgrown the Tabernacle on Temple Square, President Hinckley announced plans to construct a new Conference Center on April 6, 1996. The 1.4 million square-foot building was dedicated by President Hinckley during the general conference of the Church on October 8, 2000. The building seats 21,333 in the main Conference Center and 905 in the Little Theater, making it possibly the largest theater-type building in the world.

During the April 2000 general conference, the inaugural conference for the Conference Center, President Hinckley explained, "The building of this structure has been a bold undertaking. We worried about it. We prayed about it. We

The Conference Center in Salt Lake City.

Podium in the Conference Center made from President Hinckley's Black Walnut tree.

listened for the whisperings of the Spirit concerning it. And only when we felt the confirming voice of the Lord did we determine to go forward."[28]

PERPETUAL EDUCATION FUND

In the April 2001 general conference, President Hinckley announced a new official program of the Church, a "bold initiative" that was inspired of the Lord.[29] The Church would establish a revolving fund, similar to the Perpetual Emigration Fund in the early days of the Church, that would bless generations of people to come. From the continuing contributions of faithful Latter-day Saints, a Perpetual Education Fund (PEF) was created that extends loans to devout and ambitious young men and women so that they may borrow money to attend school. They will then repay that which they have borrowed with a small amount of interest designed as an incentive to repay the loan.[30] "It will not be a welfare effort, commendable as those

efforts are, but rather an education opportunity," said President Hinckley. "The beneficiaries will repay the money, and when they do so, they will enjoy a wonderful sense of freedom because they have improved their lives not through a grant or gift, but through borrowing and then repaying. They can hold their heads high in a spirit of independence. The likelihood of their remaining faithful and active throughout their lives will be very high."[31] It is designed to help break the cycle of poverty, lack of educational and employment opportunities, lost hope, and bleak futures. President Hinckley said of the PEF, "Young men and women in the underprivileged areas of the world, young men and women who for the most part are returned missionaries, will be enabled to get good educations that will lift them out of the slough of poverty in which their forebears for generations have struggled. They will marry and go forward with skills that will qualify them to earn well and take their places in society where they can make a substantial contribution. They will likewise grow in the Church, filling positions of responsibility and rearing families who will continue in the faith."[32]

QUORUMS OF THE SEVENTY

President Hinckley called Area Authority Seventies in the April 1997 general conference, a move toward a decentralization of the operation of the Church and greater efficiency in working with nations across the globe. Members of the Third, Fourth, and Fifth Quorums of the Seventy were called to serve for a period of years in a voluntary capacity in the area in which they reside. "We have established a pattern under which the Church may grow to any size with an organization of Area Presidencies and Area Authority Seventies, chosen and working across the world according to need."[33] Today, these three quorums, as well as three additional quorums, work under the direction of General Authorities.

TRAVELING THE WORLD

No President of the Church has traveled more miles to more lands over more years than President Hinckley. He met with the Saints in every corner of the world, traveling to more than sixty countries since becoming President. He met with leaders, people, and media around the globe. He visited scores of nations to uplift and spread the message of peace. With characteristic humor and dedication he said, "I am no longer a young man filled with energy and vitality. I am an old man trying to catch up with Brother Haight! I'm given to meditation and prayer. I would enjoy sitting in a rocker, swallowing prescriptions, listening to soft music, and contemplating the things of the universe. But such activity offers no challenge and makes no contribution. I wish to be up and doing. I wish to face each day with resolution and purpose. I wish to use every waking hour to give encouragement, to bless those whose burdens are heavy, to build faith and strength of testimony. . . . I could spend all day in my office, doing so year after year, dealing with mountains of problems, many of them of small consequence. I do spend a good deal of time there. But I feel a greater mission, a higher responsibility to be out among the people."[34] His complete commitment to helping others, spreading the restored gospel message, and witnessing of Jesus Christ took him to places and people never before visited by a prophet. He was indefatigable in his desire to be "out among the people."

President Hinckley welcomed the Winter Olympics to Salt Lake City in 2002.

MEDIA

No Church leader has been interviewed and profiled by more media outlets around the world than has Gordon B. Hinckley. He welcomed the media attention because he understood and respected journalists, and he knew that media coverage helps to spread the gospel message and continues to bring the Church out of obscurity. He was interviewed by large publications, including *Time* magazine and the *New York Times*, and by local newspapers and broadcast outlets in countries across the globe. He appeared before the National Press Club and was featured on *60 Minutes* and *Larry King Live.*

The media's deference and respect toward President Hinckley and, subsequently, the Church, are personified in these words: "Under [President Hinckley's] direction, the LDS Church made certain that Salt Lake Organizing Committee for the Olympics had sufficient support and volunteers to impress the planet. Then Hinckley understatedly led his decked-out church onto a world stage before a billion beaming viewers, readers, and spectators. . . . In those three remarkable weeks of February, the media-savvy Hinckley erased notions of cults, of peculiarity and provincialism, of proselytizing and puritanical codes, and the misplaced zeal early in 2001 that prompted the news media to temporarily nickname the Olympics 'The Mormon Games' . . . Hinckley displayed to the world an LDS Church that was mainstream, low-key, gracious, civic minded, approachable, tolerant and global."[35]

INTERFAITH OUTREACH AND TOLERANCE

One of the hallmarks of President Hinckley's presidency was his desire to reach out in love to others not of our faith and to extend a hand of friendship. Over the years he repeatedly denounced arrogance and self-righteousness among Church members, saying, "We must never forget that we live in a world of great diversity. The people of the earth are all our Father's children and are of many and varied religious persuasions. We must cultivate tolerance and appreciation and respect one another. We have differences of doctrine. This need not bring about animosity or any kind of holier-than-thou attitude."[36]

In general conference, President Hinckley commended the Pope and the Baptists for their efforts to promote chastity and morality, and he commented on the collaborative work the Church had accomplished with a Protestant minister.[37] In his opening remarks in the April 1998 general conference he said, "We can respect other religions, and must do so. We must recognize the great good they accomplish. We must teach our children to be tolerant and friendly toward those not of our faith. We can and do work with those of other religions in the defense of those values which have made our civilization great and our society distinctive."[38] As the Lord's prophet to all the world, his motivation was his love for all humankind and his desire that they may be partakers of peace in this life and eternal life in the world to come. He said, "We recognize the good that every other church in the world does. We have no quarrel with other churches. We do not argue, we do not debate, or anything of the kind. We simply say to people not of our faith, 'You bring with you all the truth that you have, and let us see if we can add to it.' That is the mission and message of this church."[39]

PUBLICATIONS

President Hinckley wrote countless articles and numerous books during his lifetime. Among his books is *Truth Restored*, a history of the Church from the Restoration to the centennial of the pioneers' entrance into the Salt Lake Valley.

Written at the request of President George Albert Smith, for decades it was a standard reference text for thousands of missionaries. His more recent publications include *Faith, The Essence of True Religion* (1998), a compilation of various general conference messages and *Ensign* articles; *Standing for Something: 10 Neglected Virtues That Will Heal Our Hearts and Homes* (2000), a nationally published book that has sold over half a million copies and appeared on the *USA Today* and *New York Times* bestseller lists; and *Way to Be: 9 Ways to Be Happy and Make Something of Your Life* (2002), another bestseller that was published by Simon & Schuster as a book of virtues for teenagers and their parents. His compelling biography, *Go Forward with Faith*, was published in 1996.

CHURCH GROWTH

In 1910, when President Hinckley was born, there were 699 wards and branches in the Church, with 398,478 members. In 1961, when he was sustained as a member of the Quorum of the Twelve, there were 3,143 wards and branches, 1.8 million members, and 11,593 missionaries serving throughout the world. As of December 31, 2007, there were 27,827 wards and branches in various locations all over the world, with 13,193,999 million members worldwide and 52,686 full-time missionaries serving all over the globe.[40] There were 19 temples in operation when President Hinckley was called to the First Presidency (as a counselor to President Spencer W. Kimball, in 1981). As of January 2008, there were 124 temples in operation, 95 of which had been dedicated by President Hinckley. Additional temples are currently being constructed and several others have been announced.

Speaking to the Los Angeles World Affairs Council on May 13, 1999, President Hinckley recalled the first time he visited Santiago, Chile, some thirty years earlier. At that time there were around one hundred members of the Church in Chile. At that first meeting in Chile, President Hinckley met with ten students in a small building that was little more than a shed. Just two weeks before this 1999 meeting with the Los Angeles World Affairs Council, President Hinckley returned from another trip to Santiago, Chile. Of that visit President Hinckley recalled, "I was back in Santiago and spoke to a congregation assembled in a large football stadium with 57,500 people in attendance. I could scarcely believe what I saw. . . . They were well-dressed, clean and attractive. They do not smoke. They do not drink. . . . They were there as families for the most part. . . . There is love and honor and respect in the family circle. This is the result of church teaching and church family programs. Every good citizen adds to the strength of a nation. With that assumption, I do not hesitate to say that the nation of Chile is better for our presence, and the same thing is happening in every other nation in South America."[41]

Commenting on the current condition of the Church, President Hinckley said, "What a miracle it is that we are able to address you out across the world. We speak here in the Conference Center in Salt Lake City. We speak in our native tongue. But many thousands of you are assembled in Church facilities in many lands, and you hear us in 56 languages. . . . I am pleased to report that the work of the Church moves forward. We continue to grow across that world. Our missionary work goes on without serious impediment. . . . Our sacrament meeting attendance gradually edges up. There is room for improvement, and I urge you to work at it constantly. . . . Faith in the payment of tithes and offerings increases despite the straitened economic circumstances in which we find ourselves. . . . We are constructing about 400 new chapels a year to accommodate the growth in the membership of the Church."[42]

Church publications have been made available in 157 languages.

TEACHINGS OF PRESIDENT
GORDON B. HINCKLEY

◆

President Hinckley spoke in hundreds of conferences and other settings since he was called as a General Authority in 1958. It would be fair to say that he spoke on scores of subjects over more years than any other General Authority. The following is a brief sampling from some of his recurring themes.

MARRIAGE AND FAMILY

Though there were occasional periods of adversity, President and Sister Hinckley enjoyed a happy marriage and family life, an example to all who knew and associated with them. Based on his own success at home, President Hinckley counseled, "The basis of a good marriage is mutual respect. . . . If a husband would think less of himself and more of his wife, we'd have happier homes throughout the Church and throughout the world. . . . Mutual respect makes all the difference in the world—having respect for one another as individuals and not trying to change your partner after your manner. You let her live her life in her way and encourage her talents and her interests."[43]

Over four decades he continually spoke on the subject of marriage and family. His counsel was always timely and timeless: "We must work at our responsibility as parents as if everything in life counted on it, because in fact everything in life does count on it. If we fail in our homes, we fail in our lives. . . . The consequences of your leadership in your home will be eternal and everlasting."[44]

President Hinckley had a grateful heart. Among his richest blessings, of which he talked on numerous occasions, was his posterity. "I don't know how anyone could have been more richly blessed than we have been. If you can live with a

President and Sister Hinckley.

Wedding Ring

Sister Hinckley: "I wear a simple gold band on my finger. It's 18-karat gold and is over a hundred years old. It belonged to my Grandmother Paxman. She told me a story—more than once—about it when I was young. She was widowed at the age of twenty-two, and this was her wedding ring. She never remarried, and the ring was precious to her because it was all she had left to remind her of her young husband. One day she was changing the straw in the mattress, which she did yearly. She lost the ring. The story goes that she felt desperate at the loss and prayed. Then she looked down on the ground, and there was the ring. Her story convinced me that prayers are heard and that prayers are answered."[16]

Young Mothers

Addressing young mothers in a Mother's Day sacrament meeting, Sister Hinckley said, "As I watched some of the young mothers come into this meeting with young children, restless from meetings that have preceded this one, I think I felt something of your frustration and challenge to be the perfect mother. Relax. There is no such thing as the perfect mother who fits all the eulogies. We just do the best we can with the help of the Lord, and who knows, these children who are struggling to be free may someday rise up and call us blessed. The trick is to enjoy it. Don't wish away your days of caring for young children. This is your great day. Sometimes we get so caught up in the physical work and trivia that we forget the big picture. We forget whose children they really are. When the house is filled with children, noise and teasing and laughter, you get the feeling this is forever. Before you know it they will be gone."[17]

"It's Too Late"

"Not long after we were married, we built our first home. We had very little money. I did much of the work myself. It would be called 'sweat equity' today. The landscaping was entirely my responsibility. The first of many trees that I planted was a thornless honey locust. Envisioning the day when its filtered shade would assist in cooling the house in the summertime, I put it in a place at the corner where the wind from the canyon to the east blew the hardest. I dug a hole, put in the bare root, put soil around it, poured on water, and largely forgot it. It was only a wisp of a tree, perhaps three-quarters of an inch in diameter. It was so supple that I could bend it with ease in any direction. I paid little attention to it as the years passed. Then one winter day, when the tree was barren of leaves, I chanced to look out the window at it. I noticed that it was leaning to the west, misshapen and out of balance. I could scarcely believe it. I went out and braced myself against it as if to push it upright. But the trunk was now nearly a foot in diameter. My strength was as nothing against it. I took from my toolshed a block and tackle. Attaching one end to the tree and another to a well-set post, I pulled the rope. The pulleys moved a little, and the trunk of the tree trembled slightly. But that was all. It seemed to say, 'You can't straighten me. It's too late. I've grown this way because of your neglect, and I will not bend.' Finally in desperation I took my saw and cut off the great heavy branch on the west side. The saw left an ugly scar, more than eight inches across. I stepped back and surveyed what I had done. I had cut off the major part of the tree, leaving only one branch growing skyward. More than half a century has passed since I planted that tree. My daughter and her family live there now. The other day I looked again at the tree. It is large. Its shape is better. It is a great asset to the home. But how serious was the trauma of its youth and how brutal the treatment I used to straighten it. When it was first planted, a piece of string would have held it in place against the forces of the wind. I could have and should have supplied that string with ever so little effort. But I did not, and it bent to the forces that came against it."[18]

good woman through your life and see your children grow to maturity as happy, able individuals who are making a contribution, then you can count your life a success."[45]

YOUTH OF THE CHURCH

President Hinckley possessed a special love and concern for the youth of the Church. In these modern times of added distractions and increasing temptations, he maintained a positive approach when counseling the youth—complimenting their virtues rather than condemning their vices. "You are wonderful and you have within you the potential to do great and marvelous and good things. Don't let anyone stop you, don't let anybody get in your way, don't get sidetracked on some venture of one kind or another that might injure you and hurt you. 'Do what is right; let the consequence follow' [*Hymns*, no. 237]. If things get going the wrong way at a party that you are attending, walk out, say good-bye. Stand tall, do what is right, count on the Lord and He will bless you in a wonderful way."[46]

Always, while praising and commending the efforts of worthy youth across the world, he sounded the clear clarion call to righteousness: "You have such a tremendous responsibility, you young men and young women. You are the products of all the generations that have gone before you. All that you have of body and mind has been passed to you through your parents. Someday you will become parents and pass on to succeeding generations the qualities of body and

Rise above the World

"You of this generation, this chosen generation . . . you cannot with impunity follow practices out of harmony with values you have been taught. I challenge you to rise above the sordid elements of the world about you. You cannot afford to drink beer and other liquors which rob you of self-control. You cannot afford to smoke cigarettes or use other forms of tobacco and live up to the values which the Lord has set for your guidance. The partaking or distribution of illegal drugs is to be shunned as you would shun a terrible disease. You cannot in any degree become involved with pornography, whatever its form. You simply cannot afford to become involved in immoral practices— or to let down the bars of sexual restraint. The emotions that stir within you which make boys attractive to girls and girls attractive to boys are part of a divine plan, but they must be restrained, subdued, and kept under control, or they will destroy you and make you unworthy of many of the great blessings which the Lord has in store for you."[19]

Interview with Mike Wallace for *60 Minutes*.

mind which you have received from the past. Do not break the chain of the generations of your family. Keep it bright and strong. So very much depends on you. You are so very precious. You mean so much to this Church. It could not be the same without you. Stand tall, proud of your inheritance as sons and daughters of God. Look to Him for understanding and guidance. Walk according to His precepts and commandments."[47]

President Hinckley spoke to countless youth all across the world. His words were always designed to inspire young people everywhere to live up to the best within them. "I am so grateful for the youth of the Church. There is so much of evil everywhere. Temptation, with all its titillating influences, is about us everywhere. We lose some to these destructive forces, unfortunately. We sorrow over every one that is lost. We reach out to help them, to save them, but in too many cases our entreaties are spurned. Tragic is the course they are following. It is the way which leads down to destruction. But there are so many, many hundreds of thousands of our young people who are faithful and true, who are straight as an arrow and as strong as a great wave of the sea in following the course they have mapped out for themselves. It is a course of righteousness and goodness, a course of accomplishment and achievement. They are making something of their lives, and the world will be so much the better for them."[48]

TEMPLE WORK

No individual has been more involved in the building of temples in this dispensation than President Gordon B. Hinckley. From the development of the multilingual film presentation of temple instructions to the announcing, building, and dedication of nearly a hundred temples, President Hinckley continued his promotion of temples and temple work by teaching these principles to the world. He said, "Vicarious temple work for the dead more nearly approaches the vicarious sacrifice of the Savior Himself than any other work of which I know. No one comes with any expectation of thanks for the work which he or she does. It is given with love, without hope of compensation, or repayment. What a glorious principle!"[49]

Saving souls and temple work is the mission of the Lord's kingdom on the earth. President Hinckley, like his prophet-predecessors, taught about the importance of temples: "We believe that the gospel of Jesus Christ is not complete without what occurs in the temples. Everything that will occur in the temple is concerned with the things of eternity. . . . We believe that the family is an eternal unit, father, mother, children; and that same relationship which exists here will exist in the life beyond. That is the basic purpose of these sacred temples for ordinances which are eternal and everlasting in behalf of those who accept them."[50]

"If temple ordinances are an essential part of the restored gospel, and I testify that they are, then we must provide the means by which they can be accomplished. All of our vast family history endeavor is directed to temple work," said President Hinckley in general conference. "There is no other purpose for it. The temple ordinances become the crowning blessings the Church has to offer."[51]

MISSIONARY WORK

Throughout his decades of service in the Church, President Hinckley said many significant and encouraging words to the missionaries that serve all over the world, and to the members who are missionaries by example. Among profound teachings, he said, "Shining through all missionary service is the reassuring faith that the work is true and that the service being given is given unto God. Missionaries serve with faith in their hearts. It is a phenomenon of great power that quietly whispers, 'This cause is true, and to you there is an obligation to serve regardless of the cost.' "[52]

On another occasion he counseled the Saints to make their lives a shining example to the world: "Bring people into the Church. Bring them in with love. Bring them in with kindness. Bring them in with the example of your lives. So live the gospel that they will see in you something of wonder and

Elder Hinckley, as a missionary in England.

beauty and be encouraged to inquire, study the gospel, and join the Church."[53] President Hinckley taught that as we do so, our lives will be blessed: "Every man or woman who goes forth in missionary service blesses the lives of all he or she teaches. Furthermore, his or her own life is enriched by this selfless labor."[54]

HOPE AND OPTIMISM

It is important that we foster a positive attitude, in spite of the adversity and trials that confront us every day. To encourage people to be hopeful and upbeat, President Hinckley said, "We have every reason to be optimistic in this world. Tragedy is around, yes. Problems everywhere, yes. . . . You can't, you don't, build out of pessimism or cynicism. You look with optimism, work with faith, and things happen."[55]

Known for his positive outlook on life, President Hinckley encouraged all to look on the bright side. Perhaps that explains another reason for his vibrant longevity—he

A major theme in the presidency of Gordon B. Hinckley was "Go forward with faith."

to others, and the cumulative, rippling effect will be tremendous."[58]

"I would just like to say that whatever happens in the world, and I think no one of us can foretell what might happen at this time, that God will be with us. He will watch over us. He will protect us. He will see that we are provided for. And we shall endure under His watchful care if we will be true and faithful and obedient and hearken to His word."[59]

PEACE

If we are committed to Christ and His kingdom, we have no need to fear. President Hinckley's life and his counsel resonate with an empowering belief about faith and peace: "As you go forward with your vocations, as you assume responsibilities of leadership, may you continue to carry in your hearts . . . a quiet and solemn faith, a faith that will carry you through every storm and difficulty and bring peace to your hearts."[60]

"May the sunlight of faith ever warm your hearts. May you grow in strength and capacity as the years pass. May your outreach to others be as that of the good Samaritan. May the service which you render be fruitful for good in the lives of others. May prayer be a part of your daily activity. . . . May you be true and faithful one to another, and may the years bring to you that peace which passeth all understanding, the peace which comes of following the precepts of the Master."[61]

"Are these perilous times? They are. But there is no need to fear. We can have peace in our hearts and peace in our homes. We can be an influence for good in this world, every one of us."[62]

LOVE AND FRIENDSHIP

More than six billion people live on this planet. There are a variety of differences that divide us and cause contention between us. There are religious differences, varying socioeconomic groups, and ethnic and cultural diversity. The dissimilarities of the people of the earth range from employment

always looked for the good and the uplifting as he counseled, "Cultivate an attitude of happiness. Cultivate a spirit of optimism. Walk with faith, rejoicing in the beauties of nature, in the goodness of those you love, in the testimony which you carry in your heart concerning things divine."[56]

"I am asking that we stop seeking out the storms and enjoy more fully the sunlight. I am suggesting that as we go through life we 'accentuate the positive.' I am asking that we look a little deeper for the good, that we still voices of insult and sarcasm, that we more generously compliment virtue and effort."[57]

"We must walk with hope and faith. We must speak affirmatively and cultivate an attitude of confidence. We all have the capacity to do so. Our strength will give strength

His Motto

President Hinckley's personal motto: "Things will work out. If you keep trying and praying and working, things will work out. They always do. If you want to die at an early age, dwell on the negative. Accentuate the positive, and you'll be around for awhile."[20]

A Painting of Two Butterflies

"A few days ago there came to my office a man from Las Vegas, Nevada. His wife and married daughter were with him. When we had accomplished the purpose of his visit, the younger woman asked if I would accept something from her thirteen-year-old daughter. She unwrapped a painting of two butterflies around a flowering shrub. The mother explained that her daughter had been struck by a car in a terrible accident when she was four years of age. Her body was badly broken. She was left paralyzed from the shoulders down, a quadriplegic without the use of arms or legs. She had painted this picture holding a brush between her teeth and moving her head. As I listened to that story, the painting grew in beauty and value before my eyes. It became more than a portrayal of butterflies. It represented remarkable courage in the face of blinding adversity; tenacious practice in holding and moving the brush; pleading prayers for help; faith—the faith of a child, nurtured by loving parents, that she could create beauty notwithstanding her handicap. . . . I will hang this small painting in my study so that during occasional hours of struggle there will come into my mind the picture of a beautiful little girl, robbed of the use of her feet and hands, gripping the handle of a paintbrush in her teeth to create a thing of beauty."[21]

"This principle of love is the basic essence of the gospel of Jesus Christ. Without love of God and love of neighbor there is little else to commend the gospel to us as a way of life."[65]

TESTIMONY

A testimony is the most precious asset, though intangible, that one can possess. It cannot be bought or sold, stolen or given away. However, it must be gained with all our hearts—through earnest study, quiet pondering, and sincere prayer. President Hinckley paid the price to acquire his heartfelt testimony of Jesus Christ and His work. About testimony, President Hinckley said, "I have a testimony—real, burning, and vital—of the truth of this work. I know that God our Eternal Father lives and that Jesus is the Christ, my Savior

and income to age and race. Independent of race, religion, age, creed, or any other gulf that divides us, President Hinckley counseled: "I hope that we will be supportive and helpful to our neighbors whatever their religious background might be. Whether it be Muslim, whether it be Buddhist, whether it be Christian, whatever. We are all sons and daughters of God. We've got to learn to live together in this world and respect and honor and help one another."[63]

The heart of this approach to life is love. President Hinckley said, "Love is of the very essence of life. It is the pot of gold at the end of the rainbow. Yet it is more than the end of the rainbow. Love is at the beginning also, and from it springs the beauty that arches across the sky on a stormy day. Love is the security for which children weep, the yearning of youth, the adhesive that binds marriage, and the lubricant that prevents devastating friction in the home; it is the peace of old age, the sunlight of hope shining through death. How rich are those who enjoy it in their associations with family, friends, church, and neighbors. I am one who believes that love, like faith, is a gift of God."[64]

Speaking from the Tabernacle on Temple Square.

and my Redeemer. It is He who stands at the head of this Church. All I desire is that I go forward with this work as He would have it go forward."[66]

"This witness, this testimony, can be the most precious of all the gifts of God. It is a heavenly bestowal when there is the right effort. It is the opportunity, it is the responsibility of every man and woman in this Church to obtain within himself or herself a conviction of the truth of this great latter-day work and of those who stand at its head, even the living God and the Lord Jesus Christ."[67]

President Hinckley has said that it is testimony that moves the work of the Lord forward. "This thing which we call testimony is the great strength of the Church. It is the wellspring of faith and activity. It is difficult to explain. It is difficult to quantify. It is an elusive and mysterious thing, and yet it is as real and powerful as any force on the earth. . . . This thing which we call testimony is difficult to define, but its fruits are plainly evident. It is the Holy Spirit testifying through us."[68]

JOSEPH SMITH

In honor of the great prophet of the Restoration and to express his love and testimony for the Prophet Joseph, President Hinckley said, "I wish to express appreciation for the birth of the prophet Joseph Smith. . . .

"How great indeed is our debt to him. His life began in Vermont and ended in Illinois, and marvelous were the things that happened between that simple beginning and that tragic ending. It was he who brought us a true knowledge of God the Eternal Father and His Risen Son, the Lord Jesus Christ. During the short time of his great vision he learned more concerning the nature of Deity than all of those who through centuries had argued that matter in learned councils and scholarly forums. He brought us this marvelous book, the Book of Mormon, as another witness for the living reality of the Son of God. To him, from those who held it anciently, came the priesthood, the power, the gift, the authority, the keys to speak and act in the name of God. He gave us the organization of the Church and its great and sacred mission.

Through him were restored the keys of the holy temples, that men and women might enter into eternal covenants with God, and that the great work for the dead might be accomplished to open the way for eternal blessings.

"He was the instrument in the hands of the Almighty. He was the servant acting under the direction of the Lord Jesus Christ in bringing to pass this great latter-day work.

"We stand in reverence before him. He is the great prophet of this dispensation. He stands at the head of this great and mighty work which is spreading across the earth. He is our prophet, our revelator, our seer, our friend. Let us not forget him. . . . God be thanked for the Prophet Joseph."[69]

JESUS CHRIST

As President of the Church, President Hinckley presided over the kingdom of God on the earth. He was the presiding high priest. The mantle of his office and the burden that accompanied it are understood by very few. One of his greatest rewards, however, was when he was out among the people, magnifying his call as a special witness of Jesus Christ to all the world. He was one who *knew* of the divinity of the Savior. He came to this absolute knowledge through personal revelation, and he bore witness of it, with strength and conviction, to the world: "I know that I am not the head of this Church. The Lord Jesus Christ is its head. He is its living head. My mission, my chief responsibility, my greatest honor comes in bearing solemn testimony of His living reality. Jesus Christ is the Son of God, who condescended to come into this world of misery, struggle and pain, to touch men's hearts for good, to teach the way of eternal life, and to give Himself as a sacrifice for the sins of all mankind. He is 'King of Kings and Lord of Lords, and He shall reign forever and ever' (Handel's *Messiah*). How different, how empty our lives would be without Him. How much truer, how much deeper is our love and appreciation and respect one for another because of Him. How infinite is our opportunity for exaltation made possible through His redeeming love. I bear solemn witness that He lives and stands on the right hand of His Father."[70]

MARJORIE PAY HINCKLEY
NOVEMBER 23, 1911–APRIL 6, 2004

Her cheerful optimism was evident in a conversation she had with Gordon: "Shortly before we were to be married, Gordon called and said, 'I think we had better go to lunch today.' So we did and he said, 'I think you should know that I only have $150 to my name.' Well, $150 sounded like a small fortune to me. I had hoped for a husband and now I was getting $150 too! I said, 'Oh, that will work out just fine; if you've got $150, we're set!"[71]

Marjorie and Gordon shared an optimistic view toward the world, a love of books, a willingness to work, and a commitment to the Church.[72] Though the physical effects of age were visible in her later years, the love they shared was equally apparent. "I sat across the table from my wife the other evening," Gordon said. "It was fifty-five years ago that we were married in the Salt Lake Temple. . . . Now, for more than half a century, we have walked together through much of storm as well as sunshine. Today neither of us stands as tall as we once did. As I looked at her across the table, I noted a few wrinkles in her face and hands. But are they less beautiful than before? No, in fact, they are more so. Those wrinkles have a beauty of their own, and inherent in their very presence is something that speaks reassuringly of strength and integrity and a love that runs more deeply and quietly than ever before."[73]

Marjorie and Gordon walked the highway of life side by side for almost sixty-seven years. She traveled the world with him, meeting members of the Church and supporting her husband in his heavy responsibilities. The dedication of the Accra Ghana Temple on January 11, 2004, was her last trip with him.

In President Hinckley's closing remarks at general conference, April 4, 2004, he said, "Some of you have noticed the absence of Sister Hinckley. For the first time in 46 years, since I became a General Authority, she has not attended general conference. Early this year we were in Africa to dedicate the Accra Ghana Temple. On leaving there we flew to Sal. . . . We then flew to St. Thomas. . . . We were on our way home when she collapsed with weariness. She's had a difficult time ever since. She's now 92, a little younger than I am. I guess the clock is winding down, and we do not know how to rewind it."[74]

Gordon B. and Marjorie Pay Hinckley.

At 5:05 PM, April 6, 2004, the hands on the clock stopped. Marjorie Pay Hinckley passed away in her home, surrounded by her family. President Hinckley described Marjorie's legacy as wife and mother in this fitting tribute: "To her I give all the credit for the virtues of our family, including our children and our grandchildren and our great-grandchildren. She holds a very bright spot in their hearts. . . . My love for her extends over a very long period of time and I expect it will go on forever."[75]

PRESIDENT GORDON B. HINCKLEY

President Hinckley died at home surrounded by family at 7 PM, Sunday, January 27, 2008, of causes incident to age. He was ninety-seven. During his nearly thirteen years as President, he led The Church of Jesus Christ of Latter-day Saints through a period of remarkable growth. No President of the Church has lived longer, traveled more, or spoken to more members of the Church around the world than President Gordon B. Hinckley.

His service was marked by significant milestones, including the creation and publication of "The Family: A Proclamation to the World," the construction of the Conference Center and dozens of temples, and the creation of six new quorums of the Seventy. Through countless media interviews, he improved the public image of the Church and helped bring it out of obscurity. Although he had many administrative duties at Church headquarters, what he wanted most was to be out among the people. He traveled nearly a million miles and spoke to hundreds of thousands of Latter-day Saints in at least 160 nations, expressing his love and faith and infectious optimism. He counseled Church members to fellowship new converts and befriend members of other faiths. He spent his life testifying of the living reality of Jesus Christ and exhorted Church members to live exemplary lives, to stand a little taller, and to avoid the evils of the world.

President Hinckley worked hard up until a few days before his death. He was known for his indefatigable energy and ability to work, his bright mind and breadth of knowledge, his endearing wit and profound wisdom, his kind and good heart, his doctrinal clarity and testimony of the restored

gospel, his compassion and warmth, and his love for his wife, his family, and the Saints spread over the earth. Above all, he will be remembered as a true prophet of the living God, a beloved and special witness of Jesus Christ.

Lloyd D. Newell

Associate Professor of Church History and Doctrine, PhD Brigham Young University

Milestones in the Presidency of Gordon B. Hinckley

During his years as President of the Church, Gordon B. Hinckley

- Saw Church membership grow from just over 9 million to 13 million.

- Dedicated or rededicated 95 of the 124 operating temples of the Church.

- Made more than 90 visits to countries outside the United States and numerous trips within the country to visit with Latter-day Saints. Traveled more than a million miles as President of the Church.

- Introduced to the Church and to the world, with the First Presidency and Quorum of the Twelve Apostles, "The Family: A Proclamation to the World" (*Liahona*, October 2004, 49; *Ensign*, November 1995, 102) and "The Living Christ: The Testimony of the Apostles" (*Liahona* and *Ensign*, April 2000, 2–3).

- Saw six quorums of the Seventy—the Third to Eighth—added to the Church's leadership.

- Saw general conference broadcast in over 80 languages, the *Liahona* published in 51 languages, and the Book of Mormon or selections from it translated into 106 languages and added to a large commercial publisher's offerings.

- Oversaw construction of and dedicated the Conference Center, which more than tripled the number of people who could watch general conference in person. He also dedicated the renovated Tabernacle.

- Met numerous times with heads of state and other government leaders from presidents of the United States to the king of Tonga and the president of Ghana.

- Instructed priesthood leaders in global leadership training sessions broadcast via satellite.

- Announced establishment of the Perpetual Education Fund.

- Appeared on nationwide television in the United States and Australia several times.

- Asked Church members to read the Book of Mormon in the final months of 2005, resulting in more people reading the book than at any other time in history.

- Authored several books.

- Longest living President of the Church.[25]

NOTES

1. Sheri Dew, *Go Forward with Faith: The Biography of Gordon B. Hinckley* (Salt Lake City: Deseret Book, 1996), 47.
2. Ibid., 24.
3. *Church News*, February 8, 1975, 4.
4. Dew, *Go Forward with Faith*, 22.
5. Leonard J. Arrington, Susan Arrington Madsen, and Emily Madsen Jones, *Mothers of the Prophets* (Salt Lake City: Bookcraft, 2001), 241.
6. Janet Peterson, "Friend to Friend," *Friend*, February 1987, 6.
7. Dew, *Go Forward with Faith*, 36.
8. Ibid., 75.
9. Ibid., 74.
10. Gordon B. Hinckley, "Be Not Afraid, Only Believe," CES Fireside for Young Adults, September 9, 2001.
11. Dew, *Go Forward with Faith*, 64.
12. Ibid., 136.
13. Francis M. Gibbons, *Dynamic Disciples, Prophets of God: Life*

Stories of the Presidents of The Church of Jesus Christ of Latter-day Saints (Salt Lake City: Deseret Book, 1996), 331.

14. "At Home with the Hinckleys," *Ensign*, October 2003, 27.

15. Jeffrey R. Holland, "President Gordon B. Hinckley: Stalwart and Brave He Stands," *Ensign*, June 1995, 2–13.

16. Dew, *Go Forward with Faith*, 114.

17. Ibid., 116.

18. Doug Robinson, "Marjorie Hinckley—'Every bit his equal,'" *Deseret News*, April 5, 2003.

19. Ibid.

20. *Church News*, May 6, 1995, 11.

21. Dew, *Go Forward with Faith*, 489.

22. Holland, "President Gordon B. Hinckley: Stalwart and Brave He Stands," 2–13.

23. Jay M. Todd, "President Gordon B. Hinckley: Fifteenth President of the Church," *Ensign*, April 1995, 6.

24. Gordon B. Hinckley, "New Temples to Provide 'Crowning Blessings' of the Gospel," *Ensign*, May 1998, 88.

25. Gordon B. Hinckley, "Benediction," *Ensign*, November 1998, 88.

26. Gordon B. Hinckley, "Thanks to the Lord for His Blessings," *Ensign*, May 1999, 89.

27. Gordon B. Hinckley, "Stand Strong against the Wiles of the World," *Ensign*, November 1995, 101.

28. Gordon B. Hinckley, "To All the World in Testimony," *Ensign*, May 2000, 4.

29. Gordon B. Hinckley, "The Perpetual Education Fund," *Ensign*, May 2001, 52.

30. Ibid.

31. Ibid.

32. Gordon B. Hinckley, "The Church Goes Forward," *Ensign*, May 2002, 4.

33. Gordon B. Hinckley, "May We Be Faithful and True," *Ensign*, May 1997, 6.

34. Gordon B. Hinckley, "Testimony," *Ensign*, May 1998, 69.

35. "2002 Utahn of the Year: Gordon B. Hinckley," *The Salt Lake Tribune*, Sunday, December 29, 2002.

36. Gordon B. Hinckley, "The Work Moves Forward," *Ensign*, May 1999, 5.

37. Gordon B. Hinckley, "We Bear Witness of Him," *Ensign*, May 1998, 4.

38. Ibid.

39. Gordon B. Hinckley, *Stand a Little Taller* (Salt Lake City: Eagle Gate, 2001), 91.

40. F. Michael Watson, "Statistical Report, 2003," *Ensign*, May 2004, 26.

41. Gordon B. Hinckley, "The International Role of The Church of Jesus Christ of Latter-day Saints," speech at the Los Angeles World Affairs Council, May 13, 1999.

42. Gordon B. Hinckley, "The Condition of the Church," *Ensign*, May 2003, 4.

43. "News of the Church," *Ensign*, June 2003, 75.

44. Gordon B. Hinckley, "Each a Better Person," *Ensign*, November 2002, 100.

45. "News of the Church," *Ensign*, June 2003, 75.

46. Gordon B. Hinckley, "Inspirational Thoughts," *Ensign*, August 1997, 5.

47. Gordon B. Hinckley, "A Prophet's Counsel and Prayer for Youth," *New Era*, January 2001.

48. Gordon B. Hinckley, "My Testimony," *Ensign*, May 2000, 69.

49. Hinckley, *Stand a Little Taller*, 25.

50. *Church News*, June 7, 2003, 2; from interview, Campinas, Brazil, May 16, 2002.

51. Gordon B. Hinckley, "New Temples to Provide 'Crowning Blessings' to the Gospel," 87.

52. Hinckley, *Stand a Little Taller*, 211.

53. Ibid., 235.

54. Ibid., 318.

55. Gordon B. Hinckley, "Words of the Prophet: The Spirit of Optimism," *New Era*, July 2001, 4.

56. Ibid.

57. Hinckley, *Stand a Little Taller*, 64.

58. Gordon B. Hinckley, *Standing for Something: 10 Neglected Virtues That Will Heal Our Hearts and Homes* (New York: Times Books, 2000), 121.

59. *Church News*, February 22, 2003, 3.

60. Devotional, Brigham Young University alumni, September 12, 2000; Gordon B. Hinckley, "Inspirational Thoughts," *Liahona*, April 2002, 3–6.

61. Devotional, Brigham Young University alumni, September 12, 2000.

62. Gordon B. Hinckley, "The Times in Which We Live," *Ensign*, November 2001, 74.

63. *Church News*, June 7, 2003, 2.

64. Gordon B. Hinckley, *Teachings of Gordon B. Hinckley* (Salt Lake City: Deseret Book, 1997), 317.

65. Ibid.

66. *Church News*, April 5, 2003, 2.

67. Ibid.

68. Hinckley, "Testimony," 69.

69. Hinckley, *Teachings of Gordon B. Hinckley*, 514.

70. Ibid., 285–86.

71. Virginia H. Pearce, *Glimpses into the Life and Heart of Marjorie Pay Hinckley* (Salt Lake City: Deseret Book, 1999), 77–78.

72. Peggy Fletcher Stack, "Partner in Faith," *Salt Lake Tribune*, April 7, 2004.

73. Pearce, *Glimpses*, 191.

74. Gordon B. Hinckley, "Concluding Remarks," *Ensign*, May 2004, 103.

75. KSL News, *Marjorie Pay Hinckley Dies at 92*, April 6, 2004.

SIDEBAR AND PHOTO NOTES

1. *Ensign*, June 1995.
2. "Take Not the Name of God in Vain," *Ensign*, November 1987.
3. Susan Arrington Madsen, *The Lord Needed a Prophet* (Salt Lake City: Deseret Book, 1996), 242.
4. *Ensign*, September 2003, 77.
5. Madsen, *The Lord Needed a Prophet*, 242.
6. Pearce, *Glimpses*, 184.
7. Ibid, 241.
8. *Gordon B. Hinckley: Man of Integrity, 15th President of the Church*, video.
9. "Special Witnesses for Christ," *Ensign*, May 1984.
10. "God Is at the Helm," *Ensign*, May 1994; see also D&C 107:22, 27, 30–31.
11. Dew, *Go Forward with Faith*, 274–75.
12. "President Hinckley: Most Caring," *Deseret News*, November 23, 2002.
13. www.lds.org/temples.
14. Hinckley, *Standing for Something*, 145–64.
15. Gordon B. Hinckley, "To All the World in Testimony," *Ensign*, May 2000, 4.
16. Pearce, *Glimpses*, 12.
17. Ibid, 60–61.
18. "Bring Up a Child in the Way He Should Go," *Ensign*, November 1993, 54.
19. "A Chosen Generation," *Ensign*, May 1992.
20. Dew, *Go Forward with Faith*, 423.
21. "Bring Up a Child in the Way He Should Go," 54.
22. *Hymns of The Church of Jesus Christ of Latter-day Saints* (Salt Lake City: The Church of Jesus Christ of Latter-day Saints, 1985) no. 135.
23. Gordon B. Hinckley, *Way to Be!* (New York: Simon and Schuster, 2002), 11.
24. See Dew, *Go Forward with Faith*, 639–40.
25. "Milestones in the Presidency of Gordon B. Hinckley," *In Memoriam: President Gordon B. Hinckley, 1910–2008* (supplement to the *Ensign*, March 2008), 13.

Author's note: The author of this chapter wishes to thank the office of the First Presidency and the Church Archives for their permission to use photos and biographical materials of Gordon B. Hinckley. In addition, the author thanks Robert Hall, a teaching assistant, for his work on this chapter.

Chapter Sixteen

THOMAS S. MONSON

LIFE AND TIMES

1927	August 21	Born to G. Spencer and Gladys Condie Monson in Salt Lake City
1944		Graduated from West High School in Salt Lake City
1945		Enlisted in Navy Reserve
1948		Graduated *cum laude* from the University of Utah in business
1948	October 7	Married Frances Beverly Johnson in the Salt Lake Temple
1948		Began work with the *Deseret News* as an advertising executive
1950–55		Served as bishop of Sixth-Seventh Ward
1952		Became assistant advertising manager of Newspaper Agency Corporation
1955–59		Served as counselor in Temple View Stake presidency
1959–62		Served as mission president of the Canadian Mission
1962		Became General Manager of Deseret News Publishing Company
1963	October 4	Ordained a member of the Quorum of the Twelve Apostles
1966		Received University of Utah Distinguished Alumni Award
1968	November 10	Made prophetic promise to the German Saints in Görlitz, German Democratic Republic
1969		Began service on National Executive Board of the Boy Scouts of America
1969	June 14	Organized Dresden Mission
1971		Received BSA's Silver Beaver Award
1974		Earned Master of Business Administration degree from BYU
1978		Received BSA's prestigious Silver Buffalo Award
1981		Awarded honorary Doctor of Laws degree at BYU
1981	December	Appointed by President Ronald Reagan to serve on Task Force for Private Sector Initiatives, aimed at increasing voluntarism
1982	August	Organized first stake in Eastern Europe
1985	June 29	Freiberg Germany Temple dedicated
1985	November 10	Ordained Second Counselor in First Presidency under President Benson
1993	October 2	Awarded International Scouting's Bronze Wolf Award
1994	June 5	Continued service as Second Counselor under President Hunter
1995	March 12	Ordained First Counselor in First Presidency under President Hinckley; also set apart as President of the Council of the Twelve
1996	June	Given honorary Doctor of Humane Letters degree by Salt Lake Community College

1997		Received Minuteman Award from the Utah National Guard
1997		Received BYU's Exemplary Manhood Award
1998		Together with Sister Monson, given the Continuum of Caring Humanitarian Award by the Sisters of Charity of St. Joseph's Villa
1998	October 7	Celebrated fiftieth wedding anniversary
2007	May	Awarded honorary Doctorate of Business degree from University of Utah
2008	February 3	Became President of The Church of Jesus Christ of Latter-day Saints

BIOGRAPHICAL HIGHLIGHTS

President Thomas Spencer Monson was ordained and set apart as the sixteenth President of the Church on February 3, 2008. Prior to his call to serve as the President of the Church, he had served in the Quorum of the Twelve Apostles for forty-four years and as a counselor to three prophets for over twenty-two years. President Monson was born and raised in Salt Lake City. He has served as the bishop of the Sixth-Seventh Ward, a counselor in the Temple View Stake presidency, and as the President of the Canadian Mission of the Church. Besides his vast leadership experience inside the Church, President Monson has played a leading role in the publishing and printing industry, serving on many boards and executive counsels including as the past president of Printing Industry of Utah and a former member of the board of directors of Printing Industry of America. Since 1969, he has served as a member of the National Executive Board of the Boy Scouts of America. He is also the recipient of Scouting's Silver Beaver and Silver Buffalo awards, and international Scouting's highest honor, the Bronze Wolf. President Monson was also appointed by President Ronald Reagan to serve on the President's Task Force for Private Sector Initiative.

TEACHINGS

President Monson is known throughout the Church for his heartwarming personal stories. More than simply teaching gospel truths through preaching, President Monson is known for bringing those truths to life through stories filled with faith, courage, and compassion. With a memory nothing short of remarkable, he fills his stories with illustrations of gospel living that bring hope and inspiration to all who hear him. President Monson is also known for using poetry, literature, and the writings of the great thinkers of the ages to add meaning to his public addresses.

LIFE OF
THOMAS S. MONSON

CHILDHOOD

Thomas Spencer Monson was born the second of six children on August 21, 1927, in Salt Lake City, Utah, to G. Spencer and Gladys Condie Monson. He grew up on the southwest corner of Fifth South and Second West in one of five homes on Condie's Terrace, a group of homes his Grandfather Condie had built for himself and each of his daughters and their families. On the day Thomas was born, his father told his mother that a new bishop was called in their home ward. Thomas's mother responded, "I have a new bishop for *you*."[1] This proved prophetic, since twenty-two years later on May 7, 1950, this son, Thomas Spencer Monson, would be sustained as a bishop of this same ward.

Tom was raised in an environment filled with hard work and family fun, surrounded by extended family on every side. He was raised during the Great Depression, a time of hardship that left an indelible impression upon his young mind. However, while many of his friends' parents were left without work, his father maintained employment as a printing manager with the Western Hotel Register Company. Economic conditions required that young Tom work at his father's side from the age of twelve. Though he gave up many extracurricular activities, this experience prepared him for early and significant success in his own career in the printing industry.

Even with hard work and economizing, there was always time for family fun. Not only would Tom spend time with his cousins on Condie's Terrace, there were many get-togethers with his Condie uncles in Granger, Utah, as well as the Monson relatives in Murray and Bountiful. A favorite part of Thomas's growing up years were summers spent at the family cabin in Vivian Park, an idyllic setting near the Provo River in Provo Canyon. These were summers filled with fishing, swimming, and carefree fun. Fishing became a lifelong hobby for Tom.

A LEGACY OF GIVING

Tom's family went without some necessities through the Depression, such as heating during winter nights. He remembers how cold his bedroom would get during those long winter months. However, Tom's parents and grandparents maintained their giving nature throughout the hard times. With his childhood home near the train tracks, homeless and needy individuals would often approach the Monsons' door asking for food. Gladys Monson never turned them away empty-handed, often inviting them in to sit down while they ate a sandwich.

His father and grandfather were also examples of selfless generosity. President Monson once said of his father,

Saving a Life at the Swimming Hole

One summer when he was twelve, Tom saved a young girl's life in the Provo River. As he floated down the river, he heard people calling desperately after her from the shore. The endangered girl had been caught in a strong whirlpool, and just before she went under for the third time, he spotted her. Maneuvering his tube toward her, he reached into the water, grabbed her by the hair, and pulled her onto his tube. The grateful relatives and friends hugged and kissed him, thanking young Tom for saving her. Though credited with a heroic rescue, President Monson humbly recalls, "I think I just happened to be in the right place at the right time in order to provide assistance."[1]

Compassion and Service

President Monson's early experiences set a pattern for a lifetime of charitable service. One experience is illustrative: "When I was about eleven and holiday time had come, we were preparing for the oven a gigantic turkey and anticipating the savory feast that awaited. I was playing with a neighborhood pal of mine in my yard when he made the observation, 'It sure smells good in your house. What are you having for dinner?' I told him we would be having a turkey dinner. He then asked a question that was startling to me: 'What does turkey taste like?'

"I responded, 'Oh, about like chicken tastes.'

"Again a question: 'What does chicken taste like?'

"It was then that I realized my friend had never eaten chicken or turkey. I asked what his family was going to have for their holiday dinner. There was no prompt response—just a downcast glance and the comment, 'I dunno. There's nothing in the house.'

"I pondered a solution. There was none. I had no turkeys, no chickens, no money. Then I remembered I did have two pet rabbits. They were the pride of my life, two beautiful New Zealand whites. I said to my friend, 'You come with me, because I've got something for your dinner.' We went to the rabbit hutch, and I opened it, placed the two rabbits in a box, and said, 'You take these home, and your dad will know what to do with them. They taste a whole lot like chicken.'

"He took the box, climbed the fence, and headed for home, a holiday dinner safely assured. Tears came easily to me as I closed the door to the empty rabbit hutch. But I was not sad. A warmth, a feeling of indescribable joy, filled my heart."[2]

Spencer, "I never heard my father speak a negative word towards another person. In fact, he would not remain in the room if anyone were speaking disrespectfully or negatively towards another person."[2] Though he worked long hours six days each week, Tom's father, Spencer, visited his aging relatives every Sunday, bringing them comfort and cheer in their times of need. Often he took them for short rides in his 1929 Oldsmobile, and sometimes young Tom went along. Tom's grandfather also set an example of selfless service. When an aged family friend shared the sad news of being evicted from his home, Grandfather Condie took the key to an empty house on Condie's Terrace and gave it to the man with a promise that he would never have to pay rent or be evicted again.[3]

This legacy of giving penetrated young Tom's heart and prompted him to similar action at an early age. Several experiences early in Tom's youth set a pattern of giving and selfless service that has persisted to this day. He recalled that when he was a rambunctious boy, his Primary teacher, Lucy Gertsch, taught him and the rest of the class a powerful lesson in giving when she asked if the class would be willing to donate the hard-earned funds that they had saved for a class party to the financially struggling family of one of their peers. They did just that, and it became a powerful witness that "it is more blessed to give than to receive." Whether in

service to an elderly neighbor or to numerous friends whose families were struggling through the Depression, Tom began a lifetime habit of concern and care for others.

EARLY CHURCH SERVICE

Along with the example and training Tom received from his family of Christlike caring and service, Tom also learned early the power of personal service inside the Lord's kingdom. While serving as a deacon, it became Tom's privilege to administer the sacrament to Louis McDonald, who, because of a palsied condition, was unable to partake of the sacrament without special assistance. Tom remembers being fearful as he approached this good brother for the first time. However, the expression of gratitude with which Brother McDonald awaited the sacrament began to change Tom's fear. Tom described how he held the sacrament tray in his left hand and pressed a small piece of bread to Brother McDonald's lips. The water was also administered in similar fashion. Tom recalled, "I felt I was on holy ground. And indeed I was. The privilege to pass the sacrament to Brother McDonald made better deacons of us all."[4]

Not long after this, when Tom was fifteen years old, he was called as the president of his teachers quorum. His adviser, a man named Harold, used Tom's interest in raising pigeons to teach the young quorum president how to minister to his quorum members' needs. Harold offered to give Tom a pair of purebred Birmingham Roller pigeons. He told Tom to keep them indoors for ten days and then release them to see if they would return. Harold knew that the young female pigeon would always make a beeline right back to his home, where Tom would have to come retrieve her. Each time Tom came over, Harold would ask him how he was going to activate one of the less active members of his quorum. Week by week passed and young Tom learned the sacred responsibility and joy of ministering to those in need. Tom credited both that pigeon, as well as Harold's loving training, for the activation of many boys in his teachers quorum. Ministering to individuals in need was to become a hallmark of Thomas Monson's lifetime service. As he later recalled, "He [Harold] had the patience and the skill to help me prepare for responsibilities which lay ahead."[5]

Tom's propensity and effectiveness in serving those around him was made possible largely through a special endowment of the gift of discernment. Elder Holland once noted that "loyalty to the still, small whisperings of the Spirit . . . may be the most conspicuous and inspiring characteristic in the life of Thomas S. Monson. 'The sweetest feeling you can have in this world is to feel the hand of the Lord upon your shoulder,' President Monson says softly and with some emotion. 'In my patriarchal blessing as a boy, I was promised that I would have the gift of discernment. I have to acknowledge that such a declaration has been abundantly fulfilled in my life.' Indeed, President Monson's life—certainly his life as an Apostle and member of the First Presidency—seems in a sense to be one long, extended chronicle of the promptings of the Holy Spirit, with the many inspirational and varied miracles which have resulted from his response to those promptings."[6]

MILITARY SERVICE

Further preparation for a life of service came through serving in the military toward the end of World War II. After graduating from West High School in 1945, Tom enlisted in the Naval Reserve, an enlistment for the duration of the war plus six months. Shortly before leaving for the service, he received the Melchizedek Priesthood and was ordained an elder. While stationed in San Diego, California, another LDS seaman asked him for a priesthood blessing. It would be the first such blessing Tom had ever participated in, let alone given. Nonetheless, after a desperate prayer and inspired guidance, he proceeded to give his friend a blessing—in front of numerous curious seamen—and his afflicted friend was completely healed.[7]

While stationed in San Diego, Tom worked diligently to earn the rank of Seaman First Class. He was also privileged to serve as personal secretary and administrative aid to the classification officer. From that experience, he learned the privileged position of commissioned officers. Thus, feeling that he might be called into action if there were another conflict, and

A Habit of Prayer

Shortly before his eighteenth birthday, during the summer of 1945, Tom had to decide which branch of the military to join. As he and forty-one other young men stood to be sworn in, the two chief petty officers said, "You men have to make a choice. You may join the regular Navy for a four-year period. You will no doubt receive schooling and extra preferences, because the Navy will have an investment in you. Or you may elect to join the Naval Reserve, which is a period of obligation for the duration of the war and six months. The Navy will not be as kind to you if you join the Reserve."

Tom conferred with his father as to what he should do, but his father answered that he did not know. At that instant, Tom sent a prayer up to heaven, pleading for guidance in this difficult decision. A question immediately entered his mind. He asked the two petty officers which branch they had joined when they had the chance to decide. Sheepishly, both admitted to choosing the Reserve. Tom said, "You men are men of experience and judgment. I'll follow your example—I'll take the Naval Reserve." He was the only young man of the forty-two to do so. It was a good thing he did, as the war ended within a few short months and he was able to return and finish his schooling. How different his life may have been had he not turned to the Lord in prayer for guidance.[3]

wanting to be a commissioned officer were that to happen, he began working toward that goal. Soon the long-awaited commission as an ensign in the United States Naval Reserve came. However, only a few days later, Tom received a call to serve in the bishopric of his ward—the same ward in which he had grown up—and scheduling conflicts between the Navy and his calling became immediately apparent.

He decided to take the matter to his former stake president, Elder Harold B. Lee of the Council of the Twelve Apostles. War was looming in Korea and Tom was sure he would be called into active duty. Elder Lee listened to his situation and, after pondering for a few moments, counseled Tom to refuse the commission and request a discharge from the Naval Reserve. When Tom expressed concern that the discharge would not be approved, Elder Lee lovingly replied, "Brother Monson, have more faith. The military is not for you." Humbly and tearfully, Tom followed Elder Lee's counsel. He was among the last group of discharges issued before the Korean War broke out in full and his Utah unit was deployed to the Far East. Of this experience President Monson later wrote: "I have often contemplated what the course of my life might have been had I not received and followed the advice of Elder Lee. I pondered the thought that the wisdom of God ofttimes appears as foolishness to men. But the greatest single lesson we can learn in mortality is that when God speaks and a man obeys, that man will always be right."[8]

EDUCATION AND FAMILY

Though Tom and Frances grew up only about a mile away from each other, he attended West High School and she attended East High School, and the two did not meet until later. It was a little while after first seeing Frances that Tom was officially introduced to her by a childhood friend at a chance meeting on Thirteenth East and Second South in Salt Lake. He later wrote: "That day I made a little note in my student directory to call on Frances Beverly Johnson, and I did. That decision, I believe, was perhaps the most important decision I have ever made."[9] The two corresponded all during his six months of active duty in the Navy and then continued to date when he returned.

While Tom and Frances were courting, Tom continued his studies in business administration at the University of Utah. Dr. O. Preston Robinson, Tom's former department head at the university remembers him as "an outstanding student."[10] He worked hard and earned excellent grades, allowing him to graduate *cum laude* from the University of Utah at twenty years old. Tom and Frances were married that very year in the Salt Lake Temple on October 7, 1948.

After graduation, Tom continued for several months at the University of Utah filling a part-time faculty role as he completed some graduate classes. However, it would be many years before he would obtain a graduate degree. Finally, in

A Family Connection

President Monson's father was a printer by trade and worked six days per week. On Sundays, his only day off, he would often visit his elderly aunts and uncles to bring them some cheer. On many occasions, he took young Tom along to visit his great uncle Elias and take him for a short ride in their Oldsmobile. His father's joy at serving and Uncle Elias's appreciation left a strong impression on Tom's young heart.

Approximately ten years later, as Tom called on his future wife, Frances, for their first date, he was met by her parents, Brother and Sister Johnson. Upon learning his name, Brother Johnson said, "Monson—that's a Swedish name!"

"Yes, sir," the young suitor replied.

At that, the man went to his room to retrieve a photo from the dresser. It was an old picture of two missionaries with the names written at the bottom. One of the names was Elias Monson.

Pointing to the missionary, Brother Johnson asked, "Are you related to that man?"

After looking at the picture, the future son-in-law answered, "Why, yes, that's my grandfather's brother."

With tears in his eyes, the future father-in-law explained that Tom's uncle Elias was one of the missionaries who had taught and converted him, his parents, and his brothers and sisters in Sweden many years before.[4]

1974, while serving in the Quorum of the Twelve, he earned his Master of Business Administration degree from Brigham Young University. Since that time he has also received three honorary degrees: a Doctor of Laws degree from Brigham Young University in 1981, a Doctor of Humane Letters degree from Salt Lake Community College in 1996, and an honorary Doctor of Business degree from the University of Utah in 2007.

Tom and Frances are the parents of three children, the grandparents of eight children, and great-grandparents of four children. They named their first son Thomas Lee in honor of the love and respect Tom held for President Harold B. Lee. Their second child was a daughter, whom they named Ann Frances. They named their final son Clark Spencer in honor of President J. Reuben Clark. Though Tom's busy professional and ecclesiastical schedule made it difficult to spend as much time at home as he wanted, he was a devoted husband and father. His children once said, "Other children's fathers seemed to be home

Frances Johnson Monson

Frances Johnson was born in Salt Lake City, Utah, after her parents immigrated from Sweden. She attended East High School in Salt Lake City and the University of Utah. Of Sister Monson, her daughter Ann Monson Dibb has said, "Mom is the other half of Dad's success story, the half no one really knows. He gave a conference address once entitled 'Anonymous' about people who serve so faithfully and give so much, yet never seek recognition. That talk applies beautifully to my mother; maybe he even wrote it with her in mind. He couldn't have done what he has done without her."

Being the wife of a prominent Church leader has come with certain sacrifices. Sister Monson recalls, "Tom was serving as ward clerk, then as superintendent of the YMMIA when we were first married, and he has gone from one assignment to another since then. Some have asked how a new bride adjusts to that, but it has never been a sacrifice to see my husband doing the Lord's work. It has blessed me, and it has blessed our children. He always knew that if it was for the Church, I expected him to do what he had to do."

President Monson lovingly remembers, "I have never known Frances to complain once of my Church responsibilities. In [all] those . . . years I have been gone many days and many nights, and I have rarely been able to sit with her in the congregation. But there is no one like her—absolutely no one. She is in every way supportive and is a woman of quiet and profoundly powerful faith."[5]

In 1981, Elder Monson received an honorary Doctor of Laws degree from Brigham Young University.

more than our dad was . . . but they didn't seem to do as much with their children as Dad did with us. We were always doing something together, and we cherish those memories."[11]

THE PRINTING BUSINESS

Shortly after graduation from the University of Utah in 1948, Tom began his career in the newspaper business. True to form, Tom soon exhibited his leadership skills, quickly becoming Assistant Classified Advertising Manager and then Classified Advertising Manager of the Newspaper Agency Corporation, an entity created jointly by the *Deseret News* and *Salt Lake Tribune*. He later moved over to the *Deseret News* press, filling the positions of

President Monson has served on the National Executive Board of the Boy Scouts of America since 1969, receiving many prestigious Scouting awards, including the Silver Beaver, the Silver Buffalo, and the Bronze Wolf, international Scouting's highest honor.

Sales Manager and Assistant Manager over the entire press, a position he held until his call as a mission president in 1959. During this ten-year period, Tom also participated in many civic printing organizations, such as the Printing Industry of America, the Printing Industry of Utah (as president), the Salt Lake Advertising Club, and the Utah Association of Sales Executives.

Soon after returning from service as mission president of the Canadian Mission in 1962, he received another promotion to general manager of Deseret News Publishing Company, one of the West's largest commercial printing firms. He continued in this capacity until his call to the Quorum of the Twelve Apostles late in 1963.[12] Since his call into the Quorum of the Twelve, President Monson has continued his association with the printing industry. He has served as a member of the Board of Directors for the Deseret News Publishing Company from May 1965 to May 1996. He was chairman of the board from 1977 to 1996.

PUBLIC SERVICE

President Monson's leadership and participation in the general public includes extensive service with the Boy Scouts. In 1969, he was asked to serve on the National Executive Board for the Boy Scouts of America. He has continued that service for almost forty years and is the longest serving member of the Board. He has been awarded many of the most prestigious Scouting awards, including the Silver Beaver, the Silver Buffalo (Scouting's highest national honor), and the Bronze Wolf (Scouting's highest international honor).

Drawing on his vast experience with the Church Welfare Program, Elder Monson was asked to serve on a Presidential Task Force for Private Sector Initiatives from 1981 to 1982 by President Ronald Reagan. The aim of the task force was to increase voluntarism nationally. With a lifetime of his own volunteer service as well as directing the volunteer service of countless other people, he had much to offer. As part of his service on this task force, President Monson developed a detailed report on the Church's philosophy, processes, and procedures in the Welfare Program as a possible model for others to use.

CONTINUING CHURCH SERVICE

Thomas Monson has always been highly active in the Church's organizations, serving in many leadership capacities, often at an unusually young age. Shortly after graduating from high school, the bishop called him to serve in his ward's Young Men's Mutual Improvement Association (YMMIA) presidency, which was the precursor to today's Young Men organization. The other two members of the presidency were fifty-nine and sixty-four years old. At the age of twenty-two, he was called first into the bishopric as a counselor, and then six weeks later as bishop of the ward he grew up in, the Sixth-Seventh Ward, which was part of the Temple View Stake.

Bishop Monson's ward consisted of more than a thousand members, including more than eighty widows. Due in part to the many widows, his ward carried the largest welfare load in the Church. However, young Bishop Monson rose to the challenge and accomplished many great things within the ward, including greatly increasing church meeting attendance and the complete renovation of their ward building.

However, perhaps his most lasting contribution as bishop was his selfless service to the many widows, in whom he took great personal interest. Each Christmas Bishop Monson would take a week of personal vacation time to visit each of those poor sisters and bring them a Christmas message. Invariably he would also take a gift, which was often a chicken raised in his own coop. Of his own volition, President Monson continued to visit and present a gift every Christmas to each of the living widows from his old ward as long as they lived. Also, as Elder Holland once commented, "These sweet folks never seem to die until Brother Monson is back in town from his many assignments, enabling him to speak at their funerals."[13] He kept track of each one while they lived and spoke at each of their funerals.

At a conference of the Temple View Stake in June 1955, President Joseph Fielding Smith presented the name of Bishop Thomas S. Monson, then twenty-seven years old, as the second counselor in the stake presidency. "Said President Smith: 'Bishop Monson knows nothing of this appointment, but if he will accept it, we will be pleased to hear from him now.' Caught unaware, Brother Monson had to improvise.

Tom was called at the young age of twenty-two to serve as the bishop of his ward. He left a legacy of love and service, especially for the many widows in his ward.

It was in this chapel that Bishop Monson presided over the Sixth-Seventh Ward for five years.

Mission President

As president of the Canadian Mission, President Monson worked very hard to strengthen the mission. The area of Kingston needed a significant change. It was the bane of the mission, a prison sentence, a place with only one convert to the Church in six years. As he prayed and pondered over what to do, Sister Monson shared with him a story she had read about Brigham Young. He had entered Kingston, Ontario, on a cold, snowy day, and after laboring for only thirty days, Elder Young baptized forty-five souls. In a flash of inspiration, President Monson removed the elders from Kingston without explanation. Then, for several weeks he circulated the word that soon he would open an area where Brigham Young had baptized forty-five souls in only thirty days. Missionaries begged to be transferred there.

At the appointed time, President Monson, backed by members' pledged support, carefully selected four missionaries to enter Kingston. In only three months, Kingston became the most successful city of the Canadian Mission. Of this experience President Monson wrote, "The gray limestone buildings stood unchanged; the city had not altered its appearance; the population remained constant. The change was one of attitude. Doubt had yielded to faith."[6]

Pausing momentarily at the pulpit, he began by referring to a song sung earlier whose lyrics admonished obedience to the Word of Wisdom: 'Have courage, my boy, to say no.' He then developed the theme 'Have Courage, My Boy, to Say Yes.' This has been a recurring theme of Thomas S. Monson's life."[14]

Four years later, at the young age of thirty-one, President Thomas S. Monson was called to preside as mission president over the Canadian Mission, which included the French-speaking province of Quebec. With only three weeks to prepare and no formal training, the young Monson family (two young children, and Frances expecting their third) set out for mission headquarters in Toronto, Ontario, Canada.

Vibrant and young—younger even than some of the missionaries over which he presided—President Monson worked hard to strengthen the mission. He identified well with the missionaries, gaining their trust and admiration. As a result, though he would never take the credit, not one of the 450 missionaries that served under him went home early or received a dishonorable release—a remarkable accomplishment by any standard. The 300th stake of the Church—and the first in the Canadian Mission—was created in Toronto during his service. More than 2,200 people attended the Sunday session, which is thought to be perhaps the largest gathering of Saints in Canada up to that point.

Upon returning from his service as mission president in 1962, Tom continued with his profession at the Deseret News Publishing Company. He also continued to serve in various capacities at Church headquarters, including on the Priesthood Missionary Committee, under Elder Spencer W. Kimball; on the Priesthood Genealogical Committee, under Elder N. Eldon Tanner; on the Adult Correlation Committee, under Elder Marion G. Romney; and on the Priesthood Home Teaching Committee, also under Elder Romney. In October of 1963, President David O. McKay called him to serve in the Council of the Twelve Apostles at age thirty-six—the youngest man called to that position since the early 1900s. Fittingly, Tom's first stake conference

Emulating the Savior

In President Monson's office is a portrait of the Savior:

"I've had that picture since I was a bishop, when it was on the wall facing me in my office for five years," he said. "I had it at home when I was a stake presidency member. I took it to Canada with me, and had it when I was a mission president. I brought it to this building when I was called as an apostle. I've occupied two or three rooms in this building, but that picture has always been on the wall facing me. There isn't a day that I'm here that I don't come up against difficult decisions, those that require wisdom beyond my own. It's very typical for me to look at that picture and ask, 'What would He do?'

"I find if I put that preamble in my mind I don't have much difficulty in providing counsel, in making decisions, in planning a course of action."[7]

Tom pauses with President J. Reuben Clark and others at the Deseret Press after the first printing of President Clark's book *Behold the Lamb of God*. Elder Mark E. Petersen is at the far right.

Mentors

While working with the Deseret Press, Brother Monson worked extensively with President J. Reuben Clark of the First Presidency in the printing of President Clark's book *Behold the Lamb of God*. They spent a great deal of time together and became so close that the Monsons' third child, Clark Spencer, was named for President Clark.

Elder Monson's first stake conference assignment as a newly called member of the Quorum of the Twelve Apostles was to Edmonton, Alberta, Canada, with his former stake president, Elder Harold B. Lee, also of the Twelve, and his former bishop, Glen L. Rudd. The Monson's first son, Thomas Lee, carries the name of Brother Monson's mentor, President Lee.

assignment after ordination to Edmonton, Canada, was with Elder Harold B. Lee, his former stake president, and Glen L. Rudd, his former bishop.

While serving as an Apostle, Thomas S. Monson continued to give leadership of the highest order in numerous capacities. He served as the chairman of the Adult Correlation Committee, the Leadership Committee, the Missionary Executive Committee, and the Church Welfare Executive Committee. He served as an executive member and on the board of trustees for both Brigham Young University as well as the Church Board of Education and served on the Melchizedek Priesthood Committee, the Internal Communications Committee, the Church's Music Committee, and as an advisor to the General Sunday School, Primary, Young Women, and Relief Society auxiliaries. He also supervised the work of missions throughout America, the South Pacific, Mexico, and Europe.

One of Thomas S. Monson's greatest legacies comes from an assignment he received in the early years of his ministry in the Quorum of the Twelve. Elder Monson received responsibilities over Eastern Europe, including the German Democratic Republic, or East Germany. At that time the East German Saints were without the full program of the Church, including wards, stakes, patriarchs, and temple blessings. On November 10, 1968, while visiting the members of the Görlitz Branch, he felt inspired to make them a dramatic

President Monson as a young Apostle with the Quorum of the Twelve.

Elder Monson was ordained and set apart as an Apostle on October 10, 1963, at the age of thirty-six. He is the youngest man called to that position since 1910, when Joseph Fielding Smith was called at age thirty-three.

promise. He declared, "If you will remain true and faithful to the commandments of God, every blessing any member of the Church enjoys in any other country will be yours."[15]

Realizing the significance of that promise and how far they seemed from receiving it, Elder Monson prayed fervently that night that the Lord would honor his words and bless the German Saints for their faithfulness. Gradually, every aspect of that promise has come true. On April 17, 1975, Elder Monson rededicated the GDR for the advancement of the work of the Church. East German leaders began attending general conferences in Salt Lake City, and the German government officials increasingly allowed for greater Church progress. He created the first stake in the GDR in Freiberg on August 29, 1982. Then, on June 29, 1985, after many years of prayer and negotiation, the Freiberg Germany Temple was dedicated, the first temple behind the Iron Curtain, and the fulfillment of his promise nearly twenty years before.

Elder Monson with two East German officials. Beginning in the late 1960s, Elder Monson was instrumental in restoring Saints' religious privileges behind the Iron Curtain.

The Suit off His Back

Elder Monson maintained the giving nature he developed as a child throughout his life and ministry. During his trips to the German Democratic Republic, he would bring two suits and two pairs of shoes, always giving the better of the two away.

Ever in search of ways to serve, he also brought small gifts to the children he would meet. For example, chewing gum did not exist in the GDR for a time, so he often brought several packages of gum to share with the children.[8]

A Gifted Memory

President Monson is well known for having excellent memorization capabilities. He has been able to put that talent to use many times. The years that Elder Monson was assigned to the German Democratic Republic were a very difficult era for the German Saints. The government placed many restrictions on building, proselyting, and shipping literature into the country. One day in the temple, Elder Monson expressed concern to Elder Spencer W. Kimball that the German Saints did not have access to the new *General Handbook of Instructions* (which he had helped revise) and that it was impossible to send them one. Elder Kimball then responded, "I have another idea, Brother Monson. Why don't you, since you've worked with the *General Handbook of Instructions*, memorize it, and then we'll put you across the border?" When he realized that Elder Kimball was indeed serious, he went to work. Though he did not memorize the voluminous manual word for word, he committed the paragraphs, chapters, and pages and their contents pretty well to memory.

Upon arriving in East Berlin, he immediately requested a typewriter, a ream of paper, and a room to work. After typing perhaps thirty pages, he stood to stretch. As he looked around the room, something caught his eye. He raced over to the shelf and took in his hands a copy, in German, of the new *General Handbook of Instructions*! Though at first he thought his work may have been in vain, for several years he was a leading authority on Church policy.[9]

When President Ezra Taft Benson was ordained President of the Church in 1985, he called Elder Thomas S. Monson as Second Counselor in the First Presidency, with President Gordon B. Hinckley continuing as First Counselor. At fifty-eight, he was the youngest person called to the First Presidency in over eighty years. Upon President Benson's death in 1994, President Howard W. Hunter asked both President Hinckley and President Monson to continue in the First Presidency. When President Hinckley became President of the Church just nine months later in March of 1995, he called President Monson as First Counselor in the First Presidency, which position President Monson held until President Hinckley's death January 27, 2008, at the age of ninety-seven. After thirteen years of service as a counselor in the First Presidency, President Thomas S. Monson became the sixteenth President of The Church of Jesus Christ of Latter-day Saints on Sunday, February 3, 2008, at the age of eighty.

THE CONSUMMATE STORYTELLER

President Monson was a consummate storyteller. Perhaps of all Church Presidents, President Monson was most likely to teach and testify through stories rather than straight didactic

The Lord Prepares Us

"He described a sign he saw some years ago at a machinery company. On the blade of an old snow plow in front of the building, the sign stated: 'You can't do today's work with yesterday's machines if you expect to be in business tomorrow.'

"President Monson added his own philosophy: 'I think we need to realize that the scriptures are sound, the doctrine is sound. The basic doctrines of the Church are in place generation after generation but the procedures whereby we achieve the Lord's objectives vary somewhat from time to time. I think if we're not careful it's an easy thing to look back at the heroes we've revered—for example, former presidents of the Church who were dear to us, whom we deeply loved—and feel that because they accomplished something in a certain way in their time that that's the way it has to be done today. That isn't good thinking because those men were pioneering in their own day solutions to problems and challenges, and were not necessarily focusing their attention in the same way as did the generation before they came on the scene.

"'That brings us to the position when we realize that the Lord has in His purposes a time when we're called to serve. He expects us to use the talents and the experiences He has given us. I'm a great believer that the Lord provides us specific experiences to prepare us to deal with some of the challenges that we're going to encounter in our own period of service.'"[10]

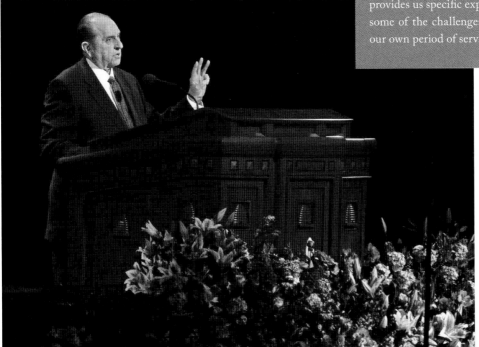

President Monson is well known for his warm and personal speaking style, filling his talks with inspiring experiences, moving quotes, poems, and humorous stories.

The First Presidency as organized on February 3, 2008.

teachings. At the time of President Monson's call, Dieter F. Uchtdorf, his second counselor, stated, "People often say, 'Well, he tells stories, . . . Well, no, I think he talks in parables, like the Savior did. He shares it in a way my grandchild can understand it.'"[16]

His remarkable memory, the loving and personal nature of his ministry, and his ability to inspire enabled President Monson to touch millions with his stories. A quick search produces numerous "favorites" lists of President Monson's stories.[17] He also loved to share quotes from literature as part of his messages. In fact, until his final general conference address in April 2017, there was not a single general

conference address that did not include either a story or a quote from literature. In fact, in the eighteen general conferences over which he presided as Church President (excluding his final conference in April 2017), he averaged almost four stories and two quotes from literature each conference. The majority of the stories President Monson shared had a direct connection to his life, adding authenticity and meaning to the narrative.[18] Though it is not possible to share a significant portion of his stories or literature quotations in this volume, the following subsample of stories from his first year as the President of the Church is representative of the stories he shared throughout his Church ministry.

A Sampling of President Thomas S. Monson's Stories and Quotes

Are You Related to This Monson?

"My father's father came from Sweden, and his wife from England. They met on the ship coming over. He waited for her to grow up, and then he proposed marriage. They were married in the Salt Lake Temple, and he wrote in his journal, 'Today is the happiest day of my life. My sweetheart and I were married for time and eternity in the holy temple.'

"Three days later, on April 23, 1898, he wrote, 'Took the train at the Rio Grande Western Depot en route eventually to Scandinavia, where I have been called as a missionary.' Off he went to Sweden, leaving his bride of three days.

"His journal, written in pencil, came to me from an uncle who somehow chose me to receive his father's journal. The most frequent entry in the journal was, 'My feet are wet.' But the most beautiful entry said: 'Today we went to the Jansson home. We met Sister Jansson. She had a lovely dinner for us. She is a good cook.' And then he said, 'The children all sang or played a harmonica or did a little dance, and then she paid her tithing. Five krona for the Lord and one for my companion, Elder Ipson, and one for me.' And then there were listed the names of the children.

"When I read that in the journal, there was my wife's father's name as one who was in that household, one who probably sang a song, one who became the father of only one daughter, the girl whom I married.

"The first day I saw Frances, I knew I'd found the right one. The Lord brought us together later, and I asked her to go out with me. I went to her home to call on her. She introduced me, and her father said, ' "Monson"—that's a Swedish name, isn't it?'

"I said, 'Yes.'

"He said, 'Good.'

"Then he went into another room and brought out a picture of two missionaries with their top hats and their copies of the Book of Mormon.

" 'Are you related to this Monson,' he said, 'Elias Monson?'

"I said, 'Yes, he's my grandfather's brother. He too was a missionary in Sweden.'

"Her father wept. He wept easily. He said, 'He and his companion were the missionaries who taught the gospel to my mother and my father and all of my brothers and sisters and to me.' He kissed me on the cheek. And then her mother cried, and she kissed me on the other cheek. And then I looked around for Frances. She said, 'I'll go get my coat.'"[11]

Your Church Is Welcome Here

"An example of such service was the missionary experience of Juliusz and Dorothy Fussek, who were called to fill a two-year mission in Poland. Brother Fussek was born in Poland. He spoke the language. He loved the people. Sister Fussek was English and knew little of Poland and its people.

"Trusting in the Lord, they embarked on their assignment. The living conditions were primitive, the work lonely, their task immense. A mission had not at that time been established in Poland. The assignment given the Fusseks was to prepare the way, that a mission could be established so that other missionaries could be called to serve, people could be taught, converts could be baptized, branches could be established, and chapels could be erected.

"Did Elder and Sister Fussek despair because of the enormity of their assignment? Not for a moment. They knew their calling was from God. They prayed for His divine help, and they devoted themselves wholeheartedly to their work. They remained in Poland not two years but five years. All of the foregoing objectives were realized.

"Elders Russell M. Nelson, Hans B. Ringger, and I, accompanied by Elder Fussek, met with Minister Adam Wopatka of the Polish government, and we heard him say, 'Your church is welcome here. You may build your buildings; you may send your missionaries. You are welcome in Poland. This man,' pointing to Juliusz Fussek, 'has served your church well. You can be grateful for his example and his work.' "[12]

Only in Good Company

"Several years ago I received a letter from a longtime friend. He bore his testimony in that letter. I would like to share part of it with you tonight, since it illustrates the strength of the priesthood in one who learned what he should learn, who did what he should do, and who always tried to be what he should be. I shall read excerpts of that letter from my friend Theron W. Borup, who passed away three years ago at the age of 90:

" 'At the age of eight, when I was baptized and received the Holy Ghost, I was much impressed about being good and able to have the Holy Ghost to be a help throughout my life. I was told that the Holy Ghost associated only in good company and that when evil entered our lives, he would leave. Not knowing when I would need his promptings and guidance, I tried to so live that I would not lose this gift. On one occasion it saved my life.

" 'During World War II, I was an engineer-gunner in a B-24 bomber fighting in the South Pacific. . . . One day there was an announcement that the longest bombing flight ever made would be attempted to knock out an oil refinery. The promptings of the Spirit told me I would be assigned on this flight but that I would not lose my life. At the time I was the president of the LDS group.

" 'The combat was ferocious as we flew over Borneo. Our plane was hit by attacking planes and soon burst into flames, and the pilot told us to prepare to jump. I went out last. We were shot at by enemy pilots as we floated down. I had trouble inflating my life raft. Bobbing up and down in the water, I began to drown and passed out. I came to momentarily and cried, "God save me!" . . . Again I tried inflating the life raft and this time was successful. With just enough air in it to keep me afloat, I rolled over on top of it, too exhausted to move.

" 'For three days we floated about in enemy territory with ships all about us and planes overhead. Why they couldn't see a yellow group of rafts on blue water is a mystery,' he wrote. 'A storm came up, and waves thirty feet high almost tore our rafts apart. Three days went by with no food or water. The others asked me if I prayed. I answered that I did pray and we would indeed be rescued. That evening we saw our submarine that was there to rescue us, but it passed by. The next morning it did [the same. We knew] this was the last day [it would] be in the area. Then came the promptings of the Holy Ghost. "You have the priesthood. Command the sub to pick you up." Silently I prayed, "In the name of Jesus Christ, and by the power of the priesthood, turn about and pick us up." In a few minutes, they were alongside of us. When on deck, the captain . . . said, "I don't know how we ever found you, for we were not even looking for you." I knew.' "[13]

Quotes

"Do your duty, that is best; leave unto the Lord the rest."[14]

"You pile up enough tomorrows, and you'll find you've collected a lot of empty yesterdays."[15]

"They do not love that do not show their love."[16]

"The bitterest tears shed over graves are for words left unsaid and deeds left undone."[17]

OUT OF OBSCURITY

When Thomas S. Monson was named the sixteenth President of The Church of Jesus Christ of Latter-day Saints, he expressed a desire to work with all who were willing and desired to do good: "As a Church we reach out not only to our own people, but also to those people of goodwill throughout the world in that spirit of brotherhood which comes from the Lord Jesus Christ."[19] At the news conference held to announce his call as Church President, he stated, "We should not be sequestered in a little cage. We should eliminate the weakness of the one standing alone and substitute it with the strength of working together to make this a better world. I believe in that spirit."[20] This desire to reach out to others and to bring the Church "forth out of obscurity and out of darkness" (D&C 1:30) was a hallmark of his time as President of the Church. As explained in a tribute to President Monson on LDS.org, under President Monson's guidance, "Church leaders worked regularly with Catholics, Evangelical Christians, and other religious and community groups in supporting moral causes such as traditional marriage. Church leaders invited other faith leaders to speak at LDS campuses and bolstered support for religious freedom with online resources."[21]

During President Monson's presidency, the Church undertook two national campaigns to help people understand the Church and its members better. In 2010, the Church launched the "I'm a Mormon" national media campaign, which included everything from television segments, to internet pieces, to ads on buses and billboards. Public figures such as Mia Love (member of Congress), Gladys Knight (singer and actress), Chad Lewis (athlete), and others shared their personal stories, always ending with the statement, "I'm a Mormon." Due to increased interest, the "I'm a Mormon" campaign was later extended internationally to locations such as Australia (2011), the United Kingdom (2013), and Ireland (2013). In the same spirit, in 2014, the Church produced a full-length documentary film, *Meet the Mormons*, which told the stories of five individuals and sought to introduce the Church to others. Such open and direct informational and promotional pieces had never been used on a national basis before.

The Kansas City Missouri Temple dedication, May 6, 2012. President Monson is standing with his back to the camera, the third person from the left. (Photo courtesy of Lori Tubbs Garcia. Used by permission.)

Under President Monson's guidance, the general Church leadership, including each member of the First Presidency and Quorum of the Twelve Apostles and each auxiliary presidency, entered the world of social media with Facebook and Instagram pages. Church leaders have likewise encouraged members of the Church to use social media to share the goodness of the gospel of Jesus Christ and His restored Church. In a Brigham Young University Campus Education Week presentation, Elder David A. Bednar explained and admonished members to greater diligence in these efforts: "My beloved brothers and sisters, what has been accomplished thus far in this dispensation communicating gospel messages through social media channels is a good beginning—but only a small trickle. I now extend to you the invitation to help transform the trickle into a flood. Beginning at this place on this day, I exhort you to sweep the earth with messages filled with righteousness and truth—messages that are authentic, edifying, and praiseworthy—and literally to sweep the earth as with a flood."[22] Clearly President Monson, whose original career revolved around newspapers and advertising, was determined to use media more effectively in an effort to build the kingdom.

The Church took strides toward greater transparency in its public pronouncements during the administration of President Monson as well. Although this effort commenced while President Monson was still an Apostle, the lion's share of the publication work for the Joseph Smith Papers project was accomplished under his watch. The Joseph Smith Papers project is an attempt to publish every manuscript or document that was created by, or written under the direction of, Joseph Smith. The first published volume, entitled *The Joseph Smith Papers, Journals, Volume 1:1832–1839*, was published in December 2008, the year President Monson was called as Church President. The Joseph Smith Papers project has been endorsed by the National Archives' Historical Publications and Records Commission (NHPRC) and has been praised for its transparency.[23]

In a further effort at transparency, beginning in 2013, the Church began publishing in-depth essays on challenging historical and doctrinal subjects. These essays were published

The Kansas City Missouri Temple was dedicated in three sessions by President Thomas S. Monson on May 6, 2012. (Photo courtesy of Lori Tubbs Garcia. Used by permission.)

online on LDS.org, and leaders were encouraged to study and use these essays in their church service. These essays have addressed several issues about which members had previously not had easy access to source material or serious scholarly interpretation. Essay topics include such subjects as becoming like God, Mother in Heaven, plural marriage, race and the priesthood, and accounts of the First Vision. Though crafted by scholars and historians, each essay has been approved by the entire First Presidency and Quorum of the Twelve.[24] These and other efforts show President Monson's and the Church's commitment to greater transparency and efforts to share the gospel with all.

President Thomas S. Monson, Kansas City Temple dedication, May 6, 2012. (Photo courtesy of Lori Tubbs Garcia. Used by permission.)

MISSIONARY WORK

President Monson will be remembered for the major changes he implemented in the missionary work of the Church. After several years of testing, President Monson announced a major restructuring of missionary service in the October 2012 general conference: "I am pleased to announce that effective immediately all worthy and able young men who have graduated from high school or its equivalent, regardless of where they live, will have the option of being recommended for missionary service beginning at the age of 18, instead of age 19. . . . I am pleased to announce that able, worthy young women who have the desire to serve may be recommended for missionary service beginning at age 19, instead of age 21."[25] The impact was felt almost immediately. At the time of the announcement, just over 58,000 missionaries were serving. That number surged to approximately 89,000 before settling down to around 67,000 missionaries serving in 2018. In order to accommodate this surge in the number of missionaries serving, the number of missions expanded from 347 in 2012 to over 421 in 2016. Another major change came in the composition of those missionaries. Sister missionaries serving full-time missions increased from 13 percent in 2012 to around 30 percent of all missionaries within a matter of a couple years.

TEMPLE WORK

Following in the footsteps of President Gordon B. Hinckley, President Monson continued efforts at bringing temples closer to the members of the Church. Thirty-seven temples were dedicated during President Monson's administration, almost a quarter of all dedicated temples worldwide. In addition, 10 more temples were under construction with 11 more temples announced during his tenure. President Monson personally dedicated 21 temples, and 14 of those were dedicated while he was serving as Church President. Only President Gordon B. Hinckley has dedicated more temples.

PROMOTING THE ETERNAL FAMILY

President Monson and the Church were involved in several high-profile efforts to promote the family as outlined in "The Family: A Proclamation to the World." During the first year of President Monson's tenure as Church President, the Church played a major role in Proposition 8, a legislative effort in California to restore the March 2000 definition of marriage between a man and a woman that voters had overwhelmingly approved but which had subsequently been overturned by the California Supreme Court. The Church joined efforts with many other faith traditions to promote the essential nature of marriage between a man and a woman. The Church produced an in-depth document explaining its stance on marriage, entitled "The Divine Institution of Marriage," and, as part of a coalition with other churches, created the website "ProtectMarriage.com" to explain the reasoning behind the effort to define marriage as a relationship between a man and a woman. Proposition 8 passed, and the California constitution was amended to state that marriage should be between a man and a woman. These efforts, however, were ultimately overturned by the United States Supreme Court Obergefell v. Hodges decision, making same-sex marriage a national, rather than state, issue.

In an effort to make clear the doctrine of the family for members of the Church, a change was also made in the Church Handbook related to same-gender marriage and children living with same-gender married parents. The new provision affirmed that "adults who choose to enter into a same-gender marriage or similar relationship commit sin that warrants a Church disciplinary council." Furthermore, the policy further stated that children whose primary residence is with parents living in a same-gender marriage are not to be baptized until they turn eighteen. The instructions made it clear that all people were welcome and invited to attend church but that priesthood ordinances in such situations were to be postponed for children until they reached the age of eighteen. Endeavoring to explain that the purpose of these efforts was to clarify doctrine on the centrality and essential nature of the eternal family—not as an attack on same-sex attracted members—the Church launched the MormonsandGays.org website. That policy has since changed, and children of parents who identify themselves as lesbian, gay, bisexual, or transgender may now be blessed as infants and baptized into The Church of Jesus Christ of Latter-day Saints without First Presidency approval.[26]

Under President Monson's leadership, Church members were encouraged to reach out to gay members and to explain the Church's position on their infinite worth and their potential for happiness in this life and the next life. The Mormons andGays.org website strongly urges understanding and compassion for all while clarifying essential and unchanging doctrines.

The site was updated in 2016, and the name was changed

President Thomas S. Monson continued to serve faithfully even as he suffered from several health challenges in the last few years of his ministry. (Photo courtesy of Rachael Van Syckel-Pancic. Used by permission.)

to MormonandGay.org. Elder Dallin H. Oaks explained, "There is no change in the Church's position of what is morally right, . . . But what is changing—and what needs to change—is helping Church members respond sensitively and thoughtfully when they encounter same-sex attraction in their own families, among other Church members, or elsewhere."[27]

PERSONAL MINISTRY AND CARE FOR THE POOR

Perhaps President Monson will be remembered best for his legacy of Christlike service. As noted earlier, from childhood, President Monson learned the importance and joy of service. His ministry to the eighty-five widows he served as a twenty-two-year-old bishop was just the beginning of his personal

President Thomas S. Monson takes time to shake hands with the youth of the Church. (Photo courtesy of Rachael Van Syckel-Pancic. Used by permission.)

ministry. Throughout his life, regardless of what official calling he held at the time, President Monson always carried on a personal ministry, reaching out to those who were most vulnerable. As Orrin Hatch, a United States senator from Utah, stated, "President Monson's example of intimate individual ministry underscored what was most remarkable about his leadership. Although he presided over a church of millions, his focus was always on the one."[28] President Monson also oversaw massive church-wide efforts to care for the poor and needy. As an example of this ministry, in 2016 alone, the Church took part in over 2,600 service projects in 147 countries and collaborated with over 1,500 other organizations to serve millions throughout the world.[29] It is only appropriate that under President Monson's ministry, the Church added a fourth component to what had become known as the "three-fold mission of the Church," as the First Presidency referred to it in 1981. To the original three emphases of proclaiming the gospel, perfecting the Saints, and redeeming the dead, President Monson added caring for the poor and needy. In the 2010 update to the Church Handbook, the following content was added: "In fulfilling its purpose to help individuals and families qualify for exaltation, the Church focuses on divinely appointed responsibilities. These include helping members live the gospel of Jesus Christ, gathering Israel through missionary work, caring for the poor and needy, and enabling the salvation of the dead by building temples and performing vicarious ordinances."[30]

A final salute to the congregation by President Thomas S. Monson. (Photo courtesy of Lori Tubbs Garcia. Used by permission.)

PRESIDENT THOMAS S. MONSON

President Monson continued to serve faithfully even as he suffered from several health challenges in the last few years of his ministry. He died at his home on January 2, 2018, surrounded by family and loved ones. Tributes poured in from national and international leaders, including the president of the United States, numerous senators, congressmen and women, leaders of industry, and the religious leaders of dozens of different faith traditions. His legacy of service, his testimony of our Savior Jesus Christ, his lifetime of selfless ministry both inside the restored gospel and to God's children everywhere, and his example of Christlike love were constant themes in these tributes. Following almost five years of separation after Sister Monson's death in 2013, President Monson and his beloved wife were reunited, never to be separated again.

Michael A. Goodman

Associate Professor of Church History and Doctrine, PhD
Brigham Young University

Temple Dedications

Thomas S. Monson oversaw the announcements or dedications of 58 temples while serving as President of the Church. He personally dedicated 21 temples while serving as an Apostle or prophet. This is the second largest number of dedicated temples after Gordon B. Hinckley (85 temples) and before Dieter F. Uchtdorf (10 temples).

Temples Dedicated by President Monson

Buenos Aires Argentina Temple	January 17, 1986
Louisville Kentucky Temple	March 19, 2000
Reno Nevada Temple	April 23, 2000
Tampico Mexico Temple	May 20, 2000
Villahermosa Mexico Temple	May 21, 2000
Mérida Mexico Temple	July 8, 2000
Veracruz Mexico Temple	July 9, 2000
Rexburg Idaho Temple	February 10, 2008
Curitiba Brazil Temple	June 1, 2008
Panama City Panama Temple	August 10, 2008
Twin Falls Idaho Temple	August 24, 2008
Draper Utah Temple	March 20, 2009
Oquirrh Mountain Utah Temple	August 21–23, 2009
Vancouver British Columbia Temple	May 2, 2010
The Gila Valley Arizona Temple	May 23, 2010
Cebu City Philippines Temple	June 13, 2010
Kiev Ukraine Temple	August 29, 2010
Kansas City Missouri Temple	May 6, 2012
Calgary Alberta Temple	October 28, 2012
Gilbert Arizona Temple	March 2, 2014
Phoenix Arizona Temple	November 16, 2014

What Others Have Said about President Monson

Jack Gallivan, member of the Roman Catholic Church, former publisher of the Salt Lake Tribune, *and community leader:*

"If he's ever met you, Tom Monson is your friend. This warm, genuine, gregarious man doesn't love his neighbor because that is the mandate; Tom Monson is your friend because he loves mankind. That's his nature."[18]

W. James Mortimer, friend and former publisher of Deseret News*:*

"I have served in business, church, and personal capacities with President Monson for the past twenty-five years. He is one of a kind. His strength is evident, but it is always blended with humility. His intellect is keen but always tempered with wisdom. The power he holds is always exercised with sound judgment. Through service and loyalty he has earned the love others have for him."[19]

Wendell J. Ashton, longtime friend:

"Tom is a man of the common people, the champion of the underdog. When he brings friends to the basketball games, it isn't the rich and famous or the leaders from the chamber of commerce. It is a handful of the ordinary folks gathered from his days 'down by the tracks.' He is like a pine tree—the top is high and ascending to heaven but the branches are broad, low to the ground, and protective of all who need shelter there."[20]

Elder James E. Faust (before he was called to the First Presidency):

"No one in this world is more loyal than Tom Monson. Once you are Tom's friend, you are his friend forever. That mind of his doesn't forget anything, but neither does his heart—especially people."[21]

Elder Boyd K. Packer:

"Few people know it, but Brother Monson is the self-appointed chaplain at a number of nursing homes around town. He visits them anytime his busy schedule will permit, and sometimes even when it doesn't permit."[22]

President Harold B. Lee, President Monson's boyhood stake president and dear friend, in the foreword of President Monson's book Pathways to Perfection:

"To listen to him is to be inspired. To work with him is to be uplifted; and to feel of his devotion and the strength of his conviction and powerful testimony is to know that there is no doubt but that his calling as a special witness as an apostle of the Lord, Jesus Christ, is well merited."[23]

Elder Joseph B. Wirthlin, then member of the Quorum of the Seventy and President of the Europe Area of the Church:

"If it weren't for Brother Monson, there would be little for our Saints in this part of Europe. Now we have stakes, wards, chapels and—miracle of miracles—a temple. Tom has given everything to those people, including the shirt off his back. I mean it! I've seen him give away his suits and his shirts and his shoes. I'll bet he's given away twenty suits to those destitute Saints in Eastern Europe. He says they were used, old ones that he was going to throw away, but they always looked brand new to me."[24]

Elder Boyd K. Packer:

"He is a genius at organization. If I were to choose someone to steer an important matter successfully through all the necessary channels and past all the necessary checkpoints, I would choose Tom Monson."[25]

President Spencer W. Kimball, in the foreword to President Monson's book Be Your Best Self:

"I regard him as one of the Lord's most able servants. He has exemplified through his years of service a steady devotion to the Lord's work that is worthy of emulation."[26]

Milestones in the Presidency of Thomas S. Monson

During his years as President of the Church, Thomas S. Monson

- Directed the Church work in defending the traditional family as typified by the Church's efforts with Proposition 8 in California in 2008.

- Oversaw an ever-increasing effort at transparency, which included the Church's work on the Joseph Smith Papers, the LDS.org Gospel Topics Essays, and the new Church History Library that was dedicated on June 20, 2009.

- Along with Elder Oaks, presented President Obama with five leather-bound volumes of his family history on July 20, 2009.

- Assigned the Quorum of the Twelve Apostles to conduct international priesthood leadership conferences and area reviews in 2010.

- Directed the writing and release of the new administrative handbooks in 2010.

- Oversaw the elimination of student wards in Utah and their replacement with single adult wards and stakes in 2010.

- Authorized the publication of *Daughters in My Kingdom: The History and Work of Relief Society* in 2011.

- Directed the public affairs work of the "I'm a Mormon" campaign in 2011 and *Meet the Mormons* in 2014.

- Was recognized by several outside organizations for his leadership, including being part of the *USA Today* top ten most admired men award (a first for a Latter-day Saint President); was also listed in *Slate* as one of the most powerful octogenarians in their "80 Over 80" survey; and was listed by Gallup as one of America's ten most admired men.

- Oversaw the massive redevelopment of downtown Salt Lake City in 2012.

- Supervised the introduction of the Come, Follow Me curriculum for Young Men and Young Women on September 12, 2012.

- Announced the missionary age change on October 6, 2012, which lowered the age of service from 19 to 18 for men and 21 to 19 for women; during his administration, over 410,000 missionaries were called—approximately one-third of all missionaries ever called to serve.

- Continued efforts at inclusiveness with the groundbreaking introduction of the Mormon and Gay website in 2012.

- Survived the passing of his eternal companion, Frances Beverly Johnson, on May 17, 2013.

- Replaced the general Relief Society session and Young Women meeting with the general women's session for women eight years and older and made it an official session of general conference.

- Became the first Church President to open a social media account, and on November 25, 2014, became the first to email members.

- Supported the 2015 Salt Lake City ordinance protecting LGBTQ individuals from discrimination on the basis of sexual orientation or gender identity in employment and housing.

- Oversaw the policy change regarding same-sex married couples and their children in 2015.

- Oversaw the announcement and/or dedication of 58 temples, 14 of which he personally dedicated while serving as Church President.

- Was part of 1.89 billion dollars of disaster relief provided while he served in the First Presidency.

- Delivered 230 general conference addresses between 1963 and 2017.

- Saw membership growth increase from 13 million to 16 million members, including the milestone of more members living outside than inside the United States. To put these numbers in perspective, there were about 650,000 members when he was born.

- Served for fifty-four years, which is longer than all but four Apostles: David O. McKay (sixty-three years), Heber J. Grant and Joseph Fielding Smith (sixty-two years), and Wilford Woodruff (fifty-nine years).

NOTES

1. Francis M. Gibbons, "President Thomas S. Monson," *Ensign*, July 1995, 6–11.

2. Gerry Avant, "On Lord's Errand," *Church News*, February 9, 2008, 5.

3. Thomas S. Monson, *Be Your Best Self* (Salt Lake City: Deseret Book, 1979), 163–64.

4. Thomas S. Monson, "Do Your Duty—That Is Best," *Ensign*, November 2005, 56–57.

5. Thomas S. Monson, "Anxiously Engaged," *Ensign*, November 2004, 56.

6. Jeffrey R. Holland, "President Thomas S. Monson: Finishing the Course, Keeping the Faith," *Ensign*, September 1994, 12–17.

7. Thomas S. Monson, "The Army of the Lord," *Ensign*, May 1979, 37.

8. Thomas S. Monson, *Inspiring Experiences That Build Faith: From the Life and Ministry of Thomas S. Monson* (Salt Lake City: Deseret Book, 1994), 199.

9. Ibid., 255.

10. Jeffrey R. Holland, "President Thomas S. Monson: Man of Action, Man of Faith, Always 'on the Lord's Errand,'" *Ensign*, February 1986, 14.

11. Ibid., 17.

12. Gerry Avant, "President Monson: Concern for Others Is Second Nature," *Church News*, March 18, 1995, 5.

13. Holland, "President Thomas S. Monson: Man of Action, Man of Faith," 11–17.

14. Gibbons, "President Thomas S. Monson," 6–11.

15. Thomas S. Monson, "Patience—A Heavenly Virtue," *Ensign*, November 1995, 60.

16. "Thomas Monson becomes Mormon leader," NBC News, Feb. 4, 2008, http://www.nbcnews.com/id/22995094/ns/us_news-faith/t/thomas-monson-becomes-mormon-leader/#.XJqzCyhKiPo.

17. The following are examples: "4 Stories of President Monson" (https://speeches.byu.edu/posts/remembering-stories-president-monson/), "6 Inspiring Stories from President Monson (That He Never Told at Conference)" (http://www.ldsliving.com/6-Stories-from-President-Monson-That-He-s-Never-Told-At-General-Conference/s/76638), "12 Stories about President Monson" (https://www.theredheadedhostess.com/blog/teach/general-conference-teach/12-stories-president-monson/), "Remembering Thomas S. Monson: 5 Favorite Stories from His Life" (http://www.alexacrckson.com/remembering-thomas-s-monson-5-favorite-stories-from-his-life/), "6 Favorite Stories from President Monson's Biography" (https://gentlyhewstone.com/2017/01/01/6-favorite-stories-from-president-monsons-biography/), "12 of the Most Memorable Talks by President Thomas S. Monson" (https://www.heraldextra.com/news/local/faith/of-the-most-memorable-talks-by-president-thomas-s-monson/collection_4d6b3c80-f65a-11e7-840d-9355c5a64076.html), "Thomas S. Monson: Mormon Faithful Recall A Great Leader Sharing Humble Stories" (https://www.kuer.org/post/thomas-s-monson-mormon-faithful-recall-great-leader-sharing-humble-stories#stream/0)

18. President Monson shared 78 stories in general conference over the period he served as Church President. Out of those 78 stories, 43 of them were directly connected to his own life.

19. Thomas S. Monson, "The Lord's Work," Church News, Feb. 9, 2008, 3.

20. "Thomas S. Monson Named 16th Church President," Mormon Newsroom, Feb. 4, 2008, https://www.mormonnewsroom.org/article/thomas-s.-monson-named-16th-church-president.

21. "President Thomas S. Monson," LDS.org, https://www.lds.org/prophets-and-apostles/biographies/president-thomas-s-monson?lang=eng.

22. David A. Bednar, "To Sweep the Earth as with a Flood," BYU Campus Education Week, Aug. 19, 2014.

23. "About the Project," The Joseph Smith Papers, https://www.josephsmithpapers.org/articles/about-the-project.

24. "Gospel Topics Essays," LDS.org, https://www.lds.org/topics/essays?lang=eng.

25. Thomas S. Monson, "Welcome to Conference," Ensign, Nov. 2012.

26. Sarah Jane Weaver, "Policy Changes Announced for Members in Gay Marriages, Children of LGBT Parents," lds.org, April 4, 2019.

27. "Church Updates Resources Addressing Same-Sex Attraction," LDS.org Church News, Oct. 25, 2016, https://www.lds.org/church/news/church-updates-resources-addressing-same-sex-attraction?lang=eng&_r=1.

28. "Public Leaders Worldwide Pay Tribute to President Monson," Mormon Newsroom, Jan. 10, 2018, https://www.mormonnewsroom.org/article/public-leaders-worldwide-tributes-president-monson.

29. "President Monson Felt Responsibility to Relieve Human Suffering," LDS.org Church News, Jan. 3, 2018, https://www.lds.org/church/news/president-monson-felt-responsibility-to-relieve-human-suffering?lang=eng.

30. "The Purpose of the Church," Handbook 2: Administering the Church, section 2.2 (2019).

SIDEBAR AND PHOTO NOTES

1. Holland, "President Thomas S. Monson: Man of Action, Man of Faith," 17.

2. Monson, *Inspiring Experiences*, 7.

3. Ibid., 105.

4. Ibid., 255.

5. Holland, "President Thomas S. Monson: Man of Action, Man of Faith," 13–14.

6. Monson, *Inspiring Experiences*, 137–38.

7. Gerry Avant, "Approaching a Milestone Event," *Church News*, August 15, 1992, 6.

8. Gerry Avant, "President Monson: Concern for Others Is Second Nature," 5.

9. Monson, *Inspiring Experiences*, 265.

10. Avant, "Approaching a Milestone Event," 6.

11. Thomas S. Monson, "Abundantly Blessed," Ensign, May 2008.

12. Thomas S. Monson, "To Learn, to Do, to Be," Ensign, Nov. 2008.

13. Monson, "To Learn, to Do, to Be."

14. Henry Wadsworth Longfellow, "A Theologian's Tale; The Legend Beautiful," Tales of a Wayside Inn, 1863.

15. Meredith Willson and Franklin Lacey, The Music Man, (1957).

16. William Shakespeare, "Two Gentlemen of Verona," 1.2.31. References are to act, scene, and line.

17. Harriet Beecher Stowe, in Gorton Carruth and Eugene Erlich, comps., The Harper Book of American Quotations (1988), 173.

18. Avant, "Approaching a Milestone Event," 15.

19. Ibid., 13.

20. Ibid., 12–13.

21. Ibid., 13.

22. Ibid.

23. Thomas S. Monson, *Pathways to Perfection* (Salt Lake City: Deseret Book, 1973), vii.

24. Holland, "President Thomas S. Monson: Man of Action, Man of Faith," 15.

25. Ibid.

26. Monson, *Be Your Best Self*, 1.

SUGGESTED READING

Thomas S. Monson, *Be Your Best Self* (Salt Lake City: Deseret Book, 1979).

Thomas S. Monson, *Conference Classics*, 3 vols. (Salt Lake City: Deseret Book, 1981–84).

Thomas S. Monson, *Faith Rewarded: A Personal Account of Prophetic Promises to the East German Saints* (Salt Lake City: Deseret Book, 1996).

Thomas S. Monson, comp., *Favorite Quotations from the Collection of Thomas S. Monson* (Salt Lake City: Deseret Book, 1985).

Thomas S. Monson, *Inspiring Experiences That Build Faith: From the Life and Ministry of Thomas S. Monson* (Salt Lake City: Deseret Book, 1994).

Thomas S. Monson, *Live the Good Life* (Salt Lake City: Deseret Book, 1988).

Thomas S. Monson, *Pathways to Perfection* (Salt Lake City: Deseret Book, 1973).

Chapter Seventeen

RUSSELL M. NELSON

LIFE AND TIMES

1924	September 9	Born in Salt Lake City, Utah
1940	November 30	Baptized at age sixteen
1945	August 31	Married Dantzel White in the Salt Lake Temple
1947	August	Graduated from the University of Utah
1947	September	Began PhD at the University of Minnesota
1951–53		Served in the Army Medical Corp during Korean War
1951	December 2	Was ordained a high priest by Elder George Q. Morris of the Quorum of the Twelve Apostles
1954		Graduated from the University of Minnesota with a PhD
1955	March	Moved back to Salt Lake City, became faculty member at the University of Utah
1955	November	Performed the first open heart surgery in the state of Utah on Vernell Worthen
1964	December 5	Called as president of the Salt Lake Bonneville Stake
1971	July 2	Set apart as the General Sunday School Superintendent
1972	April 12	Performed open heart surgery on Elder Spencer W. Kimball
1977	March 26	Parents were sealed in the Provo Temple
1984	April 12	Ordained an Apostle
1995	January 29	Daughter, Emily Nelson Wittwer, passed away at age 37
2005	February 12	Dantzel Nelson passed way
2006	April 15	Married Wendy L. Watson
2015	July 15	Set apart as President of the Quorum of the Twelve Apostles
2018	January 14	Ordained as the 17th President of The Church of Jesus Christ of Latter-day Saints
2018	April	Priesthood quorums restructured
2018	April	Ministering replaces home and visiting teaching
2018	August	Reemphasis on the correct name of the Church
2018	October	"Home-centered and Church-supported" program announced to begin in January 2019
2018	December	Changes to Primary progression, young men priesthood ordination, and youth temple recommends
2019	January 11	Daughter, Wendy Nelson Maxfield, passed away at age 67

BIOGRAPHICAL HIGHLIGHTS

Russell Marion Nelson was born and raised in Salt Lake City, Utah. He developed a strong work ethic at an early age. He worked many odd jobs, excelled academically and musically, and was involved in student government. His parents, Marion and Edna Nelson, were not active members of the Church during most of Russell's life. In 1977, however, his parents were sealed in the Provo Utah Temple.

Because of his parents' lack of interest in the gospel when he was young, Russell was not baptized into the Church until he was sixteen years old. After graduating from high school early, he attended the University of Utah, where he met Dantzel White from Brigham City, Utah. Russell and Dantzel were married in August 1945, and in 1947, Russell graduated from the University of Utah as a full-fledged medical doctor. He received a PhD from the University of Minnesota and began his professional career as a faculty member in the school of medicine at the University of Utah in 1955. That same year, he performed the first open heart surgery in the state of Utah. Russell became an internationally renowned heart surgeon, traveling the world, presenting his research at conferences, and even performing surgeries in foreign countries.

Despite his professional success, Russell's first love was his family. He and his wife Dantzel raised ten children. Russell was an involved father who made his family his top priority. Russell was also one who devoted his energy to serving in the Church and building the kingdom of God. Before being ordained an Apostle, he served in the youth program, in bishoprics, on a high council, as a stake president, as the General Sunday School President, and as a regional representative.

In April 1984 when Russell was called to the Quorum of the Twelve Apostles, he was at the apex of his professional career as a heart surgeon. President Nelson has always had a great love for the members of The Church of Jesus Christ of Latter-day Saints. He has blessed Latter-day Saints across the world with his inspiring messages, his kind words, and his personal ministry to so many of our Heavenly Father's children. He has also been instrumental in opening the doors for the gospel of Jesus Christ in many foreign lands across the globe.

CONTRIBUTIONS

Although President Russell M. Nelson has served as the President of the Church for a relatively short time, the contributions during his administration have been monumental and have come at a rapid pace. After some major changes were introduced during the April 2018 general conference, Elder Jeffrey R. Holland stood at the podium and stated, "To paraphrase Ralph Waldo Emerson, the most memorable moments of life are those in which we feel the rush of revelation. President Nelson, I don't know how many more rushes we can handle this weekend." Perhaps Elder Holland's comments capture the feelings of most members of the Church as they process and seek to incorporate the changes that have been announced.

During the priesthood session of the 188th Annual General Conference, President Russell M. Nelson announced that to accomplish the Lord's work more effectively, the high priests group and elders quorum would be merged into one quorum. At the same general conference, "home teaching" and "visiting teaching" were retired. President Nelson then referred to the new approach of caring for members of each ward and branch as "ministering."

Other changes introduced by President Nelson include the following:

- The Church's relationship with the Boy Scouts of America will end beginning December 31, 2019.
- New guidelines for youth interviews have been announced.
- The wording and length of the endowment ceremony in the temple have been adjusted.
- The Latter-day Saint hymnbook and *Children's Songbook* are being altered to meet the needs of a growing, international Church. Furthermore, members have been asked to contribute to the changes.
- In some parts of the world, mission calls will be posted online instead of through the postal service.
- Beginning in January 2020, seminary students will study the same book of scripture as the general Church membership. The study topic will be aligned with *Come, Follow Me*.

- The Mormon Tabernacle Choir has changed their name to The Tabernacle Choir at Temple Square.
- Many major Church pageants will be discontinued, except for Nauvoo, Mesa, and the British Pageant.
- Sister missionaries can now wear pants instead of dresses.
- Beginning in January 2019, children will complete primary and begin attending Sunday School, Young Men's, and Young Women's. These changes are now based on age groups, not as individual birthdays. Additionally, young men are eligible to be ordained to a priesthood office in January of the year they turn twelve, fourteen, or sixteen. For the first time in the history of the Church, there are eleven-year-old deacons and eleven-year old youth attending the temple.

Perhaps one of those most significant cultural changes was announced at the October 2018 General Conference. Beginning in January 2019, the three-hour church block was reduced to two hours. Sacrament meetings are now sixty minutes in length. Sunday School is held on the first and third Sundays of each month, and priesthood quorums, Young Women's, and Relief Society have their meetings on the second and fourth Sundays.

Another significant emphasis has been on the name of the Church. On August 16, 2018, it was announced that the Church should be referred to by its proper name—The Church of Jesus Christ of Latter-day Saints. Terms such as "LDS" or "Mormon" are now discouraged. Although attempts to make this course correction have fallen short in the past, President Nelson explained emphatically that the Lord is not pleased when we refer to the Church by any other name. In fact, he said, "When we discard the Savior's name, we are subtly disregarding all that Jesus Christ did for us—even his Atonement."

Certainly, there will be more changes to come. President Nelson told the *Church News* in November 2018, "If you think the Church has been fully restored, you're just seeing the beginning. There's much more to come." As President Nelson continues to receive revelation, more changes will come to the Church and its members. Our Prophet is determined to do all that he can to prepare the world for the Second Coming of Jesus Christ.

TEACHINGS

Before being ordained as the President of The Church of Jesus Christ of Latter-day Saints, President Russell M. Nelson served as a member of the Quorum of the Twelve Apostles for nearly thirty-four years. During that time, he delivered close to seventy major addresses during general conferences, and twenty addresses at Brigham Young University. Of course, he has delivered many additional messages at stake conferences and regional conferences across the world.

Besides speaking, President Nelson has been a prolific author, writing several books, including *Accomplishing the Impossible*, *The Power within Us*, *The Gateway We Call Death*, *Perfection Pending*, *The Magnificence of Man*, and *Hope in Our Hearts*. In 1979, Brother Nelson published his own autobiography, entitled *From Heart to Heart*. Russell wrote this book at the urging of his wife Dantzel and from President Spencer W. Kimball.

For over thirty-five years, President Nelson has inspired the general Church membership with his messages. Topics that he has addressed include the plan of salvation, the Atonement of Jesus Christ, the Book of Mormon, missionary work, the temple, marriage, family, ministering, women's roles, decisions, faith, the Sabbath day, prayer, the scriptures, covenants, and a host of others. Many of President Nelson's teachings have been recently published in *Teachings of Russell M. Nelson*.

President Nelson is a gifted speaker, addressing topics with candor, love, and encouragement. Many have been inspired by his messages that center on the plan of salvation—especially dealing with the death of loved ones. President Nelson has been transparent in his messages, as he has shared his poignant feelings about losing two of his daughters to cancer and his beloved wife Dantzel.

President Nelson has never shied away from difficult topics. He has always been a defender of the faith, and of the family. His messages have lifted the membership of the Church to greater heights and inspired them to do better and to become more devoted disciples of Jesus Christ.

LIFE OF RUSSELL M. NELSON

President Russell M. Nelson was born to Marion C. Nelson and Edna Anderson Nelson. Marion and Edna were married by their bishop Elias S. Woodruff on August 25, 1919. The next year, their first child, Marjory, was born. Five years later, on September 9, 1924, Edna Nelson gave birth to a nine-pound, eleven-ounce baby boy. It was miraculous that a five-foot, three-inch mother could deliver such a large baby. They named their baby boy Russell Marion Nelson. In a general conference, President Nelson explained, "I also owe so much to my forebears. All eight of my great-grandparents were converts to the Church in Europe. Each of these stalwart souls sacrificed everything to come to Zion. During subsequent generations, however, not all my ancestors remained so committed. As a result, I was not raised in a gospel-centered home."[1] Although Marion and Edna were not active members of The Church of Jesus Christ of Latter-day Saints, President Nelson reported:

> They made love the prevailing influence in their home. Completely absent were expressions of anger, criticism, and denigration of others. Our parents led, guided, and provided; but they were not possessive, and they did not unduly interfere in the lives of their children. The important decisions in life— choice of career, selection of marriage partner, and all other opportunities—were to be made individually, after parental counsel.[2]

However, as Russell grew up, he knew that there was something missing from his life—something big. He explained in a general conference:

An infant Russell, between 4 and 7 months old.

I adored my parents. They meant the world to me and taught me crucial lessons. I cannot thank them enough for the happy homelife they created for me and my siblings. And yet, even as a boy, I knew I was missing something. One day I jumped on the streetcar and went to an LDS bookstore to find a book about the Church. I loved learning about the gospel.

As I came to understand the Word of Wisdom, I wanted my parents to live that law. So, one day when I was very young, I went to our basement and smashed on the concrete floor every bottle of liquor! I expected my father to punish me, but he never said a word.

As I matured and began to understand the magnificence of Heavenly Father's plan, I often said to myself, "I don't want one more Christmas present. I just want to be sealed to my parents.[3]

Russell was blessed with a strong and faithful home teacher named Jonas Ryser. Brother Ryser convinced Marion and Edna that their children should be baptized, and they eventually granted their permission. On November 30, 1940, sixteen-year-old Russell was baptized by his good friend Foley C. Richards and confirmed the following day by Brother Ryser. Russell then was warmly welcomed into the ward by his bishop at the time, Sterling W. Sill. Fifty-four years later, as an Apostle, Elder Russell M. Nelson spoke at the funeral of Bishop Sill.[4] Bishop Sill ordained Russell to the office of priest in the Aaronic Priesthood on November 9, 1941, when Russell was seventeen years old, and on April 30, 1944, Bishop Joseph W. Bambrough ordained Russell an elder.[5]

Russell was always a hard worker, and his drive to excel has never left him. He began working at the age of ten as an errand boy for his father's advertising agency. Since then, he has never been without a job. He was later employed as a bank teller and then a mail sorter, and he held each of these jobs before he graduated from high school.[6]

However, other endeavors would fill Russell's time besides working for pay. He spent many hours playing the piano. He served as both the student body vice president and president at Roosevelt Junior High School. He also starred in school plays; was a member of the glee club; was involved in choir, where he sang with perfect pitch; and had his own dark room in the basement of their home, where he developed his interest in photography. He even played on the high school football team.[7] "Although Russell was successful in other activities, his football coach usually kept him on the bench during games. 'I think one of the reasons was that I always felt a little bit defensive about my hands,' he remembers. 'I was afraid somebody might step on them with their cleated shoes.' Those hands operated on the coach nearly forty years later."[8]

RUSSELL, DANTZEL, AND FAMILY

Dantzel was born on February 17, 1926, in Perry, Utah, to LeRoy Davis White and Maude Clark White. Dantzel was voted "Outstanding Senior Girl" at Box Elder High School and then attended the University of Utah on a scholarship.[9] She was a gifted singer with a beautiful soprano voice. Russell's and Dantzel's lives intersected when they met at

Dantzel White during her senior year at Box Elder High School, spring of 1941.

Russell in the University of Utah yearbook, 1942.

the University of Utah during Russell's sophomore year in 1942.[10] Some of Russell's friends tried to persuade him to try out for a university musical, *Hayfoot, Strawfoot*. Russell's response to the pressure of his friends was resistance. He said, "I was more concerned about passing biology than about being in some play."[11] On April 16, 1942,[12] Russell reluctantly attended the first rehearsal with his nose buried in a book. However, when he heard the soprano voice of a dark-haired young woman, he asked the director, "Who is that beautiful girl singing up there?" The director responded, "That's Dantzel White. She's the one you'll be performing with." Russell recalled, "I thought she was the most beautiful girl I had ever seen and sensed that she was the one I would marry." Russell then added, "That was a strange feeling, because at the time I was really not all that interested in such serious thoughts. I enjoyed dating many different girls and was concerned about pursuing my desired goal of preparing for medical school. I was only seventeen years of age, and marriage was the farthest thing from my mind."[13]

When they met, Dantzel was only sixteen years old. Nevertheless, when she went home to Perry, Utah, a short time later, she announced to her parents that she had met the man she hoped to marry.[14] After three years of courtship, Russell and Dantzel were married in the Salt Lake Temple on August 31, 1945.[15] Dantzel was accepted to attend the Julliard School of Music in New York City, but she turned the offer down to marry Russell and begin their family.[16] Russell observed, "In making the decision to marry me, she ultimately exchanged a promising future in music for the privilege of singing lullabies to her little ones in a rocker and cradle."[17] Russell and Dantzel would continue to make sacrifices throughout their lives to bless their family and build the kingdom of God.

Russell and Dantzel as a couple while attending the University of Utah.

Russell and Dantzel in the fall of 1944, before their wedding.

Russell and Dantzel on their honeymoon at the Grand Canyon, on the hike to Angels Widow, September 3–5, 1945.

May 1945, at Dantzel's sister's home in Sugarhouse, UT.

"Then in 1945, the break came that made our marriage possible. My application for the V-12 Program of the United States Naval Reserve was accepted! This meant that I would continue through medical school as an apprentice seaman in the Navy, while they would finance my tuition and books and give me a salary (as apprentice seaman) which I recall was around $125 a month. That paved the way for us, at least in part, to become financially solvent enough to proceed with our marriage" (*From Heart to Heart*, 51).

August 29, 1947. Russell graduated from the University of Utah at the top of his class with a doctor's degree, just before he and Dantzel moved to Minnesota.

Russell and Dantzel on September 5, 1947

According to Spencer J. Condie, "Following Russell's graduation from medical school, he and Dantzel stuffed all the belongings they could into a two-door, blue Chevrolet that his parents had purchased for them. In September 1947, they drove to Minneapolis, Minnesota, where Russell was to begin an internship at the University of Minnesota Hospitals" (Condie, 105).

FAMILY RITUALS

Before they had children, Russell and Dantzel found themselves having a poignant conversation in the north woods of Minnesota. Russell remembered, "We asked ourselves whether we wanted children, and if so, how many? We each timidly felt out the other's attitudes on that question. But after we had explored it a bit, we both came to the conclusion that an even dozen would do! I don't know how serious we really were at that time; we were so young and naïve."[18]

Russell and Dantzel did not have the twelve children they thought they would have, but they did have ten: Marsha, Wendy, Gloria, Brenda, Sylvia, Emily, Laurie, Rosalie, Marjorie, and Russell. Dantzel found a way to run the large Nelson household smoothly and efficiently. When asked how President Nelson accomplished everything that he did, being a stake president, surgeon, husband, father, and even a missionary on Temple Square during his prime parenting years, his daughter Sylvia responded, "One word: 'Mother.'"[19] Dantzel was supportive, never complained, and absolutely loved being a mother.

President Russell M. Nelson has many gifts, talents, and abilities, but perhaps one of his greatest strengths is his devotion to family. The first time President Spencer W. Kimball saw the Nelson family was at a stake conference in 1964. He said, "Eight daughters were singing a song, accompanied by their mother, Dantzel. I was amazed and pleased, and I thought, 'What a perfect family! What beautiful parents!

Nelson family photo, April 1978.

Front: Rosalie, Brenda, Russell Jr., Sylvia, Marsha, Laurie.
Back: Marjorie, Emily, Russell, Dantzel, Gloria, Wendy.

And what delightful children to grow up in one household.' I have known them from that time forward, and now there are nine daughters and one son. Brother Nelson has always been a family man first."[20]

Most evenings, Dantzel and the children would straighten up the house before Russell walked in the door at about 5:30 or 6:00 p.m., after a full day of work. When he came home, Russell would often turn off the television and then find Dantzel and give her a hug and a kiss. It was not unusual for Russell to say to his daughters, "Do you know how much I love your mother?"[21] On other occasions, he would say to his children, "Look how beautiful your mother looks tonight."[22] Once Dantzel was greeted affectionately, Russell would then locate each of his children and likewise greet them with verbal and physical affection.

President Nelson has always had the ability to focus on the task at hand, devoting his heart and soul to whatever needs to be done. His daughter Sylvia explained, "When he's at work, he's 100 percent at work. When he's home, he's 100 percent at home. When he's doing his Church duty, he's 100 percent Church duty. I think maybe that's how he balances things."[23] When Russell was at work, he was able to devote all of his time and energy to his patients. However, when he was home, he was able to change gears and focus solely on his family. Perhaps Russell's children were not aware of the many balls he juggled—including being a surgeon and stake president. What the Nelson children did know was that their

father loved them and made time for them. The Nelsons' daughter Emily captured something that perhaps each of their children could say: "I never felt Dad was too busy for me. . . . We spent lots of time together."[24] Despite his demanding and often unpredictable schedule, the Nelson children did not sense that their father was too busy for them or that they were neglected because of his heavy Church responsibilities.

FAMILY ACTIVITIES

As often as he could, Russell tried to give Dantzel some relief by taking their children out of the home and engaging them in some constructive play activities. On Saturdays, after the chores were done, he would often take his children to local swimming pools, ice-skating rinks, parks, the Deseret Gym, the tennis club, or even to a local park.[25]

When he was home, Russell was not one to relax and unwind in front of the television set after a long and stressful day as a surgeon. He was a dedicated husband and father, helping Dantzel with the dinner and dishes and assisting their children with homework and projects. Ever efficient, Russell even concocted

The Nelson family, Summer 1964, performing at the Bonneville Stake.

an ingenious way to bathe the children. Often he would put four of his daughters in the bathtub at the same time. "Russell would pour water and a dab of shampoo on each little girl's head and then have them massage each other's scalps until he gave the command, 'About face.' Then, amid giggles and great glee, the girls would turn around in the tub and begin to shampoo the hair of the sister who had just been working on them. The shampoo train was an elementary lesson on the Golden Rule."[26]

One of Russell's favorite hobbies was snow skiing. Throughout the lives of his children, and even grandchildren, President Nelson has believed that a *family that skis together stays together*. Spencer J. Condie observed, "Russell has never taken for granted the blessing of living close enough to the ski slopes that he can work a good forenoon and be on the lift at 1 p.m., ski until 4:30 p.m., and then return home to enjoy dinner with the family."[27] He has taught his children and grandchildren how to snow ski—sometimes five children at a time! Often, he would pull one or two of his children out of school and take them up to the resort for some afternoon skiing. This was a great stress reliever for Russell, and it provided a way for him to stay connected with his children. After he was called as an Apostle, Mondays became family ski day.

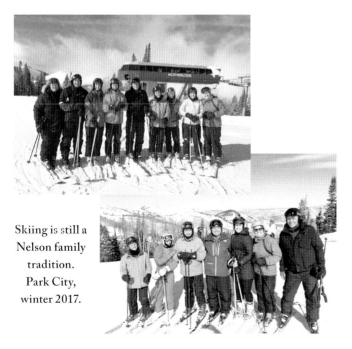

Skiing is still a Nelson family tradition. Park City, winter 2017.

RIGHTEOUS TRADITIONS

Although the Nelsons knew how to have fun, they also knew how to worship the Lord. Russell and Dantzel built their home on the foundation of the gospel of Jesus Christ. Righteous traditions became the reinforcing bars that held the foundation in place. Once, President Harold B. Lee asked Dantzel what it was like to be married to a man who was extremely busy with Church callings and professional responsibilities. Dantzel responded, "When he's home, he's home."[28] Russell understood the depth and significance of a principle that President Lee had taught: "The most important of the Lord's work you will ever do will be within the walls of your own homes."[29] Dantzel then added, "At home, he devotes his whole attention to us. . . . Rather than watching TV, he helps with the meals and the dishes, helps the children with their homework, and reads to them before they go to bed. And the two of us regularly enjoy time alone together."[30]

Besides being an involved father, Russell was a wonderful husband, always in tune to Dantzel's needs. He understood that to be an effective mother, Dantzel would need occasional breaks. Thursdays became Dantzel's days to do whatever she wanted to. On Thursday mornings, she would volunteer at the LDS Hospital. Dantzel also became a member of the Tabernacle Choir in 1967. Her choir rehearsals were on Thursday evenings. On those evenings, Russell "arranged his schedule . . . so he could be home with the children that night."[31] He was not sitting in a recliner watching television while the children were left to fend for themselves. He was actively involved in making dinner, cleaning the kitchen, helping the children with their homework and projects, and assisting them in getting prepared for the next day of school.

Every morning, after Russell's own individual religious practices, he and Dantzel would engage in consistent religious practices with their family. Daily scripture reading began at 6:30 a.m. Family prayer was at 6:45 a.m., at each meal, and at 10:00 p.m.[32] Russell had the ability to teach his children at their age level. His daughter Gloria remembered that while he and Dantzel were reading from the scriptures with their older children, Russell also read *Book of Mormon Stories* to

Attending Medical Conferences with His Children

From 1960 to 1978, Russell attended over 165 medical conferences or meetings. Russell took his children with him to those conferences thirty-six times (22 percent of his conferences), and Dantzel traveled with him thirty-five times (21 percent of his conferences). Between 1972 and 1978, Russell traveled thirty-two times in his calling as General Sunday School President of the Church. Russell took his children with him to Church events or conferences twelve times (38 percent of his conferences), and Dantzel accompanied him eleven times (34 percent of his conferences). There is no question that Russell M. Nelson enjoyed being with his family and wanted them to enjoy some of the experiences in travel that he was enjoying. Traveling became a way for Russell and his family to connect and stay bonded together.

the younger children—especially to young Russell.[33] The Nelsons also enjoyed having weekly family home evenings and attending church together. Music was also an important part of their lives. The beautiful sound of not only singing but also instruments such as the piano, violin, guitar, accordion, cello, trumpet, and flute filled the home.[34]

A righteous tradition that Russell began, with Dantzel's encouragement, was taking their children with him to medical conferences. As a busy surgeon, Russell was often gone 25–30 percent of the year attending meetings. To remedy his loneliness, one—or sometimes two—of his children would often accompany him. Having his family travel with him "kept him from getting lonesome for his loved ones, gave him a chance to listen to their problems and hopes, and provided him and family members with an opportunity to talk to each other and share ideas and experiences. The selection of which child got to go on which trip was not based on rotation but rather on which child most needed a trip with daddy."[35] President Nelson recalled, "Those trips gave me a chance to listen to their problems and their ambitions . . . and for us simply to talk to one another and share ideas and experiences with each other."[36]

Gloria remembers attending one medical conference with her father and her sister Brenda. On another occasion, Russell took Gloria with him on a trip to see where the Washington D.C. Temple was being built. Since Gloria was born in Washington, DC, that trip was a special experience for her. She also remembered a conference she attended with her father in Little Rock, Arkansas. On another trip to Denver, Gloria was excited that she and her father were able to tour the Air Force Academy together.[37] Sylvia remembered

attending a medical conference in New York City. She vividly recalled eating lasagna, one of her father's favorite meals, with him at a nice Italian restaurant and attending the opera, another one of President Nelson's favorite things to do.[38]

Once, Russell was boarding an airplane with one of his daughters when he noticed that Elder Mark E. Petersen of the Quorum of the Twelve Apostles was on the flight. Russell felt uncomfortable, so he "explained to Elder Petersen that his daughter was accompanying him to a professional meeting, adding apologetically that taking her along might be a bit extravagant. Elder Petersen responded, 'Extravagant? No Brother Nelson, it's a wise investment.'"[39]

Such investments were the kinds Russell and Dantzel most often pursued. They did not spend their money on extravagant cars or other material possessions, but they did invest their resources in spending time with their children. The payoff from their investment of time with their family continues to pay dividends today. Russell learned the significance of Elder Petersen's comment as his children grew older. He said:

I've lived to see a number of my professional colleagues regret the misdeeds of their youngsters. They've spent infinitely more money than I ever did on transportation and hotels as they have been required to pay fines, psychiatrist's fees, and other heavy penalties for the disobedience of their children to the laws of God and man. I've never had that experience. Aside from their receiving occasional parking tickets, there has never been a moment when one of our children ever gave me grief or cause for concern. Of course, I don't really credit this great blessing entirely to the occasional trips the children have taken with their dad. I'm sure the greatest share of the credit goes to their mother and to the fact that we have always reared our children in the knowledge of the Lord and his doctrines. Nonetheless, the privilege of having one or more of the family with me on my trips has been the spoonful of sugar that's helped the medicine go down—the medicine of continuing medical education that took me away from my family and loved ones while in the pursuit of excellence, that they, as well as I, might be proud of the quality of work I was doing.[40]

Despite his advancing age and global Church responsibilities, President Nelson continues to send handwritten birthday, Christmas, and anniversary cards to each member of his family—whether they be a child, grandchild, or great-grandchild.[41] When his grandchildren and great-grandchildren are born, he visits them in the hospital. He also attends as many of his grandchildren's and great-grandchildren's[42] blessings, baptisms, and temple weddings as he can. Every month, the Nelson family gathers and celebrates all of the birthdays and anniversaries of their family members for that particular month. It is not unusual to have over 150 family members in attendance.[43] President Nelson makes sure that he visits and connects with everyone present during these gatherings. He is always trying to expand his circle of love.[44]

Russell once wrote, "Dantzel and I desire each one in our family to join with us in the eternal perpetuation of our family unit. If just one is missing, our joy will be incomplete."[45] President Nelson also taught, "Our family is the focus of our greatest work and joy in this life; so it will be throughout all eternity."[46] Nothing was more important on this earth for Russell and Dantzel than their family, and today nothing is more important for Russell and Wendy than their growing family. This has been demonstrated repeatedly not only by what Russell has said but also by what he has done.

EARLY CHURCH SERVICE

Throughout his adult life, Russell has always been willing to serve in the Church and build the kingdom of God. In fact, Church service has given him much joy and satisfaction, and in some ways it became an outlet from the busy demands of medicine. We do not know much about Russell's Church callings from 1941, when he enrolled at the University of Utah, until 1947, when he and Dantzel moved to Minneapolis. What we do know is that serving a mission was not an option for him because of World War II and his enrollment in medical school.[47]

"There was never a time that Russell complained or said one derogatory remark about a leader in the Church. . . . There was never a time when a Church calling was refused or when Russell asked to be released from a Church calling."[48] Both Russell and Dantzel served in Church callings in Minneapolis; Washington, DC; Boston; and eventually Salt Lake City.

Early Church Callings

- Minneapolis years (1947–1951, 1954–1955)—Minneapolis Branch Sunday School superintendency[2]

- Washington, DC, years (1951–1953)—second counselor in the bishopric of the Washington Ward; ordained a high priest at the age of twenty-seven on December 27, 1951[3]

- Boston years (1953–1954)—secretary of the adult Aaronic Priesthood[4]; Dantzel was in the Relief Society presidency of the Cambridge Branch[5]

- Salt Lake City years (1955–1984)—priests quorum advisor in the Garden Park Ward,[6] superintendency of the Bonneville Stake YMMIA,[7] second counselor in the bishopric of the Garden Park Ward,[8] alternate high councilor in the Bonneville Stake,[9] stake president in the Bonneville Stake,[10] general Sunday School superintendent,[11] regional representative[12]

IN THE ARMY

In 1950, a new military conflict erupted halfway around the world on the Korean peninsula as North Korea invaded South Korea in an unprovoked attack. In consequence of these developments, Russell was assigned to leave the University of Minnesota and render service at the famed Walter Reed Army Medical Center in Washington, DC.

A year later, in June 1951, Russell was sent to Korea as part of a four-member surgical team of physicians that the Army deployed to visit all the MASH (Mobile Army Surgical Hospital) units in South Korea. Their purpose was to assess the care of the injured and the ill and to make recommendations for improved care where appropriate. At this time, Dantzel was in the last weeks of her second pregnancy, and since the Nelsons were new to the area and did not have many friends, they relocated to Utah to be with family while he was away.[49]

Russell's time in Korea was not without danger. On one occasion, he was fired upon while walking through the streets near a village. He and one of his traveling companions, Dr. Fiorindo A. Simeone, a devout Catholic, found prayer to be important to see them through their assignment. They prayed together for a successful mission and that their lives

would be spared. In the end, both returned home safely. In fact, several professional dividends came from his time in the war zone with the soldiers. One example is that Russell was able to document in the field the negative impact of smoking on the human circulatory system. These observations were distinct from the more overt harm smokers encountered in their lungs.

By the time he returned home from Korea, Russell weighed only about 160 pounds. Following his tours of the Korean peninsula, he returned to DC and resumed his service at Walter Reed. In 2014, he was awarded a medal "of thanks and honor" for his service in the military during the Korean Conflict.[50]

BUILDING THE KINGDOM IN SALT LAKE CITY

Once the Nelsons moved to Salt Lake City, Russell served in the priests quorum, the stake Young Men's Mutual Improvement Association (YMMIA), and eventually in the high council. Historian and General Authority Francis Gibbons observed that Russell M. Nelson "radiated a calmness and a sense of great confidence." He went on to say, "He was also one of the most naturally eloquent speakers I have ever known. When he spoke from the pulpit, he had the power to move the hearts of the people. He also was a superb delegator and had a gift for recognizing the innate talents of his fellow laborers of the Kingdom."[51]

PRESIDENT OF THE BONNEVILLE STAKE

On Wednesday, December 2, 1964, a statement made by his fellow high councilor Joseph G. Jeppson shocked Russell. Brother Jeppson said, "It has been revealed to me that you will be our new stake president." This upset Russell—he had great respect for Brother Jeppson and was "surprised at this impropriety on his part."[52] On Thursday, December 3, Russell had a similar impression—"not clearly that he would be the

July 1, 1951, Chung Ju, Korea.
Russell would get off base and mingle with locals.

stake president, but that he would somehow be involved in the reorganization."[53]

On Saturday, December 5, 1964, the Bonneville Stake presidency was reorganized. After years of service, President Frank B. Bowers was to be released, and a new stake president would be called. Two visiting Apostles, Elder Spencer W. Kimball and Elder LeGrand Richards, would interview brethren throughout the day and then prayerfully select a new stake president. The call was extended to forty-year-old Russell M. Nelson. President Nelson called Albert E. Bowen and Joseph B. Wirthlin to be his counselors, with Francis M. Gibbons as the stake executive secretary. Three of these four men later became General Authorities in The Church of Jesus Christ of Latter-day Saints.

Elder Spencer W. Kimball told President Nelson, "We feel that the Lord wants you to preside over this stake. During our many interviews, whenever your name has come up the response has been rather routine: 'Oh, he wouldn't be very good,' or 'He doesn't have time,' or both. Nonetheless, we feel that the Lord wants you. Now if you feel that you are too busy and shouldn't accept the call, then that's your privilege.'"[54] President Nelson responded to President Kimball: "I simply answered that that decision was made August 31, 1945, when Sister Nelson and I were married in the temple. We made a commitment then to 'seek . . . first the kingdom of God and his righteousness,' feeling confident that everything else would be added unto us, as the Lord promised. (See Matt. 6:33.)"[55]

Paying a Full Tithing

There is an interesting note to President Nelson's call as the stake president. During the interview with Elders Spencer W. Kimball and LeGrand Richards, "Elder Kimball showed him a figure written on a piece of paper and asked him if that was all the tithing he had paid in the previous year. Glancing at the paper, Brother Nelson said, 'Yes, it's an honest tithing.'

"'Well, I thought you were a little more prosperous than this figure might indicate,' said Elder Kimball.

"'I don't know how much I paid,' he said. 'All I can say is, it's a full tithing.'"[13]

Nevertheless, when President Nelson went home, he looked up his tithing records. During that year, the Nelsons had lived in the Garden Park Ward for eleven months and then moved to the Yale Ward. What Elder Kimball was looking at was the Nelsons' one month of tithing in the Yale Ward. "Elder Kimball did not have record of the tithing he had paid during the previous eleven months of the year!"[14] Ultimately, President Nelson's incomplete tithing records did not stop the Lord from intervening and inspiring His servants to call the young doctor.

In late 1965, just about one year after his call to be stake president, Russell was settling into his duties and adjusting to his new life and schedule. In November, he was presented with an incredible offer to accept a position as professor of surgery and chair of the Division of Thoracic and Cardiovascular Surgery at the University of Chicago. The offer appeared too good to be true: a generous salary and an arrangement to pay fully for the college education of all of his children—at any

A Doctor and Stake President?

Several weeks after Russell had been called as the stake president of the Bonneville Stake, a special meeting for stake presidents was held on Wednesday, January 13, 1965, in the Salt Lake Valley. Elder Spencer W. Kimball attended, and when he saw President Nelson, he embraced him and said, "Brother Nelson, are you still the president of the Bonneville Stake?" President Nelson responded, "Oh yes." Elder Kimball laughed and said, "After you were called to be stake president, I had all sorts of people tell me they thought you wouldn't last more than two weeks. It delights me to see that you are still serving."[15] Although Elder Kimball's comments were humorous, there was also some truth to his teasing. During this time in the Church, very few doctors held significant Church callings. The assumption was that doctors were simply too busy to serve in the Church and build the kingdom. President James E. Faust explained, "Russell Nelson changed all of that in his service as stake president. . . . We now have many fine doctors serving in the kingdom. I give Russell M. Nelson the credit for changing the stereotype that doctors are too busy to serve in the Church."[16]

university of their choice. The offer, President Nelson wrote, "made resources available to me in the way of financial support, research laboratory, and staff support that would fill the dream of any academician."[56] The dean told Dr. Nelson, "One of the reasons we want you is that we know you are a good Mormon. We want you on our faculty. We need you here to bring the influence to this University that a Mormon could bring."[57] President Dallin H. Oaks explained his role in persuading the Nelsons to move to Chicago:

> As part of his aggressive recruitment of this remarkable doctor, the dean telephoned for my help to persuade the Nelsons to move to Chicago. I was then a professor of law at the University of Chicago and knew the dean of medicine because we served together on the university's faculty senate. The dean asked me to have the Nelsons to dinner at our home. He urged me to tell them all about the Church in Chicago because he knew this was a critically important consideration for them.
>
> So it was that my late wife, June, and I met Dantzel and Russell Nelson and had them to dinner and a wonderful visit in our Chicago home on Sunday, November 21, 1965. We did our best to persuade them to move to Chicago. I later learned from his autobiography that they "were very much attracted to this offer and had even picked out a home in one of the suburbs of Chicago where [they] might raise [their] family."[58]

Dallin Oaks and his family were quite persuasive, and the Nelsons were thinking seriously about Chicago. President Nelson recalled, "To meet the Oaks family was one of the highlights of that trip to Chicago; it was a memorable experience to be with this talented and faithful family of such great ability."[59] Little did these men know that eighteen years later they would be called to serve as Apostles together.[60]

Upon returning home from Chicago, President Nelson announced to the Bonneville Stake high council that they had received an offer from the University of Chicago and would be moving. However, Joseph Anderson, a member of the high council and the secretary to the First Presidency of the Church, suggested that President Nelson might want to discuss his pending move with President David O. McKay. "The President of the Church can't be concerned about the occupational changes of stake presidents," Russell challenged. "Oh, yes he can," Brother Anderson responded. "So, at Brother Anderson's insistence, Dr. Nelson agreed to meet with the President of the Church."[61]

On December 14, 1965, Russell and Dantzel met with President David O. McKay on the tenth floor of his Hotel Utah apartment. Elder Spencer J. Condie described the details of what happened during the Nelsons' visit with a prophet:

> President McKay . . . invited Russell and Dantzel into his study, and there they reviewed the nature of the offer extended by the University of Chicago. After hearing their story, he closed his eyes, leaned his head back, and pondered the matter for a while. Then he asked, "And what would you want to do this for? To get fame? You are already famous; I know who you are!" He laughed as he said this and then continued. "How many children do you have?"
>
> "Nine daughters," the Nelsons replied.
>
> "Where is it you live in Salt Lake?" President McKay then asked.
>
> Russell told him they lived on Normandie Circle, where they had moved in the fall of 1963. Their home was just opposite the canyon where President McKay's son Llewelyn lived.
>
> Then, Russell recalled, "He laid his head back on his chair, closed his eyes, and communed with the Lord in supplicating an answer that would be a guide for us. Actually, he was nonresponsive to us for such a long time that I began to wonder if he was still alive. But then, with that keen, sharp intellect and piercing eye, he looked at me directly and said, 'Brother Nelson, if I were you I wouldn't be in a hurry to change neighborhoods. It doesn't feel good to me. No, Brother Nelson, your place is here in Salt Lake City. People will come from all over the

world to you because you are here. I don't think you should go to Chicago.'"

Russell recalled, "That was it. In a meeting lasting seventy-five minutes with President David O. McKay, the decision had been made." He called the officials in Chicago and informed them that he was declining their offer and remaining in Salt Lake City. Many of Russell's friends in academic surgery thought he had made a serious mistake, but his faith was secure. He and Dantzel had been privileged to receive a prophet's counsel, and they were going to abide by it.[62]

This experience is only one of the many that President Nelson has had in his lifetime to show his allegiance to modern prophets, seers, and revelators. The Nelsons remained in Salt Lake City, where President Nelson served faithfully as the president of the Bonneville Stake and as the chair of the division of thoracic surgery at the LDS hospital.[63] When he was set apart as a stake president, Elder Kimball blessed him that "the quality of his work as a surgeon would increase so that he would have the time to serve as stake president without jeopardizing his patients."[64] And so it was. President Nelson prospered as a surgeon and magnified his calling.

President Nelson reflected, "The call to become stake president opened up to me a wonderful opportunity to serve the Lord under the close supervision of his chosen servants in the Quorum of the Twelve."[65] During his years as the president of the Bonneville Stake, President Nelson was able to rub shoulders with, receive counsel from, and gain the trust of prophets, seers, and revelators. About three years into President Nelson's ministry as stake president, Elder Francis Gibbons recorded this in his journal on Sunday, January 14, 1968: "Should this newly emerging spirituality become his dominant characteristic, it would not be unreasonable to predict that one day Russell M. Nelson will sit in the leading councils of the Church."[66] It did not take long for Elder Gibbons's prophecy to come to fruition.

GENERAL SUNDAY SCHOOL SUPERINTENDENT

On Friday, June 4, 1971, President N. Eldon Tanner of the First Presidency contacted President Nelson. President Tanner wanted to know if President Nelson could meet with him on Monday, June 7. President Nelson explained that he would be in Hawaii on Monday for medical meetings. President Tanner then asked, "Do you think you could come right now?" During their meeting, President Tanner and President Harold B. Lee explained that David Lawrence McKay, who had been serving as the general Sunday School superintendent for the past five years, had just accepted a calling to serve as a mission president.

The Brethren then called President Nelson to serve as the head of the Sunday School organization of the Church, providing that it would not take him away from his work as a heart surgeon.[67] President Nelson recalled, "But without hesitation I replied that my work didn't matter, that if it were necessary for me to sell furniture or take up some other occupation in order to be obedient to the call they were impressed to give, that I would do."[68] Although President Nelson was willing to "straightway [leave his] nets" (Matthew 4:20) and follow the Brethren, they were insistent that the calling could only be issued if he could continue his practice as a surgeon. President Nelson called as his counselors Joseph B. Wirthlin, also from the Bonneville Stake presidency, and Richard R. Warner. The First Presidency set these men apart on Friday, July 2, 1971. Then, over a week later, on Sunday, July 11, 1971, President Nelson was released from his calling as the president of the Bonneville Stake.[69]

During his service as the Church's General Sunday School Superintendent, President Nelson was able to travel with Church leaders to area conferences throughout the world. In 1972, President Nelson was instrumental in the transition of the name from the General Sunday School Superintendency to the General Sunday School Presidency. This would allow the Sunday School presidency to line up with the other organizations with presidents and counselors. Under President Nelson's leadership, the first teacher-training manual was developed: *Teaching: No Greater Call.*[70]

Perhaps more than anything else, President Nelson's calling in the Sunday School allowed him to travel with the Brethren, see them up close and personal, and tend to their needs as a physician.

RENOWNED INTERNATIONAL HEART SURGEON

When contemplating a career, Russell was asked why he wanted to be a medical doctor, given the sacrifice and commitment it required. He explained, "I liked people. I wanted to serve them. I reasoned that the finest career that would be available to a human being would be that of mother. Inasmuch as that was out of the question for me, I reasoned that the second occupation would be medicine. There I could help people every day and teach them."[71] Russell realized early in his life that his interests were in serving people, for a "genuine desire was welling within [him] to do something of worth for them."[72] In addition, Russell recognized that his favorite subjects in school were those with exactness and precision, such as chemistry, mathematics, biology, and science, "so [he] set [his] sights on going into medicine."[73]

Russell enrolled at the University of Utah in the fall of 1941. At the University of Utah, he focused on his undergraduate requirements and at the same time began classes in pre-medicine. He earned a bachelor of arts in 1945, and two years later, at the age of twenty-two, he received his medical degree. Elder Gregory A. Schwitzer, who was also a medical doctor, said of President Nelson, "I've talked with people who were medical school classmates of his, and they always knew he would be number one in the class. When you go to medical school, there are just certain physicians who are not just confident or bright, they are brilliant, they shine. [Russell Nelson] would fit that category."[74] Russell's hard work, discipline, and keen intellect resulted in him completing a four-year MD program in three years and graduating at the top of his class. His academic achievements made him a member of honorary societies, such as Phi Beta Kappa and Alpha Omega Alpha.

A Heartbreaking Loss and Reconciliation

"Fifty-eight years ago [in 1955] I was asked to operate upon a little girl, gravely ill from congenital heart disease. Her older brother had previously died of a similar condition. Her parents pleaded for help. I was not optimistic about the outcome but vowed to do all in my power to save her life. Despite my best efforts, the child died. Later, the same parents brought another daughter to me, then just 16 months old, also born with a malformed heart. Again, at their request, I performed an operation. This child also died. This third heartbreaking loss in one family literally undid me. I went home grief stricken. I threw myself upon our living room floor and cried all night long. Dantzel stayed by my side, listening as I repeatedly declared that I would never perform another heart operation. Then, around 5:00 in the morning, Dantzel looked at me and lovingly asked, 'Are you finished crying? Then get dressed. Go back to the lab. Go to work! You need to learn more. If you quit now, others will have to painfully learn what you already know.' Oh, how I needed my wife's vision, grit, and love! I went back to work and learned more. If it weren't for Dantzel's inspired prodding, I would not have pursued open-heart surgery and would not have been prepared to do the operation in 1972 that saved the life of President Spencer W. Kimball."[17]

Almost six decades later, he recounted a moving spiritual experience that helped him reconnect with some of those girls' loved ones, who he recalled had previously "harbored lingering resentment toward [him] and the Church." In that experience, President Nelson said in April 2016, "I was awakened by those two little girls from the other side of the veil. Though I did not see or hear them with my physical senses, I felt their presence. Spiritually, I heard their pleadings. Their message was brief and clear: 'Brother Nelson, we are not sealed to anyone! Can you help us?' Soon thereafter, I learned that their mother had passed away, but their father and younger brother were still alive." President Nelson said in his retelling that he sought out the father and brother and talked about the spiritual experience, expressing to them that he would be "honored to perform sealing ordinances" for the family in an LDS temple, which later happened. President Nelson called the event "a sublime experience" and said that "many hearts were healed that day!"[18]

After completing his University of Utah degrees, Russell was admitted into the University of Minnesota for surgical training and postgraduate doctoral studies. At that time, the University of Minnesota was one of the top medical schools in the nation. Russell completed residency programs at the Walter Reed Army Hospital in Washington, DC; at the Massachusetts General Hospital in Boston; and at the University of Minnesota, where he was awarded a PhD in 1954.

While at the University of Minnesota, Russell worked on the research team responsible for developing the first heart-lung machine. Their discovery led to the first-ever human open-heart surgery using a cardiopulmonary bypass, which was performed in March 1951. This procedure "marked the important transition point in surgical history between gaining access to the open, beating heart and knowing what to do once that access had been achieved," President Nelson wrote in his autobiography. "A whole new world of the possibility of surgical repair of the heart had been opened up."[75]

Russell's numerous professional options to begin his practice as a heart surgeon were supplanted by his love of family and his Church. These were also important priorities to Dantzel. Thus, in 1955, the Nelsons returned to Salt Lake City, wanting to be of greater service to The Church of Jesus Christ of Latter-day Saints and be around family to raise their children. For the next twenty-nine years, Russell set out to accomplish his singular goal to serve others with all his heart, might, mind, and strength. Uniquely trained as a medical researcher and a heart surgeon, he accepted a faculty position at the University of Utah School of Medicine. There he built his own heart-lung bypass machine, and in 1955 he used it to support the first open-heart surgery in the state of Utah. The recipient was a thirty-nine-year-old woman from Price, Utah. With that pioneer surgery, Utah became the third state in the country where open-heart surgery had been successfully performed.[76] At the university, his professional work included the positions of research professor of surgery and director of the thoracic surgery

residency at the University of Utah, as well as chairman of the Division of Thoracic Surgery at LDS Hospital in Salt Lake City.

Reliance on God

Another contributing factor to Russell's success as a researcher and surgeon was his belief in and reliance upon God. In 1960, President Nelson treated what is called a tricuspid valve regurgitation, which at the time was a highly advanced surgical undertaking, and after successfully performing the surgery, he credited this achievement to a divine answer to his prayers. "He attributes much to inspiration," said Dr. Donald Doty, a retired heart surgeon who practiced with Russell at LDS Hospital in 1983 and 1984. One of Russell's most notable surgeries was performed on President Spencer W. Kimball, who was then a counselor in the First Presidency. A blessing given to him prior to the surgery by President Harold B. Lee indicated that Russell "had been raised up by the Lord to perform this operation."[19] It was a very risky operation. While he was operating on President Kimball, it was revealed to Russell that President Kimball would indeed survive the operation and, perhaps more important, that he would become the President of The Church of Jesus Christ of Latter-day Saints.[20]

Russell and Dantzel Nelson, Garden Park Ward at Ricky and Katie Hutchison Irion's wedding reception, August 24, 2002.

Awards and Accolades

Over the years, a host of awards and honors have come to Russell, including the Distinguished Alumni Award from the University of Utah, the Heart of Gold Award from the American Heart Association, a citation for International Service from the American Heart Association, and the Golden Plate Award from the American Academy of Achievement. To commemorate his diverse and lasting work, the American College of Cardiology and the University of Utah School of Medicine announced the establishment of the Russell M. Nelson MD, PhD Visiting Professorship in Cardiothoracic Surgery. This was an unprecedented honor for his service of fifteen years in training and schooling and twenty-nine years as a renowned international medical researcher and heart surgeon—not to mention his post-medical activities when serving in the Quorum of the Twelve.

Some of President Nelson's professional accolades include:

- President of the Thoracic Surgical Directors Association
- President of the Society for Vascular Surgery
- President of the Utah State Medical Association
- Director of the American Board of Thoracic Surgery
- Chairman of the Council on Cardiovascular Surgery for the American Heart Association
- Chairman of the Division of Thoracic Surgery at the LDS Hospital
- Vice-chairman of the board of governors at the LDS Hospital
- "Citation for International Service," American Heart Association
- "Heart of Gold Award," American Heart Association
- "Golden Plate Award," American Academy of Achievement
- "Distinguished Alumni Award," University of Utah
- "Surgical Alumnus of the Year Award," University of Minnesota Medical School
- "Governor's Medal of Science: Lifetime Achievement Award," Utah Technology Innovation Summit
- In June 2018, the University of Utah endowed a chair in cardiothoracic surgery named after Nelson and his first wife, Dantzel.

Russell lectured at various professional organizations and conferences throughout the United States, which resulted in many of his publications in medical textbooks and medical journals. It was not long before he was recognized as a renowned medical pioneer in the field of heart surgery. "He was a really, really good surgeon and impacted a lot of people's lives and families," said Dr. Craig Selzman, chief of the Division of Cardiothoracic Surgery at the University of Utah and a professor of surgery. "(He's) right up there along with the biggest legends in cardiothoracic surgery, when you think of legends."[77] On a national level, Russell has served as president of the Society for Vascular Surgery, director of the American Board of Thoracic Surgery, chairman of the Council on Cardiovascular Surgery for the American Heart Association, and president of the Utah State Medical Association. Internationally, Russell traveled abroad as a medical doctor and spoke at conferences throughout the world, including Russia, India, Africa, Latin America, and the Republic of China.

When the call came to serve as an Apostle of the Lord Jesus Christ, there was not a question as to Russell's loyalty to The Church of Jesus Christ of Latter-day Saints. Russell was in the prime of his career. In fact, in 1983—the year before he was called—"he performed 360 open heart operations and his mortality rate was about 1 percent."[78] Most likely, Russell had over twenty more years ahead of him as a heart surgeon. He had perfected his skills and developed his surgery team to an unparalleled level of expertise. Speaking to the Church the day he was sustained as an Apostle, he said, "My sweetheart, Dantzel, and I first made those covenants in the temple of the Lord over thirty-eight years ago, to consecrate our lives to the service of the Lord. Today, I reaffirm that promise, to give all I have to the building of the kingdom of God on the earth."[79] A new chapter of service in the lives of Russell and Dantzel had begun.

SEVENTEENTH PRESIDENT OF THE CHURCH

On Sunday, January 14, 2018, two days after President Monson's funeral, Russell M. Nelson was set apart as the seventeenth President of the Church. Two days later, President Nelson was introduced to the general Church membership and the media in a press conference. President Nelson announced his new counselors in the First Presidency: President Dallin H. Oaks and President Henry B. Eyring. President Nelson stated that the new First Presidency would begin its ministry "with the end in mind." That "end" would be the salvation of individuals and the sealing of families in the house of the Lord. "For this reason, we're speaking to you today from a temple [annex of the Salt Lake Temple]."[80] At the time of the announcement, President Nelson was the oldest of the past sixteen Presidents of the Church when they were called—ninety-three years old. He had served under, or had personally known, ten of the former Presidents of the Church.[81]

It is evident that President Nelson's lifetime experiences and achievements have uniquely prepared him to lead the Church. He is an accomplished speaker and writer. In fact, he speaks six different languages, and he learned all of them, other than English, after the age of sixty.[82] In particular, his love of the holy temple and scriptures is a hallmark of his life's endeavors. President Nelson is unflappable under pressure and brings a steady hand and unfailing love to his ministry.[83] Over the course of his thirty-four years as

an Apostle, he has visited 133 different nations as an ambassador for the Church. During the course of his ministry, he has exemplified diplomacy in opening doors for the Church in China, the Middle East, the Pacific, Eastern Europe, and other locations where it has been difficult for the Church to gain a foothold.

Recently in general conference, President Nelson related, "One of the things the Spirit has repeatedly impressed upon my mind since my new calling as President of the Church is how willing the Lord is to reveal His mind and will. The privilege of receiving revelation is one of the greatest gifts of God to His children. Through manifestations of the Holy Ghost, the Lord will assist us in all our righteous pursuits."[84] It is notable that President Nelson's first talk in general conference as prophet was entitled "Revelation for the Church, Revelation for Our Lives."[85] President Nelson called receiving revelation a *privilege* and one of God's greatest gifts to His children.[86] Although previous Church Presidents have emphasized that the Lord is leading the Church through revelation, President Nelson has been quite candid and specific on how revelation comes to him. "When the messages come during the dark of night, Russell M. Nelson reaches for his lighted pen and takes dictation from the Lord. 'OK dear, it's happening,' the president of The Church of Jesus Christ of Latter-day Saints tells his wife, Wendy Nelson. 'I just remain quiet and soon he's sitting up at the side of the bed, writing.'"[87]

On Sunday, March 10, 2019, President Russell M. Nelson dedicated the Rome

Dantzel Nelson passed away unexpectedly on February 12, 2005, at age 78.

Russell remarried in 2006 and is pictured here with his second wife, Wendy L. Watson.

Temple—the 162nd operating temple in the Church. Although there were many unique occurrences with the dedication of this temple, perhaps the most significant was that the entire First Presidency and Quorum of the Twelve Apostles attended the dedication. This event marks the first time in the history of the Church that the First Presidency and the Quorum of the Twelve Apostles have stood together on foreign soil. Some may have wondered why President Nelson directed all fifteen prophets, seers, and revelators to travel to the temple dedication. President Nelson explained the reason clearly when he said, "I was just following the instructions I've received. . . . It was very clear to me that I was to invite all my colleagues, and so I was just following my instructions. . . . The brethren thank me for the privilege of coming, but I thank the Lord for his letting all of us come."[88] This attitude and commitment certainly marks President Russell M. Nelson's ministry—he is going to do exactly what the Lord instructs him to do. He will follow the Spirit of the Lord, wherever it leads him. Perhaps this explains why there has been such an outpouring of spiritual directives given to President Nelson during his short term as the President of the Church.

As members of The Church of Jesus Christ of Latter-day Saints, we are witnesses to many of the revelations President Nelson has received as our prophet, seer, and revelator. President Nelson began his ministry as the President of the Church on January 14, 2017. There have been many changes in the Church since then:

- Priesthood quorums have been restructured
- Ministering has replaced home and visiting teaching
- The Church will end its relationship with the Boy Scouts
- There have been updates to the Church hymnbook and *Children's Songbook*
- New guidelines for bishop youth interviews have been established
- The name of the Church has been reemphasized
- Mission calls are now posted online
- The Mormon Tabernacle Choir is now The Tabernacle Choir at Temple Square
- The home-centered and Church-supported programs have been inaugurated, along with a two-hour Church block
- President Nelson has announced nineteen new temples
- Major Church pageants will be discontinued
- There have been major changes to Primary progression, Young Men priesthood ordination, and youth temple recommends
- Sister missionaries can now wear dress pants
- Temple ceremonies have been adjusted [89]

As President Nelson leads the Church into the future, Latter-day Saints can take great comfort in knowing that he will guide them in accordance with heaven's will. "I declare my devotion to God our Eternal Father and to His Son, Jesus Christ," he said. "I know Them, love Them, and pledge to serve Them—and you—with every remaining breath of my life."[90] If the first fourteen months is an indication of where President Nelson will lead the Church in the coming decade, then it can be expected to include more revelation that will lead to greater, inspired change.

TEACHINGS FROM PRESIDENT
RUSSELL M. NELSON

ADVERSITY AND DEATH

Throughout his career, President Nelson medically ministered to those who were going through adversity and challenges, not only in traditional hospital settings where he performed surgeries but also in the field and in such settings as the battlefront. He became intimately acquainted with trials, grief, and suffering of both of his patients as well as with close family and dear friends. He is sensitive and caring and instructs well on the subject of having patience in and enduring adversity. He has said, "The Lord has often chosen to instruct His people in their times of trial. Scriptures show that some of His lasting lessons have been taught with examples terrible as war, commonplace as childbearing, or obvious as hazards of deep water. His teachings are frequently based on common understanding, but with uncommon results. Indeed, one might say that to teach His people, the Lord employs the unlikely."[91] He acknowledges the pain but speaks of grief in hopeful ways: "You who may be momentarily disheartened, remember, life is not meant to be easy. Trials must be borne and grief endured along the way. As you remember that 'with God nothing shall be impossible' (Luke 1:37), know that He is your Father. You are a son or daughter created in His image, entitled through your worthiness to receive revelation to help with your righteous endeavors."[92] President Nelson's perspective has provided comfort for himself and his family during times of loss and grief. He stated, "Our limited perspective would be enlarged if we could witness the reunion on the other side of the veil, when doors of death open to those returning home. Such was the vision of the psalmist who wrote, 'Precious in the sight of the Lord is the death of his saints' (Psalms 116:15)."[93]

After experiencing his loved ones passing away, President Nelson testified: "I don't fear death. In fact, a scripture describes a Saint's death as 'precious in the sight of the Lord' (Psalms 116:15). It will be precious to me, too, as I am reunited with our parents and our precious daughter, Emily, who died some five years ago. Her passing left her young and righteous husband with five children. I will eagerly meet my ancestors and preceding prophets and apostles. And one day Sister Nelson and I will dwell together in the presence of our family and the Lord forevermore."[94]

AGENCY

President Nelson exemplifies the careful use of agency as he learned in his youth how to follow the Savior and educate himself about the doctrines of his Church. By the age of fifteen, he felt inclined to pursue a career in the field of medicine. He saw the enabling power of the gospel in his life. He moved into adult life and marriage with a certainty that his talents and gifts were to be used in furthering the Lord's purposes. He became an articulate and consistent messenger of the power of righteously exercising agency. He has taught:

> Even though peaceful conditions seem to prevail here, we are still at war. That war is not between nations. It is a war between the forces of God and the forces of the adversary (see Revelation 12:7–9; Doctrine and Covenants 29:40–41). This conflict began before the world was created. It began with the war in heaven. On God's side was Jesus Christ, foreordained to be the Savior of the World (see 1 Nephi 10:4). The opposing forces were and are led by Satan. Our Heavenly Father's plan has allowed for that conflict to exist. Why? It is allowed so that

we could exercise our precious gift of agency and make our own choices between good and evil. This is the conflict in which we are all enlisted.[95]

On another occasion he provided the perspective that "God wants his children to return to Him. But the amazing thing is He allows them to *choose* that course; He doesn't force them. He sends His children to earth, causing a veil of forgetfulness to come upon them. They are here to gain a body, to be tested, and to make choices. The greatest of all choices they may make is to *choose* to return to their Father."[96]

COVENANTS

There are so many ways that President Nelson has distinguished himself as a doctrinal prophet, and he has used his ministry to emphasize countless doctrines and principles. One of the ways he has chosen to reach out to Church members at all stages of mortality is through teachings of covenants. He has taught, "We . . . increase the Savior's power in our lives when we make sacred covenants and keep those covenants with precision. Our covenants bind us to Him and give us godly power."[97] Covenant keeping has become something of a theme for his ministry as exemplified in the following quote: "The greatest compliment that can be earned here in this life is to be known as a covenant keeper. The rewards for a covenant keeper will be realized both here and hereafter."[98] On another occasion he reflected, "You are one of God's noble and great spirits, held in reserve to come to earth at this time (see Doctrine and Covenants 86:8–11). In your premortal life you were appointed to help prepare the world for the great gathering of souls that will precede the Lord's Second Coming. You are one of a covenant people. You are an heir to the promise that all the earth will be blessed by the seed of Abraham and that God's covenant with Abraham will be fulfilled through his lineage in these latter days (see 1 Nephi 15:18; 3 Nephi 20:25). As a member of the Church, you have made sacred covenants with the Lord. You have taken upon yourself the name of Christ. You have promised to always remember Him and to keep His commandments. In return, He has agreed to grant His Spirit to be with you."[99]

DECISIONS

President Nelson has often taught that the decisions we make direct us on the path of a righteous destiny. Reflecting on one such decision, he shared:

Years ago, while I served as a young intern in a large medical center, I attended a Christmas party. The host was the chief of surgery. I had made a major commitment to work for and be loyal to him and his world-famous institution, which had produced many of the great surgeons, scholars, and researchers of our generation. At the party, the chief's head resident offered alcoholic beverages to Sister Nelson and me. Of course, we politely declined.

Minutes later he returned with a more persuasive pitch: "Take a drink," he said, "or the chief will be offended." Again we declined. Our refusal infuriated the head resident. Red-faced and indignant, he said, "Nelson, you take this drink or I'll make life around here mighty miserable for you!"

I simply replied, "You do what you must, doctor, but I will do what I must."

I fulfilled my promise, and he fulfilled his.

He saw to it that I had no vacation that year. His responsibility to prepare the schedule of assignments and on-call duty bore the stamp of his vitriolic vengeance against me. But now, as I reflect on this matter some forty years later, I would not trade places with him today, or ever.

. . . Remember that decisions are best made before the time of testing, whether those resolutions concern forsaking drugs, alcohol, and other addicting substances, or pornography, which can become an addiction of the mind. Resist any temptations of lust disguised as love. Instead of vice, let virtue garnish your thoughts.[100]

EDUCATION

President Nelson saw education as the key to unlocking a bright future, and he has advocated for this with the young people of the Church. He taught, "Because of our sacred regard for each human intellect, we consider the obtaining of an education to be a religious responsibility. Yet opportunities and abilities differ. I believe that in the pursuit of education, individual desire is more influential than institution and personal faith more forceful than faculty."[101] Urging the young people of the Church further still, he taught, "Take full advantage of your opportunity for an education; it will be invaluable to you. I don't think it matters much whether you study to become a librarian, a lawyer, or a musician. Complete the course you have begun, and then God can use you to bless people with the fruits of your education."[102] The fact that President Nelson pursued a career with such a challenging path and progressed so successfully makes him a model to youth even today who have dreams and the desire to pursue similar paths while at the same time maintaining a deep and abiding love for the Lord.

FAITH

It is in the spiritual DNA of prophets to be consistent in exercising faith in the day-to-day journey through mortality. President Nelson said, "Faith in Jesus Christ propels us to do things we otherwise would not do. Faith that motivates us to action gives us more access to His power."[103] Of course, the family is the primary place to plant the seeds of faith and instruction. President Nelson stresses the primary duty of parents in this regard: "Start with your children. You parents bear the primary responsibility to strengthen their faith. Let them feel your faith, even when sore trials come upon you. Let your faith be focused on our loving Heavenly Father and His Beloved Son, the Lord Jesus Christ. Teach that faith with deep conviction. Teach each precious boy or girl that he or she is a child of God, created in His image, with a sacred purpose and potential. Each is born with challenges to overcome and faith to be developed."[104]

Of course, he connects faith to pivotal moments in mortality when difficulties may call on us to show forth an abundance of faith. He once challenged the Saints, "*How* you deal with life's trials is part of the development of your faith. Strength comes when you remember that you have a divine nature, an inheritance of infinite worth. The Lord has reminded you, your children, and your grandchildren that you are lawful heirs, that you have been reserved in heaven for your specific time and place to be born, to grow and become His standard bearers and covenant people. As you walk in the Lord's path of righteousness, you will be blessed to continue in His goodness and be a light and a savior unto His people. Your rewards come not only hereafter. Many blessings will be yours in this life, among your children and grandchildren. You faithful Saints do not have to fight life's battles alone. Think of that! The Lord declared, 'I will contend with him that contendeth with thee, and I will save thy children.' Later came this promise to His faithful people: 'I, the Lord, would fight their battles, and their children's battles, and their children's children . . . to the third and fourth generation.'"[105]

MARRIAGE AND FAMILY

As a father of ten and a husband and dedicated priesthood holder, Russell knows very well the priorities that help elevate eternal values. He taught, "Brethren and sisters, material possessions and honors of the world do not endure. But your union as wife, husband, and family can. The only duration of family life that satisfies the loftiest longings of the human soul is forever. No sacrifice is too great to have the blessings of an eternal marriage. To qualify, one needs only to deny oneself of ungodliness and honor the ordinances of the temple. By making and keeping sacred temple covenants, we evidence our love for God, for our companions, and our real regard for our posterity—even those yet unborn. Our family is the focus of our greatest work and joy in this life; so will it be throughout all eternity, when we can inherit thrones, kingdoms, principalities, . . . powers, dominions, . . . exaltation and glory (Doctrine and Covenants 132:19). These priceless blessings can be ours if we set our houses in order now and faithfully cling to the gospel."[106]

He has taught that "the home is the great laboratory of love. There the raw chemicals of selfishness and greed are melded in the crucible of cooperation to yield compassionate concern and love for one another."[107] Above all, he knows and has taught that the family is the ultimate place of security for the soul. He has asserted, "There is spiritual safety in the circle of the family—the basic unit of society. The family is a sacred institution. The gospel was restored to the earth and the Church exists to exalt the family. The earth was created that each premortal spirit child of God might have this mortal experience, gain a physical body, choose a companion, form a family, and have that family sealed eternally in a temple of the Lord. If it were not so, the whole earth would be utterly wasted."[108]

Speaking to the young adults of the Church just one week before the passing of his beloved Dantzel, he said, "As Sister Nelson and I look back, we can honestly say that our family and membership in the Church are most important to us. How thankful we are that we heeded the counsel of Church leaders to marry in the temple, to invite children into our family, and to serve the Lord! If we had placed our education ahead of our family, we would not be so blessed now. Education was a lengthy process for us. Earning two doctor's degrees took me a long time. Then we struggled through many more years of surgical specialization. I did not send a bill for surgical services until I had been out of medical school for more than 12 years! By then we had five children. But somehow we managed. . . . We have tasted of life's successes and sorrows. We have dealt with disappointment, disease, and death among our children. But death cannot divide families sealed in the temple. That period of separation is only temporary. Thanks to the Lord's great plan of happiness, we can all face the future with great faith and optimism."[109]

MARRIAGE

President Russell M. Nelson is a strong advocate of marriage and the sanctity of this holy institution. He and Dantzel were married for almost sixty years and had a wonderful marriage. After Dantzel's passing in February 2005, Russell married Wendy Watson in April 2006. President Nelson and Wendy also have a strong marriage. Wendy said in an interview, "I try to do everything I can to make sure my husband feels loved, adored, wanted, and needed. We call it L.A.W.N. in our family."[110]

"The full realization of the blessings of a temple marriage is almost beyond our mortal comprehension. Such a marriage will continue to grow in the celestial realm. There we can become perfected (see Moroni 10:32). . . . Celestial marriage is a pivotal part of preparation for eternal life. It requires one to be married to the right person, in the right place, by the right authority, and to obey that sacred covenant faithfully. Then one may be assured of exaltation in the celestial kingdom of God."[111]

On another occasion, President Nelson declared, "Marriage brings greater possibilities for happiness than does any other human relationship. Yet some married couples fall short of their full potential. They let their romance become rusty, take each other for granted, allow other interests or clouds of neglect to obscure the vision of what their marriage really could be. Marriages would be happier if nurtured more carefully."[112]

President Nelson also understands the place for marriage in society. He said, "Marriage is the foundry for social order, the fountain of virtue, and the foundation for eternal exaltation. Marriage has been divinely designated as an eternal and everlasting covenant (see Doctrine and Covenants 132:19). Marriage is sanctified when it is cherished and honored in holiness. That union is not merely between husband and wife; it embraces a partnership with God (see Matthew 19:6)."[113]

FOLLOW THE PROPHET

Of course, President Nelson never expected to be the Lord's mouthpiece on earth. Still, well before he was called as an Apostle he knew of the role of a prophet in providing direction for the sons and daughters of Heavenly Father. He yearned to know prophets' counsels and to follow in faith. He reflected about his own life: "I never ask myself, 'When does the prophet speak as a prophet and when does he not?' My interest has been, 'How can I be more like him?'"[114] Measuring prophets' words against the wisdom of men, he asserted, "Surely when measured by eternal standards, teachings of the prophets are more important and enduring than the latest findings of competent researchers, even if these findings were both discovered and taught by use of modern technology and teaching aids."[115]

SABBATH DAY

President Nelson has long been an advocate of dedication to the Sabbath. He knows that blessings come through demonstrating to the Lord an attitude toward the Sabbath as a "sign" to the Lord: "How do we *hallow* the Sabbath day? In my much younger years, I studied the work of others who had compiled lists of things to do and things *not* to do on the Sabbath. It wasn't until later that I learned from the scriptures that my conduct and my attitude on the Sabbath constituted a *sign* between me and my Heavenly Father. With that understanding, I no longer needed lists of dos and don'ts. When I had to make a decision whether or not an activity was appropriate for the Sabbath, I simply asked myself, 'What *sign* do I want to give to God?' That question made my choices about the Sabbath day crystal clear. We make the Sabbath a delight when we teach the gospel to our children. Our responsibility as parents is abundantly clear. The Lord said, 'Inasmuch as parents have children in Zion . . . that teach them not to understand the doctrine of repentance, faith in Christ the Son of the living God, and of baptism and the gift of the Holy Ghost by the laying on of the hands, when eight years old, the sin be upon the heads of the parents.' I almost wish I were a young father once again. Now parents have such wonderful resources available to help them make family time more meaningful, on the Sabbath and other days as well. They have LDS.org, Mormon.org, the Bible videos, the Mormon Channel, the Media Library, the *Friend*, the *New Era*, the *Ensign*, the *Liahona*, and more—much more. These resources are so very helpful to parents in discharging their sacred duty to teach their children. No other work transcends that of righteous, intentional parenting!"[116]

Mark D. Ogletree
Craig K. Manscill
Robert C. Freeman

NOTES

1. Russell M. Nelson, "Revelation for the Church, Revelation for Our Lives," *Ensign*, May 2018.
2. Spencer J. Condie, *Russell M. Nelson: Father, Surgeon, Apostle* (Salt Lake City: Deseret Book, 2003), 24.
3. Nelson, "Revelation for the Church."
4. Condie, 34.
5. Condie, 35.
6. Condie, 38–39.
7. Condie, 41.
8. Marvin K. Gardner, "Elder Russell M. Nelson: Applying Divine Laws," *Ensign*, June 1984, 9.
9. *Mormon Newsroom*, "Sister Dantzel White Passes Away," Feb. 13, 2005, https://www.mormonnewsroom.org/article/sister-dantzel-nelson-passes-away.
10. Russell M. Nelson, *From Heart to Heart*, (1979), 44.
11. *Church News*, April 2, 1984, 4.
12. Russell recorded that he and Dantzel first kissed on May 28, 1943—over one year after they first met (see *From Heart to Heart*, 45).
13. Nelson, *From Heart to Heart*, 44.
14. Lane Johnson, "Russell M. Nelson: A Study in Obedience," *Ensign*, Aug. 1982.
15. Russell proposed to Dantzel in the summer of 1944 in the pea patch of the White Family Homestead in Perry, Utah. Russell and Dantzel expressed their love for each other and their desire to marry when they could, but financially they would not be able to marry anytime soon. Russell didn't even have enough money for an engagement ring (see *From Heart to Heart*, 50–51).
16. Peggy Fletcher Stack, "Dantzel White Nelson honored by all ages," *Salt Lake Tribune*, Feb. 19, 2005, https://archive.sltrib.com/story.php?ref=/faith/ci_2577692.
17. Condie, 54.
18. Nelson, *From Heart to Heart*, 44.
19. Interview, Sylvia Webster, Feb. 26, 2019.
20. Spencer W. Kimball, foreword to *From Heart to Heart*, [1979], vii.
21. Interview, Gloria and Richard Irion, February 15, 2019.
22. Interview, Gloria and Richard Irion.
23. Sarah Jane Weaver, "Get to Know President Russell M. Nelson, a Renaissance Man," *Church News*, https://www.lds.org/church/news/get-to-know-president-russell-m-nelson-a-renaissance-man?lang=eng.
24. Marvin K. Gardner, "Elder Russell M. Nelson: Applying Divine Laws," *Ensign*, June 1984.
25. Interview, Gloria and Richard Irion.
26. Condie, 69; see also Interview, Gloria and Richard Irion.
27. Condie, 90.
28. Johnson, "A Study in Obedience."
29. Harold B. Lee, *Teachings of President Harold B. Lee* (Salt Lake

City: Bookcraft, 1996), 280.

30. Gardner, "Applying Divine Laws."
31. Gardner, "Applying Divine Laws."
32. Gardner, "Applying Divine Laws."
33. Interview, Gloria and Richard Irion.
34. Gardner, "Applying Divine Laws."
35. Condie, 98.
36. Gardner, "Applying Divine Laws."
37. Interview, Gloria and Richard Irion.
38. Interview, Sylvia Webster.
39. Condie, 98
40. Nelson, *From Heart to Heart*, 211.
41. Weaver, "Get to Know President Russell M. Nelson."
42. As of February 15, 2019, there were 126 great-grandchildren.
43. Interview, Gloria and Richard Irion.
44. Interview, Gloria and Richard Irion.
45. Nelson, *From Heart to Heart*, 300.
46. Russell M. Nelson, "Set in Order Thy House," *Ensign*, Nov. 2001.
47. Nelson, *From Heart to Heart*, 123.
48. Nelson, *From Heart to Heart*, 4.
49. Condie, 115.
50. *Church News*, December 3, 2014.
51. Gibbons, 24.
52. Condie, 143.
53. Condie, 143.
54. Oaks, "Guided, Prepared, Committed."
55. Nelson, *From Heart to Heart*, 114.
56. Nelson, *From Heart to Heart*, 149.
57. Nelson, *From Heart to Heart*, 149.
58. Oaks, "Guided, Prepared, Committed."
59. Nelson, *From Heart to Heart*, 149.
60. Condie, 148.
61. Sheri Dew, *Insights from a Prophet's Life: Russell M. Nelson* (Salt Lake City: Deseret Book, 2019), 90–91.
62. Condie, 149.
63. Gibbons, 13.
64. Lane Johnson, "A Study in Obedience," 22.
65. Nelson, *From Heart to Heart*, 161.
66. Gibbons, 73.
67. Johnson, "A Study in Obedience," 22.
68. Nelson, *From Heart to Heart*, 125.
69. Gibbons, 15.
70. Condie, 167.
71. Condie, 39–40.
72. Nelson, *From Heart to Heart*, 42.
73. Nelson, *From Heart to Heart*, 42.
74. As cited in Dew, 14.
75. Nelson, *From Heart to Heart*, 73.
76. On November 9, 1955, Dr. Nelson operated on Mrs. Vernaell Worthen to close an atrial septal defect. All went well. She recovered without complication, and the Deseret News featured her in an article twenty-five years later titled "Utahn's Life Gets Bonus from Heart Surgery: 25 Extra Years to Love, Learn, Live."
77. Ben Lockhart, "President Nelson was 'true pioneer' of heart surgery, colleagues say," *Deseret News*, 30 January 2018; https://www.deseretnews.com/article/900008831/president-nelson-was-true-pioneer-of-heart-surgery-colleagues-say.html.
78. Lockhart, "President Nelson was 'true pioneer' of heart surgery, colleagues say."
79. Russell M. Nelson, "Call to the Holy Apostleship," *Ensign*, May 1984.
80. Tad Walch, "President Russell M. Nelson introduced as 17th," *Deseret News*, Jan. 17, 2018.
81. Dallin H. Oaks, "President Russell M. Nelson: Guided, Prepared, Committed," *Ensign Special Edition*, May 2018, 1.
82. Interview, Sylvia Webster.
83. Oaks, "Guided, Prepared, Committed," 1.
84. Nelson, "Revelation for the Church."
85. *Ensign*, May 2018.
86. Irinna Danielson, "The Most Important Change of All," blog, Mar. 29, 2019.
87. Daniel Burke, "Why the 'Mormon' Church Changed Its Name. (It's about Revelation, Not Rebranding.)," CNN, March 24, 2019, https://www.cnn.com/2019/03/22/us/mormon-lds-name-change-revelation/index.html.
88. Tad Walch, "Why President Nelson Took All Latter-day Saint Apostles to Rome, and What They Said about It," *Deseret News*, Mar. 12, 2019, https://www.deseretnews.com/article/900060133/why-president-nelson-took-all-latter-day-saint-apostles-to-rome-and-what-they-said-about-it.html.
89. Emmy Gardiner, "Review the 15 Major Church Announcements Since President Nelson became Prophet," ChurchofJesusChrist.org, Jan. 15, 2019, https://www.lds.org/church/news/review-the-15-major-church-announcements-since-president-nelson-became-prophet.
90. Oaks, "Guided, Prepared, Committed," 4.
91. Russell M. Nelson, "With God Nothing Shall Be Impossible," *Ensign*, May 1988.
92. Nelson, "With God Nothing Shall Be Impossible."
93. Russell M. Nelson, "Doors of Death," *Ensign*, May 1992.
94. Russell M. Nelson, Brigham Young University 2000–2001 Speeches, 89.
95. Russell M. Nelson, *Teachings of Russell M. Nelson*, 13–14.
96. Nelson, *Teachings of Russell M. Nelson*, 48–49.
97. Russell M. Nelson, "Drawing the Power of Jesus Christ into Our Lives," *Ensign*, May 2017.
98. Russell M. Nelson, "Covenants," *Ensign*, Nov. 2011.
99. Russell M. Nelson, "Choices," *Ensign*, Nov. 1990.
100. Russell M. Nelson, "Reflection and Resolution," BYU Speeches, Jan. 7, 1990, 5–6.

101. Russell M. Nelson, "Where is Wisdom?" *Ensign*, Nov. 1992.

102. Nelson, *Teachings of Russell M. Nelson*, 94.

103. Nelson, "Drawing the Power of Jesus Christ."

104. Russell M. Nelson, "Face the Future with Faith," *Ensign*, May 2011, 34.

105. Nelson, "Face the Future with Faith," 36.

106. Russell M. Nelson, "Set in Order Thy House," *Ensign*, Nov. 2001.

107. Russell M. Nelson, "Our Sacred Duty to Honor Women," *Ensign*, May 1999.

108. Russell M. Nelson, "Three Circles of Safety," BYU–Idaho Commencement, Apr. 29, 2006; as cited in Nelson, *Teachings of Russell M. Nelson*, 114.

109. Russell M. Nelson, "Faith and Families," CES Fireside, Feb. 6, 2005, 3–4.

110. "President Nelson: Brilliant Mind, Gentle Heart," YouTube video, 0:48, posted by KSL News, Apr. 1, 2018, https://www.youtube.com/watch?v=VKiYPK_rEPk&t=1109s.

111. Russell M. Nelson, "Celestial Marriage," *Ensign*, Nov. 2008.

112. Russell M. Nelson, in Conference Report, Apr. 2006, 37.

113. Russell M. Nelson, "Nurturing Marriage," *Ensign*, May 2006.

114. Johnson, "A Study in Obedience," 24.

115. Nelson, *Teachings of Russell M. Nelson*, 94.

116. Elder Russell M. Nelson, "The Sabbath Is a Delight," *Ensign*, May 2015.

SIDEBAR AND PHOTO NOTES

1. Interview, Gloria and Richard Irion.

2. Nelson, *From Heart to Heart*, 70.

3. Nelson, *From Heart to Heart*, 80.

4. Nelson, *From Heart to Heart*, 89.

5. Lawrence R. Flake and Elaine M. Flake, "Wilbur W. Cox: First President of the Boston Massachusetts Stake," *Regional Studies in Latter-day Saint Church History*, 36.

6. Nelson, *From Heart to Heart*, 105.

7. Nelson, *From Heart to Heart*, 105.

8. Francis M. Gibbons, *Remembering the Prophets of God: Russell M. Nelson*, (Holladay, Utah: Sixteen Stones Press, 2018), 46–47.

9. Nelson, *From Heart to Heart*, 111.

10. Dallin H. Oaks, "President Russell M. Nelson: Guided, Prepared, Committed," *Ensign*, May 2018.

11. Nelson, *From Heart to Heart*, 343.

12. Condie, 177.

13. Johnson, 21–22.

14. Johnson, 21–22.

15. Condie, 147.

16. As cited in Condie, 147.

17. Condie, 146, 153–56.

18. Russell M. Nelson, "The Price of Priesthood Power," *Ensign*, May 2016; italics in original.

19. Nelson, *From Heart to Heart*, 164.

20. Nelson, *From Heart to Heart*, 165.

INDEX